The
Crossword Phrase
Dictionary

Also by R. J. Edwards

The Crossword Anagram Dictionary

The Crossword Completion Dictionary

R. J. Edwards

The
Crossword Phrase
Dictionary

Stanley Paul
London Melbourne Sydney Auckland Johannesburg

Stanley Paul & Co. Ltd

An imprint of Century Hutchinson Ltd

62-65 Chandos Place, London WC2N 4NW

Century Hutchinson (Australia) Pty Ltd
16-22 Church Street, Hawthorn, Melbourne, Victoria 3121

Century Hutchinson Ltd (NZ) Ltd
32-34 View Road, Glenfield, Auckland 10

Century Hutchinson (SA) Pty Ltd
PO Box 337, Bergvlei 2012, South Africa

First published 1981
Reprinted 1986
© Rik Edwards 1981

Printed and bound in Great Britain by
Anchor Brendon Limited, Tiptree, Essex

British Library Cataloguing in Publication Data

Edwards, R. J.
    The crossword phrase dictionary.
    1. Crossword puzzles — Glossaries, vocabularies, etc.
    2. English language — Terms and phrases
    I. Title
    793.73′2   GV1507.C7
ISBN 0 09 143340 1

How to use the dictionary

It often happens that a crossword puzzler finds his progress halted by a single clue, the solution to which is a lengthy phrase. This book, with its comprehensive selection of some 40,000 phrases, both common and obscure, but all likely to occur in crosswords, will prove invaluable in these circumstances, as the phrases have been arranged for very quick reference.

Firstly, phrases are arranged according to the number of letters they contain. Thus, for example, all twelve-letter phrases are grouped together. Secondly, within each section, the phrases have been grouped according to the length of the separate words in the phrase. The system adopted has been to place phrases with the shortest opening word first. Where the first words are of equal length, the phrases are ordered according to the length of the second word, and so on. Within these smaller sections, phrases are ordered alphabetically. Finally, the letters have been given equal spacing, so that they line up exactly underneath one another. Thus the field can be quickly narrowed when one or more letters of the solution are known.

The following examples of crossword clues illustrate the use of the book in practice:

'Between you and me, a nervous man is lacking this (2,10)'

Suppose the seventh letter is known to be 'I'. Turn to the twelve-letter section and find the list of 2,10 phrases. Then simply scan through the seventh letter column (a transparent straight edge, such as a clear plastic ruler, may be helpful), and pick out

```
IN   CONFIDENCE
IN   DIFFICULTY
IN   PARLIAMENT
IN   PARTICULAR
```

Thus from knowing just one letter and the phrase configuration, the puzzler has reduced the field to four possible solutions – from which the correct one, IN CONFIDENCE, can easily be deduced. In some cases the solution may be a phrase in a form not included in this book. It may, for example, have -S, -ING or -ED attached to one of the words. Usually the wording of the clue will make it clear what form the solution will take. For example:

'Mate wanted to solve them (5, 8)' 'Them' suggests that the solution will be a plural phrase with an extra 's' at the end. So if the phrase is sought as a singular under 5, 7, it will be found as 'Chess problem'. Similarly:

'Collecting the cattle and exaggerating their number slightly (8, 2)'. 'Collecting' suggests that the solution contains a word ending in -ING. So if the phrase is sought under 5, 2 it will be found as 'Round up'.

After a little practice, the user will find the dictionary simple and quick to use. It should prove invaluable to crossword solvers at all levels, and will often be the difference between unfinished and finished puzzles.

1 . 1 . 5

A . A . MILNE
C . S . LEWIS
H . G . WELLS
T . S . ELIOT
T . T . RACES
W . B . YEATS
W . C . HANDY
W . G . GRACE
W . H . AUDEN

1 . 2 . 4

Á LA MODE

1 . 3 . 3

A BIT OFF
I FOR ONE

1 . 6

A LEVELS
A PRIORI
G STRING
L DRIVER
L PLATES
O LEVELS

2 . 1 . 4

AS A RULE
AT A LOSS
AT A PACE
AT A TIME
BY A HEAD
BY A MILE
BY A NECK
DO A BUNK
DO A DEAL
IN A COMA
IN A DAZE
IN A FURY
IN A HEAP
IN A LINE
IN A MESS
IN A MOOD
IN A RAGE
IN A RING
IN A RUSH
IN A SPIN
IN A SPOT
IN A STEW
IN A TRAP
IN A WEEK
IN A WORD
IN A YEAR
OF A KIND
OF A SIZE
OF A SORT

OF A TYPE
ON A DIET
TO A HAIR
TO A HEAD
TO A TURN
UP A TREE

2 . 2 . 3

DO IT ALL
GO BY AIR
GO BY BUS
GO BY SEA
GO IN FOR
GO TO BED
GO TO POT
GO TO SEA
GO TO SEE
GO TO WAR
IN NO WAY
OF AN AGE
TO NO END
UP TO BED
UP TO NOW

2 . 3 . 2

BY AND BY
BY THE BY
IN AID OF
NO LET-UP
ON AND ON
ON THE GO
ON THE UP
SO AND SO
UP AND UP

2 . 5

AS USUAL
AT FAULT
AT GRIPS
AT HEART
AT ISSUE
AT LARGE
AT LEAST
AT LUNCH
AT NIGHT
AT PAINS
AT PEACE
AT PERIL
AT SPEED
AT STAKE
AT TIMES
AT WORST
BE QUIET
BY BIRTH
BY CROOK
BY FORCE
BY HEART
BY NIGHT

BY ORDER
BY PHONE
BY PLANE
BY RADIO
BY SIGHT
BY TRAIN
BY TURNS
DA VINCI
DE FACTO
DE MILLE
DO BADLY
DO RIGHT
DO WRONG
EL GRECO
EN ROUTE
EX PARTE
GO ABOUT
GO AFTER
GO AHEAD
GO ALONG
GO BADLY
GO BELOW
GO BROKE
GO CRAZY
GO DUTCH
GO FIRST
GO FORTH
GO NORTH
GO ROUND
GO SHORT
GO SOUTH
GO SPARE
GO UNDER
GO WHITE
GO WRONG
IN ANGER
IN APRIL
IN ASHES
IN BLACK
IN BLOOM
IN CHINA
IN CLASS
IN CROWD
IN DOUBT
IN EXILE
IN FIRST
IN FOCUS
IN FORCE
IN FRONT
IN FUNDS
IN GREEK
IN HASTE
IN LATIN
IN MARCH
IN MONEY
IN ORDER
IN PAIRS
IN PARIS
IN PERIL
IN PLACE
IN POWER

IN PRINT	ST.LEGER	AIR RAID
IN RANGE	ST.LOUIS	AIR TUBE
IN REPLY	ST.PETER	ALI BABA
IN ROUGH	TO HEART	ALL EARS
IN RUINS	TO ORDER	ALL EYES
IN SCALE	TO SCALE	ALL HOPE
IN SHAPE	UP NORTH	ALL OVER
IN SHORT	UP RIVER	ALL STAR
IN SIGHT		ALL THIS
IN SPITE	3 . 1 . 3	ALL WORK
IN STATE		ANT HILL
IN STOCK	GET A JOB	ANY RATE
IN STORE	GET A TAN	ANY TIME
IN STYLE	GOT A JOB	ARC LAMP
IN TEARS	HIT A SIX	ARM LOCK
IN THIRD	LAY A BET	ART FORM
IN TOTAL	NOT A BIT	ASH TREE
IN TOUCH	PAY A FEE	ATE AWAY
IN TRAIN	RUN A CAR	ATE DIRT
IN TRUTH	TIE A BOW	ATE INTO
IN TWAIN		BAD BACK
IN WALES	3 . 2 . 2	BAD CAST
IN WHITE		BAD COLD
IT POURS	AND SO ON	BAD DEBT
LA SCALA	BIT OF IT	BAD FORM
LE HAVRE	HAM IT UP	BAD KING
MR.RIGHT	LAY IT ON	BAD LAND
MY FAULT	LET IT BE	BAD LINE
NO CLAIM	LET IT GO	BAD LUCK
NO DOUBT	LIE IN IT	BAD MOOD
NO ENTRY	OWN UP TO	BAD MOVE
NO LIMIT	RUB IT IN	BAD NAME
NO MATCH	SET EM UP	BAD NEWS
NO MEANS	SUM IT UP	BAD OMEN
NO OTHER	TRY IT ON	BAD RISK
NO POINT	WHO IS IT?	BAD ROAD
NO REPLY	WHY IS IT?	BAD SHOT
NO SWEAT		BAD SIGN
NO TASTE	3 . 3 . 1	BAD STEP
NO TRACE		BAD TIME
NO TRUMP	YOU AND I	BAD WINE
OF SORTS		BAY LEAF
OF VALUE	3 . 4	BAY TREE
ON APPRO		BED DOWN
ON BOARD	ACE HIGH	BED POST
ON EARTH	ACK EMMA	BED TIME
ON GUARD	ACT FOUR	BEE HIVE
ON LEASE	ACT WELL	BIG BAND
ON LEAVE	AGA KHAN	BIG BANG
ON OFFER	AIM HIGH	BIG CITY
ON ORDER	AIR BASE	BIG DEAL
ON PAPER	AIR CREW	BIG EARS
ON SHIFT	AIR DUCT	BIG FEET
ON SIGHT	AIR FARE	BIG FILM
ON STAGE	AIR FLUE	BIG FOUR
ON TRIAL	AIR HOSE	BIG GAME
ON TRUST	AIR LANE	BIG GIRL
SO FORTH	AIR LINE	BIG GUNS
ST.JAMES	AIR MAIL	BIG HEAD
ST.JOHNS	AIR PIPE	BIG HURT
ST.KITTS	AIR PUMP	BIG IDEA

AIR MISS

BIG NAME	EAR LOBE	GAS OVEN
BIG PART	EAR PLUG	GAS RING
BIG RACE	EAT AWAY	GET AWAY
BIG SHOT	EAT DIRT	GET BACK
BIG TALK	EAT INTO	GET COLD
BIT MUCH	EBB AWAY	GET DARK
BIT PART	EBB TIDE	GET DOWN
BOB HOPE	EGG FLIP	GET EVEN
BOW DOWN	EGG YOLK	GET HELP
BOW LEGS	ELM TREE	GET HOLD
BOX KITE	END GAME	GET INTO
BUS FARE	END SEAT	GET LOST
BUS LANE	ERE LONG	GET OVER
BUS STOP	EWE LAMB	GET RICH
BUY BACK	FAN CLUB	GET SHOT
BUY DEAR	FAR AWAY	GET SICK
CAR BOMB	FAR BACK	GET WARM
CAR PARK	FAR EAST	GET WELL
CAR PORT	FAR GONE	GET WIND
CAR WASH	FAR LESS	GIN FIZZ
CAT CALL	FAR MORE	GIN LANE
CAT SHOW	FAR SIDE	GOT AWAY
CAT SUIT	FAR WEST	GOT COLD
CAT WALK	FAT MEAT	GOT DARK
CON BRIO	FAT PART	GOT DOWN
CON MOTO	FIG LEAF	GOT EVEN
COP HOLD	FIG ROLL	GOT HELP
CRY BABY	FIG TREE	GOT HOLD
CRY WOLF	FIR CONE	GOT INTO
CUE BALL	FIR TREE	GOT LOST
CUT AWAY	FIT WELL	GOT OVER
CUT BACK	FLY AWAY	GOT RICH
CUT DEAD	FLY HALF	GOT SICK
CUT DOWN	FLY HIGH	GOT WARM
CUT OPEN	FLY HOME	GOT WELL
CUT RATE	FLY LEAF	GOT WIND
DAY BOOK	FLY OVER	GUM TREE
DAY TRIP	FLY SOLO	GUN MOLL
DIE AWAY	FOR AGES	GUN ROOM
DIE DOWN	FOR EVER	GUY ROPE
DIE HARD	FOR FREE	GYM SLIP
DIG DEEP	FOR GOOD	HAM ROLL
DIM VIEW	FOR HIRE	HAY CART
DOG CART	FOR LACK	HAY LOFT
DOG DAYS	FOR LIFE	HAY RICK
DOG RACE	FOR LOVE	HEN COOP
DOG SHOW	FOR LUCK	HIP BATH
DOG STAR	FOR SALE	HIP BONE
DON JUAN	FOR SURE	HIP ROOF
DRY CELL	FOX HUNT	HIS NIBS
DRY DOCK	FOX TRAP	HIT BACK
DRY FACT	FOX TROT	HIT HARD
DRY LAND	FUN FAIR	HIT SONG
DRY MASS	FUR COAT	HIT TUNE
DRY WINE	GAG BOOK	HOP VINE
DUE CARE	GAS BILL	HOT BATH
DUE DATE	GAS FIRE	HOT CAKE
DUE EAST	GAS LAMP	HOT DISH
DUE WEST	GAS LEAK	HOT FOOD
DUG DEEP	GAS MAIN	HOT JAZZ
EAR HOLE	GAS MASK	HOT LINE

HOT MEAL	LOW GEAR	OLD HAND
HOT MILK	LOW HEEL	OLD HEAD
HOT NEWS	LOW MARK	OLD IDEA
HOT OVEN	LOW MASS	OLD JOKE
HOT SEAT	LOW NOTE	OLD LADY
HOT SOUP	LOW RATE	OLD MAID
HOT SPOT	LOW RENT	OLD MOON
HOT WORK	LOW TIDE	OLD NICK
HOW COME ?	MAD FOOL	OLD ROPE
ICE BOAT	MAD RUSH	OLD SALT
ICE CUBE	MAE WEST	OLD SONG
ICE FLOE	MAN MADE	OLD TIME
ICE PICK	MAN TRAP	ONE CARD
ICE RINK	MAY LILY	ONE CLUB
ICH DIEN	MOB RULE	ONE DEEP
ICY WIND	MOW DOWN	ONE DOWN
IDI AMIN	MUD BATH	ONE FOOT
ILL FAME	MUD FLAT	ONE HALF
ILL LUCK	NET CORD	ONE HAND
ILL OMEN	NET GAIN	ONE HOUR
ILL WILL	NET LOSS	ONE JUMP
ILL WIND	NEW BALL	ONE KILO
INK WELL	NEW CASE	ONE LOVE
INN SIGN	NEW DEAL	ONE LUMP
JAM PUFF	NEW FACE	ONE MILE
JAM ROLL	NEW IDEA	ONE MIND
JAM TART	NEW LEAF	ONE PAGE
JOE SOAP	NEW LEFT	ONE PART
JOT DOWN	NEW LOOK	ONE PINT
JOY RIDE	NEW MOON	ONE QUID
KEY MOVE	NEW SUIT	ONE STAR
KEY NOTE	NEW TOWN	ONE TIME
KEY POST	NEW WAVE	ONE WEEK
KON TIKI	NEW WINE	ONE WORD
LAW BOOK	NEW WORD	ONE YARD
LAW LORD	NEW YEAR	ONE YEAR
LAW SUIT	NEW YORK	OUR HOPE
LAY BACK	NON ESSE	OUR LADY
LAY BARE	NOT FAIR	OUT COLD
LAY DOWN	NOT HALF	OWN GOAL
LAY FLAT	NOT HERE	PAY BACK
LEE SIDE	OAK LEAF	PAY CASH
LEE TIDE	OAK TREE	PAY LESS
LEG SIDE	ODD DATE	PAY MORE
LEG TRAP	OFF DUTY	PAY RENT
LES PAUL	OFF PEAK	PAY RISE
LET DOWN	OFF SIDE	PAY SLIP
LET DROP	OIL DRUM	PEA SOUP
LET FALL	OIL FUEL	PEN NAME
LET PAST	OIL LAMP	PEP PILL
LET SLIP	OIL PIPE	PEP TALK
LEW HOAD	OIL PUMP	PER CENT
LIE BACK	OIL WELL	PER YEAR
LIE DOWN	OLD BEAN	PET HATE
LIE FLAT	OLD BIRD	PET NAME
LOG BOOK	OLD BOYS	PET SHOP
LOG FIRE	OLD CHAP	PIE DISH
LOO ROLL	OLD FOGY	PIE SHOP
LOW BORN	OLD FOLK	PIG IRON
LOW DIVE	OLD GIRL	PIN DOWN
LOW DOWN	OLD GOLD	PIP EMMA

PIT	PONY	RUN	AMOK	TAP	ROOT
PIT	STOP	RUN	AWAY	TAX	DISC
POP	IDOL	RUN	BACK	TAX	FORM
POP	SONG	RUN	DEEP	TAX	FREE
POP	STAR	RUN	DOWN	TAX	YEAR
POT	HERB	RUN	FREE	TEA	CAKE
POT	HOLE	RUN	HARD	TEA	COSY
POT	LUCK	RUN	HIGH	TEA	GOWN
POT	SHOT	RUN	INTO	TEA	LADY
PRO	RATA	RUN	OVER	TEA	LEAF
PUB	GAME	RUN	PAST	TEA	ROSE
PUT	AWAY	RUN	RIOT	TEA	SHOP
PUT	BACK	RUN	WELL	TEA	TIME
PUT	DOWN	RUN	WILD	TEA	TRAY
PUT	OVER	SAD	NEWS	TEE	SHOT
PUT	UPON	SAD	SONG	TEL	AVIV
RAG	DOLL	SAN	JOSÉ	TEN	DAYS
RAG	WEEK	SAN	REMO	TEN	DEEP
RAM	HOME	SAT	BACK	TEN	FEET
RAN	AMOK	SAT	DOWN	TEN	FOUR
RAN	AWAY	SAW	MILL	TEN	LAPS
RAN	BACK	SAY	AMEN	TEN	PAST
RAN	DOWN	SAY	WHEN	TEN	QUID
RAN	HARD	SEA	BLUE	THE	AGES
RAN	INTO	SEA	FISH	THE	ARMY
RAN	OVER	SEA	HAWK	THE	ARTS
RAN	PAST	SEA	LINE	THE	BANK
RAN	RIOT	SEA	LION	THE	BEST
RAN	WELL	SEA	LORD	THE	BLUE
RAN	WILD	SEA	MAIL	THE	BOMB
RAT	HOLE	SEA	TRIP	THE	CITY
RAT	RACE	SEA	WALL	THE	CUBS
RAW	DEAL	SEE	LIFE	THE	DATE
RAW	MEAT	SEE	OVER	THE	DEAF
RED	ARMY	SET	BACK	THE	DEEP
RED	BALL	SET	BOOK	THE	DOGS
RED	BELT	SET	DOWN	THE	DOLE
RED	CARD	SET	FAIR	THE	EAST
RED	CENT	SET	FAST	THE	EXIT
RED	COAT	SET	FIRE	THE	FALL
RED	DEAN	SET	FOOT	THE	FLAG
RED	DEER	SET	FREE	THE	FOOL
RED	FACE	SET	SAIL	THE	FRAY
RED	FLAG	SET	UPON	THE	GODS
RED	HAIR	SEX	ORGY	THE	KILL
RED	HEAT	SEX	SHOP	THE	KING
RED	LEAD	SHY	GIRL	THE	KISS
RED	LION	SIT	BACK	THE	LADY
RED	MEAT	SIT	DOWN	THE	LIKE
RED	PINE	SIX	DAYS	THE	LINE
RED	ROSE	SIX	FEET	THE	LORD
RED	STAR	SIX	QUID	THE	MODS
RED	TAPE	SIX	RUNS	THE	MOON
RED	WINE	SKI	JUMP	THE	MOST
REP	SHOW	SKY	BLUE	THE	NAVY
RIB	CAGE	SPY	RING	THE	NAZE
ROD	HULL	SUN	DIAL	THE	NEWS
ROE	DEER	SUN	KING	THE	NILE
RON	HILL	SUN	LAMP	THE	OAKS
RUB	DOWN	SUN	SPOT	THE	OVAL
RUM	BABA	SUN	TRAP	THE	PITS

THE POPE	WAR GAME	BLOW OFF
THE RAGE	WAR HERO	BLOW OUT
THE REDS	WAR LOAN	BLUE DOT
THE RING	WAR LORD	BLUE INK
THE ROBE	WAR POEM	BLUE JAY
THE RULE	WAR POET	BLUE SKY
THE SAME	WAR SONG	BLUE TIE
THE SHAH	WAY BACK	BLUE TIT
THE SILK	WAY DOWN	BODE ILL
THE TIME	WET DOCK	BOER WAR
THE TUBE	WHO ELSE?	BOMB BAY
THE VOTE	WIN BACK	BOMB OUT
THE WASH	WIN FAME	BORE OUT
THE WEST	WIN OVER	BOWL OUT
THE WIFE	WON BACK	BRAN TUB
TIE DOWN	WON OVER	BREN GUN
TIN FOIL	YEW TREE	BRER FOX
TIN MINE		BUMP OFF
TOO COLD	**4, 1, 2**	BUNK BED
TOO DEAR		BURN OIL
TOO FAST	HALF A MO	BURN OUT
TOO GOOD	HAVE A GO	BUSY BEE
TOO HARD	JUST A MO	BUSY DAY
TOO KEEN	WAIT A MO	BUZZ OFF
TOO KIND		BUZZ SAW
TOO LATE	**4, 3**	CAKE MIX
TOO MANY		CAKE TIN
TOO MUCH	ACID DYE	CALL BOX
TOO SLOW	AGES AGO	CALL FOR
TOO SOON	ALSO RAN	CALL OFF
TOP COAT	ARMY ANT	CALL OUT
TOP DECK	ATOM ANT	CALM SEA
TOP GEAR	AWAY WIN	CAME OFF
TOP LINE	AXLE PIN	CAME OUT
TOP NOTE	BABY BOY	CAMP BED
TOP RATE	BABY KID	CAMP OUT
TOP RUNG	BACK OFF	CASE LAW
TOP SEED	BACK OUT	CASH BOX
TOP SPIN	BACK ROW	CAST OFF
TOP SPOT	BAIL OUT	CAST OUT
TOW BOAT	BALE OUT	CATS EYE
TOY SHOP	BALI HAI	CAVE MAN
TRY HARD	BALL BOY	CHEZ MOI
TUG BOAT	BARN OWL	CITY MAN
TWO ACES	BATH BUN	CLUB FEE
TWO ACTS	BATH MAT	COAL GAS
TWO BITS	BEAR OUT	COAL TIT
TWO CARS	BEAT OFF	COIN BOX
TWO DAYS	BEAT OUT	COLD AIR
TWO DEEP	BEER GUT	COLD DAY
TWO FEET	BEER MUG	COLD HAM
TWO LAPS	BELA KUN	COLD TAP
TWO LEGS	BEND LOW	COLD WAR
TWO PINS	BENT LOW	COME OFF
TWO QUID	BEST CUT	COME OUT
TWO STAR	BEST MAN	COOL OFF
TWO TWOS	BETA RAY	COPY CAT
VAN DYCK	BIRD DOG	COPY OUT
VAN DYKE	BLOT OUT	CORK TIP
VAN GOGH	BLOW DRY	CORN COB
WAR BOND	BLOW HOT	CORN LAW

COSH BOY	FEEL OUT	GOOD GOD
CÔTE DOR	FEEL SAD	GOOD JOB
CREW CUT	FELL DUE	GOOD MAN
DARE NOT	FELL FOR	GOOD TRY
DARK RED	FELL ILL	GOOD WAY
DART OUT	FELL OFF	GRAB BAG
DASH OFF	FELL OUT	GREW OLD
DASH OUT	FELT BAD	GREW OUT
DEAD END	FELT HAT	GREY FOX
DEAD SEA	FELT HOT	GREY SKY
DEAD SET	FELT ILL	GROW OLD
DEAR SIR	FELT SAD	GROW OUT
DEED BOX	FELT TIP	HAIR CUT
DEEP END	FÊTE DAY	HAIR NET
DEEP FRY	FILL OUT	HAIR OIL
DEEP SEA	FILM FAN	HALF DAY
DEEP SET	FILM SET	HALF PAY
DINE OUT	FIND OUT	HALF WAY
DISH MOP	FINE ART	HALF WIT
DISH OUT	FINE DAY	HAND OFF
DOLE OUT	FINE LEG	HAND OUT
DOOR MAT	FINE MAN	HANG HIM
DOWN BOY!	FIRE OFF	HANG OUT
DRAG OUT	FISH FLY	HARD DAY
DRAW OFF	FISH OUT	HARD HIT
DRAW OUT	FISH ROE	HARD MAN
DRAW PAY	FIVE BOB	HARD PUT
DREW OFF	FIVE MEN	HARD WAY
DRIP DRY	FLAG DAY	HAVE FUN
DROP OFF	FLAT CAP	HAVE NOT
DROP OUT	FLAT OUT	HAVE SEX
DULL BOY	FLEA PIT	BAG	HEAD BOY
DUST PAN	FORK OUT	HEAD FOR
EACH ONE	FOUR MEN	HEAD OFF
EACH WAY	FREE END	HELD OUT
EASE OFF	FREE HIT	HELP OUT
EAST END	FREE MAN	HIGH ART
EASY WIN	FULL SET	HIGH DAY
EVIL DAY	FUSE BOX	HIGH HAT
EVIL EYE	GAME PIE	HIGH PAY
EVIL MAN	GATE MAN	HIGH SEA
EVIL ONE	GAVE OUT	HIGH TEA
FADE OUT	GIFT BOX	HIND PAW
FAIR COP	GIVE EAR	HIRE OUT
FAIR SEX	GIVE OUT	HOLD OFF
FALL DUE	GIVE WAY	HOLD OUT
FALL FOR	GLAD EYE	HOLM OAK
FALL GUY	GOLD PIN	HOLY COW
FALL ILL	GOLF BAG	HOLY DAY
FALL OFF	GOLF TEE	HOLY SEE
FALL OUT	GOOD BET	HOLY VOW
FARM EGG	GOOD BOY	HOLY WAR
FARM OUT	GOOD BUY	HOME RUN
FAST CAR	GOOD DAY	HOME TIE
FAST DAY	GOOD DOG	HOME WIN
FAST DYE	GOOD EAR	HORN OWL
FAST MAN	GOOD EGG	HUNG OUT
FAUX PAS	GOOD EYE	ICED TEA
FEEL BAD	GOOD FEW	IRON AGE
FEEL HOT	GOOD FOR	IRON BAR
FEEL ILL	GOOD FUN	IRON MAN

IRON	ORE	LOCK	OUT	OPEN	AIR
IRON	OUT	LONG	AGO	OPEN	END
JACK	TAR	LONG	ARM	OPEN	OUT
JOHN	DOE	LONG	HOP	OPEN	SEA
JOHN	GAY	LONG	LEG	OPEN	WAR
JUKE	BOX	LONG	RUN	OVER	AGE
JUMP	OUT	LONG	TOM	OVER	PAR
JUNE	BUG	LONG	WAY	PAGE	BOY
JUNE	FLY	LOOK	BIG	PAGE	ONE
JURY	BOX	LOOK	FOR	PAGE	SIX
JUST	MAN	LOOK	ILL	PAGE	TEN
JUST	MEN	LOOK	OLD	PAGE	TWO
JUST	NOW	LOOK	OUT	PAIR	OFF
KEEP	FIT	LORD	GOD	PALE	ALE
KEEP	MUM	LOSE	OUT	PASS	FOR
KEEP	OFF	LOST	DOG	PASS	KEY
KEEP	OUT	LOST	OUT	PASS	OFF
KEPT	FIT	LOVE	ALL	PASS	OUT
KEPT	MUM	LUMP	SUM	PEAT	BOG
KEPT	OFF	MADE	FOR	PEEL	OFF
KEPT	OUT	MADE	HAY	PICK	AXE
KICK	OFF	MADE	OFF	PICK	OFF
KICK	OUT	MADE	OUT	PICK	OUT
KILL	OFF	MADE	WAR	PILL	BOX
KING	RAT	MADE	WAY	PINE	FOR
KING	ZOG	MAIL	VAN	PINK	GIN
KNOW	ALL	MAKE	FOR	PINT	POT
KNOW	HOW	MAKE	HAY	PLAY	OFF
LADY	DAY	MAKE	OFF	PLAY	OUT
LAID	LOW	MAKE	OUT	PLAY	PEN
LAID	OFF	MAKE	WAR	PLUM	JAM
LAID	OUT	MAKE	WAY	PLUM	PIE
LAME	DOG	MALE	SEX	POKE	FUN
LAND	TAX	MANS	MAN	POLE	CAT
LANE	ONE	MANX	CAT	POOR	BOY
LANE	SIX	MARK	OFF	POOR	DOG
LANE	TWO	MARK	OUT	POOR	LAW
LASH	OUT	MARS	BAR	POOR	MAN
LAST	ACT	MEAT	PIE	PORK	PIE
LAST	BUS	MILK	BAR	POUR	OIL
LAST	DAY	MILK	COW	POUR	OUT
LAST	LAP	MILK	JUG	PULL	OFF
LAST	MAN	MILK	RUN	PULL	OUT
LAST	MAY	MINI	CAB	PUMP	OUT
LAST	OUT	MISS	OUT	PURE	JOY
LAST	ROW	MORE	PAY	PUSH	FOR
LEAD	OFF	MOVE	OFF	PUSH	OFF
LEAK	OUT	MOVE	OUT	PUSH	OUT
LEFT	ARM	MUCH	ADO	RAIN	GOD
LEFT	EAR	MUSK	RAT	RAKE	OFF
LEFT	EYE	MUST	NOT	RARE	GAS
LEFT	LEG	NEAT	GIN	RARE	SET
LEFT	OUT	NEAT	SET	REAL	ALE
LEVY	TAX	NEED	NOT	REEL	OFF
LIFT	OFF	NEST	EGG	RENT	ACT
LIKE	MAD	NEXT	DAY	RENT	DAY
LILY	PAD	NEXT	MAY	RENT	OUT
LINO	CUT	NINE	MEN	REST	DAY
LION	CUB	NUDE	MAN	RICH	MAN
LIVE	OUT	OHMS	LAW	RICH	ORE
LOCH	TAY	ONLY	SON	RIDE	OFF

RIDE OUT	SOME DAY	TRAP SIX
RING OFF	SONG HIT	TRAP TWO
RING OUT	SORT OUT	TREE FOX
RIOT ACT	SPIN OFF	TREE TOP
RIPE AGE	SPIN OUT	TROT OFF
ROAD BED	SPIT OUT	TURF OUT
ROAD HOG	SPUN OUT	TURN OFF
ROAD MAP	STAY PUT	TURN OUT
ROAD TAX	STEN GUN	UEFA CUP
RODE OFF	STEP ONE	USED CAR
ROLL OUT	STEP OUT	VERY BAD
ROOT OUT	STEP TWO	VERY FAR
ROSE HIP	STOP KEY	VERY FEW
RUDE BOY	STOP OFF	VERY HOT
RULE OUT	STOP OUT	VERY ODD
RUSH MAT	SUSS OUT	VOTE FOR
SALT SEA	TAIL END	WAGE WAR
SAND BAG	TAIL FIN	WALK OFF
SAND BAR	TAIL OFF	WALK OUT
SAND FLY	TAIL OUT	WARD OFF
SAND PIE	TAKE AIM	WARM AIR
SANE MAN	TAKE ILL	WARM DAY
SANG OUT	TAKE OFF	WARN OFF
SEAL OFF	TAKE OUT	WASH OUT
SEEK OUT	TALK BIG	WASH TUB
SELL OFF	TALL BOY	WEAK MAN
SELL OUT	TALL MAN	WEAK TEA
SEND FOR	TAXI CAB	WEAR OFF
SEND OFF	TEAR GAS	WEAR OUT
SEND OUT	TEAR OFF	WEAR RED
SENT FOR	TEEN AGE	WEED OUT
SENT OFF	TELL ALL	WEEK OFF
SENT OUT	TELL OFF	WELL FED
SHIN PAD	TENT PEG	WELL MET
SHOW DOG	TEST RUN	WELL OFF
SHOW OFF	THIN AIR	WELL RUN
SHOW OUT	THIN CAT	WEST END
SHUT OFF	THIN END	WEST HAM
SHUT OUT	THIN MAN	WHIP TOP
SICK BAY	THIN OUT	WIDE BOY
SIDE BET	THIS DAY	WILD CAT
SIGN OFF	TICK OFF	WILD DOG
SINE DIE	TIDY SUM	WILL NOT
SING LOW	TILL NOW	WIND GOD
SING OUT	TIME LAG	WINE BAR
SITS VAC	TIME OUT	WINE GUM
SIZE ONE	TIME WAS	WING NUT
SIZE SIX	TINY BIT	WIPE DRY
SIZE TEN	TINY TIM	WIPE OFF
SIZE TWO	TINY TOT	WIPE OUT
SKID ROW	TOBY JUG	WISE GUY
SKIP OFF	TOLD ALL	WISE MAN
SKIP OUT	TOLD OFF	WISE MEN
SLIP OFF	TOOK AIM	WITS END
SLIP OUT	TOOK ILL	WOLF CUB
SLOE GIN	TOOK OFF	WORE RED
SOAP BOX	TOOK OUT	WORK FOR
SODS LAW	TOOL BOX	WORK OFF
SOFT TOY	TOOL KIT	WORK OUT
SOLD OFF	TORE OFF	WORN OFF
SOLD OUT	TRAP ONE	WORN OUT

XMAS DAY
YOKO ONO
YULE LOG

5, 1, 1

WATCH T.V.

5, 2

BLAST IT
BLOWN UP
BREAK IN
BREAK UP
BRING IN
BRING ON
BRING TO
BRING UP
BROKE IN
BROKE UP
BRUSH UP
BUILD UP
BUILT UP
BURST IN
CARRY ON
CARVE UP
CATCH IT
CATCH ON
CATCH UP
CHALK UP
CHECK IN
CHECK UP
CHEER UP
CHIME IN
CHUCK IN
CLEAN UP
CLEAR UP
CLOCK IN
CLOCK ON
CLOSE UP
COUGH UP
COUNT IN
COUNT ON
COUNT UP
COVER UP
CRACK UP
CREEP IN
CREEP UP
CREPT IN
CREPT UP
DRANK UP
DRAWN UP
DRESS UP
DRINK UP
DRIVE IN
DROVE IN
DWELL ON
ENTER IT
FENCE IN
FETCH UP
FIGHT IT

FIXED UP
FLARE UP
FRAME UP
GOING ON
GOING UP
GROWN UP
GRUBS UP
HEAVE TO
HURRY UP
KNOCK ON
KNOCK UP
LATER ON
LAUGH AT
LIGHT UP
LIVEN UP
MATCH UP
MINCE UP
MOUNT UP
OFFER UP
PATCH UP
PHONE IN
PITCH IN
PRESS ON
QUEUE UP
REFER TO
RIGHT ON
ROUGH IT
ROUND UP
SANTA FÉ
SEIZE UP
SERVE UP
SHAKE UP
SHAPE UP
SHOOK UP
SHOOT AT
SHOOT UP
SHORE UP
SLEEP IN
SLEEP ON
SLEPT IN
SLEPT ON
SMALL AD
SMASH UP
SNEAK IN
SNEAK UP
SNUFF IT
SOBER UP
SPEAK UP
SPEED UP
SPLIT UP
SPOKE UP
STAND BY
STAND IN
STAND TO
STAND UP
START UP
STEAL UP
STICK TO
STICK UP
STOCK UP
STOOD BY

STOOD IN
STOOD UP
STUCK TO
STUCK UP
SWEAR BY
SWEAR IN
SWEEP UP
SWEET ON
SWELL UP
SWEPT UP
SWORN IN
TALLY HO
THERE IS
THINK OF
THINK ON
THINK UP
THREE RS
THREW IN
THREW UP
THROW IN
THROW UP
TIMES UP
TOUCH ON
TOUCH UP
TRADE IN
TREAD ON
TRUST IN
USHER IN
WEIGH IN
WEIGH UP
WHATS UP?
WOUND UP
WRITE IN
WRITE UP
WROTE IN
WROTE UP

6, 1

MIDDLE C
TREBLE C

1, 1, 6

J.M.BARRIE
T.V.DINNER
W.C.FIELDS

1, 2, 5

À LA CARTE

1, 3, 4

A BAD TIME
A BIT MUCH
A NEW LEAF
X-RAY UNIT

1 , 4 , 3

A FAIR COP
A GOOD BUY
A GOOD FEW
A GOOD JOB
A GOOD WAY
I LOVE YOU
I THEE WED

1 , 7

À BIENTÔT

2 , 1 , 3 , 2

AS I SEE IT

2 , 1 , 5

AS A WHOLE
AT A FEAST
AT A GUESS
AT A PINCH
AT A PRICE
BE A SPORT
BY A FLUKE
DO A TRICK
IN A CHAIR
IN A CROWD
IN A DREAM
IN A FAINT
IN A FEVER
IN A FIGHT
IN A FLASH
IN A GROUP
IN A HURRY
IN A JIFFY
IN A MONTH
IN A PADDY
IN A PANIC
IN A SENSE
IN A SLING
IN A SNARE
IN A STATE
IN A SWEAT
IN A SWOON
IN A TRICE
IN A WHILE
IN A WHIRL
ON A BINGE
ON A LEASH
ON A LEVEL
ON A PLATE
ON A SLOPE
ON A VISIT
TO A FAULT

2 , 2 , 4

AS IT WERE
AT NO TIME
BE AT REST
BE IN DEBT
BE IN GOAL
BE IN LOVE
BE MY LOVE
BE NO MORE
DE LA MARE
DO BY HAND
DO IT WELL
DO NO GOOD
DO NO HARM
GO BY BOAT
GO BY FOOT
GO BY LAND
GO BY RAIL
GO BY ROAD
GO BY SHIP
GO BY TAXI
GO BY TRAM
GO BY TUBE
GO IN FEAR
GO IN RAGS
GO ON DUTY
GO ON FOOT
GO TO CAMP
GO TO GAOL
GO TO HELL
GO TO JAIL
GO TO MASS
GO TO SEED
GO TO TOWN
GO TO WORK
IN AN HOUR
IN MY VIEW
IN NO TIME
IN NO WISE
NO-GO AREA
ON MY LEFT
ON MY LIFE
SO IT GOES
TO BE SURE
TO MY MIND
UP AT DAWN
UP IN ARMS
UP TO DATE
UP TO HERE

2 , 3 , 3

AT THE BAR
AT THE END
AT THE TOP
AT THE ZOO
BY THE ARM
BY THE SEA
BY THE WAY
DO THE LOT

GO ALL OUT
GO AND SEE
GO TOO FAR
IN AND OUT
IN ANY WAY
IN MID AIR
IN OFF RED
IN ONE WAY
IN THE ACT
IN THE AIR
IN THE BAG
IN THE BAR
IN THE BOX
IN THE CUP
IN THE END
IN THE NET
IN THE RAW
IN THE RED
IN THE SEA
IN THE SUN
IN THE WAR
IN THE WAY
MY OLD MAN
NO WAY OUT
ON AND OFF
ON ONE LEG
ON THE AIR
ON THE COB
ON THE DOT
ON THE HOP
ON THE JOB
ON THE MAP
ON THE MAT
ON THE RUN
ON THE SEA
ON THE SET
ON THE SLY
ON THE TOP
ON THE WAY
ON TIP-TOE
TO AND FRO
TO THE BAD
TO THE END
TO THE TOP

2 , 4 , 2

AS GOOD AS
AS SOON AS
AS WELL AS

2 , 6

AL CAPONE
AL FRESCO
AL JOLSON
AS STATED
AT ANCHOR
AT DINNER
AT LENGTH
AT OXFORD
AT RANDOM

AT SCHOOL	IN COLOUR	MY FRIEND
AU REVOIR	IN COMMON	MY PUBLIC
BE ABSENT	IN CONVOY	NO ANSWER
BE AFRAID	IN CREDIT	NO BETTER
BE POLITE	IN DANGER	NO BOTHER
BE SEATED	IN DEMAND	NO CHANCE
BE UNKIND	IN DETAIL	NO CHANGE
BE WARNED	IN EFFECT	NO CHARGE
BY CHANCE	IN EMBRYO	NO CHOICE
BY CHEQUE	IN EUROPE	NO DESIRE
BY GEORGE	IN EXCESS	NO EFFECT
BY HALVES	IN FAVOUR	NO EFFORT
BY INCHES	IN FLAMES	NO ESCAPE
BY ITSELF	IN FLIGHT	NO EXCUSE
BY LETTER	IN FLOWER	NO LONGER
BY MYSELF	IN FOURTH	NO MATTER
BY NATURE	IN FRANCE	NO OBJECT
BY RETURN	IN FRENCH	NO OPTION
BY RIGHTS	IN FUTURE	NO REASON
BY STAGES	IN GERMAN	NO REMEDY
BY WEIGHT	IN GROUPS	NO RETURN
DE GAULLE	IN HEAVEN	NO SECRET
DE VALERA	IN HIDING	NO SLOUCH
DO BATTLE	IN HORROR	NO THANKS
DO BETTER	IN LEAGUE	NO TRUMPS
DR.JEKYLL	IN LONDON	NO WONDER
DR.WATSON	IN LUXURY	OF COURSE
EL DORADO	IN MOSCOW	ON COURSE
ET CETERA	IN MOTION	ON CREDIT
EX GRATIA	IN MUTINY	ON DEMAND
GO ABOARD	IN OFFICE	ON FRIDAY
GO ABROAD	IN PENCIL	ON MONDAY
GO ABSENT	IN PERSON	ON PARADE
GO ACROSS	IN PIECES	ON PAROLE
GO ASHORE	IN PLEDGE	ON PATROL
GO ASTERN	IN POCKET	ON RECORD
GO ASTRAY	IN PRISON	ON REMAND
GO BEFORE	IN PUBLIC	ON SAFARI
GO BEYOND	IN QUOTES	ON SKATES
GO DIRECT	IN RELIEF	ON STILTS
GO HALVES	IN REPAIR	ON STRIKE
GO HUNGRY	IN REPOSE	ON SUNDAY
GO INSIDE	IN REVOLT	ON TARGET
GO PLACES	IN RUSSIA	ON TIPTOE
GO PUBLIC	IN SAFETY	ON WHEELS
GO RACING	IN SCHOOL	OX TONGUE
GO STEADY	IN SEASON	ST.ALBANS
GO UPHILL	IN SECOND	ST.ANDREW
GO YELLOW	IN SECRET	ST.DAVIDS
IN ACCORD	IN SERIES	ST.GEORGE
IN ACTION	IN SHREDS	ST.HELENA
IN AFRICA	IN SPIRIT	ST.HELENS
IN ARREAR	IN SPRING	ST.HELIER
IN AUGUST	IN STAGES	ST.JAMESS
IN AUTUMN	IN SUMMER	ST.JOSEPH
IN CAMERA	IN TANDEM	ST.MIRREN
IN CANADA	IN TERROR	ST.MORITZ
IN CHAINS	IN THEORY	ST.PETERS
IN CHARGE	IN UNISON	ST.PIERRE
IN CHORUS	IN WINTER	
IN CLOVER	LA BOHÈME	

3, 1, 4

ACT A PART
AIM A BLOW
BUY A FLAT
CUT A DASH
CUT A DISC
DIG A HOLE
EAT A MEAL
FIX A DATE
FIX A HOLE
FIX A TIME
FLY A KITE
FOR A JOKE
FOR A LARK
FOR A SONG
FOR A TIME
GET A GOAL
GET A GRIP
GET A LIFT
GET A RISE
HIT A FOUR
HIT A SNAG
HUM A TUNE
ITS A CERT
ITS A FACT
LAY A FIRE
LAY A TRAP
NOT A SOUL
NOT A WORD
OWE A DEBT
OWE A DUTY
PAY A BILL
PAY A CALL
PAY A FINE
ROB A BANK
ROW A RACE
RUN A MILE
RUN A RACE
RUN A RISK
SEE A SHOW
SET A DATE
SET A TASK
SET A TRAP
TIE A KNOT
WIN A GAME
WIN A RACE

3, 2, 3

ACT OF GOD
ACT OF WAR
ALL AT SEA
ALL IN ALL
ALL IN ONE
ARM IN ARM
BIT BY BIT
BIT OF FUN
CAP IT ALL
COQ AU VIN
CRY OF JOY

CUP OF TEA
CUT IN TWO
CUT IT OFF
CUT IT OUT
CUT NO ICE
DAY BY DAY
EAT MY HAT
EAU DE VIE
END IT ALL
END TO END
EYE TO EYE
GOD OF WAR
HIT IT OFF
JAR OF JAM
LAY AN EGG
LET IT LIE
LET IT RIP
LET ME SEE
LIE IN BED
MAL DE MER
MAN OF GOD
MAN OF LAW
MAN OF WAR
MAN TO MAN
MEN OF OLD
NIP OF GIN
NOT AS YET
NOT AT ALL
NOT SO BAD
NOT SO FAR
OFF TO BED
OFF TO SEA
ONE BY ONE
ONE IN SIX
ONE IN TEN
ONE IN TWO
ONE OR TWO
OUT OF BED
OUT OF GAS
OUT OF OIL
OUT OF USE
OUT TO WIN
POT OF JAM
POT OF TEA
PUT TO BED
PUT TO SEA
PUT TO USE
PUT-UP JOB
RUN TO FAT
SAD TO SAY
SEE IT ALL
SEE IT OUT
SET OF SIX
SIT IT OUT
SIX TO ONE
SON OF GOD
SON OF MAN
TEA IN BED
TEN TO ONE
TEN TO SIX
TEN TO TEN

TEN TO TWO
TIP TO WIN
TOE TO TOE
TOP TO TOE
TOT OF RUM
TRY IT OUT
TRY TO SAY
TUG OF WAR
TWO BY TWO
TWO IN ONE
TWO TO ONE

3, 3, 2

ASK FOR IT
GET RID OF
GIN AND IT
HUM AND HA
NOW FOR IT
ODD GET-UP
OFF AND ON
PAY FOR IT
RUN FOR IT
TRY FOR IT
YES AND NO
YOU AND ME

3, 5

ABU DHABI
ACT THREE
ADD WATER
AGE GROUP
AIR BRAKE
AIR CARGO
AIR FORCE
AIR RIFLE
AIR ROUTE
AIR SENSE
AIR SPACE
ALE HOUSE
ALL ALIKE
ALL ALONE
ALL ALONG
ALL CLEAR
ALL FOUND
ALL FOURS
ALL HANDS
ALL HOURS
ALL KINDS
ALL NIGHT
ALL QUIET
ALL RIGHT
ALL ROADS
ALL ROUND
ALL SORTS
ALL THERE
ALL WRONG
ANN JONES
ANN MOORE
ANY EVENT

13

ARC LIGHT	BIG MONEY	DRY COUGH
ARK ROYAL	BIG MOUTH	DRY FACTS
ART CLASS	BIG NOISE	DRY GOODS
ART LOVER	BIG PRIZE	DRY PLATE
ART PAPER	BIG PUNCH	DRY TOAST
ART TATUM	BIG SCENE	DUE NORTH
ASH GROVE	BIG SCORE	DUE SOUTH
ASK LEAVE	BIG STICK	EAR PLUGS
ASK MERCY	BIG STORY	EAT LUNCH
AVE MARIA	BIG STUFF	EGG PLANT
BAD ACTOR	BIG WHEEL	EGG SALAD
BAD APPLE	BIG WORDS	EGG SPOON
BAD BLOOD	BIT FISHY	EGG TIMER
BAD BOOKS	BIT THICK	EGG WHITE
BAD CAUSE	BOB DYLAN	ELK HOUND
BAD COUGH	BOB MAJOR	EVA BRAUN
BAD DEBTS	BOB MINOR	EYE PATCH
BAD DREAM	BOG GRASS	FAN DANCE
BAD FAIRY	BOW BELLS	FAR ABOVE
BAD FAITH	BOY SCOUT	FAR AHEAD
BAD GRACE	BUN FIGHT	FAR APART
BAD HABIT	BUN PENNY	FAR NORTH
BAD HEART	BUS DEPOT	FAR SOUTH
BAD LANDS	BUS QUEUE	FAT WOMAN
BAD LIGHT	BUY CHEAP	FEW WORDS
BAD LOSER	CAR CRASH	FIT STATE
BAD MARKS	CAR FERRY	FLY ABOUT
BAD MATCH	CAR RALLY	FLY PAPER
BAD MIXER	CAR SMASH	FLY SOUTH
BAD MONEY	CON AMORE	FOB WATCH
BAD PATCH	CON ANIMA	FOG BOUND
BAD PENNY	CRY ALOUD	FOR KEEPS
BAD PRESS	CRY HAVOC	FOR KICKS
BAD SHAPE	CRY SHAME	FOR SHAME
BAD SIGHT	CUP FINAL	FOR SHORT
BAD SMELL	CUP HANDS	FUR STOLE
BAD SPORT	CUP MATCH	FUR TRADE
BAD START	CUT GLASS	GAD ABOUT
BAD STATE	CUT GRASS	GAS BOARD
BAD STORM	CUT LOOSE	GAS METER
BAD TASTE	CUT PRICE	GAS PLANT
BAD TEETH	CUT SHORT	GAS STOVE
BAD THING	DAY AFTER	GAY PARTY
BAD TIMES	DAY DREAM	GAY SPARK
BAD TOOTH	DAY NURSE	GET ABOUT
BAY HORSE	DAY SHIFT	GET AHEAD
BAY TREES	DID WRONG	GET ALONG
BED LINEN	DIE HAPPY	GET ANGRY
BEE STING	DIE YOUNG	GET BELOW
BEG LEAVE	DIM LIGHT	GET CROSS
BEN NEVIS	DOG FIGHT	GET DIRTY
BIG APPLE	DOG LATIN	GET DRUNK
BIG BREAK	DOG LOVER	GET FRESH
BIG BULLY	DOG POUND	GET GOING
BIG CHIEF	DOG TRACK	GET IDEAS
BIG CROWD	DOG WATCH	GET LUCKY
BIG FIGHT	DON REVIE	GET OLDER
BIG HEART	DOW JONES	GET READY
BIG HOUSE	DRY BONES	GET ROUGH
BIG IDEAS	DRY BREAD	GET ROUND
BIG MATCH	DRY CLEAN	GET STALE

GET STUCK	JIM LAKER	NEW BIRTH
GET THERE	JOE DAVIS	NEW BLOOD
GET TIRED	JOE LOUIS	NEW BRAND
GET TOUGH	KEY ISSUE	NEW BREAD
GET UPSET	KEY POINT	NEW BROOM
GET WORSE	KID GLOVE	NEW CROSS
GIN RUMMY	KIP KEINO	NEW DELHI
GIN SLING	LAS VEGAS	NEW DRESS
GOD BLESS	LAW AGENT	NEW HAVEN
GOD SPEED	LAW COURT	NEW HEART
GUN FIGHT	LAW LORDS	NEW HOUSE
GUN METAL	LAY ABOUT	NEW IDEAS
GYM DRESS	LAY ASIDE	NEW ISSUE
GYM SHOES	LAY CLAIM	NEW LAMPS
HAD WORDS	LAY CLERK	NEW LIGHT
HAM ACTOR	LAY JUDGE	NEW MODEL
HAM SALAD	LAY SIEGE	NEW NOVEL
HAT TRICK	LAY WASTE	NEW OWNER
HAY FEVER	LEE SHORE	NEW PENCE
HEN HOUSE	LEG BREAK	NEW PENNY
HEN PARTY	LEG DRIVE	NEW SHOES
HER GRACE	LEG STUMP	NEW START
HIP FLASK	LET ALONE	NEW STYLE
HIS GRACE	LET BLOOD	NEW TRICK
HOP ALONG	LET LOOSE	NEW WOMAN
HOT BATHS	LET SLIDE	NEW WORLD
HOT BLOOD	LEW GRADE	NOT HEARD
HOT CAKES	LIE ABOUT	NOT LEAST
HOT COALS	LIE AWAKE	NOT OFTEN
HOT CURRY	LIE DOGGO	NOT QUITE
HOT DRINK	LIE STILL	NOT THERE
HOT FLUSH	LIP SALVE	NOT TODAY
HOT GOODS	LOG CABIN	NOT VALID
HOT LUNCH	LOW BIRTH	NYE BEVAN
HOT MONEY	LOW CLASS	OAK CHEST
HOT MUSIC	LOW CLOUD	OAK RIDGE
HOT NIGHT	LOW GRADE	ODD SIGHT
HOT PLATE	LOW JOINT	ODD TRICK
HOT PUNCH	LOW MARKS	OFF BREAK
HOT SPELL	LOW PITCH	OFF DRIVE
HOT STOVE	LOW PRICE	OFF GUARD
HOT STUFF	LOW RATES	OFF PITCH
HOT TOAST	LOW SCORE	OFF SALES
HOT TODDY	LOW SOUND	OFF STAGE
HOT WATER	LOW SPEED	OFF STUMP
IAN SMITH	LOW VOICE	OIL GAUGE
ICE CREAM	LOW WAGES	OIL SLICK
ICY BLAST	LOW WATER	OIL STOVE
ICY PATCH	LUG ABOUT	OLD BONES
ICY SMILE	MAN ALIVE	OLD CROCK
ICY STARE	MAN POWER	OLD CRONY
ICY WATER	MAX BOYCE	OLD DRESS
ILL GRACE	MAY QUEEN	OLD DUTCH
INK STAIN	MON REPOS	OLD FLAME
ITS MAGIC	MOT JUSTE	OLD FOGEY
JAM TARTS	MRS.MILLS	OLD FOLKS
JAM TIGHT	NED KELLY	OLD FRUIT
JAN KODES	NET PRICE	OLD GLORY
JET BLACK	NET SALES	OLD GOBBO
JET PLANE	NET VALUE	OLD GUARD
JIM CLARK	NEW BALLS	OLD HABIT

15

OLD HANDS	PIN TABLE	SEA NYMPH
OLD HARRY	POP GROUP	SEA POWER
OLD HAUNT	POP MUSIC	SEA ROUTE
OLD SARUM	POT BLACK	SEA SCOUT
OLD SCORE	POT PLANT	SEA SNAIL
OLD SHOES	POT ROAST	SEA SPRAY
OLD SONGS	PRO FORMA	SEA WATER
OLD STORY	PUB CRAWL	SEE ABOUT
OLD STYLE	PUB GAMES	SEE AHEAD
OLD THING	PUB HOURS	SEE ROUND
OLD TIMER	PUT ABOUT	SEE STARS
OLD TIMES	PUT ASIDE	SET ABOUT
OLD TRICK	PUT FIRST	SET APART
OLD WITCH	PUT RIGHT	SET ASIDE
OLD WOMAN	QUO VADIS	SET FORTH
OLD WORLD	RAG TRADE	SET IDEAS
ONE DOZEN	RAW STEAK	SET LOOSE
ONE FIFTH	RED BERET	SET LUNCH
ONE GROSS	RED BIDDY	SET PIECE
ONE HEART	RED BLOOD	SET POINT
ONE LITRE	RED BRICK	SET RIGHT
ONE METRE	RED CHINA	SET SMILE
ONE MONTH	RED CROSS	SEX RATIO
ONE NINTH	RED DEVIL	SHY SMILE
ONE OUNCE	RED FACES	SHY THING
ONE OWNER	RED LIGHT	SHY WOMAN
ONE PENNY	RED MAPLE	SID JAMES
ONE PIECE	RED OCHRE	SIT ABOUT
ONE POINT	RED PAINT	SIT ERECT
ONE POUND	RED PERIL	SIT STILL
ONE QUART	RED QUEEN	SIT TIGHT
ONE ROUND	RED RIVER	SIX CLUBS
ONE SCORE	RED ROSES	SIX DOZEN
ONE SIXTH	RED SAILS	SIX GROSS
ONE SPADE	RED SHIRT	SIX HOURS
ONE TENTH	RED SHOES	SIX KILOS
ONE THIRD	RED STAMP	SIX MILES
ONE TRICK	RED STRIP	SIX PENCE
ONE VERSE	ROD LAVER	SIX PINTS
ONE VOICE	RUB NOSES	SIX TIMES
ONE WHEEL	RUM PUNCH	SIX WEEKS
OUR TIMES	RUN ABOUT	SIX YARDS
OWE MONEY	RUN AFTER	SIX YEARS
PAR AVION	RUN AHEAD	SKI SLOPE
PAR VALUE	RUN ALONG	SKY PILOT
PAY CLAIM	RUN AMUCK	SOB STORY
PAY CORPS	RUN ROUND	SOB STUFF
PAY COSTS	RUN SHORT	SRI LANKA
PAY EXTRA	RUY LOPEZ	SUM TOTAL
PAY OFFER	RYE BREAD	SUN PORCH
PAY PAUSE	SAD HEART	TAG ALONG
PAY PHONE	SAD SIGHT	TAJ MAHAL
PAY ROUND	SAD STORY	TAP DANCE
PAY SHEET	SAM COOKE	TAP WATER
PAY WAGES	SAM COSTA	TAX DODGE
PEA GREEN	SAN DIEGO	TAX EXILE
PEP PILLS	SAY GRACE	TAX HAVEN
PER ANNUM	SEA FEVER	TAX POINT
PER MONTH	SEA FLOOR	TEA BREAK
PIG SWILL	SEA GREEN	TEA CADDY
PIN MONEY	SEA LEVEL	TEA PARTY

TEA TABLE	THE KINKS	TOP BRASS
TED HEATH	THE KORAN	TOP FLOOR
TEN CENTS	THE LIMIT	TOP LAYER
TEN DOZEN	THE LORDS	TOP LEVEL
TEN GROSS	THE LOSER	TOP MARKS
TEN HOURS	THE MAFIA	TOP NOTCH
TEN KILOS	THE MEDIA	TOP PLACE
TEN MARKS	THE MOORS	TOP PRICE
TEN MILES	THE MUSES	TOP PRIZE
TEN PARTS	THE NADIR	TOP SCORE
TEN PENCE	THE NORTH	TOP SPEED
TEN SCORE	THE OCEAN	TOP TABLE
TEN TIMES	THE OTHER	TOY TRAIN
TEN WEEKS	THE PANEL	TRY AGAIN
TEN YEARS	THE POINT	TWO CARDS
THE ANDES	THE POOLS	TWO CLUBS
THE ASHES	THE PRESS	TWO DOZEN
THE BENCH	THE QUEEN	TWO EVILS
THE BENDS	THE RACES	TWO GROSS
THE BIBLE	THE RAINS	TWO HANDS
THE BIRDS	THE RHINE	TWO HEADS
THE BLIND	THE ROPES	TWO HOURS
THE BLITZ	THE SHEIK	TWO JACKS
THE BLUES	THE SHORE	TWO KILOS
THE BOOZE	THE SOMME	TWO KINGS
THE BRIDE	THE SOUTH	TWO LUMPS
THE BRINY	THE SPURS	TWO MILES
THE BRONX	THE STAGE	TWO MINDS
THE CHAIR	THE STARS	TWO PAGES
THE CHASE	THE STING	TWO PAIRS
THE CONGO	THE SUDAN	TWO PARTS
THE COUNT	THE SWORD	TWO PENCE
THE CREED	THE TANGO	TWO PINTS
THE CROWN	THE TENTH	TWO PUTTS
THE DALES	THE THING	TWO SCORE
THE DERBY	THE THIRD	TWO SIDES
THE DEUCE	THE TIMES	TWO TIMER
THE DEVIL	THE TOWER	TWO TIMES
THE DOWNS	THE TRIAL	TWO WEEKS
THE EARTH	THE TWIST	TWO WIVES
THE ÉLITE	THE USUAL	TWO WORDS
THE ENEMY	THE VOLGA	TWO YARDS
THE FACTS	THE WALTZ	TWO YEARS
THE FATES	THE WEALD	USE FORCE
THE FENCE	THE WELSH	VAN ALLEN
THE FIELD	THE WORKS	VIN BLANC
THE FIFTH	THE WORLD	VIN ROUGE
THE FIRST	THE WORST	WAR CRIME
THE FLEET	TIA MARIA	WAR DANCE
THE FLOOD	TIN LIZZY	WAR GRAVE
THE FRONT	TIN MINER	WAR HORSE
THE GOODS	TOM BROWN	WAR LORDS
THE GOONS	TOM JONES	WAR PAINT
THE GRAVE	TOM THUMB	WAR YEARS
THE GROOM	TOM WALLS	WAT TYLER
THE HAGUE	TOO EARLY	WAX MERRY
THE HAVES	TOO QUICK	WAX MODEL
THE IDEAL	TOO SMALL	WAY ABOVE
THE IDIOT	TOO SMART	WAY AHEAD
THE IRISH	TOO STEEP	WEE HOURS
THE JOKER	TOO YOUNG	WET NURSE

WET PAINT
WET SHEET
WET SPELL
WHY WORRY?
WIN MONEY
WRY SMILE
YET AGAIN

4, 1, 3

CALL A CAB
CARE A LOT
CAST A NET
DRAW A GUN
FILL A GAP
FIND A JOB
FIND A WAY
GIVE A FIG
GIVE A TIP
GIVE A TUG
HAIL A BUS
HAIL A CAB
HALF A CUP
HALF A MAN
HALF A TON
HAVE A BET
HAVE A FAG
HAVE A FIT
HAVE A JOB
HAVE A KIP
HAVE A NAP
HAVE A ROW
HAVE A TRY
HIRE A CAB
HIRE A CAR
JUST A BIT
JUST A FEW
JUST A KID
JUST A SEC
KEEP A DOG
LAND A JOB
LIKE A MAN
LIVE A LIE
LOSE A LEG
MAKE A BET
MAKE A BID
MAKE A BOW
MAKE A HIT
MAKE A LAW
MAKE A PUN
MAKE A VOW
MANY A ONE
NAIL A LIE
ONCE A DAY
ONLY A FEW
PACK A GUN
PASS A LAW
SHOW A LEG
SOLD A PUP
SPIN A WEB
STOP A GAP

TAKE A BET
TAKE A BOW
TAKE A BUS
TAKE A CAB
TAKE A CUT
TAKE A JOB
TAKE A NAP
TAKE A PEW
TAKE A TIP
TAKE A VOW
TALK A LOT
TELL A FIB
TELL A LIE
TOTE A GUN
WAIT A BIT
WANT A LOT

4, 2, 2

BANK ON IT
COME UP TO
FACE UP TO
FEEL UP TO
FELL AN OX
FELO DE SE
FREE TO GO
FULL OF GO
GIVE IN TO
GIVE IT UP
HAND IT IN
HANG ON TO
HARD AT IT
HERE WE GO
HOLD ON TO
JACK IT IN
JUMP AT IT
JUMP TO IT
KEEP AT IT
KEEP IT IN
KEEP IT UP
LAST TO GO
LEAD UP TO
LIVE IT UP
LIVE UP TO
LOOK IT UP
LOOK UP TO
MADE IT UP
MAKE IT UP
MAKE UP TO
OVER WE GO
PACK IT IN
PACK IT UP
PASS IT ON
PICK IT UP
PILE IT ON
PLAY UP TO
READ UP ON
STEP ON IT
STIR IT UP
TAKE IT IN
TAKE IT UP

TEAR IT UP
THIS IS IT
TIME IS UP
TIME TO GO
TURN IT IN
TURN IT ON
TURN IT UP
USED TO IT
WELL TO DO
WELL UP IN
WHAT IS IT?
WHAT OF IT?
WRAP IT UP

4, 4

ACES HIGH
ACID BATH
ACID DROP
ACID TEST
ADAM BEDE
AGED LION
ALAN BALL
ALAN LADD
ALLS FAIR
ALLS WELL
ALTO CLEF
ANDY CAPP
ANNA FORD
ANTS NEST
ARCH LOOK
ARMS RACE
ARMY CAMP
ARMY LIFE
ARMY LIST
ARMY TYPE
ARTY TYPE
ARUM LILY
ATOM BOMB
AWAY GAME
AWAY TEAM
BABE RUTH
BABY CARE
BABY DOLL
BABY FACE
BABY FOOD
BABY GIRL
BABY LOVE
BABY SHOW
BABY TALK
BABY WEAR
BACK AWAY
BACK DOOR
BACK DOWN
BACK FOUR
BACK PAGE
BACK ROOM
BACK SEAT
BACK SOON
BACK SPIN
BACK STEP

BACK YARD	BITE INTO	CAKE SHOP
BALD HEAD	BLOW AWAY	CALF LOVE
BALD PATE	BLOW COLD	CALL BACK
BALI BALI	BLOW DOWN	CALL GIRL
BALL BOYS	BLOW HARD	CALL OVER
BALL GAME	BLOW OVER	CALL TIME
BANK GIRO	BLUE BIRD	CALL UPON
BANK LOAN	BLUE BOOK	CALM DOWN
BANK NOTE	BLUE CHIP	CAME BACK
BANK RAID	BLUE COAT	CAME DOWN
BANK RATE	BLUE EYES	CAMP FIRE
BARE FEET	BLUE FILM	CAMP SITE
BARE HEAD	BLUE FUNK	CAPE HORN
BARE LEGS	BLUE JOHN	CAPE TOWN
BARE NECK	BLUE JOKE	CARD GAME
BARN DOOR	BLUE LAMP	CARD VOTE
BASE COIN	BLUE MOON	CART AWAY
BASE LINE	BLUE NILE	CASE BOOK
BASS CLEF	BLUE STAR	CASH BOOK
BASS DRUM	BLUE SUIT	CASH DOWN
BASS HORN	BOAR HUNT	CASH SALE
BASS NOTE	BOAT CLUB	CAST AWAY
BASS SOLO	BOAT RACE	CAST DICE
BATH CHAP	BOAT SHOW	CAST IRON
BATH CUBE	BODE EVIL	CAST LOTS
BATH ROBE	BODE WELL	CATS EYES
BATH SOAP	BODY BLOW	CATS HOME
BEAR ARMS	BODY HEAT	CATS TAIL
BEAR DOWN	BOIL AWAY	CHAT SHOW
BEAR LEFT	BOIL DOWN	CHEW OVER
BEAR WITH	BOIL OVER	CHEZ NOUS
BEAT BACK	BOLD DEED	CHIP SHOT
BEAT DOWN	BOLD FACE	CHOP DOWN
BEAT TIME	BOLD MOVE	CHOP SUEY
BEAU NASH	BOLD TYPE	CHOW MEIN
BEEF STEW	BOMB SITE	CITY DESK
BEER HALL	BONA FIDE	CITY GENT
BELL TENT	BONE IDLE	CITY HALL
BEND DOWN	BOOK CLUB	CITY WALL
BEND OVER	BOOK ENDS	CLAY PIPE
BEST BACK	BOOK MARK	CLUB LAND
BEST CUTS	BOOK SHOP	COAL DUST
BEST DAYS	BOOM TOWN	COAL FIRE
BEST EVER	BOOT LACE	COAL MINE
BEST LOVE	BORN DEAD	COAL SEAM
BEST PART	BORN FREE	COCA COLA
BEST ROOM	BORN RICH	CODE NAME
BEST SUIT	BOSS EYED	CODE WORD
BEST TEAM	BOTH ENDS	COKE FIRE
BEST TOGS	BOTH WAYS	COLD BATH
BEST WINE	BOWL OVER	COLD BEEF
BETA PLUS	BOYS CLUB	COLD CURE
BETA RAYS	BRIM OVER	COLD DISH
BIKE RACE	BULL NECK	COLD FEET
BIND OVER	BUMP INTO	COLD FISH
BIRD BATH	BURN DOWN	COLD FOOD
BIRD CAGE	BUSH FIRE	COLD LAMB
BIRD CALL	BUSY TIME	COLD MEAL
BIRD LIFE	BUSY TOWN	COLD MEAT
BIRD SEED	BUZZ BOMB	COLD MILK
BIRD SONG	CAFÉ NOIR	COLD PORK

COLD ROOM	DEAD SLOW	DUTY PAID
COLD SNAP	DEAD SURE	DYED HAIR
COLD SORE	DEAD WOOD	EARN MORE
COLD WAVE	DEAF EARS	EAST SIDE
COLD WIND	DEAF MUTE	EAST WIND
COME BACK	DEAL WITH	EAST WING
COME DOWN	DEAR DEAR	EASY CLUE
COME HERE	DEAR SIRS	EASY COME
COME HOME	DEED POLL	EASY GAME
COME LAST	DEEP BASS	EASY LIFE
COME NEAR	DEEP BLUE	EASY MIND
COME NEXT	DEEP COMA	EASY PACE
COME OVER	DEEP DOWN	EASY PREY
COME SOON	DEEP NOTE	EASY TASK
COME TRUE	DEEP SIGH	EASY TIME
COME UPON	DEEP SNOW	ECCE HOMO
COOL DOWN	DEEP TONE	EDGE TOOL
COOL FISH	DEER PARK	EPIC FILM
COOL HEAD	DESK WORK	EPIC POEM
COPE WITH	DICE GAME	EPIC POET
COPY DOWN	DIED AWAY	ERIC IDLE
CORN LAWS	DINE LATE	ETON CROP
COSY CHAT	DIRE NEED	ETON SUIT
COSY NOOK	DOCK LEAF	EVEN DATE
COWS MILK	DOGS HOME	EVEN KEEL
CRAP GAME	DOGS LIFE	EVEN MORE
CREW NECK	DOGS TAIL	EVEN PACE
CROW OVER	DONT CARE	EVEN TIME
CUBE ROOT	DONT KNOW	EVIL DEED
CUTS DEAD	DONT WALK	EVIL HOUR
DAMP DOWN	DOVE GREY	EVIL OMEN
DARK AGES	DOWN BEAT	EXIT LINE
DARK BLUE	DOWN HERE	EXIT SIGN
DARK DEED	DOWN TOWN	EXIT VISA
DARK GREY	DOWN WIND	EYES DOWN
DARK HAIR	DRAG DOWN	EYES LEFT
DARK LADY	DRAG HUNT	FACE CARD
DARK ROOM	DRAW AWAY	FACE DOWN
DARK SIDE	DRAW BACK	FACE EAST
DARK SKIN	DRAW LOTS	FACE LEFT
DARK SUIT	DRAW NEAR	FACE LIFT
DASH AWAY	DRAW NIGH	FACE PACK
DATE LINE	DRAW REIN	FACE RUIN
DATE PALM	DRIP FEED	FACE WEST
DAVY LAMP	DROP BACK	FADE AWAY
DAYS WORK	DROP DEAD	FAIR COPY
DEAD BALL	DROP DOWN	FAIR DEAL
DEAD BEAT	DROP GOAL	FAIR GAME
DEAD BODY	DROP KICK	FAIR HAIR
DEAD CALM	DRUM SOLO	FAIR HAND
DEAD CERT	DUCK POND	FAIR ISLE
DEAD DUCK	DUCK SOUP	FAIR LADY
DEAD EASY	DULL ACHE	FAIR MAID
DEAD FLAT	DULL PAIN	FAIR PLAY
DEAD HALT	DULL THUD	FAIR RENT
DEAD HAND	DULL WORK	FAIR SKIN
DEAD HEAT	DUMB SHOW	FAIR SWOP
DEAD KEEN	DUST BOWL	FAIR WAGE
DEAD LEAF	DUST CART	FAIR WIND
DEAD LOSS	DUTY CALL	FALL AWAY
DEAD SHOT	DUTY FREE	FALL BACK

FALL DOWN	FIRM GRIP	FOUR TENS
FALL FLAT	FIRM HAND	FOUR TWOS
FALL FOUL	FIRM HOLD	FOWL PEST
FALL OVER	FIRM HOPE	FREE BEER
FALL SICK	FIRM LINE	FREE COPY
FARM EGGS	FISH CAKE	FREE FALL
FARM HAND	FISH FORK	FREE FLOW
FARM LAND	FISH POND	FREE GIFT
FAST BALL	FISH SHOP	FREE HAND
FAST LANE	FISH TANK	FREE KICK
FAST PACE	FIVE DAYS	FREE LOVE
FAST RACE	FIVE DEEP	FREE MEAL
FAST TIME	FIVE FEET	FREE MILK
FAST WORK	FIVE PAST	FREE PASS
FEED WELL	FIVE QUID	FREE PLAY
FEEL BLUE	FIVE SETS	FREE PORT
FEEL COLD	FIVE STAR	FREE RIDE
FEEL FINE	FLAG DOWN	FREE SEAT
FEEL GOOD	FLAG POLE	FREE TIME
FEEL LAZY	FLAN CASE	FREE VOTE
FEEL LIKE	FLAT FEET	FREE WEST
FEEL PAIN	FLAT FISH	FREE WILL
FEEL SAFE	FLAT IRON	FROM AFAR
FEEL SICK	FLAT NOSE	FUEL BILL
FEEL SORE	FLAT NOTE	FUEL CELL
FEEL SURE	FLAT RACE	FUEL TANK
FEEL WARM	FLAT RATE	FULL BACK
FEEL WELL	FLAT ROOF	FULL BLUE
FELL AWAY	FLAT SPIN	FULL FACE
FELL DOWN	FLAT TYRE	FULL FARE
FELL FLAT	FLEA BITE	FULL LIFE
FEME SOLE	FLEE FROM	FULL LOAD
FILE AWAY	FLEW AWAY	FULL MEAL
FILE DOWN	FLIP SIDE	FULL MOON
FILE PAST	SLOW OVER	FULL PELT
FILM BUFF	FOLD BACK	FULL SAIL
FILM CLUB	FOLD DOWN	FULL SIZE
FILM CREW	FOLD OVER	FULL STOP
FILM IDOL	FOLK CLUB	FULL TILT
FILM SHOW	FOLK HERO	FULL TIME
FILM STAR	FOLK LORE	FULL TOSS
FIND ROOM	FOLK SONG	FULL WELL
FIND TIME	FOLK TALE	FUSE WIRE
FINE AIRS	FOND HOPE	GAIN TIME
FINE ARTS	FOOT RACE	GAME BIRD
FINE CHAP	FORT KNOX	GAME FISH
FINE EDGE	FOUL BLOW	GAME LAWS
FINE FARE	FOUL DEED	GANG SHOW
FINE FORM	FOUL MOOD	GAVE AWAY
FINE GOLD	FOUL PLAY	GAVE BACK
FINE LADY	FOUR ACES	GETS AWAY
FINE MESS	FOUR ACTS	GIFT SHOP
FINE RAIN	FOUR AWAY	GIRL TALK
FINE TIME	FOUR DAYS	GIVE AWAY
FINE VIEW	FOUR DEEP	GIVE BACK
FIRE AWAY	FOUR FEET	GIVE HEAD
FIRE BOMB	FOUR LEGS	GIVE ODDS
FIRE EXIT	FOUR QUID	GIVE OVER
FIRE RISK	FOUR RUNS	GIVE VENT
FIRE UPON	FOUR SETS	GLAD NEWS
FIRM DATE	FOUR STAR	GLAD RAGS

GLEE CLUB	GOOD NICK	HAND TOOL
GLUM FACE	GOOD OMEN	HANG BACK
GNAT BITE	GOOD PALS	HANG DOWN
GNAW AWAY	GOOD PLAN	HANG FIRE
GOAL KICK	GOOD PLAY	HANG OVER
GOAL LINE	GOOD ROAD	HARD BALL
GODS ACRE	GOOD SEAT	HARD BLOW
GODS WILL	GOOD SHOT	HARD CASE
GOES DOWN	GOOD SHOW	HARD CASH
GOES HOME	GOOD SIGN	HARD CORE
GOES SLOW	GOOD SOIL	HARD DRUG
GOES WITH	GOOD SORT	HARD FACT
GOLD COIN	GOOD TIME	HARD GAME
GOLD DUST	GOOD TRIM	HARD HEAD
GOLD FOIL	GOOD TURN	HARD LIFE
GOLD LACE	GOOD TYPE	HARD LINE
GOLD LAMÉ	GOOD VIEW	HARD LOOK
GOLD LEAF	GOOD WAGE	HARD LUCK
GOLD MINE	GOOD WIFE	HARD RAIN
GOLD RING	GOOD WILL	HARD ROAD
GOLD RUSH	GOOD WINE	HARD SEAT
GOLD VEIN	GOOD WORD	HARD SELL
GOLD WIRE	GOOD WORK	HARD SKIN
GOLF BALL	GOOD YARN	HARD TACK
GOLF CLUB	GOON SHOW	HARD TASK
GONE AWAY	GRAF SPEE	HARD TIME
GONE DOWN	GRAM ATOM	HARD UPON
GOOD BOOK	GREY COAT	HARD WORD
GOOD CASE	GREY HAIR	HARD WORK
GOOD CAST	GREY MARE	HARK BACK
GOOD CHAP	GREY SUIT	HAUL AWAY
GOOD COOK	GRIM FACE	HAVE LIFE
GOOD CROP	GRIM TASK	HAVE PITY
GOOD DEAL	GRIM VIEW	HAVE PUPS
GOOD DEED	GRIP HARD	HEAD BACK
GOOD FILM	GROW COLD	HEAD CASE
GOOD FOLK	GROW DARK	HEAD COOK
GOOD FOOD	GROW PALE	HEAD GIRL
GOOD FORM	GROW RICH	HEAD WIND
GOOD GAME	GROW WEAK	HEAR HEAR
GOOD GIRL	GROW WILD	HEAT SPOT
GOOD HAND	GULP DOWN	HEAT WAVE
GOOD HAUL	HAIL MARY	HEEL OVER
GOOD HOPE	HAIR COMB	HELD BACK
GOOD HOST	HALF BLUE	HELD OVER
GOOD IDEA	HALF DEAD	HELP DOWN
GOOD JOKE	HALF EACH	HENS EGGS
GOOD KING	HALF FARE	HERE GOES
GOOD LADY	HALF FULL	HIDE AWAY
GOOD LIFE	HALF HOUR	HIGH BALL
GOOD LOOK	HALF INCH	HIGH CARD
GOOD LORD	HALF MILE	HIGH COST
GOOD LUCK	HALF MOON	HIGH DIVE
GOOD MANY	HALF PAST	HIGH GEAR
GOOD MARK	HALF SIZE	HIGH HOPE
GOOD MEAL	HALF TERM	HIGH JUMP
GOOD MIND	HALF TIME	HIGH KICK
GOOD MOOD	HAND BACK	HIGH LIFE
GOOD MOVE	HAND DOWN	HIGH MASS
GOOD NAME	HAND OVER	HIGH NOON
GOOD NEWS	HAND PUMP	HIGH NOTE

HIGH RANK	IRON FIST	KING COLE
HIGH RATE	IRON GATE	KING DICK
HIGH RENT	IRON GRIP	KING JOHN
HIGH ROAD	IRON HAND	KING KONG
HIGH SEAS	IRON HEEL	KING LEAR
HIGH SPOT	IRON LUNG	KING PAIR
HIGH TIDE	IRON MASK	KING SIZE
HIGH TIME	IRON RULE	KISS CURL
HIGH WAGE	IRON SHOT	KNEE DEEP
HIGH WALL	IRON WILL	KNEE HIGH
HIGH WIND	JAIL BIRD	KNOW BEST
HIGH WIRE	JANE EYRE	KNOW WELL
HIND FEET	JAZZ BAND	LADY LUCK
HIND LEGS	JAZZ CLUB	LAID BARE
HIND PAWS	JEWS HARP	LAID FLAT
HOCK SHOP	JOAN BAEZ	LAKE ERIE
HOGS BACK	JOHN BULL	LAMB CHOP
HOLD BACK	JOHN CAGE	LAMB STEW
HOLD DEAR	JOHN DORY	LAME DUCK
HOLD DOWN	JOHN FORD	LAMP POST
HOLD FAST	JOHN KNOX	LAND AHOY
HOLD GOOD	JOHN PEEL	LAND ARMY
HOLD HARD	JOKE BOOK	LAND CRAB
HOLD OVER	JUMP BACK	LAND GIRL
HOLD SWAY	JUMP BAIL	LAND MILE
HOLY BOOK	JUMP DOWN	LANE FIVE
HOLY CITY	JUMP INTO	LANE FOUR
HOLY FEAR	JUMP OVER	LANG SYNE
HOLY LAND	JUNK SHOP	LAST CALL
HOLY LOCH	JURY LIST	LAST DAYS
HOLY WEEK	JUST GONE	LAST DROP
HOLY WRIT	JUST MISS	LAST FALL
HOME FARM	JUST ONCE	LAST GASP
HOME GAME	JUST THEN	LAST HOPE
HOME HELP	KARL MARX	LAST HOUR
HOME LIFE	KEEL OVER	LAST JULY
HOME NEWS	KEEN EDGE	LAST JUNE
HOME PARK	KEEP AWAY	LAST LEGS
HOME RULE	KEEP BACK	LAST LOVE
HOME TEAM	KEEP BUSY	LAST MOVE
HOME TOWN	KEEP CALM	LAST NAME
HONG KONG	KEEP COOL	LAST PAGE
HOSE DOWN	KEEP DOWN	LAST PINT
HOUR HAND	KEEP FINE	LAST POST
HOWL DOWN	KEEP GOAL	LAST RACE
HOWS THAT?	KEEP LEFT	LAST SEEN
HUGE SIZE	KEEP OPEN	LAST STEP
HULA GIRL	KEEP PACE	LAST TERM
HULA HOOP	KEEP SAFE	LAST TIME
HULL CITY	KEEP SHOP	LAST WEEK
HUNG JURY	KEEP TIME	LAST WILL
HUNT BALL	KEEP WARM	LAST WORD
HUNT DOWN	KEEP WELL	LAST YEAR
HYDE PARK	KEPT BUSY	LATE FALL
HYMN BOOK	KICK BACK	LATE HOUR
HYMN TUNE	KICK OVER	LATE NEWS
ICED CAKE	KILL TIME	LATE SHOW
IDÉE FIXE	KIND DEED	LATE WIFE
IDLE RICH	KIND FACE	LAZY SLOB
IDLE TALK	KIND SOUL	LEAD MINE
IRON DUKE	KIND WORD	LEAD PIPE

LEAD SHOT	LONG REST	MAIN ROAD
LEAK AWAY	LONG ROAD	MAKE CUTS
LEAN BACK	LONG ROOM	MAKE EASY
LEAN MEAT	LONG ROPE	MAKE EYES
LEAN OVER	LONG SHOT	MAKE FAST
LEAP OVER	LONG SPAN	MAKE FIRM
LEAP YEAR	LONG STOP	MAKE FREE
LEFT BACK	LONG TERM	MAKE GOOD
LEFT BANK	LONG TIME	MAKE LAWS
LEFT FLAT	LONG WAIT	MAKE LOVE
LEFT FOOT	LONG WALK	MAKE MOCK
LEFT HALF	LONG WAVE	MAKE NEWS
LEFT HAND	LONG WORD	MAKE OVER
LEFT HOME	LOOK AWAY	MAKE PLAY
LEFT HOOK	LOOK BACK	MAKE REAL
LEFT OVER	LOOK COLD	MAKE ROOM
LEFT SIDE	LOOK COOL	MAKE RUNS
LEFT TURN	LOOK DOWN	MAKE SAFE
LEFT WING	LOOK GOOD	MAKE SURE
LETS DOWN	LOOK GRIM	MAKE TIME
LIAR DICE	LOOK HERE	MALE LEAD
LIFE PEER	LOOK HURT	MANS CLUB
LIFE SPAN	LOOK INTO	MANS TALK
LIFE WORK	LOOK LEFT	MANY MORE
LIKE FURY	LOOK LIKE	MARK DOWN
LIKE HECK	LOOK OVER	MARK TIME
LIKE HELL	LOOK PALE	MARK WELL
LILY POND	LOOK SPRY	MARY LAMB
LILY PONS	LOOK UPON	MATA HARI
LION CUBS	LOOK WELL	MEAN TIME
LIVE BAIT	LOOM OVER	MEAN WELL
LIVE DOWN	LORD HOME	MEAT BALL
LIVE RAIL	LOSE FACE	MEAT DISH
LIVE SHOW	LOSE FORM	MEAT LOAF
LIVE WELL	LOSE HOPE	MEAT PIES
LIVE WIRE	LOSE TIME	MEAT SAFE
LOAN CLUB	LOST BALL	MELT AWAY
LOCH LONG	LOST HOPE	MELT DOWN
LOCH NESS	LOST LOVE	MERE IDEA
LOCK AWAY	LOST SOUL	MERE LUCK
LOIN CHOP	LOST TIME	MESS BILL
LONE WOLF	LOTS WIFE	MESS HALL
LONG ACRE	LOUD BANG	MILD BEER
LONG ARMS	LOUD PEAL	MILE RACE
LONG FACE	LOVE GAME	MILK MAID
LONG GONE	LOVE POEM	MILK PAIL
LONG HAIR	LOVE SONG	MILK RACE
LONG HAUL	LYRE BIRD	MILL HILL
LONG JUMP	MADE EASY	MILL POND
LONG LANE	MADE FAST	MINE HOST
LONG LAST	MADE OVER	MING VASE
LONG LEAD	MADE SURE	MINK COAT
LONG LEGS	MAIL BOAT	MINK FARM
LONG LIFE	MAIN CROP	MINK WRAP
LONG LINE	MAIN DECK	MOBY DICK
LONG LIST	MAIN DISH	MONA LISA
LONG LOST	MAIN HALL	MORE TIME
LONG NOSE	MAIN ITEM	MOST PART
LONG ODDS	MAIN LINE	MOTH BALL
LONG PLAY	MAIN MEAL	MOVE AWAY
LONG RACE	MAIN PART	MOVE BACK

MOVE FAST	OPEN DATE	PLAY DICE
MOVE OVER	OPEN DOOR	PLAY DOWN
MOWN DOWN	OPEN EARS	PLAY FAIR
MUCH LESS	OPEN EYES	PLAY GOLF
MUCH LIKE	OPEN FIRE	PLAY HARD
MUCH MORE	OPEN GAME	PLAY HELL
MUCH ROOM	OPEN GATE	PLAY HIGH
MUGS GAME	OPEN GOAL	PLAY HOST
MUSK ROSE	OPEN LATE	PLAY POLO
MUTE SWAN	OPEN MIND	PLAY SAFE
MYRA HESS	OPEN NOTE	PLAY SNAP
NAGS HEAD	OPEN PLAN	PLAY SUIT
NAIL DOWN	OPEN ROAD	PLAY WELL
NAIL FILE	OPEN SHOP	PLAY WITH
NAME PART	OPEN TOWN	PLUG AWAY
NAVY BLUE	OPEN VOTE	PLUM CAKE
NAVY LIST	OPEN WIDE	PLUM DUFF
NEAP TIDE	OVEN DOOR	PLUM TREE
NEAR EAST	OVER HERE	PLUS SIGN
NEAR HERE	PAGE FIVE	POLE JUMP
NEAR HOME	PAGE FOUR	POLE STAR
NEAR MISS	PAGE NINE	POLO NECK
NEAR SIDE	PAID BACK	POLO PONY
NEON SIGN	PALE BLUE	PONY RACE
NEON TUBE	PALE FACE	PONY TAIL
NEWS ITEM	PALL MALL	PONY TREK
NEWS ROOM	PALM TREE	POOL ROOM
NEXT BEST	PARK LANE	POOP DECK
NEXT DOOR	PART SONG	POOR CAST
NEXT JULY	PART TIME	POOR CHAP
NEXT JUNE	PART WITH	POOR CROP
NEXT MOVE	PASS AWAY	POOR DEAR
NEXT PAGE	PASS BACK	POOR FOLK
NEXT RACE	PASS BOOK	POOR GAME
NEXT STEP	PASS DOWN	POOR GIRL
NEXT TIME	PASS MARK	POOR JOHN
NEXT WEEK	PASS OVER	POOR LAWS
NEXT YEAR	PASS TIME	POOR PASS
NICE FACE	PAST HELP	POOR RISK
NICE MESS	PAST HOPE	POOR SHOT
NICE TIME	PAST LIFE	POOR SHOW
NICE WORK	PAST TIME	POOR SIDE
NINE DAYS	PAUL NASH	POOR SOIL
NINE ELMS	PAWN SHOP	POOR SOUL
NINE FEET	PEAK FORM	POOR VIEW
NINE QUID	PEAK HOUR	POOR WORK
NONE LEFT	PEAR DROP	POPE JOHN
NOTA BENE	PEAR TREE	POPE PAUL
NOTE BOOK	PEAT FIRE	POPE PIUS
NOTE DOWN	PEAT MOSS	PORE OVER
NOTE WELL	PEEP SHOW	PORK CHOP
ONCE MORE	PEER GYNT	PORT SAID
ONCE ONLY	PINE CONE	PORT SIDE
ONCE OVER	PINE TREE	PORT VALE
ONES DUTY	PINK LADY	PORT WINE
ONES WORD	PINT SIZE	POST CODE
ONLY HOPE	PIPE DOWN	POST FREE
ONLY JUST	PLAN WELL	POST PAID
ONLY ONCE	PLAY AWAY	PREY UPON
OPEN ARMS	PLAY BACK	PRIX FIXE
OPEN BOOK	PLAY BALL	PULL BACK

PULL DOWN	RISE LATE	SEND HOME
PULL HARD	ROAD FUND	SEND WORD
PULL OVER	ROAD RACE	SENT DOWN
PULL RANK	ROAD SHOW	SETS FREE
PUNK ROCK	ROAD SIGN	SHIN BONE
PURE GOLD	ROAD TEST	SHIP AHOY
PURE SILK	ROCK CAKE	SHIP OARS
PURE WOOL	ROCK HARD	SHOE SHOP
PUSH AWAY	ROCK SALT	SHOO AWAY
PUSH BACK	ROLL BACK	SHOP GIRL
PUSH DOWN	ROLL CALL	SHOT DEAD
PUSH HARD	ROLL OVER	SHOT DOWN
PUSH OVER	ROMP HOME	SHOT SILK
PUSH PAST	ROOF RACK	SHOW BOAT
QUIT RENT	ROOT BEER	SHOW CASE
QUIZ GAME	ROOT CROP	SHOW DOWN
QUIZ SHOW	ROSE BOWL	SHOW FEAR
RAIL FARE	ROSE BUSH	SHOW GIRL
RAKE OVER	ROSE PINK	SHOW OVER
RANK HIGH	ROSY GLOW	SHOW PITY
RARA AVIS	RUBY LIPS	SHUT DOWN
RARE BIRD	RUBY PORT	SICK JOKE
RARE BOOK	RUDE WORD	SICK LIST
RARE COIN	RUNS DOWN	SICK ROOM
RARE GIFT	RUSH AWAY	SIDE ARMS
RATS TAIL	RUSH HOUR	SIDE DISH
READ WELL	RUSH INTO	SIDE DOOR
REAL GOLD	RUSH MATS	SIDE DRUM
REAL LIFE	SACK RACE	SIDE LINE
REAL SILK	SAFE SEAT	SIDE ROAD
REAR EXIT	SAIL AWAY	SIDE SHOW
REAR RANK	SALE ROOM	SIDE WIND
REAR VIEW	SALT AWAY	SIDE WITH
REEF KNOT	SALT BEEF	SIGN AWAY
RELY UPON	SALT LAKE	SIGN HERE
RENT ACTS	SALT MINE	SILK GOWN
RENT BOOK	SALT PORK	SINE WAVE
RENT FREE	SAME DATE	SING FLAT
RENT ROLL	SAME KIND	SING HIGH
REST CURE	SAME MIND	SING SING
REST HOME	SAME NAME	SINK DOWN
RHUM BABA	SAME TIME	SINK UNIT
RICE CROP	SAND DUNE	SINN FEIN
RICH AUNT	SANK DOWN	SITZ BATH
RICH FOLK	SAVE FACE	SIZE FIVE
RICH FOOD	SAVE TIME	SIZE FOUR
RICH HAUL	SAXE BLUE	SIZE NINE
RICH JOKE	SCOT FREE	SKIM OVER
RICH SEAM	SEAT BELT	SKIN DEEP
RICH SOIL	SEED CAKE	SKIN GAME
RICH VEIN	SEED PLOT	SKIP OVER
RICH WIFE	SEEK WORK	SLAG HEAP
RIDE AWAY	SEEM FAIR	SLAP DOWN
RIDE OVER	SEEM REAL	SLIP AWAY
RING BACK	SELF HELP	SLIP BACK
RING DOVE	SELL DEAR	SLIP INTO
RING DOWN	SELL WELL	SLIP KNOT
RING PULL	SEND AWAY	SLIP PAST
RING ROAD	SEND BACK	SLIP ROAD
RING TRUE	SEND DOWN	SLIT OPEN
RIPE CORN	SEND HELP	SLOG AWAY

SLOP	OVER	STOP	HOME	TEST	CASE
SLOW	BALL	STOP	OVER	TEST	TUBE
SLOW	BOAT	STOP	PLAY	TEXT	BOOK
SLOW	CURE	STOP	WORK	THAI	SILK
SLOW	DOWN	STOW	AWAY	THIN	BEER
SLOW	LANE	STUD	BOOK	THIN	COAT
SLOW	PACE	STUD	FARM	THIN	EDGE
SLOW	RACE	SUCH	LIKE	THIN	SKIN
SLOW	RATE	SUCK	EGGS	THIN	TIME
SLOW	TIME	SUNS	RAYS	THIS	FALL
SLUM	AREA	SURE	SHOT	THIS	SIDE
SNAP	VOTE	SWAN	LAKE	THIS	TIME
SNOW	LINE	SWAN	SONG	THIS	WEEK
SNUB	NOSE	SWAP	NEWS	THIS	YEAR
SOAP	DISH	SWAP	OVER	TICK	OVER
SOFT	BALL	SWIM	SUIT	TIDE	MARK
SOFT	DRUG	SWOP	NEWS	TIDE	OVER
SOFT	HAIR	SWOP	OVER	TIDY	MIND
SOFT	HEAD	TAIL	AWAY	TIED	DOWN
SOFT	SEAT	TAIL	COAT	TILE	ROOF
SOFT	SKIN	TAIL	WIND	TILL	ROLL
SOFT	SOAP	TAKE	AWAY	TILL	THEN
SOFT	SPOT	TAKE	BACK	TIME	BOMB
SOLE	HEIR	TAKE	BETS	TIME	CARD
SOME	GOOD	TAKE	CARE	TIME	FUSE
SOME	HOPE	TAKE	DOWN	TIME	ZONE
SOME	MORE	TAKE	FOOD	TINY	HAND
SONG	BIRD	TAKE	HEED	TINY	TOTS
SONG	BOOK	TAKE	HOLD	TONE	DEAF
SORE	BACK	TAKE	LIFE	TONE	DOWN
SORE	EYES	TAKE	NOTE	TONE	POEM
SORE	FEET	TAKE	OVER	TORY	GAIN
SORE	HEAD	TAKE	PART	TORY	VOTE
SORE	NEED	TAKE	PITY	TOSS	AWAY
SOUL	MATE	TAKE	ROOT	TOWN	HALL
SOUR	MILK	TAKE	SICK	TRAD	JAZZ
SOUR	NOTE	TAKE	SILK	TRAP	FIVE
SOYA	BEAN	TAKE	THAT	TRAP	FOUR
SOYA	MEAT	TAKE	THIS	TRIP	OVER
SPOT	CASH	TAKE	TIME	TRUE	BILL
SPOT	KICK	TAKE	TOLL	TRUE	BLUE
SPUN	GOLD	TAKE	VOWS	TRUE	COPY
SPUN	SILK	TALK	BACK	TRUE	LOVE
SPUN	YARN	TALK	DOWN	TRUE	WORD
STAG	HUNT	TALK	OVER	TUBE	FARE
STAR	PART	TALK	SHOP	TUCK	AWAY
STAR	TREK	TALL	GIRL	TUCK	SHOP
STAR	TURN	TALL	TALK	TUNA	FISH
STAY	AWAY	TALL	TREE	TURN	AWAY
STAY	CALM	TANK	TRAP	TURN	BACK
STAY	DOWN	TAPE	DECK	TURN	BLUE
STAY	HERE	TAXI	FARE	TURN	COLD
STAY	HOME	TAXI	RANK	TURN	DOWN
STAY	NEAR	TEAM	GAME	TURN	GREY
STAY	OPEN	TEAM	MATE	TURN	INTO
STEP	BACK	TEAR	DOWN	TURN	LEFT
STEP	DOWN	TEAR	OPEN	TURN	OVER
STEP	INTO	TELL	FIBS	TURN	PALE
STEP	OVER	TELL	LIES	TURN	SOFT
STOP	DEAD	TEMP	WORK	TURN	SOUR
STOP	HERE	TERM	TIME	TURN	TAIL

TURN UPON	WASH AWAY	WISE MOVE
TWIN BEDS	WASH DOWN	WITH CARE
TWIN BOYS	WASH OVER	WITH EASE
TWIN TOWN	WAVE FORM	WITH LOVE
TYPE SIZE	WAVY HAIR	WOLF CUBS
UGLY FACE	WAVY LINE	WOLF PACK
UGLY LOOK	WEAK CHIN	WONT WASH
UPAS TREE	WEAK LINK	WOOD FIRE
USED CARS	WEAK SIDE	WOOD PULP
USED HALF	WEAK SPOT	WOOL SHOP
VAIN HOPE	WEAR AWAY	WORD FORM
VAST SIZE	WEAR BLUE	WORD GAME
VEER AWAY	WEAR DOWN	WORD PLAY
VEER LEFT	WELL AWAY	WORK HARD
VERA LYNN	WELL DONE	WORK LATE
VERY BEST	WELL HELD	WORK OVER
VERY COLD	WELL MADE	WORK WELL
VERY DEAR	WELL OVER	WORN DOWN
VERY DEEP	WELL PAID	XMAS CARD
VERY FAIR	WELL READ	YALE LOCK
VERY FAST	WELL SAID	YEAR BOOK
VERY FULL	WELL USED	YOGI BEAR
VERY GOOD	WELL WELL	YORK CITY
VERY HARD	WELL WORN	YOUR DEAL
VERY HIGH	WENT AWAY	YOUR MOVE
VERY KEEN	WENT BACK	YOUR TURN
VERY KIND	WENT DOWN	ZERO HOUR
VERY LATE	WENT EAST	ZOOM LENS
VERY LAZY	WENT WELL	ZOOT SUIT
VERY MANY	WENT WEST	
VERY MUCH	WEST SIDE	5 , 1 , 2
VERY NEAR	WEST WIND	
VERY NICE	WEST WING	WORTH A GO
VERY POOR	WHAT NEXT?	
VERY RICH	WHAT TIME?	5 , 2 , 1
VERY SLOW	WHIP HAND	
VERY SOFT	WHIT WEEK	WHERE AM I ?
VERY SOON	WHOS NEXT?	
VERY TRUE	WIDE BOYS	5 , 3
VERY WARM	WIDE GULF	
VERY WELL	WIDE OPEN	ABOVE ALL
VICE KING	WIDE ROAD	ABOVE PAR
VICE RING	WIDE VIEW	ACUTE EAR
VINE LEAF	WILD BIRD	ADAMS ALE
VIVA VOCE	WILD BOAR	ADAMS RIB
VOTE DOWN	WILD DUCK	ADMIT ONE
VOTE TORY	WILD FOWL	AFTER ALL
WAGE BILL	WILD GOAT	AFTER TAX
WAGE RATE	WILD LIFE	AFTER TEA
WAIT HERE	WILD OATS	AFTER YOU
WAIT UPON	WILD ROSE	ALLEY CAT
WALK AWAY	WILD WEST	ALPHA RAY
WALK BACK	WIND SOCK	ALTER EGO
WALK INTO	WINE GUMS	ANZAC DAY
WALK OVER	WINE LAKE	APPLE JAM
WALK PAST	WINE LIST	APPLE PIE
WALL GAME	WINE SHOP	APPLE PIP
WALL SAFE	WING HALF	ASIAN FLU
WANT MORE	WIPE AWAY	ASWAN DAM
WARM COAT	WIRE MESH	AUDIT ALE
WARM MILK	WISE HEAD	BACON FAT

BAWLS

BADLY OFF	CANON LAW	DERBY DAY
BASIC PAY	CARRY OFF	DIRTY DOG
BEACH HUT	CARRY OUT	DIRTY JOB
BEADY EYE	CARVE OUT	DIRTY MAN
BEARS OUT	CATCH OUT	DIRTY SKY
BELOW PAR	CHAIN SAW	DIVAN BED
BETEL NUT	CHECK OFF	DORIS DAY
BEVIN BOY	CHECK OUT	DRAWN OUT
BILLY CAN	CHESS SET	DREAM MAN
BIRDS EGG	CHINA CUP	DRIED EGG
BLACK ART	CHINA SEA	DRIED OUT
BLACK BOX	CHINA TEA	DRIVE MAD
BLACK CAP	CHOIR BOY	DRIVE OFF
BLACK CAT	CHOKE OFF	DRIVE OUT
BLACK DOG	CHUCK OUT	DUCKS EGG
BLACK EYE	CHURN OUT	DUMMY RUN
BLACK ICE	CIDER CUP	DUTCH HOE
BLACK INK	CIGAR ASH	DYING BED
BLACK MAN	CIGAR BOX	DYING DAY
BLACK OUT	CIVIL LAW	DYING MAN
BLACK RAT	CIVIL WAR	EAGLE EYE
BLACK ROD	CLASS WAR	EARLY AGE
BLACK SEA	CLEAN CUT	EIGHT MEN
BLACK TIE	CLEAN FUN	ELDER SON
BLESS YOU	CLEAN OUT	EMPTY BOX
BLIND DOG	CLEAR DAY	EMPTY CAN
BLIND EYE	CLEAR OFF	EMPTY TIN
BLIND MAN	CLEAR OUT	ENEMY SPY
BLOCK OUT	CLEAR SKY	ENTRY FEE
BLOOD RED	CLEAR WIN	EQUAL PAY
BLUNT END	CLOCK OUT	EVADE TAX
BLURT OUT	CLOSE FIT	EVERY BIT
BONAR LAW	CLOSE RUN	EVERY DAY
BOXER DOG	CLOTH CAP	EVERY MAN
BRAND NEW	COMES OUT	EVERY ONE
BRASS HAT	COUNT OUT	EVERY WAY
BRAVE MAN	COUNT TEN	EXTRA MAN
BREAD BIN	CREAM BUN	EXTRA PAY
BREAK OFF	CREAM JUG	FALSE GOD
BREAK OUT	CREAM TEA	FALSE RIB
BRIAN RIX	CREEP OUT	FEAST DAY
BRICK RED	CREME EGG	FIELD DAY
BRING LOW	CRIED OUT	FIERY RED
BRING OFF	CROSS NOW	FIFTH DAY
BRING OUT	CROSS OFF	FIFTH ROW
BROKE OUT	CROSS OUT	FIFTH SET
BROWN ALE	CROWD OUT	FIGHT FOR
BROWN COW	CRUDE OIL	FIGHT OFF
BROWN EGG	CRUDE ORE	FIGHT SHY
BROWN OWL	CRUEL MAN	FINAL ACT
BROWN RAT	CRUEL SEA	FINAL BID
BRUSH OFF	CUSHY JOB	FIRST ACT
BULLS EYE	DAILY USE	FIRST AID
BULLY OFF	DAIRY COW	FIRST CUT
BUNNY HUG	DANNY BOY	FIRST DAY
BURNT OAK	DAVID LOW	FIRST LAP
BURNT OUT	DAVIS CUP	FIRST MAN
BURST OUT	DEATH BED	FIRST OFF
CABIN BOY	DEATH RAY	FIRST OUT
CABLE CAR	DEATH ROW	FIRST ROW
CALLS OFF	DENSE FOG	FIRST SET

FIRST TEE	HAIRY APE	LOOSE END
FLAKE OUT	HANDS OFF	LORDS DAY
FLASH GUN	HAPPY BOY	LOUIS DOR
FLESH POT	HAPPY DAY	LOVED ONE
FLING OFF	HAPPY MAN	LOWER JAW
FLING OUT	HARMS WAY	LOWER LIP
FLOUR BIN	HAZEL NUT	LUCKY BOY
FLUFF OUT	HEAVY DEW	LUCKY DAY
FLUSH OUT	HEAVY FOG	LUCKY DIP
FOGGY DAY	HEAVY SEA	LUCKY HIT
FOOLS CAP	HEAVY TAX	LUCKY JIM
FORCE OUT	HERES HOW	LUCKY MAN
FOUND OUT	HERNE BAY	LUCKY WIN
FREAK OUT	HIRED CAR	LYNCH LAW
FRESH AIR	HIRED GUN	MAGIC BOX
FRESH EGG	HIRED MAN	MAGIC EYE
FRESH POT	HIRED OUT	MAJOR KEY
FRIED EGG	HOLED OUT	MAJOR WAR
FRONT MAN	HONEY BEE	MARCH OFF
FRONT PAW	HONEY POT	MARRY OFF
FRONT ROW	HOUND DOG	MARSH GAS
FRUIT BAT	HOUSE DOG	MAXIM GUN
FRUIT GUM	HOUSE FLY	MERRY MEN
FRUIT PIE	HURRY OFF	METAL BOX
FUNNY HAT	HURRY OUT	MILES OUT
FUNNY MAN	IDEAS MAN	MILKY WAY
GAMMA RAY	INFRA DIG	MINCE PIE
GAMMY LEG	INNER EAR	MINDS EYE
GLASS EYE	INNER MAN	MINOR KEY
GOING FAR	IRISH ELK	MINUS ONE
GOING MAD	IRISH JIG	MINUS TEN
GOING OUT	IRISH SEA	MINUS TWO
GRADE ONE	JAMES FOX	MIXED BAG
GRADE TWO	KNOCK OFF	MODEL CAR
GRAND SUM	KNOCK OUT	MORAL LAW
GRAYS INN	LANDS END	MOTOR OIL
GREAT AGE	LARGE CAR	MOURN FOR
GREAT AUK	LARGE EGG	MUSIC BOX
GREAT DAY	LARGE GIN	NAKED APE
GREAT FUN	LARGE SUM	NAKED EYE
GREAT HIT	LASER GUN	NAKED MAN
GREAT JOB	LAUGH OFF	NATAL DAY
GREAT JOY	LEAST BIT	NAVAL GUN
GREAT MAN	LEAVE OFF	NAVAL MAN
GREAT TIT	LEAVE OUT	NEWLY WED
GREAT WAR	LEGAL AID	NIGHT AIR
GREAT WIT	LEMON PIE	NIGHT CAP
GREEK ART	LEMON TEA	NIGHT OFF
GREEK GOD	LEVEL OFF	NIGHT OUT
GREEK URN	LEVEL OUT	NIGHT OWL
GREEN BAY	LEWIS GUN	NIGHT SKY
GREEN INK	LIGHT ALE	NINTH DAY
GREEN MAN	LIGHT RED	NOAHS ARK
GREEN TEA	LIONS DEN	NOBLE ART
GREEN TIE	LOCAL BOY	NORTH END
GROPE FOR	LOCAL INN	NORTH SEA
GROWN MAN	LOCAL LAW	OCEAN BED
GUARD DOG	LOCAL PUB	OLIVE OIL
GUESS WHO	LOCAL RAG	OPERA HAT
GUIDE DOG	LOOKS OUT	OPIUM DEN
GUNGA DIN	LOOSE BOX	ORDER OFF

ORDER OUT	RIGHT OFF	SIEGE GUN
ORDER TEA	RIGHT OUT	SILLY ASS
PAGAN GOD	RIGHT WAY	SIXTH DAY
PAINT BOX	RINSE OUT	SLACK OFF
PAINT OUT	RIVER CAM	SLEEP OFF
PAINT POT	RIVER DEE	SLEEP OUT
PAPER BAG	RIVER GOD	SLING OUT
PAPER HAT	RIVER TAY	SLOPE OFF
PARTY HAT	RIVER WYE	SMALL ADS
PARTY MAN	ROAST PIG	SMALL BOY
PEGGY LEE	ROBIN DAY	SMALL CAR
PENNY RED	ROMAN GOD	SMALL EGG
PETER MAY	ROMAN LAW	SMALL FRY
PETER OUT	ROPED OFF	SMALL MAN
PETER PAN	ROUGH MAP	SMALL SUM
PHASE ONE	ROUGH OUT	SMALL WAY
PHASE TWO	ROUGH SEA	SMART BOY
PHONE BOX	ROUND OFF	SMART LAD
PIANO KEY	ROUND ONE	SMART MAN
PLAIN MAN	ROUND SIX	SMASH HIT
PLANT OUT	ROUND SUM	SMOKE OUT
PLANT POT	ROUND TEN	SNACK BAR
POINT OUT	ROUND TWO	SNAKE PIT
POLKA DOT	ROYAL OAK	SNEAK OFF
POOLS WIN	RYDER CUP	SNEAK OUT
POPPY DAY	SABRE JET	SNOWY OWL
POWER CUT	SALAD OIL	SNUFF BOX
POWER SAW	SALES TAX	SNUFF OUT
PRESS BOX	SALLY ANN	SOBER MAN
PRICE CUT	SCENE ONE	SOLID OAK
PRICE WAR	SCENE TWO	SONNY BOY
PRIME CUT	SCOOP OUT	SORRY END
PROUD DAY	SCORE OFF	SOUND BET
PROUD MAN	SCOUT OUT	SOUND BOX
PUPPY FAT	SCRUB OUT	SOUND MAN
PUSSY CAT	SENNA POD	SOUND OUT
QUEEN ANT	SERVE OUT	SOUTH END
QUEEN BEE	SEVEN MEN	SOUTH PAW
QUICK EAR	SEWER RAT	SOUTH SEA
QUICK EYE	SHAKE OFF	SPACE AGE
QUICK ONE	SHAKE OUT	SPACE GUN
QUICK WIT	SHARE OUT	SPACE MAN
QUILL PEN	SHARP END	SPACE OUT
QUITE MAD	SHARP EYE	SPARE BED
RABID DOG	SHARP WIT	SPARE MAN
RADIO HAM	SHEEP DOG	SPARE RIB
RADIO ONE	SHEER OFF	SPARK OFF
RADIO SET	SHELL OUT	SPEAK FOR
RADIO TWO	SHIPS LOG	SPEAK OUT
RAINY DAY	SHOOT OFF	SPEED COP
REACH OUT	SHOOT OUT	SPELL OUT
READY CUT	SHORT CUT	SPION KOP
READY FOR	SHORT LEG	SPLIT PIN
READY PEN	SHORT MAN	SPOON FED
READY WIT	SHORT ONE	SQUAD CAR
RIGHT ARM	SHORT RUN	STAFF CAR
RIGHT EAR	SHORT TON	STAGE MOB
RIGHT EYE	SHOUT OUT	STAGE ONE
RIGHT LEG	SHOVE OFF	STAGE SET
RIGHT MAN	SHRUG OFF	STAGE TWO
RIGHT NOW	SIEGE CAP	STAIR ROD

31

STAKE OUT	THIRD LAP	WHOLE HOG
STALE BUN	THIRD MAN	WHOLE LOT
STAMP ACT	THIRD ROW	WINDY DAY
STAMP OUT	THIRD SET	WITTY MAN
STAND FOR	THOSE FOR	WORLD CUP
STAND OFF	THREE MEN	WORLD WAR
STAND OUT	THROW OFF	WORSE OFF
STAND PAT	THROW OUT	WRING DRY
START OFF	TIGER BAY	WRING OUT
START OUT	TIGER CUB	WRITE OFF
STAVE OFF	TIGHT FIT	WRITE OUT
STEAK PIE	TIRED MAN	WRONG MAN
STEEL BAR	TIRED OUT	WRONG WAY
STEEL NIB	TOMMY GUN	YEARN FOR
STICK OUT	TOTAL SUM	YEARS AGO
STIFF LEG	TOTAL WAR	YOUNG BOY
STOCK CAR	TOUGH GUY	YOUNG MAN
STOCK POT	TOUGH JOB	
STONE AGE	TOUGH NUT	**6, 1, 1**
STOOD OFF	TRADE GAP	
STOUT MAN	TRAIL OFF	COLOUR T.V.
STRAW HAT	TRAIN SET	
STRAY CAT	TRIAL RUN	**6, 2**
STRAY DOG	TROOP OFF	
STRIP OFF	TROOP OUT	ADDING UP
STUDY ART	TWICE ONE	BEATEN UP
STUDY LAW	TWICE SHY	BEYOND ME
STUNT MAN	TWICE SIX	BOOKED UP
SUGAR RAY	TWICE TEN	BOTHER IT
SUNNY DAY	TWICE TWO	BOTTLE UP
SUNNY JIM	UNCLE SAM	BOUGHT UP
SWEEP OUT	UNCLE TOM	BOUNCE UP
SWEET JAR	UNCUT GEM	BREAKS UP
SWEET PEA	UNDER AGE	BREEZE IN
SWEET TEA	UNDER PAR	BROKEN IN
SWELL OUT	UNDER WAY	BROKEN UP
SWEPT OUT	UNION MAN	BUBBLE UP
SWING LOW	UNTIL NOW	BUCKLE UP
TABBY CAT	UPPER AIR	BUNGED UP
TABLE TOP	UPPER CUT	BUTTER UP
TAKEN ILL	UPPER JAW	BUTTON UP
TAKEN OFF	UPPER LIP	CALLED IN
TAKEN OUT	UPPER TEN	CALLED UP
TAKES OFF	USHER OUT	CAUGHT ON
TAPER OFF	USUAL WAY	CAUGHT UP
TAWNY OWL	VIDEO SET	CHANCE IT
TEACH LAW	VOUCH FOR	CHANGE UP
TEDDY BOY	WATCH OUT	CLOSED IN
TELLS OFF	WATER ICE	COMING IN
TENOR SAX	WATER JUG	COMING ON
TENTH DAY	WATER RAT	COOPED UP
TENTH ROW	WHATS NEW?	COTTON ON
THANK GOD	WHEEL OUT	COVERS UP
THANK YOU	WHICH WAY?	CURLED UP
THERE NOW	WHISK OFF	DOCTOR NO
THICK EAR	WHITE ANT	DOLLED UP
THICK FOG	WHITE EGG	DOUBLE UP
THINK BIG	WHITE HOT	EXCUSE ME
THINK OUT	WHITE LIE	FATTEN UP
THIRD ACT	WHITE MAN	FENCED IN
THIRD DAY	WHITE TIE	FINISH UP

FOLLOW ON	SPRING UP	1, 4, 4
FOLLOW UP	SPRUCE UP	
FORGET IT	SQUARE UP	A DOGS LIFE
FREEZE UP	STANDS BY	A GOOD DEAL
FROZEN UP	STANDS IN	A GOOD MANY
GATHER IN	STANDS UP	I KNOW WHAT
GATHER UP	STITCH UP	
GIVING UP	STREAM BY	1, 8
GLANCE AT	STREAM IN	
GOBBLE UP	STRIKE UP	A CAPPELLA
GOINGS ON	STRING UP	I, CLAUDIUS
HAMMER IN	STROLL BY	
HAULED IN	STRUCK UP	2, 1, 3, 3
HEATED UP	STRUNG UP	
HEMMED IN	SUMMON UP	AT A LOW EBB
HIGHER UP	SWITCH ON	BE A YES-MAN
HOOKED IT	THROWN IN	DO A BAD JOB
LIMBER UP	THUMBS UP	IN A BAD WAY
LINGER ON	TODDLE UP	IN A BIG WAY
LISTEN IN	TOPPED UP	
LISTEN TO	TOSSED UP	2, 1, 6
LITTLE ME	TUCKED IN	
LITTLE MO	TURNED ON	AS A RESULT
LOCKED IN	TURNED UP	AT A CANTER
LOCKED UP	TWENTY TO	AT A GALLOP
LOOKED ON	VERSED IN	AT A GLANCE
LOOSEN UP	WALLED UP	AT A PROFIT
MAKING UP	WANGLE IT	DO A FAVOUR
MESSED UP	WARMED UP	IN A BUNKER
OPENED UP	WASHED UP	IN A CANTER
OVERDO IT	WORKED UP	IN A CIRCLE
PARDON ME		IN A CLINCH
PASSED ON	7, 1	IN A CORNER
PENCIL IN		IN A FRENZY
PICKED UP	EXHIBIT A	IN A GROOVE
PINNED UP	MALCOLM X	IN A HUDDLE
PLUNGE IN	VITAMIN A	IN A MINUTE
POLISH UP	VITAMIN B	IN A MOMENT
PONDER ON	VITAMIN C	IN A MUDDLE
PRAISE BE	VITAMIN D	IN A PICKLE
PULLED IN	VITAMIN E	IN A SCRAPE
PULLED UP		IN A SECOND
RECKON ON	1, 1, 7	IN A SPLINT
RECKON UP		IN A STUPOR
ROLLED UP	E.M.FORSTER	IN A TANGLE
SADDLE UP	J.R.TOLKIEN	IN A TEMPER
SAVING UP	T.V.LICENCE	IN A TRANCE
SCALED UP	W.S.GILBERT	IN A VACUUM
SCRAPE UP		ON A CHARGE
SEALED UP	1, 3, 2, 3	ON A STRING
SETTLE IN		TO A DEGREE
SETTLE UP	I BEG OF YOU	
SHAKEN UP		2, 2, 1, 4
SHORED UP	1, 3, 5	
SHOWED UP		GO ON A DIET
SIGNED ON	A BIT STEEP	GO TO A SHOW
SLOWED UP	A BIT THICK	
SNATCH UP	C.DAY LEWIS	2, 2, 2, 3
SNOWED IN		
SNOWED UP		BE OF AN AGE
SOFTEN UP		

2, 2, 3, 2	AT THE REAR	IN THE PARK
	AT THE SIDE	IN THE PAST
GO ON AND ON	AT THE TIME	IN THE PINK
	BE THE BEST	IN THE POST
2, 2, 5	BY AIR MAIL	IN THE RAIN
	BY SEA MAIL	IN THE REAR
AT AN ANGLE	BY THE BOOK	IN THE ROAD
BE AN ANGEL	BY THE HOUR	IN THE ROOM
BE AT FAULT	BY THE YARD	IN THE SAFE
BE AT PEACE	DO NOT BEND	IN THE SINK
BE ON GUARD	DO ONE DOWN	IN THE SNOW
BY NO MEANS	DO THE DEED	IN THE SOUP
DO AS ASKED	DO THE TOWN	IN THE SWIM
DO IT AGAIN	DO YOU MIND?	IN THE TEAM
DO TO DEATH	GO AND LOOK	IN THE VEIN
ET TU BRUTE	GO FOR GOAL	IN THE WAKE
GO BY COACH	GO FOR HELP	IN THE WARS
GO BY PLANE	GO OFF DUTY	IN THE WASH
GO BY TRAIN	HO CHI MINH	IN THE WEST
GO BY WATER	IN ANY CASE	IN THE WIND
GO IN FRONT	IN BAD FORM	IN TOP FORM
GO IT ALONE	IN BAD PART	IN TOP GEAR
GO ON BOARD	IN DRY DOCK	NO ONE ELSE
GO TO LUNCH	IN DUE TIME	OF ONE MIND
GO TO PRESS	IN NEW YORK	ON DRY LAND
GO TO SLEEP	IN ONE MOVE	ON ONE SIDE
GO TO WASTE	IN ONE WORD	ON THE BALL
IN NO DOUBT	IN THE AREA	ON THE BEAM
OF NO WORTH	IN THE ARMY	ON THE BEAT
ON MY RIGHT	IN THE BATH	ON THE BOIL
SO IT SEEMS	IN THE BOOK	ON THE BONE
SO TO SPEAK	IN THE BUSH	ON THE CART
TO BE BRIEF	IN THE CITY	ON THE CHIN
TO NO AVAIL	IN THE COLD	ON THE DOLE
UP IN SMOKE	IN THE DARK	ON THE EDGE
	IN THE DOCK	ON THE FARM
2, 3, 1, 3	IN THE EAST	ON THE FLAT
	IN THE FACE	ON THE HEAD
GO FOR A DIP	IN THE FALL	ON THE HOOF
GO FOR A JOG	IN THE FIRE	ON THE HOUR
GO FOR A RUN	IN THE FOLD	ON THE LAND
	IN THE FRAY	ON THE LEFT
2, 3, 2, 2	IN THE GODS	ON THE LINE
	IN THE HOME	ON THE LIST
UP AND AT 'EM	IN THE HUNT	ON THE MAKE
	IN THE KNOW	ON THE MARK
2, 3, 4	IN THE LEAD	ON THE MEND
	IN THE LIFT	ON THE MENU
AS YOU WISH	IN THE LOFT	ON THE MOON
AT ANY COST	IN THE MAIL	ON THE MOVE
AT ANY RATE	IN THE MAIN	ON THE NAIL
AT ANY TIME	IN THE MASS	ON THE NOSE
AT ONE TIME	IN THE MIND	ON THE PIER
AT THE BACK	IN THE MOOD	ON THE PILL
AT THE DOGS	IN THE MOON	ON THE RACK
AT THE DOOR	IN THE NAVY	ON THE ROAD
AT THE HELM	IN THE NECK	ON THE ROOF
AT THE MAIN	IN THE NEWS	ON THE SIDE
AT THE MOST	IN THE NUDE	ON THE SPOT
AT THE PEAK	IN THE OPEN	ON THE TOWN
AT THE POST	IN THE OVEN	ON THE TROT

ON THE TURN	AT LEISURE	IN BORSTAL
ON THE WALL	AT LIBERTY	IN BRITAIN
ON THE WANE	AT PRESENT	IN CAHOOTS
ON THE WING	AT WEMBLEY	IN CIRCLES
ON TWO LEGS	BE ADVISED	IN COMFORT
TO ONE SIDE	BE CAREFUL	IN COMMAND
TO THE BONE	BE CERTAIN	IN COMPANY
TO THE BRIM	BE FRIENDS	IN CONCERT
TO THE EAST	BE ONESELF	IN CONTACT
TO THE EDGE	BE PRESENT	IN CONTROL
TO THE FULL	BE PRUDENT	IN COPPERS
TO THE GOOD	BE SERIOUS	IN COSTUME
TO THE HILT	BO DIDDLEY	IN COUNCIL
TO THE LAST	BY ACCLAIM	IN CUSTODY
TO THE LEFT	BY AUCTION	IN DEFENCE
TO THE SIDE	BY COMMAND	IN DESPAIR
TO THE WEST	BY CONSENT	IN DIALECT
UP AND AWAY	BY DEFAULT	IN DISGUST
UP AND DOWN	BY DEGREES	IN DISPUTE
UP AND OVER	BY HERSELF	IN EARNEST
UP FOR SALE	BY HIMSELF	IN ECSTASY
UP THE HILL	BY NUMBERS	IN ENGLAND
UP THE LINE	BY ONESELF	IN ENGLISH
UP THE POLE	BY REQUEST	IN ESSENCE
UP THE WALL	BY THUNDER	IN FASHION
	DE RIGUEUR	IN FETTERS
2, 4, 3	DO JUSTICE	IN GENERAL
	DO NOTHING	IN GERMANY
AS THEY SAY	DO PENANCE	IN HARBOUR
BE ONES AGE	DO WITHOUT	IN HARMONY
DO ONES BIT	DO WONDERS	IN HARNESS
EN TOUT CAS	DR. KILDARE	IN INFANCY
GO FLAT OUT	DU MAURIER	IN IRELAND
GO HALF-WAY	EL ALAMEIN	IN ITALIAN
GO ONES WAY	EN PASSANT	IN ITALICS
GO OVER BIG	EX OFFICIO	IN JANUARY
IN FULL CRY	GO AGAINST	IN KEEPING
IN ONES WAY	GO AGROUND	IN NEUTRAL
IN SOME WAY	GO BEGGING	IN OCTOBER
MY DEAR BOY	GO BERSERK	IN OUTLINE
MY DEAR SIR	GO BETWEEN	IN PASSING
OF THAT ILK	GO DANCING	IN PRIVATE
ON HALF PAY	GO FISHING	IN PROFILE
ON ONES OWN	GO FORWARD	IN PROTEST
ON ONES WAY	GO HAYWIRE	IN PURSUIT
ON THIN ICE	GO INDOORS	IN REALITY
TO THIS DAY	GO MISSING	IN RESERVE
	GO OUTSIDE	IN RESPECT
2, 5, 2	GO QUIETLY	IN RETREAT
	GO SAILING	IN REVERSE
BE SWEET ON	GO SKATING	IN RUSSIAN
GO AHEAD ON	GO THROUGH	IN SERVICE
IN FRONT OF	GO TOWARDS	IN SESSION
	GO WITHOUT	IN SILENCE
2, 7	IN ADVANCE	IN SLAVERY
	IN AMERICA	IN SOCIETY
AD NAUSEAM	IN ARREARS	IN SPANISH
AD VALOREM	IN AUSTRIA	IN SUPPORT
AS ORDERED	IN BELGIUM	IN TATTERS
AS PLANNED	IN BETWEEN	IN TORMENT
AT COLLEGE	IN BLOSSOM	IN TRAFFIC

IN TRANSIT	UP AGAINST	3, 2, 4
IN TRIUMPH		
IN TROUBLE	3, 1, 5	ACT AS HOST
IN UNIFORM		ACT OF LOVE
IN WAITING	ADD A TOUCH	AIM TO KILL
IN WRITING	ALL A DREAM	ALL AT ONCE
JO GRIMOND	ASK A PRICE	ALL IN VAIN
MR. SPEAKER	BUY A DRINK	ALL IS LOST
MY DARLING	BUY A HOUSE	ALL IS WELL
MY FEELING	BUY A ROUND	ALL ON EDGE
MY HUSBAND	CAP A TOOTH	BAR OF SOAP
MY OPINION	CUT A CAPER	BIT OF LUCK
NO COMMENT	CUT A TOOTH	BUY IN BULK
NO CONTEST	DIE A DEATH	BUY ON TICK
NO DEFENCE	FIX A PRICE	CAN OF BEER
NO DEPOSIT	FOR A LAUGH	CAP IN HAND
NO FISHING	FOR A START	CRY NO MORE
NO FLOWERS	FOR A WHILE	CUP OF MILK
NO FOOLING	GET A CHILL	CUT IN HALF
NO FURTHER	GET A FIRST	CUT IT FINE
NO GROUNDS	GET A SHOCK	DAY IS DONE
NO HAWKERS	GET A START	DAY OF DOOM
NO KIDDING	ITS A CINCH	DAY OF REST
NO MANNERS	LAY A WAGER	DEN OF VICE
NO MEANING	LED A DANCE	DIE IS CAST
NO MESSING	MIX A DRINK	DIE OF FEAR
NO MISTAKE	NOT A SOUND	DRY AS DUST
NO PARKING	ONE O CLOCK	EAR OF CORN
NO PROBLEM	OWN A HOUSE	EAT AT HOME
NO QUARTER	PAY A VISIT	EAT NO LEAN
NO REGRETS	PLY A TRADE	EAT NO MEAT
NO SMOKING	SEE A GHOST	END IN GAOL
NO SPIRITS	SIX A PENNY	END IN VIEW
NO STRINGS	SIX O CLOCK	END OF TERM
NO TROUBLE	TEN A PENNY	END OF TIME
NO TURNING	TEN O CLOCK	FIT OF RAGE
NO WAITING	TRY A SAINT	FIT TO BUST
NO WARNING	TWO A PENNY	FIT TO DROP
ON ACCOUNT	TWO O CLOCK	FLY TO ARMS
ON ARRIVAL	VEX A SAINT	FOR MY PART
ON AVERAGE	WIN A FIGHT	GET AN IDEA
ON BALANCE	WIN A MATCH	GET IN LINE
ON DEPOSIT	WIN A POINT	GET IT DOWN
ON DISPLAY	WIN A PRIZE	GET ON WELL
ON DRAUGHT	WIN A TRICK	GET TO HEAR
ON HOLIDAY		GET TO KNOW
ON IMPULSE	3, 2, 1, 3	GET UP LATE
ON PURPOSE		GOD OF FIRE
ON RUNNERS	BIT OF A LAD	GOD OF LOVE
ON SUNDAYS	BUG IN A RUG	GOD OF WINE
ON TUESDAY	GET ON A BUS	HIT OR MISS
ST. ANDREWS	OUT OF A JOB	HOT AS HELL
ST. AUSTELL	SLY AS A FOX	ILL AT EASE
ST. BERNARD	SON OF A GUN	JOB IN HAND
ST. FRANCIS	TIE IN A BOW	JOB OF WORK
ST. MATTHEW	USE AS A PEG	JOT IT DOWN
ST. MICHAEL		JUG OF MILK
ST. PANCRAS	3, 2, 2, 2	LAY TO REST
ST. PATRICK		LEG OF LAMB
ST. STEPHEN	NOT UP TO IT	LEG OF PORK
ST. VINCENT		LET US PRAY

LIE AT REST	PUT UP WITH	CUT AND RUN
LIE IN WAIT	RAY OF HOPE	DOG EAT DOG
LOG OF WOOD	RIB OF BEEF	FAR TOO BIG
LOT OF GOOD	ROT IN HELL	FAR TOO FEW
MAN OF IRON	RUN OF LUCK	FIT FOR USE
MAN OF MARK	RUN TO SEED	GET THE PIP
MAN OF NOTE	RUS IN URBE	HAM AND EGG
MAN OF RANK	SAY NO MORE	HIT AND RUN
MEN AT WORK	SEE NO EVIL	HIT FOR SIX
NOT AT HOME	SET AT EASE	HIT THE BAR
NOT IN TIME	SET AT ODDS	HIT THE HAY
NOT SO FAST	SET AT REST	HOG THE LOT
NOT SO GOOD	SET OF FOUR	HOW AND WHY
ODD OR EVEN	SET ON EDGE	HOW ARE YOU?
OFF TO WORK	SET ON FIRE	HUE AND CRY
OLD AS TIME	SET ON FOOT	HUM AND HAW
ONE IN FIVE	SET TO WORK	ITS TOO BAD
ONE IN FOUR	SET UP CAMP	MID-DAY SUN
ONE IN NINE	SET UP HOME	MUM AND DAD
ONE OF MANY	SET UP SHOP	NOT FAR OFF
OUT OF DATE	SIT AT HOME	NOT TOO BAD
OUT OF DEBT	SIT UP LATE	NOT TOO FAR
OUT OF FORM	TEN TO FIVE	ODD JOB MAN
OUT OF GEAR	TEN TO FOUR	ODD MAN OUT
OUT OF HAND	TEN TO NINE	OFF THE AIR
OUT OF LINE	TIN OF SOUP	OFF THE MAP
OUT OF LOVE	TON OF COAL	OFF THE PEG
OUT OF LUCK	TON OF COKE	OLD AND NEW
OUT OF MIND	TON OF GOLD	ONE AND ALL
OUT OF PITY	TON OF LEAD	ONE AND SIX
OUT OF STEP	TOP TO TAIL	ONE AND TWO
OUT OF TIME	TRY BY JURY	ONE FOR ALL
OUT OF TOWN	TRY IN VAIN	ONE TOO FEW
OUT OF TRIM	TRY TO HELP	ONE-MAN DOG
OUT OF TRUE	TRY TO SAVE	OUT AND OUT
OUT OF TUNE	TRY TO STOP	PEN AND INK
OUT OF TURN	TWO BY FIVE	POT THE RED
OUT OF WORK	TWO BY FOUR	RIN TIN TIN
OUT ON BAIL	WAR ON WANT	RUE THE DAY
PAS DE DEUX	WAY OF LIFE	SUN AND AIR
PAY BY CASH	WEB OF LIES	SUN YAT SEN
PAY IN CASH	WIN OR LOSE	TEA FOR TWO
PAY IN FULL	YET TO COME	THE BIG ONE
PAY IN KIND		THE BIG TOP
PAY ON CALL	3, 3, 3	THE ICE AGE
PIN-UP GIRL		THE JET AGE
PUT AT EASE	AIR THE BED	THE OLD VIC
PUT IN GEAR	ALL BUT ONE	THE OLD WAY
PUT IN HAND	ALL FOR ONE	THE RED SEA
PUT IN JAIL	ALL THE DAY	THE WAY OUT
PUT IN MIND	ALL THE WAY	TIC-TAC MAN
PUT IT DOWN	ALL-OUT WAR	TIP AND RUN
PUT IT OVER	ANY DAY NOW	TIT FOR TAT
PUT ON AIRS	ASK THE WAY	TWO AND SIX
PUT ON OATH	BAD FOR ONE	TWO AND TWO
PUT ON SALE	BAG THE LOT	TWO FOR TEA
PUT ON SHOW	BAR THE WAY	WHO ARE YOU?
PUT ON TAPE	BOX AND COX	WIN THE CUP
PUT TO ROUT	CAT AND DOG	WIN THE DAY
PUT TO WORK	CHA CHA CHA	WIN THE WAR
PUT UP BAIL	CRY FOR JOY	YEA AND NAY

3, 4, 2

COP HOLD OF
EYE MAKE-UP
FAR FROM IT
GET WIND OF
GET WITH IT
GOD HELP US
HOW GOES IT?
OUT WITH IT
PUT PAID TO
SET EYES ON
SET FIRE TO
SET THEM UP

3, 6

ACT FAIRLY
ACT WISELY
ADD COLOUR
AIR BATTLE
AIR BRAKES
AIR INTAKE
AIR LETTER
AIR POCKET
AIR TRAVEL
ALF RAMSEY
ALL ABOARD
ALL ACTION
ALL AGREED
ALL AROUND
ALL BEHIND
ALL BLACKS
ALL CHANGE
ALL COMERS
ALL SAINTS
ALL SQUARE
ALL THINGS
ALL THUMBS
ANY EXCUSE
ANY MOMENT
ANY OFFERS?
ANY TAKERS?
ARC WELDER
ART CRITIC
ART DEALER
ART EDITOR
ART LESSON
ART MASTER
ART MUSEUM
ART SCHOOL
ART STUDIO
ASH BLONDE
ASK ADVICE
ASK NICELY
AYR UNITED
BAD ADVICE
BAD CREDIT
BAD DESIGN
BAD DRIVER
BAD EXCUSE

BAD HABITS
BAD HEALTH
BAD INTENT
BAD MASTER
BAD MEMORY
BAD PLAYER
BAD RECORD
BAD REPORT
BAD REVIEW
BAD SAILOR
BAD SCRAPE
BAD SECOND
BAD TEMPER
BAD TIMING
BAR MAGNET
BAS RELIEF
BAY LEAVES
BAY WINDOW
BEG PARDON
BEL ESPRIT
BEN JONSON
BEN LOMOND
BIG BERTHA
BIG CHANCE
BIG CHEESE
BIG DEMAND
BIG DIPPER
BIG EFFORT
BIG HITTER
BIG MARGIN
BIG PRIZES
BIG PROFIT
BIG TALKER
BIT PLAYER
BON CHANCE
BON MARCHÉ
BON VIVANT
BON VIVEUR
BON VOYAGE
BOW STREET
BOW WINDOW
BOX CAMERA
BOX CLEVER
BOX GIRDER
BOX NUMBER
BOX OFFICE
BOY FRIEND
BOY WONDER
BUS DRIVER
BUS STRIKE
BUS TICKET
BUY SHARES
CAB DRIVER
CAN OPENER
CAR DRIVER
CAR WINDOW
CAT FAMILY
COD FILLET
COR BLIMEY
CUB MASTER
CUP WINNER

CUT ACROSS
CUT ADRIFT
CUT CAPERS
DAN ARCHER
DAY BEFORE
DAY SCHOOL
DEI GRATIA
DES MOINES
DIM MEMORY
DOG BASKET
DOG COLLAR
DOG FAMILY
DOG KENNEL
DOG RACING
DON CARLOS
DRY GINGER
DRY HUMOUR
DRY SEASON
DRY SHERRY
DRY SUMMER
DUD CHEQUE
DUE NOTICE
DUE REWARD
EAT DINNER
EGG BEATER
EYE APPEAL
EYE DOCTOR
EYE LOTION
EYE SHADOW
EYE STRAIN
FAN DANCER
FAN HEATER
FAR AFIELD
FAR BEHIND
FAR BETTER
FAR BEYOND
FAR CORNER
FAR ENOUGH
FAT CATTLE
FAT CHANCE
FAT PROFIT
FAT WALLET
FEE SIMPLE
FIT PERSON
FOR EFFECT
FOR EXPORT
FOR VALOUR
FUN PALACE
FUR COLLAR
FUR GLOVES
FUR LINING
FUR TRADER
GAG WRITER
GAS ATTACK
GAS COOKER
GAS ENGINE
GAS ESCAPE
GAS FITTER
GAS HEATER
GAS MANTLE
GAY REVELS
GET ACROSS

GET AROUND	LEN HUTTON	NOT LIKELY
GET BEHIND	LIE AROUND	NOT PROVEN
GET BETTER	LIE ASLEEP	NOT WANTED
GET FATTER	LIE FALLOW	ODD COUPLE
GET KILLED	LIE HIDDEN	ODD MOMENT
GET MOVING	LIP READER	ODD NUMBER
GOD FORBID	LON CHANEY	ODD PERSON
GOR BLIMEY!	LOW BRIDGE	OFF CENTRE
GUM ARABIC	LOW CHURCH	OFF CHANCE
GUN BATTLE	LOW COMEDY	OFF COLOUR
GUN COTTON	LOW FELLOW	OFF COURSE
GUN RUNNER	LOW GERMAN	OFF MOMENT
GUN TURRET	LOW GROUND	OFF SEASON
GUY FAWKES	LOW INCOME	OFF TARGET
HEY PRESTO	LOW MORALE	OIL COLOUR
HIS HONOUR	LOW NUMBER	OIL CRISIS
HIT PARADE	LOW PERSON	OIL HEATER
HIT WICKET	LOW RELIEF	OIL PAINTS
HOI POLLOI	LOW RETURN	OIL STRIKE
HOP PICKER	LOW SALARY	OIL TANKER
HOT NUMBER	LOW STATUS	OIL TYCOON
HOT PEPPER	MAD HATTER	OLD BAILEY
HOT POTATO	MAD SCHEME	OLD BANGER
HOT SEASON	MAN FRIDAY	OLD BUFFER
HOT SHOWER	MAX ADRIAN	OLD CODGER
HOT SPRING	MAX MILLER	OLD COUPLE
HOT SUMMER	MAX PLANCK	OLD CUSTOM
HOT TEMPER	MRS.BEATON	OLD FAGGOT
IAN BOTHAM	MRS.GRUNDY	OLD FAMILY
ICE CORNET	NET AMOUNT	OLD FELLOW
ICE HOCKEY	NET ASSETS	OLD FRIEND
ICE SKATES	NET INCOME	OLD MASTER
ICY MANNER	NET LOSSES	OLD METHOD
ICY REMARK	NET PROFIT	OLD PEOPLE
ILL EFFECT	NET RESULT	OLD RATBAG
ILL HEALTH	NET WEIGHT	OLD RECORD
ILL HUMOUR	NEW BARNET	OLD RÉGIME
ILL REPORT	NEW DEALER	OLD SAYING
ILL REPUTE	NEW DECADE	OLD SCHOOL
INK BOTTLE	NEW ENERGY	OLD SCORES
INK ERASER	NEW FOREST	OLD STAGER
IVY LEAGUE	NEW FRIEND	OLD STREET
JAM SPONGE	NEW GROUND	ONE ACROSS
JET ENGINE	NEW GUINEA	ONE BASKET
JET FLIGHT	NEW JERSEY	ONE BETTER
JOE BUGNER	NEW LONDON	ONE CHANCE
KEW BRIDGE	NEW MEMBER	ONE DEGREE
KEY MOMENT	NEW METHOD	ONE DOLLAR
KEY WORKER	NEW MEXICO	ONE EIGHTH
KID GLOVES	NEW POTATO	ONE FATHOM
KID SISTER	NEW READER	ONE FOURTH
LAG BEHIND	NEW RECORD	ONE GALLON
LAP RECORD	NEW REGIME	ONE LENGTH
LAS PALMAS	NEW SCHOOL	ONE MINUTE
LAW REFORM	NEW THEORY	ONE MOMENT
LAW REPORT	NEW TRICKS	ONE OCTAVE
LAW SCHOOL	NEW YORKER	ONE SECOND
LED ASTRAY	NOD ASSENT	ONE STRIPE
LEG BEFORE	NOT AMUSED	ONE STROKE
LEG GLANCE	NOT GUILTY	ONE WICKET
LEG THEORY	NOT HUNGRY	OUR FATHER

PAY DEARLY	SAY PLEASE	THE ALLIES
PAY DOUBLE	SEA BATTLE	THE AMAZON
PAY FREEZE	SEA BREEZE	THE ARCTIC
PAY HOMAGE	SEA CRUISE	THE ARMADA
PAY OFFICE	SEA SHANTY	THE AUTUMN
PAY RANSOM	SEA URCHIN	THE AZORES
PEN FRIEND	SEA VOYAGE	THE BALTIC
PER CAPITA	SEE DOUBLE	THE BLACKS
PET THEORY	SEE REASON	THE BOARDS
PIT STALLS	SEE THINGS	THE BOUNTY
PIT WORKER	SET ALIGHT	THE BROADS
POP ARTIST	SET COURSE	THE BUDGET
POP RECORD	SET PHRASE	THE CHANGE
POP SINGER	SET SPEECH	THE CINEMA
POT BOILER	SET SQUARE	THE CLERGY
POT POURRI	SEX APPEAL	THE CREEPS
PRO PATRIA	SEX KITTEN	THE CRIMEA
PUT ACROSS	SEX SYMBOL	THE DANUBE
RAT POISON	SHY PERSON	THE DESERT
RAW CARROT	SIT AROUND	THE EAGLES
RAW TOMATO	SIT PRETTY	THE EMPIRE
RED CARPET	SIX HEARTS	THE FINISH
RED CHEEKS	SIX LITRES	THE FIRSTS
RED CHEESE	SIX METRES	THE FLICKS
RED CRAYON	SIX MONTHS	THE FORCES
RED DEVILS	SIX OUNCES	THE FORMER
RED DRAGON	SIX POINTS	THE FRENCH
RED DUSTER	SIX POUNDS	THE FUTURE
RED ENSIGN	SIX SPADES	THE GAMBIA
RED FLOWER	SIX TENTHS	THE GANGES
RED GROUSE	SIX TRICKS	THE GENTRY
RED GUARDS	SIX WHEELS	THE GOSPEL
RED INDIAN	SLY HUMOUR	THE GUILTY
RED LETTER	SOB SISTER	THE HILTON
RED MULLET	SUB JUDICE	THE JUNGLE
RED PENCIL	SUN BONNET	THE KAISER
RED PEPPER	SUN HELMET	THE LATEST
RED PLANET	SUN LOUNGE	THE LATTER
RED RIBBON	TAP DANCER	THE LEVANT
RED RUSSIA	TAR BARREL	THE LIZARD
RED SETTER	TAX CHARGE	THE LOUVRE
RED SPIDER	TAX DEMAND	THE MARKET
RED SQUARE	TAX FIDDLE	THE MASSES
RIO GRANDE	TAX REBATE	THE MASTER
ROY CASTLE	TAX RELIEF	THE MIGHTY
ROY ROGERS	TAX RETURN	THE MIKADO
RUB GENTLY	TAY BRIDGE	THE MORGUE
RUM BOTTLE	TEA GARDEN	THE MOVIES
RUM FELLOW	TEA KETTLE	THE OCCULT
RUM RATION	TEA LEAVES	THE ORIENT
RUM RUNNER	TEA TASTER	THE PAPERS
RUN ACROSS	TED DEXTER	THE PEOPLE
RUN AROUND	TEN LITRES	THE PLAGUE
RUN ASHORE	TEN METRES	THE PLOUGH
RYE WHISKY	TEN MONTHS	THE POLICE
SAD ENDING	TEN OUNCES	THE PRINCE
SAD PLIGHT	TEN POINTS	THE PUBLIC
SAM BROWNE	TEN POUNDS	THE REVIEW
SAN MARINO	TEN ROUNDS	THE RIVALS
SAY CHEESE	TEN TRICKS	THE SCOUTS
SAY LITTLE	THE ALBION	THE SECOND

THE SENATE	TWO TENTHS	FILL A NEED
THE SEVERN	TWO THIRDS	FIND A FLAT
THE SHAKES	TWO TRICKS	FIND A HOME
THE SOLENT	TWO VERSES	FIND A WIFE
THE SPHINX	TWO WHEELS	FIRE A SHOT
THE SPLITS	TWO WRONGS	FIVE A SIDE
THE SPOILS	UNA STUBBS	FORM A LINE
THE SPRING	VAN DRIVER	FORM A RING
THE STATES	VOX HUMANA	GIVE A DAMN
THE STICKS	VOX POPULI	GIVE A HAND
THE STOCKS	WAR DAMAGE	GIVE A HINT
THE STONES	WAR EFFORT	GIVE A LEAD
THE STRAND	WAR LEADER	GIVE A LIFT
THE SUMMER	WAR MUSEUM	GIVE A RING
THE TATLER	WAR OFFICE	GIVE A SIGN
THE THAMES	WAR RECORD	GIVE A TALK
THE TICKET	WAR VICTIM	HAIL A TAXI
THE TORIES	WAX CANDLE	HALF A KILO
THE UMPIRE	WAX EFFIGY	HALF A LOAF
THE UNSEEN	WAX FIGURE	HALF A MIND
THE WHITES	WAX STRONG	HALF A PINT
THE WINNER	WAY BEHIND	HALF A QUID
THE WINTER	WET SEASON	HALF A TICK
THE ZENITH	WET SPONGE	HALF A YARD
TIN HELMET	WET SUMMER	HAVE A BASH
TIN LIZZIE	WIN EASILY	HAVE A BATH
TIN OPENER	WIN FAVOUR	HAVE A BITE
TOM PEARSE	WIN RENOWN	HAVE A CARE
TOM SAWYER	YES PLEASE	HAVE A CASE
TON WEIGHT	ZOO INMATE	HAVE A CHAT
TOO CLEVER		HAVE A COLD
TOO LITTLE	4, 1, 4	HAVE A DATE
TOO SEVERE		HAVE A DUEL
TOO STRONG	BAKE A CAKE	HAVE A FALL
TOP DRAWER	BAKE A LOAF	HAVE A HOPE
TOP PEOPLE	BLOW A KISS	HAVE A LARK
TOP PERSON	BOOK A ROOM	HAVE A LOOK
TOP SECRET	BOOK A SEAT	HAVE A MEAL
TOP STOREY	BORE A HOLE	HAVE A PERM
TOP TWENTY	BURN A HOLE	HAVE A PLAN
TOY POODLE	CALL A HALT	HAVE A REST
TRY HARDER	CALL A TAXI	HAVE A SALE
TWO COPIES	CAST A FILM	HAVE A SEAT
TWO FIFTHS	CAST A LOOK	HAVE A SHOT
TWO HEARTS	CAST A SHOW	HAVE A STAB
TWO KNAVES	CAST A VOTE	HAVE A WORD
TWO LITRES	COIN A WORD	HOLD A SALE
TWO LOAVES	COOK A MEAL	HOLD A VIEW
TWO METRES	DEAL A BLOW	JUST A DROP
TWO MONTHS	DEAL A CARD	JUST A TICK
TWO NINTHS	DRAW A LINE	KEEP A DATE
TWO OUNCES	DRAW A VEIL	LAND A BLOW
TWO POINTS	DROP A BOMB	LEND A HAND
TWO POUNDS	DROP A HINT	LEND A QUID
TWO QUARTS	DROP A LINE	LIKE A BIRD
TWO QUEENS	EARN A NAME	LIKE A BOMB
TWO ROUNDS	EARN A WAGE	LIKE A FISH
TWO SHAKES	FEEL A FOOL	LIKE A FOOL
TWO SPADES	FEEL A NEED	LIKE A KING
TWO STOOLS	FELT A FOOL	LIKE A LAMB
TWO STROKE	FILE A SUIT	LIKE A MULE

LIKE A SHOT	SINK A WELL	CEST LA VIE
LOOK A FOOL	SLIP A DISC	CHOU EN-LAI
LOOK A MESS	SPIN A COIN	CODE OF LAW
LOSE A GAME	SPIN A YARN	COLD AS ICE
LOSE A LIMB	STOP A LEAK	COME OF AGE
MAKE A BOOK	TAKE A BATH	COME TO BED
MAKE A CAKE	TAKE A BITE	DAYS OF OLD
MAKE A CALL	TAKE A CARD	DOGS OF WAR
MAKE A DATE	TAKE A COPY	DOWN IN ONE
MAKE A DEAL	TAKE A DIVE	DRAW AN ACE
MAKE A FACE	TAKE A DROP	DROP OF TEA
MAKE A FIRE	TAKE A FALL	EASY AS PIE
MAKE A FUSS	TAKE A HAND	EASY TO SEE
MAKE A GIFT	TAKE A HINT	FAIL TO ACT
MAKE A JOKE	TAKE A LOOK	FAIL TO PAY
MAKE A KILL	TAKE A NOTE	FAIL TO SEE
MAKE A LIST	TAKE A PART	FAIL TO WIN
MAKE A LOSS	TAKE A PEEP	FALL OF MAN
MAKE A MARK	TAKE A PILL	FEAR OF GOD
MAKE A MESS	TAKE A REST	FIVE BY TWO
MAKE A MINT	TAKE A RISK	FIVE IN ONE
MAKE A MOVE	TAKE A ROOM	FIVE OR SIX
MAKE A NAME	TAKE A SEAT	FIVE TO ONE
MAKE A NOTE	TAKE A SHOT	FIVE TO SIX
MAKE A PASS	TAKE A TAXI	FIVE TO TEN
MAKE A PILE	TAKE A TEST	FIVE TO TWO
MAKE A RULE	TAKE A TRIP	FLAT TO LET
MAKE A SALE	TAKE A TURN	FOUR BY TWO
MAKE A SHOW	TAKE A VIEW	FOUR IN ONE
MAKE A SIGN	TAKE A VOTE	FOUR TO ONE
MAKE A SLIP	TAKE A WALK	FREE AS AIR
MAKE A WILL	TAKE A WIFE	FREE OF TAX
MAKE A WISH	TELL A TALE	FULL OF FUN
MANY A SLIP	TOSS A COIN	FULL OF JOY
MANY A TIME	TURN A HAIR	FULL OF PEP
MEND A FUSE	WAIT A TICK	FULL OF WOE
ONCE A WEEK	WAVE A WAND	FUND OF WIT
ONCE A YEAR	WEAR A HALO	GOES TO POT
OPEN A FILE	WEAR A MASK	GONE TO BED
OPEN A SHOP	WHAT A LIFE!	GONE TO POT
PICK A LOCK	WHAT A PITY!	GOOD AS NEW
PICK A TEAM	WITH A BANG	GOOD TO EAT
PLAY A CARD		GOOD TO SEE
PLAY A GAME	**4, 2, 1, 2**	HALF AN EYE
PLAY A JOKE		HAND IT OUT
PLAY A PART	GIVE IT A GO	HAND OF GOD
PLAY A TUNE		HANG IT ALL
PULL A FACE	**4, 2, 3**	HARD TO GET
READ A BOOK		HARD TO SAY
RENT A FLAT	ABLE TO FLY	HARD TO SEE
RIDE A BIKE	ABLE TO SEE	HAVE IT OUT
RING A BELL	BALE OF HAY	HEAD TO TOE
RING A PEAL	BEER ON TAP	HELL TO PAY
ROCK N ROLL	BEST OF ALL	HOLD AT BAY
SAIL A SHIP	BITE TO EAT	HOLE IN ONE
SEND A WIRE	BODY OF LAW	HOPE TO DIE
SHED A TEAR	BODY OF MEN	ISLE OF ELY
SHOW A SIGN	BOIL AN EGG	ISLE OF MAN
SIGN A PACT	BURY AT SEA	JOAN OF ARC
SING A SONG	CALL IT OFF	KEEP AT BAY
SINK A PUTT	CAST AN EYE	KEEP IT OUT

KEEP ON ICE
KEPT AT BAY
KEPT ON ICE
KNOW IT ALL
KNOW NO LAW
LAMB OF GOD
LAND OF NOD
LAST OF ALL
LAST OF TEN
LAST OF TWO
LEAD AN ACE
LEFT TO DIE
LEFT TO ROT
LEND AN EAR
LIFE OF SIN
LIVE IN SIN
LIVE ON AIR
LIVE OR DIE
LOSE AN ARM
LOSE AN EAR
LOSE AN EYE
LOST AT SEA
LOTS OF FUN
LOVE MY DOG
LOVE OF WAR
MAKE IT PAY
MAKE-UP MAN
MATE IN ONE
MATE IN TWO
MEAN NO ILL
MEAN TO SAY
MOST OF ALL
NEWS AT TEN
NEXT OF KIN
NICE TO SEE
NINE OR TEN
NINE TO ONE
NONE AT ALL
NUTS IN MAY
ODDS-ON BET
OPEN TO ALL
OVER TO YOU
PLAY AN ACE
PLAY BY EAR
PLAY TO WIN
PULL IT OFF
READ IN BED
RIDE IT OUT
ROLL OF FAT
ROOM TO LET
ROSS ON WYE
RULE OF LAW
SAME TO YOU
SHOP TO LET
SORT IT OUT
SOUL OF WIT
SPIT IT OUT
STAY IN BED
STOP IN BED
SUIT AT LAW
SURE TO DIE

SURE TO WIN
SUSS IT OUT
TAKE MY TIP
TAKE ON OIL
TALE OF WOE
TEAR IN TWO
TELL NO LIE
TELL NO ONE
THIN ON TOP
TIME OF DAY
TIME OF WAR
TIME TO DIE
TIME TO EAT
TIME TO PAY
TROT IT OUT
TURN IT OFF
TURN TO ICE
UGLY AS SIN
WALK ON AIR
WENT TO BED
WENT TO POT
WENT TO WAR
WILL OF GOD
WILL TO WIN
WORK IT OUT
WORK OF ART
YARD OF ALE

4, 3, 2

BACK OUT OF
COME AND GO
COME OFF IT
FALL FOR IT
FILL HER UP
FROM NOW ON
GIVE EAR TO
HALF WAY UP
LAST MAN IN
MAKE FUN OF
NEXT MAN IN
POKE FUN AT
THIS WAY IN
THIS WAY UP
TOLD YOU SO
TOSS FOR IT
WAIT FOR IT
WAIT FOR ME
WALK OUT ON
WELL SET UP
WORD FOR IT

4, 5

ACID DROPS
ADAM FAITH
ADAM SMITH
AHOY THERE
ALAN BATES
ALMA MATER
ALMS HOUSE

ANDY PANDY
ANNE FRANK
AQUA VITAE
ARAB HORSE
ARCH ENEMY
ARCH ROGUE
ARID WASTE
ARMS DEPOT
ARMS LOWER
ARMS RAISE
ARMY BOOTS
ARMY CADET
ARMY CORPS
ARMY ISSUE
ASIA MINOR
AUNT SALLY
AWAY MATCH
BABY GRAND
BABY LINEN
BACK AGAIN
BACK ALLEY
BACK BENCH
BACK COVER
BACK SLANG
BACK STAGE
BACK TEETH
BACK WATER
BACK WHEEL
BAKE BREAD
BALD EAGLE
BALD FACTS
BALD PATCH
BALD TRUTH
BALL POINT
BANK CLERK
BANK VAULT
BARE FACTS
BARE FISTS
BARE KNEES
BARE TORSO
BARE TRUTH
BARN DANCE
BASE METAL
BASS VOICE
BATH CHAIR
BATH SALTS
BATH TOWEL
BATH WATER
BEAR FRUIT
BEAR RIGHT
BEAT MUSIC
BEAU GESTE
BEEF CURRY
BEER GLASS
BEER MONEY
BEET SUGAR
BELL TOWER
BEST CHINA
BEST DRESS
BEST GRADE
BEST THING

BEST VALUE	CASH PRICE	DARK CLOUD
BÊTE NOIRE	CASH PRIZE	DARK DRESS
BILL HALEY	CASH TERMS	DARK GREEN
BILL SIKES	CAST ABOUT	DARK HORSE
BIRD BRAIN	CAST ASIDE	DARK NIGHT
BIRD TABLE	CAST DOUBT	DATE STAMP
BLUE ANGEL	CAST LOOSE	DAVE ALLEN
BLUE BLOOD	CHOP HOUSE	DAVY JONES
BLUE CHIPS	CITY STATE	DEAD AHEAD
BLUE JEANS	CLAP HANDS	DEAD DRUNK
BLUE PAINT	CLEO LAINE	DEAD FAINT
BLUE PETER	CLIP JOINT	DEAD LEVEL
BLUE RINSE	CLOG DANCE	DEAD MARCH
BLUE SHIRT	COAL BLACK	DEAD QUIET
BLUE SKIES	COAL BOARD	DEAD RIGHT
BLUE SOCKS	COAL FIELD	DEAD SLEEP
BLUE STAMP	COAL MINER	DEAD SOBER
BLUE STRIP	COCK ROBIN	DEAD STOCK
BLUE WATER	COIN MONEY	DEAD TIRED
BLUE WHALE	COLD BLAST	DEAD WATER
BOAT TRAIN	COLD BLOOD	DEAN SWIFT
BODY CHECK	COLD CREAM	DEAR HEART
BODY ODOUR	COLD DRINK	DEAR MADAM
BOIL WATER	COLD FRAME	DECK CHAIR
BOLD PRINT	COLD FRONT	DECK GAMES
BONA FIDES	COLD HANDS	DEEP GREEN
BONE CHINA	COLD HEART	DEEP RIVER
BOOK COVER	COLD LUNCH	DEEP SLEEP
BOOK LOVER	COLD NIGHT	DEEP SOUTH
BOOK SEATS	COLD SNACK	DEEP VOICE
BOOK TITLE	COLD SOBER	DEEP WATER
BOOK TOKEN	COLD SPELL	DESK CLERK
BOOK TRADE	COLD STEEL	DIET SHEET
BOOK VALUE	COLD SWEAT	DIME NOVEL
BORN ACTOR	COLD WATER	DIME STORE
BORN AGAIN	COME ABOUT	DINE EARLY
BORN COMIC	COME AGAIN	DIRT CHEAP
BORN MIMIC	COME ALIVE	DIRT TRACK
BOTH HANDS	COME ALONG	DISC BRAKE
BOTH SIDES	COME APART	DISH CLOUT
BOWL ALONG	COME CLEAN	DISH WATER
BUCK TEETH	COME CLOSE	DOCK GREEN
BULL FIGHT	COME EARLY	DONE THING
BURN ALIVE	COME FIRST	DONT WORRY
BUSH SHIRT	COME FORTH	DOOR FRAME
BUSY PLACE	COME LOOSE	DOOR PANEL
CAFÉ OWNER	COME RIGHT	DOPE FIEND
CAFÉ ROYAL	COME ROUND	DOSS HOUSE
CAKE STAND	COME THIRD	DOWN BELOW
CALL AGAIN	COME UNDER	DOWN QUILT
CALL FORTH	COOL DRINK	DOWN RIVER
CALL HEADS	COOL WATER	DOWN SOUTH
CALL TAILS	COST PRICE	DOWN STAGE
CANE CHAIR	COUP DÉTAT	DOWN THERE
CANE SUGAR	CRAB APPLE	DOWN TOOLS
CARD INDEX	CUFF LINKS	DOWN TRAIN
CARD SENSE	CURT REPLY	DOWN UNDER
CARD TABLE	DAMP PATCH	DRAW BLOOD
CARD TRICK	DAMP SQUIB	DRAW FORTH
CARL ZEISS	DARK BLUES	DRAW LEVEL
CARY GRANT	DARK BROWN	DRAW MONEY

DRAW TIGHT	FALL UNDER	FIVE KILOS
DRAW WATER	FARE STAGE	FIVE MARKS
DRAY HORSE	FARM HORSE	FIVE MILES
DROP SCONE	FAST TRAIN	FIVE PENCE
DROP SHORT	FAST WOMAN	FIVE PINTS
DRUG FIEND	FEEL ANGRY	FIVE SCORE
DRUG HABIT	FEEL AWFUL	FIVE TIMES
DRUG SQUAD	FEEL DRUNK	FIVE WEEKS
DRUG STORE	FEEL FAINT	FIVE YARDS
DRUM MAJOR	FEEL FUNNY	FIVE YEARS
DUST STORM	FEEL GIDDY	FLAT BROKE
DUTY BOUND	FEEL GREAT	FLAT EARTH
DUTY CALLS	FEEL HAPPY	FLIT ABOUT
DUTY FIRST	FEEL RIGHT	FOLK DANCE
EARN MONEY	FEEL SHAME	FOLK MUSIC
EAST COAST	FEEL SILLY	FOLK STORY
EAST END'ER	FEEL SMALL	FOOD MIXER
EAST INDIA	FEEL SORRY	FOOD STORE
EAST RIVER	FEEL TIRED	FOOD VALUE
EAST SHEEN	FEET APART	FOOL ABOUT
EASY CATCH	FEET FIRST	FOOT FAULT
EASY CHAIR	FELT SILLY	FORM FOURS
EASY CHARM	FILM ACTOR	FORT WORTH
EASY CLIMB	FILM EXTRA	FOUL CRIME
EASY FIRST	FILM STRIP	FOUL FIEND
EASY GOING	FILM STUNT	FOUL SMELL
EASY MONEY	FIND FAULT	FOUL THROW
EASY RIDER	FIND PEACE	FOUR CARDS
EASY TERMS	FIND TOUCH	FOUR CLUBS
EASY THING	FIND WORDS	FOUR DOZEN
EMIT WAVES	FINE BIRDS	FOUR FIVES
EPIC VERSE	FINE CLOTH	FOUR FOURS
ERIC SYKES	FINE GRAIN	FOUR GROSS
EVEN MONEY	FINE POINT	FOUR HOURS
EVEN SCORE	FINE SPORT	FOUR JACKS
EVER AFTER	FINE SPRAY	FOUR KILOS
EVER SINCE	FINE STYLE	FOUR KINGS
EYES FRONT	FINE TOUCH	FOUR MILES
EYES RIGHT	FINE VOICE	FOUR NINES
EZRA POUND	FINE WOMAN	FOUR PAGES
FACE CREAM	FINE WORDS	FOUR PAIRS
FACE DEATH	FIRE ALARM	FOUR PARTS
FACE FACTS	FIRE DRILL	FOUR PENCE
FACE NORTH	FIRE EATER	FOUR PINTS
FACE RIGHT	FIRE IRONS	FOUR SCORE
FACE SOUTH	FIRE POWER	FOUR SIDES
FACE TOWEL	FIRM BASIS	FOUR SIXES
FACE VALUE	FIRM FAITH	FOUR TIMES
FAIR FIGHT	FIRM GOING	FOUR WALLS
FAIR JUDGE	FIRM OFFER	FOUR WEEKS
FAIR OFFER	FIRM PRICE	FOUR WINDS
FAIR PRICE	FIRM STAND	FOUR YARDS
FAIR SHARE	FISH KNIFE	FOUR YEARS
FAIR TRADE	FISH PASTE	FRED EMNEY
FAIR TRIAL	FISH SLICE	FRED PERRY
FAIR VALUE	FISH STEAK	FREE AGENT
FAIR WORDS	FIVE CARDS	FREE BOARD
FAKE ALIBI	FIVE CLUBS	FREE DRINK
FALL ABOUT	FIVE DOZEN	FREE ENTRY
FALL APART	FIVE GROSS	FREE FIGHT
FALL SHORT	FIVE HOURS	FREE HOUSE

FREE LUNCH	GOLD FEVER	GOOD START
FREE OFFER	GOLD INGOT	GOOD STATE
FREE PRESS	GOLD MEDAL	GOOD STORY
FREE RANGE	GOLD MINER	GOOD STUFF
FREE SPACE	GOLD PAINT	GOOD TABLE
FREE STYLE	GOLD PIECE	GOOD TASTE
FREE TRADE	GOLD PLATE	GOOD THING
FREE TRIAL	GOLD PRICE	GOOD TIMES
FREE VERSE	GOLD TOOTH	GOOD TONIC
FREE WHEEL	GOLD WATCH	GOOD USAGE
FREE WORLD	GOLF CLUBS	GOOD VALUE
FROM ABOVE	GOLF LINKS	GOOD VOICE
FROM BELOW	GOLF WIDOW	GOOD WAGES
FULL BLAST	GONE UNDER	GOOD WOMAN
FULL BLOOM	GOOD ACTOR	GOOD WORKS
FULL BOARD	GOOD ANGEL	GOOD YIELD
FULL COVER	GOOD BLOKE	GORE VIDAL
FULL DRESS	GOOD BOOKS	GREY BEARD
FULL GROWN	GOOD BREAK	GREY CLOUD
FULL HOUSE	GOOD CATCH	GREY GOOSE
FULL MARKS	GOOD CAUSE	GREY HAIRS
FULL PRICE	GOOD CHEER	GREY HORSE
FULL PURSE	GOOD CLASS	GREY SHIRT
FULL QUOTA	GOOD DRINK	GREY SKIES
FULL SCOPE	GOOD EARTH	GREY SOCKS
FULL SCORE	GOOD FAIRY	GRIM DEATH
FULL SKIRT	GOOD FAITH	GRIM SMILE
FULL SPEED	GOOD FAULT	GRIM TRUTH
FULL STEAM	GOOD FIGHT	GROW ANGRY
FULL STORY	GOOD GOING	GROW APART
FULL SWING	GOOD GRACE	GROW BEANS
FULL TABLE	GOOD GRADE	GROW FRUIT
FULL VALUE	GOOD GRIEF	GROW OLDER
GAIN POWER	GOOD GUESS	GROW STALE
GAIN SPEED	GOOD HABIT	GROW TIRED
GALA NIGHT	GOOD HANDS	GROW WEARY
GALE FORCE	GOOD HEART	HAIR CREAM
GAME POINT	GOOD HOURS	HAIR SHIRT
GATE MONEY	GOOD HOUSE	HAIR TONIC
GAVE BIRTH	GOOD IMAGE	HALF AWAKE
GAZA STRIP	GOOD JUDGE	HALF BREED
GEAR LEVER	GOOD LIGHT	HALF CROWN
GENE AUTRY	GOOD LIVER	HALF DRUNK
GIFT HORSE	GOOD LOOKS	HALF EMPTY
GIFT TOKEN	GOOD LOSER	HALF HITCH
GIRL GUIDE	GOOD LUNCH	HALF LIGHT
GIVE BIRTH	GOOD MARKS	HALF OUNCE
GIVE BLOOD	GOOD MATCH	HALF POUND
GIVE CHASE	GOOD MIXER	HALF PRICE
GIVE FORTH	GOOD MONEY	HALF SHARE
GIVE TERMS	GOOD MUSIC	HALF SPEED
GIVE VOICE	GOOD OFFER	HALF TRUTH
GODS IMAGE	GOOD PATCH	HALL TABLE
GODS TRUTH	GOOD POINT	HAND BASIN
GOES ROUND	GOOD PRICE	HAND BRAKE
GOES UNDER	GOOD SCORE	HAND CREAM
GOES WRONG	GOOD SENSE	HAND ROUND
GOLD BRAID	GOOD SHAPE	HAND TOWEL
GOLD BRICK	GOOD SIGHT	HANG ABOUT
GOLD CHAIN	GOOD SPEED	HANG HEAVY
GOLD COAST	GOOD SPORT	HARD APORT

HARD CLIMB
HARD COURT
HARD COVER
HARD DRUGS
HARD FACTS
HARD FIGHT
HARD FROST
HARD FRUIT
HARD GOING
HARD GRAFT
HARD GRIND
HARD HEART
HARD KNOCK
HARD LINES
HARD MONEY
HARD STEEL
HARD STUFF
HARD TIMES
HARD WATER
HARD WORDS
HAVE FAITH
HAVE LUNCH
HAVE MERCY
HAVE SENSE
HAVE STYLE
HAVE TASTE
HAVE TWINS
HAVE VIEWS
HAVE WORDS
HEAD COUNT
HEAD FIRST
HEAP ABUSE
HEAR ABOUT
HELP ALONG
HERE BELOW
HIGH ABOVE
HIGH ALTAR
HIGH BIRTH
HIGH BOOTS
HIGH CASTE
HIGH CHAIR
HIGH CLOUD
HIGH COURT
HIGH FEVER
HIGH FLIER
HIGH FLOOR
HIGH GRADE
HIGH HEELS
HIGH HOPES
HIGH HORSE
HIGH JINKS
HIGH LEVEL
HIGH MARKS
HIGH PITCH
HIGH PRICE
HIGH RATES
HIGH SCORE
HIGH SPEED
HIGH TABLE
HIGH TOWER
HIGH VALUE

HIGH VOICE
HIGH WAGES
HIGH WATER
HOLD ALOFT
HOLD CLOSE
HOLD COURT
HOLD FORTH
HOLD HANDS
HOLD STILL
HOLD TIGHT
HOLD WATER
HOLY BIBLE
HOLY GHOST
HOLY GRAIL
HOLY MOSES
HOLY PLACE
HOLY SMOKE
HOLY WATER
HOME AGAIN
HOME FIRES
HOME FRONT
HOME GROWN
HOME GUARD
HOME LOVER
HOME MATCH
HOME TRADE
HOME TRUTH
HOPE CHEST
HURL ABUSE
HUSH MONEY
ICED DRINK
ICED WATER
IDLE BOAST
IDLE FANCY
IDLE HANDS
IDLE STORY
INTO TOUCH
IPSO FACTO
IRON CROSS
IRON FRAME
IRON GUARD
IRON HORSE
IRON OXIDE
IRON TONIC
IRON WORKS
JACK BENNY
JACK FROST
JACK HOBBS
JACK JONES
JACK KETCH
JACK LYNCH
JACK SPRAT
JACK TRAIN
JADE GREEN
JANE FONDA
JANE SHORE
JAZZ MUSIC
JEAN MARAT
JOHN ADAMS
JOHN BROWN
JOHN CABOT

JOHN CURRY
JOHN DONNE
JOHN GLENN
JOHN KEATS
JOHN LOCKE
JOHN MILLS
JOHN SMITH
JOHN WAYNE
JOIN HANDS
JUAN PERÓN
JUDI DENCH
JUDO THROW
JUMP ABOUT
JUMP AHEAD
JUMP CLEAR
JUST ABOUT
JUST CAUSE
JUST CLAIM
JUST FANCY
JUST IDEAL
JUST RIGHT
JUST SHORT
JUST THINK
KEEN BRAIN
KEEN FIGHT
KEEN MATCH
KEEN PRICE
KEEP AHEAD
KEEP ALIVE
KEEP APART
KEEP BOOKS
KEEP CLEAR
KEEP CLOSE
KEEP COUNT
KEEP FAITH
KEEP FRESH
KEEP GOING
KEEP GUARD
KEEP HOUSE
KEEP ORDER
KEEP QUIET
KEEP RIGHT
KEEP SCORE
KEEP SOBER
KEEP STILL
KEEP STOCK
KEEP TRACK
KEEP UNDER
KEEP VIGIL
KEEP WATCH
KEPT GOING
KEPT GUARD
KEPT WOMAN
KERB DRILL
KIDS STUFF
KIND HEART
KIND WORDS
KING COBRA
KING HARRY
KING HENRY
KING JAMES

KING MIDAS	LEAN YEARS	LONG WHILE
KING STORK	LEAP ABOUT	LOOK AFTER
KNEE JOINT	LEAP AHEAD	LOOK AHEAD
KURT WEILL	LEFT ALONE	LOOK ALIKE
LACK SENSE	LEFT ELBOW	LOOK ALIVE
LADY ASTOR	LEFT FLANK	LOOK BLACK
LADY DIANA	LEGS APART	LOOK FRESH
LAID WASTE	LENA HORNE	LOOK NIPPY
LAKE HURON	LEND MONEY	LOOK RIGHT
LAKE NYASA	LESS SPEED	LOOK ROUND
LAKE POETS	LIFE BLOOD	LOOK SHARP
LAMB CURRY	LIFE CYCLE	LOOK SILLY
LAMP SHADE	LIFE FORCE	LOOK SMART
LAND AGENT	LIFE STORY	LOOK THERE
LAND AHEAD	LIFE STUDY	LOOM LARGE
LAND FORCE	LIKE MAGIC	LORD BYRON
LAND ROVER	LIKE SHEEP	LORD DERBY
LAND SPEED	LIKE WATER	LORD GRADE
LANE THREE	LIME GREEN	LORD LUCAN
LARK ABOUT	LIME GROVE	LORD MAYOR
LAST APRIL	LIME JUICE	LORD NORTH
LAST DANCE	LIMP WRIST	LORD REITH
LAST DITCH	LION HEART	LOSE CASTE
LAST DREGS	LION TAMER	LOSE COUNT
LAST EVENT	LIST PRICE	LOSE FAITH
LAST FLING	LIVE AGAIN	LOSE HEART
LAST LAUGH	LIVE ALONE	LOSE MONEY
LAST LIGHT	LIVE APART	LOSE TOUCH
LAST MARCH	LIVE ROUGH	LOSE TRACK
LAST MONTH	LOAF SUGAR	LOST ANGEL
LAST NIGHT	LOCH MARIE	LOST CAUSE
LAST OFFER	LONG AFTER	LOST CHORD
LAST ORDER	LONG BEACH	LOST SHEEP
LAST PENNY	LONG BEARD	LOST SKILL
LAST PLACE	LONG CHALK	LOST TOUCH
LAST RITES	LONG DELAY	LOST TRIBE
LAST ROUND	LONG DOZEN	LOST WORLD
LAST SCENE	LONG DRESS	LOST YEARS
LAST STAGE	LONG DRINK	LOUD CHEER
LAST STAND	LONG DRIVE	LOUD KNOCK
LAST STRAW	LONG GRASS	LOUD LAUGH
LAST TANGO	LONG HAIRS	LOUD MOUTH
LAST THING	LONG HOURS	LOUD MUSIC
LAST TRAIN	LONG LEASE	LOUD NOISE
LAST VERSE	LONG MARCH	LOUD PEDAL
LAST WALTZ	LONG NIGHT	LOUD SOUND
LAST WORDS	LONG PANTS	LOUD VOICE
LATE ENTRY	LONG PURSE	LOVE APPLE
LATE EXTRA	LONG RANGE	LOVE CHILD
LATE HOURS	LONG REACH	LOVE FORTY
LATE LUNCH	LONG REIGN	LOVE MATCH
LATE NIGHT	LONG SIGHT	LOVE SCENE
LATE RISER	LONG SINCE	LOVE STORY
LATE SHIFT	LONG SKIRT	LOVE TOKEN
LATE STAGE	LONG SLEEP	LUMP SUGAR
LATE START	LONG SOCKS	LYME REGIS
LAVA BREAD	LONG SPELL	MADE WORSE
LAWN MOWER	LONG STORY	MAIL ORDER
LAZY BONES	LONG TRIAL	MAIL TRAIN
LEAD OXIDE	LONG VISIT	MAIN EVENT
LEAF MOULD	LONG VOWEL	MAIN FORCE

MAIN ISSUE	MISS WORLD	OPEN FLOOR
MAIN SEWER	MOCK TRIAL	OPEN GRATE
MAIN THEME	MOCK TUDOR	OPEN GRAVE
MAIN THING	MONT BLANC	OPEN HEART
MAKE CLEAR	MOON ABOUT	OPEN HOUSE
MAKE FACES	MOON RIVER	OPEN MOUTH
MAKE HASTE	MOOT POINT	OPEN ORDER
MAKE KNOWN	MORE HASTE	OPEN PURSE
MAKE LIGHT	MORE MONEY	OPEN SEWER
MAKE MERRY	MOSS GREEN	OPEN SHIRT
MAKE MONEY	MOVE ABOUT	OPEN SPACE
MAKE MUSIC	MOVE ALONG	OPEN WOUND
MAKE PEACE	MOVE HOUSE	OVER AGAIN
MAKE PLAIN	MOVE ROUND	OVER FIFTY
MAKE PLANS	MUCH LATER	OVER FORTY
MAKE READY	MUCH MOVED	OVER SIXTY
MAKE SENSE	MUCH SPACE	OVER THERE
MAKE TIGHT	MUCH WORSE	OWEN TUDOR
MAKE WHOLE	MULE TRAIN	PAGE EIGHT
MAKE WORSE	NAME BRAND	PAGE PROOF
MALE CHOIR	NAZI PARTY	PAGE SEVEN
MALE MODEL	NEAR OFFER	PAGE THREE
MALE NURSE	NEAR SIGHT	PALE GREEN
MALE VOICE	NEAR THING	PALM BEACH
MANY HANDS	NEAT BEARD	PARI PASSU
MANY MILES	NEAT DRINK	PARK BENCH
MANY MOONS	NEAT TRICK	PASS ALONG
MANY TIMES	NEAT VODKA	PASS ROUND
MANY WORDS	NEON LIGHT	PAST GLORY
MANY YEARS	NEWS FLASH	PAST TENSE
MARK SPITZ	NEWS SHEET	PAUL JONES
MARK TWAIN	NEXT APRIL	PAUL SIMON
MARY ASTOR	NEXT ISSUE	PICK FRUIT
MARY TUDOR	NEXT MARCH	PICK HOLES
MASS MEDIA	NEXT MONTH	PIED PIPER
MATT BUSBY	NEXT TRAIN	PIER GLASS
MATT MONRO	NEXT WORLD	PINK ICING
MATT PAINT	NICE SLEEP	PIPE DREAM
MEAN TRICK	NIKI LAUDA	PIPE MAJOR
MEAT CURRY	NILE GREEN	PIPE MUSIC
MEAT JELLY	NINE HOLES	PIPE ORGAN
MEAT PASTE	NINE HOURS	PLAN AHEAD
MEIN KAMPF	NINE KILOS	PLAY ABOUT
MERE WORDS	NINE LIVES	PLAY BINGO
MESS ABOUT	NINE MILES	PLAY BOWLS
MILD CURRY	NINE PENCE	PLAY CARDS
MILD STEEL	NINE TIMES	PLAY CHESS
MILK CHURN	NINE WEEKS	PLAY DARTS
MILK DRINK	NINE YEARS	PLAY GAMES
MILK FLOAT	NONE OTHER	PLAY GROUP
MILK PUNCH	NOTE PAPER	PLAY HAVOC
MILK ROUND	NUDE WOMAN	PLAY POKER
MILK SHAKE	NUNS HABIT	PLAY ROUGH
MILK STOUT	OAST HOUSE	PLAY RUGBY
MILK TEETH	ONCE AGAIN	PLAY RUMMY
MINE SHAFT	ONES EQUAL	PLAY WHIST
MINI SKIRT	ONLY CHILD	PLOD ALONG
MINK STOLE	ONLY HUMAN	PLUS FOURS
MINT JULEP	OPEN COURT	POGO STICK
MINT SAUCE	OPEN DRAIN	POLE VAULT
MISS RIGHT	OPEN FIELD	POOR CHILD

POOR	DEVIL	RING	AGAIN	SHOW	STYLE
POOR	JUDGE	RING	CYCLE	SHUT	TIGHT
POOR	LIGHT	RING	FALSE	SICK	LEAVE
POOR	MATCH	RING	FENCE	SIDE	ISSUE
POOR	SIGHT	RING	ROUND	SIGN	BELOW
POOR	SPORT	RIOT	SQUAD	SILK	PURSE
POOR	START	RIPE	APPLE	SILK	SCARF
POOR	TASTE	RIPE	FRUIT	SIZE	EIGHT
POOR	THING	RISE	ABOVE	SIZE	SEVEN
POOR	VALUE	RISE	EARLY	SIZE	THREE
POOR	WOMAN	ROAD	BLOCK	SKIN	DIVER
POOR	YIELD	ROAD	DRILL	SKIN	GRAFT
PORT	ELLEN	ROAD	METAL	SLIM	BUILD
POST	EARLY	ROAD	SENSE	SLIM	WAIST
POUR	FORTH	ROAD	WORKS	SLIP	COVER
PRAY	ALOUD	ROCK	MUSIC	SLIT	SKIRT
PULL	AHEAD	ROCK	PLANT	SLOP	BASIN
PULL	APART	ROLL	ALONG	SLOW	DEATH
PULL	ASIDE	ROOT	CAUSE	SLOW	MARCH
PULL	FACES	ROPE	TRICK	SLOW	MATCH
PULL	TIGHT	ROSE	MARIE	SLOW	MUSIC
PULL	WIRES	ROSE	PETAL	SLOW	PULSE
PURE	MAGIC	ROSE	WATER	SLOW	START
PURE	MATHS	RUDE	REPLY	SLOW	TEMPO
PURE	SPITE	RUDE	WORDS	SLOW	TRAIN
PURE	WATER	RUMP	STEAK	SLOW	WALTZ
PURE	WHITE	RUSH	ABOUT	SNOB	VALUE
PURE	WOMAN	SAFE	CATCH	SNOW	GOOSE
PUSH	ASIDE	SAFE	HANDS	SNOW	SCENE
RACE	AHEAD	SAFE	PLACE	SNOW	STORM
RACE	RIOTS	SAIL	ALONG	SNOW	WHITE
RACE	TRACK	SAIL	ROUND	SOAP	OPERA
RACY	STYLE	SALE	PRICE	SOAR	ABOVE
RAIN	CHECK	SALT	FLATS	SODA	WATER
RAIN	CLOUD	SALT	RIVER	SOFT	DRINK
RAIN	GAUGE	SALT	SPOON	SOFT	DRUGS
RARE	EVENT	SALT	WATER	SOFT	FRUIT
RARE	STAMP	SAME	AGAIN	SOFT	GOING
RARE	STEAK	SAME	PLACE	SOFT	GOODS
RARE	TREAT	SAME	THING	SOFT	HEART
READ	ALOUD	SAND	DUNES	SOFT	LIGHT
READ	MUSIC	SANS	SERIF	SOFT	MUSIC
READ	VERSE	SAVE	MONEY	SOFT	PEDAL
REAL	CREAM	SAVE	SPACE	SOFT	TOUCH
REAL	MCCOY	SEED	PEARL	SOFT	VERGE
REAL	SPORT	SEEK	AFTER	SOFT	VOICE
REAL	THING	SEEK	PEACE	SOFT	WATER
REAL	TONIC	SELL	SHORT	SOFT	WORDS
REAL	TRUTH	SEND	FORTH	SOLE	AGENT
REAL	WAGES	SHAM	FIGHT	SOLE	OWNER
REAL	WORLD	SHED	BLOOD	SOLO	WHIST
REAR	LIGHT	SHED	LIGHT	SONG	CYCLE
REAR	WHEEL	SHED	TEARS	SONG	SHEET
REED	ORGAN	SHOE	BRUSH	SONG	TITLE
RICE	FIELD	SHOP	FLOOR	SOON	AFTER
RICE	PAPER	SHOP	FRONT	SORE	POINT
RICH	UNCLE	SHOP	HOURS	SOUL	MATES
RICH	WIDOW	SHOW	FIGHT	SOUL	MUSIC
RICH	WOMAN	SHOW	MERCY	SOUP	LADLE
RIDE	ALONE	SHOW	ROUND	SOUP	PLATE
RIDE	ROUGH	SHOW	SIGNS	SOUP	SPOON

SOUR CREAM	TALL STORY	TWIN SCREW
SOUR TASTE	TALL WOMAN	TYRE LEVER
SOYA BEANS	TANK CORPS	UGLY BRUTE
SPIN DRIER	TASK FORCE	UGLY CROWD
SPIN ROUND	TEAM EVENT	UNIT TRUST
SPOT CHECK	TEAM STRIP	URSA MAJOR
SPOT DANCE	TEAR ABOUT	URSA MINOR
SPOT PRIZE	TEAR ALONG	VADE MECUM
STAB WOUND	TEAR APART	VAIN BOAST
STAG NIGHT	TELL TALES	VAIN GLORY
STAG PARTY	TEST DRIVE	VEER RIGHT
STAR ACTOR	TEST MATCH	VEER ROUND
STAR GAZER	TEST PAPER	VERS LIBRE
STAR PUPIL	TEST PIECE	VERY CHEAP
STAY AHEAD	TEST PILOT	VERY LIGHT
STAY ALIVE	TEST SCORE	VERY OFTEN
STAY APART	THIN BLOOD	VERY QUICK
STAY AWAKE	THIN GRUEL	VERY STEEP
STAY CLOSE	THIN SHELL	VERY SWEET
STAY SOBER	THIN SLICE	VERY WORST
STAY STILL	THIN STORY	VICE SQUAD
STAY YOUNG	THIS MONTH	VICE VERSA
STEP ASIDE	TIED HOUSE	WAGE CLAIM
STEP DANCE	TIME BEING	WAGE PAUSE
STEP THREE	TIME CHECK	WAGE SCALE
STOP LIGHT	TIME FLIES	WAIT THERE
STOP PRESS	TIME LIMIT	WAKE EARLY
STOP SHORT	TIME TAKEN	WALK ABOUT
STOP THIEF!	TINY HANDS	WALK ALONG
STOP WATCH	TITO GOBBI	WANT BADLY
STUD HORSE	TONY GREIG	WARM FRONT
STUD POKER	TOOK PLACE	WARM HANDS
SUEZ CANAL	TOOL CHEST	WARM HEART
SUNK FENCE	TORN APART	WARM NIGHT
SURE THING	TORY PARTY	WARM PLACE
TAKE ABACK	TOSS ABOUT	WARM SPELL
TAKE AFTER	TOSS ASIDE	WARM WATER
TAKE APART	TOWN CLERK	WASH CLEAN
TAKE COVER	TOWN CRIER	WASP STING
TAKE DRUGS	TOWN HOUSE	WASP WAIST
TAKE HEART	TOWN MOUSE	WAVE POWER
TAKE ISSUE	TRAP THREE	WEAK HEART
TAKE LEAVE	TREE STUMP	WEAK POINT
TAKE LUNCH	TRIM WAIST	WEAK POUND
TAKE NOTES	TROY OUNCE	WEAK SMILE
TAKE PAINS	TRUE STORY	WEAK STATE
TAKE PLACE	TRUE VALUE	WEAK VOICE
TAKE PRIDE	TRUE WORTH	WEAK WOMAN
TAKE RISKS	TUBE TRAIN	WEAR BLACK
TAKE SHAPE	TURN ABOUT	WEAR WHITE
TAKE SIDES	TURN AGAIN	WELL ABOVE
TAKE SNUFF	TURN ASIDE	WELL AHEAD
TAKE STEPS	TURN BLACK	WELL BEGUN
TAKE STOCK	TURN BROWN	WELL BELOW
TAKE TURNS	TURN GREEN	WELL OILED
TALK ABOUT	TURN LOOSE	WELL SPENT
TALK MONEY	TURN NASTY	WENT ABOUT
TALK ROUND	TURN RIGHT	WENT AHEAD
TALK SENSE	TURN ROUND	WENT NORTH
TALK TRIPE	TURN WHITE	WENT ROUND
TALL ORDER	TWIN GIRLS	WENT SOUTH

WENT UNDER	DRIVE A BUS	ADAMS WINE
WENT WRONG	DRIVE A CAR	AFTER DARK
WEST COAST	HEADS I WIN	AFTER DUSK
WEST POINT	LEAVE A GAP	AFTER NOON
WEST WALES	LEAVE A TIP	AFTER TIME
WHAT ABOUT	PLACE A BET	AGILE MIND
WHIP ROUND	QUITE A FEW	AGREE WITH
WIDE ANGLE	SCORE A HIT	ALARM BELL
WIDE APART	SCORE A RUN	ALARM CALL
WIDE AWAKE	SCORE A TRY	ALERT MIND
WIDE BERTH	SHAKE A LEG	ALFIE BASS
WIDE FIELD	SMELL A RAT	ALICE BAND
WIDE GAUGE	SMOKE A FAG	ALIEN CORN
WIDE RANGE	START A ROW	ALIEN RACE
WIDE SCOPE	START A WAR	ALLOW BAIL
WIDE SWEEP	THROW A FIT	ALPHA PLUS
WIDE WORLD	TWICE A DAY	ALPHA RAYS
WILD ABUSE	WEAVE A RUG	AMINO ACID
WILD BEAST	WEAVE A WEB	AMPLE ROOM
WILD CLAIM	WORTH A LOT	ANDRÉ GIDE
WILD GOOSE	WORTH A TRY	ANGEL CAKE
WILD GRASS		ANGEL FACE
WILD GUESS	**5 , 2 , 2**	ANGEL FISH
WILD HONEY		ANGRY LOOK
WILD HORSE	BREAK IT UP	ANKLE DEEP
WILD PARTY	BRIDE TO BE	APART FROM
WIND GAUGE	BRING IT UP	APPLE CART
WIND POWER	CEASE TO BE	APPLE TART
WIND SCALE	CHALK IT UP	APPLE TREE
WINE GLASS	CHUCK IT IN	APRIL FOOL
WIPE CLEAN	COUNT ON IT	ATTIC SALT
WIRE FENCE	DYING TO GO	AUGUR WELL
WITH GUSTO	FIRST TO GO	AZURE BLUE
WITH PRIDE	FUNNY HA-HA	BACON RIND
WITH SKILL	PATCH IT UP	BADLY DONE
WITH SUGAR	READY TO GO	BADLY HURT
WOOD GREEN	SLEEP ON IT	BALSA WOOD
WOOD NYMPH	SNEAK UP ON	BANDY LEGS
WOOL TRADE	SPEED IT UP	BARGE INTO
WORK BENCH	STAND UP TO	BARRY JOHN
WORK FORCE	START TO GO	BASIC NEED
WORK HORSE	STEAL UP ON	BASIC WAGE
WORK LOOSE	STICK AT IT	BEACH BALL
WORK PARTY	STICK EM UP	BEACH WEAR
WORK STUDY	STICK IT ON	BEECH TREE
WORK TABLE	STICK TO IT	BEGIN WELL
WRAP ROUND	SWEAR BY IT	BEGIN WORK
YOUR FAULT	THERE IT IS	BELOW COST
YOUR GRACE	THINK ON IT	BELOW DECK
ZINC PLATE	TRIED IT ON	BELOW ZERO
	VINGT ET UN	BENNY HILL
5 , 1 , 3	WHERE IS IT?	BERYL REID
	WORST OF IT	BEVIN BOYS
APPLE A DAY		BILLY BUDD
BOARD A BUS	**5 , 4**	BILLY FURY
BREAK A LEG		BILLY GOAT
CARRY A GUN	ABOUT FACE	BILLY LIAR
CATCH A BUS	ABOUT TIME	BINGO HALL
CRACK A NUT	ABOUT TURN	BIRCH TREE
CRACK A RIB	ABOVE ZERO	BIRDS NEST
DANCE A JIG	ACKER BILK	BIRTH MARK

BIRTH RATE	BREAD ROLL	CHAIN DOWN
BJORN BORG	BREAK AWAY	CHAIN GANG
BLACK ARTS	BREAK CAMP	CHAIN MAIL
BLACK BEAR	BREAK DOWN	CHASE AWAY
BLACK BELT	BREAK EVEN	CHEAP FARE
BLACK BESS	BREAK JAIL	CHEAP JACK
BLACK BOOK	BREAK OPEN	CHEAP RATE
BLACK GOLD	BRIAR PIPE	CHEAP WINE
BLACK HAIR	BRICK WALL	CHECK MATE
BLACK HOLE	BRING AWAY	CHECK OVER
BLACK JACK	BRING BACK	CHESS CLUB
BLACK KING	BRING DOWN	CHICO MARX
BLACK LACE	BRING HOME	CHIEF COOK
BLACK LIST	BRING OVER	CHIEF PART
BLACK LOOK	BRING WORD	CHIEF WHIP
BLACK MARK	BRISK WALK	CHILD CARE
BLACK MASS	BROAD BACK	CHILD STAR
BLACK MOOD	BROAD BEAM	CHINA CLAY
BLACK OPAL	BROAD BEAN	CHINA DOLL
BLACK PAWN	BROAD GRIN	CHINA ROSE
BLACK ROOK	BROAD HINT	CHINA SHOP
BLACK SPOT	BROAD MIND	CHOIR GIRL
BLACK SUIT	BROAD VIEW	CHOKE BACK
BLACK SWAN	BROKE DOWN	CHOKE DOWN
BLANK LOOK	BROOD MARE	CHUMP CHOP
BLANK MIND	BROWN BEAR	CIGAR BUTT
BLANK PAGE	BROWN BELT	CIVIC DUTY
BLANK WALL	BROWN BESS	CIVIL CASE
BLIND DATE	BROWN EYES	CIVIL CODE
BLIND MICE	BROWN HAIR	CIVIL LIFE
BLIND SIDE	BROWN LOAF	CIVIL LIST
BLIND SPOT	BROWN SUIT	CIVIL SUIT
BLOCK VOTE	BRUSH AWAY	CLAMP DOWN
BLOND HAIR	BRUSH DOWN	CLARK KENT
BLOOD BANK	BRUSH OVER	CLASH WITH
BLOOD BATH	BRUSH PAST	CLEAN AWAY
BLOOD CLOT	BUGLE CALL	CLEAN BILL
BLOOD FEUD	BUGLE HORN	CLEAN BLOW
BLOOD LUST	BULLY BEEF	CLEAR AWAY
BLOOD TEST	BUNNY GIRL	CLEAR CASE
BLOOD TYPE	BURMA ROAD	CLEAR HEAD
BLUES SONG	BURNT CORK	CLEAR LEAD
BLUNT EDGE	BURNT DOWN	CLEAR MIND
BOARD GAME	BURST OPEN	CLEAR ROAD
BOARD ROOM	BURST PIPE	CLEAR SOUP
BOMBS AWAY	BURST TYRE	CLEAR VIEW
BONNY LASS	CABIN CREW	CLIMB DOWN
BOOBY TRAP	CALFS HEAD	CLIMB OVER
BOSSA NOVA	CANNY SCOT	CLOCK CARD
BOUND OVER	CARGO SHIP	CLOCK GOLF
BOWED HEAD	CAROL REED	CLOSE CALL
BRAIN CELL	CARRY ARMS	CLOSE CROP
BRAIN WAVE	CARRY AWAY	CLOSE DOWN
BRAKE DRUM	CARRY OVER	CLOSE GAME
BRAKE SHOE	CATCH COLD	CLOSE LOOK
BRAND NAME	CATCH FIRE	CLOSE RACE
BRASS BAND	CATCH FISH	CLOSE VOTE
BRASS TACK	CATCH HOLD	CLOTH EARS
BRAVE DEED	CAUSE PAIN	CLOUD OVER
BRAVE FACE	CEASE FIRE	COACH TOUR
BREAD LINE	CEDAR TREE	COACH TRIP

COCOA BEAN	DEATH RATE	EDGED TOOL
COMIC BOOK	DEATH TRAP	EDITH PIAF
COMIC CUTS	DEATH WISH	EDSON PELE
COMIC PLAY	DECOY DUCK	EIDER DUCK
CORAL REEF	DEMOB SUIT	EIGHT DAYS
CORNY JOKE	DEPOT SHIP	EIGHT FEET
COSTA RICA	DEVIL FISH	EIGHT QUID
COUGH DROP	DIANA DORS	ELBOW ROOM
COUNT DOWN	DIANA ROSS	ELDER WINE
COUNT UPON	DIRTY DEED	ELTON JOHN
COURT CARD	DIRTY DICK	EMBER DAYS
COURT CASE	DIRTY JOKE	EMILE ZOLA
COVER GIRL	DIRTY LOOK	EMPTY ROOM
COWES WEEK	DIRTY WORD	EMPTY SACK
CRACK OPEN	DIRTY WORK	EMPTY SEAT
CRASH DIET	DODGE CITY	EMPTY SHOW
CRASH DOWN	DOING FINE	EMPTY TALK
CRAZY GANG	DOING TIME	EMPTY TANK
CREAM CAKE	DOING WELL	ENEMY CAMP
CREAM PUFF	DOLLS PRAM	ENEMY FIRE
CRIME WAVE	DOLLY BIRD	ENJOY LIFE
CROSS FIRE	DOVER SOLE	ENTER INTO
CROSS KEYS	DOZEN EGGS	ENTRY CARD
CROSS OVER	DRAIN AWAY	ENTRY FORM
CROSS WIND	DRAPE SUIT	ENTRY VISA
CROWN CORK	DRAWN GAME	EQUAL RANK
CROWN LAND	DREAM GIRL	ERNIE WISE
CROWS FEET	DRESS COAT	EVERY HOUR
CROWS NEST	DRESS DOWN	EVERY INCH
CRUDE JOKE	DRESS RING	EVERY SIDE
CRUEL BLOW	DRESS SUIT	EVERY TIME
CRUEL FATE	DRESS WELL	EVERY WEEK
CUBAN HEEL	DRIED EGGS	EVERY WORD
CUBBY HOLE	DRIED FIGS	EVERY YEAR
CUBIC FEET	DRIED MILK	EXACT COPY
CUBIC FOOT	DRIED PEAS	EXACT FARE
CUBIC INCH	DRIFT AWAY	EXACT TIME
CUBIC YARD	DRINK BEER	EXTRA FOOD
CURIO SHOP	DRIVE AWAY	EXTRA HELP
CURLY HAIR	DRIVE HARD	EXTRA ROOM
CUTTY SARK	DRIVE HOME	EXTRA SEAT
CYCLE RACE	DRIVE PAST	EXTRA TIME
CYCLE TOUR	DRURY LANE	EXTRA WELL
DAILY HELP	DUCKS BACK	EXTRA WORK
DAILY MAIL	DUCKS EGGS	FAINT HOPE
DAILY STAR	DUTCH BULB	FAINT LINE
DAILY WORK	DUTCH OVEN	FAIRS FAIR
DAIRY FARM	DUTCH WIFE	FAIRY CAKE
DAIRY HERD	DWARF STAR	FAIRY FOLK
DAIRY MAID	DWELL UPON	FAIRY KING
DALAI LAMA	DYING AWAY	FAIRY RING
DANCE BAND	DYING DUCK	FAIRY TALE
DANCE HALL	DYING RACE	FAITH CURE
DANCE STEP	DYING WISH	FALSE COIN
DANCE TUNE	EARLY BIRD	FALSE HOPE
DANNY KAYE	EARLY CALL	FALSE IDEA
DARTS TEAM	EARLY DAYS	FALSE IDOL
DEATH BLOW	EARLY FALL	FALSE MOVE
DEATH CELL	EARLY HOUR	FALSE NAME
DEATH DUTY	EARLY LIFE	FALSE NOTE
DEATH MASK	EATEN AWAY	FALSE OATH

FANCY FREE	FIRST WORD	FULLY CLAD
FANNY HILL	FIRST YEAR	FULLY PAID
FATAL BLOW	FISHY TALE	FULLY RIPE
FATAL DOSE	FIXED GAZE	FUNNY BONE
FATAL MOVE	FIXED GRIN	FUNNY FACE
FEVER HEAT	FIXED IDEA	FUNNY FARM
FIELD ARMY	FIXED ODDS	FUNNY FILM
FIELD GAME	FIXED RATE	FUNNY JOKE
FIELD TEST	FIXED STAR	FUNNY LADY
FIELD WORK	FIXED TIME	FUNNY TIME
FIFTH FORM	FIXED WAYS	GABLE ROOF
FIFTH TEST	FLARE PATH	GAMES ROOM
FIFTH TIME	FLASH BULB	GAMMA RAYS
FIFTY QUID	FLESH PINK	GENOA CAKE
FIGHT BACK	FLESH TINT	GEOFF HUNT
FIGHT FAIR	FLING AWAY	GHOST TOWN
FIGHT FIRE	FLING DOWN	GIANT CLAM
FIGHT WITH	FLIRT WITH	GIANT SIZE
FINAL BELL	FLOAT DOWN	GIDDY GOAT
FINAL BLOW	FLOOD GATE	GIDEA PARK
FINAL EXIT	FLOOD TIDE	GIPSY MOTH
FINAL HEAT	FLOOR PLAN	GIRLS CLUB
FINAL HOPE	FLOOR SHOW	GIVEN TIME
FINAL MOVE	FLOUR MILL	GLASS CASE
FINAL STEP	FOOLS GOLD	GLASS DISH
FINAL TEST	FOOLS MATE	GLASS TUBE
FINAL YEAR	FORCE FEED	GLASS VASE
FIRST BASE	FORCE OPEN	GLIDE AWAY
FIRST BLOW	FORTY DAYS	GLOAT OVER
FIRST BOOK	FORTY LOVE	GLORY HOLE
FIRST BORN	FORTY QUID	GLOSS OVER
FIRST COAT	FRANK MUIR	GOATS HAIR
FIRST COME	FRESH EGGS	GOATS MILK
FIRST COPY	FRESH FISH	GOING AWAY
FIRST COST	FRESH FOOD	GOING BACK
FIRST FOOT	FRESH LOAF	GOING BALD
FIRST FORM	FRESH MEAT	GOING DOWN
FIRST GEAR	FRESH MILK	GOING GREY
FIRST HALF	FRESH ROLL	GOING HOME
FIRST HEAT	FRESH WIND	GOING ONCE
FIRST HOME	FRIAR TUCK	GOING OVER
FIRST LADY	FRIED FISH	GOING RATE
FIRST LEAD	FRIED FOOD	GOING SLOW
FIRST LINE	FRIED RICE	GOING WELL
FIRST LORD	FROCK COAT	GOLDA MEIR
FIRST LOVE	FRONT DOOR	GOODS LIFT
FIRST MATE	FRONT LINE	GOOSE FAIR
FIRST MOVE	FRONT PAGE	GRACE NOTE
FIRST NAME	FRONT PAWS	GRAND DUKE
FIRST PAGE	FRONT ROOM	GRAND JURY
FIRST PART	FRONT SEAT	GRAND LAMA
FIRST RACE	FRONT STEP	GRAND PRIX
FIRST RATE	FRONT STUD	GRAND SLAM
FIRST RULE	FRONT VIEW	GRAND TIME
FIRST SIGN	FROWN UPON	GRAND TOUR
FIRST SLIP	FRUIT BOWL	GRASS PLOT
FIRST STEP	FRUIT CAKE	GRAVE NEWS
FIRST TEAM	FRUIT DISH	GRAVY BOAT
FIRST TERM	FRUIT GUMS	GREAT AUNT
FIRST TEST	FRUIT TART	GREAT BEAR
FIRST TIME	FRUIT TREE	GREAT BLOW

GREAT CARE	HARSH WORD	INGLE NOOK
GREAT COAT	HASTY WORD	INNER ROOM
GREAT DANE	HAZEL EYES	INNER SELF
GREAT DEAL	HEADY DAYS	INNER TUBE
GREAT DEED	HEAVY BLOW	INTER ALIA
GREAT FAME	HEAVY COLD	IRISH BULL
GREAT FEAT	HEAVY COST	IRISH EYES
GREAT FIRE	HEAVY FALL	IRISH STEW
GREAT FORM	HEAVY FINE	ITCHY PALM
GREAT GAIN	HEAVY FIRE	JAMES BOND
GREAT GOAL	HEAVY GUNS	JAMES COOK
GREAT GUNS	HEAVY HAND	JAMES DEAN
GREAT HALL	HEAVY LOAD	JAMES HUNT
GREAT HELP	HEAVY LOSS	JAMES WATT
GREAT IDEA	HEAVY MEAL	JELLY BABY
GREAT LIFE	HEAVY MIST	JENNY LIND
GREAT LOSS	HEAVY ODDS	JENNY WREN
GREAT MANY	HEAVY POLL	JESUS WEPT
GREAT MIND	HEAVY RAIN	JEWEL CASE
GREAT NAME	HEAVY SEAS	JIMMY HILL
GREAT NEWS	HEAVY SNOW	JOINT HEIR
GREAT PAIN	HEAVY SOIL	JOINT WILL
GREAT PAUL	HEAVY TANK	JOLLY GOOD
GREAT PITY	HEAVY WINE	JOLLY WELL
GREAT SEAL	HEAVY WORK	JUDAS KISS
GREAT WORK	HENRY FORD	JUDAS TREE
GREEK FIRE	HENRY HALL	KERRY BLUE
GREEK GIFT	HENRY TATE	KINGS ARMS
GREEK MYTH	HENRY WOOD	KINGS HEAD
GREEK PLAY	HIRED HAND	KINGS LYNN
GREEN BEAN	HIRED HELP	KINGS PAWN
GREEN BELT	HIRED THUG	KINGS ROAD
GREEN EYES	HITCH HIKE	KINGS ROOK
GREEN FLAG	HOARD GOLD	KIRBY GRIP
GREEN HILL	HOIST SAIL	KNEEL DOWN
GREEN LINE	HOLLY BUSH	KNEES BEND
GREEN PARK	HORSE FAIR	KNOCK BACK
GREEN PEAS	HORSE RACE	KNOCK COLD
GREEN ROOM	HORSE SHOW	KNOCK DOWN
GRILL ROOM	HOTEL BILL	KNOCK ONCE
GRIND DOWN	HOTEL ROOM	KNOCK OVER
GUARD DUTY	HOUND DOWN	KOALA BEAR
GUARD ROOM	HOURS LATE	KUBLA KHAN
GUEST ROOM	HOUSE BOAT	LADYS MAID
GUEST STAR	HOUSE FULL	LAGER BEER
GUIDE BOOK	HOUSE NAME	LAMBS WOOL
GUIDE ROPE	HOUSE PLAN	LARGE AREA
HANDS DOWN	HOUSE ROOM	LARGE ARMY
HANDS TURN	HUMAN HAND	LARGE BEER
HAPPY DAYS	HUMAN LIFE	LARGE BILL
HAPPY GIRL	HUMAN RACE	LARGE BONE
HAPPY HOME	HUMAN SOUL	LARGE CITY
HAPPY HOUR	HURRY AWAY	LARGE FLAT
HAPPY LIFE	HURRY BACK	LARGE LOAF
HAPPY MEAN	HURRY DOWN	LARGE PORT
HAPPY OMEN	HURRY HOME	LARGE ROOM
HAPPY PAIR	IDEAL GIFT	LARGE SIZE
HARPO MARX	IDEAL HOME	LARGE TOWN
HARRY LIME	IDEAL TIME	LASER BEAM
HARSH NOTE	IDEAL WIFE	LATER DATE
HARSH TONE	INERT MASS	LAUGH AWAY

LAUGH OVER	LOWER DECK	MODEL GIRL
LAYER CAKE	LOWER DOWN	MODEL WIFE
LEARN FAST	LOWER FORM	MONEY DOWN
LEASE LEND	LOWER LIMB	MONKS COWL
LEAST SAID	LUCID MIND	MORAL CODE
LEAVE HOME	LUCKY CHAP	MORAL DUTY
LEAVE OPEN	LUCKY DRAW	MORAL TONE
LEAVE ROOM	LUCKY FIND	MORAL VIEW
LEAVE WORD	LUCKY GIRL	MORSE CODE
LEAVE WORK	LUCKY MOVE	MOTOR BOAT
LEGAL CODE	LUCKY OMEN	MOTOR RACE
LEGAL HEIR	LUCKY SHOT	MOTOR SHOW
LEGAL MIND	LUCKY STAR	MOTOR TOUR
LEGAL TERM	LUNAR YEAR	MOUNT ETNA
LEGAL VIEW	LUNCH DATE	MOUSE TRAP
LEGER LINE	LUNCH HOUR	MOUTH HARP
LEMON CAKE	LUNCH TIME	MOVIE STAR
LEMON CURD	LURID PAST	MUDDY POND
LEMON PEEL	LUTON TOWN	MUSIC CASE
LEMON SOLE	LYING DOWN	MUSIC HALL
LEMON TREE	LYRIC POEM	MUSIC ROOM
LENIN PEAK	LYRIC POET	MUSIC SHOP
LEVEL BEST	MAGIC LAMP	NAKED LADY
LIBEL CASE	MAGIC RING	NANNY GOAT
LIBEL SUIT	MAGIC SIGN	NAPPY RASH
LIFES WORK	MAGIC WAND	NASAL TONE
LIGHT BLUE	MAGIC WORD	NASTY MESS
LIGHT BULB	MAINE ROAD	NASTY WORD
LIGHT DIET	MAJOR DOMO	NASTY WORK
LIGHT GREY	MAJOR PART	NAVAL BASE
LIGHT HAIR	MAJOR POET	NAVAL RANK
LIGHT LAMP	MAJOR ROAD	NAVAL TYPE
LIGHT MEAL	MAJOR ROLE	NEEDS MUST
LIGHT MIST	MAJOR SUIT	NEVER FEAR
LIGHT RAIN	MAJOR WORK	NEVER MIND
LIGHT SIDE	MAPLE LEAF	NEVER MORE
LIGHT SKIN	MAPLE TREE	NEVER STOP
LIGHT SUIT	MARCH AWAY	NEVER USED
LIGHT TANK	MARCH HARE	NIGHT CLUB
LIGHT WAVE	MARCH PAST	NIGHT DUTY
LIGHT WINE	MARCO POLO	NIGHT HAWK
LIGHT WORK	MARDI GRAS	NIGHT LIFE
LIGHT YEAR	MARES NEST	NIGHT SAFE
LILAC TIME	MARRY WELL	NIGHT SPOT
LILAC TREE	MATCH PLAY	NIGHT TIME
LIONS CAGE	MEANS TEST	NIGHT WORK
LIONS MANE	MEDAL PLAY	NOBLE LADY
LIONS TAIL	MERCY SEAT	NOBLE LINE
LIVER BIRD	MERRY HELL	NOBLE LORD
LIVID PINK	MERRY TUNE	NORTH FACE
LOCAL CALL	METAL DISC	NORTH POLE
LOCAL NEWS	METAL RING	NORTH SIDE
LOCAL TIME	METAL TUBE	NORTH STAR
LOOSE BALL	MILES AWAY	NORTH WIND
LOOSE CASH	MILLS BOMB	NORTH ZONE
LOOSE REIN	MINOR PART	NOTRE DAME
LOOSE TALK	MINOR POET	OBJET DART
LOOSE TILE	MINOR ROAD	OCEAN LANE
LOSER PAYS	MINOR ROLE	OCEAN WAVE
LOVED ONES	MINUS SIGN	OFFAS DYKE
LOWER CASE	MIXED NUTS	OGDEN NASH

OILED SILK	PITCH INTO	QUICK MEAL
OLDEN DAYS	PITCH PINE	QUICK SALE
OLIVE TREE	PIXIE RING	QUICK TIME
ONION SKIN	PLACE NAME	QUICK WORD
ONION SOUP	PLAIN CAKE	QUICK WORK
ORDER ARMS	PLAIN COOK	QUIET LIFE
ORDER BOOK	PLAIN FACT	QUIET READ
ORDER FORM	PLAIN FOOD	QUIET TOWN
ORGAN LOFT	PLAIN JANE	QUIET WORD
ORGAN STOP	PLAIN TALK	QUITE FULL
ORLOP DECK	PLANE TREE	QUITE GOOD
OTHER HALF	PLANT LIFE	QUITE NEAR
OTHER SIDE	PLATE RACK	QUITE OKAY
OUTER EDGE	PLUMB LINE	QUITE SURE
OUTER SKIN	POINT DUTY	QUITE WELL
PAINT OVER	POKER DICE	QUOTE ODDS
PALMY DAYS	POKER FACE	RADIO FOUR
PANEL GAME	POLAR BEAR	RADIO MAST
PAPAL BULL	PORTO RICO	RADIO PLAY
PAPER BACK	POUND NOTE	RADIO STAR
PAPER BILL	POWER DIVE	RAISE BAIL
PAPER CLIP	POWER GAME	RAISE CAIN
PAPER DOLL	POWER PACK	RAISE HELL
PAPER MILL	PRESS CLUB	RAPID FIRE
PAPER OVER	PRESS DATE	RAPID RATE
PAPER RACK	PRESS DOWN	REACH DOWN
PAPER WORK	PRESS GANG	REACH HOME
PARTY GAME	PRESS HARD	REACH LAND
PARTY LINE	PRESS HOME	READY CASH
PARTY MOOD	PRESS LAWS	READY MADE
PARTY WALL	PRESS SHOW	REBEL ARMY
PARTY WHIP	PRICE CUTS	RELAY RACE
PAVED ROAD	PRICE LIST	RELAY TEAM
PEACE PIPE	PRICE RING	REPLY PAID
PEACH TREE	PRICE RISE	RHINE WINE
PENAL CODE	PRIME BEEF	RIFLE FIRE
PENAL WORK	PRIME COST	RIFLE SHOT
PENNY POST	PRIME PORK	RIGHT AWAY
PENNY WISE	PRINT SHOP	RIGHT BACK
PERRY COMO	PRIVY SEAL	RIGHT BANK
PETAL SOFT	PRIZE BULL	RIGHT DOWN
PETER COOK	PRIZE CREW	RIGHT FOOL
PETER WEST	PRIZE DRAW	RIGHT FOOT
PETIT FOUR	PRIZE LIST	RIGHT GOOD
PETRI DISH	PRIZE RING	RIGHT HALF
PETTY CASH	PROOF COPY	RIGHT HAND
PETTY JURY	PROSE POEM	RIGHT HOOK
PHNOM PENH	PROVE TRUE	RIGHT IDEA
PHONE BILL	PUNCH BOWL	RIGHT LINE
PHONE BOOK	PUNCH CARD	RIGHT MIND
PHONE CALL	PUNCH LINE	RIGHT MOVE
PIANO DUET	PUNCH TAPE	RIGHT NOTE
PIANO KEYS	PUNIC WARS	RIGHT ROAD
PIANO SOLO	PUPPY LOVE	RIGHT SIDE
PIECE RATE	QUEEN ANNE	RIGHT SIZE
PIECE WORK	QUEEN BESS	RIGHT TIME
PIGGY BANK	QUEEN MARY	RIGHT TURN
PILOT FISH	QUEER COVE	RIGHT WING
PIOUS HOPE	QUEER FISH	RIGHT WORD
PITCH CAMP	QUEUE HERE	RIVAL FIRM
PITCH DARK	QUICK FIRE	RIVER AVON

RIVER BANK	ROYAL ROAD	SHIPS GUNS
RIVER BOAT	ROYAL SCOT	SHIPS MATE
RIVER FISH	ROYAL SEAL	SHOCK WAVE
RIVER KWAI	ROYAL SEAT	SHOOT DEAD
RIVER NILE	RUGBY BALL	SHOOT DOWN
RIVER OUSE	RUGBY TEAM	SHOOT POOL
RIVER STYX	RUNNY NOSE	SHORT HAIR
RIVER TRIP	RURAL DEAN	SHORT HEAD
ROAST BEEF	SAINT JOAN	SHORT LEGS
ROAST DUCK	SAINT JOHN	SHORT LIFE
ROAST LAMB	SAINT LUKE	SHORT LIST
ROAST MEAT	SAINT MARK	SHORT ODDS
ROAST PORK	SAINT PAUL	SHORT POEM
ROAST VEAL	SALAD BOWL	SHORT REST
ROBIN HOOD	SALAD DAYS	SHORT SPAN
ROMAN ARMY	SALES TALK	SHORT STAY
ROMAN BATH	SALES TEAM	SHORT STEP
ROMAN CAMP	SALLY LUNN	SHORT TERM
ROMAN COIN	SANTA CRUZ	SHORT TIME
ROMAN NOSE	SAUNA BATH	SHORT VIEW
ROMAN ORGY	SCALE DOWN	SHORT WALK
ROMAN ROAD	SCAPA FLOW	SHORT WAVE
ROMAN TOGA	SCENE FOUR	SHORT WORD
ROMAN TYPE	SCORE CARD	SHORT WORK
ROMAN WALL	SCORE DRAW	SHOUT DOWN
ROOKS NEST	SCOTS PINE	SIGHT LAND
ROOKS PAWN	SCRAP IRON	SILLY FOOL
ROUGH CAST	SCREW DOWN	SILLY TALK
ROUGH COPY	SCRUB DOWN	SILLY WALK
ROUGH EDGE	SCRUM DOWN	SIMON SAYS
ROUGH GAME	SCRUM HALF	SIREN SUIT
ROUGH IDEA	SEAMY SIDE	SIXTH FORM
ROUGH LUCK	SEIZE UPON	SIXTH TEST
ROUGH NOTE	SERVE TIME	SKATE OVER
ROUGH PLAN	SERVE WELL	SLACK ROPE
ROUGH PLAY	SEVEN AGES	SLANG WORD
ROUGH ROAD	SEVEN DAYS	SLATE CLUB
ROUGH TIME	SEVEN FEET	SLATE ROOF
ROUGH WORK	SEVEN QUID	SLAVE AWAY
ROUND ARCH	SEVEN SEAS	SLEEP WELL
ROUND FACE	SHADY DEAL	SLIDE AWAY
ROUND FIVE	SHADY NOOK	SLIDE BACK
ROUND FOUR	SHADY TREE	SLIDE DOWN
ROUND GAME	SHAKE DOWN	SLIDE RULE
ROUND HEAD	SHARP BEND	SLINK AWAY
ROUND HOLE	SHARP BLOW	SLOPE ARMS
ROUND NECK	SHARP EARS	SLOPE DOWN
ROUND NINE	SHARP EDGE	SMALL ARMS
ROUND OATH	SHARP EYES	SMALL BEER
ROUND SHOT	SHARP FALL	SMALL BORE
ROUND TOUR	SHARP NOTE	SMALL COIN
ROUND TRIP	SHARP PAIN	SMALL DOOR
ROWAN TREE	SHARP RISE	SMALL FEET
ROYAL ARMS	SHEEP FARM	SMALL FISH
ROYAL BLUE	SHEER DROP	SMALL FLAT
ROYAL LINE	SHEER FUNK	SMALL GAME
ROYAL MAIL	SHEER LUCK	SMALL GIRL
ROYAL MILE	SHEER SILK	SMALL HEAD
ROYAL MINT	SHELL PEAS	SMALL HOLE
ROYAL NAVY	SHIFT WORK	SMALL LOAF
ROYAL PARK	SHIPS BELL	SMALL MIND

SMALL PART	STAGE DOOR	STORY BOOK
SMALL ROOM	STAGE HAND	STORY LINE
SMALL SIZE	STAGE LEFT	STRAP DOWN
SMALL SLAM	STAGE NAME	STRAW POLL
SMALL TALK	STAGE PLAY	STRAW VOTE
SMALL TOWN	STAGE SHOW	STRIP BARE
SMART ALEC	STAIR RODS	STRIP CLUB
SMART GIRL	STALE CAKE	STUDY FORM
SMART PACE	STALE LOAF	STUDY HARD
SMART SUIT	STALE NEWS	SUGAR BEET
SMART WALK	STAMP DOWN	SUGAR BOWL
SMOKE BOMB	STAMP DUTY	SUGAR CANE
SMOKE DOPE	STAND AWAY	SUGAR LUMP
SMOKE RING	STAND BACK	SUGAR PLUM
SNAIL PACE	STAND BAIL	SUNNY SIDE
SNAKE BITE	STAND DOWN	SWARM OVER
SNEAK AWAY	STAND EASY	SWEAR WORD
SNEAK PAST	STAND FAST	SWEEP AWAY
SOBER FACT	STAND FIRM	SWEEP DOWN
SOLAR CELL	STAND IDLE	SWEEP PAST
SOLAR TIME	STAND OVER	SWEET CORN
SOLAR YEAR	STAND TALL	SWEET DISH
SOLID BALL	STARE DOWN	SWEET LOVE
SOLID BODY	START ANEW	SWEET NELL
SOLID FOOD	START WELL	SWEET SHOP
SOLID FUEL	START WITH	SWEET SONG
SOLID GOLD	START WORK	SWEET WINE
SOLID MASS	STATE FARM	SWELL IDEA
SOLID MEAL	STEAL AWAY	SWELL TIME
SOLID TEAK	STEAL PAST	SWING BACK
SOLID TYRE	STEAM BATH	SWING BAND
SONIC BOOM	STEAM IRON	SWING DOOR
SOTTO VOCE	STEAM OPEN	SWISS ALPS
SOUND BODY	STEEL BAND	SWISS ROLL
SOUND MIND	STEEL BLUE	SWOOP DOWN
SOUND WAVE	STEEL GREY	SWORN FOES
SOUTH BANK	STEEL GRIP	TABLE FISH
SOUTH POLE	STEEL MILL	TABLE LAMP
SOUTH SEAS	STEEL WOOL	TABLE SALT
SOUTH SIDE	STEEP HILL	TABLE TALK
SOUTH WIND	STICK FAST	TABLE WINE
SOUTH ZONE	STIFF NECK	TAKEN DOWN
SPACE RACE	STIFF TEST	TAKES PART
SPACE SHIP	STIFF WIND	TAWNY PORT
SPACE SUIT	STILL HERE	TEDDY BEAR
SPACE WALK	STILL LIFE	TEDDY BOYS
SPARE CASH	STILL MORE	TEMPT FATE
SPARE PART	STILL ROOM	TENOR CLEF
SPARE RIBS	STILL WINE	TENOR DRUM
SPARE ROOM	STINK BOMB	TENOR HORN
SPARE TIME	STOCK LIST	TENTH TIME
SPARE TYRE	STOCK PART	THATS FLAT
SPEAK WELL	STOCK SIZE	THATS LIFE
SPEED KING	STOKE CITY	THATS THAT
SPEED TRAP	STONE COLD	THEME SONG
SPEND TIME	STONE DEAD	THESE DAYS
SPILL OVER	STONE DEAF	THICK COAT
SPILT MILK	STONE WALL	THICK EDGE
SPLIT OPEN	STOOP DOWN	THICK HAIR
SPLIT VOTE	STORE AWAY	THICK HEAD
STAFF ROOM	STORM CONE	THICK MIST

THICK SKIN	TOUCH UPON	VOLTE FACE
THICK SNOW	TOUCH WOOD	WAIST HIGH
THICK SOUP	TOUGH LUCK	WAKES WEEK
THINK BACK	TOUGH MEAT	WALTZ TIME
THINK FAST	TOUGH SKIN	WALTZ TUNE
THINK HARD	TOUGH SPOT	WASPS NEST
THINK OVER	TOWER HILL	WASTE AWAY
THIRD FORM	TRACK DOWN	WASTE LAND
THIRD GEAR	TRACK SUIT	WASTE TIME
THIRD HOLE	TRADE FAIR	WATCH OVER
THIRD MATE	TRADE MARK	WATER BABY
THIRD PAGE	TRADE NAME	WATER BILL
THIRD PART	TRADE WIND	WATER FOWL
THIRD RATE	TRAIN FARE	WATER HOLE
THIRD SIDE	TREAD DOWN	WATER JUMP
THIRD TEAM	TREAT WELL	WATER LILY
THIRD TERM	TRIAL GAME	WATER MAIN
THIRD TEST	TRIAL JURY	WATER POLO
THIRD TIME	TRIAL SPIN	WATER RATE
THIRD YEAR	TRIED HARD	WATER TANK
THORA HIRD	TROOP SHIP	WEIGH DOWN
THREE ACES	TRUMP CARD	WELSH HARP
THREE ACTS	TRUMP SUIT	WHALE MEAT
THREE DAYS	TRUNK CALL	WHATS WHAT
THREE DEEP	TRUNK LINE	WHEAT GERM
THREE FEET	TRUNK ROAD	WHERE ELSE?
THREE IRON	TRUST DEED	WHITE BEAR
THREE LAPS	TRUST FUND	WHITE BELT
THREE QUID	TRUTH DRUG	WHITE CITY
THREE SETS	TUBAL CAIN	WHITE FLAG
THREE STAR	TUDOR ROSE	WHITE GOLD
THREE TENS	TULIP TREE	WHITE HAIR
THREE TWOS	TUMMY ACHE	WHITE HEAT
THROW AWAY	TWEED SUIT	WHITE HOPE
THROW BACK	TWICE FIVE	WHITE KING
THROW DOWN	TWICE FOUR	WHITE LADY
THROW OPEN	TWICE NINE	WHITE LINE
THROW OVER	TWICE OVER	WHITE LOAF
TIDAL FLOW	UNDER ARMS	WHITE MEAT
TIDAL WAVE	UNDER FIRE	WHITE MICE
TIGER LILY	UNDER OATH	WHITE NILE
TIGER MOTH	UNDER SAIL	WHITE PAWN
TIGHT GRIP	UNDER SEAL	WHITE PINE
TIGHT REIN	UNION BOSS	WHITE PORT
TIGHT SPOT	UNION CARD	WHITE ROOK
TIMES PAST	UNION FLAG	WHITE ROSE
TIPSY CAKE	UNION JACK	WHITE SPOT
TIRED EYES	UNTIL THEN	WHITE STAR
TITHE BARN	UPPER CASE	WHITE SUIT
TITLE DEED	UPPER DECK	WHITE WINE
TITLE PAGE	UPPER HAND	WIGAN PIER
TITLE ROLE	UPPER LIMB	WITCH HUNT
TOAST RACK	URIAH HEEP	WORLD BANK
TODAY WEEK	UTTER RUIN	WORLD FAIR
TOKEN VOTE	VAGUE IDEA	WORLD TOUR
TORCH SONG	VAULT OVER	WORSE LUCK
TOTAL COST	VERSE FORM	WORST PART
TOTEM POLE	VIDEO GAME	WRITE BACK
TOUCH DOWN	VILLA PARK	WRITE DOWN
TOUCH LINE	VITAL PART	WRITE HOME
TOUCH TYPE	VITAL ROLE	WRITE WELL

WRONG IDEA
WRONG MOVE
WRONG NAME
WRONG NOTE
WRONG ROAD
WRONG SIDE
WRONG TIME
WRONG TURN
WRONG VIEW
WYATT EARP
YACHT CLUB
YACHT RACE
YOUNG BIRD
YOUNG FOLK
YOUNG GIRL
YOUNG IDEA
YOUNG LADY
YOUNG LOVE
YOUTH CLUB

6 , 3

AARONS ROD
ACTING FOR
ADDLED EGG
AEGEAN SEA
ALMOST ALL
ANGORA CAT
ANIMAL FAT
ANIMAL OIL
ANNUAL FEE
APPIAN WAY
ATOMIC AGE
ATOMIC WAR
BAFFIN BAY
BAKING TIN
BALLOT BOX
BALTIC SEA
BANTRY BAY
BARBED WIT
BARROW BOY
BATTLE CRY
BECOME DUE
BECOME ONE
BEDDED OUT
BEFORE NOW
BEFORE TAX
BEFORE TEA
BETTER MAN
BETTER OFF
BETTER PAY
BEYOND ONE
BITING WIT
BITTER ALE
BITTER END
BOILED EGG
BOILED HAM
BOTANY BAY
BOUGHT OFF
BOUGHT OUT
BOWLED OUT

BOWLER HAT
BOXING DAY
BOYLES LAW
BRANCH OFF
BRANCH OUT
BRAZEN OUT
BRAZIL NUT
BRIGHT BOY
BRIGHT LAD
BRIGHT RED
BROKEN ARM
BROKEN LEG
BROKEN MAN
BROKEN RIB
BRONZE AGE
BROODY HEN
BUBBLE CAR
BUBBLE GUM
BUMBLE BEE
BUMPED OFF
CADDIE CAR
CALLED FOR
CAMERA SHY
CANCEL OUT
CARPET BAG
CASHEW NUT
CASTOR OIL
CAUGHT OUT
CEYLON TEA
CHERRY PIE
CHERRY RED
CHILDS TOY
CHOPPY SEA
CHOSEN FEW
CIRCUS ACT
CLARET CUP
CLEVER MAN
CLOUDY SKY
COCKED HAT
COFFEE BAR
COFFEE CUP
COFFEE POT
COLOUR BAR
COLWYN BAY
COMING OUT
COMMON END
COMMON LAW
COMMON LOT
COMMON MAN
CONGER EEL
CORDON OFF
COSMIC RAY
COTTON GIN
CRAFTY FOX
CRESTA RUN
CROUCH LOW
CUDDLY TOY
CUPIDS BOW
CURLED LIP
DAMSON JAM
DEADLY SIN

DESERT RAT
DEVILS OWN
DIESEL OIL
DJNING CAR
DINNER SET
DIRECT HIT
DIRECT TAX
DOCTOR WHO
DOLLAR GAP
DORSAL FIN
DOUBLE ACT
DOUBLE BAR
DOUBLE BED
DOUBLE EGG
DOUBLE GIN
DOUBLE ONE
DOUBLE PAY
DOUBLE SIX
DOUBLE TEN
DOUBLE TOP
DOUBLE TWO
DRIVEN MAD
DUFFLE BAG
DUNCES CAP
EASILY LED
EASTER DAY
EASTER EGG
EATING OUT
EIGHTH DAY
EITHER WAY
ELDEST SON
ELEVEN MEN
EMPIRE DAY
ERRAND BOY
ESKIMO DOG
ESTATE CAR
FAGGED OUT
FAIRLY NEW
FALLEN OUT
FAMILY CAR
FAMILY MAN
FAMILY PEW
FAMILY ROW
FAMOUS MAN
FAMOUS MEN
FEMALE SEX
FERRET OUT
FEUDAL LAW
FEUDAL TAX
FIGURE ONE
FIGURE OUT
FIGURE SIX
FIGURE TWO
FILTER TIP
FINISH OFF
FITTED OUT
FIZZLE OUT
FLAKED OUT
FLOWER BED
FLYING FOX
FOBBED OFF

FORAGE CAP	KOREAN WAR	MUTINY ACT
FOREST LAW	LABOUR DAY	MUTUAL AID
FORMAL BOW	LADIES DAY	MUTUAL AIM
FOSTER SON	LADIES MAN	NARROW WIN
FOURTH DAY	LASHED OUT	NATIVE WIT
FOURTH ROW	LATTER DAY	NEARLY ALL
FOURTH SET	LAUNCH PAD	NISSEN HUT
FREEZE OUT	LAWFUL ACT	NUMBER ONE
FROZEN SEA	LAWFUL AGE	NUMBER SIX
FRYING PAN	LESSON ONE	NUMBER TEN
GALLOP OFF	LESSON TEN	NUMBER TWO
GALWAY BAY	LESSON TWO	OCTANE GAS
GAMING ACT	LETTER BOX	OFFICE BOY
GATHER WAY	LEYDEN JAR	OFFICE JOB
GENTLE SEX	LIGHTS OUT	OLDEST BOY
GEORGE FOX	LIKELY LAD	OLDEST SON
GERMAN SPY	LIQUID AIR	ORANGE GIN
GIFTED MAN	LIQUOR LAW	ORANGE PIP
GINGER ALE	LITTER BIN	ORPHAN BOY
GINGER CAT	LITTER BUG	OXFORD DON
GINGER NUT	LITTLE AUK	OYSTER BED
GINGER POP	LITTLE BIT	PACKED OUT
GINGER TOM	LITTLE BOY	PANAMA HAT
GIVING OUT	LITTLE DOG	PARIAH DOG
GLANCE OFF	LITTLE MAN	PARKED CAR
GLOBAL WAR	LITTLE ONE	PATROL CAR
GLOOMY DAY	LITTLE TOE	PEAKED CAP
GOLDEN AGE	LOADED GUN	PEGGED OUT
GOLDEN BOY	LOCKED OUT	PEPPER POT
GOLDEN EGG	LONDON BUS	PETROL CAN
GOLDEN ROD	LONDON FOG	PETROL TAX
GRAVEL PIT	LONDON ZOO	PEWTER POT
GREEDY PIG	LOSING BET	PHONEY WAR
GROUND NUT	LOSING RUN	PICKED MEN
GUARDS VAN	LOUNGE BAR	PIGEON PIE
GUILTY ACT	LOVELY DAY	PILLAR BOX
GUILTY MAN	LOVERS VOW	PIPING HOT
GUINEA HEN	LOVING CUP	PISTON ROD
GUINEA PIG	MAGGIE MAY	PLEASE SIR
HAMMER OUT	MAPPED OUT	POETIC ART
HANSOM CAB	MARKED MAN	POISON GAS
HARDLY ANY	MARKET DAY	POISON IVY
HIGHER PAY	MASKED MAN	POISON PEN
HOLLOW OUT	MASTER KEY	POLICE CAR
HOMELY WIT	MASTER SPY	POLICE DOG
HONEST MAN	MEDIUM DRY	POLICE VAN
HUDSON BAY	MENTAL AGE	POLISH OFF
HUMBLE PIE	METRIC TON	POODLE CUT
HUNGRY MAN	MIDDLE AGE	POPPED OFF
HUNTED AIR	MIDDLE WAY	POWDER KEG
INCOME TAX	MIGHTY MAN	PRAYER MAT
INDIAN INK	MINUTE MAN	PRETTY BAD
INDIAN TEA	MODERN ART	PRETTY BIG
INLAND SEA	MONIED MAN	PRETTY BOY
INSIDE JOB	MONKEY NUT	PROMPT BOX
INSIDE OUT	MORTAL SIN	PROPER MAN
JERSEY COW	MOSAIC LAW	PROPER WAY
JUDGES CAP	MOTHER HEN	PUBLIC BAR
JUNGLE LAW	MOTHER WIT	PUBLIC EYE
KELLYS EYE	MUFFIN MAN	PULLED OUT
KINDLY ACT	MURDER RAP	RABBIT PIE

RACING CAR	SHRILL CRY	SUMMER DAY
RACING MAN	SIGNAL BOX	SURVEY MAP
RACING SET	SILVER CUP	SUTTON HOO
RAISED PIE	SILVER FIR	SWITCH OFF
RAPIER WIT	SILVER FOX	TEMPLE BAR
RATTLE OFF	SILVER URN	TENDER AGE
RAVING MAD	SIMPLE SUM	TENNIS NET
REASON WHY	SINGLE BED	THEYRE OFF!
RECORD BID	SINGLE MAN	THIRST FOR
RECORD SUM	SINGLE OUT	THIRTY ALL
REFUSE BIN	SKETCH MAP	THORPE BAY
RELIEF MAP	SKETCH PAD	THRASH OUT
REPAIR JOB	SLOPPY JOE	THROWN OUT
RESCUE BID	SLOUCH HAT	TINDER BOX
RESCUE DOG	SMOKED EEL	TIRING JOB
RIDING CAP	SMOKED HAM	TODDLE OFF
RIDING HAT	SMOOTH OUT	TRIBAL WAR
RISING AIR	SMOOTH SEA	TRICKY BIT
RISING SUN	SOLEMN VOW	TRICKY JOB
ROCKET MAN	SPACED OUT	TRILBY HAT
ROMANY RYE	SPARKS FLY	TROJAN WAR
ROTTEN EGG	SPEECH DAY	TSETSE FLY
ROTTEN ROW	SPONGE BAG	TUMBLE OFF
ROVING EYE	SPONGE OFF	TUMBLE OUT
SACRED COW	SPORTS CAR	TURFED OUT
SAFETY NET	SPORTS DAY	TURNED OFF
SAFETY PIN	SPOTTY DOG	TURNED OUT
SAILOR BOY	SPREAD OUT	TWELVE MEN
SAILOR HAT	SPRING OUT	UNHOLY ROW
SAINTS DAY	SQUARE JAW	URCHIN CUT
SALOON BAR	SQUARE LEG	USEFUL TIP
SALOON CAR	SQUARE OFF	VACANT LOT
SAVAGE DOG	SQUARE ONE	VANITY BAG
SAVILE ROW	SQUARE PEG	VIOLIN BOW
SCHOOL AGE	STABLE BOY	VISUAL AID
SCHOOL CAP	STANDS OUT	VOLUME ONE
SCHOOL KID	STARRY SKY	VOLUME TEN
SCHOOL TIE	STARVE OUT	VOLUME TWO
SCOTCH EGG	STATUS QUO	VOTING AGE
SCOTCH FIR	STICKY END	WALKER CUP
SCRAPE OFF	STORMY SEA	WANDER OFF
SCREAM OUT	STREAK OUT	WANDER OUT
SEALED OFF	STREAM OUT	WANTED MAN
SEARCH FEE	STREET MAP	WARNED OFF
SEARCH FOR	STRIDE OUT	WASHED OUT
SEARCH OUT	STRIKE OFF	WEAKER SEX
SECOND ACT	STRIKE OIL	WEALTH TAX
SECOND DAY	STRIKE OUT	WICKED BOY
SECOND LAP	STRIKE PAY	WICKED LIE
SECOND MAN	STRING BAG	WICKED MAN
SECOND ROW	STRING OUT	WICKED ONE
SECOND SET	STRONG ALE	WINDOW BOX
SECOND TRY	STRONG ARM	WINKLE OUT
SECRET ART	STRONG MAN	WOMANS MAN
SECURE JOB	STRONG TEA	WOMENS LIB
SEEING RED	STRUCK OFF	WONDER WHY
SELECT FEW	STRUCK OUT	WOODEN BOX
SENIOR BOY	STUPID MAN	WOODEN LEG
SHAGGY DOG	SUDDEN END	WORKED OUT
SHOVEL HAT	SUDDEN FIT	WORKER ANT
SHRIEK OUT	SUFFER TAX	WORKER BEE

WORLDS END
WORTHY AIM
YELLOW DOG
ZUIDER ZEE

7, 2

BALANCE UP
BEARING UP
BELIEVE ME
BETWEEN US
BOARDED UP
BOLSTER UP
BOTTOMS UP
BREATHE IN
BROUGHT UP
CLEANED UP
CLEARED UP
CLOSING IN
CONJURE UP
COVERED UP
CRACKED UP
CRUMPLE UP
CURTAIN UP
DOUBLED UP
DRESSED UP
FRESHEN UP
FURTHER ON
FURTHER UP
GETTING ON
GETTING UP
GROWING UP
HANGING ON
HURRIED UP
KNOCKED UP
LOOKING UP
MUFFLED UP
NOTHING ON
PACKING UP
PASSING BY
PATCHED UP
PICKING UP
PLUGGED IN
PRESSED ON
PROPPED UP
PUTTING UP
QUARTER TO
RUNNING IN
RUNNING ON
SETTLED IN
SHANGRI LA
SHRIVEL UP
SLIPPED ON
SLIPPED UP
SMARTEN UP
SMUGGLE IN
SNUGGLE UP
SOLDIER ON
SQUEEZE IN
STAGGER IN
STIRRED UP

STOPPED UP
STRETCH UP
SUMMING UP
SUPPOSE SO
SWALLOW UP
TIGHTEN UP
TOUGHEN UP
TRAMPLE ON
TRUSSED UP
TURNING IN
TURNING UP
UNHEARD OF
WELCOME IN
WINDING UP

1, 1, 8

C.S.FORESTER
E.E.CUMMINGS
T.E.LAWRENCE

1, 3, 4, 2

A BIT PAST IT

1, 4, 2, 3

I MEAN TO SAY

1, 4, 5

T-BONE STEAK

1, 5, 4

A GREAT DEAL
A GREAT MANY

2, 1, 3, 4

DO A BAD TURN
IN A BAD MOOD
UP A GUM TREE

2, 1, 4, 3

DO A GOOD JOB
GO A LONG WAY
IN A FAIR WAY
IN A GOOD WAY

2, 1, 7

AT A PREMIUM
AT A STRETCH
AT A TANGENT
DO A STRETCH
IN A DECLINE
IN A DILEMMA
IN A FASHION
IN A FLUTTER

IN A PASSION
IN A TANTRUM
IN A TURMOIL
IN A WHISPER

2, 2, 1, 5

BO TO A GOOSE
GO ON A SPREE
GO TO A DANCE
UP TO A POINT

2, 2, 2, 4

DO IT AT ONCE
UP TO NO GOOD

2, 2, 3, 3

GO IN AND OUT
GO TO THE BAR
GO TO THE ZOO
UP IN THE AIR
UP IN THE SKY

2, 2, 6

DO AN INJURY
GO ON STRIKE
GO ON TIPTOE
GO TO BLAZES!
GO TO CHURCH
GO TO GROUND
GO TO HEAVEN
GO TO PIECES
GO TO PRISON
GO TO SCHOOL
IN AN ASYLUM
IN AN UPROAR
OF NO IMPORT
OH,MR.PORTER!
ON AN ERRAND
ON MY HONOUR
TO AN EXTENT

2, 3, 1, 4

GO FOR A RIDE
GO FOR A SONG
GO FOR A SPIN
GO FOR A SWIM
GO FOR A TRIP
GO FOR A WALK

2, 3, 2, 3

MY CUP OF TEA
TO CAP IT ALL

2 . 3 . 3 . 2	IN THE KITTY	ON THE PROWL
	IN THE LOCAL	ON THE QUIET
ON THE WAY UP	IN THE LURCH	ON THE RADIO
	IN THE MONEY	ON THE RAILS
2 . 3 . 5	IN THE MOUTH	ON THE RIGHT
	IN THE NIGHT	ON THE ROCKS
AS PER USUAL	IN THE NORTH	ON THE SCENT
AT ALL COSTS	IN THE PAPER	ON THE SHELF
AT ALL TIMES	IN THE PRESS	ON THE SLANT
AT ANY PRICE	IN THE QUEUE	ON THE SLATE
AT ITS WORST	IN THE RIGHT	ON THE STAGE
AT THE FRONT	IN THE RIVER	ON THE STAND
AT THE LOCAL	IN THE ROUGH	ON THE TABLE
AT THE OPERA	IN THE ROUND	ON THE TELLY
AT THE PROMS	IN THE SHADE	ON THE TILES
AT THE READY	IN THE SLIPS	ON THE TRAIL
AT THE START	IN THE SOUTH	ON THE TRAIN
AT THE WHEEL	IN THE STAND	ON THE VERGE
AT THE WORST	IN THE STUDY	ON THE WAGON
BY ALL MEANS	IN THE SWING	ON THE WATER
BY AND LARGE	IN THE TOWER	ON THE WHOLE
BY ANY MEANS	IN THE TRADE	OX - EYE DAISY
BY THE CLOCK	IN THE VOGUE	TO THE AISLE
BY THE DOZEN	IN THE WATER	TO THE ALTAR
BY THE METRE	IN THE WILDS	TO THE DEATH
BY THE RIVER	IN THE WINGS	TO THE GRAVE
BY THE SCORE	IN THE WOODS	TO THE NORTH
DO NOT TOUCH	IN THE WORLD	TO THE PENNY
DO ONE PROUD	IN THE WRONG	TO THE POINT
DO THE DIRTY	IN TWO MINDS	TO THE QUICK
DO THE HALLS	MY OLD WOMAN	TO THE RIGHT
DO THE POLKA	NO FIT STATE	TO THE SOUTH
DO THE TANGO	OL MAN RIVER	UP ALL NIGHT
DO THE TRICK	ON ALL FOURS	UP AND ABOUT
DO THE TWIST	ON ALL HANDS	UP AND DOING
DO THE WALTZ	ON ALL SIDES	UP AND UNDER
GO ALL FUNNY	ON BAD TERMS	UP FOR GRABS
GO THE LIMIT	ON THE ALERT	UP FOR OFFER
IN ANY EVENT	ON THE BEACH	UP THE CREEK
IN BAD ODOUR	ON THE BENCH	UP THE RIVER
IN BAD SHAPE	ON THE BIBLE	UP THE SPOUT
IN BAD TASTE	ON THE BOARD	
IN HOT BLOOD	ON THE BOOZE	2 . 4 . 4
IN HOT WATER	ON THE BRAIN	
IN ITS PLACE	ON THE CARDS	AT BOTH ENDS
IN OFF WHITE	ON THE CHEAP	AT FULL TILT
IN ONE PIECE	ON THE COAST	AT HALF-MAST
IN ONE SENSE	ON THE CREST	AT LONG LAST
IN THE ATTIC	ON THE CROSS	AT ONES BEST
IN THE BLACK	ON THE FENCE	AT ONES DOOR
IN THE CHAIR	ON THE FLOOR	AT ONES EASE
IN THE CLEAR	ON THE GREEN	AT ONES FEET
IN THE DOUGH	ON THE HOUSE	AT ONES POST
IN THE DRINK	ON THE LATCH	AT ONES SIDE
IN THE DUMPS	ON THE LEVEL	AU PAIR GIRL
IN THE EVENT	ON THE LOOSE	DO AWAY WITH
IN THE FINAL	ON THE MARCH	DO ONES BEST
IN THE FLESH	ON THE OCEAN	DO ONES DUTY
IN THE FRONT	ON THE PHONE	DO ONES HAIR
IN THE GRAVE	ON THE POINT	DO SOME GOOD
IN THE HOUSE	ON THE POOLS	GO DOWN WELL

GO SCOT-FREE
IN DIRE NEED
IN FINE FORM
IN FULL VIEW
IN GOOD FORM
IN GOOD NICK
IN GOOD PART
IN GOOD TIME
IN GOOD TRIM
IN MANY WAYS
IN NAME ONLY
IN ONES HEAD
IN ONES MIND
IN ONES ROOM
IN REAL LIFE
IN SOME WAYS
IN THAT CASE
IT WONT WASH
KU KLUX KLAN
MY DEAD BODY
MY DEAR CHAP
MY DEAR GIRL
MY FAIR LADY
NO HARM DONE
NO LEFT TURN
NO LOVE LOST
NO MANS LAND
NO MEAN FEAT
NO SUCH LUCK
ON EACH SIDE
ON ONES BACK
ON ONES FEET
ON ONES LEGS
ON ONES MIND
ON ONES PINS
ON ONES TOES
ON THIS SIDE
TO ONES FACE

2 , 5 , 3

IN EVERY WAY
IT TAKES TWO
MY LUCKY DAY
NO THANK YOU

2 , 6 , 2

IN FAVOUR OF
ON BEHALF OF

2 , 8

AS ARRANGED
AS PROMISED
AS REQUIRED
AT DAYBREAK
AT GUNPOINT
AT VARIANCE
BE GRATEFUL
BE INFERIOR

BE MERCIFUL
BE MISTAKEN
BE PREPARED
BE SENSIBLE
BE SOCIABLE
BE SUPERIOR
BE YOURSELF
BY ACCIDENT
BY CONTRAST
BY DAYLIGHT
BY INSTINCT
BY SURPRISE
DO ARTICLES
DO BUSINESS
DO LIKEWISE
DO OVERTIME
DR.BARNARDO
DR.DOLITTLE
EL CORDOBES
EL SALVADOR
EX DIVIDEND
GO BACKWARD
GO BANKRUPT
GO CRACKERS
GO DOWNHILL
GO OUTDOORS
GO OVERSEAS
GO SHOOTING
GO SHOPPING
GO STRAIGHT
GO SWIMMING
GO TOGETHER
GO UPSTAIRS
IF POSSIBLE
IN ABEYANCE
IN ADDITION
IN ALLIANCE
IN ARTICLES
IN BRACKETS
IN BUSINESS
IN CHAMBERS
IN CHANCERY
IN CONCLAVE
IN CONFLICT
IN CONTRAST
IN DARKNESS
IN DAYLIGHT
IN DECEMBER
IN DEFIANCE
IN DISARRAY
IN DISGRACE
IN DISGUISE
IN DISTRESS
IN EVIDENCE
IN EXCHANGE
IN EXTREMIS
IN FEBRUARY
IN JEOPARDY
IN LONGHAND
IN MEMORIAM
IN MOURNING

IN NOVEMBER
IN PARADISE
IN PARALLEL
IN POLITICS
IN POSITION
IN PRACTICE
IN PROGRESS
IN PROSPECT
IN QUESTION
IN RESPONSE
IN ROTATION
IN SEQUENCE
IN STERLING
IN STITCHES
IN SUSPENSE
IN SYMPATHY
IN TRAINING
IN WHISPERS
LA ROCHELLE
LA TRAVIATA
MO CONNOLLY
MR.MICAWBER
MR.UNIVERSE
MY GOODNESS!
MY HEARTIES
NO APPETITE
NO DISTANCE
NO ENTRANCE
NO INTEREST
NO NONSENSE
NO PATIENCE
NO QUESTION
NO RESPONSE
NO SHORTAGE
NO STRANGER
ON APPROVAL
ON BROADWAY
ON BUSINESS
ON CRUTCHES
ON DELIVERY
ON LOCATION
ON OCCASION
ON SATURDAY
ON SCHEDULE
ON THURSDAY
ON VACATION
ST.LAWRENCE
ST.NICHOLAS

3 , 1 , 4 , 2

GET A LINE ON
GET A LOOK IN
GET A MOVE ON
GET A WORD IN
LAY A HAND ON
PUT A STOP TO

3, 1, 6	3, 2, 3, 2	
		MAN OF IDEAS
		MAN OF MEANS
ASK A FAVOUR	GET UP AND GO	MAN OF MOODS
BEG A FAVOUR	HOW DO YOU DO?	MAN OF PARTS
CUT A CORNER	OLD SO-AND-SO	MAN OF PEACE
CUT A FIGURE	PAY AS YOU GO	MAN OF STEEL
CUT A RECORD	PUT AN END TO	MAN OF STRAW
CUT A TUNNEL	TWO TO ONE ON	MAN OF TASTE
DIG A TRENCH		MAN OR MOUSE?
FOR A CHANGE	3, 2, 5	MAP OF ITALY
FOR A SEASON		MUG OF COCOA
GET A FRIGHT	ACE OF CLUBS	NOM DE PLUME
GET A THRILL	ACT AS AGENT	NOT SO DUSTY
ITS A WINNER	ACT AS GUIDE	NOT TO WORRY
NOT A CHANCE	ACT OF FAITH	NOW OR NEVER
NOT A STITCH	ACT OF GRACE	ONE IN EIGHT
NOT A STROKE	ACT OF MERCY	ONE IN FIFTY
PAY A RANSOM	ACT OF UNION	ONE IN SEVEN
PAY A REWARD	ALL IN ORDER	ONE IN THREE
RUN A MINUTE	AND SO FORTH	ONE NO-TRUMP
SAY A PRAYER	AXE TO GRIND	OUT AT ELBOW
SEE A DOCTOR	BAG OF BONES	OUT IN FORCE
SEE A LAWYER	BAG OF FLOUR	OUT IN FRONT
SET A COURSE	BAG OF NAILS	OUT OF COURT
SET A RECORD	BED OF NAILS	OUT OF DOORS
TIP A WINNER	BED OF ROSES	OUT OF FOCUS
WIN A RAFFLE	BIT OF PAPER	OUT OF FUNDS
WIN A RUBBER	BOX OF DATES	OUT OF HOURS
	BOX OF PILLS	OUT OF JOINT
3, 2, 1, 4	CAN OF DRINK	OUT OF MONEY
	CAN OF LAGER	OUT OF ORDER
ALL IN A HEAP	CUP OF COCOA	OUT OF PLACE
ALL OF A GLOW	CUP OF WATER	OUT OF PRINT
ALL OF A HEAP	CUT IN PRICE	OUT OF RANGE
BIT OF A JOKE	CUT IT SHORT	OUT OF REACH
BIT OF A MESS	CUT UP ROUGH	OUT OF SHAPE
DRY AS A BONE	DAB OF PAINT	OUT OF SIGHT
GET IN A MESS	DAY OF GRACE	OUT OF SORTS
GET IN A STEW	DEN OF LIONS	OUT OF SPITE
ONE AT A TIME	DIE OF SHOCK	OUT OF STOCK
OUT ON A LIMB	EGG ON TOAST	OUT OF TOUCH
PIG IN A POKE	END IN SIGHT	OUT OF WATER
PUT IN A WORD	END IN SMOKE	PAY ON SIGHT
PUT ON A SHOW	END IN TEARS	POT OF HONEY
RAT IN A TRAP	FIT OF ANGER	POT OF PAINT
RUN AT A LOSS	FIT TO BURST	PUT IN FRONT
RUN UP A BILL	GET IN FIRST	PUT IN IRONS
TWO AT A TIME	GET IT RIGHT	PUT IN ORDER
TWO OF A KIND	GET IT WRONG	PUT IN POWER
WIN BY A GOAL	GET TO GRIPS	PUT IN VERSE
WIN BY A HEAD	GET UP EARLY	PUT IN WORDS
WIN BY A NECK	GET UP STEAM	PUT IT ABOUT
WON BY A HEAD	HOW ON EARTH	PUT ON BOARD
	JAR OF HONEY	PUT ON PAPER
3, 2, 2, 3	LAY IN RUINS	PUT ON SPEED
	LAY IN STOCK	PUT ON TRIAL
AND SO TO BED	LET IT SLIDE	PUT TO DEATH
PUT ON AN ACT	LET IT STAND	PUT TO MUSIC
	LIE IN PEACE	PUT TO SLEEP
	LIE IN RUINS	RAY OF LIGHT
	LIE IN STATE	ROW OF BEANS

ROW OF TREES	ALL THE RAGE	HIT FOR FOUR
RUN TO EARTH	ALL THE REST	HIT THE BULL
SEA OF FACES	ALL THE SAME	HIT THE DECK
SET AT LARGE	ALL THE TIME	HIT THE MARK
SET IN ORDER	ALL THE YEAR	HIT THE POST
SET OF CLUBS	ALL TOO SOON	HIT THE TOWN
SET OF DARTS	ALL TOO WELL	HOT AND COLD
SET OF EIGHT	AND ALL THAT	HOT TIN ROOF
SET OF RULES	AND THE LIKE	IFS AND BUTS
SET OF STUDS	AND THE REST	INS AND OUTS
SET OF TEETH	ANY OLD IRON	LAY THE DUST
SET OF TOOLS	ANY OLD TIME	LAY THE ODDS
SET TO MUSIC	ASK FOR HELP	LEO THE LION
SET UP HOUSE	ASK FOR MORE	LET ONE DOWN
SIR OR MADAM	ASK TOO MUCH	MAN AND WIFE
SIX OF CLUBS	BAN THE BOMB	MAN THE GUNS
SIX OR SEVEN	BAT AND BALL	MAN THE SHIP
SUM OF MONEY	BEG FOR MORE	MAO TSE TUNG
TEN OF CLUBS	BIG BAD WOLF	MOW THE LAWN
TEN TO EIGHT	BOY AND GIRL	NOD THE HEAD
TEN TO SEVEN	BUY AND SELL	NOT FAR AWAY
TEN TO THREE	CAP AND GOWN	NOT FOR SALE
THE ST. LEGER	CRY FOR HELP	NOT THE SAME
TIE IN KNOTS	CRY OUT LOUD	NOT THE TYPE
TIN OF BEANS	CUP AND BALL	NOW AND THEN
TIN OF COCOA	CUT FOR DEAL	NUT AND BOLT
TIN OF FRUIT	CUT THE CAKE	ODD AND EVEN
TIN OF PAINT	CUT THE COST	OFF THE BALL
TWO BY THREE	CUT THE PACK	OFF THE CUFF
TWO OF CLUBS	CUT THE TAPE	OFF THE EDGE
TWO OR THREE	DIE FOR LOVE	OFF THE HOOK
USE NO HOOKS	DIG FOR GOLD	OFF THE LAND
WAD OF NOTES	DRY THE EYES	OFF THE MARK
WAR OF WORDS	EBB AND FLOW	OFF THE REEL
WAY IN FRONT	FAR AND AWAY	OLD OAK TREE
WIN AN OSCAR	FAR AND NEAR	ONE AND ONLY
WIN ON MERIT	FAR AND WIDE	ONE PER CENT
	FAR TOO MANY	ONE TOO MANY
3, 3, 1, 3	FAR TOO MUCH	ONE WAY ONLY
	FAR-OFF LAND	ONE-ACT PLAY
ALL BUT A FEW	FIT AND WELL	ONE-MAN BAND
ONE AND A BIT	FIT FOR WORK	ONE-MAN SHOW
TRY FOR A JOB	FIT THE BILL	PAY THE BILL
	FIX THE DATE	PAY THE RENT
3, 3, 2, 2	FLY THE FLAG	POT THE BLUE
	FOR ALL THAT	POT THE PINK
ALL SET TO GO	FOR ALL TIME	PUT ONE OVER
	FOR THE BEST	PUT THE SHOT
3, 3, 4	FOR TWO PINS	RED RED ROSE
	GAY OLD TIME	ROB THE TILL
ACT THE FOOL	GET THE BIRD	ROD AND LINE
ACT THE GOAT	GET THE BOOT	RUN FOR HELP
ACT THE HOST	GET THE HUMP	RUN FOR HOME
ACT THE PART	GET THE IDEA	RUN THE RISK
AID AND ABET	GET THE PUSH	RUN THE SHOW
AIM TOO HIGH	GET THE SACK	SAY THE WORD
ALL DAY LONG	GIN AND LIME	SEE THE JOKE
ALL MOD CONS	GOT THE SACK	SET THE PACE
ALL THE BEST	HAM AND EGGS	SIX PER CENT
ALL THE LUCK	HIS AND HERS	SIX-DAY WEEK
ALL THE MORE	HIT AND MISS	SON AND HEIR

69

SOW THE SEED
SUN AND MOON
SUN-RAY LAMP
TAP THE LINE
TEN PER CENT
THE BEE GEES
THE BIG FOUR
THE FAR EAST
THE HOT SEAT
THE LOW-DOWN
THE NEW LOOK
THE NEW YEAR
THE OLD FIRM
THE RED ARMY
THE RED FLAG
TIE THE KNOT
TIP THE WINK
TOE THE LINE
TOO FAR GONE
TOP AND TAIL
TOP THE BILL
TWO PER CENT
TWO-ACT PLAY
WAX AND WANE
WHY PAY MORE?
WIG AND GOWN
WIN THE GAME
WIN THE GOLD
WIN THE RACE
WIN THE TOSS
ZIG-ZAG LINE

3, 4, 3

ACT ONES AGE
ALL-TIME LOW
BIG BAND ERA
CAP GRIS-NEZ
CRY WITH JOY
DOG EATS DOG
EAT ONES HAT
HOW DARE YOU!
MAD WITH JOY
NEW-LAID EGG
NEW-MOWN HAY
NOT JUST NOW
NOT JUST YET
NOT LONG AGO
OFF ONES NUT
OLD PALS ACT
ONE FINE DAY
ONE-INCH MAP
PAY ONES SUB
PAY ONES WAY
ROW UPON ROW
RUN LIKE MAD
SEE ONES WAY
SIX-YARD BOX
TEN PAST ONE
TEN PAST SIX
TEN PAST TEN

TEN PAST TWO
THE BEST MAN
THE BOER WAR
THE COLD WAR
THE DEAD SEA
THE DEEP END
THE EAST END
THE EVIL EYE
THE EVIL ONE
THE FAIR SEX
THE GLAD EYE
THE HARD WAY
THE HIGH SEA
THE LAST LAP
THE LONG VAC
THE RIOT ACT
THE TAIL-END
THE THIN MAN
THE VERY ONE
THE WEST END

3, 5, 2

ALL KEYED UP
ALL MIXED UP
GET STUCK IN
HOW ABOUT IT?
LAY CLAIM TO
LAY HANDS ON
LAY SIEGE TO
NOT WORTH IT
SEE ABOUT IT
SET STORE BY
THE GAMES UP
THE ROYAL WE
THE THREE RS

3, 7

ABE LINCOLN
AIR COMMAND
AIR DEFENCE
AIR FREIGHT
AIR HOSTESS
AIR MARSHAL
AIR SERVICE
AIR STEWARD
AIR TRAFFIC
AIR WARFARE
ALF GARNETT
ALL CORRECT
ALL FORLORN
ALL HALLOWS
ALL PRESENT
AMY JOHNSON
ART AUCTION
ART GALLERY
ART NOUVEAU
ART ROBBERY
ART STUDENT
ART SUBJECT

BAD ACTRESS
BAD BARGAIN
BAD COMPANY
BAD CONDUCT
BAD EXAMPLE
BAD FORTUNE
BAD GRAMMAR
BAD LEARNER
BAD MANNERS
BAD MISTAKE
BAD QUALITY
BAD SERVANT
BAD TACTICS
BAD THOUGHT
BAD WEATHER
BAD WORKMAN
BAD WRITING
BID AGAINST
BIG BROTHER
BIG GEORDIE
BIG SUCCESS
BIG SWINDLE
BIG WEDDING
BOB PAISLEY
BON APPETIT
BOX BARRAGE
BOX SPANNER
BUS SHELTER
BUS STATION
BUY BRITISH
BUY CHEAPLY
CAR BATTERY
CAR LICENCE
CAT BURGLAR
CAT STEVENS
CHE GUEVARA
COR ANGLAIS
COS LETTUCE
COW PARSLEY
CUP WINNERS
CUT CORNERS
CUT FLOWERS
CUT THROUGH
DAS KAPITAL
DAY NURSERY
DAY RELEASE
DAY TRIPPER
DOG BISCUIT
DOG BREEDER
DOG LICENCE
DOG TRAINER
DOM MINTOFF
DON BRADMAN
DON CAMILLO
DON QUIXOTE
DRY BATTERY
DRY CLEANER
DRY CLIMATE
DRY MARTINI
DRY MEASURE
DRY ONESELF

DRY SHAMPOO	KEW GARDENS	ONE BILLION
DRY WEATHER	KEY WITNESS	ONE DIAMOND
DUE PROCESS	KID BROTHER	ONE FURLONG
DUE RESPECT	KID ONESELF	ONE HUNDRED
EAR TRUMPET	LAW OFFICER	ONE MILLION
EAR WITNESS	LAW SOCIETY	ONE QUARTER
EGG CUSTARD	LAW STUDENT	ONE SEVENTH
EGG SHAMPOO	LAY BROTHER	ONE SQUARED
END PRODUCT	LEE TREVINO	ONE SWALLOW
EYE WITNESS	LEO TOLSTOY	ONE TWELFTH
FAR BETWEEN	LIE DORMANT	PAN SCOURER
FLY FISHING	LIP SERVICE	PAR CONTEST
FOG WARNING	LOS ANGELES	PAY DAMAGES
FOR CERTAIN	LOW CEILING	PAY TRIBUTE
FOR EXAMPLE	LOW CUNNING	PEN PUSHING
FOR NOTHING	LOW DENSITY	PIN CUSHION
FOX HUNTING	LOW OPINION	POP CONCERT
FOX TERRIER	LOW QUALITY	POT HUNTING
GAS CHAMBER	LOW SPIRITS	PUT ASUNDER
GAS COMPANY	LOW STATION	PUT FORWARD
GAS LIGHTER	LOW STATURE	PUT THROUGH
GAS ONESELF	LOW TURNOUT	RAW RECRUIT
GAS TURBINE	MAP READING	RAY CHARLES
GAY ABANDON	MAY BLOSSOM	RED ADMIRAL
GAY COLOURS	MRS. GASKELL	RED BALLOON
GAY COMPANY	NED SHERRIN	RED CABBAGE
GAY GORDONS	NEW ADDRESS	RED CURRANT
GET DRESSED	NEW ARRIVAL	RED HERRING
GET ELECTED	NEW CHAPTER	REV COUNTER
GET ENGAGED	NEW CLOTHES	ROD STEWART
GET EXCITED	NEW COLLEGE	ROY DOTRICE
GET HITCHED	NEW CONVERT	ROY EMERSON
GET KNOTTED!	NEW EDITION	RUB AGAINST
GET MARRIED	NEW ENGLAND	RUN ABREAST
GET NOWHERE	NEW FASHION	RUN AGAINST
GET RATTLED	NEW ORLEANS	RUN AGROUND
GET STARTED	NEW RECRUIT	RUN COUNTER
GET STUFFED!	NEW RESOLVE	RUN ERRANDS
GET SUPPORT	NEW VERSION	RUN THROUGH
GET THROUGH	NEW ZEALAND	SAD FEELING
GET UPTIGHT	NOT CRICKET	SAD TIDINGS
GET WORRIED	NOT PRESENT	SAM GOLDWYN
GOD WILLING	NOT WORKING	SAN ANTONIO
GUN LICENCE	ODD NUMBERS	SAY GOODBYE
GUT FEELING	OFF BALANCE	SAY NOTHING
HER MAJESTY	OFF LICENCE	SEA ANEMONE
HIS MAJESTY	OIL COLOURS	SEA BATHING
HIS WORSHIP	OIL COMPANY	SEA CAPTAIN
HOT CLIMATE	OIL MAGNATE	SEA MONSTER
HOT PURSUIT	OIL PAINTER	SEA SERPENT
HOT WEATHER	OLD BRIGADE	SEE CLEARLY
IAN FLEMING	OLD CLOTHES	SEE NOTHING
ICE SKATING	OLD COUNTRY	SEE SERVICE
ICY SURFACE	OLD ENGLAND	SEE THROUGH
ILL FEELING	OLD ETONIAN	SEE VISIONS
ILL FORTUNE	OLD FRIENDS	SET AGAINST
ILL MANNERS	OLD ROUTINE	SET FORMULA
JAM SESSION	OLD SOLDIER	SET PURPOSE
JOE FRAZIER	OLD WARRIOR	SEX PISTOLS
JOY ADAMSON	OLD WINDBAG	SID VICIOUS
KEN RUSSELL	ONE ANOTHER	SIR GALAHAD

SIT UPRIGHT	THE ORKNEYS	WET BLANKET
SIX DOLLARS	THE PACIFIC	WET CLIMATE
SIX FIGURES	THE PLANETS	WET CLOTHES
SIX GALLONS	THE PRELUDE	WET MEASURE
SIX HUNDRED	THE PRESENT	WET SHAMPOO
SIX MINUTES	THE QUAKERS	WET THROUGH
SIX SQUARED	THE REFEREE	WET WEATHER
SIX WICKETS	THE RIVIERA	WIN FREEDOM
SUN PARLOUR	THE ROCKERS	WIN HONOURS
SUN WORSHIP	THE ROCKIES	WIN THROUGH
TAP DANCING	THE SABBATH	YUL BRYNNER
TAX EVASION	THE SEASIDE	
TEA CLIPPER	THE SEASONS	4 , 1 , 3 , 2
TEA DRINKER	THE SECONDS	
TEA PLANTER	THE SHADOWS	GIVE A LEG UP
TEA SERVICE	THE SHIVERS	
TEN DEGREES	THE SIXTIES	4 , 1 , 5
TEN DOLLARS	THE SPEAKER	
TEN FATHOMS	THE SUBURBS	BACK A HORSE
TEN GALLONS	THE TEMPEST	BACK A LOSER
TEN MILLION	THE THEATRE	BOOK A TABLE
TEN MINUTES	THE THINKER	CALL A TRUCE
TEN SECONDS	THE TITANIC	CAST A CLOUT
TEN SQUARED	THE TROPICS	CAST A SPELL
TEN WICKETS	THE UNITIES	COCK A SNOOK
THE ACCUSED	THE UNKNOWN	DRAW A BLANK
THE ANIMALS	THE VATICAN	DRAW A PRIZE
THE ARCHERS	THE VIKINGS	DRAW A SWORD
THE ARSENAL	THE WAILERS	DROP A BRICK
THE BAHAMAS	THE WEATHER	DROP A CATCH
THE BEATLES	THE WILLIES	FILE A CLAIM
THE BRITISH	THE WORKERS	FIND A PLACE
THE BRONTËS	TIN SOLDIER	FIRE A SALVO
THE CABINET	TIN WHISTLE	FIVE O CLOCK
THE CAPITAL	TOM BOWLING	FORM A QUEUE
THE CHANNEL	TOP BILLING	FOUR O CLOCK
THE COMMONS	TOP HONOURS	GIVE A CATCH
THE CRITICS	TOP QUALITY	GIVE A PARTY
THE CUSTOMS	TOY SOLDIER	GIVE A SHOUT
THE ENGLISH	TOY SPANIEL	GROW A BEARD
THE FIFTIES	TOY TERRIER	HALF A CROWN
THE FORTIES	TWO COLOURS	HALF A DOZEN
THE GALLOWS	TWO COURSES	HALF A GLASS
THE GERMANS	TWO DEGREES	HALF A METRE
THE GESTAPO	TWO DOLLARS	HALF A POUND
THE GIDEONS	TWO FATHOMS	HALF A SHAKE
THE GOODIES	TWO FINGERS	HAVE A CHAIR
THE GORBALS	TWO GALLONS	HAVE A CRACK
THE GUNNERS	TWO HUNDRED	HAVE A DREAM
THE HAMMERS	TWO LENGTHS	HAVE A DRINK
THE HORRORS	TWO MILLION	HAVE A FIGHT
THE JACKPOT	TWO MINUTES	HAVE A FLING
THE JONESES	TWO OCTAVES	HAVE A GUESS
THE KREMLIN	TWO SECONDS	HAVE A HEART
THE LANCERS	TWO SQUARED	HAVE A PARTY
THE MARINES	TWO STRIPES	HAVE A SHOCK
THE MENDIPS	TWO WICKETS	HAVE A SMOKE
THE MESSIAH	USE FINESSE	HAVE A SNACK
THE MONSOON	WAR COUNCIL	HOLD A BRIEF
THE NEEDFUL	WAR FOOTING	HOLD A PARTY
THE NEEDLES	WAR MEMOIRS	JUST A DREAM

JUST A WHILE	WELL I NEVER!	CALL TO ARMS
KEEP A DIARY	---WHAT A NERVE!	CALL TO MIND
LEAD A DANCE	WHAT A SHAME!	CASH IN HAND
LEAD A PARTY	WITH A SMILE	CASK OF WINE
LEAD A TRUMP		CHEW IT OVER
LEND A POUND	4, 2, 1, 3	COAT OF ARMS
LIKE A CHARM		COAT OF MAIL
LIKE A FLASH	BUSY AS A BEE	COME AT ONCE
LOOK A TREAT	CALL IT A DAY	COME IN LAST
LOOK A WRECK	GIVE IT A TRY	COME ON OVER
LOSE A FIGHT	HELL OF A ROW	COME TO BITS
LOSE A MATCH	KICK UP A ROW	COME TO HAND
LOSE A TRICK	MAKE IT A DAY	COME TO HARM
MAKE A BREAK	NEAT AS A PIN	COME TO HEEL
MAKE A CLAIM	PEAS IN A POD	COME TO KNOW
MAKE A GUESS	SICK AS A DOG	COME TO LIFE
MAKE A JOINT	SLIP OF A BOY	COME TO PASS
MAKE A NOISE	STAY IN A RUT	COME TO REST
MAKE A POINT	TAKE ON A JOB	COME TO STAY
MAKE A SCENE	TALE OF A TUB	DASH OF SODA
MAKE A SOUND	WHAT AM I BID?	DAWN OF LIFE
MAKE A STAND	WORD OF A LIE	DAWN OF TIME
MAKE A START		DAYS OF YORE
MAKE A STUDY	4, 2, 2, 2	DAYS TO COME
MAKE A TRUCE		DEAD ON TIME
MISS A CATCH	FACE UP TO IT	DEED OF GIFT
MISS A TRICK	FEEL UP TO IT	DEEP IN DEBT
NINE O CLOCK	LIVE UP TO IT	DINE AT HOME
ONCE A MONTH		DONT BE RUDE
PACK A PUNCH	4, 2, 4	DOOR TO DOOR
PICK A FIGHT		DOSE OF CLAP
PLAY A CHORD	ABLE TO COPE	DOWN AT HEEL
PLAY A JOKER	ABLE TO HEAR	DRAW IT FINE
PLAY A PRANK	BABE AT ARMS	DROP BY DROP
PLAY A SCALE	BABE IN ARMS	DROP OF RAIN
PLAY A TRICK	BACK TO BACK	DUKE OF KENT
PLAY A WALTZ	BACK TO WORK	DUKE OF YORK
READ A STORY	BAGS OF TIME	DUST TO DUST
RENT A HOUSE	BALL OF FIRE	DUTY OF CARE
SAIL A YACHT	BALL OF WOOL	EAST IS EAST
SEND A CABLE	BAND OF HOPE	EAST TO WEST
SING A DIRGE	BARD OF AVON	EVER SO MANY
SING A ROUND	BEAR IN MIND	EVER SO MUCH
SINK A SHAFT	BEST OF FIVE	EYES OF BLUE
SOLD A DUMMY	BEST OF LUCK	FACT OF LIFE
SUCK A LEMON	BEST OF PALS	FAIL TO MEET
TAKE A CATCH	BILL OF FARE	FAIL TO MOVE
TAKE A CHAIR	BILL OF SALE	FAIL TO PASS
TAKE A CLASS	BIRD IN HAND	FAIR OF FACE
TAKE A COUNT	BIRD OF PREY	FALL IN LINE
TAKE A GUESS	BLOW BY BLOW	FALL IN LOVE
TAKE A KNOCK	BLOW ME DOWN	FALL IN WITH
TAKE A PHOTO	BONE TO PICK	FALL OF SNOW
TAKE A PRIDE	BORN TO RULE	FALL OF TROY
TAKE A PUNCH	BOWL OF RICE	FALL TO BITS
TAKE A SHARE	BOWL OF SOUP	FEEL AT EASE
TAKE A STAND	BOYS IN BLUE	FEEL AT HOME
TAKE A THIEF	CAFÉ AU LAIT	FEEL NO PITY
TAKE A TRAIN	CAKE OF SOAP	FEET OF CLAY
TAKE A TRICK	CALL BY NAME	FILL IN TIME
TELL A STORY	CALL OF DUTY	FIVE TO FIVE

FIVE TO FOUR	INCH BY INCH	MAKE NO ODDS
FIVE TO NINE	ISLE OF DOGS	MAKE NO SIGN
FOUR BY FOUR	ISLE OF MULL	MAKE-UP ROOM
FOUR IN HAND	ISLE OF SARK	MARK OF CAIN
FOUR OR FIVE	ISLE OF SKYE	MEAN NO HARM
FREE OF COST	JUST AN IDEA	MILD AS MILK
FREE OF DUTY	JUST AS WELL	MORE OR LESS
FULL OF HATE	JUST IN CASE	MORE TO COME
FULL OF HOPE	JUST IN TIME	NEAR AT HAND
FULL OF LIFE	KEEP IN JAIL	NEXT IN LINE
FULL OF LOVE	KEEP IN MIND	NEXT TO COME
FULL OF SOUL	KEEP IN PLAY	NICE TO KNOW
FULL OF ZEAL	KEEP IN STEP	NICK OF TIME
GAME OF DICE	KEEP IN TUNE	NONE OF THAT
GIFT OF LIFE	KEEP IN VIEW	NOSE TO TAIL
GIVE AN INCH	KEEP IT DARK	NOTE OF HAND
GIVE OR TAKE	KEEP UP WITH	ONCE AN HOUR
GIVE UP HOPE	KILL OR CURE	OPEN TO VIEW
GIVE UP WORK	KING OF ARMS	PACK OF LIES
GONE TO SEED	KING OF SIAM	PAIL OF MILK
GOOD AS DEAD	KISS ME KATE	PAIR OF ACES
GOOD AS GOLD	KISS OF LIFE	PAIR OF TENS
GOOD TO HEAR	KNOT OF HAIR	PAIR OF TWOS
GOOD TO KNOW	LACK OF FOOD	PINT OF BEER
GRIP OF IRON	LACK OF TIME	PINT OF BEST
GULF OF ADEN	LAID TO REST	PINT OF MILD
GULF OF SUEZ	LAND IN JAIL	PINT OF MILK
GUST OF WIND	LAST OF FOUR	PLAT DU JOUR
HALF AN ACRE	LAST TO COME	PLAY AT HOME
HALF AN HOUR	LATE IN LIFE	PLAY IN TUNE
HALF AN INCH	LETS BE FAIR	PLAY IT COOL
HALF AS GOOD	LIFE OF EASE	PLOT OF LAND
HALF AS MUCH	LIFE ON MARS	PORT OF CALL
HALF OF MILD	LINE OF DUTY	PUFF OF WIND
HALL OF FAME	LINE OF FIRE	RIDE TO WORK
HAND IN HAND	LIVE IN DIGS	RISE IN ARMS
HAND IT OVER	LIVE IN FEAR	ROAD TO FAME
HAND OF TIME	LIVE IN HOPE	ROAD TO HELL
HAND TO HAND	LIVE IN WANT	ROAD TO RUIN
HARD AS IRON	LIVE IT DOWN	ROAR OF PAIN
HARD AT WORK	LOAD OF COAL	ROCK OF AGES
HARD TO BEAR	LOAD OF JUNK	ROOM TO MOVE
HARD TO HOLD	LOCK OF HAIR	ROOM TO TURN
HARD TO TAKE	LOCK-UP SHOP	ROPE OF SAND
HAVE AN IDEA	LORD IT OVER	SACK OF COAL
HAVE IN HAND	LOSE NO TIME	SACK OF COKE
HAVE IN MIND	LOSS OF FACE	SACK OF CORN
HAVE IN VIEW	LOSS OF LIFE	SAFE AT HOME
HAVE NO FEAR	LOSS OF TIME	SAFE AT LAST
HAVE NO HOPE	LOST TO VIEW	SALE OF WORK
HEAD OF HAIR	LOTS OF ROOM	SELL IN BULK
HEAD TO FOOT	LOTS OF TIME	SEND BY HAND
HEAD TO TAIL	LOVE IN VAIN	SEND BY MAIL
HEAP OF SAND	LUMP OF CLAY	SEND BY POST
HEAR NO EVIL	MADE BY HAND	SHAH OF IRAN
HERD OF COWS	MADE OF IRON	SHOT AT DAWN
HERD OF DEER	MADE OF WOOD	SHOW NO PITY
HERD OF PIGS	MADE TO LAST	SHOW NO SIGN
HOUR BY HOUR	MAKE AN EXIT	SHOW OF WORK
HOUR OF DOOM	MAKE IT EASY	SHUT UP SHOP
HOUR OF NEED	MAKE IT HURT	SICK OF WORK

SIDE BY SIDE	TURN TO GOLD	GAME AND SET
SIDE OF BEEF	UNIT OF HEAT	GONE TOO FAR
SIDE OF LIFE	UNIT OF TIME	GOOD AND BAD
SIDE TO SIDE	UNIT OF WORK	GOOD FOR ONE
SIGH NO MORE	UPON MY SOUL	GOOD FOR YOU
SIGN OF LIFE	UPON MY WORD	HALF THE MAN
SING IN TUNE	WAIT IN LINE	HEEL AND TOE
SINK OR SWIM	WAKE UP LATE	HERE AND NOW
SLAP-UP MEAL	WALK IN FEAR	HERE YOU ARE
SOFT AS SILK	WALK IN STEP	HIGH AND DRY
SONG OF LOVE	WALK OF LIFE	HIGH AND LOW
SPAN OF LIFE	WALK-ON PART	HOLD THE KEY
STAY AT HOME	WALL OF FIRE	HOME AND DRY
STAY UP LATE	WALL TO WALL	HOOK AND EYE
STEP BY STEP	WANT OF LOVE	JUMP FOR JOY
STOP AT HOME	WANT OF ZEAL	JUMP THE GUN
STOP AT WILL	WEEK BY WEEK	JUST FOR FUN
STOP IN TIME	WEEP NO MORE	JUST THE JOB
SUCH IS LIFE	WELL IN HAND	JUST THE MAN
SURE AS EGGS	WENT TO TOWN	KITH AND KIN
SURE AS FATE	WEST IS WEST	LAND AND SEA
SURE TO LOSE	WHEN IN ROME	LAST BUT ONE
SWAN OF AVON	WILL OF IRON	LAST MAN OUT
TAKE AN OATH	WILL TO LIVE	LEAD THE WAY
TAKE AS READ	WISH IN VAIN	LEAP FOR JOY
TAKE IN HAND	WORK IN HAND	LOCK AND KEY
TAKE IT AWAY	WORK ON HAND	LONG WAY OUT
TAKE IT BACK	WORK TO RULE	LOOK-OUT MAN
TAKE IT EASY	YARD BY YARD	LORD HAW-HAW
TAKE IT HARD	YEAR TO YEAR	LOSE THE WAY
TAKE MY HAND		LOVE AND WAR
TAKE MY WORD	**4, 3, 3**	MAKE THE BED
TAKE NO PART		MAKE THE LAW
TAKE ON FUEL	ADAM AND EVE	MAKE THE TEA
TAKE TO ARMS	BEAT THE AIR	MEAT AND VEG
TAKE TO TASK	BELL THE CAT	MEET THE EYE
TAKE UP ARMS	BILL AND COO	MELT THE ICE
TALK IT OVER	BLOW THE LOT	MICE AND MEN
TASK IN HAND	CHEW THE CUD	MISS THE BUS
TEAM OF DOGS	CHEW THE FAT	NAME THE DAY
TEAM OF FOUR	CHEW THE RAG	NEAR AND FAR
TEAR IN HALF	COME AND SEE	NEAR THE END
TEAR TO BITS	DEAD-END JOB	NEAR THE SEA
TELL NO LIES	DOWN AND OUT	NEAR THE TOP
TEST OF TIME	DOWN OUR WAY	NEXT BUT ONE
THIS OR THAT	DOWN THE PIT	ONES OWN WAY
TIME OF LIFE	DROP THE HEM	OPEN THE BOX
TIME OF YEAR	EACH AND ALL	OVER AND OUT
TIME TO COME	EACH-WAY BET	OVER THE BAR
TIME TO KILL	EASY WAY OUT	OVER THE SEA
TIME TO LOSE	ERIC THE RED	OVER THE TOP
TOUR OF DUTY	FACE THE END	OVER THE WAY
TREE OF LIFE	FEED THE CAT	PASS THE HAT
TRIP TO TOWN	FEED THE DOG	PAVE THE WAY
TRUE TO FORM	FILL THE AIR	PORK-PIE HAT
TRUE TO LIFE	FILL THE GAP	POUR THE TEA
TRUE TO TYPE	FIND THE WAY	PUSH TOO FAR
TUFT OF HAIR	FORE AND AFT	QUID PRO QUO
TURN IT DOWN	FOUR AND SIX	RIPE OLD AGE
TURN OF DUTY	FREE FOR ALL	ROOM FOR TWO
TURN TO DUST	FROM THE TOP	SAVE THE DAY

4, 3, 3

SHOW THE WAY
SINE QUA NON
SING FOR JOY
SNOW AND ICE
STIR THE POT
STOP THE BUS
STOP THE GAP
STOP THE ROT
TAKE THE AIR
TAKE THE RAP
THIS WAY OUT
TIME FOR BED
TIME FOR TEA
TURN THE KEY
VEAL AND HAM
WAIT AND SEE
WALK THE DOG
WASH AND DRY
WASH THE CAR
WEEP FOR JOY
WISE OLD OWL
WITH THE SEA

4, 4, 2

BEAR DOWN ON
BEAR WITH ME
BOIL DOWN TO
CLAP EYES ON
DAYS GONE BY
DOWN WIND OF
EASY DOES IT
FALL BACK ON
FALL FOUL OF
GIVE RISE TO
GIVE VENT TO
HARD DONE BY
KEEP TABS ON
LETS FACE IT
LOOK DOWN ON
LOOK INTO IT
MAKE EYES AT
SNAP INTO IT
TAKE PITY ON
THIS SIDE UP
WEAR MAKE-UP
WHAT GOES ON?
WHAT GOES UP

4, 6

ABLE SEAMAN
ACID TONGUE
AMEN CORNER
ANDY WARHOL
ANNA NEAGLE
ANNA SEWELL
ANNE BOLEYN
ANNE BRONTË
ANNO DOMINI
AQUA FORTIS

ARAB STATES
ARID DESERT
ARMS AKIMBO
ARMS DEALER
ARMS LENGTH
ARMY DOCTOR
AWAY DEFEAT
AXLE GREASE
BABY SITTER
BACK GARDEN
BACK MARKER
BACK NUMBER
BACK STAIRS
BACK STREET
BACK STROKE
BAND LEADER
BAND MASTER
BANK CREDIT
BANK RAIDER
BANK ROBBER
BANK VAULTS
BARE CHANCE
BASE MOTIVE
BATH OLIVER
BEAR GARDEN
BEAR MALICE
BEAR MARKET
BEAT HOLLOW
BEEF CATTLE
BEER BARREL
BEER BOTTLE
BEER CELLAR
BEER GARDEN
BENT DOUBLE
BEST BITTER
BEST CHANCE
BEST FRIEND
BEST POLICY
BEST SELLER
BEST THINGS
BEST WISHES
BING CROSBY
BLUE CHEESE
BLUE CRAYON
BLUE DANUBE
BLUE ENSIGN
BLUE FLOWER
BLUE LAGOON
BLUE MONDAY
BLUE MURDER
BLUE PENCIL
BLUE RIBBON
BLUE STREAK
BODY SWERVE
BOLD DESIGN
BOLD RELIEF
BOLD SPIRIT
BOLD STROKE
BOMB DAMAGE
BOND STREET
BOOK CRITIC

BOOK JACKET
BOOK REVIEW
BOOK RIGHTS
BOOT POLISH
BORN LEADER
BOYS SCHOOL
BRER RABBIT
BUCK RABBIT
BULK BUYING
BULL MARKET
BUMP SUPPER
BUSY LIZZIE
BUSY SEASON
BUSY STREET
BUSY WORKER
CALL TRUMPS
CAPE COLONY
CARD PLAYER
CAST ANCHOR
CATO STREET
CATS CRADLE
CINE CAMERA
CITY CENTRE
CITY EDITOR
CITY FATHER
CITY LIGHTS
CITY LIMITS
CITY OFFICE
CITY POLICE
CITY STREET
CITY WORKER
CLAY PIGEON
CLOG DANCER
CLUB MEMBER
COAL BUNKER
COAL CELLAR
COAL SHOVEL
COAT HANGER
COIN DEALER
COLD BUFFET
COLD REASON
COLD REGION
COLD SEASON
COLD SHOWER
COLD TONGUE
COLD TURKEY
COLD WINTER
COLE PORTER
COME ACROSS
COME ADRIFT
COME ASHORE
COME CLOSER
COME FOURTH
COME HITHER
COME INSIDE
COME NEARER
COME SECOND
COME UNDONE
COOL BREEZE
COPY TYPIST
CORN FLAKES

DAMP COURSE	EAST LONDON	FEEL BETTER
DARK CLOUDS	EAST RIDING	FEEL DEEPLY
DARK COLOUR	EAST SUSSEX	FEEL GROGGY
DARK CORNER	EASY ACCESS	FEEL GUILTY
DARK SECRET	EASY LESSON	FEEL HUNGRY
DAWN CHORUS	EASY LIVING	FEEL RELIEF
DAWN PATROL	EASY MANNER	FEEL SECURE
DEAD CENTRE	EASY MARKET	FEEL SLEEPY
DEAD FLOWER	EASY NUMBER	FILM ADDICT
DEAD GROUND	EASY OPTION	FILM CENSOR
DEAD LEAVES	EASY STAGES	FILM CRITIC
DEAD LETTER	EASY STREET	FILM EDITOR
DEAD MATTER	EASY TARGET	FILM REVIEW
DEAD RINGER	EASY VIRTUE	FILM RIGHTS
DEAD WEIGHT	EASY WICKET	FILM STUDIO
DEAL GENTLY	EASY WINNER	FIND FAVOUR
DEAN MARTIN	EDAM CHEESE	FIND GUILTY
DEAR FRIEND	EDDY MERCKX	FIND REFUGE
DEAR READER	EPIC POETRY	FIND RELIEF
DECK QUOITS	ETON COLLAR	FINE FELLOW
DECK TENNIS	ETON JACKET	FINE FETTLE
DEEP BREATH	EVEN BETTER	FINE FIGURE
DEEP FREEZE	EVEN CHANCE	FINE POWDER
DEEP LITTER	EVEN FASTER	FINE SHOWER
DEEP PURPLE	EVEN HIGHER	FIRE BUCKET
DEEP REGRET	EVEN NUMBER	FIRE ENGINE
DEEP SORROW	EVEN STEVEN	FIRE ESCAPE
DEER FOREST	EVEN TEMPER	FIRE SCREEN
DENY ACCESS	EVER ONWARD	FIRM ADVICE
DICK BARTON	EVIL GENIUS	FIRM BELIEF
DICK TURPIN	EVIL REPUTE	FIRM DENIAL
DISC BRAKES	EVIL SPIRIT	FIRM FRIEND
DISC JOCKEY	EVIL TEMPER	FIRM GROUND
DIVE BOMBER	EXIT PERMIT	FISH COURSE
DOCK MASTER	FACE DANGER	FISH DINNER
DOGS CHANCE	FACE DEFEAT	FISH KETTLE
DOGS DINNER	FACE POWDER	FISH MARKET
DONT FORGET	FAIR AMOUNT	FISH SUPPER
DOOR HANDLE	FAIR CHANCE	FIVE FISHES
DOPE ADDICT	FAIR ENOUGH	FIVE HEARTS
DOPE PEDLAR	FAIR EXCUSE	FIVE LITRES
DRAW BREATH	FAIR INCOME	FIVE METRES
DRAW STUMPS	FAIR SAMPLE	FIVE MONTHS
DROP ANCHOR	FAIR SHARES	FIVE NINTHS
DROP BEHIND	FAIR TACKLE	FIVE OUNCES
DRUG ADDICT	FALL ASLEEP	FIVE POINTS
DRUG PUSHER	FALL BEHIND	FIVE POUNDS
DULL AFFAIR	FALL SILENT	FIVE ROUNDS
DULL COLOUR	FARM ANIMAL	FIVE SENSES
DULL MOMENT	FARM BUTTER	FIVE SIXTHS
DUMB ANIMAL	FARM WORKER	FIVE SPADES
DUMB BLONDE	FAST ASLEEP	FIVE TENTHS
DUMB CRAMBO	FAST BOWLER	FIVE TRICKS
DUMB WAITER	FAST COLOUR	FLAT DENIAL
DUST JACKET	FAST LIVING	FLAT GROUND
DUTY ROSTER	FAST READER	FLAT RACING
EAST AFRICA	FAST RUNNER	FLAT SEASON
EAST ANGLIA	FAST WICKET	FLEA CIRCUS
EAST BERLIN	FAST WORKER	FOAM RUBBER
EAST INDIAN	FATS DOMINO	FOLK DANCER
EAST INDIES	FATS WALLER	FOLK SINGER

FOND BELIEF	GAIN HEIGHT	GOOD NATURE
FOND PARENT	GAIN WEIGHT	GOOD NOTICE
FOOD SUPPLY	GAME THEORY	GOOD NUMBER
FOOL AROUND	GAME WARDEN	GOOD PEOPLE
FORM MASTER	GARY COOPER	GOOD PERSON
FOUL STROKE	GARY PLAYER	GOOD PLAYER
FOUL TEMPER	GARY SOBERS	GOOD REASON
FOUR EIGHTS	GENE TUNNEY	GOOD RECORD
FOUR FIFTHS	GENE WILDER	GOOD REPAIR
FOUR HEARTS	GIFT COUPON	GOOD REPORT
FOUR KNAVES	GIRL FRIDAY	GOOD REPUTE
FOUR LITRES	GIRL FRIEND	GOOD RESULT
FOUR METRES	GIVE ADVICE	GOOD REVIEW
FOUR MONTHS	GIVE BATTLE	GOOD SAILOR
FOUR NINTHS	GIVE CHANGE	GOOD SALARY
FOUR OUNCES	GIVE CREDIT	GOOD SCHOOL
FOUR POINTS	GIVE FREELY	GOOD SEAMAN
FOUR POUNDS	GIVE GROUND	GOOD SECOND
FOUR QUARTS	GIVE NOTICE	GOOD SPEECH
FOUR QUEENS	GIVE ORDERS	GOOD STAYER
FOUR SEVENS	GIVE PRAISE	GOOD SUPPLY
FOUR SPADES	GIVE THANKS	GOOD TACKLE
FOUR TENTHS	GLEE SINGER	GOOD TACTIC
FOUR THREES	GLIB TONGUE	GOOD TEMPER
FOUR TRICKS	GOBI DESERT	GOOD THINGS
FOUR WHEELS	GOLD NUGGET	GOOD TIMING
FRED BASSET	GOLD RECORD	GOOD WICKET
FRED BLOGGS	GOLD SHARES	GOOD WISHES
FRED TITMUS	GOLD STATER	GREY MATTER
FREE ACCESS	GOLD STRIKE	GREY MULLET
FREE ADVICE	GOLD THREAD	GREY STREAK
FREE CHOICE	GOLF COURSE	GRID SYSTEM
FREE CHURCH	GONE ASTRAY	GROW APPLES
FREE DRINKS	GOOD ADVICE	GROW BETTER
FREE FRENCH	GOOD CHANCE	GROW BIGGER
FREE MARKET	GOOD CHOICE	GROW LARGER
FREE PARDON	GOOD CREDIT	GROW TALLER
FREE SAMPLE	GOOD DINNER	GULF STREAM
FREE SCHOOL	GOOD DRIVER	HACK WRITER
FREE SPEECH	GOOD EFFORT	HAIR LOTION
FREE TICKET	GOOD ENOUGH	HAIR RIBBON
FROM ABROAD	GOOD EXCUSE	HALF ASLEEP
FROM BEHIND	GOOD FAMILY	HALF BOTTLE
FROM MEMORY	GOOD FELLOW	HALF DOLLAR
FROM WITHIN	GOOD FIGURE	HALF LENGTH
FUEL CRISIS	GOOD FRIDAY	HALF NELSON
FULL BOTTLE	GOOD FRIEND	HALF SHARES
FULL CHORUS	GOOD GROUND	HALF SISTER
FULL CIRCLE	GOOD HABITS	HALF VOLLEY
FULL COLOUR	GOOD HEALTH	HALF YEARLY
FULL GALLOP	GOOD HIDING	HALL PORTER
FULL GROWTH	GOOD HUMOUR	HAND LOTION
FULL INSIDE	GOOD INTENT	HAND SIGNAL
FULL LENGTH	GOOD LENGTH	HANG AROUND
FULL NELSON	GOOD LIVING	HANG GLIDER
FULL PARDON	GOOD LOOKER	HARD ASTERN
FULL REPORT	GOOD LOVING	HARD CENTRE
FULL VOLUME	GOOD MASTER	HARD CHEESE
GAIN ACCESS	GOOD MEMORY	HARD DRINKS
GAIN FAVOUR	GOOD MORROW	HARD GROUND
GAIN GROUND	GOOD MOTIVE	HARD KNOCKS

HARD LABOUR	HOME MARKET	KING ALFRED
HARD LESSON	HOME MOVIES	KING ARTHUR
HARD LIQUOR	HOME OFFICE	KING CANUTE
HARD MASTER	HOME TRUTHS	KING EDWARD
HARD PENCIL	HOME WATERS	KING FAROUK
HARD TACKLE	HUGE PROFIT	KING GEORGE
HARD WINTER	ICED COFFEE	KING HAROLD
HARD WORKER	IDLE BEGGAR	KNOW BETTER
HAVE DINNER	IDLE GOSSIP	LACK BRAINS
HAVE DOUBTS	IDLE MOMENT	LACK FINISH
HAVE QUALMS	IDLE RUMOUR	LACK POLISH
HEAD HUNTER	IDLE THREAT	LACK SPIRIT
HEAD INJURY	INTO BATTLE	LADY DOCTOR
HEAD OFFICE	IRON MAIDEN	LADY GODIVA
HEAD PORTER	IRON RATION	LAKE GENEVA
HEAD WAITER	JACK HORNER	LAMB CUTLET
HEAR VOICES	JACK LONDON	LAME EXCUSE
HEAT STROKE	JACK SPRATT	LAND FORCES
HERB GARDEN	JACK WARNER	LAND REFORM
HIGH CHURCH	JANE AUSTEN	LAND TENURE
HIGH COLLAR	JEAN HARLOW	LAST AUGUST
HIGH COLOUR	JEAN RACINE	LAST AUTUMN
HIGH COMEDY	JEAN RENOIR	LAST BREATH
HIGH DEGREE	JOHN ARLOTT	LAST CHANCE
HIGH DIVING	JOHN BRIGHT	LAST COURSE
HIGH ESTEEM	JOHN BUCHAN	LAST DEMAND
HIGH FAVOUR	JOHN BUNYAN	LAST FRIDAY
HIGH FLYING	JOHN CALVIN	LAST MINUTE
HIGH GERMAN	JOHN CLEESE	LAST MOMENT
HIGH GROUND	JOHN CONTEH	LAST MONDAY
HIGH IDEALS	JOHN DALTON	LAST ORDERS
HIGH INCOME	JOHN DRYDEN	LAST PERSON
HIGH LIVING	JOHN EDRICH	LAST REFUGE
HIGH MORALE	JOHN LENNON	LAST RESORT
HIGH NUMBER	JOHN MCADAM	LAST SEASON
HIGH OCTANE	JOHN MILTON	LAST SPRING
HIGH OFFICE	JOHN NAPIER	LAST SUMMER
HIGH PLACES	JOHN RUSKIN	LAST SUNDAY
HIGH PRAISE	JOHN WESLEY	LAST SUPPER
HIGH PRIEST	JOHN WILKES	LAST WINTER
HIGH REGARD	JOIN BATTLE	LATE AUTUMN
HIGH RELIEF	JOIN FORCES	LATE DINNER
HIGH REPUTE	JUAN CARLOS	LATE GOTHIC
HIGH SALARY	JUAN FANGIO	LATE SPRING
HIGH SCHOOL	JUDO EXPERT	LATE SUMMER
HIGH SEASON	JUDY GEESON	LATE TACKLE
HIGH STAKES	JURY SYSTEM	LAWN TENNIS
HIGH STATUS	JUST BEFORE	LAZY PERSON
HIGH STREET	JUST ENOUGH	LEAD ASTRAY
HOLD GUILTY	JUST REWARD	LEAD PENCIL
HOLD OFFICE	KEEN MEMBER	LEAD PIPING
HOLY FATHER	KEEP AFLOAT	LEAD TRUMPS
HOLY GROUND	KEEP MOVING	LEAD WEIGHT
HOLY ISLAND	KEEP SECRET	LECH WALESA
HOLY ORDERS	KEEP SILENT	LEFT BEHIND
HOLY SPIRIT	KEEP TRYING	LEFT UNSAID
HOLY TEMPLE	KEEP WICKET	LEFT WINGER
HOME COUNTY	KEIR HARDIE	LEGS ELEVEN
HOME DEFEAT	KIND FRIEND	LEND WEIGHT
HOME FORCES	KIND NATURE	LIFE JACKET
HOME GROUND	KIND PERSON	LIFE MEMBER

LIFE POLICY	MAKE PUBLIC	NINE MONTHS
LIFE TENANT	MAKE TRACKS	NINE OUNCES
LIME STREET	MALE CHORUS	NINE POINTS
LOCH LOMOND	MALT LIQUOR	NINE POUNDS
LONE RANGER	MALT WHISKY	NINE TENTHS
LONG CRUISE	MANY THANKS	NINE TRICKS
LONG ISLAND	MARC ANTONY	NOEL COWARD
LONG KNIVES	MARK ANTONY	NOVA SCOTIA
LONG LADDER	MARY BARTON	OBEY ORDERS
LONG LETTER	MARY PETERS	OLGA KORBUT
LONG MEMORY	MARY STUART	ONCE BITTEN
LONG PERIOD	MASS APPEAL	ONES ELDERS
LONG PLAYER	MASS MARKET	ONLY CHANCE
LONG SHADOW	MASS MURDER	ONLY CHOICE
LONG SPEECH	MATT FINISH	OPEN CHEQUE
LONG SUMMER	MEAL TICKET	OPEN CREDIT
LONG TUNNEL	MEAN STREAK	OPEN DRAWER
LONG VOYAGE	MEAT COURSE	OPEN HEARTH
LONG WINTER	MEAT MARKET	OPEN LETTER
LOOK AROUND	MEAT RATION	OPEN MARKET
LOOK INSIDE	MESS JACKET	OPEN PRISON
LOOK LIVELY	MICK JAGGER	OPEN REVOLT
LOOK SICKLY	MILD REBUKE	OPEN SEASON
LOOK SLIPPY	MILD WINTER	OPEN SECRET
LORD ATTLEE	MILK BOTTLE	OPEN SESAME
LORD KEYNES	MISS MUFFET	OPEN WINDOW
LORD LYTTON	MOCK TURTLE	OVEN GLOVES
LORD NELSON	MOST LIKELY	OVER POLITE
LOSE COLOUR	MOST PEOPLE	PACK ANIMAL
LOSE FAVOUR	MOVE ACROSS	PALE SHERRY
LOSE GROUND	MOVE SLOWLY	PALE YELLOW
LOSE HEIGHT	MUCH BETTER	PALM SUNDAY
LOSE WEIGHT	NAIL POLISH	PARI MUTUEL
LOSS LEADER	NAZI RE¡GIME	PASS MUSTER
LOST BATTLE	NEAR ENOUGH	PASS ORDERS
LOST CHANCE	NEAR FUTURE	PAST BELIEF
LOUD CHEERS	NEAT FIGURE	PAST CARING
LOUD COLOUR	NEAT SCOTCH	PAST MASTER
LOUD PRAISE	NEAT WHISKY	PAST RECORD
LOUD REPORT	NEIL SEDAKA	PAUL KRUGER
LOVE AFFAIR	NELL GWYNNE	PAUL NEWMAN
LOVE DEARLY	NEWS AGENCY	PAUL REVERE
LOVE LETTER	NEWS EDITOR	PICK STRAWS
LOVE POTION	NEWS LETTER	PINE FOREST
LOVE THIRTY	NEWS MEDIUM	PINE MARTEN
LUIS BUÑUEL	NEWS REPORT	PINE NEEDLE
MACH NUMBER	NEXT AUGUST	PINT BOTTLE
MADE BETTER	NEXT AUTUMN	PIPE ABOARD
MAID MARION	NEXT FRIDAY	PITH HELMET
MAIL PACKET	NEXT MONDAY	PLAY ACTING
MAIL ROBBER	NEXT PLEASE	PLAY AROUND
MAIN ARTERY	NEXT SEASON	PLAY BRIDGE
MAIN CHANCE	NEXT SPRING	PLAY CENTRE
MAIN CLAUSE	NEXT SUMMER	PLAY HAMLET
MAIN COURSE	NEXT SUNDAY	PLAY HOCKEY
MAIN REASON	NEXT VICTIM	PLAY HOOKEY
MAIN STREAM	NEXT WINTER	PLAY POSSUM
MAIN STREET	NICE PEOPLE	PLAY RUGGER
MAKE AMENDS	NICE PERSON	PLAY SOCCER
MAKE BETTER	NICE THINGS	PLAY SQUASH
MAKE PASSES	NINE LITRES	PLAY STREET

PLAY	TENNIS	RIPE	TOMATO	SLOW	WICKET
PLAY	TRICKS	RISE	HIGHER	SLOW	WORKER
PLAY	TRUANT	RITA	HUNTER	SOAP	BUBBLE
PLAY	TRUMPS	ROAD	BRIDGE	SOAP	FLAKES
PLUM	BRANDY	ROAD	SAFETY	SOAP	POWDER
POLO	GROUND	ROCK	BOTTOM	SODA	SYPHON
POLO	PLAYER	ROCK	GARDEN	SOFT	ANSWER
POOR	BEGGAR	ROCK	HUDSON	SOFT	CENTRE
POOR	CHANCE	ROCK	SALMON	SOFT	COLOUR
POOR	CHOICE	ROOF	GARDEN	SOFT	GROUND
POOR	EXCUSE	ROOM	NUMBER	SOFT	NUMBER
POOR	FELLOW	ROPE	LADDER	SOFT	OPTION
POOR	HEALTH	ROSE	GARDEN	SOFT	PALATE
POOR	PEOPLE	ROSY	CHEEKS	SOFT	PENCIL
POOR	PERSON	RUDE	ANSWER	SOFT	WICKET
POOR	RELIEF	RUDE	HEALTH	SOLE	RIGHTS
POOR	RESULT	RUDE	PERSON	SOLE	TRADER
POOR	RETURN	RUDE	REMARK	SOLO	EFFORT
POOR	SECOND	RUSS	CONWAY	SOLO	FLIGHT
POOR	SINNER	SAFE	GROUND	SONG	THRUSH
POOR	SUPPLY	SAFE	METHOD	SONG	WRITER
POOR	WRETCH	SAFE	POLICY	SOON	ENOUGH
POOR	YORICK	SALT	CELLAR	SORE	THROAT
PORT	ARTHUR	SAND	CASTLE	SOUP	COURSE
PORT	ENGINE	SAUL	BELLOW	SOUR	GRAPES
PORT	TALBOT	SAVE	LABOUR	SOUR	NATURE
POST	MORTEM	SEEK	ADVICE	SPIN	BOWLER
POST	OFFICE	SEEK	ASYLUM	STAG	BEETLE
PREP	SCHOOL	SEEK	OFFICE	STAN	LAUREL
PUFF	PASTRY	SEEK	REFUGE	STAR	PLAYER
PURE	CHANCE	SELL	SHARES	STAY	AWHILE
PURE	COLOUR	SEND	FLYING	STAY	BEHIND
PURE	SILVER	SHOE	POLISH	STAY	INSIDE
PUSH	AROUND	SHOE	STRING	STEP	ASHORE
QUIZ	MASTER	SHOP	WINDOW	STEP	INSIDE
RACE	HATRED	SHOW	FAVOUR	STEP	LADDER
RAIL	STRIKE	SHOW	JUMPER	STEP	LIVELY
RAIN	FOREST	SHOW	SPIRIT	STOP	CRYING
RARE	CHANCE	SHOW	TALENT	SURE	ENOUGH
RAVE	NOTICE	SHOW	VALOUR	SURE	GROUND
RAVE	REVIEW	SICK	HUMOUR	SWIM	ACROSS
REAL	COFFEE	SICK	PARADE	TAKE	ACTION
REAL	DANGER	SICK	PERSON	TAKE	ADVICE
REAL	ESTATE	SIDE	EFFECT	TAKE	CHARGE
REAL	FRIEND	SIDE	POCKET	TAKE	CREDIT
REAL	INCOME	SIDE	STREET	TAKE	EFFECT
REAL	MADRID	SIGH	DEEPLY	TAKE	FLIGHT
REAL	PERSON	SIGN	MANUAL	TAKE	FRIGHT
REAL	SCHOOL	SILK	FABRIC	TAKE	KINDLY
REAL	TENNIS	SILK	GLOVES	TAKE	NOTICE
REAR	GUNNER	SILK	SCREEN	TAKE	OFFICE
REAR	LIGHTS	SIZE	ELEVEN	TAKE	ORDERS
REAR	WINDOW	SIZE	TWELVE	TAKE	POISON
RENT	DEMAND	SKIN	COLOUR	TAKE	REFUGE
REST	AWHILE	SKIN	DIVING	TALK	TURKEY
REST	PERIOD	SLIM	CHANCE	TAME	AFFAIR
RICH	PEOPLE	SLIM	FIGURE	TAME	ANIMAL
RICH	PERSON	SLIM	VOLUME	TAXI	DRIVER
RICH	REWARD	SLOW	BOWLER	TEAM	SPIRIT
RICH	SOURCE	SLOW	GROWTH	TELL	NOBODY
RING	FINGER	SLOW	MOTION	TEMP	AGENCY

TEST FLIGHT	WALK BEHIND	BREAK A BONE
TEST WICKET	WALK SLOWLY	BREAK A DATE
THIN EXCUSE	WALL STREET	BREAK A FALL
THIS AUTUMN	WALT DISNEY	BREAK A RULE
THIS FRIDAY	WANT WISDOM	BRING A CASE
THIS MINUTE	WARD SISTER	BRING A SUIT
THIS MOMENT	WARM FRIEND	BURST A TYRE
THIS MONDAY	WARM SEASON	CADGE A LIFT
THIS SEASON	WARM SPRING	CATCH A BALL
THIS SPRING	WEAK EXCUSE	CATCH A COLD
THIS SUMMER	WEED KILLER	CATCH A CRAB
THIS SUNDAY	WELL BEATEN	CATCH A FISH
THIS WINTER	WELL BEHIND	CAUSE A RIOT
TIDY INCOME	WELL ENOUGH	CAUSE A STIR
TIME ENOUGH	WELL PLACED	CLIMB A HILL
TIME FACTOR	WELL PLAYED	CLIMB A TREE
TIME SIGNAL	WELL SPOKEN	CLOSE A DEAL
TIME SWITCH	WELL VERSED	CRACK A CODE
TIME, PLEASE	WENT AROUND	CRACK A JOKE
TOLL BRIDGE	WEST AFRICA	FIGHT A DUEL
TONE POETRY	WEST BERLIN	FORCE A DRAW
TONY CURTIS	WEST INDIAN	GRANT A WISH
TORY LEADER	WEST INDIES	HATCH A PLOT
TORY POLICY	WEST LONDON	HEAVE A SIGH
TOWN CENTRE	WEST RIDING	HITCH A LIFT
TOWN SQUARE	WHIT MONDAY	INCUR A LOSS
TRAM DRIVER	WHIT SUNDAY	ISSUE A WRIT
TRIM FIGURE	WIDE APPEAL	LEAVE A MARK
TRIP ABROAD	WIDE CHOICE	LEAVE A NOTE
TROY WEIGHT	WIDE CIRCLE	LEAVE A WILL
TRUE BELIEF	WIDE MARGIN	LIGHT A FIRE
TRUE FRIEND	WIDE SCREEN	LIGHT A PIPE
TRUE REPORT	WIFE BEATER	ORDER A MEAL
TRUE SAMPLE	WILD ANIMAL	PITCH A TENT
TURN AROUND	WILD CHERRY	PLANT A SEED
TURN PURPLE	WILD FLOWER	PLANT A TREE
TURN TURTLE	WILD HORSES	PROVE A WILL
TURN YELLOW	WIND TUNNEL	RAISE A HAND
TWIN SISTER	WINE BIBBER	RAISE A LOAN
UGLY RUMOUR	WINE BOTTLE	RENEW A BOOK
UGLY SISTER	WINE CELLAR	REPAY A LOAN
UGLY THREAT	WINE COOLER	SCORE A BULL
VAIN EFFORT	WINE TASTER	SCORE A DUCK
VAIN PERSON	WINE WAITER	SCORE A GOAL
VAIN REGRET	WING MIRROR	SERVE A MEAL
VAST EXTENT	WIRE BASKET	SERVE A WRIT
VAST PLAINS	WISE CHOICE	SEVEN A SIDE
VEAL CUTLET	WITH EFFECT	SHARE A FLAT
VERY HUNGRY	WITH REGRET	SHOOT A LINE
VERY LIKELY	WOOD CARVER	SMOKE A PIPE
VERY LITTLE	WOOD PIGEON	SPARE A DIME
VERY NEARLY	WORD MAKING	START A FIRE
VERY SELDOM	WORD SQUARE	START A RIOT
VINE GROWER	WORK PERMIT	STATE A CASE
VOTE LABOUR	YOUR CHOICE	STEAL A KISS
WAGE FREEZE	YOUR HONOUR	THROW A KISS
WAGE PACKET		THUMB A LIFT
WAIT AROUND	**5, 1, 4**	THUMB A RIDE
WAIT AWHILE		TWICE A WEEK
WALK ACROSS	AFTER A TIME	TWICE A YEAR
WALK AROUND	BLAZE A PATH	UNTIE A KNOT

UTTER A WORD
WRITE A BOOK
WRITE A NOTE
WRITE A PLAY
WRITE A POEM
WRITE A SONG
WRITE A WILL

5, 2, 3

ABOVE IT ALL
BLACK AS INK
BLACK AS JET
BLOCK OF ICE
BREAK AN ARM
BREAK IN TWO
BREAK IT OFF
BREAK OF DAY
BRING IT OFF
CARRY IT OFF
CHEST OF TEA
CHUCK IT OUT
CLEAR AS DAY
CLEAR AS MUD
CLOSE OF DAY
COUNT ME OUT
COURT OF LAW
CROSS IT OFF
CROSS IT OUT
DANNY LA RUE
DEVIL TO PAY
EARLY TO BED
EIGHT TO ONE
FIFTH OF MAY
FIFTY TO ONE
FIGHT IT OUT
FIRST OF ALL
FIRST OF MAY
FIRST OF SIX
FIRST OF TEN
FIRST OF TWO
FIRST TO ACT
FIRTH OF TAY
FLOAT ON AIR
FORCE OF LAW
FORTY TO ONE
GLASS OF ALE
GROUP OF TEN
HATCH AN EGG
HOURS ON END
HOUSE OF GOD
HOUSE TO LET
KNOCK IT OFF
LAUGH IT OFF
LEARN TO FLY
LEAST OF ALL
LEAVE TO DIE
LEAVE TO ROT
LIGHT AS AIR
LOADS OF FUN
MARCH TO WAR

MIXED-UP KID
NINTH OF MAY
OFFER TO PAY
PIPES OF PAN
PLAIN TO SEE
POINT OF LAW
QUICK TO ACT
READY TO DIE
RIGHT OF WAY
RIGHT ON CUE
RIGHT ON TOP
RULES OF WAR
SERVE AN ACE
SEVEN TO ONE
SHAKE IT OFF
SHEET OF ICE
SHOOT IT OUT
SIXTH OF MAY
SIXTY TO ONE
SLEEP IT OFF
SORRY TO SAY
SPELL IT OUT
SPLIT IN TWO
STAND IN AWE
STAND ON END
STAND TO WIN
STAND UP FOR
STATE OF WAR
STICK IT OUT
STICK UP FOR
SWEAT IT OUT
TENTH OF MAY
THATS TO SAY
THING OR TWO
THINK IT OUT
THIRD OF MAY
THREE BY TWO
THREE IN ONE
THREE TO ONE
TIMES OF WAR
TREAD ON AIR
TRICK OR TWO
TRUSS OF HAY
TWIST MY ARM
WAGES OF SIN
WATER ON TAP
WHATS UP DOC?
WHIFF OF AIR
WHITE OF EGG
WORST OF ALL
WRITE IN INK
WRITE IT OFF
YEARS ON END

5, 3, 2

FIGHT FOR IT
FIGHT SHY OF
FIRST MAN IN
JIMLL FIX IT
READY FOR IT

RIGHT WAY UP
SILLY MID-ON
STAND FOR IT
SWING FOR IT
TOUCH AND GO
VOUCH FOR IT
WRONG WAY UP
YOUVE HAD IT

5, 5

ABOVE BOARD
ABOVE PRICE
ABOVE WATER
ACUTE ANGLE
ADAMS APPLE
ADDIS ABABA
AFTER DEATH
AFTER HOURS
AFTER LUNCH
AFTER TODAY
AIREY NEAVE
ALARM CHAIN
ALARM CLOCK
ALPHA MINUS
ALTAR CLOTH
AMBER LIGHT
AMBLE ALONG
AMPLE BELLY
AMPLE MEANS
AMPLE SCOPE
ANGEL CHILD
ANGRY SCENE
ANKLE SOCKS
APPLE GREEN
APPLE SAUCE
APRON STAGE
ARMED FORCE
ARMED GUARD
ARMED TRUCE
ASCOT RACES
ASTON VILLA
AVANT GARDE
AWAIT TRIAL
AWFUL SIGHT
BADEN BADEN
BAKED APPLE
BAKED BEANS
BANDY WORDS
BASIC TRUTH
BATON ROUGE
BEGIN AGAIN
BELOW PRICE
BETTE DAVIS
BIBLE CLASS
BLACK BEARD
BLACK BEAST
BLACK BERET
BLACK BOOKS
BLACK CLOUD
BLACK DEATH

BLACK DRESS	BRIEF VISIT	CLEAN SHIRT
BLACK HEART	BRING ABOUT	CLEAN SLATE
BLACK HORSE	BRING FORTH	CLEAN SOCKS
BLACK MAGIC	BRING ROUND	CLEAN SWEEP
BLACK MARIA	BRISK TRADE	CLEAN TOWEL
BLACK MUSIC	BROAD ARROW	CLEAN WATER
BLACK PAINT	BROAD BEANS	CLEAR IMAGE
BLACK PATCH	BROWN BOOTS	CLEAR PRINT
BLACK PEARL	BROWN BREAD	CLEAR ROUND
BLACK PIECE	BROWN PAINT	CLEAR SPACE
BLACK POWER	BROWN PAPER	CLEAR VOICE
BLACK QUEEN	BROWN SHIRT	CLEAR WATER
BLACK SHEEP	BROWN SHOES	CLEFT STICK
BLACK SHIRT	BROWN SUGAR	CLIVE JAMES
BLACK SHOES	BROWN TROUT	CLIVE LLOYD
BLACK SOCKS	BRUSH ASIDE	CLOCK TOWER
BLACK STAMP	BRUTE FORCE	CLOSE MATCH
BLACK WIDOW	BUDDY HOLLY	CLOSE RANKS
BLANK SHEET	BURNT ALIVE	CLOSE SHAVE
BLANK SPACE	BURNT AMBER	CLOSE THING
BLANK STARE	BURNT TOAST	CLOSE WATCH
BLANK VERSE	BURST FORTH	CLOVE HITCH
BLEAK HOUSE	CADET CORPS	CLUNK CLICK
BLIND ALLEY	CAMEL CORPS	COACH HORSE
BLIND DRUNK	CAMEL TRAIN	COACH HOUSE
BLIND FAITH	CANDY FLOSS	COACH PARTY
BLIND GUESS	CANIS MAJOR	COLIN DAVIS
BLOCK PRINT	CAPER SAUCE	COMFY CHAIR
BLOOD COUNT	CARRY ABOUT	COMIC OPERA
BLOOD DONOR	CASEY JONES	COMIC STRIP
BLOOD GROUP	CATCH SIGHT	COMIC VERSE
BLOOD HORSE	CHAIN SMOKE	CONAN DOYLE
BLOOD MONEY	CHAIN STORE	COSTA BRAVA
BLOOD RIVER	CHEAP SKATE	COUNT BASIE
BLOOD ROYAL	CHEAP TRICK	COUNT HANDS
BLOOD SPORT	CHEAT DEATH	COUNT HEADS
BOBBY JONES	CHECK POINT	COUNT SHEEP
BOBBY MOORE	CHESS MATCH	COURT CARDS
BOBBY RIGGS	CHESS PIECE	COURT DRESS
BONUS ISSUE	CHEVY CHASE	COURT HOUSE
BOOBY PRIZE	CHIEF CLERK	COURT ORDER
BORED STIFF	CHIEF SCOUT	COURT USHER
BOWIE KNIFE	CHINA PLATE	COVER DRIVE
BRAIN CHILD	CHINA STONE	COVER POINT
BRAIN DRAIN	CHRIS EVERT	CRAWL ABOUT
BRAIN FEVER	CHRIS LLOYD	CRÊPE PAPER
BRAIN STORM	CHUCK BERRY	CRÊPE SOLES
BRASS PLATE	CIDER APPLE	CRIME SQUAD
BRASS TACKS	CIGAR SMOKE	CRIME STORY
BRAVE FRONT	CILLA BLACK	CROSS WINDS
BREAD BOARD	CIVIC PRIDE	CROSS WORDS
BREAD FRUIT	CIVIL COURT	CROWD ROUND
BREAD KNIFE	CIVIL WRONG	CROWD SCENE
BREAD SAUCE	CLARK GABLE	CROWN AGENT
BREAK BREAD	CLASP HANDS	CROWN COURT
BREAK COVER	CLEAN BREAK	CROWN DERBY
BREAK FAITH	CLEAN FIGHT	CROWN GLASS
BREAK LOOSE	CLEAN HANDS	CROWN GREEN
BREAK RANKS	CLEAN LINEN	CROWN PIECE
BREAK ROCKS	CLEAN LIVER	CRUDE METAL
BRIAN CLOSE	CLEAN SHEET	CRUEL SHAME

CYRUS VANCE	EARLY RISER	FALSE TEETH
DAILY BREAD	EARLY STAGE	FANCY DRESS
DAILY DOZEN	EARLY START	FANCY GOODS
DAILY GRIND	EARLY TRAIN	FANCY PRICE
DAILY HABIT	EARLY TUDOR	FANNY ADAMS
DAILY PAPER	EARLY WORKS	FATAL CRASH
DAILY PRESS	EIGHT DRAWS	FATAL ERROR
DAILY ROUND	EIGHT HOURS	FATAL WOUND
DAIRY CREAM	EIGHT KILOS	FENCE ROUND
DAIRY FRESH	EIGHT MILES	FEVER PITCH
DAISY CHAIN	EIGHT PENCE	FIELD EVENT
DANCE MUSIC	EIGHT PINTS	FIELD SPORT
DARTS BOARD	EIGHT TIMES	FIERY CROSS
DARTS MATCH	EIGHT WEEKS	FIERY STEED
DAVID BOWIE	EIGHT YEARS	FIFTH FLOOR
DAVID FROST	ELLEN TERRY	FIFTH ROUND
DAVID NIVEN	EMERY CLOTH	FIFTY KILOS
DEATH KNELL	EMERY PAPER	FIFTY MILES
DEATH SCENE	EMPTY BOAST	FIFTY PENCE
DEBIT ENTRY	EMPTY CHAIR	FIFTY YEARS
DELTA WINGS	EMPTY GLASS	FINAL AUDIT
DENSE CROWD	EMPTY HOUSE	FINAL COUNT
DERBY HORSE	EMPTY PURSE	FINAL EVENT
DERBY SWEEP	EMPTY SHELL	FINAL FLING
DEVON CREAM	EMPTY SPACE	FINAL OFFER
DILLY DALLY	EMPTY WORDS	FINAL POINT
DIRTY HABIT	ENEMY AGENT	FINAL ROUND
DIRTY LINEN	ENEMY FLEET	FINAL SCENE
DIRTY MONEY	ENEMY LINES	FINAL SCORE
DIRTY STORY	ENTRY MONEY	FINAL STAGE
DIRTY TRICK	EPSOM RACES	FINAL TOUCH
DIRTY WATER	EPSOM SALTS	FIRST BLOOD
DIZZY SPELL	EQUAL PARTS	FIRST CHILD
DOLLS HOUSE	EQUAL SHARE	FIRST CLASS
DOYLY CARTE	EQUAL TERMS	FIRST DRAFT
DRAMA GROUP	EQUAL VALUE	FIRST FLOOR
DRAWN MATCH	ERNIE BEVIN	FIRST FLUSH
DRAWN SWORD	ERROL FLYNN	FIRST GRADE
DREAM HOUSE	EVERY MONTH	FIRST GUESS
DREAM LOVER	EVERY NIGHT	FIRST HOUSE
DREAM WORLD	EVERY OTHER	FIRST ISSUE
DRESS SENSE	EVERY WOMAN	FIRST LIGHT
DRESS SHIRT	EXTRA COVER	FIRST MONTH
DRIED FRUIT	EXTRA MONEY	FIRST NIGHT
DRIFT ALONG	EXTRA POWER	FIRST NOVEL
DRIFT APART	FADED YOUTH	FIRST PARTY
DRINK VODKA	FAINT HEART	FIRST PLACE
DRINK WATER	FAINT LIGHT	FIRST PRIZE
DUMMY WHIST	FAINT SOUND	FIRST ROUND
DUTCH BULBS	FAIRY QUEEN	FIRST SHIFT
DUTCH TREAT	FAIRY STORY	FIRST SIGHT
DUTCH TULIP	FALSE ALARM	FIRST STAGE
DUTCH UNCLE	FALSE ALIBI	FIRST STEPS
DYING CAUSE	FALSE BEARD	FIRST THING
DYING WORDS	FALSE CREED	FIRST VERSE
EARLS COURT	FALSE FRONT	FIRST WATER
EARLY GRAVE	FALSE IMAGE	FIRST WOMAN
EARLY HOURS	FALSE LOGIC	FISHY STORY
EARLY LIGHT	FALSE PRIDE	FIVES COURT
EARLY LUNCH	FALSE SCENT	FIXED ABODE
EARLY NIGHT	FALSE START	FIXED IDEAS

FIXED POINT
FIXED PRICE
FIXED SMILE
FIXED STARS
FLESH WOUND
FLING ASIDE
FLINT GLASS
FLOAT ABOUT
FLOOD GATES
FLOOD LEVEL
FLOOD WATER
FLOOR CLOTH
FLOOR SPACE
FLUID OUNCE
FOCAL POINT
FOGGY NIGHT
FORCE APART
FORGE AHEAD
FORTY KILOS
FORTY MILES
FORTY OVERS
FORTY PENCE
FORTY WINKS
FORTY YEARS
FRANK BOUGH
FRANZ KAFKA
FRANZ LISZT
FRAUD SQUAD
FRESH BREAD
FRESH CREAM
FRESH FRUIT
FRESH PAINT
FRESH START
FRESH WATER
FRIED BACON
FRIED BREAD
FRONT BENCH
FRONT COVER
FRONT TEETH
FRONT WHEEL
FRUIT DRINK
FRUIT JELLY
FRUIT JUICE
FRUIT SALAD
FULLY ARMED
FULLY AWARE
FULLY GROWN
FUNNY STORY
FUNNY THING
GHOST STORY
GHOST TRAIN
GIANT CRANE
GIANT PANDA
GIDDY LIMIT
GLASS BEADS
GLASS COACH
GLASS HOUSE
GLOSS PAINT
GOING BADLY
GOING CHEAP
GOING ROUND

GOING TWICE
GOING WHITE
GOODS TRAIN
GRACE KELLY
GRACE NOTES
GRADE THREE
GRAND CANAL
GRAND DUCHY
GRAND HOTEL
GRAND JUROR
GRAND MARCH
GRAND OPERA
GRAND PIANO
GRAND SCALE
GRAND STYLE
GRAND TOTAL
GRAPE JUICE
GRASS COURT
GRASS ROOTS
GRASS SKIRT
GRASS SNAKE
GRASS VERGE
GRASS WIDOW
GRAVE DOUBT
GRAVE WORDS
GRAYS ELEGY
GREAT ASSET
GREAT CRASH
GREAT HEART
GREAT HOPES
GREAT LAKES
GREAT MARCH
GREAT MERIT
GREAT MINDS
GREAT NIECE
GREAT SCOTT!
GREAT SHOCK
GREAT SPEED
GREAT THING
GREAT UNCLE
GREAT VALUE
GREAT WOMAN
GREEK CROSS
GREEK DRAMA
GREEK PROSE
GREEK VERSE
GREEN BAIZE
GREEN BEANS
GREEN BERET
GREEN CLOTH
GREEN DRESS
GREEN FIELD
GREEN FLASH
GREEN GRASS
GREEN LIGHT
GREEN PAINT
GREEN RIVER
GREEN SALAD
GREEN STUFF
GRETA GARBO
GROSS VALUE

GROWN WOMAN
GRUFF VOICE
GUESS RIGHT
GUESS WRONG
GUEST HOUSE
GUEST NIGHT
GUEST TOWEL
GYPSY QUEEN
HAPPY BREED
HAPPY CHILD
HAPPY EVENT
HAPPY KNACK
HAPPY WOMAN
HARSH SOUND
HARSH VOICE
HARSH WORDS
HEADY DRINK
HEAVY BUILD
HEAVY CLOUD
HEAVY GOING
HEAVY HEART
HEAVY METAL
HEAVY MUSIC
HEAVY PUNCH
HEAVY SLEEP
HEAVY STORM
HEAVY STUFF
HEAVY SWELL
HEAVY TOUCH
HEAVY TREAD
HEAVY WATER
HELEN WILLS
HELLO DOLLY
HELLS BELLS
HENNA RINSE
HENRY FONDA
HENRY JAMES
HENRY MOORE
HENRY TUDOR
HOBBY HORSE
HOCUS POCUS
HOLLY BERRY
HORSE LAUGH
HORSE OPERA
HORSE POWER
HORSE SENSE
HORSE THIEF
HOTEL STAFF
HOTEL SUITE
HOUSE AGENT
HOUSE ORGAN
HOUSE PARTY
HOUSE RULES
HOUSE STORK
HOVER ABOUT
HUMAN BEING
HUMAN CHAIN
HUMAN ERROR
HUMAN RIGHT
HUMAN SKILL
HUMAN VOICE

HURRY ALONG	LIGHT BLUES	MAJOR THIRD
HUSKY VOICE	LIGHT BROWN	MANOR HOUSE
ICING SUGAR	LIGHT GREEN	MAPLE SUGAR
IDEAL PLACE	LIGHT HEART	MAPLE SYRUP
INDIA PAPER	LIGHT LUNCH	MARCH WINDS
INNER HOUSE	LIGHT METER	MARIA BUENO
INNER LIGHT	LIGHT MUSIC	MARIE CURIE
INNER SPACE	LIGHT OPERA	MARIE LLOYD
IRISH LINEN	LIGHT SLEEP	MARIO LANZA
IRISH SWEEP	LIGHT SNACK	MARRY YOUNG
ISSUE FORTH	LIGHT TOUCH	MATCH POINT
IVORY BLACK	LIGHT TREAD	MELBA TOAST
IVORY COAST	LIGHT VERSE	MERRY DANCE
IVORY TOWER	LINED PAPER	MERRY HEART
JAMES JOYCE	LINEN CHEST	MERRY MONTH
JAMES MASON	LIONS MOUTH	MERRY PRANK
JAMES WOLFE	LIONS SHARE	MERRY WIDOW
JELLY MOULD	LIVER BIRDS	MERRY WIVES
JERRY BROWN	LOCAL PAPER	METAL PLATE
JERRY BUILT	LOCAL RATES	MIAMI BEACH
JERRY LEWIS	LOCAL TRAIN	MIDAS TOUCH
JESSE JAMES	LOOSE COVER	MILES APART
JESSE OWENS	LOOSE TOOTH	MINCE WORDS
JEWEL THIEF	LOOSE WOMAN	MINOR CANON
JOINT STOCK	LORDS TABLE	MINOR CHORD
JOLLY ROGER	LORNA DOONE	MINOR POINT
JULES VERNE	LOTUS EATER	MINOR SCALE
KINGS BENCH	LOUGH NEAGH	MINOR THIRD
KINGS CROSS	LOWER BERTH	MIXED BUNCH
KINKY BOOTS	LOWER CLASS	MIXED DRINK
KNIFE WOUND	LOWER HOUSE	MIXED FRUIT
KNOCK ABOUT	LOWER LEVEL	MIXED GRILL
KNOCK TWICE	LOWER LIMIT	MIXED HERBS
LARGE BUILD	LOWER SIXTH	MIXED PARTY
LARGE CROWD	LOWER THIRD	MODEL PLANE
LARGE FLEET	LOWER WAGES	MODEL TRAIN
LARGE HOUSE	LUCKY BREAK	MONEY ORDER
LARGE ORDER	LUCKY CHARM	MONEY PRIZE
LARGE PIECE	LUCKY DEVIL	MONEY TALKS
LARGE PRINT	LUCKY GUESS	MONKS HABIT
LARGE SCALE	LUCKY PATCH	MONTE CARLO
LARGE STAFF	LUCKY PENNY	MORAL FIBRE
LARGE STOCK	LUCKY STARS	MORAL ISSUE
LARGE VODKA	LUNAR MONTH	MORAL LAPSE
LARRY ADLER	LUNCH BREAK	MORAL RIGHT
LATIN PROSE	LURID STYLE	MORAL SENSE
LATIN VERSE	LYRIC DRAMA	MORAY FIRTH
LAUGH ABOUT	LYRIC VERSE	MOSHE DAYAN
LEARN MUSIC	MAGIC FLUTE	MOTOR CYCLE
LEAVE ALONE	MAGIC POWER	MOTOR RALLY
LEAVE EARLY	MAGIC SPELL	MOUNT GUARD
LEGAL CLAIM	MAGIC SWORD	MOUNT KENYA
LEGAL COSTS	MAGIC TOUCH	MOUNT SINAI
LEGAL ISSUE	MAGIC TRICK	MOUTH ORGAN
LEGAL LIMIT	MAGIC WORDS	MOVIE ACTOR
LEGAL OWNER	MAGNA CARTA	MUDDY BOOTS
LEGAL RIGHT	MAJOR ASSET	MUDDY SHOES
LEGAL TITLE	MAJOR CHORD	MUDDY WATER
LEMON DRINK	MAJOR ISSUE	MUMBO JUMBO
LEMON JUICE	MAJOR POWER	MUSIC LOVER
LEVEL SCORE	MAJOR SCALE	MUSIC NIGHT

MUSIC PAPER	PADDY FIELD	PRESS AGENT
MUSIC STAND	PAPAL COURT	PRESS AHEAD
MUSIC STOOL	PAPER CHASE	PRESS BARON
MUSIC WORLD	PAPER MONEY	PRICE INDEX
NAKED FLAME	PAPER ROUND	PRICE LABEL
NAKED LIGHT	PAPER TIGER	PRICE LEVEL
NAKED STEEL	PARIS GREEN	PRIMA DONNA
NAKED SWORD	PARTY AGENT	PRIMA FACIE
NAKED TRUTH	PARTY DRESS	PRIME CAUSE
NAKED WOMAN	PARTY FROCK	PRIME MOVER
NASAL TWANG	PARTY FUNDS	PRINT DRESS
NASAL VOICE	PARTY NIGHT	PRIOR CLAIM
NASTY HABIT	PARTY PIECE	PRIVY PURSE
NASTY SHOCK	PARTY TRICK	PRIZE COURT
NASTY SPILL	PEACE CORPS	PRIZE ESSAY
NASTY TASTE	PEACE OFFER	PRIZE FIGHT
NASTY TRICK	PEACE TERMS	PRIZE IDIOT
NAVAL CADET	PEACH MELBA	PRIZE MONEY
NAVAL CRAFT	PEARL DIVER	PROUD BOAST
NAVAL POWER	PEGGY MOUNT	PROUD HEART
NEVER AGAIN	PENNY BLACK	PROWL ABOUT
NEVER NEVER	PENNY PLAIN	PUNCH DRUNK
NEVER WAVER	PENNY STAMP	QUACK QUACK
NEVER WORRY	PERRY MASON	QUICK LUNCH
NEVER WRONG	PETER FINCH	QUICK MARCH
NEVIL SHUTE	PETER PIPER	QUICK SNACK
NIGHT NURSE	PETER SCOTT	QUICK TEMPO
NIGHT SHIFT	PETIT FOURS	QUIET START
NIGHT TRAIN	PETTY CRIME	QUITE AWFUL
NIGHT WATCH	PETTY THEFT	QUITE CLEAR
NINTH ROUND	PETTY THIEF	QUITE CLOSE
NOBEL PRIZE	PHASE THREE	QUITE HAPPY
NOBLE BIRTH	PIANO MUSIC	QUITE RIGHT
NOBLE BLOOD	PIANO SCORE	QUITE STILL
NORTH COAST	PIANO STOOL	QUITE WRONG
NORTH DOWNS	PIANO TUNER	QUOTE TERMS
NORTH KOREA	PILOT LIGHT	RADIO THREE
NORTH WALES	PIPED MUSIC	RADIO TIMES
OCEAN LINER	PITCH BLACK	RADIO WAVES
OLDEN TIMES	PLACE MONEY	RAISE ALOFT
OLIVE GREEN	PLAID CYMRU	RAISE MONEY
OLIVE GROVE	PLAIN COVER	RAISE TAXES
OMAHA BEACH	PLAIN FACTS	RALLY ROUND
OPERA GLASS	PLAIN FOLLY	RANCH HOUSE
OPERA HOUSE	PLAIN PAPER	RAPID PULSE
OPERA MUSIC	PLAIN TASTE	RAZOR BLADE
OPERA SCORE	PLAIN TERMS	RAZOR SHARP
OPIUM EATER	PLAIN TRUTH	RAZOR SHELL
OPIUM POPPY	PLAIN WORDS	RAZOR STROP
OPTIC NERVE	PLANE CRASH	READY MONEY
ORDER LUNCH	PLATE GLASS	READY REPLY
ORGAN MUSIC	PLUMB CRAZY	RHYME ROYAL
OSCAR WILDE	POINT BLANK	RIFLE RANGE
OTHER RANKS	POINT TAKEN	RIGHT ABOUT
OTHER WORLD	POLES APART	RIGHT AHEAD
OUIJA BOARD	POWER DRILL	RIGHT ANGLE
OUTER COVER	POWER HOUSE	RIGHT ELBOW
OUTER HOUSE	POWER PLANT	RIGHT FLANK
OUTER SHELL	POWER POINT	RIGHT IDIOT
OUTER SPACE	POWER PRESS	RIGHT LINES
OUTTA SIGHT!	PRAWN CURRY	RIGHT PLACE

RIGHT ROUND	RUGBY PITCH	SHORT BURST
RIGHT THING	RUGBY SCRUM	SHORT DRESS
RIGHT TRACK	RUGBY TRIAL	SHORT DRINK
RIGHT TRAIL	RUGBY UNION	SHORT DRIVE
RIGHT WOMAN	RURAL SCENE	SHORT HAIRS
RINGO STARR	SAINT JAMES	SHORT HOURS
RIVAL CAUSE	SAINT PETER	SHORT LEASE
RIVAL CLAIM	SALAD CREAM	SHORT PANTS
RIVER BASIN	SALES FORCE	SHORT PRICE
RIVER CLYDE	SALES STAFF	SHORT RANGE
RIVER CRAFT	SALLY FORTH	SHORT REIGN
RIVER FORTH	SANDY BEACH	SHORT SIGHT
RIVER LEVEL	SANTA CLAUS	SHORT SKIRT
RIVER MOUTH	SANTA MARIA	SHORT SOCKS
RIVER NIGER	SATIN DRESS	SHORT SPELL
RIVER PLATE	SAVOY HOTEL	SHORT STORY
RIVER RHINE	SCALE MODEL	SHORT VISIT
RIVER SEINE	SCENE THREE	SHOVE ASIDE
RIVER TRENT	SCOUT ROUND	SILLY BILLY
RIVER TROUT	SCRAP METAL	SILLY DEVIL
ROAST ALIVE	SCRAP PAPER	SILLY GOOSE
ROCKY COAST	SCREW LOOSE	SILLY IDIOT
ROGER BACON	SCRIP ISSUE	SILLY POINT
ROMAN FORUM	SEDAN CHAIR	SIMON PETER
ROMAN HOUSE	SEEDY JOINT	SIXTH ROUND
ROMAN RUINS	SEIZE POWER	SIXTH SENSE
ROMAN TUNIC	SENSE ORGAN	SIXTY KILOS
ROMAN VILLA	SEVEN CARDS	SIXTY MILES
ROUGH DRAFT	SEVEN CLUBS	SIXTY OVERS
ROUGH GOING	SEVEN DIALS	SIXTY PENCE
ROUGH GUESS	SEVEN HOURS	SIXTY YEARS
ROUGH GUIDE	SEVEN KILOS	SKIRT ROUND
ROUGH HOUSE	SEVEN MILES	SLAVE STATE
ROUGH NIGHT	SEVEN PENCE	SLAVE TRADE
ROUGH STONE	SEVEN PINTS	SLEEP ROUGH
ROUGH STUFF	SEVEN TIMES	SLEEP TIGHT
ROUGH TRACK	SEVEN VEILS	SLIDE VALVE
ROUGH WATER	SEVEN WEEKS	SMALL BUILD
ROUND ABOUT	SEVEN WIVES	SMALL CHILD
ROUND DANCE	SEVEN YEARS	SMALL CRAFT
ROUND DOZEN	SHAKE HANDS	SMALL CROWD
ROUND EIGHT	SHARE INDEX	SMALL FRAME
ROUND ROBIN	SHARP FROST	SMALL HOURS
ROUND SEVEN	SHARP KNIFE	SMALL HOUSE
ROUND TABLE	SHARP POINT	SMALL MEANS
ROUND THREE	SHARP TASTE	SMALL ORDER
ROUND TOWER	SHARP TWIST	SMALL PRINT
ROUTE MARCH	SHARP VOICE	SMALL SCALE
ROYAL ASCOT	SHARP WORDS	SMALL THING
ROYAL BIRTH	SHEER AGONY	SMALL VOICE
ROYAL BLOOD	SHEER FLUKE	SMALL WAIST
ROYAL FLUSH	SHEER FOLLY	SMALL WOMAN
ROYAL GUARD	SHEER FORCE	SMALL WORLD
ROYAL HOUSE	SHEET GLASS	SMART ALECK
ROYAL SCOTS	SHEET METAL	SMART WOMAN
ROYAL SUITE	SHEET MUSIC	SNEAK ABOUT
ROYAL TRAIN	SHINE FORTH	SNEAK THIEF
ROYAL VISIT	SHIPS CARGO	SNOWY WHITE
ROYAL YACHT	SHIRE HORSE	SOAPY WATER
RUGBY FIELD	SHOOT AHEAD	SOBER TRUTH
RUGBY MATCH	SHORE LEAVE	SOLAR MONTH

SOLAR POWER	STEAM POWER	TABLE DHÔTE
SOLID BUILD	STEAM RADIO	TABLE KNIFE
SOLID FACTS	STEAM TRAIN	TABLE LINEN
SOLID SENSE	STEEL WORKS	TABLE MONEY
SORRY SIGHT	STEEP CLIMB	TABLE WATER
SORRY STATE	STEEP PRICE	TAKEN ABACK
SOUND LOGIC	STEER CLEAR	TAKEN SHORT
SOUND SENSE	STERN WORDS	TASTE BLOOD
SOUND SLEEP	STEVE OVETT	TASTY SNACK
SOUND TRACK	STICK TIGHT	TEACH CLASS
SOUND WAVES	STIFF CLIMB	TEACH MATHS
SOUTH COAST	STIFF DRINK	TEENY WEENY
SOUTH DOWNS	STIFF PRICE	TENOR VOICE
SOUTH KOREA	STILL OWING	TENTH FLOOR
SOUTH WALES	STILL THERE	TENTH ROUND
SPACE PROBE	STILL WATER	TEPID WATER
SPARE PARTS	STOCK REPLY	TERRA COTTA
SPARE WHEEL	STOCK STILL	TERRA FIRMA
SPEAK ALOUD	STOKE POGES	TERRY JONES
SPEAK WELSH	STONE STEPS	TERRY WOGAN
SPEED FREAK	STONE WALLS	THEME MUSIC
SPEED GAUGE	STONY BROKE	THERE THERE
SPEED LIMIT	STONY HEART	THICK BLOOD
SPEED TRIAL	STONY STARE	THICK CLOUD
SPEND MONEY	STORM CLOUD	THICK SKULL
SPENT FORCE	STOUT HEART	THINK ABOUT
SPERM WHALE	STOUT WOMAN	THINK AGAIN
SPICY STORY	STRIP LIGHT	THINK AHEAD
SPILL BLOOD	STRIP POKER	THINK ALIKE
SPIRO AGNEW	STRIP TEASE	THINK ALOUD
SPLIT HAIRS	STUDY LEAVE	THINK TWICE
SPLIT LEVEL	STUDY MATHS	THIRD CHILD
SQUAD DRILL	STUDY MUSIC	THIRD CLASS
STAFF DANCE	SUEDE SHOES	THIRD FLOOR
STAFF NURSE	SUGAR CANDY	THIRD GRADE
STAGE FEVER	SUGAR DADDY	THIRD MONTH
STAGE THREE	SUNNY SMILE	THIRD PARTY
STAKE MONEY	SUNNY SPELL	THIRD PLACE
STALE BREAD	SURGE AHEAD	THIRD PRIZE
STAMP ALBUM	SWEAT BLOOD	THIRD REICH
STAND ABOUT	SWEAT SHIRT	THIRD ROUND
STAND ALONE	SWEEP ALONG	THIRD SHIFT
STAND ALOOF	SWEEP ASIDE	THIRD VERSE
STAND APART	SWEEP CLEAN	THIRD WORLD
STAND ASIDE	SWEET HERBS	THREE BALLS
STAND CLEAR	SWEET MUSIC	THREE BEARS
STAND ERECT	SWEET ODOUR	THREE CARDS
STAND GUARD	SWEET SMELL	THREE CLUBS
STAND READY	SWEET SMILE	THREE DARTS
STAND STILL	SWEET SOUND	THREE DOZEN
STAND TREAT	SWEET TOOTH	THREE FIVES
STAND TRIAL	SWEET WORDS	THREE FOURS
STARK NAKED	SWEPT ASIDE	THREE GROSS
START AGAIN	SWING ALONG	THREE HOURS
START POINT	SWING DOORS	THREE JACKS
START YOUNG	SWING MUSIC	THREE KILOS
STATE COACH	SWING ROUND	THREE KINGS
STATE GRANT	SWISS FRANC	THREE LUMPS
STATE TRIAL	SWORD DANCE	THREE MILES
STATE VISIT	SWORD FIGHT	THREE NINES
STEAK HOUSE	SWORN ENEMY	THREE PAGES

THREE PAIRS	UNDER COVER	WHITE BREAD
THREE PARTS	UNDER SIEGE	WHITE CHALK
THREE PENCE	UNDER STEAM	WHITE CLOUD
THREE PINTS	UNDER TRIAL	WHITE DWARF
THREE SCORE	UNDER WATER	WHITE FRIAR
THREE SIDES	UNDUE HASTE	WHITE FROST
THREE SIXES	UNION CHIEF	WHITE HAIRS
THREE STARS	UPPER BERTH	WHITE HORSE
THREE TIMES	UPPER CLASS	WHITE HOUSE
THREE WEEKS	UPPER CRUST	WHITE LIGHT
THREE WORDS	UPPER HOUSE	WHITE MAGIC
THREE YARDS	UPPER LIMIT	WHITE PAINT
THREE YEARS	UPPER SIXTH	WHITE PAPER
THROW ABOUT	UPPER THIRD	WHITE PIECE
THUMB INDEX	UPPER VOLTA	WHITE QUEEN
TIDAL BASIN	USUAL THING	WHITE ROSES
TIGER SHARK	UTTER CHAOS	WHITE SAUCE
TIGHT DRESS	UTTER TRIPE	WHITE SHARK
TIGHT GRASP	VALID POINT	WHITE SHEET
TIGHT SKIRT	VICHY WATER	WHITE SHIRT
TINNY SOUND	VITAL ERROR	WHITE SLAVE
TITLE DEEDS	VITAL FORCE	WHITE SOCKS
TITLE FIGHT	VITAL POINT	WHITE SUGAR
TITUS OATES	VITAL POWER	WHITE TOWER
TONIC WATER	VITAL SPARK	WHITE TRASH
TOTAL PEACE	VOCAL CORDS	WHOLE TRUTH
TOTAL WRECK	VOCAL MUSIC	WHOLE WORLD
TOUCH JUDGE	VOCAL ORGAN	WIELD POWER
TOUCH PAPER	VOCAL SCORE	WILLY NILLY
TOUGH BREAK	VOWEL SOUND	WITCH HAZEL
TOUGH FIGHT	WAGES CLERK	WOMAN HATER
TRACK EVENT	WAGON TRAIN	WOODY ALLEN
TRADE CYCLE	WAGON WHEEL	WORLD ATLAS
TRADE PAPER	WALTZ MUSIC	WORLD COURT
TRADE PRESS	WASTE MONEY	WORLD POWER
TRADE PRICE	WASTE PAPER	WORLD TITLE
TRADE ROUTE	WASTE WORDS	WREAK HAVOC
TRADE TERMS	WATCH CHAIN	WRIST WATCH
TRADE UNION	WATCH TELLY	WRITE ABOUT
TRAIN CRASH	WATER BOARD	WRITE BOOKS
TRAIN FERRY	WATER CLOCK	WRITE MUSIC
TREAD WATER	WATER CRESS	WRITE PLAYS
TREAT BADLY	WATER LEVEL	WRITE VERSE
TRIAL MATCH	WATER MELON	WRONG PLACE
TRIAL SCENE	WATER MUSIC	WRONG TRACK
TRULY RURAL	WATER NYMPH	WRONG WOMAN
TRUST HOUSE	WATER POWER	YIELD FRUIT
TRUTH SERUM	WATER TABLE	YOUNG BLOOD
TUDOR HOUSE	WATER TOWER	YOUNG CHILD
TUDOR STYLE	WATER WINGS	YOUNG WOMAN
TWICE DAILY	WAXED PAPER	YOURS TRULY
TWICE EIGHT	WEARY BONES	
TWICE ROUND	WELLS FARGO	6, 1, 3
TWICE SEVEN	WELSH CORGI	
TWICE THREE	WELSH HILLS	BRIDGE A GAP
TWIRL ROUND	WHATS YOURS?	IMPOSE A BAN
TYCHO BRAHE	WHEAT FIELD	ROBERT E.LEE
ULTRA VIRES	WHELK STALL	THANKS A LOT
UNCLE REMUS	WHIRL ROUND	THERES A WAY
UNCUT PAGES	WHIST DRIVE	
UNCUT STONE	WHITE BEARD	

6 , 2 , 2

ENOUGH TO DO
PLENTY TO DO
RARING TO GO
REFUSE TO GO
WIZARD OF OZ

6 , 4

ABOARD SHIP
ABRUPT EXIT
ACCESS CARD
ACCESS ROAD
ACETIC ACID
ACHING FEET
ACTING HEAD
ACTIVE DUTY
ACTIVE LIFE
ACTIVE LIST
ACTIVE MIND
ACTIVE PART
ACTIVE VERB
ACTUAL FACT
ADVICE NOTE
ADVISE WELL
AERIAL VIEW
ALBERT HALL
ALMOND CAKE
ALMOND TREE
ALMOST FULL
ALMOST OVER
ANGLED SHOT
ANGORA GOAT
ANGORA WOOL
ANIMAL FARM
ANIMAL FOOD
ANIMAL LIFE
ANSWER BACK
ARABIC RACE
ARABLE FARM
ARABLE LAND
ARCHED BACK
ARCTIC COLD
ARCTIC TERN
ARRIVE LATE
ARTHUR ASHE
ARTHUR LOWE
ASTRAL BODY
ATOMIC BOMB
ATOMIC MASS
ATOMIC PILE
AUBURN HAIR
AUTUMN WIND
BAKERS SHOP
BALLET SHOE
BALTIC PORT
BANANA SKIN
BANTAM COCK
BARBED WIRE
BARLEY WINE

BARREN LAND
BATTEN DOWN
BATTLE HYMN
BEACHY HEAD
BEARER BILL
BEAUTY SHOP
BEAUTY SPOT
BECOME LESS
BECOME SANE
BEFORE DAWN
BEFORE DUSK
BEFORE LONG
BEFORE NOON
BEFORE TIME
BEHAVE WELL
BEHIND BARS
BEHIND TIME
BELTED EARL
BENDED KNEE
BERLIN WALL
BETTER DAYS
BETTER DEAD
BETTER HALF
BETTER IDEA
BETTER PAID
BETTER SELF
BETTER THAN
BEYOND HOPE
BIGGIN HILL
BINARY FORM
BISHAN BEDI
BITING WIND
BITTER BEER
BITTER BLOW
BITTER PILL
BITTER WIND
BLONDE HAIR
BLOODY MARY
BOBBED HAIR
BODILY HARM
BODILY PAIN
BOGGED DOWN
BOILED BEEF
BOILED FISH
BOILED RICE
BOILER ROOM
BOILER SUIT
BOMBAY DUCK
BOSTON CRAB
BOSTON REEL
BOTTOM GEAR
BOTTOM LINE
BOTTOM NOTE
BOTTOM RUNG
BOUNCE BACK
BOWLED OVER
BOXING RING
BRANCH LINE
BRANDY SNAP
BREATH TEST
BRIDAL GOWN

BRIDAL VEIL
BRIDGE CLUB
BRIDGE HAND
BRIDGE ROLL
BRIDLE PATH
BRIGHT BLUE
BRIGHT EYES
BRIGHT IDEA
BRIGHT SIDE
BRIGHT SPOT
BROKEN BACK
BROKEN BONE
BROKEN DOWN
BROKEN HOME
BROKEN NECK
BROKEN NOSE
BROKEN WORD
BRONZE COIN
BUBBLE BATH
BUBBLE OVER
BUCKET SEAT
BUCKET SHOP
BUFFET MEAL
BULLET HOLE
BUMPER CROP
BUNKER HILL
BUTTER BEAN
BUTTER DISH
BYGONE DAYS
CAMDEN TOWN
CANCER WARD
CANDID VIEW
CANNED BEER
CANNON BALL
CARBON COPY
CAREER GIRL
CAROLE KING
CASUAL WARD
CATCHY TUNE
CATTLE FARM
CATTLE FOOD
CATTLE GRID
CATTLE SHED
CATTLE SHOW
CAUGHT FIRE
CELERY SALT
CENTRE HALF
CHANGE DOWN
CHANGE ENDS
CHANGE GEAR
CHANGE OVER
CHANGE STEP
CHARGE CARD
CHARGE HAND
CHEESE DISH
CHEESE ROLL
CHEQUE BOOK
CHEQUE CARD
CHERRY LIPS
CHERRY TART
CHERRY TREE

CHILDS PLAY	CREDIT NOTE	DOUBLY SURE
CHORUS GIRL	CROUCH DOWN	DREAMY LOOK
CHURCH ARMY	CRUSTY LOAF	DRIVEN SNOW
CHURCH BELL	CUCKOO PINT	DUFFEL COAT
CHURCH MICE	CUNARD LINE	DUNDEE CAKE
CINQUE PORT	CUTTLE FISH	EAGLES NEST
CIRCLE LINE	DAINTY DISH	EARTHA KITT
CITRIC ACID	DAMASK ROSE	EASILY DONE
CLEVER DICK	DAMNED LIES	EASTER TERM
CLEVER IDEA	DANGER LINE	EASTER TIME
CLEVER MOVE	DANGER LIST	EASTER WEEK
CLOSED BOOK	DANISH BLUE	ECCLES CAKE
CLOSED DOOR	DATIVE CASE	EDWARD LEAR
CLOSED EYES	DEADLY BLOW	EIGHTH ARMY
CLOSED MIND	DEADLY DULL	EIGHTH PART
CLOSED SHOP	DEATHS DOOR	EIGHTY DAYS
CLOVEN FOOT	DEATHS HEAD	ELEVEN DAYS
CLOVEN HOOF	DECREE NISI	ELEVEN FEET
CLOVER LEAF	DEEPLY FELT	ELEVEN PLUS
COARSE FISH	DEEPLY HURT	ELEVEN QUID
COARSE JOKE	DESERT RATS	ENGINE ROOM
COBALT BLUE	DESERT SONG	ENOUGH ROOM
COBALT BOMB	DEVILS LUCK	ENOUGH ROPE
COFFEE BEAN	DIESEL FUEL	ENOUGH SAID
COFFIN NAIL	DINERS CLUB	ENOUGH TIME
COLOUR FILM	DINING HALL	EOLIAN HARP
COMING SOON	DINING ROOM	EQUALS SIGN
COMMON COLD	DINNER BELL	ESTATE DUTY
COMMON FORM	DINNER DATE	EXCESS FARE
COMMON GOOD	DINNER GONG	EXCISE BILL
COMMON HERD	DINNER HOUR	EXCISE DUTY
COMMON LAND	DINNER SUIT	EXETER CITY
COMMON NAME	DINNER TIME	EXPERT SHOT
COMMON NOUN	DIRECT LINE	FAIRLY GOOD
COMMON ROOM	DIVING BELL	FAIRLY WARM
COMMON SALT	DIVING BIRD	FAIRLY WELL
COMMON SORT	DIVING SUIT	FALLEN IDOL
COMMON TALK	DOGGER BANK	FALLOW DEER
COMMON TASK	DOLLAR BILL	FALLOW LAND
COMMON TYPE	DONALD DUCK	FAMILY FEUD
COOKED MEAT	DONALD SWAN	FAMILY FIRM
COPPER COIN	DONKEY WORK	FAMILY LIFE
COPPER MINE	DORIAN GRAY	FAMILY NAME
COPPER WIRE	DOTING WIFE	FAMILY SEAT
CORDON BLEU	DOTTED LINE	FAMILY SIZE
CORNED BEEF	DOTTED NOTE	FAMILY TIES
CORNER FLAG	DOUBLE BACK	FAMILY TREE
CORNER KICK	DOUBLE BASS	FAMOUS NAME
CORNER SEAT	DOUBLE BEND	FAMOUS WORK
CORNER SHOP	DOUBLE BLUE	FATHER TIME
CORNER SITE	DOUBLE CHIN	FATTED CALF
COSMIC RAYS	DOUBLE DATE	FEEBLE JOKE
COTTON MILL	DOUBLE FIVE	FEEBLE MIND
COTTON REEL	DOUBLE FOUR	FETTER LANE
COTTON WOOL	DOUBLE LIFE	FEUDAL LORD
COUNTY CORK	DOUBLE LOCK	FIANNA FAꞮL
COUNTY DOWN	DOUBLE NINE	FIGURE FIVE
COUNTY HALL	DOUBLE ROOM	FIGURE FOUR
COUNTY TOWN	DOUBLE STAR	FIGURE NINE
CRADLE SONG	DOUBLE TAKE	FILIAL DUTY
CREDIT CARD	DOUBLE TIME	FILTHY MOOD

FINEST HOUR	GAMBLE AWAY	GUINEA FOWL
FINGER BOWL	GARAGE HAND	GUITAR SOLO
FINISH LAST	GARDEN CITY	HALTER NECK
FINITE VERB	GARDEN FÊTE	HAMMER AWAY
FIRING LINE	GARDEN FLAT	HAMMER HOME
FISCAL YEAR	GARDEN FORK	HAMMER TOES
FLAXEN HAIR	GARDEN GATE	HARDLY EVER
FLIGHT DECK	GARDEN HOSE	HEALTH FARM
FLIGHT PATH	GARDEN PATH	HEALTH FOOD
FLOWER GIRL	GARDEN PEAS	HEARTS EASE
FLOWER SHOW	GARDEN PEST	HEARTY MEAL
FLYING BOAT	GARDEN SEAT	HECTIC TIME
FLYING BOMB	GARDEN SHED	HERMIT CRAB
FLYING FISH	GARDEN WALL	HEROIC DEED
FLYING HIGH	GARLIC SALT	HIGHER RANK
FLYING JUMP	GATHER FOOD	HIGHLY PAID
FLYING KICK	GEISHA GIRL	HILARY TERM
FLYING SCOT	GENIAL HOST	HOCKEY BALL
FLYING SHOT	GENTLE PUSH	HOCKEY CLUB
FOLDED ARMS	GEORGE BEST	HOCKEY TEAM
FOLLOW SUIT	GEORGE BUSH	HOLMAN HUNT
FORCED SALE	GEORGE SAND	HOMELY GIRL
FOREST FIRE	GERALD FORD	HONEST FACE
FOREST LAND	GERMAN FLAG	HONEST LOOK
FORGED COIN	GERMAN MARK	HONEST TOIL
FORGED NOTE	GERMAN WINE	HONEST WORK
FORMAL CALL	GILDED CAGE	HOOKED NOSE
FORMIC ACID	GINGER BEER	HORNED TOAD
FOSSIL FUEL	GINGER CAKE	HORROR FILM
FOSTER HOPE	GINGER SNAP	HUMBLE FARE
FOURTH FORM	GINGER WINE	HUNGRY LOOK
FOURTH GEAR	GLANCE BACK	HURDLE RACE
FOURTH TEST	GLANCE OVER	ILKLEY MOOR
FOURTH TIME	GLASSY LOOK	IMPORT DUTY
FRAYED EDGE	GLAZED LOOK	INDIAN CLUB
FREEZE HARD	GOLDEN CALF	INDIAN CORN
FREEZE OVER	GOLDEN DAYS	INDIAN FILE
FRENCH ALPS	GOLDEN DISC	INDIAN FOOD
FRENCH BEAN	GOLDEN GATE	INDIAN HEMP
FRENCH FLAG	GOLDEN GIRL	INDIAN MEAL
FRENCH HORN	GOLDEN HAIR	INJURY TIME
FRENCH LOAF	GOLDEN HIND	INLAND PORT
FRENCH ROLL	GOLDEN HOUR	INSIDE EDGE
FRENCH WINE	GOLDEN MEAN	INSIDE LANE
FRIDAY WEEK	GOLDEN MILE	INSIDE LEFT
FRIGID TONE	GOLDEN RING	ITALIC TYPE
FRIGID ZONE	GOLDEN RULE	JAGGED EDGE
FROZEN FISH	GRAHAM HILL	JASPER WARE
FROZEN FOOD	GRANNY KNOT	JEROME KERN
FROZEN HARD	GRAVEL PATH	JERSEY CITY
FROZEN LAKE	GREASY POLE	JETHRO TULL
FROZEN MEAT	GROUND BAIT	JOCKEY CLUB
FROZEN OVER	GROUND CORN	JOHNNY CASH
FROZEN PEAS	GROUND CREW	JOKERS WILD
FROZEN POND	GROUND PLAN	JUGGED HARE
FROZEN SNOW	GROUND RENT	JUMBLE SALE
FRUGAL MEAL	GROUND RICE	JUNGLE BOOK
FUNDED DEBT	GROUSE MOOR	JUNIOR HIGH
FUTURE WIFE	GROWTH AREA	JUNIOR LEAD
GALLOP HOME	GUILTY LOOK	KAISER BILL
GALLUP POLL	GUILTY MIND	KANSAS CITY

KARATE CHOP	LLOYDS BANK	MIDDLE AGES
KENNEL CLUB	LLOYDS LIST	MIDDLE DECK
KENNEL MAID	LOADED DICE	MIDDLE EAST
KETTLE DRUM	LOCKED AWAY	MIDDLE PART
KHYBER PASS	LOCKED DOOR	MIDDLE ROAD
KIDNEY BEAN	LONDON AREA	MIDDLE TERM
KILLER BLOW	LONDON CLUB	MIGHTY FINE
KODIAK BEAR	LONDON TOWN	MILLED EDGE
KUBLAI KHAN	LONDON WALL	MINCED MEAT
LABOUR CAMP	LOSING GAME	MINERS LAMP
LABOUR CLUB	LOSING HAND	MINUTE BOOK
LABOUR VOTE	LOSING SIDE	MINUTE HAND
LADIES MAID	LOSING TEAM	MIXING BOWL
LARGER PART	LOUNGE SUIT	MOBILE HOME
LATENT HEAT	LOVELY GRUB	MODERN GIRL
LATEST NEWS	LOVELY LOOT	MODERN IDEA
LATEST WORD	LOVELY TIME	MODERN MISS
LATTER HALF	LOVERS KNOT	MOHAIR SUIT
LAVISH CARE	LOVERS LANE	MONDAY CLUB
LEADEN FEET	LOVERS LEAP	MONDAY WEEK
LEADER PAGE	LOVERS TIFF	MORBID FEAR
LEAGUE GAME	LOVERS VOWS	MORTAL BLOW
LENTIL SOUP	LOVING CARE	MORTAL COIL
LESSER EVIL	LOVING WIFE	MORTAL FEAR
LETHAL DOSE	LUXURY FLAT	MOTHER LOVE
LETTER BOMB	MAGNUM OPUS	MOTHER SHIP
LETTER CARD	MAIDEN AUNT	MOVING BELT
LETTER FILE	MAIDEN NAME	MULLED WINE
LETTER POST	MAIDEN OVER	MURDER CASE
LETTER RACK	MALTED MILK	MUTTON CHOP
LETTER RATE	MANUAL WORK	MUTUAL LOVE
LIKELY LADS	MARBLE ARCH	NAPKIN RING
LIKELY SPOT	MARCEL WAVE	NARROW DOWN
LIKELY TALE	MARINE LIFE	NARROW MIND
LIQUID DIET	MARKED DOWN	NARROW PATH
LIQUID FOOD	MARKET HALL	NARROW ROAD
LIQUID FUEL	MARKET TOWN	NARROW VIEW
LIQUOR LAWS	MARROW BONE	NATIVE LAND
LITTER LOUT	MASKED BALL	NAUTCH GIRL
LITTLE BEAR	MASTER PLAN	NEARLY OVER
LITTLE BIRD	MASTER RACE	NELSON EDDY
LITTLE DROP	MATING CALL	NESTLE DOWN
LITTLE FISH	MATTED HAIR	NITRIC ACID
LITTLE FOLK	MATURE MIND	NOBODY ELSE
LITTLE GIRL	MEADOW LARK	NORMAL LIFE
LITTLE GOOD	MEAGRE DIET	NORMAL LOAD
LITTLE HOPE	MEDIUM RARE	NORMAN ARCH
LITTLE JOHN	MEDIUM SIZE	NUDIST CAMP
LITTLE LAMB	MEDIUM WAVE	NUMBER FIVE
LITTLE MORE	MEMORY LANE	NUMBER FOUR
LITTLE NELL	MEMORY TEST	NUMBER NINE
LITTLE ROCK	MENTAL CASE	OBJECT BALL
LITTLE ROOM	MENTAL HOME	OFFICE DESK
LITTLE SLAM	MENTAL PAIN	OFFICE GIRL
LITTLE STAR	MENTAL TEST	OFFICE WORK
LITTLE TIME	MENTAL WARD	OLDEST GIRL
LITTLE USED	MERSEY BEAT	ORANGE PEEL
LIVELY MIND	METRIC UNIT	ORANGE TREE
LIVING ROOM	MEXICO CITY	ORIONS BELT
LIVING SOUL	MICKEY FINN	ORPHAN GIRL
LIVING WAGE	MIDDAY MEAL	OWNERS RISK

OXFORD BAGS	PRISON CELL	REPORT SICK
OXFORD BLUE	PRISON DIET	RESCUE TEAM
OXTAIL SOUP	PRISON FARE	RESCUE WORK
OXYGEN MASK	PRISON GATE	RETAIL SHOP
OXYGEN TENT	PRISON YARD	RETIRE HURT
PACKED JURY	PROMPT BOOK	RETURN FARE
PADDED CELL	PROPER CARE	RETURN FIRE
PADDLE BOAT	PROPER NAME	RETURN GAME
PAINED LOOK	PROPER NOUN	RETURN HOME
PARCEL POST	PROPER TIME	RETURN TRIP
PARENT SHIP	PROVEN FACT	RIDING COAT
PASTRY COOK	PUBLIC GOOD	RIDING CROP
PATROL DUTY	PUBLIC PARK	RIDING HIGH
PAVING FLAG	PUBLIC PATH	RIDING HOOD
PEARLY KING	PUBLIC ROAD	RIDING SEAT
PEDALO BOAT	PUBLIC ROOM	RIDING WHIP
PEDDLE DOPE	PUBLIC SALE	RISING COST
PENCIL CASE	PUERTO RICO	RISING DAMP
PEPPER MILL	PUPPET SHOW	RISING TIDE
PETITS POIS	PUZZLE OVER	ROBERT ASKE
PETROL PUMP	QUAINT IDEA	ROBERT OWEN
PETROL TANK	QUEENS HEAD	ROBERT PEEL
PHRASE BOOK	QUEENS PAWN	ROCKET BASE
PICKET LINE	QUEENS ROOK	ROCKET SITE
PIGEON POST	QUEENS WARE	ROLLED GOLD
PIRATE FLAG	RACING CARD	ROLLED OATS
PIRATE SHIP	RACING FORM	ROMPER SUIT
PISTOL SHOT	RADIAL TYRE	ROTARY CLUB
PLAGUE SPOT	RAGGED EDGE	ROTTEN IDEA
PLENTY MORE	RANDOM SHOT	ROTTEN LUCK
PLOUGH BACK	RATHER COLD	ROTTEN WOOD
PLUCKY CHAP	RATHER COOL	ROWING BOAT
POETIC VEIN	RATHER FINE	ROWING CLUB
POLICE BALL	RATHER FLAT	RUBBER BALL
POLICE RAID	RATHER GOOD	RUBBER BAND
POLICE TRAP	RATHER LATE	RUBBER DUCK
POPLAR TREE	RATHER MUCH	RUBBER HOSE
POSTAL RATE	RATHER NICE	RUBBER SOLE
POTATO PEEL	RATHER SLOW	RUBBER TUBE
POTATO SOUP	RATHER WARM	RUBBER TYRE
POTTED MEAT	RATION BOOK	RUDOLF HESS
POUNCE UPON	RATION CARD	RULING BODY
POWDER BLUE	RAYNES PARK	RUNNER BEAN
POWDER PUFF	REALLY MEAN	RUPERT BEAR
POWDER ROOM	RECENT DATE	RUSTIC SEAT
PRAYER BOOK	RECENT PAST	SACRED BOOK
PRETTY FACE	RECIPE BOOK	SACRED RITE
PRETTY FAIR	RECORD GATE	SACRED WRIT
PRETTY FINE	RECORD SALE	SAFETY BELT
PRETTY GIRL	RECORD SHOP	SAFETY FUSE
PRETTY GOOD	RECORD TIME	SAFETY LAMP
PRETTY MESS	REFORM BILL	SAILOR BILL
PRETTY MUCH	REFORM CLUB	SAILOR SUIT
PRETTY PASS	REFUSE BAIL	SALMON PINK
PRETTY SURE	REFUSE DUMP	SALTED BEEF
PRETTY TUNE	RELIEF FUND	SAUCER EYES
PRETTY WELL	REMAIN CALM	SAVAGE BLOW
PRIEST HOLE	REMAND HOME	SAVAGE MOOD
PRINCE IGOR	REPAIR SHOP	SAVAGE RACE
PRISON BARS	REPORT BACK	SAVING GAME
PRISON CAMP	REPORT CARD	SCHOOL BELL

SCHOOL BOOK	SHANTY TOWN	SOLEMN LOOK
SCHOOL DAYS	SHEEPS EYES	SOLEMN OATH
SCHOOL FEES	SHOWER BATH	SOVIET BLOC
SCHOOL MEAL	SHREWD IDEA	SPINAL CORD
SCHOOL SONG	SHREWD MOVE	SPIRAL DOWN
SCHOOL TERM	SHRILL NOTE	SPIRIT LAMP
SCHOOL YEAR	SHRILL TONE	SPOILT BRAT
SCOTCH KALE	SHRINK AWAY	SPOKEN WORD
SCOTCH MIST	SHRINK BACK	SPONGE CAKE
SCOTCH PINE	SIGNAL LAMP	SPONGE DOWN
SCRAPE HOME	SIGNED COPY	SPORTS CLUB
SCREEN IDOL	SIGNET RING	SPORTS COAT
SCREEN TEST	SILENT FILM	SPORTS PAGE
SEALED BOOK	SILENT TYPE	SPREAD FEAR
SEALED LIPS	SILKEN HAIR	SPRING AWAY
SECOND BEST	SILVER COIN	SPRING BACK
SECOND COAT	SILVER DISC	SPRING OPEN
SECOND CROP	SILVER FOIL	SPRING OVER
SECOND FORM	SILVER HAIR	SPRING SONG
SECOND GEAR	SILVER LAMÉ	SPRING TERM
SECOND HALF	SILVER MINE	SPRING TIDE
SECOND HAND	SILVER RING	SQUARE CHIN
SECOND HEAT	SILVER STAR	SQUARE DEAL
SECOND HOME	SILVER TRAY	SQUARE FOOT
SECOND LINE	SIMMER DOWN	SQUARE HOLE
SECOND MATE	SIMNEL CAKE	SQUARE INCH
SECOND NAME	SIMONE WEIL	SQUARE MEAL
SECOND PAGE	SIMPLE CLUE	SQUARE MILE
SECOND PART	SIMPLE DIET	SQUARE ROOT
SECOND RATE	SIMPLE FARE	SQUARE SAIL
SECOND SLIP	SIMPLE IDEA	SQUARE YARD
SECOND TEAM	SIMPLE LIFE	STABLE DOOR
SECOND TERM	SIMPLE MIND	STABLE MATE
SECOND TEST	SIMPLE SOUL	STAPLE DIET
SECOND TIME	SINGLE BLOW	STEADY FLOW
SECOND WEEK	SINGLE FARE	STEADY HAND
SECOND WIFE	SINGLE FILE	STEADY PACE
SECOND WIND	SINGLE ROOM	STEADY RAIN
SECOND YEAR	SINGLE VOTE	STEADY WIND
SECRET CODE	SISTER SHIP	STEWED BEEF
SECRET DOOR	SKETCH BOOK	STEWED LAMB
SECRET FILE	SLEIGH RIDE	STEWED MEAT
SECRET LIFE	SLICED LOAF	STICKY BOMB
SECRET PACT	SLIGHT COLD	STICKY MESS
SECRET SIGN	SMOKED FISH	STODGY FOOD
SECRET VICE	SMOOTH AWAY	STODGY MESS
SECRET VOTE	SMOOTH CHIN	STORKS NEST
SELECT CLUB	SMOOTH DOWN	STREAK PAST
SENIOR GIRL	SMOOTH FACE	STREET ARAB
SENIOR HIGH	SMOOTH OVER	STREET BAND
SENTRY DUTY	SMOOTH SKIN	STREET DOOR
SETTLE DOWN	SNAILS PACE	STREET LAMP
SEVERE BLOW	SNATCH AWAY	STRICT DIET
SEVERE LOOK	SOCCER TEAM	STRIKE BACK
SEVERE LOSS	SOCIAL CALL	STRIKE CAMP
SEVERE PAIN	SOCIAL CLUB	STRIKE DOWN
SEVERE TEST	SOCIAL EVIL	STRIKE DUMB
SEVERN BORE	SOCIAL LIFE	STRIKE GOLD
SEWAGE FARM	SOCIAL RANK	STRIKE HOME
SHABBY DEAL	SOCIAL WORK	STRING BAND
SHANKS PONY	SODIUM LAMP	STRING BEAN

STRING TRIO	THRUST OPEN	VACANT LOOK
STRING VEST	THRUST PAST	VACUUM PUMP
STROKE PLAY	THUMBS DOWN	VANITY CASE
STRONG BREW	TICKER TAPE	VANITY FAIR
STRONG CASE	TICKET VOTE	VAPOUR BATH
STRONG GRIP	TIMELY EXIT	VERBAL NOUN
STRONG HAND	TIMELY WORD	VICTOR HUGO
STRONG HEAD	TINKER WITH	VIOLIN CASE
STRONG LEAD	TINNED FISH	VIOLIN DUET
STRONG LINE	TINNED FOOD	VIOLIN SOLO
STRONG MEAT	TINNED MEAT	VIRGIN LAND
STRONG MIND	TINNED MILK	VIRGIN MARY
STRONG ROOM	TINNED SOUP	VIRGIN SOIL
STRONG SIDE	TODAYS DATE	VOLLEY BALL
STRONG SUIT	TOILET ROLL	VOLUME FOUR
STRONG WILL	TOILET SOAP	VULGAR HERD
STRONG WIND	TOMATO SOUP	VULGAR JOKE
STRUCK DOWN	TOPPLE OVER	VULGAR SORT
STRUCK DUMB	TORRID ZONE	WADING BIRD
STUDIO FLAT	TRADER HORN	WAFFLE IRON
STUFFY ROOM	TRAGIC MUSE	WALNUT TREE
STUMPY TAIL	TRAGIC NEWS	WANDER AWAY
STUPID FOOL	TRAGIC PLAY	WANING MOON
SUBTLE HINT	TRAGIC TALE	WARPED MIND
SUDDEN BLOW	TRAVEL SICK	WARSAW PACT
SUDDEN STOP	TREATY PORT	WASTED LIFE
SUFFER LOSS	TREBLE CLEF	WATERS EDGE
SUMMER CAMP	TRENCH COAT	WAXING MOON
SUMMER HEAT	TREVOR NUNN	WEBBED FEET
SUMMER SALE	TRIFLE WITH	WEDDED WIFE
SUMMER TERM	TRIPLE JUMP	WEEKLY RENT
SUMMER TIME	TRIPLE TIME	WEEKLY WAGE
SUNDAY BEST	TRUDGE PAST	WICKET GATE
SUNDAY WEEK	TRYING TIME	WIDELY HELD
SUPERB FORM	TUMBLE DOWN	WIDELY READ
SUPERB VIEW	TUMBLE OVER	WIDOWS MITE
SUPPLY BASE	TUNING FORK	WIDOWS PEAK
SUPPLY SHIP	TURKEY COCK	WILLOW TREE
SWITCH OVER	TURKEY TROT	WINDOW PANE
TAKING WAYS	TURTLE DOVE	WINDOW SASH
TALENT SHOW	TURTLE NECK	WINTER COAT
TARGET AREA	TURTLE SOUP	WINTER SALE
TARGET DATE	TWELVE DAYS	WINTER TIME
TENDER CARE	TWELVE FEET	WITHER AWAY
TENDER LOVE	TWELVE NOON	WOMANS HOUR
TENDER MEAT	TWELVE QUID	WOMANS WORK
TENDER SPOT	TWENTY DAYS	WOMENS PAGE
TENDER TRAP	TWENTY FEET	WONDER DRUG
TENNIS BALL	TWENTY PAST	WOODEN CLUB
TENNIS CLUB	TWENTY QUID	WOODEN SEAT
TENNIS STAR	TYPING POOL	WOODEN SHOE
THIRTY DAYS	UNIQUE CASE	WOOLLY MIND
THIRTY FEET	UNKIND WORD	YEARLY RENT
THIRTY LOVE	UNPAID BILL	YELLOW BELT
THIRTY QUID	UNTIDY MIND	YELLOW CARD
THOMAS COOK	UPHILL TASK	YELLOW JACK
THOMAS HOOD	UPHILL WALK	YELLOW RACE
THOMAS MANN	UPHILL WORK	YELLOW ROSE
THOMAS MORE	UPSIDE DOWN	
THRIFT CLUB	URGENT NEED	
THRONE ROOM	USEFUL HINT	

7 , 3

	COMPANY TAX	GENERAL LEE
	CONTOUR MAP	GETTING OFF
ABOUKIR BAY	COOKING FAT	GETTING OLD
ADOPTED SON	COOKING POT	GRAPHIC ART
ANILINE DYE	COPYING INK	GRAVELY ILL
ANOTHER DAY	COTTAGE PIE	GRECIAN URN
ANOTHER WAY	COUNTED OUT	GRILLED HAM
APRICOT JAM	COUNTRY INN	GROWING BOY
ARABIAN SEA	COUNTRY PUB	GROWING LAD
AUCTION OFF	COVERED WAY	GROWING OLD
AVERAGE MAN	CRICKET BAT	HACKNEY CAB
AVERAGE OUT	CRICKET CAP	HARPOON GUN
AWKWARD AGE	CRIMEAN WAR	HATCHET MAN
BALANCE DUE	CROOKED MAN	HEALING ART
BARBARY APE	CROWDED DAY	HEARING AID
BARKING DOG	CROWDED OUT	HEATHEN GOD
BATHING CAP	CRYSTAL SET	HOLIDAY PAY
BATTERY HEN	CURATES EGG	HOPPING MAD
BENEATH ONE	CURRANT BUN	HUMMING TOP
BETTING ACT	CURRENT HIT	HUNTING DOG
BETTING MAN	CURTAIN ROD	ILLEGAL ACT
BISCUIT BOX	CUSTARD PIE	IMPULSE BUY
BISCUIT TIN	CUSTOMS MAN	INVALID OUT
BLACKED OUT	DECLARE WAR	JAMAICA RUM
BLAZING ROW	DIVORCE LAW	JOCKEYS CAP
BOILING HOT	DOCTORS FEE	KEEPING FIT
BOILING OIL	DONEGAL BAY	KITCHEN BOY
BOOKING FEE	DOUGLAS FIR	KNOCKED OFF
BORSTAL BOY	DRAUGHT ALE	KNOCKED OUT
BOTTLED ALE	DRAWING PIN	LANTERN JAW
BRACING AIR	DROWNED OUT	LEADING MAN
BREATHE OUT	DROWNED RAT	LEARNED MAN
BRITISH RAJ	DRUMMED OUT	LETTING OUT
BRITISH SPY	DRUMMER BOY	LINSEED OIL
BROUGHT LOW	DRUNKEN MAN	LOADING BAY
BROWNED OFF	DUSTBIN LID	LOBSTER POT
CAPITAL SUM	EFFECTS MAN	LONGEST DAY
CARRIED OFF	ENGLISH LAW	LONGEST WAY
CARRIER BAG	FACTORY ACT	LUGGAGE VAN
CASPIAN SEA	FALLING OFF	MACHINE AGE
CASTING OFF	FARMERS BOY	MACHINE GUN
CATHODE RAY	FATHERS DAY	MARKING INK
CAUSTIC WIT	FEARFUL DIN	MARRIED MAN
CHAPTER ONE	FEATHER BED	MARRIED OFF
CHAPTER TEN	FEATHER BOA	MARTIAL ART
CHAPTER TWO	FEDERAL LAW	MARTIAL LAW
CHEESED OFF	FEELING SAD	MEASURE OUT
CHELSEA BUN	FIFTEEN ALL	MEDICAL MAN
CHEWING GUM	FIFTEEN MEN	MELTING POT
CHICKEN RUN	FINANCE ACT	MINERAL OIL
CHIMNEY POT	FISHING NET	MISERLY PAY
CHIMNEY TOP	FISHING ROD	MONEYED MAN
CHINESE BOX	FLAMING ROW	MONTEGO BAY
CLEANED OUT	FLATTEN OUT	MOORING FEE
CLOSING BID	FLOODED OUT	MORDANT WIT
CLOTHES PEG	FORMULA ONE	MORNING DEW
COCONUT OIL	FUNERAL URN	MORNING SUN
COCONUT SHY	GALLANT ACT	MORNING TEA
CODDLED EGG	GARBAGE CAN	MOTHERS BOY
COLLEGE BOY	GARBAGE MAN	MOTHERS DAY
COMPANY LAW	GATLING GUN	MUSICAL BOX

MUSICAL EAR	PUZZLED AIR	TALLEST MAN
MUSTARD GAS	QUARTER DAY	TANGLED WEB
MUSTARD POT	RADIATE JOY	TELLING OFF
MYSTERY MAN	REFINED OIL	THEATRE BAR
NATURAL GAS	REGULAR GUY	THEATRE BOX
NATURAL KEY	REMOVAL MAN	TICKING OFF
NATURAL LAW	REMOVAL VAN	TOBACCO ROW
NATURAL WIT	RETIRED MAN	TOURING CAR
NAUGHTY BOY	RICHARD ROE	TRACKER DOG
NEEDLES EYE	ROLLING PIN	TRAFFIC COP
NERVOUS TIC	RUBBISH TIP	TRAFFIC JAM
NOMINAL FEE	RUNNING OUT	TRAINED EYE
NOMINAL SUM	RUSSIAN SPY	TRAINED MAN
NOONDAY SUN	RUSSIAN TEA	TRAPEZE ACT
NOTHING BUT	SABBATH DAY	TRIGGER OFF
NOTHING NEW	SARDINE TIN	TROLLEY BUS
NUCLEAR WAR	SCALDED CAT	TWELFTH DAY
OEDIPUS REX	SCAMPER OFF	TWELFTH MAN
OPENING BAT	SCRATCH MAN	UPRIGHT MAN
OPENING BID	SCRATCH OUT	VAMPIRE BAT
OPENING DAY	SCREECH OWL	VANILLA ICE
OUTLINE MAP	SCUTTLE OFF	VANTAGE OUT
PANCAKE DAY	SEALING WAX	VARIETY ACT
PARENTS DAY	SECONDS OUT	VENTURE OUT
PARKING BAY	SERIOUS AIR	VETERAN CAR
PARKING LOT	SERVING MAN	VICTORY DAY
PASSING FAD	SESSION MAN	VIETNAM WAR
PASSING OUT	SETTING OUT	VINTAGE CAR
PAVLOVS DOG	SETTING SUN	VIOLENT END
PAYROLL TAX	SEVENTH DAY	WARMING PAN
PEEPING TOM	SEVENTH SON	WARNING CRY
PENALTY BOX	SHALLOW END	WASHING DAY
PENNINE WAY	SHALLOW FRY	WATCHED POT
PENSION OFF	SHOWING OFF	WAYSIDE INN
PERFECT FIT	SHUFFLE OFF	WEALTHY MAN
PERSIAN CAT	SIAMESE CAT	WEATHER EYE
PERSIAN MAT	SITTING OUT	WEATHER MAP
PERSIAN RUG	SKILLED MAN	WEDDING DAY
PICTURE HAT	SKITTLE OUT	WHISTLE FOR
PLASTIC BAG	SLACKEN OFF	WINNING BET
PLASTIC MAC	SMOKING CAP	WINNING HIT
POACHED EGG	SMUGGLE OUT	WINNING RUN
POLLING DAY	SOAKING WET	WINNING TRY
POMPOUS ASS	SOPPING WET	WITHOUT END
POPULAR AIR	SPANISH FLY	WITNESS BOX
PORTION OUT	SPECIAL BUS	WORKING DAY
POSTAGE DUE	SPECIAL DAY	WORKING MAN
POTTERS BAR	SPIDERS WEB	WORRIED MAN
POULTRY RUN	SPOTTED DOG	WOUNDED MAN
POURING WET	SQUEEZE BOX	WRIGGLE OUT
PRAIRIE DOG	SQUEEZE DRY	WRITTEN LAW
PRESENT DAY	SQUEEZE OUT	WRITTEN OFF
PRIVATE BAR	STAGGER OFF	YOUNGER SON
PRIVATE CAR	STARLIT SKY	
PRIVATE EYE	STATUTE LAW	8, 2
PRIVATE LAW	STIRRUP CUP	
PRIVATE WAR	STORAGE JAR	BREAKING UP
PROFITS TAX	STRANGE MAN	BRIGHTEN UP
PROVIDE FOR	STRETCH OUT	BUTTONED UP
PULLMAN CAR	SUCKING PIG	CHUCKING IT
PUTTING OUT	SUCTION PAD	CONTRACT IN

```
CRACKING    UP
CREEPING    UP
CRUMPLED    UP
GRACIOUS    ME !
PERSONAL    AD
STANDING    BY
STEALING    UP
STRAIGHT    BY
STRAIGHT    IN
STRAIGHT    ON
STRAIGHT    UP
STRUGGLE    ON
TRAMPLED    ON
WEIGHING    IN
WESTWARD    HO !
WRAPPING    UP
```

1 . 1 . 1 . 8

H.M.S.PINAFORE

1 . 1 . 9

F.D.ROOSEVELT
J.B.PRIESTLEY
P.G.WODEHOUSE

1 . 3 . 7

A JOY FOREVER
V FOR VICTORY
X-RAY MACHINE
X-RAY THERAPY

1 . 4 . 2 . 4

A BONE TO PICK
A STAR IS BORN

1 . 4 . 3 . 3

A LONG WAY OUT

1 . 5 . 2 . 3

A THING OR TWO

1 . 6 . 4

J.ARTHUR RANK

2 . 1 . 3 . 5

DO A WAR-DANCE
IN A BAD STATE
IN A FEW WORDS
IN A LOW VOICE

2 . 1 . 4 . 4

DO A GOOD TURN
IN A BLUE FUNK
IN A FLAT SPIN
IN A GOOD MOOD

2 . 1 . 5 . 3

AT A LOOSE END
IN A SMALL WAY

2 . 1 . 8

AT A DISCOUNT
AT A DISTANCE
DO A MISCHIEF
IM A DUTCHMAN
IN A HAYSTACK
IN A MINORITY

IN A NUTSHELL
IN A QUANDARY
ON A PEDESTAL

2 . 2 . 1 . 6

DO ME A FAVOUR
GO ON A BENDER
GO ON A CRUISE
GO ON-A PICNIC
UP ON A CHARGE

2 . 2 . 2 . 5

DO IT IN STYLE
GO UP IN SMOKE

2 . 2 . 3 . 4

GO BY THE BOOK
GO ON FOR EVER
GO ON THE DOLE
GO TO BED LATE
GO TO THE BALL
GO TO THE DOGS
GO TO THE FAIR
GO TO THE MOON
GO TO THE WALL
GO TO THE WARS
GO UP THE WALL
IN AT THE KILL
UP TO THE EARS
UP TO THE EYES
UP TO THE HILT
UP TO THE MARK
UP TO THE NECK

2 . 2 . 4 . 3

BE ON ONES OWN

2 . 2 . 7

BE OF SERVICE
GO BY DEFAULT
GO ON HOLIDAY
IN AN INSTANT
IN MY OPINION
IN NO RESPECT
NO.NO.NANETTE
OF NO ACCOUNT
ON NO ACCOUNT
TO NO PURPOSE
UP TO SCRATCH

2 . 3 . 1 . 5

IN FOR A PENNY
IN FOR A POUND

2 , 3 , 2 , 4

AS DRY AS DUST
GO OUT TO WORK
ME AND MY GIRL
SO FAR SO GOOD
UP AND AT THEM

2 , 3 , 3 , 3

DO ALL ONE CAN
GO ALL THE WAY
ON THE WAY OUT
UP FOR THE CUP
UP FOR THE DAY

2 , 3 , 4 , 2

AS YOU LIKE IT
DO NOT PASS GO
IN THE NAME OF
IN THE WAKE OF
TO THE TUNE OF

2 , 3 , 6

AT ALL EVENTS
AT THE BOTTOM
AT THE CINEMA
AT THE CIRCUS
AT THE DOUBLE
AT THE FINISH
AT THE HILTON
AT THE MOMENT
AT THE OUTSET
AT THE SUMMIT
AT THE WICKET
AT THE ZENITH
DO THE ROUNDS
DO THE SPLITS
GO ONE BETTER
GO THE ROUNDS
IF YOU PLEASE
IN AND AROUND
IN DUE COURSE
IN LOW RELIEF
IN THE AUTUMN
IN THE CELLAR
IN THE CENTRE
IN THE CHARTS
IN THE CINEMA
IN THE CLOUDS
IN THE CORNER
IN THE CRADLE
IN THE DESERT
IN THE FAMILY
IN THE FIELDS
IN THE FOREST
IN THE FRIDGE
IN THE FUTURE
IN THE GARAGE

IN THE GARDEN
IN THE GROOVE
IN THE GROUND
IN THE GUTTER
IN THE JUNGLE
IN THE MAKING
IN THE MARKET
IN THE MIDDLE
IN THE MIRROR
IN THE OFFING
IN THE PAPERS
IN THE PLURAL
IN THE SADDLE
IN THE SEASON
IN THE SPRING
IN THE STALLS
IN THE STATES
IN THE STOCKS
IN THE STREET
IN THE SUMMER
IN THE THROES
IN THE VALLEY
IN THE WINDOW
IN THE WINTER
IN TWO SHAKES
LE ROI SOLEIL
LO AND BEHOLD
OF ILL REPUTE
ON ALL POINTS
ON THE AGENDA
ON THE ATTACK
ON THE BOARDS
ON THE BOTTLE
ON THE BOUNTY
ON THE CARPET
ON THE CORNER
ON THE FIDDLE
ON THE FRINGE
ON THE GROUND
ON THE INSIDE
ON THE MARKET
ON THE MORROW
ON THE RAZZLE
ON THE RECORD
ON THE SCREEN
ON THE STAIRS
ON THE SWINGS
ON THE THAMES
ON THE THRONE
ON TWO WHEELS
ON - OFF SWITCH
TO THE BOTTOM
TO THE LETTER
TO THE MINUTE
TO THE RESCUE
TO THE SECOND
TO THE UTMOST
UP AND COMING
UP THE STAIRS
UP THE STREET
UP THE THAMES

2 , 4 , 1 , 4

GO LIKE A BOMB

2 , 4 , 2 , 3

AS EASY AS PIE
AS GOOD AS NEW
AS UGLY AS SIN
IN DAYS OF OLD
NO HOPE AT ALL
ST JOAN OF ARC

2 , 4 , 5

AS MUCH AGAIN
AT FULL BLAST
AT FULL SPEED
AT ONES ELBOW
AT ONES HEELS
AT ONES PERIL
AT THIS POINT
AT YOUR PERIL
BY FAIR MEANS
BY YOUR LEAVE
DE-LUXE MODEL
DO ONES WORST
DO YOUR WORST
GO DOWN BADLY
GO INTO EXILE
GO INTO ORBIT
IN COLD BLOOD
IN DEEP WATER
IN FINE STYLE
IN FINE VOICE
IN FULL BLAST
IN FULL BLOOM
IN FULL SWING
IN GODS IMAGE
IN GOOD FAITH
IN GOOD HANDS
IN GOOD HEART
IN GOOD SHAPE
IN GOOD TASTE
IN GOOD VOICE
IN ONES GRASP
IN ONES HEART
IN ONES POWER
IN ONES PRIME
IN ONES SLEEP
IN ONES TEENS
IN POOR TASTE
IN SAFE HANDS
IT WILL STAND
MY DEAR MADAM
NO PACK DRILL
ON EASY TERMS
ON GODS EARTH
ON GOOD TERMS
ON ONES GUARD
ON ONES HANDS

ON ONES KNEES
ON ONES PLATE
ON YOUR MARKS
TO ONES SHAME

2 , 5 , 1 , 3

AN APPLE A DAY

2 , 5 , 4

AT FIRST HAND
BE SHORT WITH
IN EVERY PORT
IN GREAT FORM
IN WHICH CASE
LA DOLCE VITA
NO GREAT LOSS
NO MONEY DOWN
NO RIGHT TURN
NO-SCORE DRAW
ON BOARD SHIP
ON EVERY SIDE
ON SHORT TIME
ST.JOHNS WOOD

2 , 6 , 3

ST.DAVIDS DAY

2 , 7 , 2

IT STRIKES ME
UP AGAINST IT

2 , 9

AD INFINITUM
AS REQUESTED
AT ATTENTION
AT CAMBRIDGE
AT INTERVALS
BE DIFFERENT
BE REALISTIC
BY AUTHORITY
BY MESSENGER
BY MOONLIGHT
BY TRADITION
DE PROFUNDIS
GO BACKWARDS
GO OVERBOARD
IL TROVATORE
IN AGREEMENT
IN AUTHORITY
IN CAPTIVITY
IN CHARACTER
IN COLLISION
IN COLLUSION
IN COMMITTEE
IN CONDITION
IN CONFUSION

IN DUPLICATE
IN EXISTENCE
IN FORMATION
IN GRATITUDE
IN HYSTERICS
IN MINIATURE
IN OPERATION
IN PANTOMIME
IN PRINCIPLE
IN READINESS
IN REBELLION
IN RESIDENCE
IN SECLUSION
IN SEPTEMBER
IN SHORTHAND
LE CORBUSIER
NO ADMISSION
NO AUTHORITY
NO EXCEPTION
NO GENTLEMAN
NO ILLUSIONS
NO OBJECTION
NO QUESTIONS
NO VACANCIES
ON AUTHORITY
ON HORSEBACK
ON PRINCIPLE
ON PROBATION
ON WEDNESDAY
ST.JOHNSTONE
ST MARGARETS
ST.VALENTINE

3, 1, 3, 2, 2

NOT A BIT OF IT

3, 1, 3, 4

GET A BAD NAME

3, 1, 4, 3

ITS A FAIR COP

3, 1, 5, 2

GET A ROUND IN

3, 1, 7

ADD A CODICIL
FOR A PURPOSE
GET A DIVORCE
GET A MENTION
PAY A FORFEIT
PAY A PENALTY
PAY A PREMIUM
SEE A DENTIST
SET A PROBLEM
WIN A FORTUNE

3, 2, 1, 5

ACT AS A BRAKE
ALL OF A SHAKE
ARM IN A SLING
DRY AS A STICK
LAY IN A STOCK
PUT IN A CLAIM
PUT ON A SPURT
PUT UP A FIGHT
RUN UP A SCORE
RUN UP A TOTAL
TWO OF A TRADE

3, 2, 2, 4

BUT ME NO BUTS
FIT TO BE SEEN
NOT UP TO MUCH
PAY UP OR ELSE!

3, 2, 3, 3

ALL OF THE WAY
ARM OF THE LAW
ARM OF THE SEA
DAY IN DAY OUT
DIE OF OLD AGE
END OF THE DAY
END OF THE WAR
GET IN THE WAY
GET TO THE TOP
GOD OF THE SEA
ITS IN THE BAG
LAW OF THE SEA
LET IN THE AIR
LET IN THE SUN
MAN ON THE JOB
MAN ON THE RUN
NEW TO THE JOB
NIP IN THE AIR
NIP IN THE BUD
ONE IN THE EYE
ONE OF THE FEW
OUT OF THE BAG
OUT OF THE CUP
OUT OF THE SUN
OUT OF THE WAY
PAY ON THE DOT
PIE IN THE SKY
PUT IN THE WAY
PUT ON THE MAP

3, 2, 4, 2

GET ON WITH IT

3 . 2 . 6

ACE	OF	HEARTS
ACE	OF	SPADES
ACE	OF	TRUMPS
ACT	IN	UNISON
ACT	ON	ADVICE
AGE	OF	WISDOM
AID	TO	MEMORY
AIM	TO	PLEASE
ALL	BY	MYSELF
ALL	IN	FAVOUR
ALL	IN	PIECES
BAG	OF	CRISPS
BAG	OF	NERVES
BAG	OF	SWEETS
BAG	OF	TRICKS
BAT	AN	EYELID
BAY	OF	BENGAL
BAY	OF	BISCAY
BAY	OF	NAPLES
BED	OF	THORNS
BEG	TO	DIFFER
BIT	OF	GOSSIP
BOX	OF	CIGARS
BOX	OF	PAINTS
BOX	OF	TRICKS
BUY	ON	CREDIT
CAN	OF	PETROL
CUP	OF	COFFEE
CUP	OF	POISON
CUP	OF	SORROW
CUT	IN	SALARY
CUT	TO	PIECES
DAR	ES	SALAAM
DAY	OF	PRAYER
DIE	OF	FRIGHT
DIE	OF	HUNGER
DIE	OF	THIRST
FIT	OF	NERVES
FIT	OF	TEMPER
FIT	OF	TERROR
GET	AN	ENCORE
HOT	AS	PEPPER
ILL	BE	BLOWED !
ILL	BE	DAMNED !
ILL	BE	HANGED !
JAR	OF	SWEETS
JOY	TO	BEHOLD
LAP	OF	HONOUR
LAP	OF	LUXURY
LAW	OF	NATURE
LAY	IN	AMBUSH
LEG	OF	MUTTON
LIE	AT	ANCHOR
LIE	IN	AMBUSH
MAN	IN	CHARGE
MAN	OF	ACTION
MAN	OF	GENIUS
MAN	OF	HONOUR
MAN	OF	PRAYER

MAN	OF	RENOWN
MAN	OF	REPUTE
MAN	OF	SPIRIT
MAN	OF	WEALTH
MAP	OF	CANADA
MAP	OF	EUROPE
MAP	OF	FRANCE
MAP	OF	LONDON
NIP	OF	BRANDY
NOM	DE	GUERRE
ONE	IN	TWELVE
ONE	IN	TWENTY
OUT	OF	ACTION
OUT	OF	BOUNDS
OUT	OF	BREATH
OUT	OF	DANGER
OUT	OF	FAVOUR
OUT	OF	OFFICE
OUT	OF	PETROL
OUT	OF	POCKET
OUT	OF	SCHOOL
OUT	OF	SEASON
OUT	ON	PAROLE
OUT	ON	STRIKE
PAS	DE	CALAIS
PAT	OF	BUTTER
PAY	BY	CHEQUE
PAY	ON	DEMAND
POT	OF	COFFEE
PUT	IN	CHARGE
PUT	IN	DANGER
PUT	IN	PRISON
PUT	IT	ACROSS
PUT	IT	MILDLY
PUT	ON	PAROLE
PUT	ON	RECORD
PUT	ON	WEIGHT
PUT	TO	FLIGHT
PUT	TO	RIGHTS
ROW	OF	HOUSES
RUN	AN	ERRAND
RUN	TO	GROUND
SAD	TO	RELATE
SET	IN	MOTION
SET	OF	CHAIRS
SET	OF	STAMPS
SIP	OF	BRANDY
SIX	NO-	TRUMPS
SIX	OF	HEARTS
SIX	OF	SPADES
SIX	OF	TRUMPS
TEA	OR	COFFEE
TEN	OF	HEARTS
TEN	OF	SPADES
TEN	OF	TRUMPS
TEN	OR	ELEVEN
TEN	TO	ELEVEN
TEN	TO	TWELVE
TIN	OF	SALMON
TON	OF	BRICKS
TOP	TO	BOTTOM

TOT OF WHISKY
TRY TO PLEASE
TWO NO-TRUMPS
TWO OF HEARTS
TWO OF SPADES
TWO OF TRUMPS
WAR OF NERVES
WEB OF DECEIT
WIN ON POINTS

3 . 3 . 1 . 4

ASK FOR A LOAN
ASK FOR A RISE
FIT FOR A KING
FOR ALL I CARE
FOR ALL I KNOW
ONE AND A HALF
OUT FOR A DUCK
SIX AND A HALF
TEN AND A HALF
TWO AND A HALF

3 . 3 . 2 . 3

EYE FOR AN EYE
FOR ALL TO SEE
GET OUT OF BED
PUT OUT TO SEA
RUN OUT OF GAS
RUN OUT OF OIL
SEE EYE TO EYE
SIX OUT OF TEN
TEN OUT OF TEN
YES SIR, NO SIR

3 . 3 . 3 . 2

ALL ONE CAN DO
PUT THE LID ON

3 . 3 . 5

ALL THE SIGNS
ALL THE VOGUE
ALL THE WHILE
ALL THE WORLD
ALL-OUT DRIVE
ARE YOU READY?
ASK FOR MERCY
ASK FOR MONEY
ASK THE PRICE
BAD FOR TRADE
BED AND BOARD
BEG FOR MERCY
BOW AND ARROW
CAP AND BELLS
CAT AND MOUSE
COD AND CHIPS
CUT AND DRIED
CUT THE CARDS

CUT THE GRASS
DAY AND NIGHT
DIG THE WEEDS
EAR FOR MUSIC
EAT AND DRINK
EGG AND BACON
EGG AND CHIPS
EGG AND SPOON
FAN THE FLAME
FAR TOO SMALL
FIX THE PRICE
FIX THE TERMS
FOR ONE THING
FOR THE WORSE
FOX AND GEESE
FUN AND GAMES
GET THE BENDS
GET THE FACTS
GET THE POINT
GET THE TASTE
GIN AND LEMON
GIN AND TONIC
GOG AND MAGOG
GUN THE MOTOR
HIT THE TRAIL
HOT-DOG STAND
HUG THE SHORE
LAW AND ORDER
LAY OUT MONEY
LAY THE GHOST
LAY THE TABLE
LET OFF STEAM
MAN AND BEAST
MAN AND WOMAN
MAN THE PUMPS
MAN THE WALLS
MAY THE FIFTH
MAY THE FIRST
MAY THE NINTH
MAY THE SIXTH
MAY THE TENTH
MAY THE THIRD
MEN AND WOMEN
NOT ALL THERE
NOT FAR WRONG
NOT ONE PENNY
NOT THE POINT
NOT THE THING
NOW AND AGAIN
OFF THE BOOZE
OFF THE COAST
OFF THE LEASH
OFF THE RAILS
OFF THE SCENT
OFF THE STAGE
OLD AND TRIED
OLD AND YOUNG
OLD MAN RIVER
OLD OLD STORY
OLE MAN RIVER
ONE BAD APPLE

ONE	NEW	PENNY
OUT	AND	ABOUT
OUT	FOR	BLOOD
OUT	FOR	KICKS
PAY	THE	COSTS
PAY	THE	DEVIL
PAY	THE	PIPER
PAY	THE	PRICE
PEN	AND	PAPER
POT	THE	BLACK
POT	THE	BROWN
POT	THE	GREEN
RED	AND	BLACK
RED	AND	WHITE
RED	RED	ROBIN
RED-HOT	COALS	
RED-HOT	POKER	
RUN	FOR	COVER
RUN	FOR	MAYOR
SAW	THE	LIGHT
SEE	THE	LIGHT
SEE	THE	POINT
SEE	THE	WORLD
SET	AND	MATCH
SET	THE	ALARM
SET	THE	SCENE
SET	THE	TABLE
SET	THE	TREND
SUE	FOR	LIBEL
SUE	FOR	PEACE
TAP	THE	PHONE
TEA	AND	CAKES
TEA	AND	TOAST
TEN	NEW	PENCE
THE	AIR	FORCE
THE	BIG	APPLE
THE	BIG	MATCH
THE	DAY	AFTER
THE	NEW	WORLD
THE	OLD	FOLKS
THE	OLD	GUARD
THE	OLD	WORLD
THE	TAJ	MAHAL
THE	WEE	HOURS
TIN	PAN	ALLEY
TOM	AND	JERRY
TRY	TRY	AGAIN
TWO	NEW	PENCE
UPS	AND	DOWNS
USE	AND	ABUSE
USE	THE	PHONE
WAR	AND	PEACE
WIN	THE	ASHES
WIN	THE	DERBY
WIN	THE	FIGHT
WIN	THE	MATCH
WIN	THE	POINT
WIN	THE	POOLS
WIN	THE	PRIZE
WIN	THE	TITLE
WIN	THE	TRICK

YOU AND YOURS
ZSA ZSA GABOR

3, 4, 1, 3

DIE LIKE A DOG
EAT LIKE A PIG
GET INTO A ROW
GET INTO A RUT

3, 4, 2, 2

GET DOWN TO IT
GET WISE TO IT
THE GAME IS UP
THE WELL-TO-DO

3, 4, 3, 1

THE KING AND I

3, 4, 4

ALL FALL DOWN
ALL GOES WELL
ALL HOPE GONE
ALL THAT JAZZ
ALL VERY FINE
ALL VERY WELL
ALL WEEK LONG
ALL-STAR CAST
ALL-TIME HIGH
BIG BASS DRUM
BOW ONES HEAD
BOY NEXT DOOR
CRY WITH PAIN
CUT BOTH WAYS
CUT ONES HAIR
CUT YOUR COAT
CUT-AWAY COAT
DRY ONES EYES
DYE ONES HAIR
EAT ONES FILL
END ONES DAYS
END ONES LIFE
FAR FROM HERE
FAR FROM HOME
FAR-AWAY LOOK
FLY AWAY PAUL
FOR DEAR LIFE
FOR SOME TIME
GET AWAY FROM
GET COLD FEET
GET EVEN WITH
GET INTO DEBT
GET ONES GOAT
GET ONES WISH
GET WELL SOON
INK-BLOT TEST
MAD WITH RAGE
MAN FROM MARS

MOP	ONES	BROW
NAT	KING	COLE
NEW	YORK	CITY
NEW-	BORN	BABE
NEW-	BORN	BABY
NOD	ONES	HEAD
NON-	STOP	SHOW
NOT	MUCH	GOOD
NOT	ONES	TYPE
NOT	VERY	MANY
NOT	VERY	MUCH
NOT	VERY	WELL
NOW	HEAR	THIS
NOW	LOOK	HERE
OFF	ONES	FOOD
OFF	ONES	HEAD
OFF-	PEAK	RATE
OFF-	SIDE	RULE
OLD	GREY	MARE
OLD	KENT	ROAD
OLD	KING	COLE
ONE	FOOT	TALL
ONE	GOOD	TURN
ONE	MANS	MEAT
ONE	MORE	TIME
OWN	FREE	WILL
PAY	CASH	DOWN
PIT	ONES	WITS
PUT	ONES	CASE
RUN	INTO	DEBT
RUN	INTO	FORM
SEE	NEXT	WEEK
SET	EYES	UPON
SIR	JOHN	HUNT
SIX	FEET	TALL
SOW	WILD	OATS
TAP	ONES	FEET
TAP	ONES	FOOT
TEN	PAST	FIVE
TEN	PAST	FOUR
TEN	PAST	NINE
THE	BEST	PART
THE	BOAT	RACE
THE	DARK	AGES
THE	FINE	ARTS
THE	GOLD	RUSH
THE	GOOD	BOOK
THE	GOOD	LIFE
THE	GOOD	LORD
THE	GOON	SHOW
THE	HAVE-NOTS	
THE	HIGH	SEAS
THE	HOLY	CITY
THE	HOLY	LAND
THE	LAST	GASP
THE	LAST	PAGE
THE	LAST	POST
THE	LAST	WORD
THE	MONA	LISA
THE	ONCE-OVER	
THE	OPEN	ROAD

THE	VERY	BEST
THE	VERY	FACT
THE	VERY	SAME
THE	VERY	SPOT
THE	WHIP-HAND	
TOO	MUCH	ROOM
TOO	MUCH	SALT
TRY	ONES	BEST
TRY	ONES	HAND
TRY	ONES	LUCK
TWO	LEFT	FEET
TWO-	FEET	TALL
TWO-	FOOT	RULE
USE	ONES	EARS
USE	ONES	EYES
USE	ONES	HEAD
USE	ONES	LOAF
USE	ONES	WITS
WAY	BACK	WHEN
WET	ONES	LIPS

3, 5, 3

ALL	FOOLS	DAY
ALL	SOULS	DAY
COD-LIVER		OIL
DAY	AFTER	DAY
DOG	BITES	MAN
GET	UNDER	WAY
GOD	BLESS	YOU
HOT	CROSS	BUN
HOT-WATER		TAP
ICE-CREAM		MAN
LAY	ABOUT	ONE
MAN	BITES	DOG
NEW	YEARS	DAY
NEW	YEARS	EVE
NON-STICK		PAN
OFF-SHORE		RIG
SHE	LOVES	YOU
THE	CRUEL	SEA
THE	GREAT	WAR
THE	MINDS	EYE
THE	NAKED	EYE
THE	OTHER	DAY
THE	OTHER	MAN
THE	OTHER	ONE
THE	THIRD	MAN
THE	WHOLE	HOG
THE	WHOLE	LOT
THE	WORLD	CUP

3, 6, 2

ALL WASHED UP

3, 8

ACT TOGETHER
AIR CORRIDOR
AIR MINISTER

AIR	MINISTRY	LED	ZEPPELIN
AIR	TERMINAL	LIE	DETECTOR
AIR	TERMINUS	LIE	PARALLEL
ALL	QUARTERS	LOW	ALTITUDE
ALL	STRAIGHT	LOW	COMEDIAN
ALL	TOGETHER	LOW	FOREHEAD
ART	DIRECTOR	LOW	POSITION
BAD	EYESIGHT	LOW	PRESSURE
BAD	FEELINGS	LOW	RAINFALL
BAD	JUDGMENT	LOW	STANDARD
BAD	LANGUAGE	MAD	SCRAMBLE
BAG	SNATCHER	MAX	BEERBOHM
BAR	SINISTER	MAX	BYGRAVES
BID	FAREWELL	MOB	VIOLENCE
BIG	BUSINESS	MRS.	MALAPROP
BOB	CRATCHIT	NET	PRACTICE
BUD	FLANAGAN	NET	RECEIPTS
BUS	TERMINUS	NEW	APPROACH
BUY	OUTRIGHT	NEW	BRIGHTON
CAR	INDUSTRY	NEW	EVIDENCE
CAR	SALESMAN	NEW	HEBRIDES
COW	ELEPHANT	NEW	IMPROVED
CUB	REPORTER	NEW	POTATOES
DAY	LABOURER	NEW	SENTENCE
DIE	FIGHTING	NOT	POSSIBLE
DIE	LAUGHING	NOT	SPEAKING
DRY	CLEANERS	OIL	PAINTING
DRY	CLEANING	OIL	REFINERY
EGG	SANDWICH	OIL	SHORTAGE
ENA	SHARPLES	OLD	CUSTOMER
FAR	DISTANCE	OLD	FAITHFUL
FIX	BAYONETS	OLD	MEMORIES
FOR	INSTANCE	OLD	OFFENDER
FOR	PLEASURE	OLD	TRAFFORD
FOR	STARTERS	OLD	WARHORSE
GAY	BACHELOR	ONE	FARTHING
GAY	LOTHARIO	ONE	SHILLING
GAY	NINETIES	ONE	SPOONFUL
GET	CRACKING	ONE	SYLLABLE
GET	INVOLVED	ONE	THOUSAND
GET	PROMOTED	PAY	INCREASE
GET	SUNBURNT	PAY	INTEREST
GET	TOGETHER	PAY	OVERTIME
HAM	OMELETTE	PEN	PORTRAIT
HAM	SANDWICH	PET	AVERSION
HER	HIGHNESS	PUT	STRAIGHT
HER	LADYSHIP	PUT	TOGETHER
HIS	EMINENCE	RAW	MATERIAL
HIS	HIGHNESS	RED	SQUIRREL
HIS	LORDSHIP	REX	HARRISON
HOT	CHESTNUT	RUB	TOGETHER
HOT	PROPERTY	RUN	PARALLEL
JAM	SANDWICH	RUN	SMOOTHLY
JAM	TOMORROW	RUN	STRAIGHT
JET	AIRCRAFT	SAD	FAREWELL
KEN	ROSEWALL	SAL	AMMONIAC
KEY	INDUSTRY	SAL	VOLATILE
KEY	POSITION	SEA	ELEPHANT
KEY	QUESTION	SEE	DAYLIGHT
LAW	MERCHANT	SEE	STRAIGHT
LAY	PREACHER	SET	STANDARD

SET STRAIGHT
SIR LANCELOT
SIX DIAMONDS
SIX SEVENTHS
SIX THOUSAND
SOB BITTERLY
TAM OSHANTER
TAX INCREASE
TEA CANISTER
TEA INTERVAL
TEA STRAINER
TEN THOUSAND
THE ALMIGHTY
THE ALPHABET
THE ATLANTIC
THE BARBICAN
THE BASTILLE
THE BISMARCK
THE BROWNIES
THE CENOTAPH
THE CHAMPION
THE CHEVIOTS
THE CLASSICS
THE COASTERS
THE COLONIES
THE CREATION
THE CRUCIBLE
THE CRUSADES
THE DRIFTERS
THE EIGHTIES
THE ELEMENTS
THE EPILOGUE
THE FAITHFUL
THE GREATEST
THE GUARDIAN
THE HEBRIDES
THE HUSTINGS
THE INFINITE
THE INKSPOTS
THE INNOCENT
THE INTERIOR
THE ITALIANS
THE LIBERALS
THE LISTENER
THE LOWLANDS
THE MAJORITY
THE MARATHON
THE MIDLANDS
THE MINISTRY
THE MINORITY
THE MONUMENT
THE MOUNTIES
THE NATIONAL
THE NINETIES
THE OBSERVER
THE OLYMPICS
THE PANTHEON
THE PENNINES
THE PENTAGON
THE PRISONER
THE PROLOGUE

THE PYRAMIDS
THE PYRENEES
THE RECEIVER
THE REVEREND
THE SCOTTISH
THE SERVICES
THE SORBONNE
THE SUPREMES
THE THIRTIES
THE TREASURY
THE TWENTIES
THE UNIVERSE
THE WAXWORKS
THE WINDMILL
THE WOOLSACK
TIN SOLDIERS
TOM STOPPARD
TOM WEISKOPF
TOO FAMILIAR
TOP SERGEANT
TWO BEDROOMS
TWO DIAMONDS
TWO EXTREMES
TWO FURLONGS
TWO HUSBANDS
TWO SEVENTHS
TWO SWALLOWS
TWO THOUSAND
USE VIOLENCE
VAL DOONICAN
VIV RICHARDS
WAR CRIMINAL
WAR MEMORIAL
WAR MINISTER
WAR REPORTER
WIN OUTRIGHT
ZIP FASTENER

4, 1, 2, 2, 2

MAKE A GO OF IT

4, 1, 3, 3

FIND A WAY OUT
SEEK A WAY OUT
TAKE A DAY OFF

4, 1, 4, 2

HAVE A HAIR-DO
MAKE A FOOL OF
MAKE A PASS AT

4, 1, 6

BACK A WINNER
BEAR A GRUDGE
BEAT A TATTOO
BOOK A FLIGHT

BORE	A	TUNNEL		MAKE	A	CHANGE
BOWL	A	GOOGLY		MAKE	A	CHOICE
BOWL	A	YORKER		MAKE	A	DETOUR
CALL	A	DOCTOR		MAKE	A	LIVING
CASH	A	CHEQUE		MAKE	A	PACKET
CAST	A	GLANCE		MAKE	A	PLEDGE
CAST	A	SHADOW		MAKE	A	PROFIT
COIN	A	PHRASE		MAKE	A	RECORD
COME	A	PURLER		MAKE	A	REMARK
DIAL	A	NUMBER		MAKE	A	SIGNAL
DRAW	A	CIRCLE		MAKE	A	SPEECH
DRAW	A	SALARY		MAKE	A	SPLASH
DROP	A	CURTSY		MILE	A	MINUTE
DROP	A	REMARK		MISS	A	CHANCE
DROP	A	SITTER		MISS	A	SITTER
DROP	A	STITCH		MOVE	A	MUSCLE
EARN	A	LIVING		OPEN	A	BOTTLE
FIND	A	REFUGE		OPEN	A	LETTER
FIND	A	REMEDY		PASS	A	REMARK
FIRE	A	VOLLEY		PICK	A	FLOWER
GIVE	A	LESSON		PICK	A	POCKET
GIVE	A	LITTLE		PICK	A	WINNER
GIVE	A	REASON		PLAY	A	RECORD
GIVE	A	RULING		PLOT	A	COURSE
GIVE	A	SIGNAL		POST	A	LETTER
HALF	A	BOTTLE		PULL	A	MUSCLE
HALF	A	CHANCE		READ	A	LESSON
HALF	A	DOLLAR		READ	A	SPEECH
HALF	A	GALLON		REAP	A	PROFIT
HALF	A	LEAGUE		REAP	A	REWARD
HALF	A	LENGTH		RIDE	A	TANDEM
HALF	A	MINUTE		SEND	A	LETTER
HALF	A	MOMENT		SEND	A	PARCEL
HALF	A	SECOND		SEND	A	SIGNAL
HAVE	A	CHOICE		SHOW	A	PROFIT
HAVE	A	DEFECT		STOP	A	BULLET
HAVE	A	FRIGHT		TAKE	A	CENSUS
HAVE	A	PICNIC		TAKE	A	CHANCE
HAVE	A	SECRET		TAKE	A	CORNER
HAVE	A	SHOWER		TAKE	A	COURSE
HAVE	A	SNOOZE		TAKE	A	CRUISE
HAVE	A	SQUINT		TAKE	A	DEGREE
HAVE	A	STROKE		TAKE	A	LETTER
HAVE	A	THEORY		TAKE	A	NUMBER
HAVE	A	THIRST		TAKE	A	POWDER
JUST	A	CHANCE		TAKE	A	STROLL
JUST	A	LITTLE		TAKE	A	TUMBLE
JUST	A	MINUTE		TAKE	A	WICKET
JUST	A	MOMENT		TYPE	A	LETTER
JUST	A	SECOND		WAIT	A	MINUTE
KEEP	A	SECRET		WAIT	A	MOMENT
KNOW	A	LITTLE		WAIT	A	SECOND
LEND	A	DOLLAR		WHAT	A	RELIEF!
LIFT	A	FINGER				
LIKE	A	MANIAC		4, 2, 1, 4		
LIKE	A	PARROT				
LIKE	A	STREAK		BALD	AS A	COOT
LIKE	A	TROJAN		BOLD	AS A	LION
LOOK	A	FRIGHT		BULL	AT A	GATE
LOSE	A	CHANCE		CALL	TO A	HALT
MADE	A	MEMBER		CHIT	OF A	GIRL

COME	TO	A	HALT
COME	TO	A	HEAD
COME	TO	A	STOP
DEAD	AS	A	DODO
DEAF	AS	A	POST
DONE	TO	A	TURN
DRAW	UP	A	PLAN
DROP	ME	A	LINE
FILL	IN	A	FORM
FIRM	AS	A	ROCK
FOND	OF	A	DRAM
FOUR	AT	A	TIME
FREE	AS	A	BIRD
GIVE	IT	A	MISS
GIVE	IT	A	REST
GOOD	AS	A	MILE
HELL	OF	A	MESS
HELL	OF	A	TIME
KICK	UP	A	FUSS
MISS	BY	A	MILE
SELL	AT	A	LOSS
SLIP	OF	A	GIRL
TAKE	UP	A	CASE
THIN	AS	A	LATH
THIN	AS	A	RAKE
WORK	AS	A	TEAM

4, 2, 2, 3

COME	TO	AN	END
DRAW	TO	AN	END
HANG	UP	TO	DRY
LIKE	IT	OR	NOT
PLAY	IT	BY	EAR
THAT	IS	TO	SAY
WISE	AS	AN	OWL

4, 2, 3, 2

HAVE	AN	EYE	ON
KEEP	AN	EYE	ON
MAKE	UP	FOR	IT
PACK	UP	AND	GO
TIME	TO	GET	UP

4, 2, 5

ABLE	TO	SPEAK
BACK	TO	FRONT
BAGS	OF	MONEY
BALE	OF	STRAW
BEAM	OF	LIGHT
BEST	OF	TASTE
BEST	OF	THREE
BILL	OF	COSTS
BOLD	AS	BRASS
BOOK	OF	VERSE
BOWL	OF	FRUIT
BOWL	OF	PUNCH
BURN	TO	ASHES
CALL	IT	QUITS

CALL	TO	ORDER
CASE	IN	POINT
CLAP	IN	IRONS
CLUB	TO	DEATH
COAT	OF	PAINT
COLD	AS	DEATH
COME	IN	FIRST
COME	IN	HANDY
COME	IN	THIRD
COME	TO	BLOWS
COME	TO	EARTH
COME	TO	GRIEF
COME	TO	GRIPS
COME	TO	LIGHT
COME	TO	POWER
COME	TO	TERMS
CORN	IN	EGYPT
COST	OF	MONEY
COUP	DE	GRACE
CURL	OF	SMOKE
DATE	OF	BIRTH
DAYS	OF	GRACE
DEAD	OF	NIGHT
DEAD	OR	ALIVE
DECK	OF	CARDS
DIET	OF	WORMS
DONE	TO	DEATH
DOVE	OF	PEACE
DOWN	AT	HEART
DOWN	IN	PRICE
DOWN	TO	EARTH
DRAW	TO	SCALE
DRAW	UP	PLANS
DROP	IN	PRICE
DROP	OF	BLOOD
DROP	OF	WATER
DROP	TO	DRINK
EAST	BY	NORTH
EAST	BY	SOUTH
EASY	TO	GRASP
FAIL	TO	AGREE
FAIL	TO	REPLY
FAIL	TO	SCORE
FALL	IN	PLACE
FALL	IN	PRICE
FALL	IN	RUINS
FALL	IN	VALUE
FALL	TO	EARTH
FEAR	OF	DEATH
FEAR	OF	DYING
FEAR	TO	TREAD
FEEL	NO	SHAME
FILL	AN	ORDER
FIVE	OF	CLUBS
FIVE	TO	EIGHT
FIVE	TO	SEVEN
FIVE	TO	THREE
FLAG	OF	TRUCE
FLOW	OF	WORDS
FORM	AN	IMAGE
FOUR	OF	CLUBS

FREE	OF	BLAME
FREE	OF	GUILT
FREE	ON	BOARD
FREE	TO	SPEAK
FULL	OF	BEANS
FULL	OF	FIGHT
FULL	OF	GRACE
FULL	OF	IDEAS
FULL	OF	PRIDE
GAIN	IN	VALUE
GAME	OF	BOWLS
GAME	OF	CARDS
GAME	OF	CHESS
GAME	OF	RUMMY
GAME	OF	SKILL
GAME	OF	WHIST
GIFT	OF	MONEY
GIVE	AN	ORDER
GONE	TO	EARTH
GONE	TO	LUNCH
GONE	TO	WASTE
GOOD	AT	HEART
GOOD	IN	PARTS
HAIL	OF	ABUSE
HAIL	OF	BLOWS
HALF	AN	OUNCE
HAND	IN	GLOVE
HAND	OF	DEATH
HAND	TO	MOUTH
HARD	AS	NAILS
HARD	AS	STEEL
HARD	TO	CATCH
HARD	TO	GRASP
HATE	TO	THINK
HAVE	AN	APPLE
HAVE	IN	STORE
HAVE	NO	DOUBT
HAVE	NO	MERCY
HAVE	TO	ADMIT
HEAD	OF	STATE
HELD	IN	CHECK
HELD	IN	TRUST
HELL	ON	EARTH
HERD	OF	GOATS
HERD	OF	SWINE
HOLD	IN	CHECK
HOLD	IN	TRUST
HOLD	ON	TIGHT
HOME	ON	LEAVE
HUNT	IN	PAIRS
IDES	OF	MARCH
INNS	OF	COURT
ISLE	OF	ARRAN
ISLE	OF	WIGHT
JACK	OF	CLUBS
JAWS	OF	DEATH
JOHN	OF	GAUNT
JOIE	DE	VIVRE
KEEN	TO	LEARN
KEEP	IN	CHECK
KEEP	IN	SIGHT

KEEP	IN	STOCK
KEEP	IN	TOUCH
KEEP	IT	GOING
KING	OF	BIRDS
KING	OF	CLUBS
KING	OF	KINGS
KISS	ME,	HARDY
KISS	OF	DEATH
KISS	OF	JUDAS
KNOW	BY	HEART
KNOW	BY	SIGHT
LACK	OF	FAITH
LACK	OF	FLAIR
LACK	OF	MONEY
LACK	OF	SCOPE
LACK	OF	SENSE
LACK	OF	SLEEP
LACK	OF	TASTE
LAST	OF	THREE
LAST	TO	LEAVE
LATE	AT	NIGHT
LICK	OF	PAINT
LIFE	OF	CRIME
LIFE	ON	EARTH
LIFE	OR	DEATH
LIKE	AN	ARROW
LIKE	AN	IDIOT
LINE	OF	SIGHT
LIST	OF	ITEMS
LIST	OF	NAMES
LIVE	IN	DREAD
LIVE	IN	PEACE
LIVE	ON	BOARD
LOAD	OF	TRIPE
LOAF	OF	BREAD
LOSS	OF	BLOOD
LOSS	OF	FAITH
LOSS	OF	MONEY
LOSS	OF	PRIDE
LOSS	OF	SIGHT
LOSS	OF	SMELL
LOSS	OF	SOUND
LOSS	OF	TOUCH
LOSS	OF	VOICE
LOST	TO	SIGHT
LOTS	OF	MONEY
LOVE	IS	BLIND
LOVE	OF	MONEY
LOVE	OF	TRUTH
LOVE	OR	MONEY
LUMP	OF	METAL
LUMP	OF	SUGAR
MADE	IN	ITALY
MADE	IN	JAPAN
MADE	OF	MONEY
MADE	OF	STEEL
MADE	OF	STRAW
MADE	TO	ORDER
MAKE	AN	ASIDE
MAKE	AN	ENTRY
MAKE	AN	ERROR

MAKE	AN	OFFER	PORT	OF	SPAIN
MAKE	IT	CLEAR	PORT	ST.	PETER
MAKE	IT	COUNT	POTS	OF	MONEY
MAKE	IT	KNOWN	PUFF	OF	SMOKE
MAKE	IT	PLAIN	PULL	UP	SHORT
MAKE	IT	QUICK	PURE	IN	HEART
MAKE	IT	RIGHT	PURL	OR	PLAIN
MAKE	IT	STICK	PUSS	IN	BOOTS
MAKE	IT	WORSE	RAIN	OR	SHINE
MAKE	NO	NOISE	REAM	OF	PAPER
MAKE	NO	SOUND	REST	IN	PEACE
MAKE	OR	BREAK	RING	OF	ROSES
MARK	MY	WORDS	RING	OF	TRUTH
MARK	OF	ZORRO	RISE	IN	PRICE
MATE	IN	THREE	RISE	TO	POWER
MELT	IN	TEARS	RISE	TO	SPEAK
MINT	OF	MONEY	ROBE	OF	STATE
MOVE	TO	ANGER	ROCK	TO	SLEEP
MOVE	TO	TEARS	ROLL	OF	PAPER
NAME	NO	NAMES	ROOM	TO	SPARE
NEWS	IN	BRIEF	RULE	OF	FORCE
NINE	OF	CLUBS	RULE	OF	THREE
NONE	SO	BLIND	RULE	OF	THUMB
ONCE	OR	TWICE	SACK	OF	FLOUR
ONUS	OF	PROOF	SACK	OF	WHEAT
OPEN	TO	DOUBT	SEND	AN	ORDER
OPEN	TO	ERROR	SEND	TO	SLEEP
OPEN	TO	OFFER	SHIP	OF	STATE
PACK	OF	CARDS	SHIP	TO	SHORE
PACK	OF	FOOLS	SHOW	NO	MERCY
PAIL	OF	WATER	SHOW	OF	FORCE
PAIN	OF	DEATH	SHOW	OF	HANDS
PAIR	OF	BOOTS	SICK	AT	HEART
PAIR	OF	CLOGS	SICK	TO	DEATH
PAIR	OF	FIVES	SIDE	OF	BACON
PAIR	OF	FOURS	SLAB	OF	STONE
PAIR	OF	HANDS	SLAP-UP		FEAST
PAIR	OF	HORNS	SLIP	OF	PAPER
PAIR	OF	JACKS	SLOW	TO	ANGER
PAIR	OF	KINGS	SLOW	TO	LEARN
PAIR	OF	NINES	SONG	OF	SONGS
PAIR	OF	PUMPS	STAR	OF	DAVID
PAIR	OF	SHOES	STAR	OF	INDIA
PAIR	OF	SIXES	STAY	IN	SIGHT
PAIR	OF	SOCKS	STAY	TO	LUNCH
PAIR	OF	SPATS	STEM	TO	STERN
PAIR	OF	TONGS	STOP	TO	THINK
PALE	AS	DEATH	SUIT	OF	CARDS
PANE	OF	GLASS	TAKE	AN	OFFER
PEAL	OF	BELLS	TAKE	BY	FORCE
PICK	UP	SPEED	TAKE	BY	STORM
PILE	OF	BOOKS	TAKE	NO	RISKS
PILE	OF	MONEY	TAKE	ON	BOARD
PINT	OF	BLOOD	TAKE	ON	TRUST
PINT	OF	HEAVY	TAKE	TO	COURT
PINT	OF	STOUT	TAKE	TO	DRINK
PIPE	OF	PEACE	TAKE	TO	HEART
PIPE	ON	BOARD	TELL	NO	TALES
PLAY	IT	AGAIN	TERM	OF	ABUSE
PLAY	ON	WORDS	TERM	OF	YEARS
PLUS	OR	MINUS	TEST	OF	SKILL

TIES	OF	BLOOD
TIME	IS	MONEY
TIME	IS	TIGHT
TIME	OF	DEATH
TIME	OF	NIGHT
TIME	TO	LEAVE
TIME	TO	SPARE
TIME	TO	THINK
TIME	TO	WASTE
TONE	OF	VOICE
TONS	OF	MONEY
TOUR	DE	FORCE
TOUT	DE	SUITE
TRUE	TO	SCALE
TUFT	OF	GRASS
TURN	OF	SPEED
TURN	TO	ASHES
TURN	TO	STONE
VOID	OF	SENSE
VOTE	BY	PROXY
WAIT	AT	TABLE
WAKE	UP	EARLY
WALK	IN	FRONT
WALK	ON	WATER
WALL	OF	DEATH
WALL	OF	FLAME
WARD	OF	COURT
WARM	AS	TOAST
WELL	IN	FRONT
WEST	BY	NORTH
WEST	BY	SOUTH
WINK	OF	SLEEP
WORD	OF	MOUTH
WORK	TO	DEATH
YEAR	OF	GRACE

4, 3, 1, 3

BLUE	FOR	A	BOY
EVER	AND	A	DAY
KING	FOR	A	DAY
LOOK	FOR	A	JOB
SEND	FOR	A	CAB
YEAR	AND	A	DAY

4, 3, 2, 2

KEEP	OUT	OF	IT
SNAP	OUT	OF	IT
WELL	OUT	OF	IT

4, 3, 4

AGES	AND	AGES
ARMS	AND	LEGS
AYES	AND	NOES
BAIT	THE	TRAP
BEAR	ILL-WILL	
BEAR	THE	COST
BEAR	THE	NAME
BEAT	THE	BAND

BEAT	THE	BEST
BEAT	THE	DRUM
BECK	AND	CALL
BEND	THE	KNEE
BEND	THE	MIND
BITE	THE	DUST
BLOW	FOR	BLOW
BLOW	SKY-HIGH	
BLOW	THE	GAFF
BODY	AND	SOUL
BOLT	THE	DOOR
BORN	AND	BRED
BULL	AND	BUSH
CAIN	AND	ABEL
CALL	THE	ROLL
CALL	THE	TUNE
CASH	AND	BANK
CAST	THE	DICE
CATS	AND	DOGS
COAT	THE	PILL
COCK	AND	BULL
COME	OFF	BEST
COME	OFF	WELL
COME	OUT	BEST
COME	OUT	WELL
COOL	AND	CALM
DAYS	AND	DAYS
DEAD	AND	GONE
DEAF	AND	DUMB
DEAL	THE	PACK
DEFY	THE	WHIP
DOWN	THE	HILL
DOWN	THE	LINE
DOWN	THE	MINE
DOWN	THE	ROAD
DOWN	THE	SINK
DRAW	THE	LINE
DROP	THE	CASE
DULL	THE	PAIN
EASE	THE	PAIN
EAST	AND	WEST
EVER	AND	ANON
EVER	AND	EVER
FACE	THE	ODDS
FAIL	THE	TEST
FEEL	THE	COLD
FEEL	THE	HEAT
FEEL	THE	NEED
FEEL	THE	PAIN
FEEL	THE	URGE
FIND	THE	LADY
FIND	THE	TIME
FIRE	AND	FURY
FIRE	AND	RAIN
FIRM	BUT	FAIR
FIVE	PER	CENT
FIVE-BAR	GATE	
FIVE-DAY	WEEK	
FLAT	FOR	SALE
FOOT	THE	BILL
FOUR	PER	CENT

FOUR-DAY WEEK	LIFE AND SOUL
FREE AND EASY	LIFT THE VEIL
FROM THE EAST	LIKE THE WIND
FROM THE SPOT	LIVE FOR EVER
FROM THE WEST	LOCK THE DOOR
FROM THE WOOD	LOCK THE SAFE
GILD THE LILY	LOOK FOR WORK
GILD THE PILL	LOOK THE PART
GIVE AND TAKE	LOOP THE LOOP
GIVE NEW LIFE	LORD AND LADY
GIVE THE SIGN	LOSE THE GAME
GIVE THE WORD	LOSE THE RACE
GONE FOR EVER	LOSE THE TOSS
GONE FOR GOOD	LOSE THE VOTE
GOOD AND EVIL	LOTS AND LOTS
GOOD OLD DAYS	LOVE AND HATE
HALF AND HALF	LUST FOR LIFE
HALF THE TIME	MAKE AND MEND
HALF WAY DOWN	MAKE THE NEWS
HAND AND FOOT	MAKE THE PACE
HANG THE HEAD	MARK THE SPOT
HANG-DOG LOOK	MARK YOU WELL
HARD AND FAST	MEEK AND MILD
HAVE AND HOLD	MIND AND BODY
HAVE THE VOTE	MIND THE BABY
HEAD AND TAIL	MIND THE STEP
HEAD FOR HOME	MISS THE BOAT
HEAD THE LIST	MISS THE MARK
HEAL THE SICK	MORE AND MORE
HEAR THE CALL	MUCH THE SAME
HIDE AND SEEK	MUMS THE WORD
HIGH OLD TIME	NEAR AND DEAR
HILL AND DALE	NEAR THE BONE
HOLD OUT HOPE	NEAR THE EDGE
HOLD THE BABY	NEAR THE MARK
HOLD THE FORT	NEAR THE WIND
HOLD THE LEAD	NEAT AND TIDY
HOLD THE LINE	NEAT AND TRIM
HOLD THE ROAD	NECK AND NECK
HOME AND AWAY	NICE AND COOL
HOME FOR GOOD	NICE AND EASY
HOPE AND PRAY	NICE AND EVEN
HUMS AND HAWS	NICE AND WARM
HUNT BIG GAME	NINE PER CENT
INTO THE BLUE	NONE THE LESS
INTO THE WIND	NONE TOO SOON
JACK AND JILL	NOSE FOR NEWS
JOHN AND YOKO	NULL AND VOID
JOIN THE ARMY	ODDS AND ENDS
JOIN THE NAVY	ONLY THE BEST
JUKE-BOX JURY	OPEN AND SHUT
JUST FOR ONCE	OPEN THE CASE
JUST THE SAME	OPEN THE DOOR
JUST THE WORD	OPEN THE EYES
KNOW TOO MUCH	OPEN THE GATE
LADY WHO DOES	OPEN THE SAFE
LAST BUS HOME	OPEN-AIR LIFE
LAST FOR EVER	OVER AND OVER
LATE FOR WORK	OVER SHE GOES
LESS AND LESS	OVER THE HILL
LIFE AND LIMB	OVER THE HUMP

OVER	THE	LINE	STAY	TOO	LONG
OVER	THE	MARK	STEM	THE	TIDE
OVER	THE	MOON	STOP	THE	FLOW
OVER	THE	ODDS	SUCH	AND	SUCH
OVER	THE	ROAD	TAKE	ANY	CARD
OVER	THE	WALL	TAKE	POT	LUCK
PASS	THE	BALL	TAKE	THE	BAIT
PASS	THE	BUCK	TAKE	THE	CAKE
PASS	THE	SALT	TAKE	THE	HINT
PASS	THE	TEST	TAKE	THE	LEAD
PASS	THE	TIME	TAKE	THE	LIFT
PAST	ALL	HELP	TAKE	THE	OATH
PAST	THE	POST	TAKE	THE	PILL
PICK	THE	BEST	TAKE	THE	RISE
PICK	THE	LOCK	TAKE	THE	SILK
PICK	THE	TEAM	TAKE	THE	TEST
PLAY	FOR	TIME	TAKE	THE	VEIL
PLAY	THE	BALL	TAKE	THE	VIEW
PLAY	THE	FOOL	TAKE	TOO	MUCH
PLAY	THE	GAME	TALK	TOO	MUCH
PLAY	THE	HERO	TALL	AND	SLIM
PLAY	THE	HOST	TALL	AND	THIN
PLAY	THE	LEAD	TELL	THE	TALE
PLAY	THE	PART	TELL	THE	TIME
POKE	THE	FIRE	TELL	YOU	WHAT
PONY	AND	TRAP	TEND	THE	SICK
POOR	OLD	CHAP	THIN	RED	LINE
POOR	OLD	SOUL	THIS	AND	THAT
POTS	AND	PANS	TIDE	ONE	OVER
PRAY	FOR	RAIN	TILL	THE	SOIL
PROS	AND	CONS	TIME	AND	TIDE
PURE	NEW	WOOL	TOLL	THE	BELL
PUSH	AND	PULL	TONS	AND	TONS
PUSH	THE	BELL	TOSS	AND	TURN
PUTT	THE	SHOT	TOWN	AND	GOWN
RACK	AND	RUIN	TRIM	THE	LAMP
RANK	AND	FILE	TRIM	THE	WICK
RANT	AND	RAVE	TRUE	AND	FAIR
RICH	AND	POOR	TURN	OUT	WELL
RING	THE	BELL	TURN	THE	PAGE
RISE	AND	FALL	TURN	THE	TIDE
ROCK	AND	ROLL	TYNE	AND	WEAR
ROCK	THE	BOAT	WAKE	THE	DEAD
ROLL-TOP	DESK		WALK	OFF	WITH
ROWS	AND	ROWS	WEAR	AND	TEAR
SAFE	AND	SURE	WELL	AND	GOOD
SAFE	AND	WELL	WHAT	THE	HECK
SAME	OLD	GAME	WHAT	THE	HELL
SEND	FOR	HELP	WHAT	YOU	WILL
SHOW	THE	DOOR	WIFE	AND	KIDS
SHOW	THE	FLAG	WINE	AND	DINE
SHUT	THE	DOOR	WIPE	THE	EYES
SHUT	THE	GATE	WISE	OLD	BIRD
SINK	THE	BOAT	WITH	ONE	BLOW
SKIN	AND	BONE	WITH	THE	LARK
SLAM	THE	DOOR	WITH	THE	TIDE
SLOW	AND	SURE	WITH	THE	WIND
SLOW	BUT	SURE	WORD	FOR	WORD
SODA	AND	MILK	WORK	AND	PLAY
SPOT	THE	BALL			
STAY	THE	PACE			

4, 4, 3

ANTI-TANK GUN
AWAY WITH YOU!
BACK-ROOM BOY
BITE ONES LIP
BLOW ONES TOP
BLUE-EYED BOY
COCK ONES LEG
COME WHAT MAY
CURL ONES LIP
DEEP BLUE SEA
DEEP FINE LEG
DOFF ONES CAP
DOFF ONES HAT
EDGE ONES WAY
FEEL ONES WAY
FIND ONES WAY
FIVE PAST ONE
FIVE PAST SIX
FIVE PAST TEN
FIVE PAST TWO
FULL-TIME JOB
GAIN ONES END
GIVE ONES ALL
GOOD SEND OFF
HAVE ONES DAY
HAVE ONES SAY
HAVE ONES WAY
HIGH-WIRE ACT
HOLD ONES OWN
HOME-MADE JAM
HUSH-HUSH JOB
INTO THIN AIR
JUMP WITH JOY
KNOW ONES JOB
KNOW ONES WAY
LONG LONG AGO
LONG TIME AGO
LONG WEEK-END
LOOK LIKE NEW
LOOK ONES AGE
LOSE ONES ALL
LOSE ONES WAY
MAKE MUCH ADO
MAKE ONES BED
MAKE ONES DAY
MAKE ONES WAY
MEET ONES END
MORE THAN ONE
NEAR ONES END
ONES VERY OWN
OPEN THIS END
PART-TIME JOB
PASS THIS WAY
PULL ONES LEG
RING-PULL CAN
ROAD FUND TAX
ROLL INTO ONE
SELF-MADE MAN
SHOW ONES AGE

SING WITH JOY
SOME TIME AGO
STEP THIS WAY
STIR ONES TEA
STUB ONES TOE
TAKE ONES CUE
TAKE TIME OFF
TAKE TIME OUT
TAKE-HOME PAY
THIS VERY DAY
VERY WELL OFF
WALK THIS WAY
WELL-READ MAN
WEND ONES WAY
WENT FLAT OUT
WHAT HAVE YOU
WIND ONES WAY
WING ONES WAY
WORK ONES WAY
WORM ONES WAY
YOUR VERY OWN

4, 5, 2

GOOD WRITE-UP
HEAP ABUSE ON
KEEP RIGHT ON
KEEP SIGHT OF
LOSE SIGHT OF
MAKE LIGHT OF
MAKE SPORT OF
PICK HOLES IN
SHED LIGHT ON
STEP RIGHT UP
WELL WORTH IT
WHAT ABOUT IT?
WHAT ABOUT ME.
WITH KNOBS ON

4, 7

AIDE MEMOIRE
ALAN BENNETT
ALAN WHICKER
ANDY ROBERTS
ANNA PAVLOVA
ARCH VILLAIN
ARMS TRAFFIC
ARMY OFFICER
ARMY RESERVE
ARMY SURPLUS
ARTS COUNCIL
ARTS SUBJECT
BABY BUNTING
BACK HEAVILY
BACK PAYMENT
BALL BEARING
BANK ACCOUNT
BANK BALANCE
BANK CASHIER
BANK CHARGES

BANK	DEPOSIT
BANK	HOLIDAY
BANK	MANAGER
BANK	ROBBERY
BARE	MIDRIFF
BARE	MINIMUM
BEAR	BAITING
BEAR	WITNESS
BEEF	EXTRACT
BEEF	SAUSAGE
BEER	SHAMPOO
BEER	TANKARD
BEND	FORWARD
BEST	CIRCLES
BEST	CLOTHES
BEST	QUALITY
BEST	REGARDS
BILL	POSTERS
BILL	SHANKLY
BIRD	FANCIER
BIRD	WATCHER
BLOW	BUBBLES
BODY	POLITIC
BOLD	ATTEMPT
BOLD	OUTLINE
BOLT	UPRIGHT
BOMB	SHELTER
BORN	ACTRESS
BOYS	BRIGADE
BULL	BAITING
BULL	MASTIFF
BULL	TERRIER
BURY	ONESELF
CAKE	MIXTURE
CALL	COLLECT
CALM	WEATHER
CAPE	KENNEDY
CASE	HISTORY
CASH	ACCOUNT
CASH	ADVANCE
CASH	PAYMENT
CATS	CONCERT
CATS	WHISKER
CAVE	DRAWING
CAVE	DWELLER
CITY	COUNCIL
CITY	FATHERS
CLAM	CHOWDER
CLUB	COLOURS
COAL	SCUTTLE
COCK	SPARROW
COLD	CHICKEN
COLD	CLIMATE
COLD	COMFORT
COLD	STORAGE
COLD	WEATHER
COLD	WELCOME
COME	BETWEEN
COME	DANCING
COME	FORWARD
COME	OUTSIDE
COME	QUIETLY
COME	THROUGH
COME	UNSTUCK
COOK	ISLANDS
COOL	MILLION
CORN	PLASTER
CROP	FAILURE
DAME	FORTUNE
DARK	CLOTHES
DARK	GLASSES
DARK	LANTERN
DART	FORWARD
DASH	THROUGH
DAYS	JOURNEY
DEAD	AGAINST
DEAD	CERTAIN
DEAD	EARNEST
DEAD	SILENCE
DEAR	BELOVED
DEAR	FRIENDS
DEAR	OCTOPUS
DEBS	DELIGHT
DEEP	CONCERN
DEEP	FEELING
DEEP	INSIGHT
DEEP	MYSTERY
DEEP	REMORSE
DEEP	THINKER
DEEP	THOUGHT
DICK	BENTLEY
DIRE	STRAITS
DIRE	TROUBLE
DIRK	BOGARDE
DOPE	PEDDLER
DOWN	PAYMENT
DRUG	PEDDLER
DRUG	PROBLEM
DRUG	TRAFFIC
DUAL	CONTROL
DUAL	PURPOSE
DULL	READING
DULL	ROUTINE
DULL	WEATHER
DUMB	CHARADE
DUMB	FRIENDS
DUTY	OFFICER
EARL	MARSHAL
EAST	GERMANY
EAST	LOTHIAN
EASY	VICTORY
ECHO	CHAMBER
ETON	COLLEGE
EVEN	NUMBERS
EVIL	CONDUCT
EVIL	THOUGHT
EWAN	MACCOLL
FACE	MASSAGE
FACE	REALITY
FAIR	COMMENT
FAIR	HEARING
FAIR	WARNING

FAIR WEATHER
FALL THROUGH
FARM MANAGER
FARM PRODUCE
FAST BOWLING
FAST COLOURS
FAST FRIENDS
FATA MORGANA
FEEL ASHAMED
FEEL CERTAIN
FEEL EMOTION
FEEL NOTHING
FEEL PECKISH
FEEL REMORSE
FEEL STRANGE
FILM ACTRESS
FILM CENSORS
FILM COMPANY
FIND COMFORT
FIND ONESELF
FIND SHELTER
FINE SOLDIER
FINE WEATHER
FINE WRITING
FIRE BRIGADE
FIRE CURTAIN
FIRE DAMAGED
FIRE HYDRANT
FIRE SERVICE
FIRE STATION
FIRM CONTROL
FIRM FRIENDS
FIRM OPINION
FIRM PROMISE
FIRM RESOLVE
FISH FINGERS
FIVE DEGREES
FIVE DOLLARS
FIVE EIGHTHS
FIVE FATHOMS
FIVE FIGURES
FIVE GALLONS
FIVE HUNDRED
FIVE MILLION
FIVE MINUTES
FIVE SECONDS
FIVE SQUARED
FIVE WICKETS
FLAG CAPTAIN
FLAG OFFICER
FLAT HUNTING
FLAT REFUSAL
FLAT SURFACE
FLOW THROUGH
FLOW TOWARDS
FOLK DANCING
FOND EMBRACE
FOND PARENTS
FOND REGARDS
FOOD COUNTER
FOOT SOLDIER

FORT WILLIAM
FOUL WEATHER
FOUR COLOURS
FOUR CORNERS
FOUR COURSES
FOUR DEGREES
FOUR DOLLARS
FOUR FATHOMS
FOUR FIGURES
FOUR GALLONS
FOUR HUNDRED
FOUR MILLION
FOUR MINUTES
FOUR SEASONS
FOUR SECONDS
FOUR SQUARED
FOUR WICKETS
FRED ASTAIRE
FREE COUNTRY
FREE ECONOMY
FREE ONESELF
FREE PARKING
FREE PASSAGE
FREE SERVICE
FREE THINKER
FREE THOUGHT
FROM SCRATCH
FROM WITHOUT
FULL ACCOUNT
FULL ADDRESS
FULL APOLOGY
FULL CONSENT
FULL DETAILS
FULL FLAVOUR
FULL FRONTAL
FULL GENERAL
FULL MEASURE
FULL REGALIA
FULL RETREAT
FULL SERVICE
FULL STRETCH
FULL SUPPORT
GAIN CONTROL
GAIN MASTERY
GALA EVENING
GALE WARNING
GAME LICENCE
GAME RESERVE
GANG WARFARE
GERM CARRIER
GERM WARFARE
GIFT VOUCHER
GIVE DETAILS
GIVE LESSONS
GIVE OFFENCE
GIVE QUARTER
GIVE SUPPORT
GIVE TROUBLE
GIVE WARNING
GLAD TIDINGS
GLEE SINGERS

GLIB	SPEAKER	HANG	ONESELF
GOLD	BULLION	HANS	HOLBEIN
GOLD	COINAGE	HARD	BARGAIN
GOLD	FILLING	HARD	CONTEST
GONE	FISHING	HARD	DRINKER
GOOD	ACCOUNT	HARD	DRIVING
GOOD	ACTRESS	HARD	PRESSED
GOOD	ADDRESS	HARD	SURFACE
GOOD	BARGAIN	HAVE	ANOTHER
GOOD	BEATING	HAVE	COMPANY
GOOD	CITIZEN	HAVE	FRIENDS
GOOD	COMPANY	HAVE	KITTENS
GOOD	CONDUCT	HAVE	REGRETS
GOOD	DEFENCE	HAVE	TROUBLE
GOOD	DICTION	HEAD	TEACHER
GOOD	EVENING	HEAL	THYSELF
GOOD	EXAMPLE	HEAR	NOTHING
GOOD	FEELING	HEAT	BARRIER
GOOD	FORTUNE	HEAT	THERAPY
GOOD	FRIENDS	HELD	CAPTIVE
GOOD	GRAMMAR	HELD	HOSTAGE
GOOD	HARVEST	HELP	ONESELF
GOOD	HEARING	HERO	WORSHIP
GOOD	HEAVENS	HIGH	CALLING
GOOD	HUNTING	HIGH	CEILING
GOOD	HUSBAND	HIGH	CIRCLES
GOOD	INNINGS	HIGH	COMMAND
GOOD	LEARNER	HIGH	DENSITY
GOOD	MANAGER	HIGH	DUDGEON
GOOD	MANNERS	HIGH	FASHION
GOOD	MEASURE	HIGH	FINANCE
GOOD	MORNING	HIGH	HOLBORN
GOOD	OFFICES	HIGH	MOTIVES
GOOD	OPENING	HIGH	OPINION
GOOD	OPINION	HIGH	QUALITY
GOOD	QUALITY	HIGH	SHERIFF
GOOD	READING	HIGH	SOCIETY
GOOD	SCHOLAR	HIGH	SPIRITS
GOOD	SERVANT	HIGH	STATION
GOOD	SERVICE	HIGH	TENSION
GOOD	SOCIETY	HIGH	TREASON
GOOD	SOLDIER	HIGH	TURNOUT
GOOD	SPEAKER	HIGH	VOLTAGE
GOOD	SPIRITS	HIGH	WYCOMBE
GOOD	SWIMMER	HILL	COUNTRY
GOOD	TACTICS	HOLD	CLASSES
GOOD	TEMPLAR	HOLY	TRINITY
GOOD	TIDINGS	HOLY	UNCTION
GOOD	WEATHER	HOLY	WEDLOCK
GOOD	WORKMAN	HOME	AFFAIRS
GRIM	OUTLOOK	HOME	COOKING
GROW	SMALLER	HOME	COUNTRY
GROW	UPWARDS	HOME	SERVICE
GROW	YOUNGER	HOME	STRETCH
GUNS	BLAZING	HOMO	SAPIENS
HAIR	STYLIST	HORS	DOEUVRE
HALF	BROTHER	HUGE	EXPENSE
HALF	HOLIDAY	HUGE	SUCCESS
HALF	MEASURE	IDLE	THOUGHT
HAND	GRENADE	ILIE	NASTASE
HANG	GLIDING	IRIS	MURDOCH

RON CURTAIN	LAST CHAPTER
RON FILINGS	LAST JANUARY
RON FOUNDRY	LAST JOURNEY
RON PYRITES	LAST OCTOBER
RON RATIONS	LAST QUARTER
VOR NOVELLO	LAST REQUEST
ACK DEMPSEY	LAST TUESDAY
ACK HAWKINS	LAST VESTIGE
ACK KENNEDY	LATE ARRIVAL
ACK KEROUAC	LATE EDITION
ANE SEYMOUR	LATE EVENING
AZZ SESSION	LATE HUSBAND
EAN ANOUILH	LATE MORNING
EAN COCTEAU	LATE STARTER
EAN SIMMONS	LAZY HOLIDAY
EFF THOMSON	LEAD BALLOON
IMI HENDRIX	LEAN AGAINST
OAN HAMMOND	LEAN FORWARD
OBS COMFORT	LEAN TOWARDS
OHN GIELGUD	LECH WALENSE
OHN KENNEDY	LEFT LUGGAGE
OHN OGROATS	LEFT OUTSIDE
OHN OSBORNE	LEIF ERICSON
OHN TENNIEL	LEND SUPPORT
UDY GARLAND	LEON TROTSKY
URY SERVICE	LÈSE MAJESTÉ
UST DESERTS	LESS TROUBLE
UST IMAGINE	LIFE HISTORY
UST MARRIED	LIFE PEERAGE
UST VISIBLE	LIFE SAVINGS
UST WILLIAM	LIME CORDIAL
EEN CONTEST	LIME FLAVOUR
EEN HEARING	LINE DRAWING
EEN STUDENT	LION PASSANT
EEP ABREAST	LION RAMPANT
EEP COMPANY	LIVE THEATRE
EEP COUNSEL	LIVE THROUGH
EEP SMILING	LOCK FORWARD
EEP WAITING	LONG ACCOUNT
ICK AGAINST	LONG HOLIDAY
ILL ONESELF	LONG INNINGS
IND GESTURE	LONG JOURNEY
IND REGARDS	LONG MEASURE
IND THOUGHT	LONG OVERDUE
ING CHARLES	LONG PLAYING
ING HUSSEIN	LONG SERVICE
ING PENGUIN	LONG STRETCH
ING RICHARD	LONG STRIDES
ING SOLOMON	LONG VEHICLE
ING WILLIAM	LONG VERSION
IRK DOUGLAS	LONG WEEKEND
NOW THYSELF	LOOK ASKANCE
ACK COURAGE	LOOK DAGGERS
ACK MANNERS	LOOK FOOLISH
ACK SPARKLE	LOOK FORWARD
ADY ALMONER	LOOK GHASTLY
ADY MACBETH	LOOK OUTSIDE
AKE LUCERNE	LOOK PLEASED
AND MEASURE	LOOK THROUGH
AST BASTION	LOOK WORRIED
AST CENTURY	LORD BOOTHBY
	LORD DENNING

LORD	JUSTICE	NAZI	GERMANY
LORD	PROVOST	NAZI	REGALIA
LORD	RUSSELL	NEAR	PERFECT
LOSE	CONTROL	NEWS	CAPTION
LOSE	FRIENDS	NEWS	CONTENT
LOSE	ONESELF	NEWS	SUMMARY
LOST	HORIZON	NEXT	CENTURY
LOUD	PROTEST	NEXT	CHAPTER
LOUD	SPEAKER	NEXT	JANUARY
LOVE	FIFTEEN	NEXT	OCTOBER
MACK	SENNETT	NEXT	TUESDAY
MADE	WELCOME	NICE	MANNERS
MAIN	ELEMENT	NICE	WEATHER
MAIN	FEATURE	NINE	DOLLARS
MAIN	PROBLEM	NINE	GALLONS
MAIN	PURPOSE	NINE	HUNDRED
MAKE	BELIEVE	NINE	MINUTES
MAKE	CERTAIN	NINE	SQUARED
MAKE	CHANGES	NINE	WICKETS
MAKE	CONTACT	ODDS	AGAINST
MAKE	DEMANDS	OMAR	KHAYYAM
MAKE	ENEMIES	ONCE	REMOVED
MAKE	EXCUSES	ONES	BETTERS
MAKE	FRIENDS	OPEN	ACCOUNT
MAKE	HEADWAY	OPEN	CIRCUIT
MAKE	HISTORY	OPEN	COUNTRY
MAKE	INROADS	OPEN	INWARDS
MAKE	STRIDES	OPEN	MEETING
MAKE	TROUBLE	OPEN	VERDICT
MAKE	WELCOME	OPEN	WARFARE
MAKE	WHOOPEE	OTIS	REDDING
MALE	DESCENT	OVER	ANXIOUS
MALT	VINEGAR	PAGE	HEADING
MASS	EMOTION	PAID	HOLIDAY
MASS	MEETING	PAID	SERVANT
MASS	SUICIDE	PALM	SPRINGS
MATT	SURFACE	PART	COMPANY
MEAN	NOTHING	PART	FRIENDS
MEAT	CLEAVER	PART	PAYMENT
MEAT	EXTRACT	PASS	COMMENT
MEET	HALFWAY	PASS	THROUGH
MERE	NOTHING	PAST	HISTORY
MERE	THOUGHT	PAUL	CÉZANNE
MEWS	COTTAGE	PAUL	GAUGUIN
MIKE	YARWOOD	PAUL	ROBESON
MILD	CLIMATE	PHIL	SILVERS
MILD	REPROOF	PICK	FLOWERS
MILD	WEATHER	PICK	POCKETS
MILK	PUDDING	PINE	NEEDLES
MINT	FLAVOUR	PINK	PANTHER
MISS	ENGLAND	PINT	MEASURE
MISS	NOTHING	PINT	TANKARD
MOON	GODDESS	PIPE	CLEANER
MOON	LANDING	PIPE	TOBACCO
MOVE	FORWARD	PLAY	AGAINST
MOVE	QUICKLY	PLAY	COWBOYS
MOVE	TOWARDS	PLAY	CRICKET
MUCH	OBLIGED	PLAY	MACBETH
MUCH	TROUBLE	PLAY	MARBLES
NAIL	VARNISH	PLAY	PONTOON
NAME	DROPPER	PLAY	SNOOKER

*LUM	PUDDING	SAGO	PUDDING
*OLE	VAULTER	SAME	CHANNEL
*ONY	EXPRESS	SAME	FOOTING
OOR	CALIBRE	SAME	PATTERN
*OOR	DICTION	SAVE	NOTHING
*OOR	HARVEST	SAVE	ONESELF
OOR	OPINION	SCAT	SINGING
OOR	OUTLOOK	SEAM	BOWLING
*OOR	QUALITY	SEAN	CONNERY
*OOR	SWIMMER	SEAT	ONESELF
OPE	GREGORY	SELF	CONTROL
*ORK	BUTCHER	SELF	DEFENCE
ORK	SAUSAGE	SELL	TICKETS
*ORT	GLASGOW	SEND	PACKING
*ROP	FORWARD	SENT	PACKING
ULL	STRINGS	SHEA	STADIUM
ULL	THROUGH	SHOE	LEATHER
*ULP	FICTION	SHOP	COUNTER
*URE	ALCOHOL	SHOP	STEWARD
URE	FICTION	SHOT	THROUGH
URE	SCIENCE	SHOW	ABILITY
USH	FORWARD	SHOW	COURAGE
*USH	THROUGH	SHOW	FEELING
ACE	MEETING	SHOW	JUMPING
ACE	PROBLEM	SHOW	ONESELF
ARE	EXAMPLE	SHOW	PROMISE
ARE	QUALITY	SHOW	RESPECT
ASH	PROMISE	SHOW	RESULTS
AVI	SHANKAR	SHOW	WILLING
EAD	BRAILLE	SHUN	COMPANY
EAD	THROUGH	SIDE	AGAINST
EAL	MEANING	SIDE	TURNING
EAR	ADMIRAL	SKIM	THROUGH
EED	BUNTING	SKIN	DISEASE
ENT	ASUNDER	SKYE	TERRIER
ENT	CONTROL	SLIM	WHITMAN
EST	ASSURED	SLIP	THROUGH
ICE	PUDDING	SLOT	MACHINE
ICH	HARVEST	SLOW	BOWLING
ICH	HUSBAND	SLOW	DECLINE
ISE	AGAINST	SLOW	FOXTROT
OAD	HAULAGE	SLOW	PROCESS
OAD	REPAIRS	SLOW	STARTER
OAD	SURFACE	SLUM	DWELLER
OAD	SWEEPER	SNOW	LEOPARD
OAD	TRAFFIC	SOAP	BUBBLES
OCK	CONCERT	SOFT	LANDING
OOM	SERVICE	SOIL	EROSION
OSY	PICTURE	SOLE	SUPPORT
UBY	WEDDING	SONG	CONTEST
UDE	GESTURE	SONG	RECITAL
UIN	ONESELF	SORE	PRESSED
USH	FORWARD	SOUP	KITCHEN
USH	THROUGH	STAR	BILLING
AFE	CONDUCT	STAR	CHAMBER
AFE	CUSTODY	STAR	CLUSTER
AFE	DEPOSIT	STAR	QUALITY
AFE	JOURNEY	STAR	STUDDED
AFE	KEEPING	STAR	VEHICLE
AFE	LANDING	STAY	INDOORS
AFE	PASSAGE	STAY	NEUTRAL

STAY	OUTSIDE	TUBE	STATION
STEP	FORWARD	TURN	AGAINST
STEP	OUTSIDE	TURN	CRIMSON
STOP	OUTSIDE	TURN	TRAITOR
STOP	PAYMENT	TWIN	BROTHER
STOP	SMOKING	TWIN	SISTERS
STOP	TALKING	TWOS	COMPANY
STOP	WORKING	UGLY	SISTERS
SUET	PUDDING	UGLY	THOUGHT
SUIT	ONESELF	UGLY	WEATHER
SURE	FOOTING	VAIN	ATTEMPT
TAKE	ACCOUNT	VAST	ACREAGE
TAKE	CAPTIVE	VAST	EXPANSE
TAKE	CHANCES	VAST	EXPENSE
TAKE	COMFORT	VERY	PLEASED
TAKE	COMMAND	VERY	SPECIAL
TAKE	CONTROL	VERY	STRANGE
TAKE	COUNSEL	VERY	WEALTHY
TAKE	COURAGE	VERY	WELCOME
TAKE	CUSTODY	VERY	WORRIED
TAKE	HOSTAGE	VOTE	AGAINST
TAKE	LESSONS	VOTE	LIBERAL
TAKE	LIGHTLY	WADE	THROUGH
TAKE	OFFENCE	WALK	QUICKLY
TAKE	SHELTER	WALK	TOWARDS
TAKE	UMBRAGE	WARM	CLIMATE
TAKE	WARNING	WARM	CLOTHES
TALK	QUIETLY	WARM	COUNTRY
TALK	RUBBISH	WARM	WEATHER
TALK	TWADDLE	WARM	WELCOME
TANK	WARFARE	WASH	LEATHER
TAPE	MACHINE	WAVE	GOODBYE
TAPE	MEASURE	WEAK	STOMACH
TATE	GALLERY	WELL	CONTENT
TEAM	CAPTAIN	WELL	GROOMED
TEAM	COLOURS	WELL	MATCHED
TEAM	SUPPORT	WELL	WRITTEN
TEAR	ASUNDER	WENT	THROUGH
TEST	CRICKET	WEST	CENTRAL
THIS	CENTURY	WEST	COUNTRY
THIS	ENGLAND	WEST	GERMANY
THIS	INSTANT	WEST	LOTHIAN
THIS	MORNING	WIDE	READING
THIS	TUESDAY	WIDE	VARIETY
TIED	COTTAGE	WILD	COUNTRY
TIME	MACHINE	WILD	DELIGHT
TONY	HANCOCK	WILD	FLOWERS
TONY	JACKLIN	WINE	TASTING
TORY	VICTORY	WINE	VINEGAR
TOWN	COUNCIL	WING	FORWARD
TOWN	DWELLER	WISE	VIRGINS
TOWN	PLANNER	WITH	ABANDON
TREE	DWELLER	WITH	HONOURS
TREE	SURGEON	WITH	MEANING
TREE	SURGERY	WITH	RESPECT
TRIP	LIGHTLY	WOLF	WHISTLE
TRUE	ACCOUNT	WOOD	CARVING
TRUE	COLOURS	WORD	PAINTER
TRUE	MEANING	WORD	PERFECT
TRUE	PICTURE	WORD	PICTURE
TRUE	READING	WORK	AGAINST

WORK WONDERS
YARD MEASURE
YORK MINSTER
YOUR MAJESTY
YOUR OPINION
YOUR WORSHIP
YURI GAGARIN
YVES MONTAND
ZERO GRAVITY

5, 1, 3, 2

FORCE A WAY IN

5, 1, 5

ADOPT A CHILD
AFTER A WHILE
BLAZE A TRAIL
BREAK A HABIT
BUILD A HOUSE
CARRY A TORCH
CATCH A CHILL
CATCH A PLANE
CATCH A THIEF
CATCH A TRAIN
CAUSE A SCENE
CROWN A TOOTH
DANCE A TANGO
DANCE A WALTZ
DRINK A PINTA
DRINK A TOAST
DRIVE A TRAIN
EIGHT O CLOCK
ENTER A PHASE
FLASH A SMILE
GRANT A TRUCE
LEARN A TRADE
LEAVE A SPACE
LEAVE A TRAIL
LIGHT A MATCH
MOUNT A HORSE
OFFER A PRICE
ORDER A DRINK
POINT A MORAL
PRESS A CLAIM
PROVE A POINT
RAISE A CHEER
RAISE A LAUGH
RENEW A LEASE
RIGHT A WRONG
SCORE A POINT
SERVE A FAULT
SEVEN O CLOCK
SHINE A LIGHT
SMOKE A CIGAR
SPARE A PENNY
SPEND A PENNY
STAKE A CLAIM
STAND A DRINK
STAND A ROUND
START A FIGHT

STEAL A MARCH
THREE A PENNY
THREE O CLOCK
THROW A PARTY
THROW A PUNCH
THROW A STONE
TWICE A MONTH
UNDER A CLOUD
UNDER A CURSE
UNDER A SPELL
WEAVE A SPELL
WRITE A LYRIC
WRITE A NOVEL
WRITE A STORY
YIELD A POINT

5, 2, 1, 3

BLIND AS A BAT
BROTH OF A BOY
GIANT OF A MAN
STICK IN A RUT

5, 2, 2, 2

LEAVE IT TO ME

5, 2, 4

AHEAD OF TIME
ALIVE OR DEAD
BARON OF BEEF
BASED ON FACT
BEAST OF PREY
BEGIN TO PALL
BLACK AS COAL
BLACK AS SOOT
BLACK TO MOVE
BLACK TO PLAY
BLESS MY SOUL!
BLOCK OF WOOD
BREAD OF LIFE
BRING TO BEAR
BRING TO BOOK
BRING TO HEEL
BRING TO LIFE
BRING TO MIND
BRING TO REST
BUILD ON SAND
BUILT ON SAND
BUILT TO LAST
BUILT-UP AREA
BUNCH OF KEYS
BURST OF FIRE
CEASE TO LIVE
CHEEK BY JOWL
CLAIM TO FAME
CLEAR OF DEBT
CLOSE AT HAND
CLOSE OF PLAY
CLOTH OF GOLD

CLOUD	OF	DUST		LEARN	TO	READ
CRACK	OF	DAWN		LEARN	TO	RIDE
CRACK	OF	DOOM		LEARN	TO	TALK
CROCK	OF	GOLD		LEARN	TO	WALK
CYCLE	TO	WORK		MAKES	NO	ODDS
DEATH	BY	FIRE		MARCH	IN	STEP
DRESS	TO	KILL		MARCH	OF	TIME
DRIVE	TO	WORK		MIGHT	AS	WELL
EARLY	IN	LIFE		MONEY	TO	BURN
EARLY	TO	RISE		NINTH	OF	JULY
EIGHT	OR	NINE		NINTH	OF	JUNE
FACTS	OF	LIFE		NORTH	BY	EAST
FIELD	OF	PLAY		NORTH	BY	WEST
FIFTH	OF	JULY		OFFER	NO	HOPE
FIFTH	OF	JUNE		PAINT	IN	OILS
FIRST	IN	LINE		PEACE	OF	MIND
FIRST	OF	FIVE		PHONE	IN	SICK
FIRST	OF	FOUR		PIECE	OF	CAKE
FIRST	OF	JULY		PIECE	OF	LAND
FIRST	OF	JUNE		PIECE	OF	LUCK
FIRST	OF	MANY		PINCH	OF	SALT
FIRST	TO	COME		PLACE	OF	REST
FIRST	TO	LAST		PLACE	TO	LIVE
FLASK	OF	WINE		POINT	IN	TIME
FLEET	OF	CABS		POINT	OF	FACT
FLEET	OF	CARS		POINT	OF	SALE
FLEET	OF	FOOT		POINT	OF	TIME
FLEET	OF	VANS		POINT	OF	VIEW
FLUSH	OF	HOPE		POWER	OF	GOOD
FORCE	OF	ARMS		POWER	OF	LOVE
FRAME	OF	MIND		POWER	OF	VETO
GLASS	OF	BEER		PRICE	OF	FAME
GLASS	OF	MILK		PRICE	OF	GOLD
GLASS	OF	PORT		PRIME	OF	LIFE
GLASS	OF	WINE		QUITE	AT	HOME
GLEAM	OF	HOPE		RAISE	ON	HIGH
GRAIN	OF	SALT		READY	TO	DROP
GRAIN	OF	SAND		READY	TO	HAND
GRIND	TO	BITS		READY	TO	WEAR
GRIND	TO	DUST		RIGHT	AS	RAIN
GROUP	OF	FIVE		RIGHT	ON	TIME
GROUP	OF	FOUR		RIGHT	TO	VOTE
HANDS	ON	HIPS		RIGHT	TO	WORK
HAVEN	OF	REST		ROUGE	ET	NOIR
HEART	OF	GOLD		ROUND	OF	FIRE
HEAVY	AS	LEAD		ROUND	OF	GOLF
HELEN	OF	TROY		SANDS	OF	TIME
HOURS	OF	WORK		SEEDS	OF	TIME
HOUSE	OF	KEYS		SENSE	OF	DUTY
HOUSE	OF	YORK		SENSE	OF	LOSS
HOUSE	ON	FIRE		SENSE	OF	PAIN
JOINT	OF	BEEF		SHEAF	OF	CORN
JOINT	OF	LAMB		SHOAL	OF	FISH
JOINT	OF	MEAT		SHOCK	OF	HAIR
JOINT	OF	PORK		SHOOT	TO	KILL
KNOCK	IT	BACK		SHORT	OF	CASH
KNOCK	ON	WOOD		SHORT	OF	FOOD
LAPSE	OF	TIME		SHORT	OF	TIME
LARGE	AS	LIFE		SHORT	OF	WORK
LEARN	TO	HATE		SIEGE	OF	TROY
LEARN	TO	LOVE		SIGNS	OF	WEAR

SIXTH	OF	JULY
SIXTH	OF	JUNE
SLICE	OF	CAKE
SLICE	OF	LUCK
SLICE	OF	MEAT
SOUND	IN	MIND
SOUTH	BY	EAST
SOUTH	BY	WEST
SPACE	OF	TIME
SPATE	OF	NEWS
SPEAK	NO	EVIL
SPECK	OF	DUST
SPELL	OF	DUTY
SPICE	OF	LIFE
STACK	OF	WORK
STAFF	OF	LIFE
STAND	AT	EASE
STAND	IN	LINE
STAND	IN	NEED
STAND	OR	FALL
STAND	TO	GAIN
STAND	TO	LOSE
STATE	OF	FLUX
STATE	OF	MIND
STATE	OF	PLAY
STICK	OF	ROCK
STILL	TO	COME
STOCK	IN	HAND
STORE	OF	NUTS
STRIP	OF	LAND
SWARM	OF	ANTS
SWARM	OF	BEES
SWEAR	AN	OATH
SWEAR	ON	OATH
SWIFT	OF	FOOT
SWORD	IN	HAND
SYRUP	OF	FIGS
TEACH	TO	READ
TEACH	TO	RIDE
TEACH	TO	SWIM
TEARS	OF	PITY
TEARS	OF	RAGE
TEETH	ON	EDGE
TENTH	OF	JULY
TENTH	OF	JUNE
THIEF	OF	TIME
THINK	IT	OVER
THIRD	OF	JULY
THIRD	OF	JUNE
THREE	OR	FOUR
TIRED	OF	LIFE
TIRED	OF	WORK
TOKEN	OF	LOVE
TOWER	OF	PISA
TRAIL	OF	DUST
TRAIL	OF	SAND
TRIAL	BY	JURY
TRIED	BY	JURY
TRUST	TO	LUCK
TRUTH	TO	TELL
TWICE	AS	FAST

TWICE	AS	GOOD
TWICE	AS	MUCH
TWIST	OF	FATE
VASCO	DA	GAMA
VENUS	DE	MILO
VICAR	OF	BRAY
VOICE	OF	DOOM
WASTE	OF	TIME
WATER	OF	LIFE
WHATS	MY	LINE?
WHITE	AS	SNOW
WHITE	TO	MOVE
WHITE	TO	PLAY
WOMEN	IN	LOVE
WORLD	OF	GOOD
WORSE	TO	COME
WRITE	IT	DOWN
YEARS	TO	COME

5, 3, 3

ABOVE	THE	LAW
AFTER	THE	WAR
APPLE-PIE		BED
BACON	AND	EGG
BILLY	THE	KID
BLACK	AND	TAN
BLOCK	THE	WAY
BRACE	AND	BIT
BREAD	AND	JAM
BREAK	FOR	TEA
BREAK	THE	ICE
BREAK	THE	LAW
BRING	AND	BUY
BULLY	FOR	YOU
CAKES	AND	ALE
CARRY	THE	CAN
CARRY	THE	DAY
CARRY	TOO	FAR
CATCH	THE	SUN
CLEAR	THE	AIR
CLEAR	THE	WAY
CLOSE	THE	GAP
COSTA	DEL	SOL
CROSS	THE	SEA
DANCE	FOR	JOY
DRIVE	ONE	MAD
EMPTY	THE	BAG
EVADE	THE	LAW
FELIX	THE	CAT
FIGHT	FOR	AIR
FIRST	BUT	ONE
FIRST-AID		BOX
GRAND	OLD	AGE
GRAND	OLD	MAN
INFRA-RED		RAY
LIGHT	THE	GAS
LIGHT	THE	WAY
MONEY	FOR	JAM
NEVER	SAY	DIE
NIGHT	AND	DAY

129

NORTH	SEA	GAS	AGONY	COLUMN
POINT	THE	WAY	ALARM	SIGNAL
PRIDE	AND	JOY	ALLOW	CREDIT
RAISE	THE	BID	ALTER	COURSE
REACH	THE	END	ALVAR	LIDELL
REACH	THE	TOP	ANDRÉ	PREVIN
READY	FOR	BED	ANNIE	BESANT
RIGHT	YOU	ARE	ANNIE	OAKLEY
ROSES	ARE	RED	ANVIL	CHORUS
SEVEN	AND	SIX	APRIL	SHOWER
SHORT	AND	FAT	ARMED	BANDIT
SHORT	WAY	OFF	ARMED	COMBAT
SHOUT	FOR	JOY	ARMED	ESCORT
SPARE	THE	ROD	ARMED	FORCES
SPOIL	THE	FUN	ARMED	ROBBER
START	THE	DAY	AUDIO	TYPIST
TABLE	FOR	TWO	AVOID	DEFEAT
THATS	THE	WAY	BACON	SLICER
THERE	YOU	ARE	BADEN	POWELL
THREE	AND	SIX	BADLY	PLACED
TWICE	THE	MAN	BADLY	SHAKEN
TWIST	THE	ARM	BAKED	POTATO
UNDER	THE	MAT	BAKER	STREET
UNDER	THE	SEA	BARRY	LYNDON
UNDER	THE	SUN	BASIC	RIGHTS
UNFIT	FOR	USE	BATED	BREATH
WIDEN	THE	GAP	BELLY	DANCER
WIELD	THE	BAT	BELOW	GROUND
WORLD	WAR	ONE	BELOW	STAIRS
WORLD	WAR	TWO	BETTY	GRABLE
YOUNG	AND	OLD	BIBLE	SCHOOL
			BILLY	BUNTER

5, 4, 2

ABIDE	WITH	ME
FOOLS	RUSH	IN
FULLY	PAID-UP	
OTHER	SIDE	UP
RIGHT	SIDE	UP
STAGE	MAKE-UP	
SUNNY	SIDE	UP
THATS	DONE	IT
THATS	TORN	IT
THINK	MUCH	OF
WORDS	FAIL	ME
YEARS	GONE	BY

(continued right column)

BILLY	GRAHAM
BILLY	WILDER
BLACK	BEAUTY
BLACK	BEETLE
BLACK	BISHOP
BLACK	CASTLE
BLACK	CLOUDS
BLACK	COFFEE
BLACK	COMEDY
BLACK	FOREST
BLACK	FRIDAY
BLACK	KNIGHT
BLACK	LETTER
BLACK	MARKET
BLACK	MONDAY
BLACK	PEPPER
BLACK	PRINCE
BLACK	SQUARE
BLACK	VELVET
BLANK	CHEQUE
BLIND	CHANCE
BLIND	CORNER
BLIND	FLYING
BLOOD	SAMPLE
BLOOD	SPORTS
BLOOD	STREAM
BLOOD	VESSEL
BLUES	SINGER
BLUNT	REMARK

5, 6

ABOVE	GROUND
ABOVE	NORMAL
ACUTE	ACCENT
ACUTE	ATTACK
ADDED	RELISH
ADMIT	BEARER
ADMIT	DEFEAT
ADOLF	HITLER
AFTER	DINNER
AFTER	SCHOOL
AFTER	SUNSET
AFTER	SUPPER

BOARD SCHOOL	CIVVY STREET
BONNE BOUCHE	CLASS HATRED
BONUS SCHEME	CLEAN BOWLED
BOSOM FRIEND	CLEAN BREAST
BOXER SHORTS	CLEAN COLLAR
BRAIN DAMAGE	CLEAN FORGOT
BRAIN INJURY	CLEAN RECORD
BRAIN TUMOUR	CLEAR MARGIN
BRASS MONKEY	CLEAR PROFIT
BRAVE EFFORT	CLEFT PALATE
BRAVE PERSON	CLIFF HANGER
BREAD BASKET	CLOSE BEHIND
BREAD RATION	CLOSE COMBAT
BREAD WINNER	CLOSE FINISH
BREAK GROUND	CLOSE FRIEND
BRIAN CLOUGH	CLOSE SEASON
BRIEF MOMENT	CLOSE SECOND
BRIEF SKETCH	CLOSE SECRET
BROAD ACCENT	COMIC RELIEF
BROAD COMEDY	CONEY ISLAND
BROAD STREET	CORAL ISLAND
BROWN BOMBER	COUNT DOUBLE
BUNNY RABBIT	COURT JESTER
BURNT ALMOND	COVER CHARGE
BURNT EFFIGY	COVER GROUND
BURNT SIENNA	CRACK TROOPS
CABIN WINDOW	CRANE DRIVER
CABLE STITCH	CRASH COURSE
CAGED ANIMAL	CRASH HELMET
CANDY KISSES	CRAZY NOTION
CANDY STRIPE	CRAZY PAVING
CAREY STREET	CREAM CHEESE
CARGO VESSEL	CROSS SWORDS
CAROL SINGER	CROWN COLONY
CARRY ACROSS	CROWN JEWELS
CARRY WEIGHT	CROWN PRINCE
CATCH PHRASE	CRUEL NATURE
CATTY REMARK	CRUEL TYRANT
CAUSE DAMAGE	CURRY FAVOUR
CECIL BEATON	CURRY POWDER
CECIL RHODES	CUSHY NUMBER
CELLO PLAYER	CYCLE RACING
CHAIN LETTER	DAILY MIRROR
CHAIN SMOKER	DAILY RECORD
CHAIN STITCH	DAILY REPORT
CHARM SCHOOL	DAILY SKETCH
CHEAP LABOUR	DAIRY BUTTER
CHEAP REMARK	DAIRY CATTLE
CHEAP RETURN	DAMON RUNYON
CHEAP THRILL	DANCE TROUPE
CHEAP TICKET	DARTS PLAYER
CHEER LEADER	DAVID BROOME
CHESS PLAYER	DEATH DUTIES
CHIEF STOKER	DEATH NOTICE
CHILD GENIUS	DEATH RATTLE
CHILD LABOUR	DEATH THROES
CHOIR MASTER	DEMON BOWLER
CIVIL ACTION	DENIS HEALEY
CIVIL ARREST	DENSE FOREST
CIVIL RIGHTS	DENSE JUNGLE
CIVIL TONGUE	DEPTH CHARGE

DERBY	COUNTY	EQUAL	RIGHTS
DERBY	STAKES	EQUAL	SHARES
DERBY	WINNER	ERECT	FIGURE
DILYS	POWELL	EVERY	DETAIL
DIRTY	HABITS	EVERY	FRIDAY
DIZZY	HEIGHT	EVERY	MINUTE
DOING	NICELY	EVERY	MONDAY
DOLLY	VARDEN	EVERY	SUNDAY
DONNY	OSMOND	EXACT	AMOUNT
DOVER	CASTLE	EXTRA	CHARGE
DRAMA	CRITIC	EXTRA	STRONG
DRAMA	SCHOOL	FADED	BEAUTY
DREAM	DREAMS	FAINT	PRAISE
DRESS	CIRCLE	FAIRY	CIRCLE
DRINK	SHERRY	FAIRY	LIGHTS
DRINK	WHISKY	FAITH	HEALER
DRIVE	AROUND	FALSE	ARREST
DRIVE	INSANE	FALSE	BOTTOM
DRIVE	SLOWLY	FALSE	CHARGE
DUSTY	MILLER	FALSE	FRIEND
DUTCH	CHEESE	FALSE	REPORT
DUTCH	GUIANA	FALSE	VALUES
DUTCH	TULIPS	FALSE	VANITY
DYING	BREATH	FARES	PLEASE
DYING	EMBERS	FATAL	INJURY
DYLAN	THOMAS	FATTY	TISSUE
EAGER	BEAVER	FEMME	FATALE
EARLY	AUTUMN	FIBRE	OPTICS
EARLY	CHURCH	FIDEL	CASTRO
EARLY	DINNER	FIELD	COURSE
EARLY	GOTHIC	FIELD	EVENTS
EARLY	SPRING	FIELD	SPORTS
EARLY	STAGES	FIERY	SPEECH
EARLY	SUMMER	FIERY	SPIRIT
EARTH	TREMOR	FIERY	TEMPER
EDITH	CAVELL	FIFTH	AVENUE
EIGHT	LITRES	FIFTH	COLUMN
EIGHT	METRES	FIFTH	STOREY
EIGHT	MONTHS	FIFTH	WICKET
EIGHT	NINTHS	FIFTY	METRES
EIGHT	OUNCES	FIFTY	POINTS
EIGHT	POINTS	FIFTY	POUNDS
EIGHT	POUNDS	FINAL	ANSWER
EIGHT	ROUNDS	FINAL	BATTLE
EIGHT	TENTHS	FINAL	CHOICE
EIGHT	TRICKS	FINAL	DEFEAT
ELBOW	GREASE	FINAL	DEMAND
ELDER	SISTER	FINAL	NOTICE
EMILY	BRONTË	FINAL	REPORT
EMLYN	HUGHES	FINAL	RESULT
EMPTY	BOTTLE	FIRST	CHOICE
EMPTY	LARDER	FIRST	COURSE
EMPTY	POCKET	FIRST	COUSIN
EMPTY	THREAT	FIRST	CUCKOO
ENEMY	ACTION	FIRST	DEGREE
ENEMY	PATROL	FIRST	ELEVEN
ENEMY	TROOPS	FIRST	FIDDLE
ENOCH	POWELL	FIRST	FINGER
ENTRY	PERMIT	FIRST	FLIGHT
EQUAL	CHANCE	FIRST	FRUITS
EQUAL	HEIGHT	FIRST	GLANCE

FIRST LESSON	GRAND CANYON
FIRST LETTER	GRAND COULEE
FIRST PERSON	GRAND FELLOW
FIRST RECORD	GRAND FINALE
FIRST SERIES	GRAND MANNER
FIRST SERVED	GRAND MASTER
FIRST SINGLE	GRAND RAPIDS
FIRST STOREY	GRAND VIZIER
FIRST STROKE	GRANT ACCESS
FIRST VIOLIN	GRANT ASYLUM
FIRST VOLUME	GRAVE ACCENT
FIRST WICKET	GRAVE AFFAIR
FIXED AMOUNT	GRAVE CRISIS
FIXED ASSETS	GRAVE DOUBTS
FIXED CHARGE	GRAVE MATTER
FIXED INCOME	GRAVE ROBBER
FIXED SALARY	GRAVE SPEECH
FLAKY PASTRY	GREAT AMOUNT
FLANK ATTACK	GREAT ARTIST
FLEET STREET	GREAT AUTHOR
FLESH COLOUR	GREAT BEAUTY
FLOOD DAMAGE	GREAT BURDEN
FLOOR POLISH	GREAT CAESAR
FLORA ROBSON	GREAT CHANCE
FLUID INTAKE	GREAT CIRCLE
FOOLS ERRAND	GREAT DANGER
FORTH BRIDGE	GREAT DARING
FORTY METRES	GREAT DEBATE
FORTY NIGHTS	GREAT DETAIL
FORTY POUNDS	GREAT DIVIDE
FORTY THIRTY	GREAT EFFORT
FOUND GUILTY	GREAT FAVOUR
FRESH BREEZE	GREAT FRIEND
FRESH BUTTER	GREAT HEALER
FRESH FIELDS	GREAT HEIGHT
FRESH GROUND	GREAT HONOUR
FRESH SALMON	GREAT IMPORT
FRESH TROOPS	GREAT NEPHEW
FRIED ONIONS	GREAT NUMBER
FRIED TOMATO	GREAT PLAGUE
FRONT GARDEN	GREAT REGRET
FRONT LIGHTS	GREAT RELIEF
FRONT WINDOW	GREAT SINGER
FRUIT MARKET	GREAT SORROW
FRUIT PICKER	GREAT STRAIN
FULLY BOOKED	GREAT TALKER
FUNNY AFFAIR	GREAT THINGS
FUNNY PERSON	GREAT WEALTH
GAMES MASTER	GREAT WEIGHT
GHOST WRITER	GREEK CHORUS
GIANT KILLER	GREEK CHURCH
GIANT STRIDE	GREEK COMEDY
GIRLS SCHOOL	GREEK LEGEND
GLASS BLOWER	GREEK STATUE
GLASS HOUSES	GREEN BOTTLE
GLENN MILLER	GREEN CHEESE
GLOSS FINISH	GREEN FIELDS
GLOVE PUPPET	GREEN GINGER
GOING STEADY	GREEN MONKEY
GOING STRONG	GREEN PEPPER
GOUDA CHEESE	GREER GARSON

GROSS	INCOME	JAMES GALWAY
GROSS	PROFIT	JAMES GARNER
GUEST	ARTIST	JESUS CHRIST
HAPPY	CHANCE	JIMMY CAGNEY
HAPPY	COUPLE	JIMMY CARTER
HAPPY	ENDING	JIMMY SAVILE
HAPPY	FAMILY	JOINT APPEAL
HAPPY	MEDIUM	JOINT EFFORT
HAPPY	MEMORY	JOINT TENANT
HAPPY	VALLEY	JOLLY HUNGRY
HARDY	ANNUAL	KERRY PACKER
HARRY	LAUDER	KEVIN KEEGAN
HARRY	TRUMAN	KHAKI SHORTS
HASTY	TEMPER	KINGS BISHOP
HEART	ATTACK	KINGS BOUNTY
HEAVY	BOMBER	KINGS KNIGHT
HEAVY	BURDEN	KINGS MUSICK
HEAVY	CLOUDS	KINGS PARDON
HEAVY	OBJECT	KINGS RANSOM
HEAVY	SMOKER	KNOCK AROUND
HEAVY	WEIGHT	KUALA LUMPUR
HELLS	ANGELS	LAPIS LAZULI
HENRY	COOPER	LARGE AMOUNT
HENRY	ESMOND	LARGE BRANDY
HENRY	IRVING	LARGE FAMILY
HENRY	MORGAN	LARGE INCOME
HIRED	KILLER	LARGE NUMBER
HORSE	DEALER	LARGE PROFIT
HORSE	DOCTOR	LARGE SALARY
HORSE	GUARDS	LARGE SCOTCH
HORSE	PISTOL	LARGE SCREEN
HORSE	RACING	LARGE SHERRY
HORSE	TRADER	LARGE VOLUME
HOTEL	KEEPER	LARGE WHISKY
HOTEL	LOUNGE	LARRY HAGMAN
HOTEL	PORTER	LATIN MASTER
HOUSE	ARREST	LATIN PRIMER
HOUSE	HUNTER	LEAVE BEHIND
HOUSE	MARTIN	LEAVE FALLOW
HOUSE	MASTER	LEAVE SCHOOL
HOUSE	NUMBER	LEAVE UNDONE
HUMAN	DYNAMO	LEAVE UNSAID
HUMAN	EFFORT	LEEDS UNITED
HUMAN	NATURE	LEGAL ACTION
HUMAN	RIGHTS	LEGAL ADVICE
INDEX	FINGER	LEGAL BATTLE
INDIA	RUBBER	LEGAL ENTITY
INNER	CIRCLE	LEGAL ESTATE
INNER	TEMPLE	LEGAL JARGON
IRISH	BROGUE	LEGAL MATTER
IRISH	COFFEE	LEGAL NICETY
IRISH	GUARDS	LEGAL REFORM
IRISH	SETTER	LEGAL REMEDY
IRISH	WHISKY	LEGAL TENDER
ISAAC	ASIMOV	LEMON BARLEY
ISAAC	NEWTON	LEMON SQUASH
ISSUE	SHARES	LEMON YELLOW
IZAAK	WALTON	LIBEL ACTION
JAFFA	ORANGE	LIGHT BOMBER
JAMES	BARRIE	LIGHT BREEZE
JAMES	CAGNEY	LIGHT COLOUR

LIGHT	COMEDY	MIXED	SPICES
LIGHT	DUTIES	MOLLY	MALONE
LIGHT	RELIEF	MONEY	LENDER
LIGHT	SWITCH	MONEY	MARKET
LIGHT	WEIGHT	MONEY	MATTER
LINEN	BASKET	MONEY	SPIDER
LINEN	DRAPER	MONTY	PYTHON
LLOYD	GEORGE	MORAL	DEFECT
LOCAL	BRANCH	MORAL	IMPACT
LOCAL	COLOUR	MORAL	LESSON
LOCAL	CUSTOM	MORSE	SIGNAL
LOCAL	GOSSIP	MOTOR	LAUNCH
LOCAL	TALENT	MOTOR	RACING
LOCUM	TENENS	MOUNT	ARARAT
LOFTY	HEIGHT	MURKY	DEPTHS
LOOSE	CHANGE	MUSIC	CRITIC
LOOSE	LIVING	MUSIC	LESSON
LOOSE	MORALS	MUSIC	MASTER
LOOSE	THREAD	MUSIC	SCHOOL
LORDS	PRAYER	NASAL	ACCENT
LORDS	SUPPER	NASTY	PEOPLE
LORRY	DRIVER	NASTY	PERSON
LOWER	REMOVE	NASTY	TEMPER
LOWER	SCHOOL	NAVAL	BATTLE
LUCID	MOMENT	NAVAL	RATING
LUCKY	BEGGAR	NAVEL	ORANGE
LUCKY	CHANCE	NERVE	CENTRE
LUCKY	ESCAPE	NEVER	BEFORE
LUCKY	FELLOW	NEVER	ENDING
LUCKY	MASCOT	NEVER	FORGET
LUCKY	NUMBER	NIGHT	CURFEW
LUCKY	STREAK	NIGHT	EDITOR
LUCKY	STRIKE	NIGHT	FLIGHT
LUCKY	WINNER	NIGHT	FLYING
LUNDY	ISLAND	NIGHT	PORTER
LURID	DETAIL	NIGHT	SCHOOL
LYRIC	POETRY	NIGHT	SISTER
MAGIC	CARPET	NIGHT	WORKER
MAGIC	CIRCLE	NINTH	WICKET
MAGIC	MOMENT	NOBLE	EFFORT
MAGIC	NUMBER	NOBLE	FAMILY
MAGIC	POTION	NOBLE	FIGURE
MAGIC	REMEDY	NOBLE	SAVAGE
MAGIC	SQUARE	NORTH	AFRICA
MAINS	SWITCH	NORTH	BORNEO
MAJOR	CRISIS	NORTH	DAKOTA
MAJOR	PLANET	NORTH	ISLAND
MALAY	STATES	NORTH	LONDON
MANLY	FIGURE	NORTH	RIDING
MANLY	SPIRIT	NOSEY	PARKER
MARIA	CALLAS	NOTTS	COUNTY
MARIE	STOPES	NOTTS	FOREST
MATHS	LESSON	ODDLY	ENOUGH
MATHS	MASTER	OFFER	ADVICE
MEDAL	RIBBON	OLDER	SISTER
MERRY	ANDREW	OLIVE	BRANCH
METAL	POLISH	ONION	SELLER
MINOR	DETAIL	OPERA	BOUFFE
MINOR	INJURY	OPERA	SINGER
MINOR	MATTER	OPIUM	ADDICT
MINOR	PLANET	OPIUM	SMOKER

ORDER	DINNER	QUART	BOTTLE
ORIEL	WINDOW	QUEEN	MOTHER
ORSON	WELLES	QUEER	PERSON
OTHER	PEOPLE	QUEER	STREET
OUTER	CIRCLE	QUEUE	JUMPER
OWNER	DRIVER	QUICK	ANSWER
PABLO	CASALS	QUICK	FREEZE
PANEL	DOCTOR	QUICK	GLANCE
PANTY	GIRDLE	QUICK	PROFIT
PAPER	PROFIT	QUICK	RETURN
PARTY	LEADER	QUICK	TALKER
PARTY	MEMBER	QUICK	TEMPER
PARTY	SPIRIT	QUICK	TONGUE
PARTY	SYSTEM	QUICK	WORKER
PATER	NOSTER	QUIET	PLEASE
PEACE	TREATY	QUITE	ENOUGH
PEACH	BRANDY	QUITE	LIKELY
PEARL	HARBOR	RADAR	SCREEN
PENAL	COLONY	RADIO	BEACON
PENAL	REFORM	RADIO	LONDON
PENAL	SYSTEM	RADIO	SIGNAL
PENNY	BAZAAR	RAINY	SEASON
PETER	OTOOLE	RAISE	MORALE
PETTY	TYRANT	RAISE	PRICES
PHONE	NUMBER	RAITH	ROVERS
PHOTO	FINISH	RAPID	CHANGE
PIANO	LESSON	RAPID	GLANCE
PIANO	PLAYER	RAPID	GROWTH
PILOT	SCHEME	RAPID	MOTION
PITHY	REMARK	REACH	SAFETY
PLAIN	ANSWER	READY	ACCESS
PLAIN	FIGURE	READY	ANSWER
PLAIN	PEOPLE	READY	ENOUGH
PLAIN	SPEECH	READY	RUBBED
PLAIN	STUPID	REBEL	LEADER
PLATE	ARMOUR	RHETT	BUTLER
PLEAD	GUILTY	RHODE	ISLAND
POETS	CORNER	RIGHT	ANGLES
POKER	PLAYER	RIGHT	ANSWER
POLAR	CIRCLE	RIGHT	INSIDE
POLAR	LIGHTS	RIGHT	MOMENT
POLAR	REGION	RIGHT	NUMBER
POOLS	COUPON	RIGHT	PERSON
POWER	SOURCE	RIGHT	WINGER
POWER	SUPPLY	RIGOR	MORTIS
PRESS	NOTICE	RIVER	AMAZON
PRESS	OFFICE	RIVER	DANUBE
PRESS	ONWARD	RIVER	JORDAN
PRICE	FREEZE	RIVER	MEDWAY
PRICE	TICKET	RIVER	MERSEY
PRIME	FACTOR	RIVER	PATROL
PRIME	NUMBER	RIVER	POLICE
PRIZE	CATTLE	RIVER	SEVERN
PROBE	DEEPLY	RIVER	THAMES
PROOF	READER	ROAST	MUTTON
PROOF	SPIRIT	ROAST	POTATO
PROSE	POETRY	ROAST	TURKEY
PROUD	FATHER	ROHAN	KANHAI
PROVE	GUILTY	ROMAN	CANDLE
QUACK	DOCTOR	ROMAN	CHURCH
QUACK	REMEDY	ROMAN	EMPIRE

ROUGH	GROUND	SHIFT	WORKER
ROUGH	MANNER	SHIPS	DOCTOR
ROUGH	SKETCH	SHIPS	MASTER
ROUGH	TONGUE	SHIPS	STOKER
ROUND	FIGURE	SHOCK	HORROR
ROUND	NUMBER	SHOCK	TROOPS
ROUND	OBJECT	SHOOT	GROUSE
ROYAL	ASSENT	SHORT	ANSWER
ROYAL	FAMILY	SHORT	CHANGE
ROYAL	GUARDS	SHORT	JACKET
ROYAL	PALACE	SHORT	LESSON
ROYAL	PARDON	SHORT	LETTER
ROYAL	SALUTE	SHORT	MEMORY
ROYAL	TENNIS	SHORT	NOTICE
RUGBY	LEAGUE	SHORT	PASTRY
RUGBY	PLAYER	SHORT	PERIOD
RUGBY	TACKLE	SHORT	SHRIFT
SADLY	MISSED	SHORT	SPEECH
SAINT	ANDREW	SHORT	SUPPLY
SAINT	GEORGE	SHORT	TEMPER
SAINT	JOSEPH	SHORT	WEIGHT
SALES	LEDGER	SILAS	MARNER
SATIN	FINISH	SILLY	ANSWER
SATIN	STITCH	SILLY	DUFFER
SAUDI	ARABIA	SILLY	PERSON
SCENE	CHANGE	SILLY	REMARK
SCENT	BOTTLE	SILLY	SEASON
SCORE	FREELY	SIXTH	WICKET
SCORE	SLOWLY	SIXTY	METRES
SCOTS	ACCENT	SIXTY	POUNDS
SCOTS	GUARDS	SLACK	SEASON
SCOTT	JOPLIN	SLATE	PENCIL
SCOUT	AROUND	SLAVE	DRIVER
SCOUT	MASTER	SLAVE	LABOUR
SCRAP	DEALER	SLAVE	MARKET
SERVE	DINNER	SLAVE	TRADER
SERVE	NOTICE	SMALL	AMOUNT
SEVEN	BRIDES	SMALL	CHANCE
SEVEN	DWARFS	SMALL	CHANGE
SEVEN	HEARTS	SMALL	CHARGE
SEVEN	LITRES	SMALL	FAMILY
SEVEN	METRES	SMALL	FARMER
SEVEN	MONTHS	SMALL	INCOME
SEVEN	NINTHS	SMALL	MATTER
SEVEN	OUNCES	SMALL	NUMBER
SEVEN	POINTS	SMALL	PARCEL
SEVEN	POUNDS	SMALL	PROFIT
SEVEN	SPADES	SMALL	SCREEN
SEVEN	TENTHS	SMALL	SHERRY
SEVEN	TRICKS	SMALL	TRADER
SHARP	ANSWER	SMALL	WONDER
SHARP	ATTACK	SMART	PEOPLE
SHARP	CORNER	SMART	PERSON
SHARP	LESSON	SMART	RETORT
SHARP	REBUFF	SMART	SAYING
SHARP	TEMPER	SMART	TALKER
SHARP	TONGUE	SMELL	DANGER
SHEEP	FARMER	SMILE	PLEASE
SHEER	LUNACY	SMOKE	SCREEN
SHEER	MURDER	SMOKE	SIGNAL
SHEET	ANCHOR	SNAKE	POISON

SOBER	COLOUR	STILL	WATERS
SOBER	PERSON	STOCK	EXCUSE
SOLAR	PLEXUS	STOCK	MARKET
SOLAR	SYSTEM	STOCK	PHRASE
SOLID	FIGURE	STONE	QUARRY
SOLID	GROUND	STONY	GROUND
SOLID	MATTER	STORM	CENTRE
SOLID	SILVER	STORM	CLOUDS
SONNY	LISTON	STORM	SIGNAL
SORRY	EXCUSE	STORM	TROOPS
SORRY	FELLOW	STORY	TELLER
SORRY	FIGURE	STORY	WRITER
SORRY	PLIGHT	STOUT	FELLOW
SOUND	ADVICE	STRAY	BULLET
SOUND	ASLEEP	STUDY	FRENCH
SOUND	EFFECT	STUMP	ORATOR
SOUND	PLAYER	STUNT	FLYING
SOUND	POLICY	SUAVE	MANNER
SOUND	REASON	SUEDE	JACKET
SOUTH	AFRICA	SUNNY	PERIOD
SOUTH	DAKOTA	SUSAN	GEORGE
SOUTH	ISLAND	SWEET	DREAMS
SOUTH	LONDON	SWEET	PICKLE
SOUTH	RIDING	SWEET	POTATO
SPACE	FLIGHT	SWEET	SHERRY
SPACE	ROCKET	SWEET	TEMPER
SPACE	TRAVEL	SWEET	THINGS
SPADE	GUINEA	SWIFT	GLANCE
SPEAK	FREELY	SWISS	CHALET
SPEAK	FRENCH	SWISS	CHEESE
SPEAK	GERMAN	SWISS	GUARDS
SPEAK	MILDLY	SWORD	THRUST
SPEAK	OPENLY	TABLE	NAPKIN
SPEAK	SLOWLY	TABLE	TENNIS
SPEAK	SOFTLY	TARRY	AWHILE
SPEED	RECORD	TASTY	MORSEL
SPELL	DANGER	TEACH	FRENCH
SPLIT	SECOND	TEACH	GERMAN
STAGE	EFFECT	TENSE	MOMENT
STAGE	FRIGHT	TENTH	STOREY
STAGE	PLAYER	TENTH	WICKET
STAGE	SCHOOL	TERRY	THOMAS
STAGE	STRUCK	TERSE	SPEECH
STAIR	CARPET	THANK	HEAVEN
STAMP	DEALER	THICK	ACCENT
STAND	AGHAST	THIRD	CHOICE
STAND	AROUND	THIRD	COURSE
START	AFRESH	THIRD	DEGREE
START	SAVING	THIRD	FINGER
STATE	PRISON	THIRD	LESSON
STATE	SCHOOL	THIRD	LETTER
STATE	SECRET	THIRD	PERSON
STEAM	ENGINE	THIRD	STOREY
STEAM	LAUNCH	THIRD	VOLUME
STEEL	GIRDER	THIRD	WICKET
STEEL	HELMET	THREE	CHEERS
STERN	REBUKE	THREE	EIGHTS
STICK	INSECT	THREE	FIFTHS
STIFF	BREEZE	THREE	GRACES
STIFF	COLLAR	THREE	HEARTS
STILL	HOPING	THREE	KNAVES

THREE	LITRES	UNDER	ARREST
THREE	METRES	UNDER	ATTACK
THREE	MONTHS	UNDER	CANVAS
THREE	OUNCES	UNDER	DURESS
THREE	POINTS	UNDER	GROUND
THREE	POUNDS	UNDER	NOTICE
THREE	QUARTS	UNDER	ORDERS
THREE	QUEENS	UNDER	REVIEW
THREE	ROUNDS	UNDER	STRAIN
THREE	SEVENS	UNDER	STRESS
THREE	SPADES	UNION	LEADER
THREE	TENTHS	UPPER	CIRCLE
THREE	THREES	UPPER	REMOVE
THREE	TRICKS	UPPER	SCHOOL
THREE	VERSES	UPPER	STOREY
THREE	WHEELS	URINE	SAMPLE
THREE	WISHES	USUAL	CUSTOM
THROW	STONES	UTTER	DEFEAT
TIDAL	WATERS	UTTER	MISERY
TIGHT	BUDGET	VALID	REASON
TIGHT	CORNER	VICHY	FRANCE
TIMES	CHANGE	VITAL	ENERGY
TITLE	HOLDER	VIVID	COLOUR
TOKEN	STRIKE	VIVID	DETAIL
TOMMY	ATKINS	VOCAL	CHORDS
TOMMY	COOPER	VOCAL	EFFORT
TOMMY	STEELE	VOCAL	NUMBER
TOMMY	TUCKER	VOCAL	TALENT
TOOTH	POWDER	WAGON	WHEELS
TORCH	SINGER	WASTE	GROUND
TOTAL	AMOUNT	WATCH	POCKET
TOTAL	DEFEAT	WATER	BABIES
TOTAL	NUMBER	WATER	CLOSET
TOTAL	OUTPUT	WATER	COLOUR
TOUCH	BOTTOM	WATER	GARDEN
TOUCH	GROUND	WATER	HEATER
TOUCH	TYPING	WATER	PISTOL
TOUCH	TYPIST	WATER	SKIING
TOWER	BRIDGE	WATER	SPORTS
TRADE	GOSSIP	WATER	SPRITE
TRADE	SECRET	WATER	SUPPLY
TRAIL	BEHIND	WATER	VAPOUR
TRAIN	ROBBER	WEEKS	NOTICE
TRAIN	TICKET	WEIGH	ANCHOR
TREAD	SOFTLY	WELSH	ACCENT
TREAD	WARILY	WELSH	BORDER
TREND	SETTER	WELSH	RABBIT
TRENT	BRIDGE	WELSH	WIZARD
TRIAL	PERIOD	WENDY	HILLER
TRICK	RIDING	WHITE	BISHOP
TRITE	REMARK	WHITE	CASTLE
TROUT	STREAM	WHITE	CLIFFS
TRUCK	DRIVER	WHITE	COFFEE
TRULY	SPOKEN	WHITE	COLLAR
TUDOR	PERIOD	WHITE	COTTON
TWEED	JACKET	WHITE	DRAGON
TWICE	ELEVEN	WHITE	ENSIGN
TWICE	TWELVE	WHITE	GLOVES
TWICE	WEEKLY	WHITE	HORSES
TWICE	YEARLY	WHITE	KNIGHT
ULTRA	VIOLET	WHITE	PEPPER
		WHITE	POWDER

WHITE RABBIT
WHITE RUSSIA
WHITE SQUARE
WILLI BRANDT
WITCH DOCTOR
WITTY REMARK
WITTY RETORT
WITTY SPEECH
WOMAN DRIVER
WORKS OUTING
WORLD CRUISE
WORLD EVENTS
WORLD RECORD
WORLD SERIES
WORTH SEEING
WOVEN FABRIC
WRITE POETRY
WRONG ANSWER
WRONG CHANGE
WRONG COURSE
WRONG MOMENT
WRONG NUMBER
WRONG PERSON
YACHT RACING
YOUNG PEOPLE
YOUNG PERSON
YOUNG RASCAL
YOUNG SHAVER
YOURE JOKING!
YOURS ALWAYS
YOUTH CENTRE
YOUTH HOSTEL
YOUTH LEADER

6, 1, 4

ASSUME A ROLE
BEYOND A JOKE
BORROW A BOOK
BORROW A QUID
CHOOSE A WIFE
CLINCH A DEAL
CREATE A NEED
CREATE A STIR
DIRECT A PLAY
ELEVEN A SIDE
EXPECT A BABY
FOLLOW A LEAD
FOLLOW A PLAN
IMPOSE A DUTY
LABOUR A JOKE
REFUSE A GIFT
RETURN A BLOW
RETURN A CALL
SCRAPE A PASS
SPRING A LEAK
SPRING A TRAP
STIFLE A YAWN
STRIKE A BLOW
STRIKE A NOTE
STRIKE A POSE

SUFFER A BLOW
SUFFER A LOSS
UNFOLD A TALE

6, 2, 3

BETTER BY FAR
BOTTLE OF GIN
BOTTLE OF INK
BOTTLE OF RUM
BRAZEN IT OUT
BREATH OF AIR
BUNDLE OF FUN
BUNDLE OF HAY
BURIAL AT SEA
CHANGE OF AIR
CHEMIN DE FER
CHOICE OF TWO
COMING OF AGE
DIVIDE BY SIX
DIVIDE BY TEN
DIVIDE BY TWO
DOCTOR OF LAW
DOOMED TO DIE
EIGHTH OF MAY
FIGURE IT OUT
FIGURE OF FUN
FORGET ME NOT
FOURTH OF MAY
FRIEND OR FOE
GALLON OF OIL
GLANCE TO LEG
LIKELY AS NOT
OFFICE TO LET
PACKET OF TEN
PATRON OF ART
PLENTY TO EAT
PUZZLE IT OUT
REFUSE TO ACT
REFUSE TO PAY
RETIRE TO BED
SCHOOL OF ART
SECOND OF MAY
SINEWS OF WAR
SPOILS OF WAR
SWITCH IT OFF
THIRTY TO ONE
THRASH IT OUT
THREAT OF WAR
TIPPED TO WIN
TRAVEL BY AIR
TRAVEL BY SEA
TWENTY TO ONE
UNABLE TO PAY
WALLOW IN MUD
WITHIN AN ACE

6, 3, 2

RUMOUR HAS IT

6 , 5

AARONS BEARD
ACHING HEART
ACHING TOOTH
ACTIVE VOICE
AFGHAN HOUND
ALBERT CAMUS
ALFRED MARKS
ALFRED NOBEL
ALMOND PASTE
ALMOST THERE
ANIMAL LOVER
ANIMAL WORLD
ANNUAL EVENT
ANNUAL LEAVE
APPEAL COURT
APPEAL JUDGE
ARCTIC OCEAN
ARMOUR PLATE
ARRIVE EARLY
ARTFUL DODGE
ARTHUR ASKEY
ARTHUR NEGUS
ASKING PRICE
ASSIZE COURT
ASTRAL PLANE
ATOMIC CLOCK
ATOMIC POWER
AUTUMN MISTS
BAKERS DOZEN
BALLOT PAPER
BANANA SPLIT
BARBED ARROW
BARBED WORDS
BARLEY SUGAR
BARLEY WATER
BARREL ORGAN
BARREN HEATH
BARREN WASTE
BASKET CHAIR
BASSET HOUND
BATTLE ARRAY
BATTLE ORDER
BATTLE ROYAL
BEATEN TRACK
BEAUTY QUEEN
BEAUTY SALON
BEAUTY SLEEP
BECOME AWARE
BEFORE LUNCH
BEHAVE BADLY
BESSIE SMITH
BETTER TIMES
BETTER VALUE
BETTER WAGES
BEYOND DOUBT
BITTER ENEMY
BITTER GRIEF
BITTER IRONY
BITTER LEMON

BITTER SWEET
BITTER TASTE
BITTER TEARS
BLOODY TOWER
BOGNOR REGIS
BOILED SHIRT
BOILED SWEET
BOMBER PILOT
BORROW MONEY
BOSTON BEANS
BOTTLE GREEN
BOTTLE PARTY
BOTTOM MARKS
BOTTOM TEETH
BOXING BOOTH
BOXING GLOVE
BOXING MATCH
BRAINS TRUST
BRANDY GLASS
BREEZE BLOCK
BRIDAL SUITE
BRIDAL TRAIN
BRIDGE DRIVE
BRIDGE FIEND
BRIDGE PARTY
BRIDGE TABLE
BRIGHT CHILD
BRIGHT DRESS
BRIGHT GREEN
BRIGHT LIGHT
BRIGHT PUPIL
BRIGHT SMILE
BRIGHT SPARK
BROGUE SHOES
BROKEN ANKLE
BROKEN BONES
BROKEN GLASS
BROKEN HEART
BRONZE MEDAL
BUDGET PRICE
BUENOS AIRES
BUFFER STATE
BULLET HOLES
BULLET WOUND
BURIAL PLACE
BURIED ALIVE
BUTTER BEANS
BUTTER KNIFE
BUYING PRICE
BUYING SPREE
BYGONE TIMES
CALLOW YOUTH
CANCEL LEAVE
CANINE TEETH
CANINE TOOTH
CANNED DRINK
CANNED FRUIT
CANNED GOODS
CANNED MUSIC
CANVAS SHOES
CARBON PAPER

CAREER WOMAN	COMMON THIEF
CARMEN JONES	COMMON TOUCH
CASTER SUGAR	COMMON USAGE
CATTLE RANCH	COPPER BEECH
CATTLE THIEF	CORNER HOUSE
CAUGHT SHORT	CORNER TABLE
CELTIC CROSS	COTTON DRESS
CEMENT MIXER	COTTON FIELD
CENTRE COURT	COTTON FROCK
CENTRE PARTY	COTTON PLANT
CHANGE BUSES	COTTON SOCKS
CHANGE HANDS	COUNTY CLARE
CHANGE ROUND	COUNTY COURT
CHANGE SIDES	COUNTY MATCH
CHAPEL ROYAL	CREATE HAVOC
CHARGE SHEET	CREDIT ENTRY
CHEESE BOARD	CREDIT TERMS
CHEESE SALAD	CREDIT TITLE
CHEVAL GLASS	CRYING SHAME
CHURCH BELLS	CUCKOO CLOCK
CHURCH CHOIR	CUPIDS ARROW
CHURCH MOUSE	CUPPED HANDS
CHURCH MUSIC	CUSTOM HOUSE
CHURCH ORGAN	DAMPER PEDAL
CHURCH SPIRE	DANGER MONEY
CINDER TRACK	DANIEL BOONE
CINEMA QUEUE	DANIEL DEFOE
CINEMA USHER	DANISH BACON
CINQUE PORTS	DARNED SIGHT
CIRCUS RIDER	DASHED HOPES
CITRUS FRUIT	DEADLY CRIME
CLAUDE MONET	DEADLY ENEMY
CLEVER DODGE	DEADLY PERIL
CLEVER STUFF	DEEPLY MOVED
CLEVER TRICK	DEMAND CURVE
CLOSED DOORS	DESERT SANDS
COARSE CLOTH	DESERT WASTE
COARSE GRAIN	DEVILS ELBOW
COARSE GRASS	DIESEL TRAIN
COARSE VOICE	DINING TABLE
COFFEE BEANS	DINNER DANCE
COFFEE BREAK	DINNER DRESS
COFFEE CREAM	DINNER PARTY
COFFEE HOUSE	DINNER PLATE
COFFEE TABLE	DINNER TABLE
COLOUR BLIND	DIRECT ROUTE
COLOUR CHART	DIRECT STYLE
COLOUR PHOTO	DIVINE BEING
COLOUR PLATE	DIVINE GRACE
COLOUR PRINT	DIVINE RIGHT
COMEDY ACTOR	DIVING BOARD
COMEDY DRAMA	DIVING CATCH
COMELY WENCH	DOUBLE AGENT
COMMON CAUSE	DOUBLE BERTH
COMMON CHORD	DOUBLE BLANK
COMMON ENEMY	DOUBLE CHECK
COMMON FAULT	DOUBLE CREAM
COMMON FRONT	DOUBLE CROSS
COMMON PLEAS	DOUBLE DOORS
COMMON SENSE	DOUBLE DUTCH
COMMON STOCK	DOUBLE EAGLE

DOUBLE EIGHT	FERRIS WHEEL
DOUBLE ENTRY	FIDDLE ABOUT
DOUBLE EVENT	FIERCE GLARE
DOUBLE FAULT	FIGURE EIGHT
DOUBLE FIRST	FIGURE SEVEN
DOUBLE MARCH	FIGURE THREE
DOUBLE SEVEN	FILING CLERK
DOUBLE SHARE	FILLET STEAK
DOUBLE THREE	FILTER PAPER
DOUBLE TRACK	FILTHY LUCRE
DOUBLE VODKA	FINGER BOARD
DUDLEY MOORE	FINISH EARLY
DULCET TONES	FINISH FIRST
EARTHS CRUST	FINISH THIRD
EATING APPLE	FIRING PARTY
EATING HOUSE	FIRING SQUAD
EDIBLE FUNGI	FLARED JEANS
EDMUND BURKE	FLIMSY PAPER
EDWARD ELGAR	FLORAL DANCE
EDWARD HEATH	FLORID STYLE
EIFFEL TOWER	FLYING CORPS
EIGHTH ROUND	FLYING SPEED
EIGHTY KILOS	FLYING SQUAD
EIGHTY MILES	FLYING START
EIGHTY PENCE	FLYING VISIT
EIGHTY YEARS	FOLLOW AFTER
ELEVEN HOURS	FORCED ENTRY
ELEVEN MILES	FORCED ERROR
ELEVEN PENCE	FORCED LAUGH
ELEVEN TIMES	FORCED MARCH
ELEVEN YEARS	FORCED SMILE
EMPIRE STATE	FORMAL DRESS
ENGINE HOUSE	FORMAL OFFER
ENGINE POWER	FORMAL VISIT
ERNEST BEVIN	FORMER PUPIL
ESCAPE DEATH	FORMER TIMES
ESCAPE HATCH	FOSTER CHILD
ESCAPE ROUTE	FOURTH FLOOR
ESTATE AGENT	FOURTH ROUND
EVELYN WAUGH	FREEZE DRIED
EXEUNT OMNES	FRENCH BEANS
EXPORT DRIVE	FRENCH BREAD
EXPORT ORDER	FRENCH CHALK
EXPORT TRADE	FRENCH COAST
FADING HOPES	FRENCH CONGO
FADING LIGHT	FRENCH FRANC
FAIRLY CLOSE	FRENCH FRIED
FALLEN ANGEL	FRENCH LEAVE
FAMILY ALBUM	FRIDAY NIGHT
FAMILY BIBLE	FROSTY SMILE
FAMILY HOTEL	FROZEN BEANS
FAMILY MOTTO	FROZEN NORTH
FAMILY PRIDE	FROZEN SOLID
FAMINE PRICE	FROZEN STIFF
FAMOUS WOMAN	FROZEN WATER
FAMOUS WOMEN	FRUITY VOICE
FARMER GILES	FUTURE PLANS
FATHER IMAGE	FUTURE TENSE
FEEBLE GRASP	GALLEY PROOF
FEEBLE VOICE	GALLEY SLAVE
FEMALE VOICE	GAMING HOUSE

GAMING	TABLE
GAMMON	STEAK
GARDEN	CHAIR
GARDEN	FENCE
GARDEN	PARTY
GARDEN	SPADE
GARDEN	TOOLS
GATHER	ROSES
GATHER	ROUND
GATHER	SPEED
GENTLE	CLIMB
GENTLE	SLOPE
GENTLE	TOUCH
GENTLE	VOICE
GEORGE	BROWN
GEORGE	BURNS
GEORGE	CROSS
GEORGE	ELIOT
GEORGE	MEDAL
GEORGE	MELLY
GIFTED	WOMAN
GILDED	YOUTH
GINGER	GROUP
GLIDER	PILOT
GLOSSY	PAINT
GOLDEN	APPLE
GOLDEN	ARROW
GOLDEN	BOUGH
GOLDEN	BROWN
GOLDEN	CURLS
GOLDEN	EAGLE
GOLDEN	GOOSE
GOLDEN	SANDS
GOLDEN	SYRUP
GOLDEN	TOUCH
GORDON	BANKS
GORDON	RIOTS
GOSPEL	MUSIC
GOSPEL	TRUTH
GOTHIC	STYLE
GRANNY	SMITH
GRAVEN	IMAGE
GREASE	PAINT
GRETNA	GREEN
GROUND	FLOOR
GROUND	FROST
GROUND	SPEED
GROUND	SPICE
GROUND	SWELL
GUILTY	PARTY
GUMMED	LABEL
GUSTAV	HOLST
GUTTER	PRESS
HAMMER	THROW
HANKER	AFTER
HAROLD	LLOYD
HARRIS	TWEED
HARVEY	SMITH
HEARTH	BRUSH
HEARTY	CHEER
HEARTY	EATER
HEARTY	LAUGH
HEATED	WORDS
HECTIC	FLUSH
HENRIK	IBSEN
HERALD	ANGEL
HEROIC	VERSE
HIDDEN	MERIT
HIDDEN	PANEL
HIDING	PLACE
HIGHER	CLASS
HIGHER	COURT
HIGHER	LEVEL
HIGHER	POWER
HIGHER	WAGES
HILTON	HOTEL
HITLER	YOUTH
HOARSE	LAUGH
HOARSE	VOICE
HOBBLE	SKIRT
HOCKEY	MATCH
HOCKEY	STICK
HOLLOW	BOAST
HOLLOW	LAUGH
HOLLOW	SOUND
HOLLOW	TRUCE
HOLLOW	TRUTH
HONEST	INJUN
HONEST	PENNY
HONEST	SWEAT
HONEST	TRUTH
HONEST	WOMAN
HONOUR	BOUND
HORNED	VIPER
HORROR	COMIC
HORSES	MOUTH
HUGHIE	GREEN
HUMBLE	BIRTH
HUNGER	MARCH
HUSHED	TONES
HUSHED	VOICE
INDIAN	BRAVE
INDIAN	CLUBS
INDIAN	OCEAN
INDIAN	SQUAW
INDIAN	TRIBE
INDOOR	GAMES
INSIDE	RIGHT
INSIDE	STORY
INSIDE	TRACK
JINGLE	BELLS
JOKING	APART
JOSHUA	NKOMO
JULIAN	BREAM
JUNGLE	FEVER
JUNGLE	JUICE
KIDNEY	BEANS
KILLER	WHALE
LABOUR	FORCE
LABOUR	PARTY
LADIES	FIRST
LATEST	CRAZE

LATEST ISSUE	MENTAL LAPSE
LATEST MODEL	MENTAL POWER
LATEST SCORE	MENTAL SHOCK
LATEST STYLE	MENTAL STATE
LATEST THING	MERSEY SOUND
LEAGUE MATCH	METHOD ACTOR
LEAGUE TABLE	MICKEY MOUSE
LEDGER CLERK	MIDDLE CLASS
LESSER BREED	MIDDLE STUMP
LIKELY STORY	MILTON OBOTE
LIQUID LUNCH	MINNIE MOUSE
LITMUS PAPER	MINUTE STEAK
LITTLE ANGEL	MINUTE WALTZ
LITTLE BOXES	MIRROR IMAGE
LITTLE CHILD	MISTER RIGHT
LITTLE DEVIL	MODERN DANCE
LITTLE EXTRA	MODERN DRESS
LITTLE KNOWN	MODERN HOUSE
LITTLE THING	MODERN IDIOM
LITTLE WHILE	MODERN MUSIC
LITTLE WOMEN	MODERN NOVEL
LIVELY PARTY	MODERN STYLE
LIVING DEATH	MODERN TIMES
LIVING IMAGE	MODERN TREND
LIVING PROOF	MODERN YOUTH
LIVING SPACE	MODEST HOPES
LIVING THING	MODEST MEANS
LIVING WATER	MOLTEN METAL
LIZARD POINT	MONDAY NIGHT
LONDON CRIES	MONEYS WORTH
LONDON DOCKS	MONKEY ABOUT
LONDON IRISH	MORRIS DANCE
LONDON PRIDE	MORTAL AGONY
LONDON STAGE	MORTAL ENEMY
LONDON WELSH	MORTAL PERIL
LOUNGE ABOUT	MORTAL WOUND
LOVELY MONEY	MOTHER EARTH
LOVELY SIGHT	MOTHER IMAGE
LUXURY GOODS	MOTIVE FORCE
LUXURY HOTEL	MOTIVE POWER
LUXURY SUITE	MOTLEY CROWD
MADRAS CURRY	MOULIN ROUGE
MAGGIE SMITH	MOVING FORCE
MARINE CORPS	MOVING PARTS
MARKED CARDS	MOVING SCENE
MARKET OVERT	MOVING SIGHT
MARKET PLACE	MOVING STORY
MARKET PRICE	MOVING WORDS
MARKET RASEN	MURDER TRIAL
MARKET TREND	MUSEUM PIECE
MARKET VALUE	MYSTIC RITES
MASSED BANDS	NARROW GAUGE
MASSED RANKS	NARROW SHAVE
MATURE YEARS	NATIVE CHIEF
MAUNDY MONEY	NATIVE DRESS
MEDIUM BUILD	NATIVE HEATH
MEDIUM STEAK	NATIVE TRIBE
MELODY MAKER	NATURE LOVER
MENDIP HILLS	NATURE STUDY
MENTAL GRASP	NEARLY READY
MENTAL IMAGE	NEARLY THERE

NEEDLE	MATCH	POLICE	FORCE
NEEDLE	POINT	POLICE	STATE
NETHER	WORLD	POLICY	MAKER
NEWTON	ABBOT	POSTAL	ORDER
NINETY	KILOS	POTATO	CHIPS
NINETY	MILES	POTATO	CRISP
NINETY	PENCE	POTATO	SALAD
NINETY	YEARS	POTTED	PLANT
NORMAL	STATE	POTTER	ABOUT
NORMAN	STYLE	PRANCE	ABOUT
NOTICE	BOARD	PRETTY	AWFUL
NUMBER	EIGHT	PRETTY	PENNY
NUMBER	PLATE	PRETTY	POLLY
NUMBER	SEVEN	PRETTY	SIGHT
NUMBER	THREE	PRETTY	SMART
OBITER	DICTA	PRETTY	STATE
OBTUSE	ANGLE	PRIMUS	STOVE
OFFICE	BLOCK	PRISON	GATES
OFFICE	CLERK	PRISON	GUARD
OFFICE	HOURS	PRISON	WALLS
OFFICE	PARTY	PRIVET	HEDGE
OFFICE	STAFF	PROMPT	REPLY
OLIVER	TWIST	PROPER	PLACE
ORANGE	DRINK	PROPER	SENSE
ORANGE	JUICE	PROPER	TITLE
ORPHAN	CHILD	PUBLIC	BATHS
OXFORD	SHOES	PUBLIC	ENEMY
OXFORD	UNION	PUBLIC	FUNDS
PACKED	HOUSE	PUBLIC	HOUSE
PACKED	LUNCH	PUBLIC	IMAGE
PALACE	GUARD	PUBLIC	MONEY
PAMPAS	GRASS	PUBLIC	PURSE
PANAMA	CANAL	PUBLIC	TASTE
PAPIER	MACHÉ	PUBLIC	WORKS
PARISH	CLERK	PUMICE	STONE
PASTEL	SHADE	PURPLE	HEART
PATENT	AGENT	PURPLE	PATCH
PATRON	SAINT	PYJAMA	PARTY
PAVING	STONE	QUARTO	PAPER
PAYING	GUEST	QUARTZ	CLOCK
PEARLY	GATES	QUARTZ	WATCH
PEARLY	QUEEN	QUEENS	AWARD
PEBBLE	BEACH	QUEENS	BENCH
PENCIL	SKIRT	QUOTED	PRICE
PERIOD	DRESS	RABBIT	HUTCH
PERIOD	HOUSE	RABBIT	PUNCH
PERIOD	PIECE	RACING	MODEL
PETROL	FUMES	RACING	WORLD
PETROL	GAUGE	RACING	YACHT
PETULA	CLARK	RAGGED	EDGES
PICKET	FENCE	RAGGED	ROBIN
PICNIC	PARTY	RAISED	VOICE
PILLOW	FIGHT	RAISIN	BREAD
PIRATE	RADIO	RAISON	DÊTRE
PLANET	EARTH	RANSOM	MONEY
PLAYER	PIANO	RAQUEL	WELCH
POCKET	GUIDE	RARITY	VALUE
POCKET	MONEY	RECENT	ISSUE
POETIC	STYLE	RECENT	YEARS
POLICE	CADET	RECORD	ALBUM
POLICE	COURT	RECORD	CROWD

RECORD	SCORE
RECORD	TOKEN
REDUCE	SPEED
REFLEX	ANGLE
REMAIN	ALOOF
REPORT	STAGE
RESCUE	PARTY
RETAIL	PRICE
RETAIL	TRADE
RETURN	FIGHT
RETURN	MATCH
RETURN	VISIT
RIDING	BOOTS
RIDING	HABIT
RISING	COSTS
RITUAL	DANCE
ROBBIE	BURNS
ROBERT	BOYLE
ROBERT	BURNS
ROBERT	CLIVE
ROBERT	FROST
ROCKET	RANGE
ROLLER	TOWEL
ROTARY	POWER
ROTARY	PRESS
ROTARY	VALVE
ROTTEN	APPLE
RUBBER	PLANT
RUBBER	SOLES
RUBBER	STAMP
RUGGER	MATCH
RUGGER	SCRUM
RUINED	HOUSE
RULING	CLASS
RULING	PARTY
RULING	POWER
RULING	PRICE
RUNNER	BEANS
SACRED	HEART
SACRED	MUSIC
SAFETY	CATCH
SAFETY	FIRST
SAFETY	MATCH
SAFETY	RAZOR
SAFETY	VALVE
SAINTS	ALIVE
SALMON	STEAK
SALMON	TROUT
SAMUEL	MORSE
SAMUEL	PEPYS
SANCHO	PANZA
SAVAGE	BEAST
SAVAGE	TRIBE
SAVING	GRACE
SAVOIR	FAIRE
SCARED	STIFF
SCHOOL	BADGE
SCHOOL	BOARD
SCHOOL	CHILD
SCHOOL	HOURS
SCHOOL	HOUSE
SCHOOL	LUNCH
SCHOOL	MEALS
SCILLY	ISLES
SCOTCH	BROTH
SEARCH	PARTY
SECOND	CHILD
SECOND	CLASS
SECOND	FLOOR
SECOND	FRONT
SECOND	GRADE
SECOND	HOUSE
SECOND	MONTH
SECOND	PARTY
SECOND	PLACE
SECOND	PRIZE
SECOND	ROUND
SECOND	SHIFT
SECOND	SIGHT
SECOND	STAGE
SECOND	VERSE
SECRET	AGENT
SECRET	ENEMY
SECRET	HAUNT
SECRET	PANEL
SECRET	PLACE
SECURE	GRASP
SENATE	HOUSE
SENILE	DECAY
SENIOR	PUPIL
SERIAL	STORY
SEVERE	FROST
SEVERE	SHOCK
SEWAGE	WORKS
SEWING	CLASS
SEXTON	BLAKE
SHABBY	TRICK
SHAGGY	BEARD
SHEILA	SCOTT
SHERRY	GLASS
SHERRY	PARTY
SHODDY	GOODS
SHREWD	GUESS
SHRILL	SOUND
SHRILL	VOICE
SICKLY	SMILE
SIERRA	LEONE
SIGNAL	CORPS
SIGNAL	LIGHT
SILENT	NIGHT
SILVER	BIRCH
SILVER	CROWN
SILVER	MEDAL
SILVER	MONEY
SILVER	PAPER
SILVER	PENNY
SILVER	PERCH
SILVER	PLATE
SILVER	SPOON
SIMPLE	HEART
SIMPLE	SIMON
SIMPLE	STYLE

SIMPLE TASTE	STOLEN GOODS
SIMPLE TRUTH	STONES THROW
SIMPLY AWFUL	STORMY NIGHT
SINGLE BERTH	STREAM FORTH
SINGLE CREAM	STREET CRIES
SINGLE ENTRY	STREET LEVEL
SINGLE PIECE	STREET LIGHT
SINGLE STATE	STREET PARTY
SINGLE TRACK	STREET SCENE
SINGLE VOICE	STRICT ORDER
SINGLE WOMAN	STRICT TEMPO
SLEIGH BELLS	STRICT TRUTH
SLICED BREAD	STRIKE BLIND
SLIGHT DOUBT	STRIKE FORCE
SLIGHT PAUSE	STRIKE LUCKY
SLINKY DRESS	STRING ALONG
SLOUCH ALONG	STRING BEANS
SMOKED GLASS	STRING MUSIC
SMOKED TROUT	STRONG DRINK
SNAKES ALIVE!	STRONG FAITH
SNOWED UNDER	STRONG LIGHT
SOCCER MATCH	STRONG POINT
SOCCER PITCH	STRONG POUND
SOCIAL CLASS	STRONG SMELL
SOCIAL GROUP	STRONG STUFF
SOCIAL ROUND	STRONG TASTE
SOCIAL SCALE	STRONG VIEWS
SOCIAL WHIRL	STRONG WORDS
SOILED GOODS	STUDIO COUCH
SOILED LINEN	STUPID WOMAN
SOLEMN MUSIC	STURDY BUILD
SOLEMN TRUTH	STURDY FRAME
SOLWAY FIRTH	SUCKER PUNCH
SOPHIA LOREN	SUDDEN BREAK
SORELY TRIED	SUDDEN DEATH
SOVIET UNION	SUDDEN SHOCK
SPIRIT LEVEL	SUMMER DRESS
SPOILT CHILD	SUMMER HOUSE
SPORTS ARENA	SUMMIT LEVEL
SPORTS MODEL	SUMMIT TALKS
SPORTS SHIRT	SUNDAY JOINT
SPREAD GLOOM	SUNDAY LUNCH
SPRING APART	SUNDAY NIGHT
SPRING CLEAN	SUNDAY PAPER
SPRING FEVER	SUNDAY TIMES
SPRING ONION	SUNSET STRIP
SPRING WATER	SUPPER PARTY
SQUARE DANCE	SUPPER TABLE
SQUARE METRE	SUPPLY DEPOT
SQUARE WORLD	SWANEE RIVER
SQUASH COURT	SWIVEL CHAIR
STARRY NIGHT	TALENT SCOUT
STEADY FLAME	TARTAN CLOTH
STEADY PULSE	TARTAN SKIRT
STEADY TREND	TEMPUS FUGIT
STEWED FRUIT	TENDER HEART
STICKY LABEL	TENDER MERCY
STICKY PAPER	TENDER STEAK
STICKY PATCH	TENDER YEARS
STICKY STUFF	TENNIS COURT
STICKY SWEET	TENNIS DRESS

TENNIS ELBOW
TENNIS MATCH
TENNIS SHOES
TESSIE OSHEA
THAMES BASIN
THIRST AFTER
THIRTY FORTY
THIRTY KILOS
THIRTY MILES
THIRTY PENCE
THIRTY YEARS
THOMAS HARDY
THOMAS MOORE
THRASH ABOUT
THRUST ASIDE
TICKET AGENT
TICKLE TROUT
TIMBER TRADE
TINNED BEANS
TINNED FRUIT
TINNED GOODS
TINNED PEARS
TISSUE PAPER
TOFFEE APPLE
TOILET PAPER
TOILET WATER
TOMATO JUICE
TOMATO SAUCE
TOTTER ABOUT
TRAGIC DEATH
TRAGIC EVENT
TRAGIC IRONY
TRAGIC SCENE
TRAVEL ABOUT
TRAVEL AGENT
TRAVEL ALONG
TRAVEL LIGHT
TRENCH FEVER
TRIPLE CROWN
TRIPLE EVENT
TROJAN HORSE
TRUSTY STEED
TRUSTY SWORD
TRYING TIMES
TWELVE DOZEN
TWELVE GROSS
TWELVE HOURS
TWELVE MILES
TWELVE PENCE
TWELVE TIMES
TWELVE YEARS
TWENTY GROSS
TWENTY HOURS
TWENTY KILOS
TWENTY MILES
TWENTY PENCE
TWENTY WEEKS
TWENTY YEARS
TYPING ERROR
TYPING SPEED
UNBORN CHILD

UNEASY PEACE
UNEASY TRUCE
UNFAIR MEANS
UNHOLY NOISE
UNITED FRONT
UPHILL CLIMB
UPHILL FIGHT
UTMOST SPEED
VACANT STARE
VACUUM FLASK
VAPOUR TRAIL
VELVET GLOVE
VIRGIN BIRTH
VIRGIN QUEEN
VIVIEN LEIGH
VOLUME THREE
VOTING PAPER
VULGAR TASTE
WAKING HOURS
WALTER HAGEN
WALTER MITTY
WALTER SCOTT
WANDER ABOUT
WANING LIGHT
WATERY GRAVE
WEDDED BLISS
WEEKLY PAPER
WICKED FAIRY
WICKED UNCLE
WICKED WITCH
WICKER CHAIR
WIDOWS WEEDS
WINDOW BLIND
WINDOW FRAME
WINDOW LEDGE
WINGED HORSE
WINTER SLEEP
WISDOM TOOTH
WITCHS SPELL
WITHIN RANGE
WITHIN REACH
WITHIN SIGHT
WOBURN ABBEY
WONDER WOMAN
WOODEN BENCH
WOODEN CHAIR
WOODEN FRAME
WOODEN HORSE
WOODEN SPOON
WORLDS APART
WORTHY CAUSE
YELLOW FEVER
YELLOW OCHRE
YELLOW PAGES
YELLOW PAINT
YELLOW PERIL
YELLOW PRESS
YELLOW RIVER

7 , 1 , 3

CONVERT A TRY
HARBOUR A SPY

7 , 2 , 2

HUSBAND TO BE
NOTHING TO DO
NOTHING TO IT
NOWHERE TO GO
ROLLING IN IT

7 , 4

ABANDON HOPE
ABANDON SHIP
ACCOUNT BOOK
ACCOUNT PAID
ADDRESS BOOK
ADVANCE COPY
AEOLIAN HARP
AGAINST TIME
AMATEUR SIDE
AMATEUR TEAM
ANCIENT CITY
ANCIENT ROME
ANCIENT RUIN
ANGELIC HOST
ANGLING CLUB
ANISEED BALL
ANOTHER TIME
ANTHONY EDEN
ANTIQUE SHOP
ANXIOUS TIME
APPLIED MATH
AQUATIC LIFE
ARTHURS SEAT
ASIATIC RACE
ASSUMED NAME
ATTACHÉ CASE
AUCTION ROOM
AUCTION SALE
AUTHORS NOTE
AVERAGE TYPE
AVERAGE WAGE
AVOCADO PEAR
AWKWARD TIME
BALCONY SEAT
BANBURY CAKE
BARBERS POLE
BARBERS SHOP
BARGAIN SALE
BARKING DOGS
BARRACK ROOM
BARRIER REEF
BATHING POOL
BATHING SUIT
BATTING SIDE
BEARDED LADY
BEDSIDE LAMP

BEGGING BOWL
BERNARD SHAW
BETTING SHOP
BETTING SLIP
BICYCLE BELL
BICYCLE PUMP
BICYCLE RACE
BISHOPS PAWN
BLAZING FIRE
BOATING SONG
BOOKING HALL
BOTTLED BEER
BRAISED BEEF
BREATHE FIRE
BREATHE HARD
BREWERS DRAY
BRISTOL CITY
BRISTOL MILK
BRITISH ARMY
BRITISH CAMP
BRITISH FILM
BRITISH FLAG
BRITISH LION
BRITISH MADE
BRITISH NAVY
BRITISH RAIL
BRITISH RULE
BRITISH ZONE
BRONZED SKIN
BROTHER LOVE
BROUGHT BACK
BROUGHT DOWN
BROUGHT HOME
BUDDING POET
BUFFALO BILL
BULGING EYES
BURNING BUSH
CABARET STAR
CABBAGE LEAF
CABBAGE MOTH
CABBAGE ROSE
CABINET POST
CAESARS WIFE
CALLING CARD
CAMPING SITE
CANDIED PEEL
CAPITAL CITY
CAPITAL GAIN
CAPITAL IDEA
CAPTAIN COOK
CAPTAIN HOOK
CAPTAIN KIDD
CAPTAIN NEMO
CAPTAIN WEBB
CARAVAN SITE
CARDIFF CITY
CAREFUL LOOK
CARLTON CLUB
CARRIED AWAY
CARRION CROW
CASSIUS CLAY

CASTILE SOAP	CRICKET CLUB
CASTING VOTE	CRICKET PADS
CATHODE RAYS	CRICKET TEAM
CAUSTIC SODA	CRIMSON LAKE
CAVALRY UNIT	CROOKED MILE
CENTRAL ASIA	CROOKED PATH
CENTRAL HALL	CROPPED HAIR
CENTRAL LINE	CROQUET BALL
CENTRAL PARK	CROQUET HOOP
CERTAIN CURE	CROQUET LAWN
CERTAIN GAIN	CROWDED HOUR
CHAFING DISH	CROWDED ROOM
CHANNEL SWIM	CROWNED HEAD
CHAPTER FIVE	CRUCIAL TEST
CHAPTER FOUR	CRUCIAL TIME
CHARIOT RACE	CRUMBLE AWAY
CHARLES LAMB	CRYPTIC CLUE
CHARMED LIFE	CRYSTAL BALL
CHICKEN COOP	CURDLED MILK
CHICKEN FARM	CURLING IRON
CHICKEN FEED	CURRANT LOAF
CHICKEN SOUP	CURRENT DATE
CHICKEN WIRE	CURRENT NEWS
CHIMNEY TOPS	CURRENT YEAR
CHINESE FOOD	CURTAIN CALL
CHINESE JUNK	CURTAIN HOOK
CHINESE MEAL	CURTAIN RAIL
CITIZEN KANE	CUSTARD TART
CLARION CALL	CUSTOMS DUTY
CLASSIC RACE	CUTTING EDGE
CLEARLY SEEN	CUTTING WIND
CLOSING DATE	CYCLING CLUB
CLOSING TIME	DANCING BEAR
CLOTHES LINE	DANCING GIRL
COASTAL ROAD	DARKEST HOUR
COCONUT PALM	DARTING PAIN
COLLECT DUST	DEATHLY HUSH
COLLEGE GIRL	DEATHLY PALE
COMPOST HEAP	DEBORAH KERR
CONCERT HALL	DEFENCE WORK
CONTACT LENS	DESSERT FORK
CONTACT MINE	DEVOTED WIFE
CONTOUR LINE	DIAMOND MINE
COOKERY BOOK	DIAMOND RING
COPPERS NARK	DISPLAY UNIT
CORRECT TIME	DISTAFF SIDE
COSTUME BALL	DISTANT PAST
COSTUME PLAY	DIVORCE CASE
COTTAGE LOAF	DIVORCE RATE
COUNCIL FLAT	DIVORCE SUIT
COUNTRY CLUB	DOLEFUL LOOK
COUNTRY CODE	DRAUGHT BEER
COUNTRY LANE	DRAWING ROOM
COUNTRY LIFE	DRESSED CRAB
COUNTRY ROCK	DREYFUS CASE
COUNTRY SEAT	DRIVING IRON
COUNTRY TOWN	DRIVING RAIN
COUNTRY WALK	DRIVING TEST
COWSLIP WINE	DROPPED GOAL
CREAMED RICE	DRUNKEN ORGY
CRICKET BALL	DWINDLE AWAY

EASTERN BLOC	FOREIGN NEWS
ECONOMY SIZE	FOREIGN RULE
EJECTOR SEAT	FOREIGN SOIL
ELASTIC BAND	FORLORN HOPE
ELEANOR BRON	FORSYTE SAGA
EMERALD ISLE	FORWARD GEAR
EMERALD RING	FORWARD LINE
ENDLESS BELT	FORWARD PASS
ENDLESS TIME	FORWARD PLAY
ENGAGED TONE	FRANTIC PACE
ENGLISH HORN	FRESNEL LENS
ENGLISH ROSE	FRITTER AWAY
ENLARGE UPON	FUNERAL HYMN
ETERNAL CITY	FUNERAL PILE
ETERNAL LIFE	FUNERAL PYRE
ETERNAL REST	FUNERAL SONG
EVENING GOWN	FURIOUS MOOD
EVENING MEAL	FURIOUS PACE
EVENING NEWS	FURTHER DOWN
EVENING STAR	GENERAL IDEA
EXHAUST PIPE	GENERAL POST
EXPLAIN AWAY	GENERAL RATE
EXPRESS LIFT	GENERAL RULE
EXPRESS POST	GENERAL VIEW
EXTREME CASE	GENERIC NAME
EXTREME PAIN	GENGHIS KHAN
FACTORY ACTS	GENUINE CASE
FACTORY GATE	GETTING WELL
FACTORY HAND	GHASTLY MESS
FALLING DOWN	GLAMOUR GIRL
FALLING STAR	GLEEFUL MOOD
FARMERS WIFE	GLEEFUL NEWS
FASHION SHOW	GNAWING PAIN
FATIGUE DUTY	GORDIAN KNOT
FEARFUL BORE	GORGONS HEAD
FEATURE FILM	GRAPHIC ARTS
FEEDING TIME	GREATER PART
FEELING GOOD	GRECIAN NOSE
FERTILE LAND	GREGORY PECK
FERTILE MIND	GRILLED CHOP
FERTILE SOIL	GRILLED FISH
FERVENT HOPE	GRILLED PORK
FESTIVE MOOD	GRILLED SOLE
FEVERED BROW	GRIMSBY TOWN
FIFTEEN LOVE	GRIZZLY BEAR
FINANCE BILL	GROUCHO MARX
FINGALS CAVE	GROWING GIRL
FISHING BIRD	GROWING PAIN
FISHING BOAT	GUIDING HAND
FISHING LINE	GUIDING STAR
FITTING ROOM	HAGGARD LOOK
FIXTURE LIST	HAIRPIN BEND
FLAMING JUNE	HALCYON DAYS
FLOWING HAIR	HALFWAY LINE
FLUTTER DOWN	HALIFAX TOWN
FONDEST LOVE	HALTING GAIT
FOOLISH IDEA	HAMPTON WICK
FOOLISH TALK	HARICOT BEAN
FOREIGN BODY	HARVEST HOME
FOREIGN COIN	HARVEST MOON
FOREIGN LAND	HARVEST TIME

HATEFUL TASK	KNITTED BROW
HEALTHY BODY	KNOCKED DOWN
HEALTHY MIND	KNOWING LOOK
HELPING HAND	KNUCKLE DOWN
HERRING GULL	LAMBETH WALK
HIGHWAY CODE	LANDING GEAR
HISTORY BOOK	LARGEST PART
HOLIDAY CAMP	LATTICE WORK
HOLIDAY HOME	LAUNDRY MAID
HOLIDAY MOOD	LEADING EDGE
HOLIDAY SNAP	LEADING LADY
HOLIDAY TASK	LEADING NOTE
HOLIDAY TIME	LEADING PART
HONITON LACE	LEADING ROLE
HONOURS EVEN	LEADING WREN
HONOURS LIST	LEATHER BELT
HOPEFUL SIGN	LEATHER COAT
HORNETS NEST	LEATHER SOLE
HOWLING WIND	LEAVING HOME
HUMMING BIRD	LECTURE HALL
HUNDRED DAYS	LECTURE TOUR
HUNDRED FEET	LEISURE TIME
HUNDRED QUID	LENDING RATE
HUNTERS MOON	LETTERS PAGE
HUNTING HORN	LIBERAL ARTS
HUNTING PINK	LIBERAL VIEW
HURRIED MEAL	LIBRARY BOOK
IGNEOUS ROCK	LIDDELL HART
ILLICIT LOVE	LIGHTER FUEL
INITIAL MOVE	LIGHTER SIDE
INJURED BACK	LIGHTER VEIN
INJURED LOOK	LIMITED TIME
INSTANT CURE	LINCOLN CITY
INTENSE COLD	LOGICAL MIND
INTENSE HEAT	LOGICAL STEP
IPSWICH TOWN	LOOKING GOOD
ITALIAN ALPS	LUGGAGE RACK
ITALIAN WINE	MACHINE HAND
JACQUES TATI	MACHINE MADE
JEALOUS WIFE	MACHINE SHOP
JELLIED EELS	MACHINE TOOL
JUBILEE LINE	MADEIRA CAKE
JUBILEE YEAR	MADEIRA WINE
JUGULAR VEIN	MADONNA LILY
JUMPING BEAN	MAGINOT LINE
JUMPING JACK	MAILING LIST
JUNIPER TREE	MANSARD ROOF
KELLOGG PACT	MARRIED LIFE
KEMPTON PARK	MARRIED NAME
KENNETH MORE	MARSHAL TITO
KENTISH TOWN	MARSTON MOOR
KILLING PACE	MARTIAL ARTS
KINDRED SOUL	MASONIC HALL
KINGDOM COME	MATINÉE IDOL
KISSING GATE	MAXIMUM FINE
KITCHEN FIRE	MEASURE TIME
KITCHEN HAND	MEDICAL CARE
KITCHEN MAID	MEDICAL CASE
KITCHEN SINK	MEDICAL TEST
KITCHEN UNIT	MEMBERS ONLY
KNIGHTS PAWN	MICHAEL FOOT

MICHAEL	YORK	OPINION	POLL
MIDLAND	BANK	ORDERLY	DUTY
MINERAL	SALT	ORDERLY	ROOM
MINERAL	VEIN	ORGANIC	LIFE
MINIMUM	WAGE	OUTDOOR	GAME
MINUTES	LATE	OUTDOOR	LIFE
MIRACLE	DRUG	OUTSIDE	LANE
MIRACLE	PLAY	OUTSIDE	LEFT
MISSING	LINK	OUTSIDE	WORK
MOCKING	BIRD	OUTWARD	SHOW
MONTHLY	RENT	OUTWARD	SIGN
MORNING	CALL	PACKAGE	DEAL
MORNING	COAT	PACKAGE	TOUR
MORNING	ROOM	PAINTED	FACE
MORNING	STAR	PAINTED	LADY
MORNING	SUIT	PAINTED	SHIP
MORTICE	LOCK	PANCAKE	RACE
MOSELLE	WINE	PARKING	FINE
MOTHERS	HELP	PARLOUR	GAME
MOTHERS	MILK	PARLOUR	MAID
MOTHERS	RUIN	PARSONS	NOSE
MOVABLE	TYPE	PARTING	GIFT
MUSICAL	NOTE	PARTING	SHOT
MUSICAL	SHOW	PASSING	SHOW
MUSICAL	WORK	PASSING	TIME
MUSTARD	SEED	PASSING	WHIM
MUSWELL	HILL	PASSION	PLAY
MYSTERY	PLAY	PASSION	WEEK
MYSTERY	SHIP	PASSIVE	ROLE
MYSTERY	TOUR	PASSIVE	VERB
MYSTERY	TRIP	PEACOCK	BLUE
NAGGING	PAIN	PELTING	RAIN
NAGGING	WIFE	PENALTY	AREA
NATURAL	BENT	PENALTY	GOAL
NATURAL	GIFT	PENALTY	KICK
NATURAL	LIFE	PENALTY	LINE
NATWEST	BANK	PENALTY	SPOT
NAUGHTY	GIRL	PENSION	FUND
NAUGHTY	WORD	PENSIVE	MOOD
NETBALL	TEAM	PERFECT	CASE
NEUTRAL	ZONE	PERFECT	FOOL
NOBODYS	FOOL	PERFECT	HOST
NOMADIC	RACE	PERFECT	LADY
NOMINAL	HEAD	PERFECT	WIFE
NOMINAL	RATE	PERSIAN	GULF
NOMINAL	RENT	PERSIAN	LAMB
NORFOLK	SUIT	PHANTOM	SHIP
NORWICH	CITY	PHINEAS	FINN
NOTHING	ELSE	PHOENIX	PARK
NOTHING	LEFT	PICTURE	BOOK
NOTHING	LIKE	PICTURE	POST
NOTHING	MUCH	PICTURE	RAIL
NOWHERE	NEAR	PICTURE	SHOW
NUCLEAR	BOMB	PIERCED	EARS
NURSERY	MAID	PIGEONS	MILK
NURSERY	TALE	PILLION	RIDE
NURSING	HOME	PILLION	SEAT
OLYMPIC	TEAM	PIRANHA	FISH
ONEROUS	TASK	PLASTER	CAST
OPENING	MOVE	PLASTIC	DISC
OPENING	TIME	PLASTIC	TUBE

PLAYING CARD	REGULAR ARMY
POPULAR HERO	REGULAR HERO
POPULAR NAME	REGULAR VERB
POPULAR SONG	RELEASE DATE
POPULAR TUNE	RENEWED HOPE
POSTAGE FREE	REQUEST STOP
POSTAGE PAID	REQUIEM MASS
POSTERN GATE	RESERVE TEAM
POTTERS CLAY	RETIRED HURT
POTTING SHED	REVERSE GEAR
POULTRY FARM	RHENISH WINE
POURING RAIN	RHUBARB TART
POVERTY LINE	RINGING TONE
PRAIRIE FIRE	RIPPING YARN
PRAIRIE WOLF	ROARING FIRE
PRECISE TIME	ROLLING GAIT
PREMIUM BOND	ROLLING HOME
PRESENT ARMS	ROUSING SONG
PRESENT TIME	ROWLAND HILL
PRESSED BEEF	RUBBISH DUMP
PRESTER JOHN	RUBBISH HEAP
PRICKLY HEAT	RUMMAGE SALE
PRICKLY PEAR	RUNNING COLD
PRIESTS HOLE	RUNNING COST
PRINTED PAGE	RUNNING FIRE
PRINTED WORD	RUNNING JUMP
PRIVATE BILL	RUNNING KNOT
PRIVATE HELL	RUNNING RIOT
PRIVATE LIFE	RUNNING SORE
PRIVATE ROAD	RUNNING WILD
PRIVATE ROOM	SAILING BOAT
PRIVATE SALE	SAILING CLUB
PRIVATE WARD	SAILING SHIP
PROBATE DUTY	SAILING TIME
PROBLEM PLAY	SAILORS KNOT
PROMISE WELL	SANDOWN PARK
PROTEST VOTE	SAUSAGE MEAT
PRUSSIC ACID	SAUSAGE ROLL
PUDDING BOWL	SAVINGS BANK
QUARTER DECK	SAVOURY FOOD
QUARTER MILE	SCAFELL PIKE
QUARTER PAST	SCENTED SOAP
QUIETEN DOWN	SCRAPPY MEAL
RABBITS FOOT	SCRATCH CREW
RADIANT HEAT	SCRATCH SIDE
RADICAL CURE	SCRATCH TEAM
RADICAL VIEW	SEASIDE TOWN
RAGTIME BAND	SECONDS AWAY
RAILWAY LINE	SECONDS LATE
RAMBLER ROSE	SECURED LOAN
READING DESK	SERIOUS LOOK
READING GAOL	SERIOUS LOSS
READING LAMP	SERIOUS MIND
READING LIST	SERIOUS MOOD
READING ROOM	SERIOUS STEP
RECEIPT BOOK	SERIOUS TALK
REDUCED FARE	SERIOUS VEIN
REDUCED RATE	SERIOUS VIEW
REFUGEE CAMP	SERVANT GIRL
REGATTA WEEK	SERVICE FLAT
REGENTS PARK	SERVICE LIFT

SERVICE LINE	SURFACE AREA
SERVICE ROAD	SURFACE MAIL
SERVING TIME	SURPLUS CASH
SHALLOW DISH	SWALLOW DIVE
SHANKSS MARE	SWANSEA CITY
SHANKSS PONY	SWEENEY TODD
SHAVING SOAP	SWINDON TOWN
SHINING HOUR	SWOLLEN HEAD
SILVERY MOON	TALKING BIRD
SIMPLON PASS	TALKING DOLL
SINGING BIRD	TAMMANY HALL
SINGING SAND	TEDIOUS WORK
SINKING FUND	TEEMING RAIN
SINKING SHIP	TESTING TIME
SITTING BULL	THEATRE CLUB
SITTING DOWN	THEATRE LAND
SITTING DUCK	THEATRE SEAT
SITTING ROOM	THEATRE SHOW
SKATING RINK	THERMAL UNIT
SKILLED WORK	THIRSTY WORK
SKIMMED MILK	THROUGH ROAD
SLENDER HOPE	TICKLED PINK
SLIDING DOOR	TINKERS CUSS
SLIDING ROOF	TOBACCO ROAD
SLIDING RULE	TORPEDO BOAT
SLIDING SEAT	TOURING CLUB
SLIPPED DISC	TOURING SHOW
SLOPING EDGE	TOUSLED HAIR
SLOPING ROOF	TRADING POST
SMOKING ROOM	TRAFFIC DUTY
SOCIETY LADY	TRAFFIC LANE
SOCIETY NEWS	TRAMPLE DOWN
SOCIETY PAGE	TREACLE TART
SOLDIER KING	TRINITY HALL
SOMEONE ELSE	TRIUMPH OVER
SPANISH GOLD	TROUBLE FREE
SPANISH MAIN	TROUBLE SPOT
SPANISH WINE	TROUSER SUIT
SPARTAN FARE	TRUMPET CALL
SPECIAL CARE	TUESDAY WEEK
SPECIAL CASE	TUITION FEES
SPECIAL DIET	TURKISH BATH
SPECIAL DUTY	TWELFTH HOUR
SPECIAL GIFT	TYPICAL CASE
SPECIAL NOTE	UNDYING LOVE
SPOTTED DICK	UNIFORM SIZE
STATELY HOME	UNLUCKY STAR
STATUTE BOOK	UNSOUND MIND
STATUTE MILE	UNUSUAL NAME
STEAMED FISH	VARIETY SHOW
STIRRUP PUMP	VATICAN CITY
STOMACH ACHE	VAULTED ROOF
STRANGE LAND	VICTORY ROLL
STUDENT BODY	VICTORY SIGN
STUDENT DAYS	VILLAGE FÊTE
STUFFED BIRD	VILLAGE HALL
STUMBLE OVER	VILLAGE LIFE
STUMBLE UPON	VILLAGE POND
SUICIDE NOTE	VILLAGE PUMP
SUICIDE PACT	VILLAGE SHOP
SUPPORT LIFE	VINTAGE PORT

VINTAGE WINE
VINTAGE YEAR
VIOLENT BLOW
VIOLENT RAGE
VITAMIN PILL
WAILING WALL
WAITING GAME
WAITING LIST
WAITING ROOM
WALKING PACE
WALKING RACE
WALKING TOUR
WARNING LOOK
WARNING NOTE
WARNING SHOT
WASHING LINE
WASHING SOAP
WASHING SODA
WATERED SILK
WEAKEST LINK
WEATHER SIDE
WEDDING CAKE
WEDDING CARD
WEDDING GIFT
WEDDING RING
WEDDING VOWS
WELCOME BACK
WELCOME HOME
WELCOME NEWS
WELCOME SIGN
WELFARE WORK
WESTERN ROLL
WHITSUN WEEK
WHITTLE DOWN
WILLIAM CODY
WILLIAM PENN
WILLIAM PITT
WILLIAM TAFT
WILLIAM TELL
WILLING HAND
WILLING HELP
WINDING ROAD
WINNING CARD
WINNING GAME
WINNING GOAL
WINNING HAND
WINNING LEAD
WINNING MOVE
WINNING POST
WINNING SHOT
WINNING SIDE
WINNING TEAM
WINNING TIME
WINNING WAYS
WINTERS TALE
WISHING WELL
WITCHES BREW
WITHOUT FAIL
WITHOUT LOSS
WITHOUT PEER
WITHOUT PITY

WORKING GIRL
WORKING LIFE
WORKING WEEK
WORKING WIFE
WORKING YEAR
WORLDLY WISE
WORRIED LOOK
WRESTLE WITH
WRITING DESK
WRITTEN WORD
WROUGHT IRON

8, 3

ABSTRACT ART
ADRIATIC SEA
ADVANCED AGE
ALISTAIR SIM
ALMIGHTY GOD
AMERICAN LAW
AMERICAN SPY
AMERICAN WAR
ARMCHAIR JOB
ARMOURED CAR
BACHELOR PAD
BACKROOM BOY
BACKWARD BOY
BASEBALL BAT
BEARSKIN RUG
BILLIARD CUE
CALCUTTA CUP
CAMBRIAN AGE
CAPTAINS LOG
CARDIGAN BAY
CARDINAL RED
CARDINAL SIN
CHANCERY INN
CHESHIRE CAT
CIRCULAR SAW
COCKTAIL BAR
COLONIAL WAR
COLOURED MAN
COMPLETE ASS
COMPLETE LIE
COMPLETE SET
CONSTANT USE
CONTRACT LAW
CONTRACT OUT
CRIMINAL LAW
CULINARY ART
DAZZLING WIT
DEFERRED PAY
DEFERRED TAX
DELICATE BOY
DELIVERY MAN
DISPATCH BOX
DIVINING ROD
DIVISION ONE
DIVISION SUM
DIVISION TWO
DOMESTIC PET

DOMINANT KEY	MARITIME LAW
DRAMATIC ART	MARRYING MAN
DRIPPING WET	MATCHING SET
DROWNING MAN	MEDICINE MAN
ECONOMIC AID	MEMORIAL DAY
ECONOMIC LAW	MENTALLY ILL
EDUCATED MAN	MIDNIGHT OIL
EGYPTIAN GOD	MIDNIGHT SUN
ELECTION DAY	MILITARY AID
ELECTRIC EEL	MILITARY LAW
ELECTRIC EYE	MILITARY MAN
ELECTRIC FAN	MINSTREL BOY
ELECTRIC RAY	MORTALLY ILL
ELEPHANT GUN	MOSQUITO NET
ELEVENTH DAY	MOUNTAIN ASH
ENABLING ACT	MOUNTAIN DEW
ENLISTED MAN	MOUNTAIN TOP
ENTRANCE FEE	MUHAMMAD ALI
ESCAPING GAS	NINETEEN TEN
EUROPEAN CUP	OPPOSITE SEX
FAINTING FIT	ORDINARY MAN
FAITHFUL FEW	ORDNANCE MAP
FIGHTING FIT	ORIENTAL ART
FIGHTING MAN	ORIGINAL SIN
FLOATING RIB	ORTHODOX JEW
FOOTBALL FAN	OUTRIGHT WIN
FOUNTAIN PEN	OVERCAST SKY
FRIENDLY ACT	OVERTIME PAY
FRIENDLY TIP	PANDORAS BOX
FRIGHTEN OFF	PEACEFUL END
GAMBLING DEN	PILTDOWN MAN
GAMBLING MAN	PLEASANT DAY
GLORIOUS DAY	PRACTICE RUN
GLORIOUS FUN	PRACTISE LAW
GLORIOUS MUD	PRINTERS INK
GRESHAMS LAW	PRINTING INK
GUERILLA WAR	PRODIGAL SON
HANDSOME BOY	PROPERTY TAX
HANDSOME MAN	PROVIDED FOR
HANDSOME SUM	PURCHASE TAX
HANDSOME TIP	QUICKEST WAY
HERMETIC ART	RAINBOWS END
HOSPITAL BED	RALLYING CRY
IGNITION KEY	RETIRING AGE
IGNORANT MAN	ROADSIDE INN
IMPROPER USE	ROASTING HOT
INDIRECT TAX	ROMANTIC ART
INNOCENT MAN	SANDWICH BAR
JAUNTING CAR	SAUCEPAN LID
JOURNEYS END	SCOTTISH LAW
JUDGMENT DAY	SCOURING PAD
JUGGLING ACT	SEETHING MOB
KILKENNY CAT	SENSIBLE BOY
LAUGHING GAS	SENSIBLE MAN
LINCOLNS INN	SETTLING DAY
LITERARY MAN	SHEPHERD BOY
LIVELONG DAY	SHOOTING BOX
LOLLIPOP MAN	SHOOTING WAR
MACASSAR OIL	SHOPPING BAG
MACKEREL SKY	SHORTEST DAY
MANICURE SET	SHORTEST WAY

SHOULDER BAG
SIXPENNY BIT
SKELETON KEY
SLEEPING BAG
SLEEPING CAR
SLEEPING DOG
SLIPPERY EEL
SOLDIERS KIT
SOLDIERS PAY
SOLITARY MAN
SPELLING BEE
SPINNING TOP
SPORTING DOG
SPORTING GUN
SPORTING MAN
STANDARD EGG
STARTERS GUN
STARTING GUN
STEAMING HOT
STRAIGHT BAT
STRAIGHT HIT
STRAIGHT MAN
STRAIGHT OFF
STRAIGHT RUN
STRAIGHT SET
STRAIGHT TIP
STRAIGHT WIN
STUBBORN MAN
STUDENTS RAG
SUPERIOR AIR
TACTICAL WAR
TAKEOVER BID
TEACHERS PET
TEACHING AID
TELEGRAM BOY
THESPIAN ART
THINKING CAP
TOBOGGAN RUN
TRANSFER FEE
TROPICAL SEA
TROPICAL SUN
ULTIMATE END
UNBROKEN RUN
UNCALLED FOR
UNLAWFUL ACT
UNTIMELY END
VAGRANCY ACT
VENETIAN RED
VISITING DAY
VOLATILE OIL
VOLATILE WIT
VOLCANIC ASH
WATCHFUL EYE
WATERING CAN
WHACKING LIE
WHIPPING BOY
WHOPPING LIE
WIGHTMAN CUP
WIRELESS SET
WRETCHED MAN
WRINGING WET

YACHTING CAP
YOUNGEST BOY
YOUNGEST SON

1 , 1 , 10

G.K.CHESTERTON
P.T.INSTRUCTOR

1 , 4 , 1 , 6

A MILE A MINUTE

1 , 4 , 3 , 4

A LONG WAY AWAY

1 , 4 , 4 , 3

A LONG TIME AGO

1 , 4 , 7

A FINE ROMANCE

1 , 6 , 5

A LITTLE EXTRA

2 , 1 , 4 , 5

BY A LONG CHALK
IN A COLD SWEAT
IN A GOOD LIGHT

2 , 1 , 5 , 4

AT A LATER DATE
BY A SHORT HEAD
DO A HANDS TURN
IN A SHORT TIME
ON A LEVEL WITH

2 , 1 , 9

DO A HANDSTAND
ON A STRETCHER

2 , 2 , 1 , 7

GO TO A WEDDING

2 , 2 , 2 , 6

DO IT BY HALVES
GO ON AN ERRAND
GO UP IN FLAMES

2 , 2 , 3 , 5

```
DO  NO  MAN  WRONG
GO  BY  THE  BOARD
GO  ON  ALL  FOURS
GO  ON  THE  STAGE
GO  TO  BED  EARLY
GO  TO  THE  DEVIL
GO  TO  THE  FRONT
GO  TO  THE  OPERA
GO  TO  THE  POLLS
GO  TO  THE  RACES
IN  AT  THE  DEATH
UP  TO  THE  NINES
UP  TO  THE  WAIST
```

2 , 2 , 4 , 4

```
DO  AS  ONES  TOLD
DO  AS  ROME  DOES
GO  TO  ONES  HEAD
JE  NE  SAIS  QUOI
ON  AN  EVEN  KEEL
UP  TO  ONES  EYES
UP  TO  ONES  NECK
```

2 , 2 , 6 , 2

```
DO  AS  OTHERS  DO
```

2 , 2 , 8

```
DO  IT  YOURSELF
GO  TO  EXTREMES
IN  AN  ACCIDENT
TO  BE  EXPECTED
UP  TO  STANDARD
UP  TO  STRENGTH
```

2 , 3 , 1 , 6

```
DO  ONE  A  FAVOUR
GO  FOR  A  BURTON
GO  FOR  A  STROLL
```

2 , 3 , 2 , 1 , 4

```
AS  FAR  AS  I  KNOW
BY  WAY  OF  A  JOKE
```

2 , 3 , 2 , 3 , 2

```
ON  THE  UP - AND - UP
```

2 , 3 , 2 , 5

```
NO  BED  OF  ROSES
NO  END  IN  SIGHT
NO  END  OF  MONEY
TO  ERR  IS  HUMAN
```

2 , 3 , 3 , 4

```
BY  FAR  THE  BEST
GO  FOR  THE  BULL
GO  HOT  AND  COLD
IF  THE  CAP  FITS
IN  FOR  THE  KILL
IN  OFF  THE  POST
IN  THE  OLD  DAYS
ON  THE  FAR  SIDE
ON  THE  LEE  SIDE
ON  THE  LEG - SIDE
ON  THE  OFF - SIDE
ON  THE  ONE  HAND
ON  THE  TOP  RUNG
ON  THE  WAY  DOWN
```

2 , 3 , 4 , 3

```
AT  THE  DEEP  END
BE  OFF  WITH  YOU
GO  THE  LONG  WAY
GO  THE  SAME  WAY
IN  THE  DEEP  END
IN  THE  LONG  RUN
IN  THE  OPEN  AIR
IN  THE  VERY  ACT
ON  THE  LOOK - OUT
TO  THE  LAST  MAN
```

2 , 3 , 7

```
AT  ALL  HAZARDS
AT  THE  SEASIDE
AT  THE  STATION
AT  THE  THEATRE
BY  THE  SEASIDE
BY  THE  WAYSIDE
DO  NOT  DISTURB
DO  THE  HONOURS
DO  THE  WASHING
GO  FOR  NOTHING
IN  ALL  HONESTY
IN  ANY  RESPECT
IN  HOT  PURSUIT
IN  ITS  INFANCY
IN  LOW  SPIRITS
IN  ONE  RESPECT
IN  OUR  OPINION
IN  THE  BALANCE
IN  THE  BALCONY
IN  THE  BEDROOM
IN  THE  CABINET
IN  THE  COMMONS
IN  THE  COUNTRY
IN  THE  DAYTIME
IN  THE  EVENING
IN  THE  EXTREME
IN  THE  INTERIM
IN  THE  KITCHEN
IN  THE  MORNING
```

IN THE PARLOUR
IN THE PICTURE
IN THE RUNNING
IN THE SHADOWS
IN THE SLAMMER
IN THE SUBURBS
IN THE TROPICS
IT ALL DEPENDS
ON THE BALCONY
ON THE COUNTER
ON THE DECLINE
ON THE DEFENCE
ON THE HORIZON
ON THE OUTSIDE
ON THE PAYROLL
ON THE RAMPAGE
ON THE REBOUND
ON THE RETREAT
ON THE SUBJECT
ON THE SURFACE
ON THE WARPATH
TO ALL INTENTS
UP FOR AUCTION
UP THE CHIMNEY

2, 4, 1, 5

GO WITH A SWING

2, 4, 2, 1, 3

AS BUSY AS A BEE

2, 4, 2, 4

AS GOOD AS DEAD
AS GOOD AS EVER
AS GOOD AS GOLD
AS SURE AS EGGS
AS SURE AS FATE
GO BACK TO WORK
IN CASE OF NEED
IN DAYS OF YORE
IN NEED OF HELP
IT CAME TO PASS
MY TIME OF LIFE
NO TIME TO LOSE

2, 4, 3, 3

GO ONES OWN WAY
GO OVER THE TOP
IN LOVE AND WAR
IN ONES OLD AGE
OF MICE AND MEN
ON WITH THE JOB
UP WITH THE SUN

2, 4, 4, 2

AS TIME GOES BY
BE DONE WITH IT
TO HELL WITH IT!

2, 4, 6

AT ARMS LENGTH
AT FULL LENGTH
AT SOME LENGTH
BY EASY STAGES
DO ONES UTMOST
GO INTO ACTION
GO INTO BATTLE
GO INTO DETAIL
GO INTO EUROPE
GO INTO HIDING
GO-SLOW POLICY
IN EASY STAGES
IN FINE FETTLE
IN GOOD HEALTH
IN GOOD HUMOUR
IN GOOD REPAIR
IN GOOD SUPPLY
IN HIGH RELIEF
IN HOLY ORDERS
IN LIKE MANNER
IN ONES FAVOUR
IN ONES HEYDAY
IN ONES STRIDE
IN ONES WISDOM
IN OPEN REVOLT
IN POOR HEALTH
IN SLOW MOTION
MY BLUE HEAVEN
MY DEAR FELLOW
MY DEAR WATSON
MY GOOD FRIEND
ON FIRM GROUND
ON FOUR WHEELS
ON ONES HONOUR
ON ONES METTLE
ON SAFE GROUND
TO ONES CREDIT
UP ONES SLEEVE
UP ONES STREET

2, 5, 2, 3

AS BLACK AS INK
AS CLEAR AS DAY
AS CLEAR AS MUD
AS LIGHT AS AIR
NO DOUBT AT ALL
NO FLIES ON HIM

2, 5, 5

AT FIRST SIGHT
AT WHICH PLACE

AT WHICH POINT
GO FIFTY-FIFTY
IN OTHER WORDS
IN SHORT PANTS
NO FIXED ABODE
NO-CLAIM BONUS
ON EQUAL TERMS
ST. VITUS DANCE
WE NEVER CLOSE
WE THREE KINGS

2, 6, 4

AT DEATHS DOOR
IN BOTTOM GEAR
IN LEAGUE WITH
IN RECORD TIME
IN SINGLE FILE
ON BENDED KNEE
ST.JAMESS PARK

2, 7, 3

EX-SERVICE MAN
NO EARTHLY USE
ST.ANDREWS DAY
ST.GEORGES DAY

2, 10

AS UNDERSTOOD
AT UNIVERSITY
BY COMPARISON
GO DOWNSTAIRS
GO SWIMMINGLY
IN APPEARANCE
IN ATTENDANCE
IN CONCLUSION
IN CONFERENCE
IN CONFIDENCE
IN CONTENTION
IN DIFFICULTY
IN MODERATION
IN OPPOSITION
IN PARLIAMENT
IN PARTICULAR
IN POSSESSION
IN PROPORTION
IN QUARANTINE
IN RETROSPECT
IN SILHOUETTE
IN SUCCESSION
IN TRIPLICATE
NO ADMITTANCE
NO COMPARISON
NO DIFFERENCE
NO IMPORTANCE
NO OBLIGATION
NO PREFERENCE
OF ASSISTANCE
ON REFLECTION

ON TELEVISION
ST.PETERSBURG

3, 1, 3, 5

ADD A FEW WORDS
HIT A BAD PATCH
SAY A FEW WORDS

3, 1, 4, 2, 2

PUT A SOCK IN IT
PUT A STOP TO IT

3, 1, 4, 4

ITS A DEAD CERT
PAY A FAIR WAGE
SAY A GOOD WORD

3, 1, 5, 3

FOR A RAINY DAY

3, 1, 6, 2

LAY A FINGER ON
PUT A FINISH TO

3, 1, 8

ASK A QUESTION
FOR A LIFETIME
GET A MORTGAGE
GET A PUNCTURE
HIT A BOUNDARY
ITS A PLEASURE
PAY A DIVIDEND
PUT A QUESTION
SET A STANDARD

3, 2, 1, 6

ALL OF A DITHER
ALL OF A QUIVER
ALL OF A SUDDEN
DOG IN A MANGER
EYE OF A NEEDLE
FIT AS A FIDDLE
MAD AS A HATTER
SEE AT A GLANCE
SEW ON A BUTTON
WIN AT A CANTER
WIN BY A LENGTH

3, 2, 2, 5

BIT OF AN UPSET
LAY IT ON THICK
TIE UP IN KNOTS

3, 2, 3, 2, 2

PUT AN END TO IT

3, 2, 3, 4

ACE IN THE HOLE
ADD TO THE LIST
AIM AT THE MOON
ALL IN THE GAME
ALL IN THE MIND
ALL IS NOT LOST
ALL MY OWN WORK
ALL OF THE TIME
ALL ON ONE SIDE
ALL TO THE GOOD
BAY AT THE MOON
BET ON THE SIDE
BOB UP AND DOWN
BOX ON THE EARS
CUT TO THE BONE
DAY OF THE LORD
DAY OF THE WEEK
DIG IN THE RIBS
DIG UP THE PAST
END OF THE LINE
END OF THE ROAD
END OF THE WEEK
END OF THE YEAR
FAT OF THE LAND
FLY ON THE WALL
FUN OF THE FAIR
HIT ON THE HEAD
ITS AN ILL WIND
KEY OF THE DOOR
KEY TO THE DOOR
LAP OF THE GODS
LAW OF THE LAND
LIE OF THE LAND
MAN IN THE DOCK
MAN IN THE MOON
MAN OF HIS WORD
MAN OF THE HOUR
MAN ON THE MOON
MAN ON THE SPOT
MAN-TO-MAN TALK
NOT IN THE MOOD
ONE OF THE BEST
ONE OF THE BOYS
ONE OF THE GANG
ONE OF THE LADS
ONE-UP ONE-DOWN
OUT IN THE COLD
OUT IN THE OPEN
OUT OF THE BLUE
OUT OF THE RACE
OUT OF THE RAIN
OUT OF THE ROOM
OUT OF THE WIND
OUT OF THE WOOD
PAT ON THE BACK

PAT ON THE HEAD
PAY AS YOU EARN
PAY ON THE NAIL
PIP AT THE POST
PUT ON ONE SIDE
PUT ON THE LIST
PUT ON THE RACK
PUT ON THE SPOT
PUT TO THE TEST
PUT TO THE VOTE
PUT UP FOR SALE
RED IN THE FACE
RUN OF BAD LUCK
RUN OF THE MILL
RUN ON THE BANK
RUN ON THE SPOT
RUN UP THE FLAG
SEE IN THE DARK
SIT AT THE BACK
SIT IN THE BACK
SIX OF THE BEST
TAP AT THE DOOR
TAP ON THE HEAD
TOP OF THE BILL
TOP OF THE FORM
TOP OF THE HILL
TOP OF THE MILK
TOP OF THE POPS
TOP OF THE TREE
TWO IN THE BUSH
TWO-UP TWO-DOWN
WAR TO END WARS
WET TO THE SKIN

3, 2, 4, 3

ALL ON ONES OWN
ALL TO PLAY FOR
CUT OF ONES JIB
DIE IN ONES BED
GOD BE WITH YOU
MUD IN YOUR EYE
OUT OF ONES WAY
PUT TO GOOD USE

3, 2, 5, 2

LEG TO STAND ON

3, 2, 7

ACT IN CONCERT
ACT OF COURAGE
ACT OF TREASON
ACT OF WORSHIP
ACT ON IMPULSE
AGE OF CONSENT
AIR OF MYSTERY
AIR OF TRIUMPH
ALL BY ONESELF
ALL OR NOTHING

ASK ME ANOTHER
ASK NO FAVOURS
ASK NO QUARTER
BAG OF TOFFEES
BED OF NETTLES
BIT OF SCANDAL
BIT OF TROUBLE
BOX OF MATCHES
CRY OF DESPAIR
CUT TO RIBBONS
DAY OF FASTING
DAY OF LEISURE
DAY OF WORSHIP
DEN OF THIEVES
EAU DE COLOGNE
END IN FAILURE
END OF CHAPTER
FIT OF MADNESS
GOD BE PRAISED
GOD OF THUNDER
LAW OF GRAVITY
LED TO BELIEVE
MAN OF DESTINY
MAN OF FORTUNE
MAN OF LEISURE
MAN OF LETTERS
MAN OF MYSTERY
MAN OF SCIENCE
MAP OF AMERICA
MAP OF BRITAIN
MAP OF ENGLAND
MAP OF GERMANY
MAP OF IRELAND
MEN OF HARLECH
NOT IN KEEPING
OIL OF VITRIOL
OLD AS HISTORY
OUT OF BALANCE
OUT OF CONTEXT
OUT OF CONTROL
OUT OF EARSHOT
OUT OF FASHION
OUT OF HARMONY
OUT OF KEEPING
OUT OF SERVICE
OUT OF TROUBLE
OUT OF UNIFORM
OUT OF WEDLOCK
PAY IN ADVANCE
PUT IN WRITING
PUT IT BLUNTLY
PUT IT CRUDELY
RAS AL-KHAIMAH
RAY OF COMFORT
RIO DE JANEIRO
SEA OF GALILEE
SEE IT THROUGH
SET AN EXAMPLE
SET AT LIBERTY
SIT IN COUNCIL
SON ET LUMIÈRE

VOW OF SILENCE

3, 3, 2, 4

FAT LOT OF GOOD
GET OUT OF HAND
GET OUT OF JAIL
SET ONE AT EASE
THE DIE IS CAST
THE JOB IN HAND
TOO HOT TO HOLD

3, 3, 3, 3

CUT OFF THE GAS
LET THE CAT OUT
MAN FOR THE JOB
ONE FOR HIS NOB
PUT OUT THE CAT
PUT THE CAT OUT
THE OLD ONE-TWO

3, 3, 4, 2

GET THE WIND·UP
PUT THE PLUG IN
PUT THE WIND UP
THE ROT SETS IN

3, 3, 6

AIR-SEA RESCUE
ALL AND SUNDRY
ALL THE BETTER
ALL THE FAMILY
ALL THE OTHERS
ALL-OUT STRIKE
ASK FOR ADVICE
ASK FOR CREDIT
BIB AND TUCKER
BIG AND LITTLE
BOW AND SCRAPE
CAT AND FIDDLE
CUP AND SAUCER
CUT AND THRUST
CUT FOR TRUMPS
CUT THE CACKLE
CUT THE CORNER
DIG THE GARDEN
DUM-DUM BULLET
EAR AND THROAT
EYE FOR BEAUTY
EYE FOR COLOUR
FAN THE EMBERS
FAN THE FLAMES
FIT AND PROPER
FIT FOR HEROES
FOR THE BETTER
FOR THE MOMENT
FOR THE RECORD
FOX AND HOUNDS

GET THE CREDIT
GET THE NEEDLE
GET THE STITCH
GIN AND ORANGE
HAM AND TONGUE
HIP HIP HOORAY!
HIT THE BOTTLE
HIT THE STUMPS
HIT THE TARGET
HOT AND STRONG
JIG-SAW PUZZLE
JOG THE MEMORY
MAY THE EIGHTH
MAY THE FOURTH
MAY THE SECOND
OFF HIS ROCKER
OFF THE RECORD
OFF THE SCREEN
OIL THE WHEELS
ONE-DAY STRIKE
ONE-WAY STREET
PAW THE GROUND
PAY THE BEARER
PEN AND PENCIL
POT THE YELLOW
RED FOR DANGER
RIG THE MARKET
RIP VAN WINKLE
RUN FOR OFFICE
RUN FOR SAFETY
SEE THE SIGHTS
SIN AND MISERY
SUN-TAN LOTION
TEN-TON TESSIE
THE ALL-BLACKS
THE BOY FRIEND
THE DAY BEFORE
THE MAD HATTER
THE NEW FOREST
THE OLD BAILEY
THE OLD SCHOOL
THE TOP DRAWER
TIP THE SCALES
TIP THE WINNER
TWO FAT LADIES
TWO-CAR FAMILY
TWO-WAY STREET
VIM AND VIGOUR
WAG THE FINGER
WIN THE BATTLE
WIN THE BRONZE
WIN THE SILVER
WIT AND WISDOM

3, 4, 1, 4

ACT LIKE A FOOL
BUT ONCE A YEAR
CRY LIKE A BABY
FLY INTO A RAGE
FLY LIKE A BIRD

GET INTO A MESS
GET INTO A RAGE
OFF LIKE A SHOT
RUN LIKE A HARE

3, 4, 2, 3

FOR GOOD OR ILL
ONE LUMP OR TWO?
RUN AWAY TO SEA
THE FALL OF MAN
THE LAND OF NOD
THE WILL TO WIN

3, 4, 3, 2

GET ONES EYE IN
PUT ONES OAR IN

3, 4, 5

AIR ONES VIEWS
ALL OVER AGAIN
ANY MORE FARES
BED-TIME STORY
BIG-TIME CROOK
CRY ONES WARES
CUT ONES NAILS
CUT ONES TEETH
DIG ONES GRAVE
EAT ONES WORDS
FLY AWAY PETER
GET ONES CARDS
GET RICH QUICK
GET WELL-OILED
LET WELL ALONE
LOW-DOWN TRICK
MAN-MADE FIBRE
NEW YORK STATE
NON-STOP TRAIN
OFF ONES CHUMP
OFF ONES GUARD
OFF ONES HANDS
OLD MANS BEARD
OLD-TIME DANCE
ONE FELL SWOOP
ONE JUMP AHEAD
ONE MOVE AHEAD
ONE STEP AHEAD
PAY ONES SHARE
PIN ONES FAITH
PIN ONES HOPES
PLY ONES TRADE
PUT INTO FORCE
PUT INTO SHAPE
PUT INTO WORDS
RUB ONES HANDS
SAY ONES PIECE
SET ONES TEETH
SIR TOBY BELCH
SIX FEET UNDER

TEA-TIME SCORE
TEN PAST EIGHT
TEN PAST SEVEN
TEN PAST THREE
TEN-CENT STORE
TEN-MILE LIMIT
THE BEES KNEES
THE BLUE ANGEL
THE DARK BLUES
THE DEEP SOUTH
THE DONE THING
THE FOUR WINDS
THE HARD STUFF
THE HOLY BIBLE
THE LAST LAUGH
THE LAST STRAW
THE LAST TRAIN
THE LAST WALTZ
THE LION HEART
THE LOST CHORD
THE REAL MCCOY
THE REAL THING
THE SAME THING
THE VERY DEVIL
THE VERY IMAGE
THE VERY PLACE
THE VERY THING
TIE ONES HANDS
TOO MANY COOKS
TRY ONES SKILL
USE ONES BRAIN
USE ONES HANDS
WAY WITH WOMEN
WHO GOES THERE?
WIN ONES SPURS

3, 5, 2, 2

THE THING TO DO
THE WORST OF IT

3, 5, 4

AIR-FORCE BLUE
ALL NIGHT LONG
AND THATS FLAT!
BOY MEETS GIRL
FOR PITYS SAKE
FOR QUICK SALE
FUR-LINED COAT
GET CLEAN AWAY
GET CLEAR AWAY
HOT CROSS-BUNS
HOT-WATER PIPE
ICE-CREAM CONE
ICE-CREAM SODA
ILL-TIMED JEST
LOW BIRTH-RATE
MAN ABOUT TOWN
MUM KNOWS BEST
OLD FOLKS HOME

OLD WIVES TALE
ONE-HORSE TOWN
ONE-SIDED VIEW
ONE-TRACK MIND
OUT FIRST BALL
SIR HENRY WOOD
TEN-POUND NOTE
THE APPLE-CART
THE FRONT LINE
THE GREAT FIRE
THE MARCH HARE
THE NORTH-EAST
THE NORTH-WEST
THE OTHER SIDE
THE SEVEN SEAS
THE SOUTH-EAST
THE SOUTH-WEST
THE STORY GOES
THE UPPER HAND
THE WASTE LAND
THE WHOLE TIME
THE YOUNG IDEA
TWO-PIECE SUIT
WIN HANDS DOWN

3, 6, 3

ALL SAINTS DAY
ANY MINUTE NOW
ANY MOMENT NOW
ANY SECOND NOW
EAT HUMBLE PIE
LET THINGS RIP
OLD BATTLE-AXE
OLD SCHOOL TIE
ONE-LEGGED MAN
RED-LETTER DAY
TEN-GALLON HAT
THE BALTIC SEA
THE BITTER END
THE DEVILS OWN
THE GENTLE SEX
THE PIPERS SON
THE STATUS QUO
THE WEAKER SEX

3, 7, 2

ALL DRESSED UP
ALL STEAMED UP
ALL SYSTEMS GO
DIG ONESELF IN
LET ONESELF GO
RUN COUNTER TO

3, 9

ACT FOOLISHLY
AIR COMMODORE
AIR PASSENGER
AIR TRANSPORT

AIR	TRAVELLER	PAY	ATTENTION
ANY	QUESTIONS	PAY	DIVIDENDS
APT	QUOTATION	RAW	MATERIALS
ART	TREASURES	RED	CORPUSCLE
ASH	WEDNESDAY	RED	LEICESTER
ASK	QUESTIONS	RUB	SHOULDERS
BAD	BEGINNING	SAN	FRANCISCO
BAD	BEHAVIOUR	SAN	SEBASTIAN
BAD	CHARACTER	SAW	SHARPENER
BAD	CONDUCTOR	SAY	GOODNIGHT
BAD	INFLUENCE	SAY	SOMETHING
BAD	QUALITIES	SET	PROGRAMME
BAD	TREATMENT	TAX	AVOIDANCE
BAR	BILLIARDS	TAX	COLLECTOR
BOB	MONKHOUSE	TAX	EXEMPTION
BOY	ARTIFICER	TAX	INSPECTOR
BUS	CONDUCTOR	TEN	SHILLINGS
CUP	FINALISTS	THE	ACROPOLIS
DIE	INTESTATE	THE	AFTERLIFE
DUE	DEFERENCE	THE	ALCHEMIST
FAR	DIFFERENT	THE	AMERICANS
FOR	GALLANTRY	THE	ANTARCTIC
GAS	POISONING	THE	ANTIPODES
GET	PLASTERED	THE	ARGENTINE
GET	PROMOTION	THE	BOSPHORUS
GET	RELEGATED	THE	CAVALIERS
HIS	REVERENCE	THE	CHILTERNS
HOT	CHOCOLATE	THE	CONQUEROR
HOT	FAVOURITE	THE	CONTINENT
HOT	GOSPELLER	THE	COTSWOLDS
ICY	RECEPTION	THE	DOLOMITES
JAM	YESTERDAY	THE	EXCEPTION
KEY	SIGNATURE	THE	FALKLANDS
LIE	PROSTRATE	THE	FOLLOWING
LOW	COUNTRIES	THE	GRAMPIANS
LOW	FREQUENCY	THE	HAYMARKET
LOW	VALUATION	THE	HEREAFTER
MAN	OVERBOARD	THE	HIGHLANDS
MID	GLAMORGAN	THE	HIMALAYAS
NEW	AMSTERDAM	THE	LIMELIGHT
NEW	BRUNSWICK	THE	MAYFLOWER
NEW	DEPARTURE	THE	MOUSETRAP
NEW	HAMPSHIRE	THE	PALLADIUM
NEW	INVENTION	THE	PARTHENON
NEW	PARAGRAPH	THE	PERISHERS
NEW	STATESMAN	THE	POTTERIES
NEW	TECHNIQUE	THE	PROVINCES
NEW	TESTAMENT	THE	SEARCHERS
NEW	ZEALANDER	THE	SEVENTIES
NOT	AVAILABLE	THE	SHETLANDS
ODD	SENSATION	THE	SPECTATOR
OLD	FASHIONED	THE	THIRTIETH
OLD	FAVOURITE	TOM	COURTENAY
OLD	GENTLEMAN	TOP	EXECUTIVE
OLD	HARROVIAN	TWO	SHILLINGS
OLD	PRETENDER	TWO	SYLLABLES
OLD	SHOULDERS	VIN	ORDINAIRE
OLD	TESTAMENT		
ONE	CONDITION		
ONE	KILOMETRE		
OWE	OBEDIENCE		

4, 1, 3, 2, 2

MAKE A DAY OF IT

4, 1, 3, 4

HAVE A BAD TIME
HAVE A WAY WITH
HEAR A PIN DROP
LEAD A GAY LIFE
MAKE A BEE-LINE
TAKE A DIM VIEW
TAKE A POT-SHOT
WILL O THE WISP

4, 1, 4, 3

COME A LONG WAY
KEEP A LOOK-OUT
MAKE A DEAD SET
MAKE A FAUX PAS
MANY A LONG DAY
PULL A FAST ONE
TAKE A LOOK-SEE
TAKE A WEEK OFF
TURN A DEAF EAR

4, 1, 5, 2

HAVE A CRUSH ON

4, 1, 7

BEAT A RETREAT
BLOW A WHISTLE
BOOK A PASSAGE
BOOK A SLEEPER
CALL A MEETING
COME A CROPPER
DRAW A PENSION
DRAW A PICTURE
DROP A CLANGER
DROP A CURTSEY
FILE A LAWSUIT
FILL A VACANCY
FIND A FORMULA
FIND A HUSBAND
GAIN A HEARING
GAIN A VICTORY
GIVE A CONCERT
GIVE A LECTURE
GIVE A PRESENT
GIVE A SUMMARY
HAVE A FEELING
HAVE A FLUTTER
HAVE A HAIRCUT
HAVE A RELAPSE
HAVE A VACANCY
HOLD A MEETING
JOHN F.KENNEDY
KEEP A PROMISE

KNIT A SWEATER
LIKE A TROOPER
MAKE A BARGAIN
MAKE A BEQUEST
MAKE A BONFIRE
MAKE A CENTURY
MAKE A CURTSEY
MAKE A FORTUNE
MAKE A GESTURE
MAKE A GETAWAY
MAKE A HUNDRED
MAKE A KILLING
MAKE A MISTAKE
MAKE A PROMISE
MAKE A PROTEST
MAKE A REQUEST
PICK A QUARREL
PLAY A BLINDER
POSE A PROBLEM
RENT A CARAVAN
RENT A COTTAGE
RIDE A BICYCLE
SEAL A BARGAIN
SEEK A QUARREL
SEND A MESSAGE
TAKE A BEATING
TAKE A HOLIDAY
TAKE A HUSBAND
TAKE A LIBERTY
TAKE A PENALTY
TAKE A READING
TELL A WHOPPER
TOSS A PANCAKE
WHAT A LIBERTY
WHAT A WHOPPER!
WITH A PURPOSE
WORK A MIRACLE

4, 2, 1, 5

BLOW UP A STORM
COME TO A CLOSE
COME TO A POINT
COOK UP A STORY
DRAW TO A CLOSE
FOND OF A GLASS
GIVE IT A SHAKE
GIVE IT A TWIST
GIVE IT A WHIRL
GONE IN A FLASH
HELL OF A NOISE
LIVE IN A DREAM
ONCE IN A WHILE
PALE AS A GHOST
PILE UP A SCORE
PORT IN A STORM
SLIP OF A THING
SONG OF A SHIRT
TAKE UP A STAND
TELL ME A STORY

4 . 2 . 2 . 1 . 3

SLIP UP ON A JOB

4 . 2 . 2 . 4

BANG UP TO DATE
COME IN TO LAND
COME TO NO GOOD
COME TO NO HARM
GERM OF AN IDEA
KEEP UP-TO-DATE
SEEN TO BE FAIR
TAKE IT AS READ
TIME TO GO HOME

4 . 2 . 3 . 3

BASK IN THE SUN
BEST OF THE LOT
BLUE AS THE SKY
CALL OF THE SEA
CALL TO THE BAR
CAST IN THE EYE
COME TO THE END
COME UP FOR AIR
CORN ON THE COB
CURL OF THE LIP
CURL UP AND DIE
EASY ON THE EYE
EYES OF THE LAW
FALL BY THE WAY
FREE AS THE AIR
GIFT OF THE GAB
HAIR OF THE DOG
HEAD IN THE AIR
HEAT OF THE DAY
HEAT OF THE SUN
HIGH IN THE AIR
HOUR OF THE DAY
JOIN IN THE FUN
JUST AS YOU SAY
LATE IN THE DAY
LEAP IN THE AIR
LEFT IN THE AIR
LIMB OF THE LAW
NICE TO SEE YOU
PART OF THE ACT
PART OF THE WAY
POKE IN THE EYE
RING IN THE NEW
RISE TO THE TOP
ROOM AT THE TOP
SHOT IN THE ARM
SLIP OF THE PEN
SOUP OF THE DAY
STAY TO THE END
STEP ON THE GAS
SWAY TO AND FRO
TAKE TO THE AIR
TURN ON THE GAS

TURN ON THE TAP
WELL ON THE WAY
WHAT DO YOU SAY?

4 . 2 . 4 . 2

HARD TO COME BY
TAKE IT FROM ME

4 . 2 . 6

ANNE OF CLEVES
ARCH OF HEAVEN
BACK OF BEYOND
BACK TO MOTHER
BACK TO NATURE
BACK TO NORMAL
BACK TO SCHOOL
BALL OF STRING
BALM OF GILEAD
BAND OF HEROES
BANG ON TARGET
BEST OF HEALTH
BILL OF HEALTH
BILL OF LADING
BILL OF RIGHTS
BLOW TO PIECES
BODY OF PEOPLE
BODY OF TROOPS
BOOK OF EXODUS
BOOK OF PSALMS
BOOK OF STAMPS
CALL TO PRAYER
CANT BE HELPED
CASE OF MURDER
CASE OF SCOTCH
CASE OF WHISKY
CASE TO ANSWER
CASH ON DEMAND
CEST LA GUERRE
CITY OF LONDON
CODE OF HONOUR
COME IN SECOND
COME IN USEFUL
COME ON STRONG
COME TO NAUGHT
COME TO PIECES
COME UP TRUMPS
CORN IN ISRAEL
COST OF LIVING
COST OF UPKEEP
CZAR OF RUSSIA
DASH TO PIECES
DEAD AS MUTTON
DEAD OF WINTER
DEAF TO REASON
DROP OF BRANDY
DROP OF LIQUID
DROP OF SCOTCH
DROP OF WHISKY
EASY TO PLEASE

EDGE	OF	BEYOND
EVER	SO	LITTLE
FAIL	TO	PPEAR
FAIL	TO	ARRIVE
FAIL	TO	FINISH
FAIR	TO	MEDIUM
FALL	IN	PRICES
FALL	TO	PIECES
FIRE	AT	RANDOM
FIRE	OF	LONDON
FIVE	NO-TRUMPS	
FIVE	OF	HEARTS
FIVE	OF	SPADES
FIVE	OF	TRUMPS
FIVE	TO	ELEVEN
FIVE	TO	TWELVE
FOUR	NO-TRUMPS	
FOUR	OF	HEARTS
FOUR	OF	SPADES
FOUR	OF	TRUMPS
FREE	OF	CHARGE
FREE	TO	CHOOSE
FULL	OF	ENER Y
FULL	OF	SORROW
FULL	OF	SPIRIT
GAME	OF	BRIDGE
GAME	OF	CHANCE
GAME	OF	SOCCER
GAME	OF	TENNIS
GIVE	AN	ENCORE
GIVE	UP	OFFICE
GIVE	UP	TRYING
GONE	TO	GROUND
GULF	OF	MEXICO
GULF	OF	PANAMA
HACK	TO	PIECES
HALF	OF	BITTER
HARD	TO	HANDLE
HARD	TO	PLEASE
HAVE	NO	CHOICE
HAVE	NO	DOUBTS
HAVE	NO	OPTION
HEAD	OF	CATTLE
HEAT	OF	BATTLE
HERD	OF	CATTLE
HIRE	AN	ESCORT
HOLD	IN	COMMON
HOLD	IN	ESTEEM
HOLD	IN	PLEDGE
HOLD	TO	RANSOM
HOLY	OF	HOLIES
HORN	OF	PLENTY
HORS	DE	COMBAT
HOUR	OF	DANGER
HUNK	OF	CHEESE
HYMN	OF	PRAISE
JACK	IN	OFFICE
JACK	OF	HEARTS
JACK	OF	SPADES
JACK	OF	TRUMPS
KEEP	IN	PRISON
KEEP	IT	SECRET
KEEP	ON	TRYING
KILO	OF	APPLES
KILO	OF	BUTTER
KING	OF	BEASTS
KING	OF	FRANCE
KING	OF	HEARTS
KING	OF	SPADES
KING	OF	TRUMPS
KNOW	NO	BETTER
KNOW	NO	BOUNDS
LACK	OF	BRAINS
LACK	OF	ENERGY
LACK	OF	FINISH
LACK	OF	HEIGHT
LACK	OF	POLISH
LACK	OF	SPIRIT
LACK	OF	WISDOM
LAND	OF	PLENTY
LAST	TO	ARRIVE
LAWS	OF	MOTION
LEAD	IN	PRAYER
LEFT	OF	CENTRE
LEFT	TO	CHANCE
LIFE	OF	LUXURY
LINE	OF	ACTION
LINE	OF	BATTLE
LINE	OF	VISION
LIVE	IN	CLOVER
LIVE	IN	LUXURY
LOCK-UP	GARAGE	
LORD	OF	APPEAL
LOSS	OF	HEALTH
LOSS	OF	HONOUR
LOSS	OF	MEMORY
LOSS	OF	MORALE
LOSS	OF	SPEECH
LOSS	OF	VISION
LOSS	OF	WEIGHT
LOST	IN	WONDER
LOVE	ME	TENDER
LOVE	OF	NATURE
MADE	IN	FRANCE
MAID	OF	HONOUR
MAKE	AN	APPEAL
MAKE	AN	ARREST
MAKE	AN	EFFORT
MAKE	AN	ESCAPE
MAKE	IT	SNAPPY
MAKE	NO	PROFIT
MAKE	UP	LEEWAY
MAKE-UP	ARTIST	
MAKE-UP	MIRROR	
MARK	OF	GENIUS
MASS	OF	NERVES
MEET	IN	SECRET
MODE	OF	LIVING
MOOR	OF	VENICE
MOVE	UP-MARKET	
MUCH	IN	DEMAND
NAME	IN	LIGHTS

NEST	OF	TABLES	SOFT	AS	BUTTER
NINE	OF	HEARTS	SONG	OF	PRAISE
NINE	OF	SPADES	SOUL	OF	HONOUR
NINE	OF	TRUMPS	SPOT	OF	BOTHER
ODDS-ON	CHANCE		STAY	TO	DINNER
OPEN	TO	ATTACK	STOP-GO	POLICY	
OPEN	TO	CHANCE	SUCK	AN	ORANGE
OPEN	TO	CHOICE	SUIT	OF	ARMOUR
PACK	OF	HOUNDS	SURE	TO	PLEASE
PACK	OF	WOLVES	TAKE	MY	ADVICE
PAID-UP	MEMBER		TAKE	NO	NOTICE
PAIR	OF	BRACES	TAKE	TO	FLIGHT
PAIR	OF	EIGHTS	TAKE	TO	PIECES
PAIR	OF	GLOVES	TAKE	UP	OFFICE
PAIR	OF	PLIERS	TALK	AT	LENGTH
PAIR	OF	QUEENS	TALK	TO	NOBODY
PAIR	OF	SCALES	TEAM	OF	ELEVEN
PAIR	OF	SEVENS	TEAM	OF	HORSES
PAIR	OF	SHORTS	TEAR	IN	PIECES
PAIR	OF	SKATES	TEAR	TO	PIECES
PAIR	OF	SLACKS	TEAR	TO	SHREDS
PAIR	OF	THREES	TERM	OF	OFFICE
PAIR	OF	TIGHTS	TIDE	OF	EVENTS
PAIR	OF	TRUNKS	TORN	TO	SHREDS
PART	OF	SPEECH	TOUR	DE	FRANCE
PINT	OF	BITTER	TRUE	TO	NATURE
PINT	OF	WALLOP	TSAR	OF	RUSSIA
PLAN	OF	ACTION	TURN	OF	EVENTS
PLAN	OF	ATTACK	TURN	OF	PHRASE
PLEA	OF	GUILTY	TURN	UP	TRUMPS
POOL	OF	LABOUR	UNIT	OF	ENERGY
POOL	OF	LONDON	UNIT	OF	LENGTH
POOR	IN	SPIRIT	UNIT	OF	VOLUME
PORT	OF	LONDON	UNIT	OF	WEIGHT
PULL	TO	PIECES	UPON	MY	HONOUR
RACE	OF	GIANTS	VOTE	OF	THANKS
RAGS	TO	RICHES	WALK	ON	STILTS
RATE	OF	CHANGE	WALK	ON	TIPTOE
RATE	OF	GROWTH	WANT	OF	TRYING
REEL	OF	COTTON	WILL	OF	HEAVEN
RIDE	AT	ANCHOR	WIND	OF	CHANGE
RIDE	TO	HOUNDS	WITH	AN	ACCENT
RIOT	OF	COLOUR	WORD	IN	SEASON
RISE	IN	REVOLT	WORD	OF	ADVICE
RITE	OF	SPRING	WORD	OF	HONOUR
ROLL	OF	HONOUR			
ROOM	TO	EXPAND	**4, 3, 1, 4**		
RULE	OF	TERROR			
SAFE	AS	HOUSES	FILL	OUT	A FORM
SALE	OR	RETURN	FIVE	AND	A HALF
SELL	ON	CREDIT	FOUR	AND	A HALF
SEND	TO	PRISON	GIVE	ONE	A LIFT
SENT	TO	SCHOOL	HOLD	OUT	A HAND
SHAH	OF	PERSIA	JUST	FOR	A LARK
SHOT	TO	PIECES	KNOW	FOR	A FACT
SIDE	OF	MUTTON	MAKE	OUT	A CASE
SIGH	OF	RELIEF	MILK	AND	A DASH
SIGN	OF	DANGER	NINE	AND	A HALF
SING	IN	CHORUS	PICK	OUT	A TUNE
SING	IN	UNISON	PINK	FOR	A GIRL
SLOW	OF	SPEECH	PLAY	FOR	A DRAW

RIDE FOR A FALL
SELL FOR A SONG
TAKE FOR A FOOL
TAKE FOR A RIDE
TAKE FOR A WALK
TIME AND A HALF
YARD AND A HALF
YEAR AND A HALF

4 , 3 , 2 , 3

COME OUT ON TOP
FIVE OUT OF TEN
FROM DAY TO DAY
FROM END TO END
FROM TOP TO TOE
HEAD OUT TO SEA
NINE OUT OF TEN
WAIT FOR NO MAN

4 , 3 , 3 , 2

BEST ONE CAN DO
COME AND GET IT
MIND HOW YOU GO
TURN THE GAS ON
TURN THE TAP ON
WASH AND DRY UP

4 , 3 , 5

ALAS AND ALACK
ARMY PAY CORPS
BACK AND FORTH
BACK AND FRONT
BACK AND SIDES
BACK THE LOSER
BALL AND CHAIN
BEAR THE BLAME
BEAR THE BRUNT
BEAT THE CLOCK
BEAT THE COUNT
BEEF AND ONION
BEND THE ELBOW
BLOW OFF STEAM
BOYS AND GIRLS
BURN THE CAKES
BURN THE TOAST
CALL THE BANNS
CASE THE JOINT
CASH AND CARRY
CHOP AND CHIPS
CLIP THE WINGS
COCO THE CLOWN
COMB AND PAPER
COME OFF WORST
COOK THE BOOKS
COST THE EARTH
DAMN AND BLAST !
DEAL THE CARDS
DEAR OLD THING

DEEP-SEA DIVER
DIVE FOR COVER
DOWN THE AISLE
DOWN THE DRAIN
DOWN THE HATCH
DOWN THE RIVER
DOWN THE SPOUT
DRAW THE BLIND
EACH AND EVERY
EGGS AND BACON
FACE THE ENEMY
FACE THE FACTS
FACE THE FRONT
FACE THE ISSUE
FACE THE MUSIC
FACE THE TRUTH
FACT AND FANCY
FAST AND LOOSE
FEAR THE WORST
FEED THE BIRDS
FEEL THE PINCH
FIND THE MONEY
FINE AND DANDY
FIRE AND SWORD
FIRE AND THEFT
FIRE AND WATER
FISH AND CHIPS
FIVE NEW PENCE
FIVE-DAY MATCH
FOOD AND DRINK
FOOT AND MOUTH
FOUR NEW PENCE
FROM ALL SIDES
FROM THE FIRST
FROM THE NORTH
FROM THE SOUTH
FROM THE START
GAME AND MATCH
GATE-LEG TABLE
GIVE THE ALARM
GIVE THE EARTH
GIVE THE FACTS
GOOD AND READY
HANS VON BÜLOW
HARE AND HOUND
HAVE THE FLOOR
HAVE THE KNACK
HAVE THE MEANS
HAVE THE MONEY
HERE AND THERE
HIDE THE TRUTH
HOLD OUT HOPES
HOLD THE CARDS
HOLD THE REINS
HOLD THE STAGE
IRON AND STEEL
JOIN THE DANCE
JOIN THE ENEMY
JOIN THE QUEUE
JULY THE FIFTH
JULY THE FIRST

JULY	THE	NINTH		ODDS	AND	EVENS
JULY	THE	SIXTH		ONCE	TOO	OFTEN
JULY	THE	TENTH		ONES	BIG	BREAK
JULY	THE	THIRD		ONES	OWN	FAULT
JUMP	THE	QUEUE		ONLY	ONE	OWNER
JUNE	THE	FIFTH		OPEN	ALL	HOURS
JUNE	THE	FIRST		OPEN	ALL	NIGHT
JUNE	THE	NINTH		OVER	AND	ABOVE
JUNE	THE	SIXTH		OVER	AND	UNDER
JUNE	THE	TENTH		OVER	THE	COALS
JUNE	THE	THIRD		OVER	THE	HILLS
JUST	ADD	WATER		OVER	THE	LIMIT
JUST	THE	THING		OVER	THE	OCEAN
KEEP	THE	BOOKS		OVER	THE	WATER
KEEP	THE	PEACE		OVER	THE	WORST
KEEP	THE	SCORE		OVER	THE	YEARS
KEEP-FIT		CLASS		PASS	THE	SAUCE
KICK	THE	HABIT		PITT	THE	ELDER
KING	AND	QUEEN		PLAY	FOR	KEEPS
KNOW	THE	DRILL		PLAY	FOR	MONEY
KNOW	THE	FACTS		PLAY	ONE	FALSE
KNOW	THE	ROPES		PLAY	THE	CLOWN
KNOW	THE	SCORE		PLAY	THE	FIELD
KNOW	THE	TRUTH		PLAY	THE	HALLS
KNOW	THE	WORST		PLAY	THE	ORGAN
LEAD	THE	FIELD		PLAY	THE	PIANO
LEFT	AND	RIGHT		PLEA	FOR	MERCY
LICK	THE	PLATE		PLUS	AND	MINUS
LIFE	AND	DEATH		PORK	AND	BEANS
LIKE	HOT	CAKES		POST-WAR		WORLD
LIKE	THE	DEVIL		PRAY	FOR	MERCY
LIVE	AND	LEARN		PRAY	FOR	PEACE
LIVE	FOR	TODAY		PURL	AND	PLAIN
LONG	WAY	ROUND		QUIT	THE	SCENE
LOSE	THE	ASHES		QUIT	THE	STAGE
LOSE	THE	MATCH		RAGS	AND	BONES
LOSE	THE	SCENT		READ	AND	WRITE
LOST	AND	FOUND		READ	THE	CARDS
LOST	FOR	WORDS		READ	THE	SIGNS
LOUD	AND	CLEAR		READ	THE	STARS
LUST	FOR	POWER		READ	THE	TAROT
MAKE	THE	GRADE		RIDE	THE	STORM
MAKE	THE	POINT		RISE	AND	SHINE
MAKE	THE	RULES		ROLL	THE	PITCH
MARK	THE	CARDS		ROOM	FOR	DOUBT
MEAN	THE	WORLD		ROSE	AND	CROWN
MEAT	AND	DRINK		RULE	THE	ROOST
MEET	THE	TRAIN		SAFE	AND	SOUND
MELT	THE	HEART		SAGE	AND	ONION
MILK	AND	HONEY		SAME	OLD	THING
MILK	AND	SUGAR		SAVE	OUR	SOULS
MISS	THE	PLANE		SEEK	THE	TRUTH
MISS	THE	POINT		SICK	AND	TIRED
MISS	THE	TRAIN		SING	THE	BLUES
MOON	AND	STARS		SKIN	AND	BONES
NEAR	THE	COAST		SLIP	AND	SLIDE
NEAR	THE	TRUTH		SOAP	AND	WATER
NICE	AND	HANDY		SONG	AND	DANCE
NONE	THE	WISER		SPIN	THE	WHEEL
NONE	THE	WORSE		STAY	THE	NIGHT
NUTS	AND	BOLTS		STIR	THE	BLOOD

STOP AND START
STOP THE CLOCK
STOP THE FIGHT
STOP THE NIGHT
TAKE THE BLAME
TAKE THE COUNT
TAKE THE FIELD
TAKE THE FLOOR
TAKE THE MONEY
TAKE THE POINT
TAKE THE REINS
TAKE THE STAGE
TAKE THE STAND
TAKE THE TRAIN
TELL THE TRUTH
TELL THE WORLD
THEN AND THERE
TILL ALL HOURS
TIME AND AGAIN
TIME AND MONEY
TIME AND PLACE
TIME AND SPACE
TIME FOR LUNCH
TOSS FOR SIDES
TOSS THE CABER
TRIM THE SAILS
TURN THE PAGES
TURN THE SCREW
UNDO THE CATCH
WALK THE PLANK
WARM THE HEART
WAYS AND MEANS
WEAR THE CLOTH
WEAR THE CROWN
WEEK-END LEAVE
WELL AND TRULY
WEST-END STAGE
WHAT THE DEUCE?
WHEN AND WHERE
WIND THE CLOCK
WINE AND WOMEN
WIPE THE FLOOR
WITH ALL HASTE
WITH ALL SPEED
WITH ONE VOICE
WORK FOR PEACE
WORK OFF STEAM

4, 4, 1, 3

COME DOWN A PEG
HOLD DOWN A JOB
MOVE LIKE A CAT
SPIN LIKE A TOP
TAKE DOWN A PEG
WORK LIKE A DOG

4, 4, 2, 2

KNOW WHAT TO DO
THIN TIME OF IT

WHAT TIME IS IT?

4, 4, 4

ARCH ONES BACK
AULD LANG SYNE
AWAY DULL CARE!
AWAY FROM HOME
BACK ROOM BOYS
BANG ONES HEAD
BARE ONES HEAD
BEAR DOWN UPON
BIDE ONES TIME
BITE ONES LIPS
BLOW ONES HORN
BLUE WITH COLD
BOLT ONES FOOD
BURY ONES HEAD
CALL INTO PLAY
CAST AWAY FEAR
CAST ONES VOTE
CAST-IRON CASE
COMB ONES HAIR
COME BACK HOME
COME BACK SOON
COME INTO LINE
COME INTO PLAY
COME INTO VIEW
COME OVER HERE
DAME MYRA HESS
DEAD WITH COLD
DEAD-BALL LINE
DEEP-LAID PLOT
DONT TALK BACK
DRAG ONES FEET
DUCK ONES HEAD
EARN ONES KEEP
EASE ONES MIND
ETON WALL-GAME
EVER-OPEN DOOR
FACE BOTH WAYS
FAIR DAYS WORK
FALL BACK UPON
FALL INTO LINE
FALL INTO RUIN
FARE THEE WELL
FEEL ONES FEET
FIND ONES FEET
FIND ONES LEGS
FIVE FEET TALL
FIVE PAST FIVE
FIVE PAST FOUR
FIVE PAST NINE
FIVE-YEAR PLAN
FOLD ONES ARMS
FOUR FEET TALL
FREE FROM CARE
FREE FROM DEBT
FREE FROM FEAR
FREE FROM PAIN
FREE FROM VICE

FREE	FROM	WANT
FUME	WITH	RAGE
GAIN	ONES	ENDS
GIRL	NEXT	DOOR
GIVE	ONES	BEST
GIVE	ONES	LIFE
GIVE	ONES	WORD
GOAL-LESS		DRAW
GOOD	DAYS	WORK
GOOD	LONG	REST
GOOD-TIME		GIRL
HALF	SEAS	OVER
HAND	OVER	FIST
HAND	OVER	HAND
HANG	ONES	HEAD
HAVE	COLD	FEET
HAVE	ONES	FILL
HAVE	ONES	WILL
HIDE	ONES	FACE
HIDE	ONES	HEAD
HOME	FROM	HOME
HOME-MADE		CAKE
HOME-MADE		SOUP
JUST	LIKE	THAT
JUST	THIS	ONCE
KEEP	GOOD	TIME
KEEP	ONES	HEAD
KEEP	ONES	SEAT
KEEP	ONES	WORD
KEEP	PACE	WITH
KNIT	ONES	BROW
KNOW	FULL	WELL
KNOW	ONES	MIND
LADY	JANE	GREY
LEFT-HAND		BEND
LEFT-HAND		SIDE
LEFT-HAND		TURN
LESS	THAN	COST
LICK	ONES	LIPS
LIFT	ONES	HAND
LIKE	UNTO	LIKE
LIMB	FROM	LIMB
LINE	UPON	LINE
LIVE	ONES	LIFE
LONG	HARD	LOOK
LONG-FELT		NEED
LONG-FELT		WANT
LONG-LIFE		MILK
LONG-TERM		LOAN
LONG-TERM		VIEW
LOOK	BOTH	WAYS
LOOK	DOWN	UPON
LOOK	ONES	BEST
LOSE	ONES	FORM
LOSE	ONES	GRIP
LOSE	ONES	HAIR
LOSE	ONES	HEAD
LOSE	ONES	LIFE
LOSE	ONES	SEAT
LOSE	ONES	WITS
MAKE	ENDS	MEET

MAKE	GOOD	TIME
MAKE	ONES	EXIT
MAKE	ONES	MARK
MAKE	ONES	PILE
MAKE	ONES	WILL
MEET	ONES	FATE
MEND	ONES	WAYS
MERE	FLEA-BITE	
MILE	UPON	MILE
MIND	YOUR	HEAD
MIND	YOUR	STEP
MORE	THAN	EVER
MORE	THAN	ONCE
NEWS	FROM	HOME
NINE	NINE	NINE
NINE	TILL	FIVE
NUMB	WITH	COLD
ONES	BORN	DAYS
ONES	FAIR	NAME
ONES	LAST	WORD
OPEN	ONES	EYES
OPEN	THIS	SIDE
OPEN-CAST		MINE
OVER	ONES	HEAD
PACK	ONES	BAGS
PACK	ONES	CASE
PART	ONES	HAIR
PART-TIME		WORK
PAST	ONES	BEST
PELT	WITH	RAIN
PICK	ONES	NOSE
PING-PONG		BALL
PLAY	LEAP-FROG	
PLAY	ONES	PART
PLAY	ONES	ROLE
PLAY	WITH	FIRE
POPE	JOHN	PAUL
POUR	WITH	RAIN
PUSH	ONES	LUCK
QUIT	ONES	POST
READ	ONES	PALM
REAR	ONES	HEAD
REST	ONES	CASE
REST	ONES	EYES
REST	ONES	LEGS
RIDE	BARE-BACK	
RISK	ONES	LIFE
RISK	ONES	NECK
ROAR	WITH	PAIN
ROAR	WITH	RAGE
ROLL	ONES	EYES
SALT	LAKE	CITY
SAVE	ONES	FACE
SAVE	ONES	LIFE
SAVE	ONES	NECK
SAVE	ONES	SKIN
SELL	ONES	SOUL
SHED	ONES	LOAD
SHOT	ONES	BOLT
SHOW	ONES	CARD
SHOW	ONES	FACE

SHOW	ONES	HAND
SHUT	ONES	EYES
SHUT	THAT	DOOR!
SHUT	YOUR	TRAP!
SIGN	ONES	NAME
SKYE	BOAT	SONG
SLIP	ONES	MIND
SOME	TIMe	BACK
STAY	OPEN	LATE
STEP	INTO	LINE
TAKE	GOOD	CARE
TAKE	ONES	EASE
TAKE	ONES	LIFE
TAKE	ONES	NAME
TAKE	ONES	PICK
TAKE	ONES	TIME
TAKE	ONES	TURN
TAKE	ONES	WORD
TAKE	YOUR	PICK
TAKE-HOME		WAGE
TEAR	ONES	HAIR
TEEM	WITH	RAIN
TELL-TALE		SIGN
TEST-TUBE		BABY
THIS	VERY	ROOM
TILL	NEXT	TIME
TIME	WILL	TELL
TOOT	ONES	HORN
TOSS	ONES	HEAD
TURN	INTO	CASH
TURN	INTO	GOLD
TURN	ONES	BACK
TURN	ONES	HEAD
VENI	VIDI	VICI
VICE-LIKE		GRIP
WAIT	ONES	TURN
WASH	ONES	FACE
WASH	ONES	HAIR
WELL-MADE		SUIT
WENT	DOWN	WELL
WILD-WEST		SHOW
WIPE	ONES	EYES
WIPE	ONES	FEET
WITH	OPEN	ARMS
WITH	THIS	RING
YELL	WITH	PAIN

4, 5, 3

BALL-POINT		PEN
BLUE-BLACK		INK
COLD-WATER		TAP
COME	ALONG	NOW
EVEN-MONEY		BET
GIVE	FIRST	AID
GOOD	CLEAN	FUN
GOOD	ROUND	SUM
GOOD	WATCH-DOG	
LONG	DRAWN-OUT	
MANY	YEARS	AGO
ONES	MINDS	EYE

OPEN	OTHER	END
PIGS	MIGHT	FLY
SHOE-SHINE		BOY
WELL-TIMED		ACT

4, 6, 2

WELL VERSED IN

4, 8

ABEL	MUZOREWA
ALEC	GUINNESS
ANDY	WILLIAMS
ANNA	KARENINA
ANNE	HATHAWAY
ANTE	MERIDIAN
ARAB	EMIRATES
ARMY	CHAPLAIN
ARMY	EXERCISE
ARMY	QUARTERS
BABY	CARRIAGE
BABY	SNATCHER
BACK	ENTRANCE
BACK	STRAIGHT
BALL	BEARINGS
BAND	TOGETHER
BANK	INTEREST
BARE	CUPBOARD
BASS	CLARINET
BEAU	BRUMMELL
BEEF	SANDWICH
BEEF	SAUSAGES
BEND	BACKWARD
BEND	SINISTER
BIND	TOGETHER
BIRD	WATCHING
BLUE	MAGAZINE
BLUE	STOCKING
BODY	BUILDING
BODY	SNATCHER
BODY	STOCKING
BOMB	DISPOSAL
BOOK	LEARNING
BOOK	REVIEWER
BORN	OPTIMIST
BULL	ELEPHANT
BURT	REYNOLDS
CAMP	FOLLOWER
CASH	CUSTOMER
CASH	REGISTER
CATS	WHISKERS
CAVE	PAINTING
CITY	ALDERMAN
CITY	BOUNDARY
CLUB	SANDWICH
CLUB	TOGETHER
COAL	INDUSTRY
COAL	MERCHANT
COAL	SHORTAGE
CODE	NAPOLEON

COLD COMPRESS
COLD SHOULDER
COME TOGETHER
COME UPSTAIRS
COOL CUSTOMER
COOL JUDGMENT
COOL THOUSAND
CORN EXCHANGE
COST ACCOUNTS
CROP ROTATION
DARK STRANGER
DARK THOUGHTS
DEAD LANGUAGE
DEAD STRAIGHT
DEAR DEPARTED
DEEP FEELINGS
DEEP INTEREST
DEEP THOUGHTS
DESK CALENDAR
DIRE DISTRESS
DRAW TOGETHER
DULL MONOTONY
DUMB CREATURE
EARN INTEREST
EAST KILBRIDE
EASY PAYMENTS
EASY SOLUTION
ERIC ROBINSON
FACE DISGRACE
FAIR DECISION
FAIR EXCHANGE
FAIR PROSPECT
FAIR QUESTION
FAIT ACCOMPLI
FALL HEADLONG
FARM BUILDING
FARM LABOURER
FAST THINKING
FEEL DOUBTFUL
FEEL HELPLESS
FEEL HOMESICK
FEEL RELIEVED
FEEL STRONGLY
FEEL SYMPATHY
FEET TOGETHER
FILM DIRECTOR
FILM FESTIVAL
FILM INDUSTRY
FILM MAGAZINE
FILM PREMIERE
FILM PRODUCER
FIND PLEASURE
FINE FEATHERS
FINE FEATURES
FINE PROSPECT
FINE SPECIMEN
FIRE PRACTICE
FIRM DECISION
FIRM MEASURES
FIRM PRESSURE
FIRM PROPOSAL

FIVE BEDROOMS
FIVE DIAMONDS
FIVE SEVENTHS
FIVE THOUSAND
FIVE TWELFTHS
FOAM MATTRESS
FOOD SHORTAGE
FOOD SUPPLIES
FOOT REGIMENT
FORM MISTRESS
FOUL LANGUAGE
FOUR BEDROOMS
FOUR DIAMONDS
FOUR FREEDOMS
FOUR FURLONGS
FOUR SEVENTHS
FOUR THOUSAND
FREE CHURCHES
FREE DELIVERY
FREE FACILITY
FREE QUARTERS
FREE THINKING
FREE TRANSFER
FUEL MERCHANT
FULL CAPACITY
FULL DAYLIGHT
FULL PRESSURE
FULL STRENGTH
FUME CUPBOARD
GAIN STRENGTH
GALA OCCASION
GAME PRESERVE
GIFT WRAPPING
GIVE CREDENCE
GIVE EVIDENCE
GIVE JUDGMENT
GIVE PLEASURE
GOLD BRACELET
GOLD RESERVES
GOLD STANDARD
GOOD APPETITE
GOOD BREEDING
GOOD BUSINESS
GOOD EYESIGHT
GOOD FEATURES
GOOD GRACIOUS
GOOD JUDGMENT
GOOD LIKENESS
GOOD LISTENER
GOOD PHYSIQUE
GOOD PRACTICE
GOOD PROGRESS
GOOD QUESTION
GOOD RIDDANCE
GOOD SHEPHERD
GOOD SHOOTING
GOOD SPANKING
GOOD SPECIMEN
GOOD THINKING
GOOD THRILLER
GRAF ZEPPELIN

GRAM	MOLECULE	JOHN	CLEMENTS
GREG	CHAPPELL	JOHN	NEWCOMBE
GREY	EMINENCE	JOHN	WILLIAMS
GREY	SQUIRREL	JOHN	WYCLIFFE
GRIM	LAUGHTER	JOIN	TOGETHER
GROW	POTATOES	JOMO	KENYATTA
GROW	TOGETHER	JONI	MITCHELL
GUYS	HOSPITAL	KEEN	APPETITE
HAIR	RESTORER	KEEN	INTEREST
HALF	FARTHING	KEEP	ACCOUNTS
HALF	MEASURES	KEEP	PRISONER
HANG	TOGETHER	KILL	OUTRIGHT
HANK	WILLIAMS	KING	ETHELRED
HANS	ANDERSON	KNEE	BREECHES
HARD	CURRENCY	KNIT	TOGETHER
HARD	DRINKING	LACK	INTEREST
HARD	EVIDENCE	LADY	HAMILTON
HARD	FEELINGS	LADY	SUPERIOR
HARD	MATTRESS	LAKE	DISTRICT
HARD	QUESTION	LAKE	MICHIGAN
HARD	SHOULDER	LAKE	SUPERIOR
HARD	THINKING	LAKE	VICTORIA
HARD	TRAINING	LAND	SURVEYOR
HAVE	FEELINGS	LAND	TRANSFER
HAVE	PATIENCE	LAST	DECEMBER
HAVE	SCRUPLES	LAST	DELIVERY
HEAD	GARDENER	LAST	FEBRUARY
HEAD	SHRINKER	LAST	FRONTIER
HEIR	APPARENT	LAST	JUDGMENT
HELP	YOURSELF	LAST	NOVEMBER
HERD	INSTINCT	LAST	SATURDAY
HIGH	ALTITUDE	LAST	THURSDAY
HIGH	BUILDING	LATE	LAMENTED
HIGH	ESTIMATE	LEFT	SHOULDER
HIGH	FIDELITY	LEFT	STANDING
HIGH	FOREHEAD	LEGS	TOGETHER
HIGH	INTEREST	LEIF	ERICSSON
HIGH	MOUNTAIN	LIFE	INTEREST
HIGH	OFFICIAL	LIFE	SENTENCE
HIGH	POSITION	LIKE	SARDINES
HIGH	PRESSURE	LIKE	WILDFIRE
HIGH	RAINFALL	LINK	TOGETHER
HIGY	STANDARD	LIVE	AUDIENCE
HIGH	STANDING	LIVE	TOGETHER
HIGH	VELOCITY	LONG	ANCESTRY
HIRE	PURCHASE	LONG	DISTANCE
HOLD	TOGETHER	LONG	DIVISION
HOLY	ALLIANCE	LONG	SENTENCE
HOLY	MACKEREL	LONG	STANDING
HOME	COMFORTS	LONG	TROUSERS
HOME	COUNTIES	LONG	VACATION
HOME	INDUSTRY	LOOK	SHEEPISH
HOME	STRAIGHT	LOOK	SIDEWAYS
HUGE	QUANTITY	LOOK	SUPERIOR
HURL	DEFIANCE	LORD	ADVOCATE
JACK	CHARLTON	LORD	ALMIGHTY
JACK	NICKLAUS	LORD	NUFFIELD
JAIL	SENTENCE	LORD	TENNYSON
JAZZ	FESTIVAL	LOSE	INTEREST
JAZZ	MUSICIAN	LOSE	MOMENTUM
JOHN	BETJEMAN	LOSE	PATIENCE

LOSE	STRENGTH	PIGS	TROTTERS
LOSS	ADJUSTER	PINK	ELEPHANT
LOST	PROPERTY	PLAY	DOMINOES
LOUD	APPLAUSE	PLAY	DRAUGHTS
LUMP	TOGETHER	PLAY	FOOTBALL
MAIN	DRAINAGE	PLAY	OPPOSITE
MAIN	ENTRANCE	PLAY	ROULETTE
MAIN	SEQUENCE	PLAY	SKITTLES
MAKE	ABSOLUTE	POET	LAUREATE
MAKE	ADVANCES	PONS	ASINORUM
MAKE	BANKRUPT	POOR	CREATURE
MAKE	DELIVERY	POOR	LIKENESS
MAKE	PROGRESS	POOR	PHYSIQUE
MANY	RESPECTS	POOR	RELATION
MARK	PHILLIPS	POOR	RELATIVE
MARX	BROTHERS	POOR	SPECIMEN
MARY	PICKFORD	POPE	INNOCENT
MASS	HYSTERIA	PORK	SANDWICH
MASS	MOVEMENT	PORK	SAUSAGES
MASS	MURDERER	PORT	ADELAIDE
MEAN	BUSINESS	PORT	SUNLIGHT
MEAT	SANDWICH	POST	MERIDIAN
MERE	PITTANCE	PULL	TOGETHER
MIKE	BREARLEY	PURE	ACCIDENT
MINE	DETECTOR	PURE	NONSENSE
MISS	UNIVERSE	RACE	QUESTION
MOLL	FLANDERS	RAIL	TERMINUS
MOOT	QUESTION	RAKE	TOGETHER
MOST	GRACIOUS	RANK	OUTSIDER
MOST	REVEREND	RARE	OCCASION
MOVE	SIDEWAYS	REAL	PROPERTY
MUCH	IMPROVED	REAR	ENTRANCE
MUCH	MISTAKEN	RENT	TRIBUNAL
NAIL	CLIPPERS	RICH	PICKINGS
NAIL	SCISSORS	RICH	RELATION
NEAR	DISTANCE	RICH	RELATIVE
NEAR	RELATION	ROAD	ACCIDENT
NEON	LIGHTING	ROAD	JUNCTION
NEWS	BULLETIN	ROCK	FESTIVAL
NEWS	HEADLINE	ROSY	PROSPECT
NEXT	DECEMBER	RUDE	REMINDER
NEXT	FEBRUARY	RUSH	HEADLONG
NEXT	NOVEMBER	SAFE	CROSSING
NEXT	QUESTION	SAFE	DISTANCE
NEXT	SATURDAY	SEED	MERCHANT
NEXT	THURSDAY	SEEK	GUIDANCE
NINE	THOUSAND	SHOE	REPAIRER
ONLY	DAUGHTER	SHOW	BUSINESS
OPEN	CHAMPION	SHOW	COURTESY
OPEN	CONFLICT	SHOW	INTEREST
OPEN	OUTWARDS	SIDE	ENTRANCE
OPEN	QUESTION	SIGN	LANGUAGE
OPEN	SANDWICH	SILK	STOCKING
OVER	EIGHTEEN	SLOW	MOVEMENT
PART	EXCHANGE	SLOW	PROGRESS
PASS	JUDGMENT	SLUM	DWELLING
PASS	SENTENCE	SNAP	DECISION
PAST	HISTORIC	SNAP	JUDGMENT
PAST	MIDNIGHT	SODA	FOUNTAIN
PAUL	VERLAINE	SOFT	CURRENCY
PEAK	DISTRICT	SOFT	HANDLING

SOFT MATTRESS
SOLE OCCUPANT
SOLE SURVIVOR
SORE KNUCKLES
STAR MATERIAL
STEP BACKWARD
STOP DRINKING
STOP FIGHTING
STOP LAUGHING
STOP WORRYING
SUIT YOURSELF
SWIM UPSTREAM
TAKE BEARINGS
TAKE DELIVERY
TAKE DISCOUNT
TAKE MEASURES
TAKE PLEASURE
TAKE PRIORITY
TAKE PRISONER
TALK BUSINESS
TALK NONSENSE
TALK POLITICS
TALK STRAIGHT
TAPE RECORDER
TELL EVERYONE
THIN DISGUISE
THIN MATERIAL
THIS SATURDAY
THIS THURSDAY
TILL DOOMSDAY
TIME EXPOSURE
TORY MAJORITY
TOWN PLANNING
TRUE BELIEVER
TRUE FEELINGS
TWIN BROTHERS
TYRE PRESSURE
UGLY CUSTOMER
UGLY DUCKLING
VAST QUANTITY
VERY REVEREND
WAGE INCREASE
WALK SIDEWAYS
WALK STRAIGHT
WALK TOGETHER
WALL PAINTING
WARM FEELINGS
WEAK ARGUMENT
WEAK SOLUTION
WEAR BLINKERS
WELL ADVANCED
WELL DESERVED
WELL DISPOSED
WELL EDUCATED
WEST BROMWICH
WEST MIDLANDS
WEST VIRGINIA
WILD APPLAUSE
WILD HYACINTH
WILD LAUGHTER
WILL SCARLETT

WINE MERCHANT
WISE DECISION
WITH EMPHASIS
WITH IMPUNITY
WITH INTEREST
WITH PLEASURE
WOOD SHAVINGS
WORD PAINTING
WORK MIRACLES
WORK OVERTIME
WORK TOGETHER
YOUR EMINENCE
YOUR HIGHNESS
YOUR LORDSHIP

5, 1, 6

BREAK A RECORD
BRING A CHARGE
BUILD A BRIDGE
CATCH A TARTAR
CLAIM A REWARD
CLIMB A LADDER
FORGE A CHEQUE
GIVEN A CHANCE
HARRY S. TRUMAN
ISSUE A THREAT
LEARN A LESSON
LEAVE A LEGACY
LIGHT A CANDLE
MOUNT A LADDER
OFFER A CHOICE
OFFER A REWARD
RAISE A FAMILY
SHOOT A GLANCE
SPARE A COPPER
STAGE A STRIKE
STAND A CHANCE
START A RUMOUR
TABLE A MOTION
TEACH A LESSON
THROW A SWITCH
UNDER A BUSHEL
UNDER A LADDER
UNDER A STRAIN
UTTER A THREAT
WORTH A PACKET
WRITE A CHEQUE
WRITE A LETTER
WRITE A REPORT

5, 2, 1, 4

BRAVE AS A LION
CLEAR AS A BELL
DEVIL OF A MESS
DEVIL OF A TIME
DRUNK AS A LORD
GRIND TO A HALT
HAPPY AS A LARK
NEVER AT A LOSS

SERVE UP A MEAL
SOUND AS A BELL
THREE AT A TIME
WHALE OF A TIME

5, 2, 2, 3

BRING TO AN END
COUNT UP TO TEN
MEANS TO AN END
WHITE OF AN EGG

5, 2, 3, 2

THREE TO ONE ON

5, 2, 5

AGREE TO TERMS
ALLOW TO STAND
ALPHA TO OMEGA
ANGEL OF DEATH
ANGEL OF MERCY
APPLE OF SODOM
ASHES TO ASHES
BADGE OF MERIT
BEANS ON TOAST
BLACK AS NIGHT
BLACK AS PITCH
BLACK OR WHITE
BLADE OF GRASS
BLAZE OF GLORY
BLAZE OF LIGHT
BLOCK OF FLATS
BLOCK OF STONE
BLOOM OF YOUTH
BOARD OF TRADE
BORED TO DEATH
BORED TO TEARS
BRACE OF BIRDS
BRICK BY BRICK
BRING TO EARTH
BRING TO LIGHT
BRING TO TRIAL
BUILT OF STONE
BUNCH OF ROSES
BURNT TO ASHES
BURST OF ANGER
BURST OF SPEED
CEASE TO EXIST
CHEAT AT CARDS
CHEEK TO CHEEK
CHIEF OF STAFF
CLASH OF STEEL
CLASH OF VIEWS
CLERK OF WORKS
CLIMB TO POWER
CLIVE OF INDIA
CLOSE TO DEATH
CLOUD OF SMOKE
CLOUD OF STEAM

CLUMP OF TREES
COAST TO COAST
COULD BE WORSE
CRÊPE DE CHINE
CROSS OF DAVID
CRUST OF BREAD
DANCE OF DEATH
DEATH OR GLORY
DRAWN TO SCALE
DREAM OF YOUTH
DRINK OF WATER
DRIVE TO DRINK
DRIVE-IN MOVIE
DRUNK OR SOBER
EIGHT OF CLUBS
EVERY SO OFTEN
FIELD OF WHEAT
FIFTH OF APRIL
FIFTH OF MARCH
FIRST OF APRIL
FIRST OF MARCH
FIRST OF THREE
FIRST TO LEAVE
FIRTH OF CLYDE
FIRTH OF FORTH
FLEET OF SHIPS
FLEET OF TAXIS
FLOCK OF BIRDS
FLOCK OF GEESE
FLOCK OF SHEEP
FLOOD OF TEARS
FLUSH OF YOUTH
FORCE AN ENTRY
FORCE OF HABIT
FORTY OR FIFTY
FRESH AS PAINT
GLASS OF WATER
GLEAM OF LIGHT
GRAIN OF SENSE
GRAIN OF TRUTH
GROUP OF THREE
HAVEN OF PEACE
HEADS OR TAILS
HEAPS OF MONEY
HEART OF STONE
HEART TO HEART
HEAVY AT HEART
HOUND TO DEATH
HOUSE OF CARDS
HOUSE OF LORDS
HOUSE OF PEERS
HOUSE OF TUDOR
HOUSE TO HOUSE
KNAVE OF CLUBS
LAUGH TO SCORN
LEARN BY HEART
LEARN TO DRIVE
LEARN TO WRITE
LEAVE IT ALONE
LEAVE NO DOUBT
LEAVE NO TRACE

LIGHT	OF	HEART
LUCKY	AT	CARDS
LYING	IN	STATE
MARRY	IN	HASTE
MIGHT	IS	RIGHT
MONEY	TO	SPARE
MONTH	BY	MONTH
MOUNT	OF	VENUS
MOUTH	TO	MOUTH
MOVED	TO	TEARS
NIGHT	OF	BLISS
NINTH	OF	APRIL
NINTH	OF	MARCH
NORTH	TO	SOUTH
ORDER	IN	COURT
ORDER	OF	MERIT
OUNCE	OF	FLESH
OUNCE	OF	SENSE
PARTY	IN	POWER
PEACE	ON	EARTH
PIECE	BY	PIECE
PIECE	OF	BREAD
PIECE	OF	CHALK
PIECE	OF	EIGHT
PIECE	OF	MAGIC
PIECE	OF	MUSIC
PIECE	OF	PAPER
PINCH	OF	SNUFF
PLACE	AN	ORDER
PLACE	IN	ORDER
PLACE	OF	BIRTH
POINT	AT	ISSUE
POINT	BY	POINT
POINT	OF	ISSUE
POINT	OF	ORDER
POINT	TO	POINT
POUND	OF	FLESH
POUND	OF	SUGAR
PRICE	OF	MONEY
PRIDE	OF	LIONS
PRIDE	OF	PLACE
PROOF	OF	GUILT
PROUD	AS	PUNCH
QUEEN	OF	CLUBS
QUEEN	OF	SCOTS
QUEEN	OF	SHEBA
QUICK	TO	ANGER
QUITE	IN	ORDER
RANGE	OF	HILLS
READY	TO	BURST
READY	TO	LEAVE
READY	TO	START
RIGHT	OF	ENTRY
RIGHT	OR	WRONG
RIVER	OF	BLOOD
ROUND	OF	TOAST
SCRAP	OF	PAPER
SEEDS	OF	DOUBT
SENSE	OF	GUILT
SENSE	OF	SHAME
SENSE	OF	SIGHT

SENSE	OF	SMELL
SENSE	OF	TASTE
SENSE	OF	TOUCH
SERVE	AT	TABLE
SEVEN	OF	CLUBS
SEVEN	OR	EIGHT
SHAFT	OF	LIGHT
SHALL	WE	DANCE?
SHEAF	OF	WHEAT
SHEET	OF	FLAME
SHEET	OF	GLASS
SHEET	OF	PAPER
SHEIK	OF	ARABY
SHORE	TO	SHORE
SHORT	OF	FUNDS
SHORT	OF	MONEY
SHORT	OF	SPACE
SHORT	OF	STAFF
SIEGE	OF	PARIS
SIXTH	OF	APRIL
SIXTH	OF	MARCH
SKEIN	OF	GEESE
SLAVE	TO	DRINK
SLAVE	TO	DRUGS
SLICE	OF	BREAD
SLICE	OF	TOAST
SOUND	OF	MUSIC
SPARE	NO	PAINS
SPEED	OF	LIGHT
SPEED	OF	SOUND
SPORT	OF	KINGS
SPURN	AN	OFFER
STAND	IN	FRONT
STAND-UP		FIGHT
STATE	OF	BLISS
STATE	OF	PEACE
STATE	OF	SHOCK
STATE	OF	SIEGE
STICK	NO	BILLS
STICK	OF	CHALK
STICK	OR	TWIST
STICK-ON		SOLES
STILL	OF	NIGHT
STOCK	IN	TRADE
STOKE	ON	TRENT
STONE	OF	SCONE
STONE	TO	DEATH
STOUT	OF	HEART
STRIP	OF	PAPER
SUGAR	IS	SWEET
SUITE	OF	ROOMS
SWARM	OF	FLIES
SWEET	AS	HONEY
SWEET	AS	SUGAR
SWIFT	TO	ANGER
TASTE	OF	HONEY
TEARS	OF	GRIEF
TEARS	OF	SHAME
TENTH	OF	APRIL
TENTH	OF	MARCH
TERMS	OF	TRADE

THIRD OF APRIL
THIRD OF MARCH
THREE BY THREE
THREE OF CLUBS
TOUCH OF CLASS
TOUCH OF FROST
TOUGH AS STEEL
TOWER OF BABEL
TREAT IN STORE
TRUSS OF STRAW
TWICE AS HEAVY
TWICE AS QUICK
WASTE OF MONEY
WHICH IS WHICH?
WOMAN TO WOMAN
WORLD OF SPORT
WRITE AN ESSAY
YEARS OF STUDY
YOUNG AT HEART
YOURS IN HASTE
YOUTH OF TODAY

5, 3, 1, 3

APPLY FOR A JOB

5, 3, 4

ABOVE THE LINE
AFTER THE BALL
AFTER THE FACT
ALONG THE ROAD
APPLY FOR BAIL
ARGUE THE CASE
ARGUE THE TOSS
AWAKE THE DEAD
BACON AND EGGS
BEARD THE LION
BELOW THE BELT
BELOW THE KNEE
BELOW THE LINE
BIRDS-EYE VIEW
BLACK AND BLUE
BLACK AND TANS
BLOOD AND IRON
BLOOD AND SAND
BONNY WEE LASS
BREAD AND MILK
BREAD AND WINE
BREAK THE BANK
BREAK THE NEWS
BREAK THE RULE
BREAK THE SEAL
BRUIN THE BEAR
BRUSH AND COMB
CATCH THE POST
CATCH THE TUBE
CHEAP-DAY FARE
CHECK THE TILL
CLEAR THE DECK
CLEAR THE PATH

CLEAR THE ROAD
CLOSE THE DOOR
CLOSE THE FILE
CLOSE THE GATE
COACH AND FOUR
COACH AND PAIR
COUNT THE COST
COUNT THE DAYS
COVER THE COST
CRACK THE CODE
CRACK TYE WHIP
CRACK-POT IDEA
CROSS THE LINE
CROSS THE ROAD
CURDS AND WHEY
DARBY AND JOAN
DEVIL MAY CARE
DEVIL YOU KNOW
EIGHT PER CENT
EVERY MAN JACK
FIFTY PER CENT
FIGHT FOR LIFE
FIGHT THE CUTS
FIRST AND LAST
FIRST SEA-LORD
FIRST-AID POST
FORCE THE PACE
FORTY PER CENT
GIRLS AND BOYS
GIVEN THE BIRD
GIVEN THE BOOT
GIVEN THE CANE
GIVEN THE PUSH
GIVEN THE SACK
GIVEN THE SLIP
HANDS AND FEET
HAPPY NEW YEAR
HEART AND SOUL
HOIST THE FLAG
HORSE AND CART
HORSE AND TRAP
HOUSE AND HOME
HOUSE FOR SALE
INFRA-RED LAMP
INFRA-RED RAYS
JUDGE AND JURY
KNIFE AND FORK
KNOCK OFF WORK
LAGER AND LIME
LAUGH OUT LOUD
LEAVE FOR DEAD
LEAVE FOR WORK
LEAVE THE NEST
LEAVE THE ROOM
LEGAL AID FUND
LIGHT AND DARK
LIGHT THE LAMP
LIGHT THE OVEN
LOWER THE FLAG
MANYS THE TIME
MERRY OLD SOUL

MIGHT AND MAIN
MILES PER HOUR
MINOR SET-BACK
MONEY FOR ROPE
MORES THE PITY
NEVER THE SAME
NEVER TOO LATE
NEVER YOU MIND!
OFFER FOR SALE
PAINT THE LILY
PAINT THE WALL
PAPER THE ROOM
PAPER THE WALL
PITCH AND PUTT
PITCH AND TOSS
PLAIN AND PURL
PORGY AND BESS
POUND THE BEAT
PRESS THE BELL
PROVE THE RULE
PUNCH AND JUDY
RAISE THE CASH
RAISE THE DEAD
RAISE THE DUST
RAISE THE FLAG
RAISE THE ROOF
RIGHT AND LEFT
ROUND THE BACK
ROUND THE BEND
ROUND THE FIRE
ROUND THE TOWN
SCOOP THE POOL
SEVEN PER CENT
SHAKE THE HEAD
SHARE THE LOAD
SHARE THE LOOT
SHARE THE WORK
SHOUT FOR HELP
SHOUT THE ODDS
SHOWN THE DOOR
SIXTY PER CENT
SLICE THE BALL
SMASH AND GRAB
SMOKE THE WEED
SMOKE TOO MUCH
SOUND AND FURY
SPADE AND FORK
SPICK AND SPAN
SPIKE THE GUNS
SPILL THE SALT
SPLIT THE ATOM
SPLIT THE VOTE
SPOON AND FORK
STALL FOR TIME
STAND THE HEAT
STAND THE PACE
STAND THE TEST
START TOO LATE
START TOO SOON
STEAL THE SHOW
SUGAR THE PILL

SWEEP THE DECK
SWEET AND SOUR
SWING THE LEAD
TAILS YOU LOSE
THERE AND BACK
THERE AND THEN
THICK AND FAST
THICK AND THIN
THREE PER CENT
THREE-ACT PLAY
THREE-DAY WEEK
THREE-PLY WOOD
TOOTH AND CLAW
TOOTH AND NAIL
TRUST AND OBEY
TWICE THE SIZE
TWIST AND TURN
UNDER AND OVER
UNDER ONE ROOF
UNDER THE FLAG
UNDER THE HEEL
UNDER THE ROSE
UNDER THE SKIN
UNFIT FOR WORK
VENUS FLY-TRAP
VISIT THE SICK
WATCH AND PRAY
WHATS THE ODDS?
WHERE AND WHEN
WHILE YOU WAIT
WORMS EYE VIEW
WORSE FOR WEAR

5 , 4 , 3

ABOUT TIME TOO
ADMIT ONES AGE
ASCOT GOLD CUP
BLACK-EYED PEA
BLUFF KING HAL
BREAK ONES ARM
BREAK ONES LEG
CAKED WITH MUD
CARRY ONES BAT
CLING LIKE IVY
DANCE WITH JOY
DIRTY WEEK-END
ELBOW ONES WAY
FIGHT ONES WAY
FIRST-BORN SON
FORCE ONES WAY
GRAND SEND-OFF
GREEN-LINE BUS
GRIND ONES AXE
GROPE ONES WAY
HOARY WITH AGE
MUSIC-HALL ACT
PRESS HAND-OUT
RAISE ONES HAT
RIGHT-HAND MAN
SHARP LOOK-OUT

SHORT TIME AGO
SPARE-TIME JOB
THREE WISE MEN
TOUCH ONES CAP
TRUTH WILL OUT
TWIST ONES ARM
UNDER ONES HAT

5, 5, 2

CATCH SIGHT OF
SAMMY DAVIS JR
STEER CLEAR OF
THINK ABOUT IT
THROW LIGHT ON

5, 7

ABOUT AVERAGE
ABOVE AVERAGE
ABUSE ONESELF
ACTOR MANAGER
ADMIT NOTHING
AFTER SUNRISE
ALICE SPRINGS
ALIGN ONESELF
AMONG FRIENDS
AMUSE ONESELF
ANDRÉ MALRAUX
ANDRÉ MAUROIS
ANGRY SILENCE
ANTON CHEKHOV
APPLE BLOSSOM
APPLE CRUMBLE
APPLE FRITTER
APPLE ORCHARD
APPLE STRUDEL
APPLY ONESELF
APRIL SHOWERS
APRON STRINGS
ARMED ROBBERY
AWAIT PAYMENT
AWARD CUSTODY
AWARD DAMAGES
BADLY BEHAVED
BADLY DAMAGED
BADLY WOUNDED
BASIC ENGLISH
BELOW AVERAGE
BENNY GOODMAN
BIBLE THUMPER
BIRTH CONTROL
BLACK CLOTHES
BLACK COUNTRY
BLACK DESPAIR
BLACK DIAMOND
BLACK PUDDING
BLAST FURNACE
BLEAK OUTLOOK
BLIND BARGAIN
BLIND IMPULSE

BLOCK CAPITAL
BLOCK LETTERS
BLOOD BROTHER
BOARD MEETING
BOBBY FISCHER
BORIS GODUNOV
BORIS KARLOFF
BOSOM FRIENDS
BOUND EDITION
BRACE ONESELF
BRAIN SURGEON
BRAIN SURGERY
BRASS RUBBING
BRASS SECTION
BRAVE ATTEMPT
BRAVE WARRIOR
BREAD PUDDING
BREAK CONTACT
BREAK RECORDS
BREAK SURFACE
BREAK THROUGH
BRIEF HOLIDAY
BRIEF OUTLINE
BRIEF SUMMARY
BRING CHARGES
BRING FORWARD
BRING THROUGH
BROAD OUTLINE
BROAD OUTLOOK
BROWN WINDSOR
BRUCE FORSYTH
BRUSH AGAINST
BURMA RAILWAY
BURNT ALMONDS
BURNT FINGERS
CABIN CRUISER
CABIN STEWARD
CABLE RAILWAY
CAIRN TERRIER
CAROL CONCERT
CAROL SINGERS
CARRY FORWARD
CARRY THROUGH
CARTE BLANCHE
CATCH NAPPING
CAUSE CÉLÈBRE
CAUSE OFFENCE
CAUSE TROUBLE
CHASE SHADOWS
CHEAP COMMENT
CHEAP TWISTER
CHESS PROBLEM
CHIEF CASHIER
CHIEF JUSTICE
CHIEF MOURNER
CHIEF OFFICER
CHIEF SKIPPER
CHIEF STEWARD
CHIEF SUSPECT
CHIEF WITNESS
CHILD WELFARE

CHINA	CABINET
CIVIC	WELCOME
CIVIL	DEFENCE
CIVIL	LIBERTY
CIVIL	OFFENCE
CIVIL	SERVANT
CIVIL	SERVICE
CLAIM	DAMAGES
CLARE	COLLEGE
CLASS	WARFARE
CLEAN	LICENCE
CLEAR	ONESELF
CLEAR	PASSAGE
CLEAR	THOUGHT
CLEAR	WARNING
CLIFF	RICHARD
CLIMB	EVEREST
CLINK	GLASSES
CLOCK	WATCHER
CLOSE	CONTACT
CLOSE	CONTEST
CLOSE	FIELDER
CLOSE	HARMONY
CLOUD	CHAMBER
COACH	STATION
CODED	MESSAGE
COLIN	COWDREY
CONIC	SECTION
COUGH	MIXTURE
COUNT	DRACULA
COUPE	JACQUES
COURT	MARTIAL
COURT	OFFICER
COURT	PLASTER
COURT	SUMMONS
CRACK	SOLDIER
CRASH	LANDING
CREAM	CRACKER
CRÊPE	SUZETTE
CROSS	ONESELF
CROSS	SECTION
CROWN	WITNESS
CRUDE	METHODS
CUBIC	MEASURE
DAILY	EXPRESS
DAILY	ROUTINE
DAILY	SERVICE
DAIRY	FARMING
DAIRY	PRODUCE
DANCE	HOSTESS
DANCE	SESSION
DAVID	COLEMAN
DAVID	GARRICK
DAVID	KOSSOFF
DEATH	CHAMBER
DEATH	PENALTY
DEATH	WARRANT
DEBIT	BALANCE
DENIS	COMPTON
DEVIL	WORSHIP
DIANA	SPENCER
DIRTY	WEATHER

DIZZY	HEIGHTS
DRESS	CLOTHES
DRESS	UNIFORM
DRINK	HEAVILY
DRIVE	FORWARD
DRIVE	THROUGH
DROWN	ONESELF
DUTCH	AUCTION
DUTCH	COURAGE
EARLY	CLOSING
EARLY	EDITION
EARLY	ENGLISH
EARLY	MORNING
EARLY	PROMISE
EARLY	WARNING
EDDIE	COCHRAN
EDGAR	WALLACE
EIGHT	DOLLARS
EIGHT	GALLONS
EIGHT	HUNDRED
EIGHT	MINUTES
EIGHT	SQUARED
EIGHT	WICKETS
ELDER	BROTHER
ELGIN	MARBLES
ÉLITE	CIRCLES
ELVIS	PRESLEY
EMPTY	FEELING
EMPTY	STOMACH
ENJOY	ONESELF
EQUAL	CONTEST
EVERY	MORNING
EVERY	TUESDAY
EXACT	ACCOUNT
EXACT	DETAILS
EXACT	MEANING
EXACT	SCIENCE
EXCEL	ONESELF
EXERT	ONESELF
EXTRA	EDITION
EXTRA	SPECIAL
FAINT	ATTEMPT
FAITH	HEALING
FALSE	ACCOUNT
FALSE	ADDRESS
FALSE	COLOURS
FALSE	ECONOMY
FALSE	HORIZON
FALSE	MODESTY
FALSE	PROPHET
FALSE	READING
FALSE	VERDICT
FALSE	WITNESS
FANCY	ONESELF
FARNE	ISLANDS
FAROE	ISLANDS
FATAL	BLUNDER
FATAL	DISEASE
FATAL	MISTAKE
FIELD	GLASSES
FIELD	KITCHEN

FIELD MARSHAL	GLASS TUMBLER
FIELD OFFICER	GLOBE THEATRE
FIELD STUDIES	GOING BEGGING
FIFTH CENTURY	GOING CONCERN
FIFTY DOLLARS	GRACE DARLING
FIFTY MINUTES	GRAIN HARVEST
FIGHT AGAINST	GRAND CENTRAL
FINAL ACCOUNT	GRAND DUCHESS
FINAL ATTEMPT	GRAND GUIGNOL
FINAL CURTAIN	GRAND LARCENY
FINAL EDITION	GRAND OPENING
FINAL EPISODE	GRAPE HARVEST
FINAL OUTCOME	GRAVE MISTAKE
FINAL PAYMENT	GRAVE OFFENCE
FINAL VICTORY	GREAT BRAVERY
FINAL WARNING	GREAT BRITAIN
FINAL WHISTLE	GREAT EASTERN
FINER FEELING	GREAT EXPENSE
FIRST ATTEMPT	GREAT FRIENDS
FIRST CENTURY	GREAT MALVERN
FIRST CHAPTER	GREAT MYSTERY
FIRST EDITION	GREAT PAINTER
FIRST HELPING	GREAT RESPECT
FIRST INNINGS	GREAT SOLDIER
FIRST OFFENCE	GREAT STATURE
FIRST OFFICER	GREAT SUCCESS
FIRST PAYMENT	GREAT THINKER
FIRST QUARTER	GREAT TRAGEDY
FIRST READING	GREAT TRIUMPH
FIRST REFUSAL	GREAT VARIETY
FIRST RESERVE	GREAT VICTORY
FIRST SERVICE	GREAT WESTERN
FIRST THOUGHT	GREEK ISLANDS
FIRST VIOLINS	GREEK SCHOLAR
FIXED CAPITAL	GREEK THEATRE
FIXED PAYMENT	GREEK TRAGEDY
FLUID MEASURE	GREEN FINGERS
FOGGY WEATHER	GROSS NEGLECT
FORCE FEEDING	GROSS TONNAGE
FORTY DOLLARS	GROUP CAPTAIN
FORTY FIFTEEN	GROUP THERAPY
FORTY MINUTES	GUARD AGAINST
FORTY THIEVES	GUEST SPEAKER
FOUND WANTING	GUILT COMPLEX
FRANK SINATRA	HABIT FORMING
FRANK WHITTLE	HAIRS BREADTH
FRANK WORRELL	HANDS BREADTH
FRESH CHAPTER	HAPPY HOLIDAY
FRESH FLOWERS	HAPPY LANDING
FRESH OUTLOOK	HAPPY OUTCOME
FRONT PARLOUR	HAPPY RETURNS
FRUIT MACHINE	HAPPY THOUGHT
FULLY DRESSED	HARRY CORBETT
FULLY ENGAGED	HARRY HOUDINI
FULLY SECURED	HARRY SECOMBE
FUNNY FEELING	HARRY WHARTON
GENTS BICYCLE	HASTY PUDDING
GEOFF BOYCOTT	HASTY RETREAT
GIDDY HEIGHTS	HAUTE COUTURE
GLASS FACTORY	HEADY MIXTURE
GLASS SLIPPER	HEADY PERFUME

HEART	DISEASE
HEART	FAILURE
HEART	SURGERY
HEART	TROUBLE
HEAVY	BRIGADE
HEAVY	DRINKER
HEAVY	PENALTY
HEAVY	PETTING
HEAVY	READING
HEAVY	SLEEPER
HEAVY	VEHICLE
HEDGE	SPARROW
HENRY	PURCELL
HENRY	STANLEY
HEROS	WELCOME
HILLY	COUNTRY
HIRED	SERVANT
HORSE	BLANKET
HORSE	MARINES
HORSE	SOLDIER
HORSE	TRADING
HORSE	TRAINER
HOTEL	MANAGER
HOUSE	PAINTER
HOUSE	SPARROW
HOUSE	SURGEON
HOUSE	TRAINED
HUMAN	ELEMENT
HUMAN	FAILING
HUMAN	FRAILTY
HUMAN	REMAINS
HUMAN	SPECIES
IDEAL	HUSBAND
INNER	SANCTUM
INNER	TURMOIL
IRISH	TERRIER
IRISH	WHISKEY
JACOB	EPSTEIN
JAMES	BOSWELL
JAMES	HERRIOT
JAMES	MADISON
JAMES	STEWART
JAMES	THURBER
JESUS	COLLEGE
JIMMY	CONNORS
JIMMY	DURANTE
JIMMY	EDWARDS
JIMMY	GREAVES
JIMMY	STEWART
JOINT	ACCOUNT
JOINT	CONCERN
JOINT	HOLDING
JOINT	TENANCY
JOINT	TRUSTEE
JULIE	ANDREWS
KEBLE	COLLEGE
KEMAL	ATATURK
KENNY	EVERETT
KHAKI	UNIFORM
KINGS	COLLEGE
KINGS	COUNSEL
KINGS	ENGLISH
KINGS	HIGHWAY
KINGS	PROCTOR
KNIFE	GRINDER
KNOCK	AGAINST
LADYS	BICYCLE
LARGE	EXPANSE
LARGE	HELPING
LARGE	PORTION
LARGE	VARIETY
LARGE	WRITING
LARRY	GRAYSON
LATIN	AMERICA
LATIN	GRAMMAR
LATIN	QUARTER
LATIN	SCHOLAR
LEAVE	OUTSIDE
LEGAL	ADVISER
LEGAL	CUSTODY
LEGAL	FICTION
LEGAL	HISTORY
LEGAL	OPINION
LEGAL	PROCESS
LEMON	FLAVOUR
LEMON	PUDDING
LEVEL	PEGGING
LEWIS	CARROLL
LIGHT	BRIGADE
LIGHT	CAVALRY
LIGHT	CLOTHES
LIGHT	CRUISER
LIGHT	DRAGOON
LIGHT	FINGERS
LIGHT	FITTING
LIGHT	READING
LIGHT	SLEEPER
LIVER	SAUSAGE
LOCAL	AFFAIRS
LOCAL	DIALECT
LOOSE	CLOTHES
LOOSE	GARMENT
LOTUS	BLOSSOM
LOUIS	BLÉRIOT
LOUIS	BRAILLE
LOUIS	PASTEUR
LOWER	BRACKET
LOWER	CHAMBER
LOWER	CLASSES
LOWER	ONESELF
LOWER	REGIONS
LOYAL	SUBJECT
LOYAL	SUPPORT
LUCKY	VENTURE
LUTON	AIRPORT
MAGIC	FORMULA
MAGIC	LANTERN
MAJOR	BARBARA
MAJOR	GENERAL
MAJOR	PROBLEM
MAJOR	PROPHET
MAJOR	SURGERY

MARIA THERESA	NORTH VIETNAM
MARIE CELESTE	OLDER BROTHER
MARTY FELDMAN	ONION FLAVOUR
MENAI STRAITS	OPERA COMIQUE
MERCY KILLING	OPERA GLASSES
MERRY ENGLAND	OPIUM TRAFFIC
MERRY MONARCH	ORGAN BUILDER
METAL FATIGUE	ORGAN GRINDER
MEZZO SOPRANO	ORGAN RECITAL
MINCE MATTERS	OUTER COATING
MINOR AILMENT	OUTER GARMENT
MINOR OFFENCE	PABLO PICASSO
MINOR PROPHET	PARTY MACHINE
MINOR SURGERY	PEACH BLOSSOM
MIXED BATHING	PEARL FISHERS
MIXED COMPANY	PEARL FISHING
MIXED DOUBLES	PEARL HARBOUR
MIXED ECONOMY	PEARL WEDDING
MIXED MOTIVES	PEASE PUDDING
MODEL HUSBAND	PEDAL PUSHERS
MODEL PATIENT	PENNY WHISTLE
MODEL RAILWAY	PETER CUSHING
MODUS VIVENDI	PETER SELLERS
MOIRA SHEARER	PETER USTINOV
MONEY CHANGER	PETTY DETAILS
MONEY MATTERS	PETTY LARCENY
MONEY TROUBLE	PETTY OFFENCE
MORAL CONDUCT	PETTY OFFICER
MORAL COURAGE	PIANO RECITAL
MORAL SUPPORT	PLAIN CLOTHES
MORAL VICTORY	PLAIN COOKING
MORTE DARTHUR	PLAIN DEALING
MOTOR LICENCE	PLAIN ENGLISH
MOTOR SCOOTER	PLAIN SAILING
MOTOR VEHICLE	PLAIN SPEAKER
MOUNT EVEREST	PLAIN WRAPPER
MOUNT OLYMPUS	PLANE SPOTTER
MUGGY WEATHER	PLEAD POVERTY
MUSIC TEACHER	POLES ASUNDER
MUTED STRINGS	POUND FOOLISH
NAVAL ACADEMY	POWER STATION
NAVAL ATTACHÉ	PREEN ONESELF
NAVAL COLLEGE	PRESS COUNCIL
NAVAL COMMAND	PRESS CUTTING
NAVAL OFFICER	PRESS FORWARD
NAVAL RESERVE	PRESS GALLERY
NAVAL SERVICE	PRESS OFFICER
NAVAL UNIFORM	PRESS ONWARDS
NAVAL WARFARE	PRESS RELEASE
NEVER DESPAIR	PRICE CONTROL
NEWLY MARRIED	PRICE RIGGING
NIGHT CLASSES	PRIDE ONESELF
NIGHT CLOTHES	PRIME SUSPECT
NIGHT FIGHTER	PRIVY COUNCIL
NINTH CENTURY	PUPIL TEACHER
NOBLE BEARING	QUEEN CONSORT
NOBLE DESCENT	QUEEN JULIANA
NOBLE GESTURE	QUEUE JUMPING
NORTH AMERICA	QUIET WEDDING
NORTH COUNTRY	QUIET WEEKEND
NORTH SHIELDS	QUITE CERTAIN

QUITE	CORRECT	SARAH	VAUGHAN
RADAR	STATION	SAUCE	TARTARE
RADIO	MESSAGE	SCALE	DIAGRAM
RADIO	NETWORK	SCALE	DRAWING
RADIO	STATION	SCENE	SHIFTER
RAINY	CLIMATE	SCENE	STEALER
RAINY	WEATHER	SEVEN	DOLLARS
RAPID	DECLINE	SEVEN	EIGHTHS
RAPID	STRIDES	SEVEN	GALLONS
RAPID	TRANSIT	SEVEN	HUNDRED
REACH	FORWARD	SEVEN	MINUTES
REACH	PUBERTY	SEVEN	SISTERS
REACH	WEMBLEY	SEVEN	SQUARED
REACT	AGAINST	SEVEN	WICKETS
REACT	SHARPLY	SEVEN	WONDERS
REIGN	SUPREME	SHADY	RETREAT
RIDER	HAGGARD	SHARE	CAPITAL
RIGHT	CHARLIE	SHEER	TORTURE
RIGHT	FORWARD	SHIPS	BISCUIT
RIGHT	THROUGH	SHIPS	CAPTAIN
RIVER	SHANNON	SHIPS	COMPASS
RIVER	TRAFFIC	SHIPS	STEWARD
ROAST	CHICKEN	SHIRT	SLEEVES
ROAST	VENISON	SHOCK	TACTICS
ROMAN	EMPEROR	SHOCK	THERAPY
ROMAN	HISTORY	SHOOT	ONESELF
ROMAN	NUMBERS	SHORT	ACCOUNT
ROMAN	NUMERAL	SHORT	CIRCUIT
ROMAN	REMAINS	SHORT	COMMONS
ROMAN	SOLDIER	SHORT	EXTRACT
ROUGH	DIAMOND	SHORT	JOURNEY
ROUGH	DRAUGHT	SHORT	MEASURE
ROUGH	DRAWING	SHORT	PASSAGE
ROUGH	JUSTICE	SHORT	ROMANCE
ROUGH	MANNERS	SHORT	SESSION
ROUGH	OUTLINE	SHORT	SUMMARY
ROUGH	PASSAGE	SHORT	VERSION
ROUGH	SURFACE	SHOVE	HAPENNY
ROUGH	WEATHER	SIEGE	WARFARE
ROUND	FIFTEEN	SIMON	BOLIVAR
ROUND	FIGURES	SIXTH	CENTURY
ROYAL	ACADEMY	SIXTY	DOLLARS
ROYAL	ARSENAL	SIXTY	MINUTES
ROYAL	CHARTER	SIXTY	SECONDS
ROYAL	COLOURS	SLAVE	TRAFFIC
ROYAL	COMMAND	SLEEP	SOUNDLY
ROYAL	CONSENT	SLEEP	SWEETLY
ROYAL	DESCENT	SMALL	COMFORT
ROYAL	MARINES	SMALL	FORTUNE
ROYAL	WARRANT	SMALL	HELPING
ROYAL	WEDDING	SMALL	LETTERS
ROYAL	WELCOME	SMALL	MEASURE
SAINT	BERNARD	SMALL	MERCIES
SAINT	FRANCIS	SMALL	PARCELS
SAINT	MATTHEW	SMALL	PORTION
SAINT	PATRICK	SMALL	WRITING
SAINT	STEPHEN	SMART	CLOTHES
SALES	FIGURES	SMILE	SWEETLY
SALES	GIMMICK	SMOKE	SIGNALS
SALES	MANAGER	SNAKE	CHARMER
SANTA	BARBARA	SNEAK	PREVIEW

SOLAR BATTERY	STRIP CARTOON
SOLAR ECLIPSE	STUDY CLOSELY
SOLID CITIZEN	STUDY ENGLISH
SONIC BARRIER	STUFF ONESELF
SOUND BARRIER	SUGAR COATING
SOUND EFFECTS	SUGAR CONTENT
SOUND FOOTING	SUGAR REFINER
SOUND SLEEPER	SUNNY WEATHER
SOUND TACTICS	SURGE FORWARD
SOUTH AFRICAN	SWEEP THROUGH
SOUTH AMERICA	SWEET CHARIOT
SOUTH GEORGIA	SWEET MARTINI
SOUTH PACIFIC	SWEET PERFUME
SOUTH SHIELDS	SWEET REVENGE
SOUTH VIETNAM	SWEET SIXTEEN
SPACE CAPSULE	SWEET SUCCESS
SPACE FICTION	SWEET WILLIAM
SPACE STATION	SWIFT CURRENT
SPARE BEDROOM	SWISS COTTAGE
SPEAK CLEARLY	SWORN ENEMIES
SPEAK ENGLISH	SWORN FRIENDS
SPEAK ITALIAN	TABLE MANNERS
SPEAK PLAINLY	TEACH ENGLISH
SPEAK RAPIDLY	TEACH SCIENCE
SPEAK RUSSIAN	TEMPT FORTUNE
SPEAK SPANISH	TENTH CENTURY
SPEAK VOLUMES	TERRY GILLIAM
SPEED WRITING	THANK HEAVENS!
SPOIL ONESELF	THINK QUICKLY
STAFF COLLEGE	THINK THROUGH
STAFF OFFICER	THIRD CENTURY
STAFF PROBLEM	THIRD CHANNEL
STAGE EFFECTS	THIRD CHAPTER
STAGE MANAGER	THIRD OFFICER
STAGE SETTING	THIRD QUARTER
STAGE WHISPER	THIRD READING
STAMP AUCTION	THOSE AGAINST
STAND ACCUSED	THREE COLOURS
STAND AGAINST	THREE COURSES
STAND BETWEEN	THREE DEGREES
STAND UPRIGHT	THREE DOLLARS
STARK REALITY	THREE EIGHTHS
START PACKING	THREE FATHOMS
START TALKING	THREE FIGURES
STATE CONTROL	THREE GALLONS
STATE FUNERAL	THREE GUESSES
STATE LOTTERY	THREE HUNDRED
STATE PENSION	THREE LENGTHS
STATE SUBSIDY	THREE MILLION
STEAK PUDDING	THREE MINUTES
STEAM TURBINE	THREE OCTAVES
STEAM WHISTLE	THREE SECONDS
STEEL ONESELF	THREE SISTERS
STERN REALITY	THREE SQUARED
STEVE CAUTHEN	THREE STOOGES
STIFF PENALTY	THREE STRIPES
STILL WAITING	THREE UNITIES
STOCK COMPANY	THREE WICKETS
STORM BREWING	THREE WITCHES
STORM TROOPER	TIGHT SQUEEZE
STORM WARNING	TOKEN GESTURE

TOKEN	PAYMENT	WOODY	GUTHRIE
TOMMY	HANDLEY	WORKS	CANTEEN
TOMMY	TRINDER	WORKS	COUNCIL
TOTAL	ECLIPSE	WORKS	MANAGER
TRADE	DEFICIT	WORTH	NOTHING
TRADE	JOURNAL	WRONG	ADDRESS
TRADE	SURPLUS	WRONG	MEANING
TRAIN	JOURNEY	WRONG	TURNING
TRAIN	ROBBERY	YOUNG	ENGLAND
TRAIN	SERVICE	YOUNG	HOPEFUL
TRAIN	SPOTTER		
TRAMP	STEAMER		

6, 1, 3, 2

THERES A WAR ON

TREAD	LIGHTLY
TREAT	LIGHTLY
TRIAL	BALANCE

6, 1, 5

TRICK	CYCLIST		
TRITE	COMMENT		
TROOP	CARRIER	BEYOND	A DOUBT
TROUT	FISHING	BORROW	A FIVER
TRUST	COMPANY	BORROW	A POUND
TWICE	NIGHTLY	CEMENT	A UNION
TWICE	REMOVED	COMMIT	A CRIME
UNCUT	DIAMOND	CREATE	A SCENE
UNDER	CONTROL	ELEVEN	O CLOCK
UNDER	ENQUIRY	HAZARD	A GUESS
UNDER	LICENCE	MÉNAGE	À TROIS
UNDER	PROTEST	RETURN	A VISIT
UNION	MEETING	SETTLE	A SCORE
UPPER	CHAMBER	STRAIN	A POINT
UPPER	CLASSES	STRIKE	A CHORD
UPPER	REGIONS	STRIKE	A LIGHT
URBAN	RENEWAL	STRIKE	A MATCH
UTTER	FAILURE	THREES	A CROWD
UTTER	RUBBISH	TWELVE	O CLOCK
UTTER	THREATS		

6, 2, 2, 2

STRONG AS AN OX

VITAL	CONCERN		
VIVID	PICTURE		
WASTE	NOTHING		
WASTE	PRODUCT		

6, 2, 4

WATCH	CLOSELY		
WATER	BISCUIT		
WATER	BUFFALO	APPEAL	TO ARMS
WATER	COLOURS	ARRIVE	ON TIME
WATER	DIVINER	BARREL	OF BEER
WATER	HYDRANT	BATTLE	OF WITS
WATER	MEASURE	BEREFT	OF HOPE
WATER	SPANIEL	BEREFT	OF LIFE
WATER	TORTURE	BOTTLE	OF BEER
WEIGH	HEAVILY	BOTTLE	OF MILK
WEIGH	ONESELF	BOTTLE	OF PORT
WEIRD	SISTERS	BOTTLE	OF WINE
WELSH	DRESSER	BREATH	OF LIFE
WELSH	RAREBIT	CARAFE	OF WINE
WELSH	TERRIER	CHANGE	OF FACE
WHATS	COOKING?	CHANGE	OF LIFE
WHITE	FEATHER	CHANGE	OF LUCK
WHITE	HEATHER	CHANGE	OF MIND
WHITE	RUSSIAN	CHANGE	OF PLAN
WHITE	WEDDING	CHURCH	OF ROME
WIDOW	TWANKEY	CLUTCH	OF EGGS
WINDY	WEATHER	COLONY	OF ANTS

COMMON	AS	DIRT	REVERT	TO	TYPE
COURSE	OF	DUTY	SEARCH	IN	VAIN
COURSE	OF	LOVE	SECOND	OF	JULY
COURSE	OF	TIME	SECOND	OF	JUNE
DEVOID	OF	FEAR	SECOND	TO	NONE
DEVOID	OF	HOPE	SHOWER	OF	RAIN
DIVIDE	BY	FIVE	SPIRIT	OF	EVIL
DIVIDE	BY	FOUR	SPLASH	OF	SODA
DIVIDE	BY	NINE	SPOKEN	IN	JEST
EIGHTH	OF	JULY	SPRING	TO	MIND
EIGHTH	OF	JUNE	STITCH	IN	TIME
ELIXIR	OF	LIFE	STRAND	OF	HAIR
ESSAYS	OF	ELIA	STREAK	OF	LUCK
FILLET	OF	SOLE	STRIKE	IT	RICH
FLAGON	OF	WINE	STRIKE	ME	DEAD!
FOREST	OF	DEAN	STRING	OF	LIES
FOURTH	OF	JULY	STRIVE	IN	VAIN
FOURTH	OF	JUNE	STROKE	OF	FATE
FRIEND	IN	NEED	STROKE	OF	LUCK
GALLON	OF	MILK	STROKE	OF	WORK
GARDEN	OF	EDEN	TABLET	OF	SOAP
GENIUS	IS	PAIN	THINGS	TO	COME
GROUND	TO	DUST	TISSUE	OF	LIES
HEIGHT	OF	FAME	TRAVEL	BY	LAND
HOTBED	OF	VICE	TREATY	OF	ROME
KETTLE	OF	FISH	TUNNEL	OF	LOVE
LABOUR	IN	VAIN	TURNED-UP		NOSE
LABOUR	OF	LOVE	TWINGE	OF	PAIN
LENGTH	OF	TIME	UNABLE	TO	COPE
MAQUIS	DE	SADE	UNABLE	TO	MOVE
MASTER	OF	ARTS	WRITHE	IN	PAIN
MATTER	OF	FACT			
MOMENT	IN	TIME	**6, 3, 3**		
MOTHER	OF	MINE			
OBJECT	OF	PITY	ACROSS	THE	SEA
ORDEAL	BY	FIRE	ACROSS	THE	WAY
PAYING-IN		BOOK	ATTILA	THE	HUN
PAYING-IN		SLIP	BEFORE	THE	WAR
PERIOD	OF	TIME	BEHIND	THE	BAR
PERMIT	TO	LAND	BESIDE	THE	SEA
PERSON	OF	NOTE	BEYOND	THE	LAW
PILLAR	OF	SALT	BRIDGE	THE	GAP
PILLAR	TO	POST	COLLAR	AND	TIE
PLATES	OF	MEAT	DOMBEY	AND	SON
PLENTY	OF	CASH	DURING	THE	DAY
PLENTY	OF	ROOM	DURING	THE	WAR
PLENTY	OF	ROPE	FATHER	AND	SON
PLENTY	OF	TIME	FINISH	THE	JOB
PRINCE	OF	TYRE	JACKET	AND	TIE
RECALL	TO	LIFE	LITTLE	TIN	GOD
REDUCE	TO	DUST	MIDDLE	AND	LEG
REDUCE	TO	PUMP	MOTHER	AND	SON
REDUCE	TO	SIZE	NARROW	THE	GAP
REFUSE	TO	MOVE	PILLAR-BOX		RED
REFUSE	TO	PLAY	SECURE	OLD-AGE	
REFUSE	TO	SIGN	SMOOTH	THE	WAY
REFUSE	TO	WORK	SPIDER	AND	FLY
REMAIN	AT	HOME	STRIKE	THE	EYE
RESORT	TO	ARMS	STROKE	THE	CAT
RETURN	OF	POST	STROKE	THE	DOG
RETURN	TO	BASE	STRONG-ARM		MAN

193

THERES THE RUB
WITHIN THE LAW

6, 4, 2

GENTLY DOES IT
HEAVEN HELP US!
POWERS THAT BE
TWENTY-FIVE TO

6, 6

ABJECT SPIRIT
ABRUPT MANNER
ABSURD MANNER
ACCEPT ADVICE
ACCEPT DEFEAT
ACCEPT OFFICE
ACTIVE MEMBER
AESOPS FABLES
ALBERT BRIDGE
ALBERT FINNEY
ALDOUS HUXLEY
ALKALI METALS
ALLIED FORCES
ALLIED TROOPS
ALPINE FLOWER
ALPINE GARDEN
ANCIEN RÉGIME
ANGELA RIPPON
ANIMAL DOCTOR
ANNUAL BUDGET
ANNUAL DINNER
ANNUAL INCOME
ANNUAL OUTING
ANNUAL REPORT
ANNUAL RETURN
ANNUAL SALARY
APOLLO ELEVEN
ARCTIC CIRCLE
ARCTIC REGION
ARCTIC WINTER
ARDENT SPIRIT
ARNOLD PALMER
ARNOLD WESKER
ARTFUL DODGER
ARTHUR MILLER
ATOMIC ENERGY
ATOMIC FUSION
ATOMIC NUMBER
ATOMIC THEORY
ATOMIC WEIGHT
ATTEND CHURCH
AUTUMN CROCUS
AUTUMN LEAVES
BAFFIN ISLAND
BAILEY BRIDGE
BAKING POWDER
BALLAD SINGER
BALLET DANCER
BALLET MASTER

BALLET SCHOOL
BALTIC STATES
BAMBOO SHOOTS
BARREN DESERT
BAYERN MUNICH
BEARER CHEQUE
BEATEN HOLLOW
BECOME PUBLIC
BECOME SILENT
BEFORE CHRIST
BEFORE DINNER
BEFORE SUPPER
BENGAL LANCER
BENIGN MANNER
BERING STRAIT
BETTER THINGS
BEYOND BELIEF
BEYOND BOUNDS
BEYOND RECALL
BEYOND REPAIR
BIASED SAMPLE
BITCHY REMARK
BITTER ALMOND
BITTER ATTACK
BITTER ORANGE
BITTER SHANDY
BITTER STRIFE
BLAISE PASCAL
BLITHE SPIRIT
BOILED SWEETS
BOTTLE OPENER
BOTTOM DOLLAR
BOTTOM DRAWER
BOUNTY HUNTER
BOXING GLOVES
BRANCH OFFICE
BRANDY BOTTLE
BRANDY BUTTER
BREAST POCKET
BREAST STROKE
BREEZY MANNER
BRIDGE PLAYER
BRIGHT COLOUR
BRIGHT LIGHTS
BRIGHT PERIOD
BRIGHT PURPLE
BRIGHT YELLOW
BROKEN ACCENT
BROKEN GROUND
BROKEN SPIRIT
BROKEN WINDOW
BRUTAL MURDER
BUDGET SPEECH
BUNSEN BURNER
BURIAL GROUND
BUSTER KEATON
BUYERS MARKET
CABLES LENGTH••
CANARY YELLOW
CANDID CAMERA
CANDLE GREASE

CANNON	FODDER
CANNON	STREET
CANVEY	ISLAND
CARBON	DATING
CARPET	BEATER
CARPET	KNIGHT
CASUAL	GLANCE
CASUAL	LABOUR
CASUAL	REMARK
CASUAL	WORKER
CATTLE	DEALER
CATTLE	FARMER
CATTLE	MARKET
CAUGHT	BEHIND
CAVEAT	EMPTOR
CELTIC	FRINGE
CENTRE	POCKET
CEREAL	PACKET
CHAISE	LONGUE
CHANCE	REMARK
CHANGE	AROUND
CHANGE	COLOUR
CHANGE	COURSE
CHANGE	HORSES
CHANGE	PLACES
CHANGE	PLANES
CHANGE	TRAINS
CHEEKY	MONKEY
CHEERY	MANNER
CHEESE	STRAWS
CHERRY	BRANDY
CHILLI	PEPPER
CHOICE	MORSEL
CHOOSE	FREELY
CHOOSE	TRUMPS
CHOSEN	CAREER
CHOSEN	PEOPLE
CHROME	YELLOW
CHURCH	BAZAAR
CHURCH	LIVING
CHURCH	MEMBER
CHURCH	PARADE
CHURCH	SCHOOL
CINEMA	SCREEN
CINEMA	STUDIO
CLEVER	MANNER
CLEVER	SPEECH
CLEVER	STROKE
CLEVER	WHEEZE
CLOSED	CIRCLE
COARSE	FABRIC
COARSE	MANNER
COILED	SPRING
COLOUR	SCHEME
COMBAT	TROOPS
COMING	EVENTS
COMMIT	MURDER
COMMON	ACCENT
COMMON	FACTOR
COMMON	FRIEND
COMMON	GOSSIP
COMMON	OROUND
COMMON	HATRED
COMMON	LAWYER
COMMON	MARKET
COMMON	ORIGIN
COMMON	PEOPLE
COMMON	PERSON
COMMON	PRAYER
COMMON	SAYING
COMMON	SPEECH
COMPOS	MENTIS
CONVEX	MIRROR
COPPER	KETTLE
CORNER	POCKET
COTTON	THREAD
COUNTY	ANTRIM
COURSE	RECORD
COUSIN	GERMAN
COVENT	GARDEN
CREDIT	RATING
CREDIT	TITLES
CYPRUS	SHERRY
DAINTY	HABITS
DANGER	SIGNAL
DANISH	PASTRY
DEADLY	DANGER
DEADLY	POISON
DEADLY	SECRET
DEADLY	WEAPON
DECENT	LIVING
DENNIS	LILLEE
DEPUTY	LEADER
DESERT	ISLAND
DESIGN	CENTRE
DEVILS	ISLAND
DIESEL	ENGINE
DINING	SALOON
DINNER	JACKET
DIRECT	ACTION
DIRECT	COURSE
DIRECT	OBJECT
DIRECT	SPEECH
DIVINE	NATURE
DIVINE	RIGHTS
DIVING	BEETLE
DOCTOR	FOSTER
DOCTOR	JEKYLL
DOCTOR	WATSON
DOMINO	THEORY
DONALD	SINDEN
DONALD	WOLFIT
DONKEY	ENGINE
DONKEY	JACKET
DORMER	WINDOW
DOTTED	QUAVER
DOUBLE	BARREL
DOUBLE	BRANDY
DOUBLE	DEALER
DOUBLE	DECKER
DOUBLE	ELEVEN
DOUBLE	SCOTCH

195

DOUBLE TWELVE	FIRMLY ROOTED
DOUBLE TWENTY	FISCAL POLICY
DOUBLE VISION	FITTED CARPET
DOUBLE WHISKY	FLIGHT NUMBER
DUNDEE UNITED	FLIMSY EXCUSE
DUNMOW FLITCH	FLOWER BORDER
EALING COMEDY	FLOWER GARDEN
EARNED INCOME	FLOWER SELLER
EASTER BONNET	FLUENT FRENCH
EASTER ISLAND	FLUENT GERMAN
EASTER MONDAY	FLUTED COLUMN
EASTER PARADE	FLYING CARPET
EASTER RISING	FLYING CIRCUS
EASTER SUNDAY	FLYING COLUMN
EDIBLE FUNGUS	FLYING DOCTOR
EDWARD GIBBON	FLYING LIZARD
EDWARD JENNER	FLYING OBJECT
EIGHTH WICKET	FLYING SAUCER
EIGHTY METRES	FLYING TACKLE
EIGHTY POUNDS	FOLLOW ADVICE
ELDEST SISTER	FORCED GAIETY
ELEVEN MONTHS	FORCED LABOUR
ELEVEN OUNCES	FORMAL GARDEN
ELEVEN POUNDS	FORMAL SPEECH
ELEVEN TRICKS	FOSTER FATHER
ENGINE DRIVER	FOSTER MOTHER
ENRICO CARUSO	FOSTER PARENT
ERRANT KNIGHT	FOSTER SISTER
ESCAPE CLAUSE	FOURTH ESTATE
ESCAPE NOTICE	FOURTH LETTER
ESCORT AGENCY	FOURTH STOREY
EXCESS DEMAND	FOURTH WICKET
EXCESS PROFIT	FRENCH ACCENT
EXCESS WEIGHT	FRENCH CUSTOM
EXPERT ADVICE	FRENCH LESSON
EXPORT MARKET	FRENCH MASTER
EXTEND CREDIT	FRENCH PASTRY
FABLED ANIMAL	FRENCH POLISH
FALLEN ARCHES	FRENCH POODLE
FALLEN LEAVES	FRENCH WINDOW
FAMILY AFFAIR	FRIARS BALSAM
FAMILY CIRCLE	FRIEND INDEED
FAMILY DOCTOR	FROZEN ASSETS
FAMILY FRIEND	FUTILE EFFORT
FAMILY LAWYER	FUTURE EVENTS
FAMILY MATTER	GARDEN ROLLER
FAMINE RELIEF	GARDEN SUBURB
FATHER FIGURE	GARDEN TROWEL
FATHER THAMES	GENTLE BREEZE
FAULTY SWITCH	GENTLE NATURE
FEEBLE ATTACK	GENTLE READER
FEEBLE EFFORT	GEORGE FORMBY
FEEBLE EXCUSE	GEORGE ORWELL
FELLOW MEMBER	GERMAN ACCENT
FEUDAL SYSTEM	GERMAN CUSTOM
FIERCE ATTACK	GERMAN LESSON
FIERCE HATRED	GINGER BRANDY
FIERCE TEMPER	GINGER ROGERS
FIGURE SKATER	GLOOMY ASPECT
FILING SYSTEM	GOLDEN FLEECE
FINISH SECOND	GOLDEN GUINEA

GOLDEN NEEDLE	INDOOR SPORTS
GOLDEN NUMBER	INFANT SCHOOL
GOLDEN SUNSET	INSANE ASYLUM
GOSSIP COLUMN	IRVING BERLIN
GOSSIP WRITER	ITALIC SCRIPT
GOTHIC SCRIPT	JACKET POTATO
GRACIE FIELDS	JACOBS LADDER
GRAHAM GREENE	JOHNNY MATHIS
GRATED CHEESE	JOHNNY ROTTEN
GROUND COFFEE	JOKING MATTER
GROUND GINGER	JOSEPH CONRAD
GROUSE SEASON	JOSEPH STALIN
GUILTY PERSON	JULIAN HUXLEY
GUILTY SECRET	JULIUS CAESAR
GUITAR PLAYER	JUNIOR SCHOOL
GUITAR STRING	KARATE EXPERT
GUSTAV MAHLER	KNIGHT ERRANT
HABEAS CORPUS	LABOUR LEADER
HANDLE GENTLY	LABOUR MARKET
HARLEY STREET	LABOUR POLICY
HAROLD PINTER	LANDED GENTRY
HAROLD WILSON	LATENT ENERGY
HARROW SCHOOL	LATENT TALENT
HEALTH CENTRE	LATEST REPORT
HEALTH RESORT	LAUREL WREATH
HEARTS DESIRE	LAUREN BACALL
HEARTY ASSENT	LAVISH PRAISE
HEAVEN FORBID!	LAVISH SPREAD
HERALD ANGELS	LEADER WRITER
HERBAL REMEDY	LETHAL WEAPON
HEROIC FIGURE	LETTER OPENER
HEROIC POETRY	LETTER WRITER
HIDDEN DANGER	LIQUID ASSETS
HIDDEN DEPTHS	LIQUID OXYGEN
HIDDEN TALENT	LITTER BASKET
HIDDEN WEALTH	LITTLE CHANCE
HIGHER BIDDER	LITTLE DEMAND
HIGHER DEGREE	LITTLE DORRIT
HIGHLY AMUSED	LITTLE FINGER
HIGHLY STRUNG	LITTLE HITLER
HIGHLY VALUED	LITTLE MONKEY
HOCKEY PLAYER	LITTLE PEOPLE
HOLLOW CHEEKS	LITTLE SISTER
HOLLOW SQUARE	LITTLE SQUIRT
HOLLOW THREAT	LITTLE TERROR
HOMELY PERSON	LITTLE THINGS
HOMING PIGEON	LITTLE WONDER
HONEST FELLOW	LIVELY DEBATE
HONEST LABOUR	LIVELY PERSON
HONEST LIVING	LIVING MEMORY
HOUSEY HOUSEY	LIVING TISSUE
HUMANE KILLER	LONDON BRIDGE
HUMBLE ORIGIN	LONDON EDITOR
HUMPTY DUMPTY	LONDON SUBURB
HUNGER STRIKE	LOSING BATTLE
INCHES TALLER	LOSING HAZARD
INDIAN EMPIRE	LOSING STREAK
INDIAN MUTINY	LOUNGE LIZARD
INDIAN SUMMER	LOVELY FIGURE
INDIRA GANDHI	LOVING COUPLE
INDOOR AERIAL	LOWEST DEPTHS

LUMBER JACKET	MOVING APPEAL
LUXURY CRUISE	MOVING FINGER
MADAME BOVARY	MOVING SPEECH
MAIDEN FLIGHT	MOVING TARGET
MAIDEN SPEECH	MURDER CHARGE
MAIDEN STAKES	MURDER VICTIM
MAIDEN VOYAGE	MURDER WEAPON
MAITRE DHÔTEL	MUTUAL FRIEND
MANUAL LABOUR	MUTUAL HATRED
MANUAL WORKER	MUTUAL REGARD
MARCEL PROUST	NARROW DEFEAT
MARINE ANIMAL	NARROW ESCAPE
MARINE ENGINE	NARROW MARGIN
MARIUS GORING	NARROW STREET
MARKET GARDEN	NATIVE CUSTOM
MARKET SQUARE	NATIVE TONGUE
MARLON BRANDO	NATIVE TROOPS
MARTIN LUTHER	NEUTER GENDER
MASSED CHOIRS	NICELY PLACED
MASTER GUNNER	NICELY POISED
MASTER STROKE	NICKEL SILVER
MASTER TAILOR	NINETY METRES
MATING SEASON	NINETY POUNDS
MEDIUM HEIGHT	NORMAN MAILER
MELTED BUTTER	NORMAN WISDOM
MELTED CHEESE	NOTARY PUBLIC
MENTAL ASYLUM	NUDIST COLONY
MENTAL DEFECT	NUMBER ELEVEN
MENTAL EFFORT	NUMBER THIRTY
MENTAL ENERGY	NUMBER TWELVE
MENTAL HEALTH	NUMBER TWENTY
MENTAL STRAIN	NUMBER, PLEASE
MERSEY TUNNEL	NUTMEG GRATER
METEOR SHOWER	OBITER DICTUM
METHOD ACTING	OBJECT LESSON
METRIC SYSTEM	ORANGE PIPPIN
MICKEY ROONEY	ORANGE SQUASH
MIDDLE COURSE	OSWALD MOSLEY
MIDDLE FINGER	OXFORD CIRCUS
MIDDLE POCKET	OXFORD STREET
MIDDLE SCHOOL	OXFORD UNITED
MIDDLE WICKET	PARADE GROUND
MIGHTY EFFORT	PARISH CHURCH
MILTON KEYNES	PARISH PRIEST
MINERS STRIKE	PARISH SCHOOL
MINING RIGHTS	PASTEL COLOUR
MISSED CHANCE	PATENT OFFICE
MOBILE COLUMN	PATENT RIGHTS
MODERN SCHOOL	PATROL LEADER
MODEST INCOME	PAYING GUESTS
MODEST PERSON	PEANUT BUTTER
MONKEY JACKET	PENCIL RUBBER
MONKEY PUZZLE	PENCIL SKETCH
MONKEY TRICKS	PETROL RATION
MONKEY WRENCH	PHILIP SIDNEY
MONTHS NOTICE	PICKED TROOPS
MORRIS DANCER	PICNIC BASKET
MORTAL DANGER	PICNIC HAMPER
MORTAL TERROR	PLOUGH MONDAY
MOTHER NATURE	POINTS SYSTEM
MOTHER TONGUE	POLICE CORDON

POLICE ESCORT	RECENT EVENTS
POLICE PATROL	RECITE POETRY
POLICE PERMIT	RECORD HOLDER
POLICE RECORD	RECORD OFFICE
POLITE PHRASE	RECORD PLAYER
PORTLY FIGURE	REEFER JACKET
POTATO CRISPS	REFLEX ACTION
POTATO FAMINE	REFORM SCHOOL
POWDER MONKEY	REFUSE CREDIT
PRETTY SPEECH	REGENT STREET
PRETTY USEFUL	RELIEF WORKER
PRINCE ALBERT	REMAIN SEATED
PRINCE ANDREW	REMAIN SILENT
PRINCE EDWARD	REMAIN SINGLE
PRINCE PHILIP	REMOTE CHANCE
PRINCE REGENT	REMOVE BODILY
PRINCE RUPERT	RENDER THANKS
PRISON RECORD	REPAIR OUTFIT
PRISON REFORM	RESCUE WORKER
PRISON SYSTEM	RESIDE ABROAD
PRISON WARDER	RETAIL TRADER
PROFIT MARGIN	RETURN TICKET
PROFIT MOTIVE	RETURN VOYAGE
PROFIT TAKING	RHESUS MONKEY
PROMPT ACTION	RHYTHM METHOD
PROMPT ANSWER	RICHIE BENAUD
PROMPT RETORT	RIDING LESSON
PROPER COFFEE	RIDING MASTER
PROPER PERSON	RIDING SCHOOL
PROVEN GUILTY	RIDING STABLE
PUBLIC AFFAIR	RISING GROUND
PUBLIC DEMAND	RISING PRICES
PUBLIC FIGURE	RITUAL MURDER
PUBLIC HEALTH	ROBERT DUDLEY
PUBLIC NOTICE	ROBERT MORLEY
PUBLIC OFFICE	ROBERT MUGABE
PUBLIC ORATOR	ROBUST HEALTH
PUBLIC OUTCRY	ROLLER SKATES
PUBLIC SCHOOL	RONALD REAGAN
PUBLIC SECTOR	RONNIE BARKER
PUBLIC SPEECH	ROTARY ACTION
PUBLIC SPIRIT	ROTARY ENGINE
PUFFIN ISLAND	ROTTEN BRANCH
PUTNEY BRIDGE	RUBBER CHEQUE
QUEENS BISHOP	RUBBER DINGHY
QUEENS KNIGHT	RUBBER GLOVES
QUEENS MUSICK	RUGGER PLAYER
QUEENS SPEECH	RUINED CASTLE
RABBIT WARREN	RUPERT BROOKE
RACIAL HATRED	SACRED PLEDGE
RACING DRIVER	SAFETY DEVICE
RACING PIGEON	SAFETY FACTOR
RACING SEASON	SAFETY MARGIN
RACING STABLE	SAHARA DESERT
RAFFLE TICKET	SAILOR BEWARE
RAGING TEMPER	SALLOW CHEEKS
RAGLAN SLEEVE	SALTED BUTTER
RAISED VOICES	SAMUEL BUTLER
RANDOM SAMPLE	SAVAGE ATTACK
RAPIER THRUST	SAVING CLAUSE
RATHER POORLY	SCHOOL BLAZER

SCHOOL	DINNER	SIMPLE	PERSON
SCHOOL	FRIEND	SIMPLE	REMEDY
SCHOOL	OUTING	SINGLE	BRANDY
SCHOOL	REPORT	SINGLE	COMBAT
SCOTCH	WHISKY	SINGLE	PERSON
SCOUTS	HONOUR	SINGLE	SCOTCH
SEALED	ORDERS	SINGLE	TICKET
SEASON	TICKET	SINGLE	WHISKY
SECOND	CHANCE	SLIGHT	CHANCE
SECOND	CHOICE	SLIGHT	CHANGE
SECOND	COMING	SLIGHT	DAMAGE
SECOND	COURSE	SLIGHT	INJURY
SECOND	COUSIN	SLINKY	NUMBER
SECOND	DEGREE	SLOANE	SQUARE
SECOND	ELEVEN	SMOKED	SALMON
SECOND	FIDDLE	SMOKED	TONGUE
SECOND	FINGER	SMOOTH	MANNER
SECOND	GLANCE	SMOOTH	TALKER
SECOND	LEAGUE	SMOOTH	TONGUE
SECOND	LESSON	SOCIAL	CIRCLE
SECOND	LETTER	SOCIAL	CREDIT
SECOND	NATURE	SOCIAL	MISFIT
SECOND	PERSON	SOCIAL	STATUS
SECOND	SERIES	SOCIAL	SURVEY
SECOND	STOREY	SOCIAL	UNREST
SECOND	STRING	SOCIAL	WORKER
SECOND	VIOLIN	SOFTLY	SPOKEN
SECOND	VOLUME	SOLEMN	PLEDGE
SECOND	WICKET	SOLEMN	THREAT
SECRET	BALLOT	SOVIET	RUSSIA
SECRET	ERRAND	SPEECH	DEFECT
SECRET	POLICE	SPEEDY	ANSWER
SECRET	WEAPON	SPINAL	COLUMN
SEEDED	PLAYER	SPORTS	EDITOR
SENIOR	MEMBER	SPORTS	GROUND
SENIOR	PURSER	SPORTS	JACKET
SENIOR	SCHOOL	SPORTS	MASTER
SERENE	NATURE	SPORTS	TROPHY
SERIAL	NUMBER	SPRING	BUDGET
SERIAL	RIGHTS	SPRING	GREENS
SEVERE	ATTACK	SPRING	ONIONS
SEVERE	CRITIC	SQUARE	NUMBER
SEVERE	STRAIN	STATEN	ISLAND
SEVERE	WINTER	STATUS	SYMBOL
SEVERN	BRIDGE	STEADY	DEMAND
SHADOW	BOXING	STEADY	INCOME
SHERRY	TRIFLE	STEVIE	WONDER
SIDNEY	SUSSEX	STEWED	APPLES
SIGNAL	DEFEAT	STEWED	PRUNES
SILENT	LETTER	STICKY	TOFFEE
SILENT	PRAYER	STICKY	WICKET
SILVER	BULLET	STORMY	CAREER
SILVER	DOLLAR	STORMY	DEBATE
SILVER	LINING	STORMY	PETREL
SILVER	SALVER	STRAIT	JACKET
SILVER	SCREEN	STREET	ARTIST
SILVER	TEAPOT	STREET	CORNER
SIMPLE	ANSWER	STREET	MARKET
SIMPLE	BEAUTY	STREET	SINGER
SIMPLE	DEVICE	STREET	TRADER
SIMPLE	MATTER	STREET	URCHIN

STREET	VENDOR	TREVOR	HOWARD
STRICT	ORDERS	TRIBAL	CUSTOM
STRIKE	ACTION	TRIBAL	SYSTEM
STRIKE	BOTTOM	TROPHY	HUNTER
STRIKE	TERROR	TRUMAN	CAPOTE
STRIKE	WEAPON	TRUSTY	FRIEND
STRONG	DEMAND	TUNNEL	VISION
STRONG	DENIAL	TWELVE	MONTHS
STRONG	DESIRE	TWELVE	OUNCES
STRONG	NERVES	TWELVE	POUNDS
STUPID	ANSWER	TWELVE	ROUNDS
STUPID	FELLOW	TWELVE	TRICKS
SUDDEN	ATTACK	TWENTY	METRES
SUDDEN	CHANGE	TWENTY	POINTS
SUDDEN	TWITCH	TWENTY	POUNDS
SUFFER	DAMAGE	UNEVEN	CHANCE
SUFFER	DEFEAT	UNFAIR	CHOICE
SUMMER	MONTHS	UNITED	ACTION
SUMMER	RESORT	UNITED	STATES
SUMMER	SCHOOL	UNPAID	LABOUR
SUMMER	SEASON	UNPAID	WORKER
SUNDAY	DINNER	UNTOLD	DAMAGE
SUNDAY	DRIVER	UNTOLD	WEALTH
SUNDAY	MIRROR	UPWARD	STROKE
SUNDAY	PEOPLE	URGENT	DEMAND
SUNDAY	SCHOOL	URGENT	MATTER
SUNKEN	GARDEN	VACANT	OFFICE
SUNTAN	LOTION	VALUED	FRIEND
SUPERB	FINISH	VEILED	THREAT
SUPPLY	TROOPS	VERBAL	ATTACK
TALCUM	POWDER	VESTAL	VIRGIN
TALLOW	CANDLE	VIOLET	CARSON
TANNOY	SYSTEM	VIOLIN	PLAYER
TENANT	FARMER	VIOLIN	STRING
TENNIS	PLAYER	VIRGIN	FOREST
TENNIS	RACKET	VOODOO	DOCTOR
THAMES	DITTON	VOODOO	PRIEST
THAMES	VALLEY	VOTING	RIGHTS
THINLY	SPREAD	WALLED	GARDEN
THIRTY	METRES	WANTED	PERSON
THIRTY	POUNDS	WARPED	NATURE
THOMAS	ARNOLD	WARREN	BEATTY
THOMAS	EDISON	WASTED	EFFORT
THOMAS	HUGHES	WEDDED	COUPLE
THOMAS	WOLSEY	WEEKLY	COLUMN
TICKET	HOLDER	WEEKLY	REPORT
TICKET	OFFICE	WEEKLY	RETURN
TICKET	POCKET	WHISKY	BOTTLE
TIMELY	ADVICE	WICKER	BASKET
TINNED	SALMON	WICKET	KEEPER
TITLED	PERSON	WIDELY	SPACED
TITTLE	TATTLE	WILBUR	WRIGHT
TRACER	BULLET	WILFUL	DAMAGE
TRAGIC	ENDING	WILFUL	MURDER
TRAVEL	ABROAD	WILLIE	CARSON
TRAVEL	AGENCY	WINGED	INSECT
TRAVEL	AGENTS	WINTER	GARDEN
TRAVEL	BUREAU	WINTER	MONTHS
TREBLE	CHANCE	WINTER	SEASON
TREBLE	TWENTY	WINTER	SPORTS
TRENCH	MORTAR	WITHIN	BOUNDS

WITHIN LIMITS
WITHIN REASON
WOMENS RIGHTS
WOOLLY JUMPER
YANKEE DOODLE
YELLOW FLOWER
YELLOW HAMMER
YELLOW RIBBON
YELLOW STREAK
ZIGZAG COURSE

7, 1, 4

ARRANGE A DATE
EXPRESS A VIEW
PREPARE A CASE
PREPARE A MEAL
SUPPORT A WIFE
SUSTAIN A LOSS
WITHOUT A BEAN
WITHOUT A CARE
WITHOUT A CENT
WITHOUT A HOPE
WITHOUT A WORD

7, 2, 3

ABILITY TO MIX
COUNCIL OF WAR
CURRENT OF AIR
CUSHION OF AIR
DESCENT OF MAN
DRESSED IN RED
EXPANSE OF SKY
HANDFUL OF MEN
HUNDRED TO ONE
MILLION TO ONE
NOTHING AT ALL
NOTHING TO ADD
NOTHING TO EAT
NOTHING TO PAY
NOTHING TO SAY
PROMISE TO PAY
PROPHET OF WOE
QUARTER TO ONE
QUARTER TO SIX
QUARTER TO TEN
QUARTER TO TWO
SEVENTH OF MAY
STRANGE TO SAY
STUDENT OF LAW
TANKARD OF ALE
THEATRE OF WAR
TWELFTH OF MAY
VENTURE TO SAY
WHETHER OR NOT

7, 3, 2

NOTHING FOR IT
WHISTLE FOR IT

7, 5

ACADEMY AWARD
ACCOUNT PAYEE
ADOPTED CHILD
ADVANCE GUARD
ADVANCE PARTY
AERATED WATER
AFRICAN QUEEN
AMATEUR ACTOR
AMATEUR BOXER
AMATEUR STAGE
AMOROUS DITTY
ANCIENT HOUSE
ANCIENT ROMAN
ANCIENT RUINS
ANCIENT TIMES
ANCIENT WORLD
ANEURIN BEVAN
ANGELIC SMILE
ANOTHER GUESS
ANOTHER PLACE
ANOTHER STORY
ANOTHER THING
ANOTHER WORLD
ANTHONY QUINN
APOSTLE SPOON
APPLIED MATHS
AQUATIC PLANT
AQUATIC SPORT
ARTISTS MODEL
ARTISTS PROOF
ASSUMED TITLE
AUCTION ROOMS
AVERAGE CHILD
AVERAGE SPEED
AWKWARD SQUAD
BALANCE SHEET
BALANCE WHEEL
BALCONY SCENE
BANBURY CROSS
BANKERS DRAFT
BANKERS ORDER
BANKING HOURS
BARBARY COAST
BARBARY SHEEP
BARBERS CHAIR
BARGAIN PRICE
BARNABY RUDGE
BAROQUE STYLE
BATHING BEACH
BATHING DRESS
BATTING ORDER
BEAMING SMILE
BECHERS BROOK
BEDSIDE LIGHT
BEDSIDE TABLE
BEDTIME STORY
BEGGARS OPERA
BELGIAN CONGO

BENARES BRASS
BENEFIT MATCH
BERNARD MILES
BERTRAM MILLS
BETHNAL GREEN
BETWEEN MEALS
BETWEEN TIMES
BEVERLY HILLS
BICYCLE CHAIN
BICYCLE CLIPS
BICYCLE THIEF
BISHOPS APRON
BLARNEY STONE
BLIGHTY WOUND
BOILING POINT
BOILING WATER
BONFIRE NIGHT
BOOKING CLERK
BOTTLED CIDER
BOTTLED FRUIT
BOTTLED WATER
BOUQUET GARNI
BOWLING ALLEY
BOWLING GREEN
BRAISED STEAK
BRAMBLE JELLY
BREATHE AGAIN
BRIGADE MAJOR
BRISTOL CREAM
BRITISH ISLES
BRITISH STEEL
BROUGHT FORTH
BUDDING ACTOR
BUDDING YOUTH
BULLDOG BREED
BURGLAR ALARM
BURNHAM SCALE
BURNING GLASS
BURNING ISSUE
BURNING SHAME
CABBAGE PATCH
CABBAGE WHITE
CABINET MAKER
CANNING PLANT
CAPABLE HANDS
CAPITAL CRIME
CAPITAL GAINS
CAPITAL GOODS
CAPITAL RADIO
CAPTAIN BLIGH
CAPTAIN OATES
CAPTAIN SCOTT
CARAWAY SEEDS
CAREFUL STUDY
CARTOON STRIP
CARVING KNIFE
CAUTION MONEY
CAVALRY TWILL
CERTAIN DEATH
CHAMBER MUSIC
CHANNEL FERRY

CHAPTER HOUSE
CHAPTER THREE
CHARING CROSS
CHARITY MATCH
CHARLES BOYER
CHARNEL HOUSE
CHARTER PARTY
CHARTER PLANE
CHEDDAR GORGE
CHERISH HOPES
CHEVIOT HILLS
CHICKEN CURRY
CHIMING CLOCK
CHIMNEY STACK
CHIMNEY SWEEP
CHINESE WHITE
CIRCUIT COURT
CIRCUIT JUDGE
CLASPED HANDS
CLASSIC STYLE
CLIPPED HEDGE
CLOSING PRICE
CLOTHES BRUSH
CLOTHES HORSE
CLOTHES SENSE
CLOTTED CREAM
COLLECT TAXES
COLLEGE SCARF
COLONEL BLIMP
COLONEL BOGEY
COMPARE NOTES
COMPASS POINT
COMPOSE MUSIC
CONCERT GRAND
CONCERT MUSIC
CONCERT PARTY
CONCERT PITCH
CONSOLE TABLE
CONTACT SPORT
CONTOUR LINES
CONTROL PANEL
CONTROL TOWER
COOKERY CLASS
COOKING APPLE
COOLING AGENT
COOLING TOWER
COPIOUS NOTES
CORNISH CREAM
CORNISH PASTY
CORRECT DRESS
CORRECT STYLE
COSTUME PIECE
COTTAGE PIANO
COUNCIL HOUSE
COUNTRY DANCE
COUNTRY HOUSE
COUNTRY MOUSE
COUNTRY MUSIC
COUNTRY SPORT
COVERED COURT
COVERED DRAIN

CRESTED GREBE
CRICKET MATCH
CRICKET PITCH
CRICKET SCORE
CRICKET STUMP
CROSSED LINES
CROSSED WIRES
CROWNED HEADS
CRYSTAL CLEAR
CRYSTAL GLASS
CUMULUS CLOUD
CURIOUS SIGHT
CURIOUS SOUND
CURIOUS THING
CURRENT CRAZE
CURRENT ISSUE
CURRENT PRICE
CURRENT TREND
CUSHION COVER
CUSTOMS UNION
CUTTING WORDS
CYNICAL SMILE
DAGGERS DRAWN
DAMAGED GOODS
DANCING GIRLS
DAYTONA BEACH
DEAREST HEART
DEATHLY WHITE
DECIMAL POINT
DEFENCE BONDS
DEFENCE MEDAL
DESSERT SPOON
DEVIOUS MEANS
DIAMOND CLASP
DIAMOND TIARA
DICTATE TERMS
DISTANT TIMES
DIVIDED SKIRT
DIVORCE COURT
DONKEYS YEARS
DOUBLES MATCH
DRAGONS BLOOD
DRAUGHT CIDER
DRAUGHT HORSE
DRAWING BOARD
DRAWING PAPER
DRESDEN CHINA
DRIVING FORCE
DROPPED CATCH
DRUNKEN BRAWL
DRUNKEN STATE
DUCKING STOOL
DURABLE GOODS
DYNAMIC FORCE
EASTERN FRONT
EASTERN WORLD
ECONOMY DRIVE
ELEGANT DRESS
ELEGANT LINES
EMERALD GREEN
ENDLESS CHAIN

ENGLISH VERSE
ENQUIRE AFTER
ENQUIRY AGENT
ERUDITE STYLE
ESPARTO GRASS
ETERNAL SHAME
ETERNAL YOUTH
EVENING CLASS
EVENING DRESS
EVENING PAPER
EXACTLY RIGHT
EXPOSED NERVE
EXPRESS SPEED
EXPRESS TRAIN
EXTREME VIEWS
EXTREME YOUTH
FAILING LIGHT
FAILING SIGHT
FALLING ROCKS
FALLING SALES
FASCIST PARTY
FASHION HOUSE
FASHION MODEL
FASHION PLATE
FATIGUE PARTY
FEARFUL SIGHT
FEATURE STORY
FEDERAL AGENT
FEDERAL COURT
FEDERAL UNION
FERTILE BRAIN
FESTIVE BOARD
FIFTEEN FORTY
FIFTEEN HOURS
FIFTEEN KILOS
FIFTEEN MILES
FIFTEEN PENCE
FIFTEEN YEARS
FIGHTER PILOT
FIGHTER PLANE
FISHING FLEET
FISHING SMACK
FLODDEN FIELD
FLOUNCE ABOUT
FLOWERY STYLE
FLOWING LOCKS
FLOWING WATER
FOLDING CHAIR
FOLDING DOORS
FOLDING STOOL
FOOLISH PRIDE
FOREIGN AGENT
FOREIGN MONEY
FOREIGN PARTS
FOREIGN STAMP
FOREIGN TRADE
FORWARD MARCH
FRANCIS BACON
FRANCIS DRAKE
FRANTIC HASTE
FREDDIE MILLS

FREDDIE STARR	ILLEGAL ENTRY
FREIGHT TRAIN	ILLICIT GAINS
FRIDAYS CHILD	ILLICIT STILL
FROSTED GLASS	INJURED PARTY
FULLERS EARTH	INJURED PRIDE
FUNERAL MARCH	INVALID CHAIR
FUNERAL RITES	INVERSE ORDER
FURTHER DELAY	INVOICE CLERK
GENERAL ALERT	IRONING BOARD
GENERAL GRANT	ITCHING PALMS
GENERAL ISSUE	JANUARY SALES
GENERAL STAFF	KENNETH HORNE
GENERAL STORE	KENNETH TYNAN
GENERAL TERMS	KITCHEN RANGE
GENERAL TREND	KITCHEN STOVE
GENERAL USAGE	KITCHEN TABLE
GENERAL WOLFE	KNUCKLE UNDER
GHOSTLY WHITE	LACKING FAITH
GLARING ERROR	LACKING SENSE
GLOWING TERMS	LAISSEZ FAIRE
GOLDERS GREEN	LANDING CRAFT
GRATING VOICE	LANDING PARTY
GRILLED BACON	LANDING PLACE
GRILLED STEAK	LANDING STRIP
GRILLED TROUT	LANTERN SLIDE
GROCERY CHAIN	LASTING PEACE
GROCERY STORE	LEADING ACTOR
GROWING CHILD	LEADING LIGHT
GROWING PAINS	LEANING TOWER
GUARDED REPLY	LEARNED JUDGE
GUIDING LIGHT	LEATHER GOODS
GUNSHOT WOUND	LEATHER SOLES
HACKING COUGH	LEGALLY BOUND
HALFWAY HOUSE	LEONARD COHEN
HALLEYS COMET	LIBERAL PARTY
HAMBURG STEAK	LIBERAL SHARE
HAMPTON COURT	LIBERAL VIEWS
HANGING JUDGE	LIMITED MEANS
HARBOUR LIGHT	LIMITED SPACE
HARICOT BEANS	LINCOLN GREEN
HARVEST MOUSE	LITERAL TRUTH
HAUNTED HOUSE	LOBSTER PATTY
HEALING POWER	LODGING HOUSE
HEALING TOUCH	LOGICAL CHAIN
HEAVENS ABOVE!	LOGICAL ERROR
HEINOUS CRIME	LOGICAL ORDER
HERMANN HESSE	LONGEST NIGHT
HIDEOUS CRIME	LUCIFER MATCH
HIGHEST SCORE	LUGGAGE LABEL
HOLIDAY HAUNT	MACHINE TOOLS
HOSTILE CROWD	MADDING CROWD
HOSTILE PRESS	MALTESE CROSS
HUMMING SOUND	MANILLA PAPER
HUNDRED KILOS	MANSION HOUSE
HUNDRED MILES	MARRIED BLISS
HUNDRED PENCE	MARRIED WOMAN
HUNDRED YARDS	MARTIAL MUSIC
HUNDRED YEARS	MASONIC LODGE
HUNTING LODGE	MAXIMUM PRICE
HUNTING SPEAR	MAXIMUM SPEED
HURRIED VISIT	MAYPOLE DANCE

MEDICAL	CHECK
MEDICAL	STAFF
MEETING	HOUSE
MEETING	PLACE
MELTING	POINT
MICHAEL	ASPEL
MICHAEL	PALIN
MILFORD	HAVEN
MILKING	STOOL
MILLION	MILES
MILLION	YEARS
MINCING	STEPS
MINERAL	WATER
MINIMUM	PRICE
MISSING	PIECE
MISSION	HOUSE
MONDAYS	CHILD
MOONLIT	NIGHT
MORNING	AFTER
MORNING	DRESS
MORNING	GLORY
MORNING	PAPER
MOTHERS	UNION
MUFFLED	TONES
MUFFLED	VOICE
MUSICAL	PIECE
MUSICAL	SCALE
MUSICAL	SCORE
MUSICAL	SOUND
MYSTERY	STORY
NAGGING	DOUBT
NAPIERS	BONES
NATURAL	BREAK
NATURAL	CHARM
NATURAL	CHILD
NATURAL	DEATH
NATURAL	ENEMY
NATURAL	FIBRE
NATURAL	PRIDE
NATURAL	STATE
NAUGHTY	CHILD
NEAREST	OFFER
NEAREST	POINT
NERVOUS	STATE
NERVOUS	WRECK
NEUTRAL	STATE
NIAGARA	FALLS
NOBODYS	CHILD
NOBODYS	FAULT
NODDING	TERMS
NOMINAL	PRICE
NOMINAL	RULER
NOMINAL	VALUE
NOTHING	AMISS
NOTHING	DOING
NOUVEAU	RICHE
NUCLEAR	POWER
NURSERY	CLASS
NURSERY	RHYME
NURSERY	STORY
OBLIQUE	ANGLE
OFFICER	CADET
OLYMPIC	GAMES
OLYMPIC	MEDAL
OLYMPIC	TORCH
OPENING	HOURS
OPENING	NIGHT
OPENING	PRICE
OPENING	SCENE
OPENING	VERSE
OPTICAL	GLASS
OUTDOOR	GAMES
OUTDOOR	SPORT
OUTSIDE	RIGHT
OUTSIDE	TRACK
OUTWARD	BOUND
PACIFIC	OCEAN
PAINFUL	DEATH
PAINTED	OCEAN
PAISLEY	SHAWL
PALETTE	KNIFE
PARKING	METER
PARKING	PLACE
PARKING	SPACE
PARLOUS	STATE
PARQUET	FLOOR
PARTIAL	TRUTH
PARTING	WORDS
PASSING	FANCY
PASSING	PHASE
PASSING	PLACE
PASSION	FRUIT
PASSIVE	VOICE
PATTERN	MAKER
PEPPERS	GHOST
PERFECT	FIFTH
PERFECT	IMAGE
PERFECT	MATCH
PERFECT	PEACE
PERFECT	SIGHT
PERFECT	TENSE
PERSONA	GRATA
PICKLED	ONION
PICTURE	FRAME
PICTURE	HOUSE
PICTURE	STORY
PILLION	RIDER
PIONEER	CORPS
PLASTER	SAINT
PLAYING	CARDS
PLAYING	FIELD
PLEATED	DRESS
PLEATED	SKIRT
POLLING	BOOTH
POPULAR	BRAND
POPULAR	FRONT
POPULAR	MUSIC
POPULAR	NOVEL
POPULAR	PRESS
POPULAR	SPORT
PORTERS	LODGE
POSTAGE	STAMP

POTTERS WHEEL	ROUSING CHEER
PREMIUM BONDS	ROUTINE CHECK
PRESENT TENSE	RUINOUS FOLLY
PRICKLY PLANT	RUNAWAY HORSE
PRIVATE BEACH	RUNAWAY LORRY
PRIVATE FIGHT	RUNAWAY TRAIN
PRIVATE HOTEL	RUNAWAY TRUCK
PRIVATE HOUSE	RUNNING BOARD
PRIVATE LIVES	RUNNING COSTS
PRIVATE MEANS	RUNNING FIGHT
PRIVATE NURSE	RUNNING FLUSH
PRIVATE PARTY	RUNNING TRACK
PRIVATE VISIT	RUNNING WATER
PROBATE COURT	RUSSIAN DANCE
PROBLEM CHILD	RUSSIAN NOVEL
PROTEST MARCH	RUSSIAN SALAD
PRUNING KNIFE	SADLERS WELLS
PUDDING BASIN	SAILING BARGE
PUFFING BILLY	SALIENT ANGLE
PURSUIT PLANE	SALIENT POINT
PUTTING GREEN	SATURNS RINGS
QUALITY GOODS	SAVINGS STAMP
QUARTER FINAL	SCARLET FEVER
QUENTIN CRISP	SCENTED PAPER
RADIANT SMILE	SELLING PRICE
RADICAL VIEWS	SERIOUS OFFER
RAILWAY GUIDE	SERIOUS RIVAL
RAILWAY HOTEL	SERIOUS WOUND
RAILWAY TRAIN	SERRIED RANKS
RAINBOW TROUT	SERVICE DEPOT
RASPING VOICE	SERVICE DRESS
RATABLE VALUE	SERVICE RIFLE
RATCHET WHEEL	SERVING HATCH
READING GLASS	SEVENTH ROUND
REDUCED FARES	SEVENTY KILOS
REDUCED PRICE	SEVENTY MILES
REDUCED SPEED	SEVENTY PENCE
REFINED SUGAR	SEVENTY YEARS
REFINED TASTE	SEVERAL TIMES
REGENCY HOUSE	SHALLOW WATER
REGENCY STYLE	SHAVING BRUSH
REGULAR HABIT	SHAVING STICK
REGULAR HOURS	SHINING LIGHT
REGULAR MEALS	SHORTER HOURS
RESERVE PRICE	SHORTLY AFTER
RESTING PLACE	SIAMESE TWINS
RESTORE ORDER	SIGMUND FREUD
RESTORE PEACE	SINGING VOICE
REVERSE ORDER	SINGLES MATCH
RHYMING SLANG	SIRLOIN STEAK
RICHARD BAKER	SIXTEEN MILES
RICHARD NIXON	SIXTEEN PENCE
RINGING LAUGH	SIXTEEN YEARS
RINGING SOUND	SKIFFLE GROUP
ROARING TRADE	SKITTLE ALLEY
ROASTED ALIVE	SLACKEN SPEED
ROCKING CHAIR	SLENDER MEANS
ROCKING HORSE	SLENDER WAIST
ROLLING STOCK	SLIDING DOORS
ROLLING STONE	SLIDING PANEL
ROSETTA STONE	SLIDING SCALE

SLOPING SIDES	TINKERS CURSE
SMOKERS COUGH	TINTERN ABBEY
SOCIETY WOMAN	TOBACCO PLANT
SOPRANO VOICE	TOBACCO POUCH
SPANISH ONION	TOBACCO SMOKE
SPECIAL AGENT	TOBACCO STAIN
SPECIAL GUEST	TOURIST CLASS
SPECIAL ISSUE	TOURIST TRADE
SPECIAL OFFER	TRACING PAPER
SPECIAL ORDER	TRADING STAMP
SPECIAL PRICE	TRAFFIC LIGHT
SPECIAL TERMS	TRAINED NURSE
SPECIAL TRAIN	TRAINED VOICE
SPENCER TRACY	TRESTLE TABLE
SPOILED CHILD	TRIBUNE GROUP
STAINED GLASS	TRIGGER HAPPY
STARLIT NIGHT	TRINITY HOUSE
STATION HOTEL	TROUBLE AHEAD
STATION WAGON	TROUSER PRESS
STAYING POWER	TRUMPET BLAST
STERNER STUFF	TRUNDLE ALONG
STORAGE SPACE	TRUSTEE STOCK
STRANGE PLACE	TUESDAY NIGHT
STRANGE SIGHT	TURKISH TOWEL
STRANGE SOUND	TURNING POINT
STRANGE THING	TWELFTH NIGHT
STRANGE WOMAN	TYPHOID FEVER
STREAKY BACON	TYPISTS ERROR
STREETS AHEAD	UMPTEEN TIMES
STRETCH TIGHT	UPRIGHT GRAND
STUDENT NURSE	UPRIGHT PIANO
STUFFED OLIVE	VALIANT HEART
STUFFED SHIRT	VANTAGE POINT
SUBDUED LIGHT	VARIETY STAGE
SUCCESS STORY	VARSITY MATCH
SUFFOLK PUNCH	VENTURE FORTH
SULTANS WIVES	VICTORY BONDS
SUNDAYS CHILD	VICTORY MEDAL
SUPREME COURT	VILLAGE GREEN
SUPREME POWER	VILLAGE IDIOT
SURGERY HOURS	VINCENT PRICE
SURPLUS FLESH	VIOLENT DEATH
SURPLUS GOODS	VIOLENT STORM
SURPLUS STOCK	VISIBLE MEANS
SWALLOW WHOLE	WAITING WOMAN
TAILORS DUMMY	WALDORF SALAD
TAINTED GOODS	WALKING SHOES
TALKING POINT	WARLIKE TRIBE
TARTARE SAUCE	WARNING LIGHT
TEARING HURRY	WARNING SOUND
TEENAGE DREAM	WAYWARD CHILD
TEENAGE YEARS	WEAKEST POINT
THEATRE QUEUE	WEALTHY WIDOW
THEATRE ROYAL	WEATHER CHART
THEATRE USHER	WEATHER GAUGE
THERMOS FLASK	WEATHER GLASS
THROATY COUGH	WEDDING BELLS
THROATY LAUGH	WEDDING DRESS
THROUGH TRAIN	WEDDING FEAST
THYROID GLAND	WEDDING GUEST
TIMOTHY LEARY	WEDDING MARCH

WEDDING RITES	ABSTRACT TERM
WELCOME BREAK	ACCIDENT SPOT
WELCOME EVENT	ACHILLES HEEL
WELCOME GUEST	ACOUSTIC BASS
WELCOME SIGHT	ADDITION SIGN
WELCOME SOUND	ADHESIVE TAPE
WELFARE STATE	ADJUTANT BIRD
WESTERN FRONT	ADVANCED IDEA
WESTERN ISLES	ALADDINS CAVE
WESTERN WORLD	ALADDINS LAMP
WHIPPED CREAM	ALLOTTED TASK
WILLIAM BLAKE	AMERICAN FILM
WILLIAM BOOTH	AMERICAN FLAG
WILLIAM RUFUS	ANTONIUS PIUS
WILLING HANDS	ANYTHING GOES
WILLING PARTY	APPROACH ROAD
WILLING SLAVE	APPROACH SHOT
WINDING TRAIL	APPROVED LIST
WINDSOR CHAIR	APTITUDE TEST
WINNING HORSE	AQUILINE NOSE
WINNING SCORE	ARTERIAL ROAD
WINNING SMILE	ARTESIAN WELL
WINSOME SMILE	ARTISTIC WORK
WISTFUL SMILE	ASBESTOS SUIT
WITCHES COVEN	ASSEMBLY HALL
WITHOUT CAUSE	ASSEMBLY LINE
WITHOUT DELAY	ASSEMBLY ROOM
WITHOUT DOUBT	ATHLETES FOOT
WITHOUT FAULT	ATLANTIC CITY
WITHOUT LEAVE	AUDIENCE HALL
WITHOUT LIMIT	BACHELOR FLAT
WITHOUT SUGAR	BACHELOR GIRL
WORKING CLASS	BACKROOM BOYS
WORKING HOURS	BACKWARD GIRL
WORKING LUNCH	BACKWARD STEP
WORKING MODEL	BAKERLOO LINE
WORKING ORDER	BAKEWELL TART
WORKING PARTY	BALANCED DIET
WORLDLY CARES	BALANCED MIND
WORLDLY GOODS	BARCLAYS BANK
WORRIED FROWN	BARNYARD FOWL
WOUNDED PRIDE	BASEBALL TEAM
WRITERS CRAMP	BASEMENT FLAT
WRITING PAPER	BELIEVED DEAD
WRITING TABLE	BILLIARD BALL
WRITTEN ORDER	BILLIARD HALL
WRITTEN REPLY	BILLIARD ROOM
YANGTSE RIVER	BIRDCAGE WALK
YAWNING ABYSS	BIRTHDAY CAKE
ZAMBEZI RIVER	BIRTHDAY CARD
	BIRTHDAY GIFT
8 . 4	BIRTHDAY SUIT
	BITTERLY COLD
ABLATIVE CASE	BORROWED TIME
ABSOLUTE COLD	BOUNCING BABY
ABSOLUTE FOOL	BOUNDARY LINE
ABSOLUTE RULE	BRADFORD CITY
ABSOLUTE VETO	BRANDING IRON
ABSOLUTE ZERO	BRIDGING LOAN
ABSTRACT IDEA	BRIGHTON PIER
ABSTRACT NOUN	BRIGHTON ROCK

BRIMMING OVER	CRIMINAL SUIT
BUBBLING OVER	CRIMINAL TYPE
BUDDHIST MONK	CRITICAL LIST
BUILDERS MATE	CRITICAL MASS
BUILDING LAND	CRITICAL PATH
BUILDING PLOT	CRITICAL TIME
BUILDING SITE	CRUSHING BLOW
BUSINESS DEAL	CULLODEN MOOR
BUSINESS LIFE	CUPBOARD LOVE
BUSINESS TRIP	CURRENCY NOTE
BUTCHERS SHOP	CURRENCY UNIT
CALAMITY JANE	CYLINDER HEAD
CALENDAR YEAR	DAYLIGHT RAID
CARBOLIC ACID	DECIDING VOTE
CARBOLIC SOAP	DEFINITE TIME
CARELESS TALK	DELICATE HINT
CARNEGIE HALL	DELIVERY DATE
CARNIVAL WEEK	DELIVERY NOTE
CARRIAGE PAID	DEPONENT VERB
CASSETTE DECK	DESPATCH CASE
CASSETTE TAPE	DESPATCH NOTE
CASUALTY LIST	DETACHED MIND
CASUALTY WARD	DETACHED VIEW
CAUTIOUS MOVE	DETAILED PLAN
CAUTIOUS TYPE	DIAGONAL LINE
CHANGING ROOM	DIALLING CODE
CHARLESS WAIN	DIALLING TONE
CHARLEYS AUNT	DISAGREE WITH
CHASTITY BELT	DISASTER AREA
CHEERFUL MOOD	DISPATCH CASE
CHEMICAL TEST	DISPENSE WITH
CHEMISTS SHOP	DISTRICT LINE
CHESTNUT TREE	DIVIDING WALL
CHILDISH WAYS	DIVISION BELL
CIRCULAR TOUR	DIVISION FOUR
CIVILIAN LIFE	DIVISION SIGN
CLEARING BANK	DOMESDAY BOOK
CLENCHED FIST	DOMESTIC HELP
CLERICAL WORK	DOOMSDAY BOOK
CLIMBING ROPE	DOWNWARD PATH
COMMANDO RAID	DRAMATIC FORM
COMMANDO UNIT	DRAMATIC PLAY
COMPLETE FOOL	DRAMATIC POEM
COMPLETE LIST	DRAMATIC POET
COMPOUND TIME	DREADFUL BORE
CONCRETE PATH	DRESSING CASE
CONCRETE POST	DRESSING DOWN
CONFUSED MIND	DRESSING GOWN
CONVEYOR BELT	DRESSING ROOM
CORONERS JURY	DRINKING BOUT
COVENTRY CITY	DRINKING ORGY
CRACKING PACE	DRINKING SONG
CRACKPOT IDEA	EASTERLY GALE
CRASHING BORE	EASTERLY WIND
CREAKING GATE	ELECTION DATE
CREATIVE MIND	ELECTION YEAR
CREATIVE MOOD	ELECTRIC BELL
CREATIVE WORK	ELECTRIC BLUE
CRESCENT MOON	ELECTRIC BULB
CRIMINAL CASE	ELECTRIC FIRE
CRIMINAL CODE	ELECTRIC HARE

ELECTRIC IRON	GRACIOUS LADY
ELECTRIC LAMP	GRIEVOUS PAIN
ELECTRIC OVEN	GRIPPING TALE
ELECTRIC PLUG	GUESSING GAME
ELECTRIC WIRE	HABITUAL LIAR
ELEVENTH HOUR	HADRIANS WALL
ENDURING FAME	HANDICAP RACE
ENDURING LOVE	HANGMANS ROPE
ENTRANCE FREE	HEADLINE NEWS
ENTRANCE HALL	HEAVENLY BODY
ETERNITY RING	HEAVENLY HOST
EXCHANGE RATE	HEINRICH BÖLL
EXCITING BOOK	HIGHLAND REEL
EXCITING FILM	HITCHING POST
EXCITING NEWS	HOPELESS CASE
EXCITING PLAY	HOPELESS TASK
EXERCISE BOOK	HOSPITAL CASE
EXERCISE YARD	HOSPITAL SHIP
EXTENDED PLAY	HOSPITAL WARD
EXTERIOR WALL	HUMOROUS VEIN
FAMILIAR FACE	HUMPHREY DAVY
FAMILIAR RING	HYDROGEN ATOM
FESTIVAL HALL	HYDROGEN BOMB
FEVERISH COLD	IDENTITY CARD
FIELDING SIDE	IDENTITY DISC
FIGHTING COCK	IMMANUEL KANT
FIGHTING FISH	IMMORTAL FAME
FIGHTING TALK	IMMORTAL NAME
FINISHED WORK	IMMORTAL SOUL
FINSBURY PARK	IMPERIAL PINT
FIREMANS LIFT	IMPERIAL RULE
FIRESIDE CHAT	INCHCAPE ROCK
FLANDERS MARE	INCOMING SHIP
FLASHING EYES	INCOMING TIDE
FLOATING DEBT	INFANTRY UNIT
FLOATING DOCK	INTEGRAL PART
FLOATING FUND	INTEREST FREE
FLOATING MINE	INTEREST RATE
FLOATING VOTE	INTERIOR WALL
FOOTBALL CLUB	INVERTED SNOB
FOOTBALL TEAM	INVERTED TURN
FOURTEEN DAYS	ISOLATED CASE
FREEZING COLD	JUDGMENT SEAT
FREUDIAN SLIP	JUDICIAL OATH
FRIENDLY CHAT	JULIENNE SOUP
FRIENDLY FACE	JUVENILE LEAD
FRIENDLY WORD	KEYSTONE COPS
FRIGHTEN AWAY	KINGSLEY AMIS
FRONTIER POST	KNACKERS YARD
GAMBLING DEBT	LAVENDER BLUE
GAMBLING GAME	LITERARY HACK
GARRISON TOWN	LITERARY LION
GENITIVE CASE	LITERARY WORK
GLANCING BLOW	LONSDALE BELT
GLORIOUS TIME	LUNCHEON MEAT
GLORIOUS VIEW	MAGAZINE RACK
GOLDFISH BOWL	MAGNETIC MINE
GOLDFISH POND	MAGNETIC POLE
GOODISON PARK	MAGNETIC TAPE
GOODWOOD PARK	MAJORITY RULE
GRACEFUL EXIT	MAJORITY VOTE

MANDARIN	DUCK
MARATHON	RACE
MARCHING	SONG
MARGINAL	COST
MARGINAL	LAND
MARGINAL	SEAT
MARRIAGE	KNOT
MARRIAGE	RATE
MARRIAGE	VOWS
MARSHALL	PLAN
MATCHING	PAIR
MATERIAL	GAIN
MATERNAL	LOVE
MEASURED	MILE
MEDICINE	BALL
MEMORIAL	HALL
MENTALLY	SICK
MERCHANT	BANK
MERCHANT	NAVY
MERCHANT	SHIP
METEORIC	RISE
METRICAL	UNIT
MIDNIGHT	BLUE
MIDNIGHT	HOUR
MIDNIGHT	MASS
MILITARY	BAND
MILITARY	BASE
MILITARY	BODY
MILITARY	CAMP
MILITARY	DUTY
MILITARY	RANK
MILITARY	UNIT
MINORITY	VOTE
MINSTREL	SHOW
MISTAKEN	IDEA
MONASTIC	VOWS
MONETARY	UNIT
MORALITY	PLAY
MOSQUITO	BITE
MOTHERLY	LOVE
MOUNTAIN	GOAT
MOUNTAIN	LAKE
MOUNTAIN	LINE
MOUNTAIN	LION
MOUNTAIN	PASS
MOUNTAIN	PEAK
MOUNTAIN	ROAD
MOUNTAIN	TARN
MULBERRY	BUSH
MUSHROOM	SOUP
NATIONAL	BANK
NATIONAL	DEBT
NATIONAL	FLAG
NATIONAL	GAME
NATIONAL	GRID
NATIONAL	HERO
NATIONAL	HUNT
NATIONAL	NEWS
NATIONAL	PARK
NATIONAL	STUD
NATIVITY	PLAY
NAUTICAL	LIFE
NAUTICAL	MILE
NEGATIVE	SIGN
NEGATIVE	VOTE
NORTHERN	LINE
NOTIONAL	RATE
OBSTACLE	RACE
OFFICERS	MESS
OFFICIAL	DUTY
OFFICIAL	FORM
OFFICIAL	LINE
OFFICIAL	VIEW
OFFICIAL	LIST
OKLAHOMA	CITY
OPERATIC	ARIA
OPERATIC	WORK
OPPOSING	SIDE
OPPOSING	TEAM
OPPOSITE	CAMP
OPPOSITE	SIDE
ORDINARY	FOLK
ORIGINAL	COPY
ORIGINAL	COST
ORIGINAL	IDEA
ORIGINAL	PLAN
ORIGINAL	WORK
OUTGOING	SHIP
OUTGOING	TIDE
PADDLING	POOL
PAINTING	BOOK
PARADISE	LOST
PARAFFIN	LAMP
PARALLEL	BARS
PARTHIAN	SHOT
PASTORAL	POEM
PATERNAL	LOVE
PEACOCKS	TAIL
PERSONAL	CALL
PERSONAL	GAIN
PERSONAL	LOAN
PERSONAL	NOTE
PHARAOHS	TOMB
PHYSICAL	PAIN
PIERCING	NOTE
PLATONIC	LOVE
PLEASANT	TIME
PLEASANT	TRIP
PLEASURE	BOAT
PLEASURE	TRIP
PLIMSOLL	LINE
PLIMSOLL	MARK
PLOUGHED	LAND
PLUMBERS	MATE
POISONED	DART
PORTLAND	BILL
POSITIVE	SIGN
POWDERED	MILK
PRACTICE	GAME
PRECIOUS	BANE
PRECIOUS	VASE
PREPARED	TEXT

PRESSING NEED	SPEAKING PART
PRIMROSE PATH	SPECIFIC HEAT
PRINCESS ANNE	SPECIMEN COPY
PROMISED LAND	SPELLING BOOK
PROPERTY DEAL	SPIRITED AWAY
PRUSSIAN BLUE	SPLENDID TIME
QUESTION MARK	SPORTING LIFE
QUESTION TIME	STABBING PAIN
RAMBLING ROSE	STANDARD LAMP
RECKLESS FOOL	STANDARD RATE
REGIONAL NEWS	STANDARD SIZE
REIGNING KING	STANDARD TIME
RELEVANT FACT	STANDARD WORK
RESEARCH TEAM	STANDING ARMY
RESEARCH WORK	STANDING JOKE
RESERVED SEAT	STANDING ONLY
RICHMOND PARK	STANDING ROOM
RIGHTFUL HEIR	STARRING ROLE
RINGSIDE SEAT	STARTING POST
ROADSIDE CAFÉ	STEERING GEAR
ROGATION DAYS	STERLING AREA
ROGATION WEEK	STINGING BLOW
ROMANTIC FOOL	STIRLING MOSS
ROMANTIC IDEA	STIRRING NEWS
SALUTING BASE	STIRRING TALE
SALVADOR DALI	STRAIGHT AWAY
SANDWICH CAKE	STRAIGHT BACK
SAPPHIRE RING	STRAIGHT CASH
SARDONIC GRIN	STRAIGHT DEAL
SATURDAY WEEK	STRAIGHT DOWN
SCANTILY CLAD	STRAIGHT FACE
SCEPTRED ISLE	STRAIGHT HAIR
SCOTLAND YARD	STRAIGHT LEFT
SCOTTISH REEL	STRAIGHT LINE
SCULLERY MAID	STRAIGHT NOSE
SEALSKIN COAT	STRAIGHT PART
SECLUDED SPOT	STRAIGHT PAST
SECURITY RISK	STRAIGHT PATH
SEETHING MASS	STRAIGHT PLAY
SEPARATE WAYS	STRAIGHT ROAD
SERVANTS HALL	STRAIGHT SETS
SHEEPISH GRIN	STRAIGHT TALK
SHETLAND PONY	STRICTLY TRUE
SHIPPING LANE	STRONGLY MADE
SHIPPING LINE	STRUGGLE HARD
SHOCKING COLD	STUNNING BLOW
SHOCKING MOOD	STUNNING VIEW
SHOCKING PINK	SUNSHINE ROOF
SHOOTING PAIN	SUPERIOR RANK
SHOOTING STAR	SURGICAL WARD
SHOPPING DAYS	SURPRISE MOVE
SHOPPING LIST	SUSANNAH YORK
SHOULDER ARMS	SWIMMING BATH
SKELETON CREW	SWIMMING CLUB
SKIPPING ROPE	SWIMMING GALA
SLEEPING DOGS	SWIMMING POOL
SLEEPING PILL	SYCAMORE TREE
SLIMMING DIET	TAILORED SUIT
SMALLEST ROOM	TERRIBLE TIME
SOLOMONS SEAL	THATCHED ROOF
SPARKING PLUG	THURSDAY WEEK

TIMBERED ROOF	BESETTING SIN
TOASTING FORK	BILLYCOCK HAT
TOMORROW WEEK	BREAKFAST CUP
TOREADOR SONG	BRILLIANT WIT
TOWERING RAGE	BUTTERFLY NET
TRAINING SHIP	CARDBOARD BOX
TRAITORS GATE	CARDINALS HAT
TRAPPIST MONK	CARIBBEAN SEA
TREASURE HUNT	CENTURIES OLD
TREASURY BILL	CERTAINLY NOT
TREASURY BOND	CHALLENGE CUP
TREASURY NOTE	CHAMPAGNE CUP
TROPICAL BIRD	CHEMISTRY SET
TROPICAL FISH	CHOCOLATE BAR
TROPICAL HEAT	CHOCOLATE BOX
TROPICAL RAIN	CHOCOLATE EGG
TROPICAL WIND	CHRISTIAN AID
TROPICAL ZONE	CHRISTIAN ERA
TROUBLED MIND	CHRISTMAS BOX
TUBELESS TYRE	CHRISTMAS DAY
UMBRELLA BIRD	CHRISTMAS EVE
UNBROKEN LINE	CIGARETTE ASH
UNTIMELY JEST	CIGARETTE END
UPSTAIRS ROOM	CLASSICAL ART
VARIABLE GEAR	CLOCKWORK TOY
VARIABLE RATE	CLOUDLESS SKY
VARICOSE VEIN	COMPANIES ACT
VERONICA LAKE	CONDEMNED MAN
VERTICAL LINE	CONVICTED MAN
VICTORIA LINE	COURTEOUS ACT
VICTORIA PLUM	CRIPPLING TAX
VIRGINIA REEL	DANGEROUS JOB
VIRGINIA WADE	DANGEROUS MAN
VISITING CARD	DEAFENING ROW
VISITING TEAM	DESPERATE BID
VISITING TIME	DESPERATE DAN
VISITORS BOOK	DESPERATE MAN
VOCATIVE CASE	DIFFICULT JOB
VOLCANIC ROCK	DIFFICULT SUM
WATERING CART	DIRECTORS BOX
WEDGWOOD BLUE	DISHONEST ACT
WESTERLY GALE	DOWNRIGHT LIE
WESTERLY WIND	DUPLICATE KEY
WHATEVER NEXT?	EDWARDIAN AGE
WHIPPING POST	EDWARDIAN ERA
WITCHING HOUR	EINSTEINS LAW
WORRYING TIME	ELIZABETH FRY
YACHTING CLUB	ESSENTIAL OIL
YOUNGEST GIRL	EVERYBODY OUT
	EXTRACTOR FAN
9 . 3	FARMHOUSE TEA
	FINANCIAL AID
AFTERNOON NAP	FLOWERPOT MEN
AFTERNOON TEA	FOURPENNY ONE
AMBULANCE MAN	FRACTURED ARM
ARMISTICE DAY	FRACTURED LEG
ASCENSION DAY	FRACTURED RIB
BALANCING ACT	FURNITURE VAN
BAREFACED LIE	GENTLEMAN JIM
BATTERING RAM	GLADSTONE BAG
BEAUTIFUL DAY	GUERRILLA WAR

HOUSEHOLD GOD
HYDRAULIC RAM
INCREASED PAY
INDELIBLE INK
INVALIDED OUT
INVISIBLE INK
INVISIBLE MAN
JAUNDICED EYE
LAUNCHING PAD
LICENSING LAW
LIGHTNING ROD
MARMALADE CAT
MESSENGER BOY
MIDSUMMER DAY
MINIATURE DOG
MORECAMBE BAY
MUNICIPAL LAW
ORCHESTRA PIT
OVERNIGHT BAG
PENSIONED OFF
PERMANENT JOB
PICTORIAL ART
PLAINTIVE CRY
POLITICAL MAP
POLYTHENE BAG
PRIMITIVE ART
PRIMITIVE MAN
PRINCIPAL BOY
RASPBERRY JAM
RECEIVING END
RELIGIOUS WAR
RETAINING FEE
SCORCHING HOT
SCRAMBLED EGG
SEAFARING MAN
SEBASTIAN COE
SEDENTARY JOB
SENSITIVE EAR
SERIOUSLY ILL
SEVERANCE PAY
SHEEPSKIN RUG
SHEPHERDS DOG
SHEPHERDS PIE
SHRIMPING NET
SOMETHING NEW
SOMETHING OLD
SPARKLING WIT
STRAPPING LAD
TELEGRAPH BOY
TELEPHONE BOX
TEMPORARY JOB
TRENCHANT WIT
UNKINDEST CUT
UNMARRIED MAN
UNWRITTEN LAW
VEGETABLE FAT
VEGETABLE OIL
VICTORIAN AGE
VICTORIAN ERA
WANDERING JEW
WHIPSNADE ZOO

10, 2

CLASSIFIED AD
STRAIGHTEN UP

1, 3, 9

X-RAY APPARATUS

1, 4, 3, 5

A LONG WAY AHEAD

1, 4, 5, 3

A LONG WHILE AGO

1, 5, 3, 4

X MARKS THE SPOT

1, 6, 2, 4

A FRIEND IN NEED
A STITCH IN TIME

1, 7, 2, 3

I PROMISE TO PAY

2, 1, 3, 7

ON A WAR FOOTING

2, 1, 4, 6

IN A GOOD TEMPER
ON A SHOE-STRING
TO A HIGH DEGREE

2, 1, 5, 5

DO A BRISK TRADE
IN A CLEFT STICK
IN A SORRY STATE
IN A STILL VOICE
ON A GRAND SCALE
ON A SMALL SCALE

2, 1,10

AT A STANDSTILL
ON A BROOMSTICK

2, 2, 2, 3, 2, 2

TO BE OR NOT TO BE

2, 2, 3, 6

DO AS YOU PLEASE
GO AS YOU PLEASE
GO ON THE RAZZLE
GO TO THE BOTTOM
GO TO THE CINEMA
GO TO THE MOVIES
GO TO THE OFFICE
GO TO THE RESCUE
IN AT THE FINISH
UP IN THE CLOUDS
UP TO THE ANKLES
UP TO THE ELBOWS
UP TO THE MINUTE

2, 2, 4, 5

BE OF GOOD CHEER
BE OF GOOD HEART
BE ON ONES GUARD
IN SO MANY WORDS
UP TO ONES KNEES

2, 2, 9

AT AN ADVANTAGE
BE MY VALENTINE
IN AN EMERGENCY
TO BE CONTINUED
UP TO SOMETHING

2, 3, 2, 2, 4

AS FAR AS IT GOES

2, 3, 2, 6

GO OUT ON STRIKE
TO PUT IT MILDLY

2, 3, 3, 2, 3

AN EYE FOR AN EYE

2, 3, 3, 5

GO AND EAT WORMS
GO OFF THE RAILS
IN THE AIR FORCE
IN THE DOG-HOUSE

2, 3, 4, 2, 2

ON THE FACE OF IT

2, 3, 4, 4

AT THE LAST GASP
AT THE SAME TIME
GO AND SUCK EGGS

GO OFF ONES HEAD
IF ALL GOES WELL
IF YOU DONT MIND
IN THE SAME BOAT
IN THE SAME CAMP
OF THE SAME MIND
ON ITS LAST LEGS
ON THE DOOR-STEP
ON THE HIGH SEAS
ON THE LEFT SIDE
ON THE NEAR-SIDE
ON THE OPEN ROAD
ON THE ROOF-TOPS
ON THE SAFE SIDE
ON THE SICK LIST

2, 3, 5, 3

GO THE WHOLE HOG
IN THE LIONS DEN
IN THE MINDS EYE
IN THE USUAL WAY

2, 3, 8

AT THE CONTROLS
AT THE RINGSIDE
BY ALL ACCOUNTS
GO THE DISTANCE
IN ALL FAIRNESS
IN ALL RESPECTS
IN ALL WEATHERS
IN ONE MOVEMENT
IN THE AUDIENCE
IN THE BUSINESS
IN THE CORRIDOR
IN THE DAYLIGHT
IN THE DISTANCE
IN THE DOLDRUMS
IN THE INTERVAL
IN THE MAJORITY
IN THE MEANTIME
IN THE MINORITY
IN THE NEGATIVE
IN THE RESERVES
IN THE SINGULAR
IN THE STRAIGHT
IN THE SUNSHINE
IN THE TRENCHES
IN THE VANGUARD
IN THE VICINITY
ON THE CONTRARY
ON THE DOORSTEP
ON THE FRONTIER
ON THE INCREASE
ON THE PREMISES
ON THE SCAFFOLD
ON THE WIRELESS
TO THE BACKBONE
UP THE MOUNTAIN

2, 4, 1, 6

GO INTO A TRANCE
TO COIN A PHRASE

2, 4, 2, 1, 4

AS BOLD AS A LION
AS GOOD AS A MILE
AS GOOD AS A REST
AS THIN AS A LATH

2, 4, 2, 2, 3

AS LONG AS MY ARM

2, 4, 2, 3, 2

AS SURE AS CAN BE

2, 4, 2, 5

AS BOLD AS BRASS
AS DARK AS NIGHT
AS HARD AS NAILS
AS PALE AS DEATH
AS WARM AS TOAST
BY WORD OF MOUTH
ON PAIN OF DEATH

2, 4, 3, 2, 2

UP BOYS AND AT EM!

2, 4, 3, 4

AT ONES OWN RISK
GO LIKE THE WIND
GO WITH THE TIDE
GO WITH THE WIND
IN ONES OWN NAME
ON ONES OWN FEET
UP WITH THE DAWN
UP WITH THE LARK

2, 4, 4, 3

AT ONES WITS END

2, 4, 7

AT FULL STRETCH
AT ONES LEISURE
AT YOUR SERVICE
DE-LUXE EDITION
DO ONES BIDDING
GO INTO DETAILS
IN COLD STORAGE
IN DEAD EARNEST
IN DIRE STRAITS
IN DIRE TROUBLE

IN FULL MEASURE
IN FULL RETREAT
IN HIGH SPIRITS
IN ONES ELEMENT
IN SAFE KEEPING
IN SELF-DEFENCE
IN SOME MEASURE
IN TOWN TONIGHT
IN VINO VERITAS
NO HAND SIGNALS
TO SOME PURPOSE

2, 5, 2, 1, 3

AS BLIND AS A BAT

2, 5, 2, 4

AS HEAVY AS LEAD
AS LARGE AS LIFE
AS RIGHT AS RAIN
IN POINT OF FACT
IN TIMES OF YORE
ON WINGS OF SONG

2, 5, 6

AT GREAT LENGTH
AT RIGHT-ANGLES
AT SHORT NOTICE
IN EVERY DETAIL
IN GREAT DEMAND
IN SHORT SUPPLY
LA BELLE FRANCE
NO EXTRA CHARGE
NO GREAT SHAKES
NO HOLDS BARRED
ON SOLID GROUND

2, 6, 2, 3

AS LIKELY AS NOT

2, 6, 5

IN MORTAL PERIL
NO HIDING PLACE
OF LITTLE WORTH
ON BENDED KNEES
ST.VITUSS DANCE

2, 7, 4

DO ONESELF WELL
IN CAHOOTS WITH
NO THROUGH ROAD

2, 8, 3

ST.CRISPINS DAY
ST.PATRICKS DAY

ST. SWITHINS DAY

2, 11

AT LOGGERHEADS
BY APPOINTMENT
BY ARRANGEMENT
BY CANDLELIGHT
BY INSTALMENTS
DR. LIVINGSTONE
GO UNDERGROUND
IN CIRCULATION
IN COMPETITION
IN CONSEQUENCE
IN DESPERATION
IN INSTALMENTS
IN LIQUIDATION
IN PERSPECTIVE
IN TREPIDATION
NO ALTERNATIVE
NO EXPECTATION
ON TENTERHOOKS

3, 1, 3, 6

CUT A SAD FIGURE
SET A NEW RECORD

3, 1, 4, 5

CAT O NINE TAILS

3, 1, 5, 4

SIX O CLOCK NEWS
TEN O CLOCK NEWS

3, 1, 9

AIR A GRIEVANCE
ASK A POLICEMAN

3, 2, 1, 1, 6

AIR ON A G-STRING

3, 2, 1, 3, 4

BIT OF A LET-DOWN

3, 2, 1, 4, 3

PUT IN A WORD FOR

3, 2, 1, 7

ALL OF A TREMBLE
MAN IN A MILLION
OFF AT A TANGENT
ONE IN A HUNDRED

ONE IN A MILLION
RED AS A LOBSTER
RUN UP A DEFICIT

3, 2, 2, 1, 5

SAY BO TO A GOOSE

3, 2, 2, 3, 3

GET IN ON THE ACT

3, 2, 3, 1, 4

PUT IN FOR A RISE

3, 2, 3, 2, 3

NOT MY CUP OF TEA

3, 2, 3, 5

ALL IN ONE PIECE
CUT TO THE QUICK
END OF THE MONTH
END OF THE STORY
END OF THE WORLD
GET AT THE FACTS
GET AT THE TRUTH
GET IT ALL WRONG
GET TO THE POINT
HOT ON THE SCENT
HOT ON THE TRAIL
LAY IN THE GRAVE
LED TO THE ALTAR
LET GO THE REINS
MAN AT THE WHEEL
MAN OF FEW WORDS
MAN OF THE WORLD
MAP OF THE WORLD
NOT IN THE LEAST
OLD AS THE HILLS
ONE OF THE CROWD
ONE OR THE OTHER
OUT OF THE HOUSE
PAY AS YOU ENTER
PUT IN THE SHADE
PUT ON THE BRAKE
PUT ON THE LIGHT
OUT ON THE STAGE
PUT TO THE SWORD
PUT UP THE MONEY
PUT UP THE PRICE
RUB OF THE GREEN
RUN IN THE BLOOD
RUN OF THE GREEN
RUN OF THE HOUSE
SIT AT THE FRONT
SIT IN THE FRONT
SIT ON THE FENCE
SIT ON THE FLOOR

TOP OF THE CLASS
TOP OF THE SCALE
TOP OF THE TABLE
TOP OF THE WORLD
WAR TO THE DEATH
WAY OF ALL FLESH
WAY OF THE CROSS
WAY OF THE WORLD
WIN ON THE POOLS

3 . 2 . 4 . 2 . 2

OFF TO WORK WE GO

3 . 2 . 4 . 4

ALL IN GOOD TIME
ALL IN ONES MIND
DIE AT ONES POST
DIG IN ONES TOES
GET IT OVER WITH
GET TO ONES FEET
LIE ON ONES BACK
LIE TO ONES FACE
NOT ON YOUR LIFE
OUT OF ONES HAND
OUT OF ONES HEAD
OUT OF ONES MIND
OUT ON ONES FEET
TOP OF ONES HEAD

3 . 2 . 5 . 3

OUT OF HARMS WAY

3 . 2 . 6 . 2

ACT ON BEHALF OF

3 . 2 . 8

ACE OF DIAMONDS
ACT AS CHAIRMAN
ACT OF COURTESY
ACT OF KINDNESS
ACT OF VIOLENCE
AGE OF CHIVALRY
ALL-IN WRESTLER
ARC DE TRIOMPHE
BIT OF NONSENSE
BOX OF BISCUITS
BOX OF CRACKERS
BUY ON APPROVAL
CRY OF DERISION
DAY OF JUDGMENT
DAY OF MOURNING
DAY TO REMEMBER
DEN OF INIQUITY
DIE OF EXPOSURE
DIE OF LAUGHING
END IN DISASTER

END OF MOTORWAY
EYE TO BUSINESS
FIT OF COUGHING
FIT OF LAUGHTER
GET IT STRAIGHT
GET ON TOGETHER
HUB OF INDUSTRY
LAW OF AVERAGES
LAW OF CONTRACT
LAW OF PROPERTY
LET IN DAYLIGHT
LOW IN CALORIES
MAN OF BREEDUNG
MAN OF BUSINESS
MAN OF LEARNING
MAN OF PROPERTY
MAP OF SCOTLAND
NOT SO HANDSOME
OUT OF BUSINESS
OUT OF INTEREST
OUT OF KINDNESS
OUT OF MISCHIEF
OUT OF PATIENCE
OUT OF PRACTICE
OUT OF SYMPATHY
OUT OF TRAINING
PAR OF EXCHANGE
PUT IN JEOPARDY
PUT IT TOGETHER
PUT ON PRESSURE
RAY OF SUNSHINE
RUN TO MILLIONS
SEA OF TROUBLES
SET AT VARIANCE
SIT IN JUDGMENT
SIX OF DIAMONDS
SOP TO CERBERUS
TEN OF DIAMONDS
TIN OF SARDINES
TWO OF DIAMONDS
WAY OF THINKING
WEB OF INTRIGUE

3 . 3 . 1 . 6

CUT OFF A CORNER
LET OUT A SECRET
PUT OUT A FEELER

3 . 3 . 2 . 1 . 4

ONE DAY AT A TIME
RED RAG TO A BULL

3 . 3 . 2 . 2 . 3

GET OUT OF MY WAY
THE LAW IS AN ASS

3, 3, 2, 5

GET OUT OF SIGHT
PUT OUT OF JOINT
PUT OUT TO GRASS
PUT PEN TO PAPER
RED SKY AT NIGHT
RUN OUT OF FUNDS
RUN OUT OF MONEY
RUN OUT OF STEAM
WAY OUT IN FRONT

3, 3, 3, 2, 2

PUT THE LID ON IT

3, 3, 3, 4

ALL FOR THE BEST
ALL FOR THE GOOD
ALL HOT AND HOLD
ASK FOR THE MOON
CAT-AND-DOG LIFE
CRY FOR THE MOON
CUT FOR THE LEAD
FIT FOR THE GODS
NOW SEE THE FILM
NOW THE BAD NEWS
OFF THE-PEG SUIT
ONE AND THE SAME
ONE FOR THE ROAD
SPY OUT THE LAND
THE BIG BAD WOLF
THE INS AND OUTS

3, 3, 4, 3

OFF THE DEEP END
OLD FOR ONES AGE
RAG-AND-BONE MAN
SEE HOW THEY RUN
TAN THE HIDE OFF

3, 3, 5, 2

PUT THE BRAKE ON

3, 3, 7

ALL THE ANSWERS
ALL-DAY SESSION
ASK FOR NOTHING
ASK FOR TROUBLE
BAG AND BAGGAGE
BEG FOR FAVOURS
BID FOR FREEDOM
DIG FOR VICTORY
FED AND WATERED
FIT FOR NOTHING
FOR AND AGAINST
FOR THE PRESENT

GET OFF LIGHTLY
GET THE GIGGLES
GET THE MESSAGE
GET THE PICTURE
GET THE SHIVERS
HIT THE JACKPOT
ITS NOT CRICKET
MAY THE SEVENTH
MAY THE TWELFTH
OFF THE SUBJECT
OLD BOY NETWORK
OLD-AGE PENSION
ONE-WAY TRAFFIC
ORB AND SCEPTRE
OUT FOR THRILLS
PAY LIP-SERVICE
PAY THE PENALTY
PIG AND WHISTLE
PUT OUT FEELERS
RUN FOR SHELTER
SEE FOR ONESELF
SEE ONE THROUGH
SET THE FASHION
SIR DON BRADMAN
SUE FOR DAMAGES
SUE FOR DIVORCE
TAR AND FEATHER
THE GAY GORDONS
THE OLD BRIGADE
THE TWO RONNIES
TWO-WAY TRAFFIC
WIN THE JACKPOT
WIN TOP HONOURS

3, 4, 1, 5

ACT LIKE A CHILD
ACT LIKE A TONIC
CRY LIKE A CHILD
FIT LIKE A GLOVE
OUT LIKE A LIGHT

3, 4, 2, 1, 3

TWO PEAS IN A POD

3, 4, 2, 4

CUT DOWN TO SIZE
THE BEST OF LUCK
THE HOUR IS NIGH
THE ROAD TO HELL
THE ROAD TO RUIN
THE TEST OF TIME
THE TIME IS RIPE
THE WILL TO LIVE
TOO GOOD BY HALF
TOO GOOD TO LAST
TOY WITH AN IDEA

3, 4, 3, 3

GET ONES OWN WAY

AY DOWN THE LAW
FF ONES OWN BAT
IT THIS ONE OUT

3, 4, 4, 2

IG ONES TOES IN
ET AWAY WITH IT
UT ONES BACK UP
UT ONES FEET UP
UT ONES MIND TO
HE AYES HAVE IT
HE NOES HAVE IT

3, 4, 6

IR-RAID WARDEN
LL GOOD THINGS
LL-TIME RECORD
EG ONES PARDON
IG GAME HUNTER
RY BLUE MURDER
UP THAT CHEERS
UT ONES LOSSES
UT ONES THROAT
IT ROCK-BOTTOM
OG ONES MEMORY
EW BOND STREET
ON-FAST COLOUR
ON STOP TALKER
OT GOOD ENOUGH
FF ONES ROCKER
FF-HAND MANNER
NE GOOD REASON
NE MORE CHANCE
ED STAR PARCEL
UN INTO DANGER
ET ONES SIGHTS
IR NOEL COWARD
IT-DOWN STRIKE
EN PAST ELEVEN
EN PAST TWELVE
HE BEST PEOPLE
HE BEST POLICY
HE BLUE DANUBE
HE LAST MOMENT
HE LAST SUPPER
HE MAIN CHANCE
HE NEAR FUTURE
HE VERY LATEST
IE WITH STRING
WO EASY STAGES
SE ONES BRAINS
SE ONES WEIGHT
AG ONES FINGER

3, 5, 2, 3

HE DEVIL TO PAY

3, 5, 5

ALL ABOVE BOARD
BIG WHITE CHIEF
DOW-JONES INDEX
GAY YOUNG THING
GET THERE FIRST
HOT-HOUSE PLANT
ICE-CREAM WAFER
MRS.DALES DIARY
NEW SOUTH WALES
OLD PENNY STAMP
OLD WIVES TALES
RUN RINGS ROUND
SIR COLIN DAVIS
THE BLACK DEATH
THE BLACK TULIP
THE COSTA BRAVA
THE DOLLS HOUSE
THE GIDDY LIMIT
THE GREAT CRASH
THE GREAT MARCH
THE LIGHT BLUES
THE LIONS SHARE
THE MAGIC FLUTE
THE MERRY WIDOW
THE OTHER WOMAN
THE RIGHT LINES
THE RIVER PLATE
THE SMALL HOURS
THE SOUTH DOWNS
THE THIRD REICH
THE THREE BEARS
THE UPPER CRUST
THE WHITE HOUSE
THE WHOLE TRUTH
THE WHOLE WORLD
TWO-EDGED SWORD
WIN FIRST PRIZE

3, 6, 2, 2

THE WIZARD OF OZ

3, 6, 4

ALL CHANGE HERE
ALL THINGS NICE
FOR MERCYS SAKE
GET BOGGED DOWN
LET THINGS SLIP
LOW-CALORY DIET
OFF-SEASON RATE
OLD CROCKS RACE
OLD FATHER TIME
ONE WICKET DOWN
PIN-STRIPE SUIT
RED RIDING HOOD
SIR ROBERT PEEL
SIR THOMAS MORE
TEN-DOLLAR BILL

THE BOTTOM LINE
THE BRIGHT SIDE
THE COMMON COLD
THE COMMON HERD
THE FATTED CALF
THE FLYING SCOT
THE GARDEN PATH
THE GOLDEN RULE
THE JUNGLE BOOK
THE MIDDLE EAST
THE PUBLIC GOOD
THE SECOND BEST
THE SECOND-RATE
THE SIMPLE LIFE
THE SPOKEN WORD
THE TENDER TRAP
TOO LITTLE ROOM
TOP-SECRET FILE
TWO-COURSE MEAL
TWO-LETTER WORD

3 , 7 , 3

ALL HALLOWS EVE
CUP-WINNERS CUP
OLD-CLOTHES MAN
PUT ONESELF OUT
SUB-MACHINE GUN
THE BRITISH RAJ
THE SHALLOW END
THE WINSLOW BOY

3 , 10

ART COLLECTION
ART EXHIBITION
ASK PERMISSION
BAD CONNECTION
BAD IMPRESSION
BAD MANAGEMENT
BAD REPUTATION
BAD UPBRINGING
BEG PERMISSION
DIE FLEDERMAUS
GAY LIBERATION
HER EXCELLENCY
HIS EXCELLENCY
JET PROPULSION
LES MISÉRABLES
LOW VISIBILITY
NEW MANAGEMENT
NEW REGULATION
NEW RESOLUTION
NOT IMPOSSIBLE
NOT NEGOTIABLE
OLD CAMPAIGNER
ONE CENTIMETRE
PAR EXCELLENCE
RED CORPUSCLES
SIX KILOMETRES
TAX CONCESSION

TEA PLANTATION
TEN CIGARETTES
TEN KILOMETRES
THE CHALLENGER
THE CHARLESTON
THE EISTEDDFOD
THE EMBANKMENT
THE FOOTLIGHTS
THE GONDOLIERS
THE GOVERNMENT
THE GUILLOTINE
THE INEVITABLE
THE MATTERHORN
THE METROPOLIS
THE MILLENNIUM
THE OPPOSITION
THE RESISTANCE
THE ROUNDHEADS
THE SERPENTINE
THE UNDERWORLD
THE UNEXPECTED
THE UNFORESEEN
THE WILDERNESS
TWO KILOMETRES
WAR DEPARTMENT

4 , 1 , 3 , 1 , 4

GIVE A DOG A BONE

4 , 1 , 3 , 5

HAVE A BAD NIGHT
JUST A FEW LINES
LIKE A BAD PENNY
MAKE A BAD START
MAKE A NEW START
WITH A BAD GRACE

4 , 1 , 4 , 2 , 2

MAKE A MESS OF IT

4 , 1 , 4 , 4

DRAW A VEIL OVER
GIVE A FIRM DATE
HAVE A FIRM HOLD
HAVE A GOOD MIND
HAVE A GOOD TIME
HAVE A THIN TIME
HAVE A WORD WITH
KEEP A COOL HEAD
LEAD A DOGS LIFE
MAKE A COME-BACK
MAKE A GOOD WIFE
MANY A TRUE WORD
PLAY A LONE HAND
PULL A LONG FACE
TAKE A BACK SEAT
TAKE A FIRM HOLD

TAKE A FIRM LINE
TAKE A HARD LINE
TAKE A LONG TIME
TELL A GOOD TALE
TELL A GOOD YARN

4 , 1 , 5 , 3

HAVE A QUICK ONE
HAVE A TOOTH OUT
PULL A TOOTH OUT
TAKE A SHORT CUT
TURN A BLIND EYE

4 , 1 , 6 , 2

TAKE A LIKING TO

4 , 1 , 8

DRAW A PARALLEL
EARN A DIVIDEND
FIND A LOOPHOLE
FIND A SOLUTION
FIRE A QUESTION
FROM A DISTANCE
GIVE A REPRIEVE
HAVE A BREATHER
LAST A LIFETIME
MAKE A CONQUEST
MAKE A DECISION
MAKE A FOURSOME
MAKE A PROPOSAL
MEET A DEADLINE
MEND A PUNCTURE
PLAY A FRIENDLY
POSE A QUESTION
RIDE A TRICYCLE
SEEK A SOLUTION
SEND A POSTCARD
SEND A REMINDER
SEND A TELEGRAM
TAKE A BREATHER
TAKE A NIGHTCAP
TAKE A SNAPSHOT
WITH A FLOURISH

4 , 2 , 1 , 3 , 3

BEST OF A BAD JOB
COME TO A BAD END
DAWN OF A NEW ERA

4 , 2 , 1 , 6

BURN TO A CINDER
COME TO A CLIMAX
GIVE IT A CHANCE
GLAD OF A CHANCE
HANG BY A THREAD
KICK UP A SHINDY

PALE AS A CORPSE
SELL AT A PROFIT
SHIP IN A BOTTLE
TAKE IN A LODGER
TELL AT A GLANCE
WEAK AS A KITTEN
WORK UP A LATHER

4 , 2 , 2 , 5

TAKE IT IN TURNS
TAKE IT TO COURT
TAKE IT TO HEART
TIED UP IN KNOTS
WANT TO BE ALONE

4 , 2 , 3 , 4

BACK IN THE FOLD
BACK OF THE HAND
BACK OF THE NECK
BACK TO THE LAND
BACK TO THE WALL
BANG ON THE HEAD
BEND IN THE ROAD
BEST OF ITS KIND
BIRD IN THE HAND
BIRD OF ILL OMEN
BIRD ON THE WING
BLUE IN THE FACE
BOOK OF THE FILM
BOOK OF THE PLAY
BOOK OF THE YEAR
CALL OF THE WILD
CASH IN THE BANK
CASH ON THE NAIL
CAST AN EYE OVER
CLAP ON THE BACK
COCK OF THE WALK
COIN IN THE SLOT
COLD IN THE HEAD
COME ON YOU REDS
COME TO THE FAIR
COME TO THE FORE
COME UP FOR MORE
DOWN ON THE FARM
DYED IN THE WOOL
FEAR OF THE DARK
FILM OF THE BOOK
FLAT OF THE HAND
FREE AS THE WIND
FULL IN THE FACE
FULL TO THE BRIM
GIVE UP ALL HOPE
GIVE UP THE IDEA
GONE TO THE DOGS
GOOD OF ITS KIND
HAIR OF THE HEAD
HEAD IN THE SAND
HEAD OF THE FORM
HOLE IN THE ROAD

JUST AS YOU LIKE
JUST AS YOU WISH
KEEP IN THE DARK
KEEP TO THE LEFT
KEEP UP THE PACE
KEPT IN THE DARK
KEYS OF THE CITY
KISS IN THE RING
LADY OF THE LAKE
LADY OF THE LAMP
LAND IN THE SOUP
LAND OF THE FREE
LAND ON THE MOON
LEAD BY THE HAND
LEAD BY THE NOSE
LEAP IN THE DARK
LEFT AT THE POST
LEFT IN THE DARK
LIVE IN THE PAST
LOOK IN THE FACE
LOOK UP AND DOWN
LOST IN THE POST
LOVE OF THE GAME
LUCK OF THE DRAW
LUCK OF THE GAME
MAID OF ALL WORK
MAKE DO AND MEND
NEXT ON THE LIST
PACE UP AND DOWN
PAID BY THE HOUR
PAIN IN THE ARSE
PAIN IN THE NECK
PART OF THE PLAN
PART OF THE SHOW
PART OF THE TIME
PAWN IN THE GAME
RAKE UP THE PAST
RISE TO THE BAIT
ROLL IN THE DUST
ROOT OF ALL EVIL
RULE OF THE ROAD
SAVE AS YOU EARN
SHIP OF THE LINE
SHOT IN THE DARK
SIGN ON THE LINE
SLAP IN THE FACE
SLAP ON THE BACK
SOFT IN THE HEAD
SOME OF THE TIME
STAB IN THE BACK
STAR OF THE SHOW
SWAY IN THE WIND
TAKE BY THE HAND
TAKE TO THE ROAD
TALK OF THE TOWN
TOAD IN THE HOLE
TRUE TO THE LAST
TURN OF THE TIDE
TURN ON THE HEAT
TURN TO THE LEFT
VEER TO THE LEFT

WALK ON THE MOON
WALK UP AND DOWN
WARM TO THE TASK
WAVE OF THE HAND
WEAK IN THE HEAD
WELL TO THE FORE
WHAT DO YOU KNOW?
WIDE OF THE MARK
WOLF AT THE DOOR

4, 2, 4, 3

FLEA IN ONES EAR
GIVE UP ONES JOB
HANG UP ONES HAT
MIND OF ONES OWN
TAKE TO ONES BED
WEEK IN, WEEK OUT
WILL OF ONES OWN
WORD IN ONES EAR
YEAR IN YEAR OUT

4, 2, 7

AWAY ON HOLIDAY
BACK IN HARNESS
BAND OF ROBBERS
BANK OF ENGLAND
BANK OF IRELAND
BEST OF FRIENDS
BEST OF MOTIVES
BIRD OF PASSAGE
BODY OF OPINION
BOOK OF GENESIS
BOOK OF TICKETS
BORN IN WEDLOCK
BOUT OF ILLNESS
CALL TO WITNESS
CLAP OF THUNDER
CODE OF CONDUCT
COME IN CONTACT
COME TO NOTHING
COME TO ONESELF
COME UP SMILING
DEEP IN THOUGHT
DOWN TO BEDROCK
DUKE OF NORFOLK
DUKE OF WINDSOR
FACT OR FICTION
FAIL TO CONNECT
FALL OF JERICHO
FEAR OF HEIGHTS
FEAT OF COURAGE
FEEL NO EMOTION
FLOW OF TRAFFIC
FORM AN OPINION
FORM OF ADDRESS
FULL OF MEANING
FULL OF ONESELF
FULL OF PROMISE
FULL OF REGRETS

FUND	OF	STORIES	LOSS	OF	BALANCE
GAIN	IN	STATURE	LOSS	OF	CONTROL
GAME	OF	CRICKET	LOSS	OF	FREEDOM
GANG	OF	ROBBERS	LOSS	OF	HEARING
GANG	OF	THIEVES	LOST	IN	THOUGHT
GIVE	AN	ACCOUNT	LOST	IN	TRANSIT
GIVE	AN	EXAMPLE	MADE	IN	ENGLAND
GIVE	AN	OPINION	MADE	IN	GERMANY
GIVE	NO	QUARTER	MADE	TO	MEASURE
GIVE	NO	TROUBLE	MAID	OF	ORLEANS
GIVE	UP	SMOKING	MAKE	AN	ADVANCE
GOOD	AT	FIGURES	MAKE	AN	ATTEMPT
HAIL	OF	BULLETS	MAKE	NO	DEMANDS
HALL	OF	MIRRORS	MAKE	NO	MISTAKE
HARD	AS	GRANITE	MARK	OF	RESPECT
HARD	OF	HEARING	MEET	AS	FRIENDS
HARD	ON	SOMEONE	MESS	OF	POTTAGE
HARD	TO	BELIEVE	MODE	OF	ADDRESS
HARD	TO	IMAGINE	NECK	OR	NOTHING
HARD	TO	SWALLOW	NEXT	TO	NOTHING
HAVE	NO	REGRETS	NOTE	OF	CENSURE
HAVE	NO	SECRETS	NOTE	OF	TRIUMPH
HAVE	NO	TROUBLE	NOTE	OF	WARNING
HOLD	AN	ENQUIRY	OBEY	AN	IMPULSE
HOLD	AN	INQUEST	OMIT	TO	MENTION
HOLD	AN	INQUIRY	OPEN	AN	ACCOUNT
HOLD	AN	OPINION	PACK	OF	THIEVES
HOLD	AS	HOSTAGE	PAIR	OF	BELLOWS
HOLD	IN	BONDAGE	PAIR	OF	GARTERS
HOOK	OF	HOLLAND	PAIR	OF	GLASSES
HOST	OF	FRIENDS	PAIR	OF	PYJAMAS
HOUR	OF	TRIUMPH	PAIR	OF	SANDALS
JUST-SO	STORIES		PANG	OF	REMORSE
KEEN	AS	MUSTARD	PART	OF	HISTORY
KEEP	IN	CUSTODY	PEAL	OF	THUNDER
KEEP	IN	RESERVE	PULL	NO	PUNCHES
KEEP	TO	ONESELF	PURE	IN	THOUGHT
KILL	BY	DEGREES	RENT	IN	ADVANCE
KING	OF	DENMARK	RENT	IN	ARREARS
KING	OF	ENGLAND	ROAD	TO	SUCCESS
KNOW	IN	ADVANCE	ROOM	TO	BREATHE
LACK	OF	CAUTION	SALE	BY	AUCTION
LACK	OF	MEANING	SELL	BY	AUCTION
LACK	OF	RESPECT	SHOW	NO	RESPECT
LADY	IN	WAITING	SICK	OF	WAITING
LADY	OF	LEISURE	SIGN	OF	EMOTION
LADY	OF	SHALOTT	SIGN	OF	FAILURE
LANE	OF	TRAFFIC	SIGN	OF	FATIGUE
LEFT	TO	ONESELF	SIGN	OF	SUCCESS
LIFE	OF	LEISURE	SING	IN	HARMONY
LINE	OF	ADVANCE	SLOW	OF	THOUGHT
LINE	OF	COUNTRY	SONG	OF	SOLOMON
LINE	OF	DEFENCE	SPOT	OF	TROUBLE
LINE	OF	DESCENT	STIR	UP	TROUBLE
LINE	OF	THOUGHT	STOP	AT	NOTHING
LIST	OF	RUNNERS	SUIT	OF	CLOTHES
LIVE	IN	COMFORT	SURE	OF	ONESELF
LIVE	IN	HARMONY	SURE	OF	SUCCESS
LIVE	IN	POVERTY	TAKE	AN	AVERAGE
LIVE	IN	SQUALOR	TAKE	IN	LODGERS
LOAD	OF	RUBBISH	TAKE	IN	WASHING

TAKE NO CHANCES
TALK IN RIDDLES
TALK TO ONESELF
TEAM OF EXPERTS
TEAR TO RIBBONS
TELL ME ANOTHER
TIDE OF AFFAIRS
TIME OF ARRIVAL
TOUR OF BRITAIN
TRUE TO ONESELF
TURN TO ACCOUNT
VALE OF EVESHAM
VEIL OF SECRECY
VOTE OF CENSURE
WANT OF THOUGHT
WISE AS SOLOMON
WITH OR WITHOUT
WORD OF COMFORT
WORD OF COMMAND
WORD OF WARNING
WORK OF FICTION

4, 3, 1, 5

GOOD FOR A LAUGH
JUST FOR A LAUGH
LEAD ONE A DANCE
TEAR OFF A STRIP
TORN OFF A STRIP

4, 3, 2, 4

GIVE HIM AN INCH
STEP OUT OF LINE
TALK OUT OF TURN

4, 3, 3, 3

ARMS AND THE MAN
GIVE ONE THE LIE
GIVE ONE THE PIP
LIVE FOR THE DAY
MEAT AND TWO VEG
ONCE AND FOR ALL
POUR OUT THE TEA
RATE FOR THE JOB
RING OUT THE OLD
TAKE THE DAY OFF
TURN OFF THE GAS
TURN OFF THE TAP
VEAL AND HAM PIE
WIPE OFF THE MAP

4, 3, 4, 2

GRIN AND BEAR IT
KISS AND MAKE UP

4, 3, 6

AIRS AND GRACES
ARTS AND CRAFTS
BACK THE WINNER
BEAR THE BURDEN
BEAT ALL-COMERS
BEAT ONE HOLLOW
BEAT THE RECORD
BITS AND PIECES
CALL THE DOCTOR
CALL THE POLICE
CHOP AND CHANGE
COME OUT EASILY
DAYS AND NIGHTS
DEAD AND BURIED
DEEP-SEA DIVING
DENY THE CHARGE
DIAL THE NUMBER
DIAL THE POLICE
DONE FOR EFFECT
DOTS AND DASHES
DOWN THE STAIRS
DOWN THE STREET
DOWN THE THAMES
DRAW THE BLINDS
DULL AND DREARY
EACH-WAY DOUBLE
EASE THE BURDEN
ETON AND HARROW
FAIR AND SQUARE
FIND THE REMEDY
FITS AND STARTS
FOOD AND WARMTH
FOUL THE CARPET
FOUR AND TWENTY
FROM ALL ANGLES
FROM THE CRADLE
FROM THE OUTSET
FUSS AND BOTHER
GASP FOR BREATH
GIVE THE SIGNAL
GOLD AND SILVER
GOOD AND PROPER
HALE AND HEARTY
HALF THE BATTLE
HALF THE NUMBER
HANG THE KAISER
HARE AND HOUNDS
HAVE THE ANSWER
HAVE THE CHOICE
HAVE THE HONOUR
HAVE THE OPTION
HEAL THE BREACH
HIGH AND MIGHTY
HOLD THE RECORD
HOLD THE SCALES
HOLE AND CORNER
INTO THE BREACH
INTO THE SUNSET
JACK THE RIPPER

JEAN-LUC	GODARD	
JULY	THE	EIGHTH
JULY	THE	FOURTH
JULY	THE	SECOND
JUNE	THE	EIGHTH
JUNE	THE	FOURTH
JUNE	THE	SECOND
JUST	ONE	MOMENT
JUST	THE	TICKET
KEEP	THE	CHANGE
KICK	THE	BUCKET
KISS	AND	CUDDLE
KISS	THE	GROUND
KNOW	THE	ANSWER
LADS	AND	LASSES
LATE	FOR	DINNER
LATE	FOR	SCHOOL
LEAD	ONE	ASTRAY
LEAN	AND	HUNGRY
LIKE	THE	BLAZES
LIKE	THE	PLAGUE
LONG	WAY	BEHIND
LORD	AND	MASTER
LOSE	THE	BATTLE
LOSE	THE	RUBBER
LOSE	THE	THREAD
LOVE	AND	KISSES
MAKE	THE	EFFORT
MAKE	THE	WEIGHT
MALE	AND	FEMALE
MISS	THE	TARGET
MUST	TRY	HARDER
NEAR	THE	GROUND
NICE	AND	TENDER
NOOK	AND	CRANNY
NOSE	AND	THROAT
OPEN	THE	DRAWER
OPEN	THE	WINDOW
OVER	THE	STICKS
OVER	THE	WICKET
PART	AND	PARCEL
PASS	THE	BUTTER
PICK	AND	CHOOSE
PICK	AND	SHOVEL
PICK	THE	WINNER
PLAY	THE	FIDDLE
PLAY	THE	GUITAR
PLAY	THE	MARKET
PLAY	THE	MARTYR
PLAY	THE	SYSTEM
PLAY	THE	VIOLIN
POOR	BUT	HONEST
PRIM	AND	PROPER
PURE	AND	SUMPLE
RAID	THE	LARDER
READ	THE	FUTURE
READ	THE	SERMON
REAP	THE	REWARD
RIDE	THE	WINNER
ROCK	THE	CRADLE
ROLL	AND	BUTTER

ROLL	THE	WICKET
ROOT	AND	BRANCH
ROPE	AND	PULLEY
SAGE	AND	ONIONS
SALT	AND	PEPPER
SING	THE	CHORUS
SLAP	AND	TICKLE
SLOW	AND	STEADY
SOAP-BOX	ORATOR	
SONS	AND	LOVERS
SPIT	AND	POLISH
STAR	AND	GARTER
STAY	THE	COURSE
TAKE	FOR	GOSPEL
TAKE	THE	CREDIT
TAKE	THE	MICKEY
TAKE	THE	PLUNGE
TAKE	THE	SALUTE
TAKE	THE	STRAIN
TAKE	THE	WATERS
TEST-BAN	TREATY	
TILT	THE	SCALES
TIME	AND	MOTION
TIME	FOR	DINNER
TIME	FOR	SUPPER
TOUT	FOR	CUSTOM
TURN	THE	CORNER
TURN	THE	TABLES
TWOS	AND	THREES
WAIT	FOR	ORDERS
WASH	THE	DISHES
WEED	THE	GARDEN
WEST	HAM	UNITED
WIFE	AND	FAMILY
WILD	AND	WOOLLY
WILD-CAT	STRIKE	
WITH	ONE	ACCORD
WITH	THE	STREAM
WORK	THE	ORACLE

4, 4, 1, 4

EYES	LIKE	A	HAWK
FALL	INTO	A	TRAP
HAVE	HALF	A	MIND
ONCE	UPON	A	TIME
ROOM	WITH	A	VIEW
SING	LIKE	A	BIRD
SING	LIKE	A	LARK
SWIM	LIKE	A	FISH
WALK	INTO	A	TRAP
WORK	WITH	A	WILL

4, 4, 2, 3

AWAY	FROM	IT	ALL
LONG	TIME	NO	SEE
PLAY	HARD	TO	GET

4, 4, 3, 2

HANG ONES HAT UP
KEEP ONES END UP
KEEP ONES EYE IN
KEEP ONES EYE ON
KEEP ONES HAT ON
WORK ONES WAY UP

4, 4, 5

BACK ONES FANCY
BARE ONES TEETH
BITE ONES NAILS
BOBS YOUR UNCLE!
BURN ONES BOATS
BURN WITH ANGER
CAWL ONES BLUFF
CAST-IRON ALIBI
CLAP ONES HANDS
CLIP ONES WINGS
COME BACK AGAIN
COME INTO BEING
COME INTO FORCE
COME INTO MONEY
COME INTO SIGHT
COOK ONES GOOSE
COOL ONES HEELS
DASH ONES HOPES
DEAD MANS CHEST
DEAD MANS SHOES
DICE WITH DEATH
DING-DONG FIGHT
DRAW ONES SWORD
DROP ONES GUARD
EARN GOOD MONEY
EYES LIKE STARS
FALL FROM GRACE
FALL INTO ERROR
FALL INTO PLACE
FEEL ONES PULSE
FILL ONES GLASS
FIND ONES LEVEL
FIVE PAST EIGHT
FIVE PAST SEVEN
FIVE PAST THREE
FIVE-MILE LIMIT
FIVE-STAR HOTEL
FLOW LIKE WATER
FREE FROM BLAME
FREE FROM FAULT
FREE FROM GUILT
FROM BOTH SIDES
FROM ONES HEART
GLOW WITH PRIDE
GRIT ONES TEETH
HALF-TIME SCORE
HARD DAYS NIGHT
HARD-LUCK STORY
HAVE ONES FLING
HEAD OVER HEELS

HEAR BOTH SIDES
HELL UPON EARTH
HELP EACH OTHER
HOLD ONES PEACE
HOME-MADE BREAD
HURT ONES PRIDE
JOHN PAUL JONES
KEEP LATE HOURS
KEEP OPEN HOUSE
KICK INTO TOUCH
KICK ONES HEELS
KNIT ONES BROWS
KNOW ONES PLACE
KNOW ONES STUFF
LEFT-HAND DRIVE
LEFT-HAND SCREW
LICK INTO SHAPE
LICK ONES CHOPS
LONE-STAR STATE
LONG LAST SLEEP
LOOK OVER THERE
LOSE ONES FAITH
LOSE ONES HEART
LOSE ONES LOOKS
LOSE ONES MONEY
LOSE ONES NERVE
LOSE ONES SHIRT
LOSE ONES SIGHT
LOSE ONES TOUCH
LOSE ONES VOICE
LOVE ONES ENEMY
MAIN LINE TRAIN
MAKE ONES DEBUT
MAKE ONES PEACE
MAKE ONES POINT
MAKE ONES STAND
MEET ONES MAKER
MEET ONES MATCH
NAME ONES PRICE
NEXT BEST THING
ONES HIGH HORSE
OPEN ONES HEART
OPEN ONES MOUTH
PAST ONES PRIME
PING-PONG TABLE
PLAY ONES CARDS
PLAY UPON WORDS
PULL INTO SHAPE
RACK ONES BRAIN
REAL-LIFE STORY
REST ONES BONES
RICH MANS TABLE
RISK ONES MONEY
ROAR WITH ANGER
RUSH INTO PRINT
SAVE ONES BACON
SHOW ONES CARDS
SHOW ONES PACES
SHOW ONES TEETH
SHUT YOUR MOUTH!
SING-SONG VOICE

SLIP INTO PLACE
SOIL ONES HANDS
SOME TIME LATER
SUCK ONES THUMB
TAKE ONES FANCY
TAKE ONES LEAVE
TAKE ONES PLACE
TAKE-HOME WAGES
THIS VERY PLACE
TRUE UNTO DEATH
TRUE-LIFE STORY
WASH ONES HANDS
WELL MEET AGAIN
WEST SIDE STORY
WIPE ONES HANDS
WITH BOTH HANDS
WORK LIKE MAGIC

4, 5, 2, 2

BEST THING TO DO

4, 5, 4

BARE-FACED LIAR
BUCK STOPS HERE
COME UNDER FIRE
FINE TOOTH-COMB
FIVE-POUND NOTE
FREE TRADE AREA
FREE-RANGE EGGS
GALE-FORCE WIND
GOOD QUEEN BESS
HAVE WORDS WITH
HIGH BIRTH-RATE
HIGH-WATER MARK
HOME SWEET HOME
HOUR AFTER HOUR
KNOW WHATS WHAT
LATE-NIGHT NEWS
LIKE MEETS LIKE
LORD PRIVY SEAL
LOSE HANDS DOWN
MAKE SHORT WORK
MAKE SMALL TALK
MILE AFTER MILE
ONES LEVEL BEST
ONES RIGHT MIND
OPEN OTHER SIDE
PLAY EXTRA TIME
RIDE ROUGH-SHOD
SALT-WATER FISH
SHED LIGHT UPON
SOME OTHER TIME
STOP-PRESS NEWS
TAKE GREAT CARE
TIME AFTER TIME
WEEK AFTER NEXT
WEEK AFTER WEEK
WELL-AIMED SHOT
YEAR AFTER YEAR

4, 6, 3

EVEN THINGS OUT
FOUR-POSTER BED
HARD-BOILED EGG
MAKE THINGS HUM
OVER TWENTY-ONE
POST OFFICE BOX
POST OFFICE VAN
POST-OFFICE RED
SORT THINGS OUT
THIS LITTLE PIG
TURN INSIDE OUT
WELL TURNED OUT

4, 7, 2

DONT BELIEVE IT
DONT MENTION IT
GIVE ONESELF UP
GOOD TALKING-TO
LOOK FORWARD TO
TAKE ACCOUNT OF
TIME MARCHES ON
WELL BROUGHT UP
WELL THOUGHT OF
YOUR NUMBERS UP

4, 9

AJAX AMSTERDAM
ARMS PROGRAMME
ARMY COMMANDER
BALD STATEMENT
BANK MESSENGER
BANK OVERDRAFT
BANK STATEMENT
BARE NECESSITY
BEST BEHAVIOUR
BEST FORGOTTEN
BIRD SANCTUARY
BODY CORPORATE
BOON COMPANION
BORN YESTERDAY
BUSH TELEGRAPH
CAPE CANAVERAL
COLD RECEPTION
COOL RECEPTION
DARK CONTINENT
DEAD CERTAINTY
DEAD RECKONING
DEBT COLLECTOR
DEEP BREATHING
DEEP GRATITUDE
DIRE NECESSITY
DRAW ATTENTION
DUKE ELLINGTON
DUMB INSOLENCE
EAST GRINSTEAD
ERIC MORECAMBE

EVIL	INFLUENCE	HOLY	MATRIMONY
FAIL	MISERABLY	HOME	ECONOMICS
FAIR	CONDITION	HOME	PROGRAMME
FAIR	TREATMENT	HOME	SECRETARY
FAKE	JEWELLERY	HUGH	GAITSKELL
FALL	OVERBOARD	JOBS	COMFORTER
FEEL	EXHAUSTED	JOHN	BARRYMORE
FILM	PROJECTOR	JOHN	COCKCROFT
FIND	SALVATION	JOHN	CONSTABLE
FINE	CHARACTER	JOHN	MASEFIELD
FINE	SITUATION	JOHN	STEINBECK
FINE	TOOTHCOMB	JUMP	OVERBOARD
FIRE	INSURANCE	KING	WENCESLAS
FIRE	QUESTIONS	KNOW	BACKWARDS
FIRM	FAVOURITE	LADY	BOUNTIFUL
FIRM	HANDSHAKE	LAST	CHRISTMAS
FIRM	PRINCIPLE	LAST	SEPTEMBER
FIVE	SHILLINGS	LAST	WEDNESDAY
FOOD	POISONING	LATE	AFTERNOON
FORK	LIGHTNING	LATE	BREAKFAST
FOUR	FARTHINGS	LEAD	POISONING
FOUR	SHILLINGS	LEAN	BACKWARDS
FOUR	SYLLABLES	LIFE	ASSURANCE
FREE	ADMISSION	LIFE	HEREAFTER
FULL	PROGRAMME	LIFE	INSURANCE
FULL	TREATMENT	LIKE	CLOCKWORK
GAIN	ADMISSION	LIKE	LIGHTNING
GAIN	NOTORIETY	LIMP	HANDSHAKE
GAIN	SUPREMACY	LIVE	BROADCAST
GIVE	UTTERANCE	LIVE	PROGRAMME
GOLD	MEDALLIST	LIVE	RECORDING
GOOD	AFTERNOON	LONG	PARAGRAPH
GOOD	AUTHORITY	LOOK	DANGEROUS
GOOD	BEGINNING	LOOK	DIFFERENT
GOOD	BEHAVIOUR	LOOK	EXPECTANT
GOOD	CHARACTER	LOOK	SURPRISED
GOOD	CONDITION	LORD	LIVERPOOL
GOOD	CONDUCTOR	LORD	PRESIDENT
GOOD	GROUNDING	LORD	PROTECTOR
GOOD	HOUSEWIFE	LOUD	EXPLOSION
GOOD	INFLUENCE	MADE	REDUNDANT
GOOD	NEIGHBOUR	MAIN	CHARACTER
GOOD	PROSPECTS	MAKE	ALLOWANCE
GOOD	QUALITIES	MAKE	ECONOMIES
GOOD	RECEPTION	MAKE	INQUIRIES
GOOD	SAMARITAN	MAKE	MINCEMEAT
GOOD	SPORTSMAN	MAKE	PROVISION
GOOD	THRASHING	MAKE	REDUNDANT
GOOD	WALLOPING	MARY	MAGDALENE
GROW	DESPERATE	MASS	FORMATION
GROW	DOWNWARDS	MERE	BAGATELLE
HALF	SOVEREIGN	MERE	EXISTENCE
HAVE	BREAKFAST	MILD	EXPLETIVE
HAVE	DELUSIONS	MILK	CHOCOLATE
HAVE	HYSTERICS	MINT	CONDITION
HEAT	TREATMENT	MOST	DESIRABLE
HIGH	CHURCHMAN	MOST	EXCELLENT
HIGH	EXPLOSIVE	MOVE	MOUNTAINS
HIGH	FREQUENCY	MUCH	REGRETTED
HIGH	VALUATION	NEAR	NEIGHBOUR
HOLY	COMMUNION	NEIL	ARMSTRONG

NEXT CHRISTMAS		TAPE RECORDING	
NEXT SEPTEMBER		TEST CRICKETER	
NEXT WEDNESDAY		THIS WEDNESDAY	
ONES RELATIVES		TORY CANDIDATE	
OPEN HOSTILITY		TOUR CONDUCTOR	
OPEN REBELLION		TRAM CONDUCTOR	
OTTO KLEMPERER		TRUE STATEMENT	
OTTO PREMINGER		TURN CLOCKWISE	
OWEN GLENDOWER		UGLY SITUATION	
PALE IMITATION		VERY DIFFERENT	
PARK ATTENDANT		VERY IMPORTANT	
PASS UNNOTICED		VERY REWARDING	
PAST BEHAVIOUR		WAIT PATIENTLY	
PAUL MCCARTNEY		WALK BACKWARDS	
PINK CHAMPAGNE		WARM HANDSHAKE	
PLAY BILLIARDS		WARM RECEPTION	
POOL RESOURCES		WEAK CHARACTER	
POOR CONDITION		WELL ORGANISED	
POOR PROSPECTS		WELL PRESERVED	
POOR RECEPTION		WEST GLAMORGAN	
PORT ELIZABETH		WEST YORKSHIRE	
QUIZ PROGRAMME		WIDE INTERESTS	
RACE PREJUDICE		WIDE KNOWLEDGE	
RAPT ATTENTION		WING COMMANDER	
RASH STATEMENT		WISH OTHERWISE	
RATE COLLECTOR		WITH AUTHORITY	
RENÉ DESCARTES		WITH CERTAINTY	
RENT COLLECTOR		WITH RESTRAINT	
ROAD DIVERSION		WOOD ENGRAVING	
ROAD TRANSPORT			
ROOF ORCHESTRA		5, 1, 2, 5	
ROOT VEGETABLE			
RUDE AWAKENING		CECIL B.DE MILLE	
RULE BRITANNIA			
SEEK ADMISSION		5, 1, 3, 4	
SHOP ASSISTANT			
SHOP DETECTIVE		REACH A NEW HIGH	
SHOW ANIMOSITY			
SHOW DEFERENCE		5, 1, 4, 3	
SHOW GRATITUDE			
SHOW RESTRAINT		REACH A DEAD END	
SIDE ELEVATION		5, 1, 5, 2	
SILK STOCKINGS			
SKIN TREATMENT		STEAL A MARCH ON	
SLUM CLEARANCE			
SOLE OWNERSHIP		5, 1, 7	
SOON FORGOTTEN			
STAR PERFORMER		AFTER A FASHION	
STAR TREATMENT		BREAK A PROMISE	
STAY OVERNIGHT		BRING A LAWSUIT	
STEP BACKWARDS		CATCH A GLIMPSE	
STOP BREATHING		CATCH A WHOPPER	
TAKE ADVANTAGE		CAUSE A FLUTTER	
TAKE EXCEPTION		CAUSE A SCANDAL	
TAKE LIBERTIES		DRIVE A BARGAIN	
TAKE SANCTUARY		ERECT A BARRIER	
TAKE SERIOUSLY		FLOAT A COMPANY	
TAKE SHORTHAND		FORCE A PASSAGE	
TAKE SOUNDINGS		FRAME A PICTURE	
TALK GIBBERISH		GRANT A DIVORCE	
TALK PRIVATELY		GRANT A REQUEST	

```
INCUR  A  PENALTY        SLEEP  ON  THE  JOB
ISSUE  A  SUMMONS        SMACK  IN  THE  EYE
ISSUE  A  WARNING        STAND  IN  THE  WAY
LEAVE  A  FORTUNE        STICK  IN  THE  MUD
LEAVE  A  MESSAGE        TEACH  AN  OLD  DOG
LIGHT  A  BONFIRE        THROW  IN  THE  AIR
MARRY  A  FORTUNE        TOUCH  OF  THE  SUN
PAINT  A  PICTURE        TOUGH  AT  THE  TOP
REACH  A  VERDICT        WEAVE  IN  AND  OUT
SCORE  A  CENTURY        WHITE  OF  THE  EYE
SCORE  A  HUNDRED        WHOLE  OF  THE  DAY
SERVE  A  PURPOSE
SOLVE  A  PROBLEM
SOUND  A  FANFARE            5 , 2 , 4 , 2
SPARE  A  THOUGHT
SPEND  A  FORTUNE        WHERE  WE  CAME  IN
START  A  QUARREL
THROW  A  TANTRUM            5 , 2 , 6
WORTH  A  FORTUNE
WORTH  A  MILLION        AGREE  TO  DIFFER
                        BADGE  OF  HONOUR
                        BADGE  OF  OFFICE
     5 , 2 , 1 , 5       BEAST  OF  BURDEN
                        BEGIN  TO  WEAKEN
BRING  TO  A  CLOSE      BLAZE  OF  COLOUR
FRESH  AS  A  DAISY      BREAK  IT  GENTLY
QUICK  AS  A  FLASH      BRING  AN  ACTION
QUIET  AS  A  MOUSE      BROOK  NO  DENIAL
SERVE  AS  A  MODEL      BUNCH  OF  GRAPES
SHARP  AS  A  KNIFE      BURST  OF  ENERGY
SHARP  AS  A  RAZOR      CAUSE  OF  INJURY
SOBER  AS  A  JUDGE      CHAIN  OF  EVENTS
STIFF  AS  A  BOARD      CHAIN  OF  OFFICE
STIFF  AS  A  POKER      CHIEF  OF  POLICE
TIMID  AS  A  MOUSE      CHILD  OF  NATURE
WHITE  AS  A  GHOST      CHOSE  IN  ACTION
WHITE  AS  A  SHEET      CLOSE  TO  NATURE
                        COULD  BE  BETTER
                        COURT  OF  APPEAL
     5 , 2 , 2 , 4       CRÉME  DE  MENTHE
                        CRIES  OF  LONDON
BRING  UP  TO  DATE      CROWD  OF  PEOPLE
LIGHT  OF  MY  LIFE      CROWN  OF  THORNS
RIGHT  UP  TO  DATE      CRUSH  TO  PIECES
                        DEATH  BY  INCHES
     5 , 2 , 3 , 3       DRINK  TO  EXCESS
                        DRIVE-IN  CINEMA
ABIDE  BY  THE  LAW      DROVE  OF  CATTLE
APPLE  OF  THE  EYE      EAGER  TO  PLEASE
BIRDS  OF  THE  AIR      EAMON  DE  VALÉRA
BLIND  IN  ONE  EYE      EIGHT  OF  HEARTS
CLIMB  TO  THE  TOP      EIGHT  OF  SPADES
DODGE  IN  AND  OUT      EIGHT  OF  TRUMPS
FLASH  IN  THE  PAN      FIELD  OF  ACTION
LEAVE  IN  THE  AIR      FIELD  OF  BATTLE
MATCH  OF  THE  DAY      FIELD  OF  VISION
ORDER  OF  THE  DAY      FIFTH  OF  AUGUST
PLACE  IN  THE  SUN      FIRST  OF  AUGUST
POINT  OF  THE  JAW      FLASH  OF  GENIUS
POWER  OF  THE  LAW      FLEET  OF  TRUCKS
RIGHT  AT  THE  END      FOUNT  OF  WISDOM
RIGHT  ON  THE  DOT      FREAK  OF  NATURE
RIGHT  TO  THE  END
```

GIVEN	IN	CHARGE
GIVEN	TO	EXCESS
GLASS	OF	BRANDY
GLASS	OF	SHERRY
GLASS	OF	WHISKY
GRIND	TO	PIECES
GRIND	TO	POWDER
GROUP	OF	PEOPLE
GUARD	OF	HONOUR
GUEST	OF	HONOUR
HAVEN	OF	REFUGE
HEART	OF	HEARTS
HOUSE	OF	ORANGE
HOUSE	OF	PRAYER
HOUSE	OF	STUART
HOUSE	ON	WHEELS
KNAVE	OF	HEARTS
KNAVE	OF	SPADES
KNAVE	OF	TRUMPS
LAPSE	OF	MEMORY
LAUGH	AT	DANGER
LEAVE	NO	CHOICE
LEAVE	NO	OPTION
LEAVE	TO	APPEAL
LEAVE	TO	CHANCE
LODGE	AN	APPEAL
MEALS	ON	WHEELS
MEANS	OF	ESCAPE
MEANS	OF	SAFETY
MONEY	NO	OBJECT
MOUNT	OF	OLIVES
NEVER	ON	SUNDAY
NIGHT	OF	TERROR
NINTH	OF	AUGUST
ORDER	OF	BATTLE
ORDER	OF	THINGS
PANEL	OF	JUDGES
PANGS	OF	HUNGER
PAPER	OF	RECORD
PEARL	OF	WISDOM
PIECE	OF	ADVICE
PIECE	OF	STRING
PLACE	OF	HONOUR
PLACE	OF	REFUGE
PLACE	ON	RECORD
POINT	IN	FAVOUR
POINT	OF	HONOUR
POUND	OF	APPLES
POUND	OF	BUTTER
POWER	OF	SPEECH
QUEEN	OF	HEARTS
QUEEN	OF	SPADES
QUEEN	OF	TRUMPS
RANGE	OF	COLOUR
READY	TO	POUNCE
READY	TO	SPRING
REFER	TO	DRAWER
REIGN	OF	TERROR
REPEL	AN	ATTACK
REPLY	BY	RETURN
RHYME	OR	REASON

RIGHT	OF	ACCESS
RIGHT	OF	APPEAL
RIGHT	OF	CHOICE
ROUND	OF	DRINKS
SENSE	OF	DANGER
SENSE	OF	HUMOUR
SENSE	OF	RELIEF
SENSE	OF	TIMING
SENSE	OF	VALUES
SERVE	UP	DINNER
SEVEN	NO-	TRUMPS
SEVEN	OF	HEARTS
SEVEN	OF	SPADES
SEVEN	OF	TRUMPS
SHORT	OF	BREATH
SHORT	OF	CHANGE
SIXTH	OF	AUGUST
SMASH	TO	PIECES
SONGS	OF	PRAISE
SOUTH	OF	FRANCE
SOUTH	OF	RUSSIA
SPARE	NO	EFFORT
SPEAK	AT	LENGTH
STAND	ON	TIPTOE
STAND	TO	REASON
STAND-	BY	TICKET
START	TO	FINISH
STATE	OF	CHANGE
STATE	OF	FRENZY
STATE	OF	REPAIR
STATE	OF	UNREST
STICK	OF	CELERY
TEARS	OF	SORROW
TENTH	OF	AUGUST
THANE	OF	CAWDOR
THING	OF	BEAUTY
THIRD	OF	AUGUST
THOSE	IN	FAVOUR
THREE	NO-	TRUMPS
THREE	OF	HEARTS
THREE	OF	SPADES
THREE	OF	TRUMPS
TIMES	OF	STRESS
TIMON	OF	ATHENS
TIRED	OF	LIVING
TOKEN	OF	ESTEEM
TOUCH	OF	COLOUR
TOUCH	OF	GENIUS
TOWER	OF	LONDON
TRAIN	OF	EVENTS
TRIAL	BY	COMBAT
TRIAL	BY	ORDEAL
TRUST	TO	CHANCE
VOICE	OF	REASON
WASTE	OF	BREATH
WASTE	OF	EFFORT
WHITE	AS	MARBLE
WORDS	OF	WISDOM
WRITE	AT	LENGTH
WRITE	IN	PENCIL

5 , 3 , 1 , 4

APPLY FOR A LOAN
EIGHT AND A HALF
GOING FOR A SONG
REACH OUT A HAND
SEVEN AND A HALF
STAND OUT A MILE
STICK OUT A MILE
TAKEN FOR A RIDE
THREE AND A HALF

5 , 3 , 2 , 3

EIGHT OUT OF TEN
PLACE END TO END
SEVEN OUT OF TEN

5 , 3 , 5

ABOVE SEA-LEVEL
ACHES AND PAINS
AFTER THE EVENT
AFTER THE FLOOD
AFTER THE STORM
AGAIN AND AGAIN
ALONG THE COAST
ALPHA AND OMEGA
APPLE-PIE ORDER
APPLY FOR LEAVE
APRIL THE FIFTH
APRIL THE FIRST
APRIL THE NINTH
APRIL THE SIXTH
APRIL THE TENTH
APRIL THE THIRD
ARGUE THE POINT
AVOID THE ISSUE
BANKS AND BRAES
BELOW SEA-LEVEL
BLACK AND WHITE
BLAZE THE TRAIL
BLESS THE BRIDE
BOARD THE TRAIN
BRAVE NEW WORLD
BREAD AND WATER
BREAK ITS BANKS
BREAK THE BREAD
BREAK THE HABIT
BREAK THE PEACE
BREAK THE RULES
BREAK THE SPELL
BREAK THE TRUCE
BRIDE AND GROOM
CARRY THE BLAME
CARVE THE JOINT
CATCH THE TRAIN
CAUSE FOR ALARM
CAUSE FOR PANIC
CECIL DAY LEWIS
CHEAP AND NASTY

CHILI CON CARNE
CLAIM THE CROWN
CLEAN THE SLATE
CLEAR THE DECKS
CLEAR THE FENCE
CLEAR THE TABLE
CLOSE THE RANKS
CLOSE-RUN THING
CLOUD THE ISSUE
COUNT THE HOURS
CRASH THE GEARS
CROSS THE FLOOR
CROSS THE OCEAN
CURSE AND SWEAR
DANCE THE POLKA
DANCE THE TANGO
DEATH AND GLORY
DODGE THE ISSUE
DRAIN THE DREGS
DRIBS AND DRABS
DRINK AND DRIVE
EVADE THE ISSUE
EVERY FEW WEEKS
EVERY FEW YEARS
FETCH AND CARRY
FIFTY NEW PENCE
FIFTY-ONE PENCE
FIFTY-SIX PENCE
FIFTY-TWO PENCE
FIFTY-TWO WEEKS
FLESH AND BLOOD
FLORA AND FAUNA
FLOUR AND WATER
FORCE THE ISSUE
FORTY-ONE PENCE
FORTY-SIX PENCE
FORTY-TWO PENCE
FRESH-AIR FIEND
FRUIT AND CREAM
GIVEN THE WORKS
GOODY TWO-SHOES
GREAT AND SMALL
GRIND THE TEETH
HANDS AND KNEES
HENRY THE FIFTH
HENRY THE FIRST
HENRY THE SIXTH
HENRY THE THIRD
HORSE AND GROOM
HOURS AND HOURS
INFRA-RED LIGHT
JAMES THE FIRST
JERRY LEE LEWIS
KNEAD THE DOUGH
LARGE AND SMALL
LEARN THE ROPES
LEARN THE TRUTH
LEVEL THE SCORE
LIGHT AND SHADE
LIGHT THE STOVE
LIVER AND BACON

LOWER AND LOWER	STAND AND FIGHT
LOWER THE PRICE	STAND AND STARE
MARCH THE FIFTH	STEAK AND CHIPS
MARCH THE FIRST	STONE THE CROWS!
MARCH THE NINTH	STUDY ALL SIDES
MARCH THE SIXTH	STUDY FOR EXAMS
MARCH THE TENTH	STUDY THE FACTS
MARCH THE THIRD	STUDY THE PLANS
MATCH-BOX LABEL	STUDY THE STARS
MILES AND MILES	SUGAR AND SPICE
MUMMY AND DADDY	SWEEP THE BOARD
NEVER JAM TODAY	SWEEP THE FLOOR
NORTH AND SOUTH	SWEET AND JUICY
OLDER AND WISER	SWELL THE RANKS
OTHER WAY ROUND	TEMPT THE DEVIL
PAPER THE WALLS	THATS ALL FOLKS
PEACE AND QUIET	THATS THE LIMIT
PICTS AND SCOTS	THINK THE WORST
PINKY AND PERKY	THREE NEW PENCE
PLEAD THE CAUSE	THREE-DAY MATCH
POINT FOR POINT	THUMP THE TABLE
POWER AND GLORY	TOUCH THE HEART
QATAR AND DUBAI	TRACK AND FIELD
QUEER THE PITCH	TRIAL AND ERROR
QUITE THE THING	TWIST AND SHOUT
RAISE THE ALARM	UNDER THE TABLE
RAISE THE FUNDS	UNDER THE THUMB
RAISE THE MONEY	VALUE FOR MONEY
RAISE THE PRICE	VOTES FOR WOMEN
RAISE THE TEMPO	WATCH AND CHAIN
REACH THE FINAL	WATCH THE TELLY
RENEW THE LEASE	WEEKS AND WEEKS
RIGHT ALL ALONG	WHATS THE POINT?
RIGHT AND WRONG	WIELD THE BATON
ROUGH AND READY	WINED AND DINED
ROUND AND ABOUT	WORDS AND MUSIC
ROUND AND ROUND	WORLD WAR THREE
ROUND THE BLOCK	WORSE AND WORSE
ROUND THE CLOCK	WRONG WAY ROUND
ROUND THE EARTH	YARDS AND YARDS
ROUND THE TABLE	YEARS AND YEARS
ROUND THE TWIST	
ROUND THE WAIST	5, 4, 1, 3
ROUND THE WORLD	
ROYAL AIR FORCE	BREAK INTO A RUN
SEIZE THE CROWN	CLIMB LIKE A CAT
SERVE ONE RIGHT	SLEEP LIKE A LOG
SHAME THE DEVIL	SLEEP LIKE A TOP
SHARE AND ENJOY	TAKEN DOWN A PEG
SHARE THE BLAME	
SHIFT THE BLAME	5, 4, 4
SHORT AND SWEET	
SIXTY-ONE PENCE	ABOUT ONES EARS
SIXTY-SIX PENCE	ABOVE ONES HEAD
SIXTY-TWO PENCE	ARGUE ONES CASE
SOUND THE ALARM	AVERT ONES EYES
SPEAK THE TRUTH	BIRDS-NEST SOUP
SPILL THE BEANS	BLIND MANS BUFF
SPOIL THE BROTH	BREAK INTO SONG
SPOIL THE CHILD	BREAK ONES BACK
STACK THE CARDS	BREAK ONES DUCK

BREAK ONES FALL
BREAK ONES NECK
BREAK ONES WORD
BRING INTO LINE
BRING INTO PLAY
BRUSH ONES HAIR
CARVE ONES NAME
CATHY COME HOME
CEASE-FIRE LINE
CHASE ONES TAIL
CLEAR ONES NAME
CLOSE ONES EYES
CRICK ONES NECK
CROSS ONES LEGS
CROSS ONES MIND
CROSS ONES PALM
CROSS ONES PATH
DADDY LONG-LEGS
DANCE WITH RAGE
DOING VERY WELL
DRINK ONES FILL
DRIVE WITH CARE
FACED WITH RUIN
FEAST ONES EYES
FORCE ONES HAND
FORTY-HOUR WEEK
FRONT-PAGE NEWS
GLASS WITH CARE
GREAT SALT LAKE
GREEN WITH ENVY
GRIND INTO DUST
JOLLY GOOD CHAP
LEAVE ONES CARD
LEAVE ONES POST
LIVID WITH RAGE
MUSIC-HALL JOKE
MUSIC-HALL STAR
MUSIC-HALL TURN
NEVER LOOK BACK
NORTH-EAST WIND
NORTH-WEST WIND
OLDER THAN TIME
PAINT ONES FACE
PAVED WITH GOLD
PITCH ONES TENT
PRESS ONES SUIT
PROVE ONES CASE
PURSE ONES LIPS
RAISE ONES HAND
REACH ONES GOAL
READY MADE SUIT
RIGHT-HAND BEND
RIGHT-HAND SIDE
RIGHT-HAND TURN
SERVE ONES TIME
SEVEN-YEAR ITCH
SHAKE ONES FIST
SHAKE ONES HEAD
SHAKE WITH FEAR
SHOOT ONES BOLT
SHORT-TERM LOAN

SHORT-TERM VIEW
SMACK ONES LIPS
SOUND ONES HORN
SOUTH EAST WIND
SOUTH-WEST WIND
SPEAK ONES MIND
SPIKE ONES GUNS
SPITE ONES FACE
STAKE ONES LIFE
STATE ONES CASE
STICK LIKE GLUE
STRAY FROM HOME
SWING ONES ARMS
THREE BAGS FULL
THREE FEET TALL
THREE-FOOT RULE
THREE-LINE WHIP
THROW INTO JAIL
THUMB ONES NOSE
TOUCH ONES TOES
TREAT LIKE DIRT
TREAT WITH CARE
TWICE-TOLD TALE
UNDER MILK WOOD
UNDER ONES NOSE
UNDER ONES SKIN
UNDER ONES WING
UNTIL NEXT TIME
VALUE ONES LIFE
WALLS HAVE EARS
— WATCH ONES STEP
WATCH YOUR STEP
WHATS YOUR GAME?
WHATS YOUR NAME?
WHITE HART LANE
WHITE WITH RAGE
WORLD-WIDE FAME
WORSE THAN EVER
WORTH ONES SALT
WRITE ONES NAME

5 , 5 , 3

ANGRY YOUNG MAN
APRIL FOOLS DAY
BLIND-ALLEY JOB
BROWN PAPER BAG
EDGAR ALLAN POE
EVERY OTHER DAY
EVERY WHICH WAY
FIRST WORLD WAR
KNOCK SPOTS OFF
LARGE-SCALE MAP
ROBIN HOODS BAY
ROUND-ABOUT WAY
SEVEN YEARS WAR
STIFF UPPER LIP
THIRD WORLD WAR
TRULY GREAT MAN
UNDER-COVER MAN
VALUE ADDED TAX

5, 6, 2

DEATH WARMED UP
LIVEN THINGS UP
READY STEADY GO
THINK LITTLE OF

5, 8

ABOVE REPROACH
ACUTE DISTRESS
ADDED PLEASURE
ADDED STRENGTH
AFTER MIDNIGHT
ALLEN GINSBERG
APPLE DUMPLING
APPLE TURNOVER
APPLY PRESSURE
ARMED CONFLICT
ARMED UPRISING
BACON SANDWICH
BAGGY TROUSERS
BALLY NUISANCE
BARRY RICHARDS
BASIC INSTINCT
BASSO PROFUNDO
BELOW FREEZING
BELOW STANDARD
BELOW STRENGTH
BILLY CONNOLLY
BLOCK CAPITALS
BLOOD BROTHERS
BLOOD PRESSURE
BLOOD RELATION
BLUNT QUESTION
BOBBY CHARLTON
BONNY SCOTLAND
BRASS BEDSTEAD
BRASS FARTHING
BREAD SHORTAGE
BRIEF INTERVAL
BRING TOGETHER
BROAD DAYLIGHT
BROWN ENVELOPE
BRUTE STRENGTH
BURNT OFFERING
CATCH UNAWARES
CHAIN REACTION
CHARM BRACELET
CHESS CHAMPION
CHEST EXPANDER
CHIEF ARMOURER
CHIEF ENGINEER
CHOIR PRACTICE
CIVIL AVIATION
CIVIL ENGINEER
CLASS STRUGGLE
CLING TOGETHER
CLINT EASTWOOD
CLOSE FIGHTING
CLOSE QUARTERS

CLOSE RELATIVE
CLOSE TOGETHER
CORAL NECKLACE
COURT DISASTER
COURT INTRIGUE
COURT REPORTER
CRACK REGIMENT
CRAZY BUSINESS
CRAZY PAVEMENT
CRIME REPORTER
CROWD TOGETHER
CRUDE ESTIMATE
CUBIC CAPACITY
CUBIC CONTENTS
CYRIL FLETCHER
DAILY DELIVERY
DAILY PRACTICE
DEATH SENTENCE
DEATH STRUGGLE
DIRTY POSTCARD
DRAMA FESTIVAL
DREAM SEQUENCE
DRESS DESIGNER
DRESS MATERIAL
DRESS OPTIONAL
DRILL SERGEANT
EARLY DECISION
EIGHT FURLONGS
EIGHT THOUSAND
ELDER DAUGHTER
EMPTY CUPBOARD
EMPTY PLEASURE
EMPTY PROMISES
ENEMY AIRCRAFT
ENJOY IMMUNITY
EQUAL DIVISION
EQUAL QUANTITY
EVERY SATURDAY
EVERY THURSDAY
EXACT LIKENESS
EXERT PRESSURE
FAIRY PRINCESS
FALSE CLAIMANT
FALSE EVIDENCE
FALSE IDENTITY
FALSE OPTIMISM
FALSE TEACHING
FATAL ACCIDENT
FATAL CASUALTY
FATAL DECISION
FEIGN SICKNESS
FIELD HOSPITAL
FIFTH SYMPHONY
FIFTY THOUSAND
FIGHT PROMOTER
FINAL DECISION
FINAL ESTIMATE
FINAL JUDGMENT
FINER FEELINGS
FIRST BIRTHDAY
FIRST DIVIDEND

FIRST DIVISION	HEATH ROBINSON
FIRST LANGUAGE	HEAVY EXPENSES
FIRST OFFENDER	HEAVY INDUSTRY
FIRST SYMPHONY	HEAVY RAINFALL
FIRST THOUGHTS	HEAVY SENTENCE
FIXED BAYONETS	HELLO STRANGER
FIXED DOMICILE	HENRY FIELDING
FIZZY LEMONADE	HIRED ASSASSIN
FLOCK TOGETHER	HORSE CHESTNUT
FOOLS PARADISE	HOTLY DISPUTED
FORTY THOUSAND	HOUSE MAGAZINE
FRANK RICHARDS	HUMAN ACTIVITY
FRANZ SCHUBERT	HUMAN CREATURE
FRESH APPROACH	HUMAN INTEREST
FRESH EVIDENCE	HUMAN KINDNESS
FRIED POTATOES	HUMAN PROGRESS
FRIED TOMATOES	HUMAN WEAKNESS
FRONT ENTRANCE	INNER CONFLICT
FULLY EQUIPPED	INNER HEBRIDES
FULLY LICENSED	IRISH REGIMENT
FULLY PREPARED	JAMES GARFIELD
FULLY RESTORED	JAMES WHISTLER
FUNNY BUSINESS	JEWEL MERCHANT
FUNNY PECULIAR	JOINT PARTNERS
GAMES MISTRESS	JOYCE GRENFELL
GIANT TORTOISE	JUDAS ISCARIOT
GOING STRAIGHT	JUDGE ADVOCATE
GRAND ENTRANCE	JUDGE JEFFREYS
GRAND JUNCTION	JULIE CHRISTIE
GRAND NATIONAL	KENNY DALGLISH
GRANT IMMUNITY	KINGS BIRTHDAY
GRAVE DECISION	KINGS CHAMPION
GREAT DICTATOR	KINGS EVIDENCE
GREAT DISTANCE	KINGS PLEASURE
GREAT INTEREST	KINGS SHILLING
GREAT KINDNESS	KNOCK SIDEWAYS
GREAT MAJORITY	LARGE AUDIENCE
GREAT OCCASION	LARGE MAJORITY
GREAT PATIENCE	LARGE MINORITY
GREAT PLEASURE	LARGE QUANTITY
GREAT STRENGTH	LARGE TURNOVER
GREAT THOUGHTS	LATIN AMERICAN
GREAT YARMOUTH	LEAVE HOSPITAL
GREEK ALPHABET	LEAVE STANDING
GREEK LANGUAGE	LEGAL CURRENCY
GREEK ORTHODOX	LEGAL DOCUMENT
GREEN PASTURES	LEGAL GUARDIAN
GROSS RECEIPTS	LEGAL POSITION
GROUP ACTIVITY	LEGAL TRICKERY
HAILE SELASSIE	LEMON MERINGUE
HAPPY ACCIDENT	LEMON SQUEEZER
HAPPY BIRTHDAY	LEVEL CROSSING
HAPPY FAMILIES	LIGHT INDUSTRY
HAPPY MARRIAGE	LIGHT INFANTRY
HAPPY MEMORIES	LIGHT SENTENCE
HAPPY WANDERER	LOCAL CURRENCY
HARSH CONTRAST	LOCAL ELECTION
HARSH DECISION	LOCAL LANDMARK
HARSH SENTENCE	LOCAL PREACHER
HASTY DECISION	LOFTY AMBITION
HEADS TOGETHER	LORDS TEMPORAL

LOUIS	QUATORZE	PLAIN	LANGUAGE
LOWER	REGISTER	PLAIN	SPEAKING
LOYAL	DEVOTION	PLEAD	INNOCENT
LUCID	ARGUMENT	POLAR	EXPLORER
LUCKY	TALISMAN	POSTE	RESTANTE
LUNCH	INTERVAL	POUND	STERLING
MAJOR	DISASTER	POWER	POLITICS
MAJOR	INCIDENT	PRAWN	COCKTAIL
MERCI	BEAUCOUP	PRESS	CAMPAIGN
MESSY	BUSINESS	PRESS	CUTTINGS
METAL	DETECTOR	PRICE	INCREASE
MINOR	COUNTIES	PRIME	MINISTER
MINOR	INCIDENT	PRIZE	SPECIMEN
MIXED	BLESSING	QUEEN	BOADICEA
MIXED	FEELINGS	QUEEN	MARGARET
MIXED	MARRIAGE	QUEEN	VICTORIA
MIXED	METAPHOR	QUEER	CUSTOMER
MODEL	AIRCRAFT	QUICK	MOVEMENT
MODEL	PRISONER	QUICK	RECOVERY
MODUS	OPERANDI	QUICK	THINKING
MORAL	PRESSURE	QUITE	POSSIBLE
MORAL	STRENGTH	RADIO	CAROLINE
MORAL	WEAKNESS	RADIO	OPERATOR
MOTOR	MECHANIC	RADIO	RECEIVER
MOUNT	PLEASANT	RAISE	CHILDREN
MOUNT	VESUVIUS	RAKES	PROGRESS
MUSIC	BUSINESS	RAPID	PROGRESS
MUSIC	FESTIVAL	RAPID	TURNOVER
MUSIC	MISTRESS	REACH	MATURITY
NADIA	COMANECI	READY	RECKONER
NASTY	BUSINESS	READY	RESPONSE
NAVAL	EXERCISE	REPEL	BOARDERS
NIGHT	EXERCISE	RIGHT	APPROACH
NIGHT	WATCHMAN	RIGHT	DECISION
NINTH	SYMPHONY	RIGHT	REVEREND
NOBLE	AMBITION	RIGHT	SHOULDER
NORTH	AMERICAN	RISKY	BUSINESS
NORTH	ATLANTIC	RIVAL	BUSINESS
NORTH	CAROLINA	ROAST	CHESTNUT
OUTER	HEBRIDES	ROAST	POTATOES
OUTER	MONGOLIA	ROCKY	MARCIANO
OWNER	OCCUPIER	ROGUE	ELEPHANT
PAGAN	FESTIVAL	ROMAN	ALPHABET
PANIC	MEASURES	ROMAN	CATHOLIC
PANIC	STATIONS	ROMAN	NUMERALS
PAPER	CURRENCY	ROMAN	POLANSKI
PARIS	FASHIONS	ROUGH	CROSSING
PARTY	POLITICS	ROUGH	CUSTOMER
PEACE	OFFERING	ROUGH	ESTIMATE
PEARL	NECKLACE	ROUGH	EXTERIOR
PEGGY	ASHCROFT	ROUGH	HANDLING
PENNY	DREADFUL	ROWAN	ATKINSON
PENNY	FARTHING	ROYAL	FUNCTION
PENNY	PINCHING	ROYAL	HIGHNESS
PETTY	OFFICIAL	ROYAL	MARRIAGE
PETTY	SESSIONS	ROYAL	OCCASION
PIANO	CONCERTO	ROYAL	STANDARD
PIECE	TOGETHER	RUGBY	FOOTBALL
PITCH	DARKNESS	RURAL	DISTRICT
PLAIN	ENVELOPE	RURAL	INDUSTRY
PLAIN	FEATURES	SAINT	AUGUSTUS

SAINT LAWRENCE	STERN MEASURES
SAINT NICHOLAS	STICK TOGETHER
SALAD DRESSING	STIFF SENTENCE
SAUTÉ POTATOES	STILL LEMONADE
SCARE HEADLINE	STOCK EXCHANGE
SCRAP MERCHANT	STOCK QUESTION
SEVEN BROTHERS	STRAW MATTRESS
SEVEN DIAMONDS	STRIP LIGHTING
SEVEN THOUSAND	STUDY MEDICINE
SEVEN TWELFTHS	SUGAR REFINERY
SHADY BUSINESS	SUNIL GAVASKAR
SHARP CONTRAST	SWEET CHESTNUT
SHARP FEATURES	SWEET LAVENDER
SHARP PRACTICE	SWEET NOTHINGS
SHEER NONSENSE	SWEET POTATOES
SHIPS CORPORAL	SWEET THOUGHTS
SHIPS REGISTER	SWORN EVIDENCE
SHOCK ABSORBER	TABLE FOOTBALL
SHOOT STRAIGHT	TABLE MOUNTAIN
SHORT DISTANCE	TAKEN PRISONER
SHORT SENTENCE	TAKEN UNAWARES
SHORT SYNOPSIS	TEACH CLASSICS
SHORT TROUSERS	THANK GOODNESS!
SHORT VACATION	THINK STRAIGHT
SILLY QUESTION	THIRD DIVISION
SIXTH SYMPHONY	THIRD ENGINEER
SIXTY THOUSAND	THIRD SYMPHONY
SLICK OPERATOR	THREE BEDROOMS
SMALL BUSINESS	THREE DIAMONDS
SMALL DIVIDEND	THREE FURLONGS
SMALL INVESTOR	THREE QUARTERS
SMALL QUANTITY	THREE SEVENTHS
SMART TROUSERS	THREE THOUSAND
SMEAR CAMPAIGN	TIGHT SECURITY
SOBER ESTIMATE	TOMMY DOCHERTY
SOUND ARGUMENT	TOTAL DARKNESS
SOUND DOCTRINE	TOTAL DEADLOCK
SOUND JUDGMENT	TOUGH CUSTOMER
SOUND STRATEGY	TRADE DISCOUNT
SOUTH AMERICAN	TRADE ENTRANCE
SOUTH CAROLINA	TRADE MAGAZINE
SPACE INVADERS	TRADE UNIONIST
SPEED MERCHANT	TRAIN SPOTTING
SPELL DISASTER	TRICK QUESTION
SPIKE MILLIGAN	TRULY GRATEFUL
SPINY ANTEATER	TWEED TROUSERS
SPLIT DECISION	UNDER CONTRACT
STAFF ENTRANCE	UNDER PRESSURE
STAFF PROBLEMS	UNDER SENTENCE
STAFF SERGEANT	UNDER STRENGTH
STAND TOGETHER	UNDER TRAINING
STARK CONTRAST	UPPER REGISTER
START THINKING	URBAN DISTRICT
START TOGETHER	URBAN GUERILLA
STATE BOUNDARY	USUAL CHANNELS
STATE CRIMINAL	UTTER CONTEMPT
STATE FUNCTION	UTTER DEVOTION
STATE MONOPOLY	UTTER NONSENSE
STATE OCCASION	VALID CONTRACT
STATE PRISONER	VALUE RECEIVED
STEEL INDUSTRY	VEXED QUESTION

VIDEO RECORDER
VINYL EMULSION
VITAL QUESTION
VOCAL MINORITY
VOICE TRAINING
WATER SHORTAGE
WATER SOFTENER
WELSH LANGUAGE
WELSH REGIMENT
WHITE ELEPHANT
WHITE FLANNELS
WIGAN ATHLETIC
WORLD CHAMPION
WORLD PREMIERE
WORST POSSIBLE
WORTH MILLIONS
WRONG APPROACH
WRONG DECISION
YOUNG CHILDREN
YOUTH MOVEMENT
ZEBRA CROSSING

6, 1, 3, 3

BECOME A NEW MAN

6, 1, 6

BECOME A MEMBER
BOUNCE A CHEQUE
COMMIT A FELONY
CREATE A MARKET
CREATE A RUMPUS
CREATE A VACUUM
JEROME K. JEROME
OBLIGE A FRIEND
PLOUGH A FURROW
REDEEM A PLEDGE
REFUSE A CHANCE
RETURN A FAVOUR
RETURN A PROFIT
SCRAPE A LIVING
SPREAD A RUMOUR
STRAIN A MUSCLE
SUBMIT A REPORT
SUFFER A STROKE
TAUGHT A LESSON
THOMAS À BECKET
THREAD A NEEDLE
UNVEIL A STATUE

6, 2, 1, 4

CAUGHT IN A TRAP
GENTLE AS A LAMB
PISSED AS A NEWT
SONATA IN A FLAT
STEADY AS A ROCK
STRIKE UP A TUNE

6, 2, 3, 2

ALWAYS ON THE GO

6, 2, 5

ACCEPT AN OFFER
AFRAID TO SPEAK
APPEAR IN COURT
ASSUME AN ALIAS
BATTLE OF WORDS
BETTER OR WORSE
BOTTLE OF SCENT
BOTTLE OF STOUT
BOTTLE OF WATER
BREACH OF FAITH
BREACH OF TRUST
BRIDGE OF SIGHS
BUCKET OF WATER
BURDEN OF GUILT
BURDEN OF PROOF
BURTON ON TRENT
CAREER OF CRIME
CASTLE IN SPAIN
CHANGE OF HEART
CHANGE OF PLACE
CHANGE OF SCENE
CHANGE OF VENUE
CHEESE ON TOAST
CHOICE OF THREE
CHOICE OF WORDS
CHORUS OF ABUSE
CLIFFS OF DOVER
COLUMN OF SMOKE
COMMIT AN ERROR
COMMIT TO PAPER
COURSE OF STUDY
COWARD AT HEART
CRADLE TO GRAVE
DEGREE OF SKILL
DEVOID OF SENSE
DEVOID OF TRUTH
DIVIDE BY EIGHT
DIVIDE BY SEVEN
DIVIDE BY THREE
DOCTOR OF MUSIC
DOUBLE OR QUITS
DRIVEN TO DRINK
EDITOR IN CHIEF
EIGHTH OF APRIL
EIGHTH OF MARCH
ERRAND OF MERCY
ESPRIT DE CORPS
EXCUSE-ME DANCE
FIGURE OF EIGHT
FILLET OF STEAK
FLIGHT OF BIRDS
FLIGHT OF FANCY
FLIGHT OF STEPS
FLITCH OF BACON
FLOWER OF YOUTH

241

FOREST	OF	ARDEN
FOURTH	OF	APRIL
FOURTH	OF	MARCH
FREEZE	TO	DEATH
FRIEND	AT	COURT
FROZEN	TO	DEATH
GAGGLE	OF	GEESE
GRAPES	OF	WRATH
HEAVEN	ON	EARTH
HEIGHT	OF	FOLLY
LITTLE	TO	SPARE
LYTHAM	ST.	ANNES
MARGIN	OF	ERROR
MOMENT	OF	TRUTH
MOTHER	OF	PEARL
NERVES	OF	STEEL
NOBODY	ON	EARTH
OBJECT	OF	MIRTH
OBJECT	OF	SCORN
OPENED	IN	ERROR
ORDEAL	BY	WATER
PIECES	OF	EIGHT
PLENTY	OF	MONEY
PLENTY	TO	SPARE
PRINCE	OF	WALES
RASHER	OF	BACON
REDUCE	TO	ASHES
REDUCE	TO	TEARS
REFUSE	AN	OFFER
REFUSE	TO	SPEAK
REJECT	AN	OFFER
REMAIN	AT	PEACE
RESORT	TO	FORCE
RETURN	TO	EARTH
SCARED	OF	DYING
SCARED	TO	DEATH
SECOND	OF	APRIL
SECOND	OF	MARCH
SHADOW	OF	DEATH
SHADOW	OF	DOUBT
SISTER	OF	MERCY
SMOOTH	AS	GLASS
SOONER	OR	LATER
SOURCE	OF	LIGHT
SOURCE	OF	POWER
SOURCE	OF	PRIDE
SOURCE	OF	WORRY
SPIRIT	OF	YOUTH
STACKS	OF	MONEY
STARVE	TO	DEATH
STREAM	OF	LIGHT
STREAM	OF	WATER
STRIKE	IT	LUCKY
STRING	OF	BEADS
STRING	OF	NAMES
STRING	OF	OATHS
TEMPLE	OF	DIANA
THIRTY	OR	FORTY
TONGUE	IN	CHEEK
TRAVEL	BY	COACH
TRAVEL	BY	TRAIN

TURNED	TO	STONE
UNITED	IN	DEATH
UNITED	WE	STAND
VALLEY	OF	DEATH
WRITHE	IN	AGONY

6, 3, 4

ACROSS	THE	ROAD
ANSWER	THE	BELL
ANSWER	THE	DOOR
APPEAL	FOR	HELP
AROUND	THE	TOWN
BATTLE	FOR	LIFE
BEFORE	THE	FACT
BEFORE	THE	WIND
BEHIND	THE	VEIL
BETTER	OFF	DEAD
BEYOND	THE	PALE
BOUGHT	AND	SOLD
BREACH	THE	WALL
BREAST	THE	TAPE
CHANGE	THE	LOCK
CHARGE	TOO	MUCH
CHEESE	AND	WINE
CHIANG	KAI	SHEK
CLINCH	THE	DEAL
DEFRAY	THE	COST
EIGHTY	PER	CENT
ELEVEN	PER	CENT
EXPECT	TOO	MUCH
FINISH	THE	RACE
FOLLOW	THE	FLAG
FOLLOW	THE	HERD
FOLLOW	THE	ROAD
FUMBLE	THE	BALL
GREASE	THE	PALM
HEARTH	AND	HOME
HEAVEN	AND	HELL
HONOUR	AND	OBEY
INCOME - TAX		FORM
JEKYLL	AND	HYDE
KILROY	WAS	HERE
LABOUR	THE	JOKE
LITTLE	BOY	BLUE
MAIMED	FOR	LIFE
MUSCAT	AND	OMAN
NINETY	PER	CENT
NUMBER	ONE	SEED
OCCUPY	THE	MIND
PEPPER	AND	SALT
PLOUGH	THE	LAND
POWDER	AND	SHOT
PROFIT	AND	LOSS
PUSHED	FOR	TIME
REGAIN	THE	LEAD
REMAIN	THE	SAME
REPORT	FOR	DUTY
ROTATE	THE	CROP
RUINED	FOR	LIFE
SALUTE	THE	FLAG

SAVILE ROW SUIT
SCOTCH AND SODA
SCRIMP AND SAVE
SILVER AND GOLD
SOFTEN THE BLOW
SPREAD THE LOAD
SPREAD THE NEWS
SPRING THE TRAP
STRAIN THE EYES
STRESS THE FACT
STRIKE THE BALL
STRIKE THE HOUR
TAURUS THE BULL
THIRTY PER CENT
THIRTY-ONE DAYS
TWELVE PER CENT
TWENTY PER CENT
TWENTY-ONE DAYS
UNBOLT THE DOOR
UNFURL THE FLAG
UNLOCK THE DOOR
WATTLE AND DAUB
WHISKY AND SODA
WINNIE THE POOH

6, 4, 3

ANOINT WITH OIL
BETTER THAN ONE
BEYOND ONES KEN
BUTTON YOUR LIP
CHANCE ONES ARM
FAIRLY WELL OFF
GENIUS WILL OUT
MIDDLE-AGED MAN
PLEASE GIVE WAY
REMOVE ONES HAT
ROLLED INTO ONE
SECOND-HAND CAR
TALENT WILL OUT
TWELVE GOOD MEN
YELLOW WITH AGE

6, 5, 2

LITTLE SHORT OF
USEFUL STAND-BY

6, 7

ABJECT APOLOGY
ABJECT POVERTY
ABRUPT DESCENT
ABSENT FRIENDS
ACCEPT PAYMENT
ACCUSE FALSELY
ACROSS COUNTRY
ACTING MANAGER
ACTION PICTURE
ACTIVE PARTNER
ACTIVE SERVICE

ACTIVE VOLCANO
ADDING MACHINE
ADESTE FIDELES
AERIAL TORPEDO
AERIAL WARFARE
ALFRED DREYFUS
ALLIED LANDING
ANDREW JACKSON
ANDREW JOHNSON
ANIMAL KINGDOM
ANIMAL SPIRITS
ANIMAL TRAINER
ANNUAL FIXTURE
ANNUAL HOLIDAY
ANNUAL MEETING
ANNUAL PREMIUM
ARCTIC REGIONS
ARDENT ADMIRER
ARNOLD BENNETT
ARTHUR BALFOUR
ARTHUR RANSOME
ARTHUR RIMBAUD
ASSERT ONESELF
ASSUME COMMAND
ATOMIC FISSION
ATOMIC REACTOR
ATOMIC WARFARE
ATOMIC WARHEAD
AUDREY HEPBURN
AUGEAN STABLES
AUTUMN COLOURS
BALLET DANCING
BANANA FRITTER
BARBER SURGEON
BATTER PUDDING
BATTLE CRUISER
BATTLE HONOURS
BATTLE STATION
BEAUTY CONTEST
BEAUTY CULTURE
BEAUTY PARLOUR
BECOME ENGAGED
BECOME EXTINCT
BECOME FRIENDS
BEFORE SUNRISE
BEHAVE ONESELF
BELLES LETTRES
BERTIE WOOSTER
BESIDE ONESELF
BETTER ONESELF
BEYOND COMPARE
BEYOND CONTROL
BEYOND DISPUTE
BEYOND MEASURE
BILLIE HOLIDAY
BITING SARCASM
BITTER FLAVOUR
BITTER QUARREL
BITTER REMORSE
BLOODY ASSIZES
BOMBER COMMAND

BORDER COUNTRY
BOSTON TERRIER
BRANCH LIBRARY
BRANCH MEETING
BRIDGE PROBLEM
BROKEN ENGLISH
BROKEN PROMISE
BROKEN ROMANCE
BRONTË SISTERS
BUMPER HARVEST
BURIAL SERVICE
BURKES PEERAGE
CAMERA OBSCURA
CANARY ISLANDS
CANDID OPINION
CARBON DIOXIDE
CARPET CLEANER
CARPET SWEEPER
CASUAL CLOTHES
CASUAL MEETING
CASUAL VISITOR
CATTLE BREEDER
CAUGHT NAPPING
CAYMAN ISLANDS
CEMENT MIXTURE
CENTRE FORWARD
CHAMPS ÉLYSÉES
CHANCE MEETING
CHARGE ACCOUNT
CHEESE BISCUIT
CHEESE FLAVOUR
CHERRY BLOSSOM
CHERRY ORCHARD
CHILLY WELCOME
CHORAL CONCERT
CHORAL SINGING
CHORAL SOCIETY
CHURCH SERVICE
CHURCH STEEPLE
CHURCH WEDDING
CLAUDE DEBUSSY
CLOSED CIRCUIT
CLOUDY WEATHER
COARSE FISHING
COCKER SPANIEL
COFFEE GRINDER
COFFEE GROUNDS
COFFEE PLANTER
COLOUR PICTURE
COLOUR PROBLEM
COMEDY ACTRESS
COMING SHORTLY
COMMIT ONESELF
COMMIT PERJURY
COMMIT SUICIDE
COMMON ASSAULT
COMMON CONSENT
COMMON FEATURE
COMMON GROUNDS
COMMON MEASURE
COMMON MISTAKE

COMMON PURPOSE
COMMON SOLDIER
CONSUL GENERAL
CORPUS CHRISTI
COSTLY FAILURE
COSTLY VENTURE
COTTON PLANTER
COUNTY BOROUGH
COUNTY COUNCIL
COUNTY CRICKET
COUNTY DONEGAL
COURSE BETTING
CREATE DISCORD
CREDIT ACCOUNT
CREDIT BALANCE
CREDIT CONTROL
CREDIT SQUEEZE
DANDIE DINMONT
DANIEL DERONDA
DANTÉS INFERNO
DARING ATTEMPT
DEARLY BELOVED
DECIDE AGAINST
DEEPLY TOUCHED
DEFEND ONESELF
DELUDE ONESELF
DEMAND JUSTICE
DEMAND PAYMENT
DENNIS COMPTON
DENTAL SURGEON
DENTAL SURGERY
DEPUTY PREMIER
DEPUTY SHERIFF
DERIVE BENEFIT
DEVILS KITCHEN
DEVOUT ADMIRER
DINNER SERVICE
DIRECT CONTACT
DIRECT CURRENT
DIRECT DESCENT
DISMAL FAILURE
DIVINE SERVICE
DOCTOR JOHNSON
DOCTOR KILDARE
DOLLAR PREMIUM
DONALD BRADMAN
DOTING HUSBAND
DOTING PARENTS
DOUBLE BASSOON
DOUBLE DEALING
DOUBLE FIFTEEN
DOUBLE FIGURES
DOUBLE HELPING
DOUBLE MEANING
DOUBLE PORTION
DOUBLE SIXTEEN
DOUBLE TROUBLE
DOUBLE WEDDING
DRYING MACHINE
DUSTIN HOFFMAN
EAMONN ANDREWS

EASILY AROUSED
EASILY PLEASED
EDMUND HILLARY
EDWARD KENNEDY
EIGHTH CENTURY
EIGHTY DOLLARS
ELDEST BROTHER
ELEVEN MINUTES
ELEVEN SQUARED
ENGINE FAILURE
ENGINE TROUBLE
ERNEST MARPLES
ESTATE MANAGER
EUGENE IONESCO
EUSTON STATION
EXCESS BAGGAGE
EXCESS LUGGAGE
EXCESS PROFITS
EXCUSE ONESELF
EXPERT OPINION
EXPERT TUITION
EXPERT WITNESS
FABIAN SOCIETY
FACIAL MASSAGE
FAIRLY CERTAIN
FAMILY BUTCHER
FAMILY CONCERN
FAMILY FAILING
FAMILY MATTERS
FAMILY QUARREL
FAMILY REUNION
FAMOUS VICTORY
FEEBLE ATTEMPT
FEEBLE GESTURE
FELLOW CITIZEN
FELLOW FEELING
FELLOW SOLDIER
FIGURE SKATING
FILING CABINET
FILTER THROUGH
FLORAL PATTERN
FLORAL TRIBUTE
FLUENT ENGLISH
FLUENT SPANISH
FLYING COLOURS
FLYING MACHINE
FLYING OFFICER
FLYING TRAPEZE
FOLIES BERGÈRE
FOLLOW THROUGH
FORCED LANDING
FORGET ONESELF
FORMAL PROTEST
FORMAL REQUEST
FOSTER BROTHER
FOURTH CENTURY
FOURTH CHANNEL
FOURTH OFFICER
FRENCH ACADEMY
FRENCH CRICKET
FRENCH CUISINE

FRENCH GRAMMAR
FRENCH MUSTARD
FRENCH PERFUME
FRENCH TEACHER
FRENCH WINDOWS
FRIDAY EVENING
FRIDAY MORNING
FRIDGE FREEZER
FRINGE BENEFIT
FROSTY WEATHER
FROSTY WELCOME
FRYING TONIGHT
FUTILE ATTEMPT
FUTURE HUSBAND
FUTURE OUTLOOK
FUTURE PERFECT
GALINA ULANOVA
GARDEN PRODUCE
GATHER FLOWERS
GENTLE MANNERS
GEORGE CANNING
GEORGE FOREMAN
GEORGE WALLACE
GERMAN MEASLES
GERMAN SAUSAGE
GIRTON COLLEGE
GLENDA JACKSON
GLOOMY OUTLOOK
GLOOMY PICTURE
GLORIA SWANSON
GOLDEN HAMSTER
GOLDEN JUBILEE
GOLDEN TRESSES
GOLDEN WEDDING
GROUND CONTROL
GUIDED MISSILE
GUILTY FEELING
GYPSYS WARNING
HANDLE ROUGHLY
HARDEN ONESELF
HATTIE JACQUES
HEALTH SERVICE
HEALTH VISITOR
HEARTS CONTENT
HEARTY DISLIKE
HEARTY WELCOME
HEATED DISPUTE
HEATED QUARREL
HECTOR BERLIOZ
HENLEY REGATTA
HIDDEN MEANING
HIDDEN RESERVE
HIGHER CLASSES
HOLLOW FEELING
HOLLOW MOCKERY
HOLLOW VICTORY
HONEST ATTEMPT
HUMANE SOCIETY
HUMBLE ADMIRER
HUMBLE APOLOGY
HUMBLE OPINION

HUMBLE SERVANT	MENTAL THERAPY
HUMBLE STATION	MENTAL TORMENT
IMPOSE ONESELF	MENTAL TORTURE
INCOME BRACKET	MENTAL TROUBLE
INFANT PRODIGY	MERRIE ENGLAND
INFORM AGAINST	MERTON COLLEGE
INGMAR BERGMAN	METRIC MEASURE
INGRID BERGMAN	MIDDLE AMERICA
INLAND REVENUE	MIDDLE CLASSES
INNATE ABILITY	MOBILE CANTEEN
INSIDE FORWARD	MOBILE LIBRARY
INVITE TENDERS	MODERN COSTUME
ISSUED CAPITAL	MODERN ENGLISH
JACKIE STEWART	MODERN FASHION
JEREMY BENTHAM	MODERN HISTORY
JOHANN STRAUSS	MODERN METHODS
JUNGLE WARFARE	MODERN PAINTER
JUNIOR PARTNER	MODERN SOCIETY
KAISER WILHELM	MODERN WARFARE
KNOTTY PROBLEM	MODEST FORTUNE
LABOUR TROUBLE	MONDAY EVENING
LABOUR VICTORY	MONDAY MORNING
LATEST EDITION	MORBID CRAVING
LATEST FASHION	MORTAL REMAINS
LAWFUL WEDLOCK	MOTHER COUNTRY
LESTER PIGGOTT	MOTHER HUBBARD
LILLIE LANGTRY	MOTHER SHIPTON
LINEAR MEASURE	MOTHER THERESA
LIQUID MEASURE	MOTION PICTURE
LITTLE BIGHORN	MOVING PICTURE
LITTLE BROTHER	MUDDLE THROUGH
LITTLE COMFORT	MURDER MYSTERY
LITTLE RICHARD	MUTUAL BENEFIT
LIVERY COMPANY	MUTUAL CONSENT
LIVING THEATRE	MUTUAL FRIENDS
LONDON AIRPORT	MUTUAL RESPECT
LONDON SUBURBS	NARROW OUTLOOK
LONNIE DONEGAN	NARROW VICTORY
LOVELY WEATHER	NATIVE QUARTER
LOVING HUSBAND	NATURE RESERVE
LUXURY HOLIDAY	NETHER REGIONS
LYNDON JOHNSON	NEWTON STEWART
MADAME TUSSAUD	NIMBLE FINGERS
MARGOT FONTEYN	NINETY DEGREES
MARINE OFFICER	NINETY DOLLARS
MARKET DRAYTON	NINETY MINUTES
MASTER BUILDER	NORMAL SERVICE
MASTER MARINER	NUMBER ENGAGED
MATURE STUDENT	OFFICE CLEANER
MATURE THOUGHT	OFFICE MANAGER
MEDIUM QUALITY	OFFICE ROUTINE
MELTON MOWBRAY	ORANGE BITTERS
MENTAL BALANCE	ORANGE BLOSSOM
MENTAL CALIBRE	ORANGE FLAVOUR
MENTAL CRUELTY	ORKNEY ISLANDS
MENTAL DISEASE	OXFORD ENGLISH
MENTAL FATIGUE	PARISH COUNCIL
MENTAL ILLNESS	PARROT FASHION
MENTAL PATIENT	PARTLY COVERED
MENTAL PICTURE	PASTEL COLOURS
MENTAL PROCESS	PATENT LEATHER

PATENT	PENDING
PEBBLE	GLASSES
PERIOD	COSTUME
PETROL	LIGHTER
PETROL	STATION
PEWTER	TANKARD
PIERRE	TRUDEAU
PIGEON	FANCIER
PILOTS	LICENCE
PLEASE	ONESELF
PLEDGE	ONESELF
POCKET	EDITION
POETIC	JUSTICE
POETIC	LICENCE
POETRY	READING
POLICE	OFFICER
POLICE	STATION
POLICE	WHISTLE
POLITE	COMPANY
POLITE	REFUSAL
POLITE	SOCIETY
POORLY	DRESSED
POSTAL	ADDRESS
POSTER	COLOURS
POTTED	SHRIMPS
POWDER	COMPACT
PRAYER	MEETING
PRETTY	COLOURS
PRETTY	PICTURE
PRINCE	CHARLES
PRINCE	CONSORT
PROFIT	SHARING
PROMPT	PAYMENT
PROMPT	SERVICE
PROPER	CHARLIE
PUBLIC	ADDRESS
PUBLIC	AFFAIRS
PUBLIC	AUCTION
PUBLIC	COMMENT
PUBLIC	COMPANY
PUBLIC	ENQUIRY
PUBLIC	GALLERY
PUBLIC	HANGING
PUBLIC	HIGHWAY
PUBLIC	HOLIDAY
PUBLIC	INQUIRY
PUBLIC	LIBRARY
PUBLIC	MEETING
PUBLIC	OPINION
PUBLIC	RECORDS
PUBLIC	SCANDAL
PUBLIC	SERVANT
PUBLIC	SERVICE
PUBLIC	SPEAKER
PUBLIC	TRUSTEE
PUBLIC	WARNING
PUBLIC	WORSHIP
PUPPET	THEATRE
PURPLE	HEATHER
PURPLE	PASSAGE
QUEENS	COLLEGE
QUEENS	COUNSEL
QUEENS	ENGLISH
RACIAL	TENSION
RACING	TIPSTER
RACING	TRAINER
RAGING	TEMPEST
RAGING	TORRENT
RATING	OFFICER
RAVING	LUNATIC
RECENT	ARRIVAL
RECENT	HISTORY
RECORD	ATTEMPT
RECORD	BREAKER
RECORD	SESSION
REFUSE	PAYMENT
REGAIN	CONTROL
REMAIN	HOPEFUL
REMAIN	NEUTRAL
REMAIN	UPRIGHT
REMAIN	VISIBLE
REMOTE	CONTROL
REMOTE	VILLAGE
REPEAT	ONESELF
RESIGN	ONESELF
RETURN	JOURNEY
RETURN	SERVICE
REVOLT	AGAINST
REWARD	OFFERED
RITUAL	KILLING
ROBERT	KENNEDY
ROBERT	MENZIES
ROBERT	MITCHUM
ROBERT	REDFORD
ROBERT	SOUTHEY
ROBERT	WALPOLE
ROGUES	GALLERY
ROLLER	COASTER
ROLLER	SKATING
ROMNEY	MARSHES
RONNIE	CORBETT
ROTTEN	BOROUGH
RUBBER	PLANTER
RULING	CLASSES
RULING	PASSION
RUPERT	MURDOCH
SACRED	EDIFICE
SAFETY	CURTAIN
SAFETY	MATCHES
SAFETY	MEASURE
SALMON	FISHING
SALTED	PEANUTS
SAMUEL	BECKETT
SAMUEL	JOHNSON
SCHOOL	EDITION
SCHOOL	HOLIDAY
SCHOOL	PREFECT
SCHOOL	UNIFORM
SCILLY	ISLANDS
SCOTCH	TERRIER
SCRAPE	THROUGH
SCREEN	VERSION

SEALED VERDICT	SOCIAL WELFARE
SEARCH WARRANT	SOLEMN PROMISE
SECOND ATTEMPT	SOLEMN WARNING
SECOND CENTURY	SORDID DETAILS
SECOND CHAMBER	SPEECH THERAPY
SECOND CHAPTER	SPONGE PUDDING
SECOND EDITION	SPORTS EDITION
SECOND HELPING	SPORTS STADIUM
SECOND HUSBAND	SPRING BALANCE
SECOND INNINGS	SPRING BLOSSOM
SECOND OFFICER	SPRING CHICKEN
SECOND OPINION	SPRING MADNESS
SECOND READING	SPRING MEETING
SECRET FORMULA	SQUARE BASHING
SECRET INQUIRY	SQUARE MEASURE
SECRET MEETING	SQUASH RACKETS
SECRET MISSION	STATIC WARFARE
SECRET PASSAGE	STEADY ADVANCE
SECRET SERVICE	STORMY PASSAGE
SECRET SOCIETY	STORMY SESSION
SECRET THOUGHT	STORMY WEATHER
SECURE FOOTING	STRAIN ONESELF
SELECT CIRCLES	STREET CLOTHES
SELECT COMPANY	STRING QUARTET
SENIOR CITIZEN	STRONG CURRENT
SENIOR PARTNER	STRONG DEFENCE
SENIOR SERVICE	STRONG DISLIKE
SEVERE ILLNESS	STRONG EMOTION
SEVERE WEATHER	STRONG FEELING
SEWING MACHINE	STRONG PROTEST
SHADOW CABINET	STRONG STOMACH
SHERPA TENSING	STRONG SWIMMER
SHERRY COBBLER	SUDDEN IMPULSE
SHROVE TUESDAY	SUDDEN THOUGHT
SIGNAL FAILURE	SUFFER TORMENT
SIGNAL SUCCESS	SUMMER HOLIDAY
SIGNAL VICTORY	SUMMER MADNESS
SILENT PARTNER	SUMMER VISITOR
SILENT PROTEST	SUMMIT MEETING
SILENT SERVICE	SUNDAY CLOTHES
SILVER COINAGE	SUNDAY EVENING
SILVER JUBILEE	SUNDAY EXPRESS
SILVER PLATTER	SUNDAY MORNING
SILVER TANKARD	SUNDAY SERVICE
SILVER WEDDING	SUPPLY TEACHER
SIMPLE PROBLEM	SWANEE WHISTLE
SIMPLE REQUEST	SYDNEY HARBOUR
SIMPLY FURIOUS	TALENT CONTEST
SINGLE THOUGHT	TALENT SPOTTER
SKIING HOLIDAY	TENDER FEELING
SMOKED HADDOCK	TENDER PASSION
SMOOTH PASSAGE	TENPIN BOWLING
SMOOTH SAILING	THIRTY DOLLARS
SMOOTH SURFACE	THIRTY FIFTEEN
SMOOTH TEXTURE	THIRTY MINUTES
SOCIAL CLIMBER	THIRTY SECONDS
SOCIAL EVENING	THOMAS ADDISON
SOCIAL OUTCAST	THOMAS AQUINAS
SOCIAL PROBLEM	THOMAS BEECHAM
SOCIAL SCIENCE	THOMAS CRAMNER
SOCIAL SERVICE	THOMAS FAIRFAX

THORNY SUBJECT
TICKET MACHINE
TIMELY WARNING
TINNED PEACHES
TOMATO KETCHUP
TONGUE TWISTER
TRENCH WARFARE
TRIBAL WARFARE
TRICKY PROBLEM
TRUSTY SERVANT
TUNNEL THROUGH
TWELVE DOLLARS
TWELVE MINUTES
TWELVE SQUARED
TWENTY DOLLARS
TWENTY MINUTES
TWENTY SECONDS
UNEASY FEELING
UNEVEN CONTEST
UNEVEN SURFACE
UNFAIR VERDICT
UNITED ARTISTS
UNITED KINGDOM
UNITED NATIONS
UNKIND THOUGHT
UNPAID SERVANT
USEFUL PURPOSE
VACUUM CLEANER
VERBAL QUIBBLE
VERNAL EQUINOX
VESTAL VIRGINS
VIOLIN RECITAL
VIRGIN ISLANDS
VOLUME CONTROL
VULGAR DISPLAY
WALTER BAGEHOT
WALTER MATTHAU
WALTER RALEIGH
WARREN HARDING
WEEKLY PAYMENT
WIDOWS PENSION
WILKIE COLLINS
WILLIE RUSHTON
WILLOW PATTERN
WINDOW CLEANER
WINDOW DRESSER
WINDOW SHOPPER
WINGED VICTORY
WINTER GARDENS
WINTER HOLIDAY
WINTER WEATHER
WINTRY WEATHER
WITHIN EARSHOT
WITHIN HEARING
WOOLLY SWEATER
YEHUDI MENUHIN
YELLOW BUNTING
YELLOW WAGTAIL

7, 1, 5

ARRANGE A MATCH
CHARTER A PLANE
CONCEDE A POINT
DISPUTE A POINT
EXTRACT A TOOTH
PERFORM A STUNT
PERFORM A TRICK
PROPOSE A TOAST
STRETCH A POINT
SUSPECT A TRICK
THROUGH A STRAW
WITHOUT A DOUBT
WITHOUT A HITCH

7, 2, 2, 2

NOTHING TO GO ON

7, 2, 4

ABSENCE OF MIND
BALANCE OF MIND
BAPTISM OF FIRE
BATTERY OF GUNS
BLANKET OF SNOW
BREADTH OF MIND
BRISKET OF BEEF
CHERISH AN IDEA
COLLEGE OF ARMS
COMRADE IN ARMS
CURIOUS TO KNOW
DELIVER BY HAND
DEPRIVE OF LIFE
DIVIDED WE FALL
DRESSED IN BLUE
DRESSED IN RAGS
DRESSED TO KILL
DUCHESS OF KENT
ELEMENT OF LUCK
ELEMENT OF RISK
EXPOSED TO VIEW
EYELESS IN GAZA
FACULTY OF ARTS
FLICKER OF HOPE
GLIMMER OF HOPE
GODDESS OF LOVE
LETTERS OF FIRE
MARQUIS DE SADE
MEASURE OF LAND
NOTHING TO GAIN
NOTHING TO LOSE
NOTHING TO WEAR
PASSAGE OF ARMS
PASSAGE OF TIME
PAYMENT IN KIND
PISTOLS AT DAWN
PLEASED TO COME
PLEASED TO HELP
PROVIDE AN HEIR

QUALITY	OF	LIFE
QUARTER	TO	FIVE
QUARTER	TO	FOUR
QUARTER	TO	NINE
RAVAGES	OF	TIME
RECEIVE	IN	FULL
RELEASE	ON	BAIL
RESTORE	TO	LIFE
RICHARD	OF	YORK
SCRATCH	MY	BACK
SEVENTH	OF	JULY
SEVENTH	OF	JUNE
SIRLOIN	OF	BEEF
SLEIGHT	OF	HAND
STATION	IN	LIFE
STRETCH	OF	ROAD
TANKARD	OF	BEER
TORRENT	OF	RAIN
TWELFTH	OF	JULY
TWELFTH	OF	JUNE
UNLUCKY	IN	LOVE

7, 3, 3

AGAINST	THE	LAW
COMFORT	AND	JOY
ENFORCE	THE	LAW
EXTREME	OLD	AGE
HUNDRED	AND	ONE
HUNDRED	AND	SIX
HUNDRED	AND	TEN
HUNDRED	AND	TWO
OUTSIDE	THE	LAW
PREPARE	FOR	WAR
PREPARE	THE	WAY
RESPECT	THE	LAW
REYNARD	THE	FOX
SHAMPOO	AND	SET
STEPTOE	AND	SON
VIOLATE	THE	LAW

7, 4, 2

NOTHING LIKE IT

7, 6

ADIPOSE TISSUE
ADMIRAL NELSON
ADVANCE NOTICE
AIRPORT LOUNGE
AMATEUR BOXING
AMATEUR GOLFER
AMATEUR PLAYER
AMATEUR SLEUTH
AMATEUR STATUS
ANCIENT BRITON
ANCIENT CUSTOM
ANCIENT GREECE
ANCIENT LIGHTS
ANCIENT WISDOM

ANGULAR FIGURE
ANOTHER CHANCE
ANOTHER MATTER
ANTHONY QUAYLE
ANTIQUE DEALER
ANXIOUS MOMENT
APRICOT BRANDY
AQUATIC SPORTS
ARABIAN DESERT
ARABIAN NIGHTS
ARTISTS STUDIO
AUCTION BRIDGE
AVERAGE FIGURE
AVERAGE HEIGHT
AVERAGE PERSON
AVERAGE WEIGHT
BALLOON ASCENT
BAPTIST CHURCH
BARGAIN HUNTER
BARNARD CASTLE
BASHFUL MANNER
BATHING BEAUTY
BATHING TRUNKS
BATTING WICKET
BEATRIX POTTER
BEDSIDE MANNER
BEGGING LETTER
BELATED EFFORT
BELISHA BEACON
BENEATH NOTICE
BERMUDA SHORTS
BERNARD BRADEN
BERTOLT BRECHT
BISCUIT BARREL
BOLSHOI BALLET
BOOKING OFFICE
BOOMING MARKET
BOWLERS WICKET
BOWLING CREASE
BREATHE DEEPLY
BREATHE FREELY
BRENDAN FOSTER
BRISTOL ROVERS
BRITISH COLONY
BRITISH CONSUL
BRITISH EMPIRE
BRITISH LEGION
BRITISH MUSEUM
BRITISH PUBLIC
BRUSQUE MANNER
BUBONIC PLAGUE
BUCKING BRONCO
BUDDING AUTHOR
BUDDING GENIUS
BUDDING WRITER
BULLION MARKET
BURNING DESIRE
BURNING THIRST
BUTLERS PANTRY
CABARET SINGER
CABINET MEMBER

CAMPING GROUND
CAPITAL FELLOW
CAPITAL LETTER
CAPITAL OUTLAY
CARDIAC ARREST
CAREFUL DRIVER
CARNABY STREET
CARRIER PIGEON
CAUSTIC REMARK
CAVALRY CHARGE
CAYENNE PEPPER
CENTRAL AFRICA
CENTRAL EUROPE
CENTRAL FIGURE
CENTRAL LONDON
CENTRAL OFFICE
CERTAIN DEFEAT
CERTAIN PERSON
CHANGED PERSON
CHANNEL TUNNEL
CHARLES DARWIN
CHARLIE MINGUS
CHARLIE PARKER
CHARMED CIRCLE
CHARTER FLIGHT
CHEDDAR CHEESE
CHELSEA BRIDGE
CHICKEN FARMER
CHIMNEY CORNER
CLAPHAM COMMON
CLEMENT ATTLEE
CLIPPED SPEECH
CLOSING SPEECH
CLOSING STAGES
CLOTHES BASKET
COASTAL RESORT
COASTAL WATERS
COBBLED STREET
COCAINE ADDICT
COCKNEY ACCENT
COLLECT STAMPS
COLONEL GADAFY
COMBINE FORCES
COMPANY LAWYER
COMPANY REPORT
COMPARE PRICES
COMPASS NEEDLE
COMPLEX NUMBER
COMPLEX SYSTEM
CONCEDE DEFEAT
CONCERT TICKET
CONTACT LENSES
CONVENT SCHOOL
COOKERY LESSON
COOKING SHERRY
COOLING BREEZE
CORRECT ANSWER
CORRECT SPEECH
COTTAGE CHEESE
COUNCIL ESTATE
COUNTRY COUSIN

COUNTRY CUSTOM
COUNTRY GARDEN
COUNTRY SQUIRE
COVERED MARKET
CRICKET ELEVEN
CRICKET GROUND
CRICKET SEASON
CRICKET STUMPS
CROCHET NEEDLE
CROQUET MALLET
CROSSED CHEQUE
CROWDED STREET
CRUCIAL MOMENT
CRUCIAL PERIOD
CRYSTAL PALACE
CUNNING FELLOW
CURIOUS EFFECT
CURRENT ASSETS
CURRENT EVENTS
CURRENT REPORT
CURRENT RUMOUR
CURSORY GLANCE
CURTAIN RAISER
CUTTING REMARK
CUTTING RETORT
DANCING LESSON
DANCING MASTER
DARKEST AFRICA
DEBTORS PRISON
DECIMAL SYSTEM
DELAYED ACTION
DELPHIC ORACLE
DESIRED EFFECT
DESMOND MORRIS
DEVIOUS MANNER
DIAMOND BROOCH
DIAMOND CUTTER
DISOBEY ORDERS
DISTANT COUSIN
DISTANT FUTURE
DISTANT MEMORY
DIVORCE DECREE
DOCTORS ORDERS
DOWNING STREET
DRAGOON GUARDS
DRASTIC REMEDY
DRAWING MASTER
DREADED MOMENT
DRIVING LESSON
DRIVING MIRROR
DRIVING SCHOOL
DRUNKEN SAILOR
DRUNKEN STUPOR
DUBIOUS HONOUR
DUBIOUS MANNER
DUSTING POWDER
DYNAMIC ENERGY
EARTHLY THINGS
EASTERN CHURCH
EASTERN EUROPE
ELUSIVE PERSON

ELYSIAN FIELDS
ENGAGED COUPLE
ENGLISH ACCENT
ENGLISH GARDEN
ENGLISH LESSON
ENGLISH MASTER
ENGLISH SETTER
ENOUGHS ENOUGH
EVASIVE ACTION
EVASIVE ANSWER
EVENING PRAYER
EXEMPLI GRATIA
EXPRESS LETTER
EXPRESS REGRET
EXPRESS SORROW
EXTINCT ANIMAL
EXTREME BEAUTY
EXTREME DANGER
EXTREME HATRED
EYEBROW PENCIL
FACTORY WORKER
FACULTY MEMBER
FAILING HEALTH
FALLING LEAVES
FALLING MARKET
FALLING PRICES
FALLING VALUES
FARAWAY PLACES
FASCIST RÉGIME
FASHION LEADER
FASHION PARADE
FEARFUL RACKET
FEATHER DUSTER
FEATHER PILLOW
FEDERAL STATES
FEEDING BOTTLE
FENCING MASTER
FERTILE GROUND
FERTILE REGION
FERVENT DESIRE
FESTIVE SEASON
FESTIVE SPIRIT
FICTION WRITER
FIFTEEN METRES
FIFTEEN OUNCES
FIFTEEN POUNDS
FIFTEEN ROUNDS
FIFTEEN THIRTY
FISHING RIGHTS
FISHING TACKLE
FLOWERY SPEECH
FOOLISH PERSON
FOOLISH VIRGIN
FOREIGN ACCENT
FOREIGN EDITOR
FOREIGN LEGION
FOREIGN MARKET
FOREIGN OFFICE
FOREIGN POLICY
FOREIGN SHORES
FOREIGN TONGUE

FOREIGN TRAVEL
FORTUNE HUNTER
FORTUNE TELLER
FOUNDER MEMBER
FRANKIE HOWERD
FRANTIC APPEAL
FRONTAL ATTACK
FUNERAL SERMON
FURIOUS TEMPER
FURTHER NOTICE
GARBLED REPORT
GENERAL CUSTER
GENERAL DEALER
GENERAL FRANCO
GENERAL GORDON
GENERAL PARDON
GENERAL PUBLIC
GENERAL STORES
GENERAL STRIKE
GENUINE REGARD
GLASGOW CELTIC
GLOWING CHEEKS
GLOWING EMBERS
GLOWING HEALTH
GLOWING REPORT
GRAMMAR SCHOOL
GRAPHIC DETAIL
GREATER LONDON
GREATLY MISSED
GRILLED TOMATO
GRUYÈRE CHEESE
HALTING SPEECH
HANGING GARDEN
HANGING MATTER
HANOVER SQUARE
HARBOUR LIGHTS
HARBOUR MASTER
HARLECH CASTLE
HARVEST SUPPER
HEALING SPIRIT
HEAVILY LOADED
HELPFUL ADVICE
HERBERT HOOVER
HERCULE POIROT
HIGHEST BIDDER
HIGHEST ESTEEM
HIGHWAY PATROL
HIGHWAY ROBBER
HILAIRE BELLOC
HISTORY LESSON
HISTORY MASTER
HOBSONS CHOICE
HOLIDAY CHALET
HOLIDAY RESORT
HOLIDAY SEASON
HONOURS DEGREE
HORATIO NELSON
HOSTILE CRITIC
HOSTILE MANNER
HOUSING ESTATE
HOUSING SCHEME

HUNDRED	METRES
HUNDRED	POUNDS
HUNTING	SEASON
HURRIED	GLANCE
HURRIED	SPEECH
IDEALLY	SUITED
INCOMES	POLICY
INITIAL	LETTER
INITIAL	OUTLAY
INITIAL	STAGES
INSTANT	COFFEE
INTERIM	REPORT
ISADORA	DUNCAN
KENNETH	KAUNDA
KINDRED	SPIRIT
KINETIC	ENERGY
KNAVISH	TRICKS
KNOWING	GLANCE
LAMBETH	PALACE
LANDING	GROUND
LATTICE	WINDOW
LAUNDRY	BASKET
LEADING	ARTIST
LEADING	SEAMAN
LEADING	STOKER
LEARNED	FRIEND
LEARNER	DRIVER
LEATHER	GLOVES
LEATHER	JACKET
LEATHER	UPPERS
LETTERS	PATENT
LIBERAL	LEADER
LIBRARY	TICKET
LICENCE	HOLDER
LIMITED	AMOUNT
LIMITED	APPEAL
LIMITED	CHOICE
LIMITED	NUMBER
LIMITED	PERIOD
LIMITED	SUPPLY
LIQUEUR	BRANDY
LIQUEUR	WHISKY
LOGICAL	ACTION
LOGICAL	RESULT
LOMBARD	STREET
LOTTERY	TICKET
LUNATIC	ASYLUM
LUNATIC	FRINGE
LYRICAL	POETRY
MACHINE	GUNNER
MADISON	AVENUE
MADISON	SQUARE
MAHATMA	GANDHI
MALTESE	FALCON
MARILYN	MONROE
MARRIED	COUPLE
MARSHAL	PÉTAIN
MAXIMUM	AMOUNT
MAXIMUM	CHARGE
MAXIMUM	POINTS
MAXIMUM	VOLUME
MEDICAL	ADVICE
MEDICAL	SCHOOL
MERTHYR	TYDFIL
MIDLAND	ACCENT
MIDLAND	COUNTY
MILLION	POUNDS
MINIMUM	AMOUNT
MINIMUM	CHARGE
MIRACLE	WORKER
MISSING	PERSON
MONTHLY	REPORT
MONTHLY	SALARY
MORNING	COFFEE
MORNING	PRAYER
MOUNTED	POLICE
MOUNTED	TROOPS
MUSICAL	CHAIRS
MUSICAL	COMEDY
MUSTARD	YELLOW
MYSTERY	WRITER
NAGGING	TONGUE
NANETTE	NEWMAN
NATURAL	BEAUTY
NATURAL	CAUSES
NATURAL	COURSE
NATURAL	HAZARD
NATURAL	TALENT
NELSONS	COLUMN
NERVOUS	ENERGY
NERVOUS	SYSTEM
NERVOUS	TWITCH
NESTING	SEASON
NEUTRAL	COLOUR
NEUTRAL	GROUND
NEWGATE	PRISON
NEWPORT	COUNTY
NOMINAL	CHARGE
NOMINAL	LEDGER
NORFOLK	BROADS
NORFOLK	JACKET
NOTHING	GAINED
NUCLEAR	ENERGY
NUCLEAR	FUSION
NUCLEAR	WEAPON
NURSERY	GARDEN
NURSERY	SCHOOL
NURSING	SISTER
OFFHAND	MANNER
OLYMPIC	RECORD
OMNIBUS	VOLUME
OPENING	BOWLER
OPENING	GAMBIT
ORDERLY	MANNER
ORDINAL	NUMBER
ORGANIC	MATTER
ORVILLE	WRIGHT
OTTOMAN	EMPIRE
OUTSIDE	CHANCE
PACIFIC	ISLAND
PASSING	GLANCE
PASSING	REMARK

PASSION	FLOWER
PENALTY	CLAUSE
PENSION	SCHEME
PERFECT	CIRCLE
PERFECT	FRIGHT
PERFECT	SQUARE
PERFECT	TIMING
PERFECT	WICKET
PERSIAN	CARPET
PICTURE	PALACE
PIONEER	SPIRIT
PITCHED	BATTLE
POINTED	REMARK
POMPOUS	MANNER
PONTIUS	PILATE
PONTOON	BRIDGE
POPPING	CREASE
POPULAR	APPEAL
POPULAR	BALLAD
POPULAR	CHOICE
POPULAR	DECREE
POPULAR	DEMAND
POPULAR	FIGURE
POPULAR	RESORT
POPULAR	SINGER
POULTRY	FARMER
PRAIRIE	OYSTER
PRAYING	MANTIS
PRECISE	MOMENT
PRESENT	EVENTS
PRESENT	MOMENT
PRESSED	FLOWER
PRIMARY	COLOUR
PRIMARY	SCHOOL
PRINCES	STREET
PRINTED	LETTER
PRINTED	MATTER
PRIVATE	AFFAIR
PRIVATE	INCOME
PRIVATE	LESSON
PRIVATE	MATTER
PRIVATE	MEMBER
PRIVATE	PERSON
PRIVATE	REASON
PRIVATE	SCHOOL
PRIVATE	SECTOR
PRIVATE	SOURCE
PROFANE	PERSON
PROFUSE	THANKS
QUALITY	STREET
QUANTUM	MERUIT
QUANTUM	THEORY
QUARTER	DOLLAR
RADICAL	CHANGE
RADICAL	REFORM
RAILWAY	BRIDGE
RAILWAY	ENGINE
RAILWAY	SIDING
RAILWAY	SIGNAL
RAILWAY	SYSTEM
RAILWAY	TICKET
RAILWAY	TUNNEL
RAYMOND	MASSEY
READERS	DIGEST
READING	MATTER
READING	PUBLIC
RECEIVE	NOTICE
RECEIVE	ORDERS
REFINED	ACCENT
REGULAR	FORCES
REGULAR	HABITS
REGULAR	INCOME
REGULAR	PERSON
REGULAR	READER
REGULAR	SALARY
REGULAR	TROOPS
REGULAR	VISITS
RENEWED	VIGOUR
RESERVE	ELEVEN
RETIRED	PEOPLE
RETIRED	PERSON
RHONDDA	VALLEY
RICHARD	BURTON
RICHARD	TAUBER
RICHARD	WAGNER
RIOTOUS	LIVING
ROLLING	STONES
ROUGHLY	SPOKEN
ROUNDLY	ABUSED
ROUSING	CHEERS
ROUSING	CHORUS
ROUSING	SERMON
ROUTINE	MATTER
RUNNING	BATTLE
RUNNING	STREAM
RUSSIAN	BALLET
SAFFRON	WALDEN
SAILING	MASTER
SCARLET	RIBBON
SCARLET	RUNNER
SCIENCE	LESSON
SCIENCE	MASTER
SCIENCE	MUSEUM
SCORING	STROKE
SEASIDE	RESORT
SELFISH	MOTIVE
SELLERS	MARKET
SERIOUS	CHARGE
SERIOUS	DAMAGE
SERIOUS	DANGER
SERIOUS	INJURY
SERIOUS	MATTER
SERIOUS	PERSON
SERIOUS	THREAT
SERVICE	CHARGE
SETTING	LOTION
SEVENTH	HEAVEN
SEVENTH	WICKET
SEVENTY	METRES
SEVENTY	POUNDS
SEVILLE	ORANGE
SHALLOW	VESSEL

SHAPELY FIGURE	TRADING STAMPS
SHEPTON MALLET	TRAFFIC ISLAND
SHINING ARMOUR	TRAFFIC LIGHTS
SHINING KNIGHT	TRAFFIC SIGNAL
SHIRLEY BASSEY	TRAFFIC WARDEN
SHIRLEY TEMPLE	TRAINED SINGER
SHORTLY BEFORE	TRAPEZE ARTIST
SIGNIFY ASSENT	TREACLE TOFFEE
SIMPLON TUNNEL	TRIGGER FINGER
SISTINE CHAPEL	TRINITY SUNDAY
SITTING MEMBER	TRIVIAL MATTER
SITTING PRETTY	TROUSER BUTTON
SITTING TARGET	TROUSER POCKET
SITTING TENANT	TRUMPET PLAYER
SIXTEEN OUNCES	TRUSTED FRIEND
SIXTEEN POUNDS	TWISTED NATURE
SKILLED LABOUR	UNARMED COMBAT
SKILLED WORKER	UNIFORM HEIGHT
SLANDER ACTION	UNIFORM LENGTH
SLENDER CHANCE	UNIFORM WEIGHT
SLIDING TACKLE	UNKNOWN ORIGIN
SLOPING GROUND	UNLUCKY CHOICE
SMOKING JACKET	UNLUCKY NUMBER
SNOOKER PLAYER	UPRIGHT FELLOW
SOARING PRICES	UPRIGHT PERSON
SOCIETY COLUMN	UTOPIAN SCHEME
SOCIETY GOSSIP	VALIANT EFFORT
SOCIETY PERSON	VANTAGE GROUND
SOLOMON GRUNDY	VARIETY ARTIST
SOONEST MENDED	VICIOUS ATTACK
SORTING OFFICE	VICIOUS CIRCLE
SPANISH ARMADA	VICIOUS GOSSIP
SPANISH GUITAR	VICTORY PARADE
SPARTAN RÉGIME	VIEWING PUBLIC
SPECIAL BITTER	VILLAGE BEAUTY
SPECIAL BRANCH	VILLAGE CHURCH
SPECIAL FRIEND	VILLAGE SCHOOL
SPECIAL SCHOOL	VILLAGE SMITHY
STATION MASTER	VILLAGE STREET
STILTON CHEESE	VIOLENT ATTACK
STRANGE MANNER	VIOLENT EFFORT
STUFFED OLIVES	VIOLENT NATURE
STUFFED TURKEY	VIOLENT TEMPER
STUMBLE ACROSS	VISIBLE EFFECT
STUNTED GROWTH	VITAMIN TABLET
SUBJECT MATTER	WAGGING TONGUE
SUCCESS SYMBOL	WARDOUR STREET
SUGARED ALMOND	WARLIKE MANNER
SUNBURN LOTION	WARLIKE PEOPLE
SURPLUS ENERGY	WARNING GLANCE
TALKING PARROT	WARNING SIGNAL
TAXABLE INCOME	WARNING SYSTEM
TELLING EFFECT	WASHING POWDER
THEATRE CRITIC	WATLING STREET
THEATRE TICKET	WEATHER BUREAU
TICKETS PLEASE	WEATHER EXPERT
TOASTED CHEESE	WEATHER REPORT
TORQUAY UNITED	WEEPING WILLOW
TOURIST AGENCY	WEIGHTY MATTER
TOURIST SEASON	WELCOME RELIEF
TRADING ESTATE	WELFARE WORKER

WESTERN CHURCH
WESTERN EUROPE
WESTERN POWERS
WILDCAT STRIKE
WILLIAM CAXTON
WILLIAM COWPER
WILLIAM MORRIS
WILLING HELPER
WILLING WORKER
WINDING COURSE
WINDING STAIRS
WINDSOR CASTLE
WINNING DOUBLE
WINNING GAMBIT
WINNING HAZARD
WINNING NUMBER
WINNING STREAK
WINNING STROKE
WINNING TICKET
WINNING TREBLE
WITHOUT CHARGE
WITHOUT EFFECT
WITHOUT MALICE
WITHOUT NOTICE
WITHOUT NUMBER
WITHOUT REASON
WITHOUT REGARD
WOODROW WILSON
WOOLLEN GLOVES
WORKING DINNER
WORLDLY WISDOM
WRITTEN ANSWER
WRITTEN PERMIT
YOUNGER SISTER

8, 2, 3

ARTICLES OF WAR
ATTORNEY AT LAW
BACHELOR OF LAW
CONFINED TO BED
DESCRIBE AN ARC
ELEVENTH OF MAY
GOODWILL TO MEN
MINISTER OF WAR
MULTIPLY BY SIX
MULTIPLY BY TEN
MULTIPLY BY TWO
NEEDLESS TO SAY
OUTBREAK OF WAR
PATIENCE OF JOB
PRISONER OF WAR
SKETCHES BY BOZ
THOUSAND TO ONE
TOMORROW WE DIE

8, 3, 2

WHATEVER YOU DO

8, 5

ABRAHAMS BOSOM
ABSOLUTE PITCH
ABSOLUTE POWER
ABSOLUTE PROOF
ABSOLUTE TRUST
ABSTRACT TERMS
ACCEPTED TRUTH
ACCIDENT PRONE
ACCOUNTS CLERK
ACQUIRED TASTE
ADEQUATE CAUSE
ADVANCED GUARD
ADVANCED LEVEL
ADVANCED PUPIL
ADVISORY BOARD
AFFECTED VOICE
ALBRECHT DÜRER
ALISTAIR COOKE
ALLUVIAL PLAIN
AMERICAN DREAM
AMERICAN EAGLE
AMERICAN NEGRO
AMERICAN SLANG
ANYBODYS GUESS
APOSTLES CREED
ARTICLED CLERK
ASSEMBLY ROOMS
ATLANTIC LINER
ATLANTIC OCEAN
AVENGING ANGEL
AWAITING TRIAL
BABBLING BROOK
BACKWARD CHILD
BANKRUPT STOCK
BARBECUE PARTY
BAREBACK RIDER
BARONESS ORCZY
BARTERED BRIDE
BEAUFORT SCALE
BILLIARD TABLE
BIRTHDAY PARTY
BIRTHDAY TREAT
BLEEDING HEART
BLINDING LIGHT
BLISSFUL STATE
BLOTTING PAPER
BLUSHING BRIDE
BOARDING HOUSE
BOARDING PARTY
BORROWED MONEY
BOUNDARY FENCE
BREAKING POINT
BRIGHTON BELLE
BROTHERS GRIMM
BUILDING BLOCK
BUILDING BRICK
BUSINESS HOURS
BUSINESS LUNCH
BUSINESS TERMS

BUTTERED TOAST	DESPATCH CLERK
CALENDAR MONTH	DESPATCH RIDER
CAPACITY CROWD	DETACHED HOUSE
CAPACITY HOUSE	DIFFUSED LIGHT
CAPTAINS TABLE	DISCOUNT HOUSE
CARNIVAL QUEEN	DISCOUNT PRICE
CASHMERE SHAWL	DISPUTED POINT
CATERING CORPS	DISTRICT COURT
CATHOLIC FAITH	DISTRICT JUDGE
CHAMPION BOXER	DISTRICT NURSE
CHEERFUL SIGHT	DIVISION LOBBY
CHEMICAL AGENT	DIVISION THREE
CHESTNUT BROWN	DOMESTIC BLISS
CHILDISH PRANK	DOMESTIC TRADE
CHILTERN HILLS	DOWNWARD CURVE
CHOPPING BLOCK	DOWNWARD SLOPE
CIVILIAN DRESS	DOWNWARD TREND
CLEARING HOUSE	DRAINING BOARD
CLENCHED TEETH	DREADFUL SIGHT
CLERICAL DRESS	DREADFUL STATE
CLERICAL ERROR	DREADFUL STORY
CLERICAL STAFF	DRESSING TABLE
CLICKETY CLICK	DRINKING PARTY
CLIMBING IRONS	DRINKING STRAW
CLIMBING PLANT	DRINKING WATER
COCKTAIL DRESS	DUODENAL ULCER
COCKTAIL PARTY	DWELLING HOUSE
COCKTAIL STICK	ECONOMIC VALUE
COLONIAL STYLE	EGYPTIAN MUMMY
COLORADO RIVER	EIGHTEEN HOLES
COLOURED CHALK	EIGHTEEN MILES
COMPLETE IDIOT	EIGHTEEN PENCE
COMPLETE WORKS	EIGHTEEN YEARS
CONFINED SPACE	EJECTION ORDER
CONGRESS PARTY	ELECTION NIGHT
CONISTON WATER	ELECTRIC CABLE
CONSTANT USAGE	ELECTRIC CHAIR
CONSUMER GOODS	ELECTRIC CLOCK
COTSWOLD HILLS	ELECTRIC DRILL
COURTESY TITLE	ELECTRIC FENCE
CRIBBAGE BOARD	ELECTRIC LIGHT
CRIMINAL CLASS	ELECTRIC METER
CRIMINAL COURT	ELECTRIC MOTOR
CRIMINAL LIBEL	ELECTRIC ORGAN
CRIMINAL TRIAL	ELECTRIC PIANO
CRIMINAL WORLD	ELECTRIC RAZOR
CRITICAL ANGLE	ELECTRIC SHOCK
CRITICAL STAGE	ELECTRIC STOVE
CROWNING GLORY	ELECTRIC TRAIN
CRUISING SPEED	ELEVENTH ROUND
DAZZLING SMILE	EMULSION PAINT
DEBATING POINT	ENGAGING SMILE
DEFINITE MAYBE	ENTRANCE LOBBY
DEFINITE PROOF	ENTRANCE MONEY
DELICATE CHILD	EUROPEAN COURT
DELICATE POINT	EXCHANGE BLOWS
DELICATE SHADE	EXCHANGE IDEAS
DELICATE TOUCH	EXCHANGE JOKES
DEMERARA SUGAR	EXCHANGE SHOTS
DENTISTS CHAIR	EXCHANGE VALUE
DENTISTS DRILL	EXCHANGE VIEWS

EXCITING MATCH	HAVELOCK ELLIS
EXCITING STORY	HEAVENLY CHOIR
EXERCISE POWER	HIGHLAND CHIEF
EXTERIOR ANGLE	HIGHLAND DRESS
FABULOUS BEAST	HIGHLAND FLING
FABULOUS STORY	HIGHLAND GAMES
FALSETTO VOICE	HISTORIC SCENE
FAMILIAR SIGHT	HISTORIC TENSE
FAMILIAR STYLE	HOMEWARD BOUND
FAMILIAR VOICE	HONEYDEW MELON
FAREWELL PARTY	HONOURED GUEST
FARTHEST POINT	HOPELESS CAUSE
FEMININE CHARM	HOPELESS STATE
FEMININE LOGIC	HORRIBLE CRIME
FEMININE WILES	HORRIBLE DEATH
FEVERISH HASTE	HORRIBLE NOISE
FEVERISH STATE	HOSPITAL NURSE
FIDDLERS THREE	HOSPITAL STAFF
FIGHTING DRUNK	IGNORANT WOMAN
FIGHTING FORCE	IMPERIAL CROWN
FIREWORK PARTY	IMPERIAL EAGLE
FLASHING SMILE	IMPERIAL GUARD
FLOATING VOTER	IMPUDENT ROGUE
FOOLSCAP PAPER	INCLINED PLANE
FOOTBALL BOOTS	INDECENT HASTE
FOOTBALL FIELD	INDIRECT ROUTE
FOOTBALL MATCH	INFERIOR GOODS
FOOTBALL PITCH	INFINITE SPACE
FOOTBALL POOLS	INFLATED IDEAS
FOOTBALL SCARF	INFLATED PRICE
FOURTEEN HOURS	INFORMAL DRESS
FOURTEEN MILES	INFORMAL PARTY
FOURTEEN PENCE	INNOCENT PARTY
FOURTEEN YEARS	INSPIRED GUESS
FRAGRANT SMELL	INSPIRED WORDS
FREEZING POINT	INTEREST RATES
FRICTION MATCH	INTIMATE TERMS
FRIENDLY MATCH	JONATHAN SWIFT
FRIENDLY TERMS	JUDICIAL COURT
GENEROUS GIVER	JUVENILE COURT
GENEROUS OFFER	KENTUCKY DERBY
GENEROUS SHARE	KNOCKOUT PUNCH
GEORGIAN HOUSE	LATCHKEY CHILD
GERTRUDE STEIN	LAUGHING HYENA
GIUSEPPE VERDI	LAUGHING STOCK
GIVEAWAY PRICE	LEOPARDS SPOTS
GLOATING SMILE	LICENSED TRADE
GLORIOUS MUSIC	LIFELONG ENEMY
GLORIOUS REIGN	LIFELONG HABIT
GLORIOUS YEARS	LITERARY AGENT
GRATEFUL HEART	LITERARY GUILD
GRIPPING STORY	LITERARY STYLE
GUARDIAN ANGEL	LITERARY WORKS
GUTTERAL VOICE	LITERARY WORLD
HALLOWED PLACE	LOCKABLE DIARY
HANDSOME OFFER	LUKEWARM WATER
HANDSOME THING	LUMINOUS PAINT
HANGMANS NOOSE	LUNCHEON TABLE
HARDWARE STORE	MAGAZINE STORY
HARMONIC SCALE	MAGNETIC FIELD
HATFIELD HOUSE	MAGNETIC NORTH

MAGNETIC STORM	OVERHEAD CABLE
MARGARET COURT	OVERHEAD WIRES
MARRIAGE BELLS	OVERLAND ROUTE
MARRIAGE FEAST	OVERSEAS TRADE
MARRIAGE LINES	PARAFFIN STOVE
MARRIAGE RITES	PARALLEL LINES
MARTELLO TOWER	PATHETIC SIGHT
MATCHBOX LABEL	PECULIAR SMELL
MATERIAL GOODS	PENDULUM CLOCK
MATERIAL POINT	PENTLAND FIRTH
MEASURED TREAD	PERSONAL ABUSE
MEDICINE CHEST	PERSONAL CHARM
MEDICINE GLASS	PERSONAL GUEST
MEMORIAL STONE	PERSONAL LEVEL
MENTALLY ALERT	PERSONAL PRIDE
MENTALLY SOUND	PERSONAL STYLE
MESSINES RIDGE	PERSONAL TOUCH
METALLIC PAINT	PERVERSE LOGIC
METALLIC SOUND	PHYSICAL JERKS
MILITARY CROSS	PHYSICAL POWER
MILITARY DRESS	PHYSICAL WRECK
MILITARY FORCE	PLATFORM SOLES
MILITARY MUSIC	PLOUGHED FIELD
MILITARY STAFF	POETICAL WORKS
MISSPENT YOUTH	POISONED ARROW
MODERATE PRICE	POLISHED ACTOR
MODERATE SKILL	PORTABLE RADIO
MODERATE SPEED	PORTLAND STONE
MODERATE VIEWS	POSITIVE PROOF
MONETARY VALUE	POSTMANS KNOCK
MOONLESS NIGHT	POUNDING HEART
MOUNTAIN GUIDE	POWERFUL VOICE
MOUNTAIN RANGE	PRACTICE ROUND
MOUNTAIN SHEEP	PRECIOUS JEWEL
MOUNTAIN SLOPE	PRECIOUS METAL
MULTIPLE STORE	PRECIOUS STONE
MUSCULAR SPASM	PRESSING CLAIM
MUSHROOM CLOUD	PRESSURE GAUGE
NATIONAL DRESS	PRESSURE GROUP
NATIONAL DRINK	PRIMEVAL SLIME
NATIONAL FRONT	PRINCESS GRACE
NATIONAL GUARD	PRINCESS ROYAL
NATIONAL PRIDE	PRINTERS DEVIL
NATIONAL SPORT	PRINTERS ERROR
NATIONAL TRUST	PRINTING ERROR
NATIONAL UNITY	PRINTING PRESS
NEGATIVE REPLY	PRINTING WORKS
NINETEEN FIFTY	PROFOUND SLEEP
NINETEEN FORTY	PROGRESS CHART
NINETEEN MILES	PROPERTY OWNER
NINETEEN PENCE	PULITZER PRIZE
NINETEEN SIXTY	PURCHASE PRICE
NINETEEN YEARS	RALLYING POINT
NONSENSE VERSE	RATEABLE VALUE
OPPOSITE CAMPS	RECKLESS YOUTH
OPPOSITE SIDES	REDUCING PILLS
OPPOSITE VIEWS	REIGNING QUEEN
ORDINARY LEVEL	RELATIVE VALUE
ORDINARY SHARE	RELATIVE WORTH
ORIGINAL MODEL	RESERVED TABLE
OUTBOARD MOTOR	RESTLESS NIGHT

RETARDED BRAIN	SPITTING IMAGE
RETARDED CHILD	SPLINTER GROUP
RIGHTFUL OWNER	SPLINTER PARTY
ROMANTIC MUSIC	SPORTING EVENT
ROMANTIC NOVEL	SPORTING GOODS
ROMANTIC STORY	SPORTING PRESS
ROULETTE TABLE	SPORTING PRINT
ROULETTE WHEEL	SPORTING WORLD
SATURDAY NIGHT	SPRAINED ANKLE
SCARCITY VALUE	STALKING HORSE
SCARLETT OHARA	STANDARD GAUGE
SCORCHED EARTH	STANDARD MODEL
SECURITY CHECK	STANDARD PRICE
SENSIBLE WOMAN	STANDING ORDER
SEPARATE COVER	STANDING START
SEPARATE ROOMS	STANDING WATER
SERGEANT MAJOR	STARTING POINT
SERPENTS TOOTH	STARTING PRICE
SHETLAND ISLES	STEERING WHEEL
SHIFTING SANDS	STEPPING STONE
SHILLING PIECE	STERLING WORTH
SHIPPING AGENT	STICKING POINT
SHOCKING STATE	STILETTO HEELS
SHOOTING MATCH	STIRRING MUSIC
SHOOTING PARTY	STIRRING TIMES
SHOOTING RANGE	STOPPING PLACE
SHOPPING SPREE	STRAIGHT ACTOR
SHORTEST NIGHT	STRAIGHT AHEAD
SHORTEST ROUTE	STRAIGHT DRAMA
SHORTEST WOMAN	STRAIGHT DRIVE
SHOULDER BLADE	STRAIGHT FIGHT
SHOULDER STRAP	STRAIGHT FLUSH
SHOUTING MATCH	STRAIGHT RIGHT
SHREDDED WHEAT	STRICTLY LEGAL
SIXPENNY PIECE	STRIKING CLOCK
SKELETON STAFF	STRIKING FORCE
SKIRTING BOARD	STRUGGLE ALONG
SLANGING MATCH	SUBURBAN HOUSE
SLEEPING BERTH	SUITABLE MATCH
SLIGHTLY BUILT	SUPERIOR BEING
SLIPPERY SLOPE	SUPERIOR COURT
SMELLING SALTS	SUPERIOR FORCE
SNOWBALL FIGHT	SURGEONS KNIFE
SOMERSET HOUSE	SURGICAL KNIFE
SOOTHING MUSIC	SURPRISE PARTY
SOOTHING TOUCH	SURPRISE VISIT
SOOTHING WORDS	SWEEPING CLAIM
SOUNDING BOARD	SWIMMING BATHS
SOUNDING BRASS	TANGIBLE ASSET
SOUTHERN CROSS	TEACHING STAFF
SOUTHERN STATE	TELEGRAM CLAIM
SPEAKERS NOTES	TEMPTING OFFER
SPEAKING TERMS	TENEMENT HOUSE
SPEAKING VOICE	TENPENNY PIECE
SPEEDWAY TRACK	TENPENNY STAMP
SPELLING ERROR	TERRACED HOUSE
SPENDING POWER	TERRIBLE CHILD
SPENDING SPREE	TERRIBLE CRIME
SPINNING JENNY	TERRIBLE HAVOC
SPINNING WHEEL	TERRIBLE SIGHT
SPIRITED REPLY	TERRIBLE TWINS

THIRTEEN	CARDS	
THIRTEEN	HOURS	
THIRTEEN	MILES	
THIRTEEN	PENCE	
THIRTEEN	WEEKS	
THIRTEEN	YEARS	
THOUSAND	MILES	
THOUSAND	YEARS	
THURSDAY	NIGHT	
TIRESOME	CHORE	
TOGETHER	AGAIN	
TOMORROW	NIGHT	
TOUCHING	SCENE	
TRANQUIL	SCENE	
TRANSFER	PRICE	
TREASURE	CHEST	
TREASURE	TRAIL	
TREASURE	TROVE	
TRIFLING	ERROR	
TROPICAL	FRUIT	
TROPICAL	PLANT	
TROPICAL	STORM	
TUESDAYS	CHILD	
TWOPENNY	PIECE	
TWOPENNY	STAMP	
UMBRELLA	STAND	
UNBROKEN	FRONT	
UNIONIST	PARTY	
UNLAWFUL	ENTRY	
UNSOLVED	CRIME	
UNTIMELY	DEATH	
UNWANTED	CHILD	
UNWORTHY	CAUSE	
VARICOSE	VEINS	
VAULTING	HORSE	
VENETIAN	BLIND	
VENOMOUS	SNAKE	
VERTICAL	PLANE	
VICTORIA	CROSS	
VICTORIA	FALLS	
VIENNESE	WALTZ	
VINDALOO	CURRY	
VIRGINIA	WATER	
VIRGINIA	WOOLF	
VISITING	HOURS	
WATCHING	BRIEF	
WATERING	PLACE	
WHIRLING	ROUND	
WHOOPING	COUGH	
WIRELESS	WAVES	
WRAPPING	PAPER	
WRETCHED	WOMAN	
YOUNGEST	CHILD	

9, 2, 2

SOMETHING TO DO

9, 4

ADMISSION	CARD
ADMISSION	FREE
AFTERNOON	REST
ALLIGATOR	SKIN
ALUMINIUM	FOIL
AMUSEMENT	PARK
ANCESTRAL	HALL
ANCESTRAL	HOME
ANNOTATED	TEXT
ANONYMOUS	GIFT
APPALLING	RUSH
APPOINTED	TIME
ARMAMENTS	RACE
ARTILLERY	FIRE
ASPARAGUS	TIPS
AUTOGRAPH	BOOK
AUTOMATIC	LIFT
AUTOMATIC	LOCK
AUXILIARY	VERB
BAREFACED	LIAR
BATTERSEA	PARK
BAYSWATER	ROAD
BEAUTIFUL	BODY
BEAUTIFUL	FACE
BEAUTIFUL	VIEW
BEGINNERS	LUCK
BLACKPOOL	ROCK
BLINDMANS	BUFF
BLOODSHOT	EYES
BREAKFAST	DISH
BREAKFAST	FOOD
BREAKFAST	TIME
BREATHING	ROOM
BRILLIANT	IDEA
BRILLIANT	MIND
BRILLIANT	PLAN
BROTHERLY	LOVE
BURLESQUE	SHOW
BURNISHED	GOLD
CAMBRIDGE	BLUE
CARTRIDGE	CASE
CATHEDRAL	CITY
CATHERINE	PARR
CELESTIAL	BODY
CELESTIAL	CITY
CHANTILLY	LACE
CHARACTER	PART
CHILDHOOD	DAYS
CHILDRENS	BOOK
CHILDRENS	HOME
CHILDRENS	HOUR
CHOCOLATE	CAKE
CHOCOLATE	DROP
CHRISTIAN	DIOR
CHRISTIAN	NAME
CHRISTMAS	CAKE
CHRISTMAS	CARD
CHRISTMAS	GIFT
CHRISTMAS	LIST

CHRISTMAS	ROSE
CHRISTMAS	TERM
CHRISTMAS	TREE
CIGARETTE	CARD
CIGARETTE	CASE
CIGARETTE	GIRL
CLEARANCE	SALE
COMMUNIST	BLOC
COMPOSING	ROOM
CONDEMNED	CELL
CONDENSED	FORM
CONDENSED	MILK
CONDUCTED	TOUR
CONFIRMED	CASE
CONFIRMED	LIAR
CONTENTED	MIND
CORPORATE	BODY
CRIPPLING	BLOW
CURIOSITY	SHOP
DANDELION	WINE
DANGEROUS	BEND
DANGEROUS	DRUG
DANGEROUS	GAME
DANGEROUS	WORK
DASTARDLY	DEED
DAUNTLESS	HERO
DECIDUOUS	TREE
DEPRESSED	AREA
DESERVING	CASE
DESERVING	POOR
DESPERATE	MOVE
DETECTIVE	WORK
DIFFERENT	KIND
DIFFERENT	VIEW
DIFFICULT	CASE
DIFFICULT	TASK
DIFFICULT	TIME
DISTURBED	MIND
DORMITORY	TOWN
DOWNRIGHT	LIAR
EDWARDIAN	DAYS
EIGHTSOME	REEL
ELECTORAL	ROLL
ELEPHANTS	TUSK
EMERGENCY	CALL
EMERGENCY	EXIT
EMERGENCY	STOP
EMERGENCY	WARD
EMINENTLY	FAIR
EMOTIONAL	LIFE
ENDURANCE	TEST
ENQUIRING	MIND
ESSENTIAL	PART
ESTIMATED	COST
ESTIMATED	TIME
EVERGREEN	TREE
EXCELLENT	SHOT
EXCLUSIVE	CLUB
EXPENSIVE	ITEM
EXPENSIVE	LINE
EXTREMELY	GOOD

FAVOURITE	SONG
FAVOURITE	TUNE
FINANCIAL	NEWS
FINANCIAL	PAGE
FINANCIAL	RUIN
FINANCIAL	YEAR
FINISHING	POST
FOLLOWING	WIND
FORTIFIED	TOWN
FRIGHTFUL	BORE
FRIGHTFUL	TIME
FRUITLESS	TASK
FURNISHED	FLAT
GOVERNING	BODY
GRAPPLING	IRON
GREENWOOD	TREE
GREETINGS	CARD
GREYHOUND	RACE
GRUELLING	HEAT
GRUELLING	PACE
GRUELLING	RACE
GUNPOWDER	PLOT
HARROWING	TALE
HERCULEAN	TASK
HOLLYWOOD	BOWL
HORSESHOE	BEND
HOUSEHOLD	HINT
HOUSEHOLD	WORD
HURRICANE	LAMP
HYDRAULIC	LIFT
IDENTICAL	TWIN
IMAGINARY	LINE
IMPENDING	DOOM
IMPORTANT	POST
INCREASED	WAGE
INQUIRING	MIND
INSURANCE	RISK
IRREGULAR	VERB
ISOLATION	WARD
JAILHOUSE	ROCK
JAUNDICED	VIEW
JEWELLERS	SHOP
LAUNCHING	SITE
LEASEHOLD	FLAT
LEICESTER	CITY
LICENSING	LAWS
LIFETIMES	WORK
LIGHTNING	MOVE
LINGERING	LOOK
LISTENING	POST
LUCRATIVE	DEAL
MANSFIELD	TOWN
MATERNITY	WARD
MEASURING	TAPE
MODELLING	CLAY
MOONLIGHT	FLIT
MORTALITY	RATE
MUNICIPAL	PARK
NARRATIVE	POEM
NECESSARY	EVIL
NEWSPAPER	RACK

NORTHERLY WIND	SHEPHERDS BUSH
OBJECTIVE CASE	SIEGFRIED LINE
OPERATIVE WORD	SIGNATURE TUNE
OVERNIGHT CASE	SINCERELY FELT
PAPERBACK BOOK	SMOKELESS FUEL
PARACHUTE JUMP	SMOKELESS ZONE
PASSENGER LIST	SMOOTHING IRON
PASSENGER SHIP	SOLITAIRE RING
PATERNITY SUIT	SOMETHING BLUE
PATRIOTIC SONG	SOMETHING ELSE
PECUNIARY LOSS	SOMETHING GOOD
PERISHING COLD	SOMETHING LIKE
PERMANENT HOME	SOMETHING NICE
PERMANENT POST	SOMEWHERE ELSE
PERMANENT WAVE	SOMEWHERE NEAR
PETTICOAT LANE	SPARKLING WINE
PETTICOAT LINE	SPECTACLE CASE
PISTACHIO NUTS	SPIRITUAL LIFE
PLAUSIBLE TALE	SPIRITUAL SELF
PNEUMATIC TYRE	STARBOARD SIDE
POISONOUS DART	STARTLING NEWS
POLITICAL NEWS	STATUTORY MILE
POLITICAL VIEW	STRAPPING GIRL
PRACTICAL JOKE	STREAMING COLD
PRACTICAL TEST	STRETCHER CASE
PRACTISED LIAR	SUBMARINE BASE
PRECISION TOOL	SUBMARINE CREW
PRESIDENT TITO	SULPHURIC ACID
PRIMITIVE FORM	SUSPENDER BELT
PRINCIPAL PART	SUSTAINED NOTE
PRINCIPAL TOWN	TECHNICAL TERM
PRISONERS BASE	TELEGRAPH POLE
PROMENADE DECK	TELEGRAPH POST
PROMISING IDEA	TELEGRAPH WIRE
PUBLISHED WORK	TELEPHONE BILL
PUNISHING WORK	TELEPHONE BOOK
QUARTERLY RENT	TELEPHONE CALL
QUOTATION MARK	TELEPHONE LINE
RASPBERRY FOOL	TELEPHOTO LENS
RASPBERRY TART	TEMPERATE ZONE
RECEPTION DESK	TEMPORARY HALT
RECEPTIVE MIND	TEMPORARY HOME
RECLAIMED LAND	TEMPORARY LOAN
REFERENCE BOOK	TEMPORARY STOP
REHEARSAL ROOM	TERRORIST ARMY
REJECTION SLIP	TERRORIST BAND
RETAINING WALL	THANKLESS TASK
REVOLVING DOOR	TRANSPORT CAFÉ
SALVATION ARMY	TRIUMPHAL ARCH
SATELLITE TOWN	TWINKLING EYES
SCRAMBLED EGGS	TWINKLING FEET
SCRIBBLED NOTE	UNANIMOUS VOTE
SECRETARY BIRD	UNCROWNED KING
SEDENTARY LIFE	UNIVERSAL AUNT
SENSELESS TALK	UNIVERSAL RULE
SERIOUSLY HURT	UNSECURED DEBT
SERVIETTE RING	UNSECURED LOAN
SHEEPSKIN COAT	UNSKILLED WORK
SHELTERED LIFE	VALENTINE CARD
SHELTERED SIDE	VEGETABLE DIET
SHELTERED SPOT	VEGETABLE DISH

VEGETABLE SOUP
VENERABLE BEDE
VOLUNTARY ARMY
VOLUNTARY WORK
VOLUNTEER ARMY
WANDERING MIND
WEDNESDAY WEEK
WHOLESOME FOOD
WITHERING LOOK
WONDERFUL NEWS
WONDERFUL TIME
WORTHLESS JUNK

10, 3

ABYSSINIAN CAT
ALTOGETHER BAD
ARTIFICIAL ARM
ARTIFICIAL LEG
BLACKBERRY PIE
BOTTOMLESS PIT
CHELTENHAM SPA
COLLECTION BOX
COMMERCIAL ART
COMMERCIAL LAW
COMPRESSED AIR
CONNECTING ROD
CRITICALLY ILL
DARJEELING TEA
DECORATIVE ART
DELIBERATE LIE
DEMOLITION JOB
DIPLOMATIC BAG
EXORBITANT FEE
GENERATION GAP
GOOSEBERRY JAM
HONOURABLE MAN
LEAMINGTON SPA
LIBERATION DAY
MECHANICAL AID
MICHAELMAS DAY
MIDSUMMERS DAY
MONOTONOUS JOB
NEAPOLITAN ICE
PARKINSONS LAW
PERCUSSION CAP
PHYSICALLY FIT
POLICEMANS LOT
PROSPEROUS MAN
REASONABLE MAN
REMARKABLE BOY
REMARKABLE MAN
REPETITIVE JOB
RESTAURANT CAR
ROUNDABOUT WAY
SCIENTIFIC AGE
SETTLEMENT DAY
STRAIGHTEN OUT
STRAWBERRY ICE
STRAWBERRY JAM
SUCCESSFUL MAN

SUGGESTION BOX
SWELTERING SUN
TELEVISION SET
THREEPENNY BIT
TRAVELLERS JOY
TREMENDOUS JOB
UNDERCOVER MAN
UNFRIENDLY ACT
UNIVERSITY RAG
VALENTINES DAY
VAUDEVILLE ACT

1, 3, 2, 3, 5

A DAY AT THE RACES

1, 3, 4, 6

I BEG YOUR PARDON

1, 4, 2, 2, 5

I WANT TO BE ALONE

1, 4, 2, 3, 4

A BIRD IN THE HAND

1, 4, 2, 7

A BOOK AT BEDTIME

1, 4, 4, 5

A TOWN LIKE ALICE

2, 1, 4, 7

BY A LONG STRETCH

2, 1, 5, 2, 4

IN A STATE OF FLUX

2, 1, 5, 6

TO A GREAT EXTENT
TO A LARGE DEGREE

2, 1, 6, 5

IN A LITTLE WHILE
ON A HIGHER PLANE

2, 1, 7, 4

AS A GENERAL RULE

2, 2, 1, 4, 5

ON TO A GOOD THING

2, 2, 2, 1, 7

GO UP IN A BALLOON

2, 2, 2, 3, 5

GO UP IN THE WORLD

2, 2, 3, 4, 3

DO IT THE HARD WAY
IN AT THE DEEP END

2, 2, 3, 7

GO TO ANY LENGTHS
GO TO THE COUNTRY
GO TO THE SEASIDE
GO TO THE THEATRE

2, 2, 5, 5

BY NO MEANS LEAST

2, 2, 10

BE OF ASSISTANCE
GO TO CONFESSION

2, 3, 2, 1, 6

AS FIT AS A FIDDLE
AS MAD AS A HATTER

2, 3, 2, 4, 3

GO OUT OF ONES WAY

2, 3, 3, 2, 4

TO THE END OF TIME

2, 3, 3, 3, 3

BE-ALL AND END-ALL

2, 3, 3, 6

GO OFF THE HANDLE
ON THE OFF CHANCE
WE ARE NOT AMUSED

2, 3, 4, 1, 4

GO OFF WITH A BANG

2, 3, 4, 2, 3

IN THE NAME OF GOD

2, 3, 4, 3, 2

AS THE CASE MAY BE

2, 3, 4, 5

AS THE CROW FLIES
AT ONE FELL SWOOP
BY THE SAME TOKEN
IN THE SAME CLASS
ON THE BAND-WAGON
ON THE HOME FRONT
TO THE BACK TEETH

2, 3, 5, 2, 2

IN THE THICK OF IT

2, 3, 5, 4

AT THE RIGHT TIME
ON THE OCEAN WAVE
ON THE OTHER HAND
ON THE OTHER SIDE
ON THE RIGHT SIDE
ON THE SHORT LIST
ON THE SMALL SIDE
ON THE TOUCH-LINE
ON THE WRONG FOOT
ON THE WRONG SIDE
ON THE WRONG TACK
SO THE STORY GOES

2, 3, 6, 3

IN THE PUBLIC EYE
TO THE BITTER END

2, 3, 7, 2

DO THE WASHING-UP

2, 3, 9

AT THE THRESHOLD
IN ALL INNOCENCE
IN THE AFTERNOON
IN THE ASCENDANT
IN THE BEGINNING
IN THE FOREFRONT
IN THE HEADLINES
IN THE LIMELIGHT
IN THE MOONLIGHT
IN THE NEWSPAPER
ON ONE CONDITION
ON THE BANDWAGON
ON THE CONTINENT

ON THE DEFENSIVE
ON THE OFFENSIVE
ON THE OUTSKIRTS
ON THE TELEPHONE
ON THE THRESHOLD
ON THE TOUCHDOWN

2, 4, 1, 7

GO INTO A DECLINE

2, 4, 2, 1, 5

AS HARD AS A STONE
AS PALE AS A GHOST

2, 4, 2, 2, 4

MY WORD IS MY BOND

2, 4, 2, 3, 3

AS FAST AS YOU CAN
AS SOON AS ONE CAN
NO ROOM AT THE INN

2, 4, 2, 6

AS SAFE AS HOUSES
AS SOFT AS BUTTER
NO CASE TO ANSWER

2, 4, 3, 5

GO LIKE HOT CAKES
GO WITH THE TIMES
IN ONES BAD BOOKS
IN ONES OWN RIGHT
NO ROOM FOR DOUBT
ON ONES OWN TERMS
ON WITH THE DANCE
SO MUCH THE WORSE

2, 4, 4, 4

IN ONES BORN DAYS
ON ONES BEAM-ENDS
ON ONES HIND LEGS
ON ONES LAST LEGS

2, 4, 5, 3

GO WEST YOUNG MAN
IN ONES MINDS EYE
ON ONES DEATH-BED

2, 4, 8

AT FULL STRENGTH
DO ONES ARTICLES
DO THOU LIKEWISE

GO DOWN FIGHTING
GO INTO BUSINESS
GO INTO HOSPITAL
GO INTO MOURNING
GO INTO RAPTURES
IN LOCO PARENTIS
IN MANY RESPECTS
NO HARD FEELINGS

2, 5, 2, 1, 4

AS BRAVE AS A LION
AS DRUNK AS A LORD
AS SOUND AS A BELL

2, 5, 2, 5

AS BLACK AS NIGHT
AS BLACK AS PITCH
AS FRESH AS PAINT
AS GREEN AS GRASS
AS SWEET AS HONEY
AS SWEET AS SUGAR
IN ORDER OF MERIT

2, 5, 3, 4

GO ROUND THE BEND

2, 5, 7

AN IDEAL HUSBAND
AT GREAT EXPENSE
IN EVERY RESPECT
IN ROUND NUMBERS
NO FIXED ADDRESS
OF HUMAN BONDAGE

2, 6, 2, 4

BY RETURN OF POST
IN COURSE OF TIME

2, 6, 6

IN MORTAL COMBAT
NO JOKING MATTER
ST.JAMESS PALACE

2, 7, 2, 3

NO TROUBLE AT ALL

2, 7, 3, 2

NO STOMACH FOR IT

2, 7, 5

BY DEVIOUS MEANS
DO ONESELF PROUD

IN ANCIENT TIMES
IN ANOTHER WORLD
NO VISIBLE MEANS
OR NEAREST OFFER

2, 8, 4

DO BUSINESS WITH
IN STRAIGHT SETS
ON BORROWED TIME

2, 12

IN ANTICIPATION
IN DIFFICULTIES
NO THOROUGHFARE
ON SUBSCRIPTION

3, 1, 3, 2, 1, 4

BUY A PIG IN A POKE

3, 1, 3, 7

SET A BAD EXAMPLE

3, 1, 4, 2, 1, 3

NOT A WORD OF A LIE

3, 1, 4, 6

CUT A FINE FIGURE
CUT A POOR FIGURE

3, 1, 5, 3, 2

GET A TASTE FOR IT

3, 1, 5, 5

ITS A SMALL WORLD

3, 1, 6, 2, 2

PUT A FINISH TO IT

3, 1, 10

PAY A COMPLIMENT
WAG A FOREFINGER

3, 2, 1, 3, 5

PUT IN A BAD LIGHT

3, 2, 1, 4, 4

ALL IN A DAYS WORK
BIT OF A COME-DOWN
PUT IN A GOOD WORD

PUT ON A BOLD FACE
PUT UP A GOOD SHOW

3, 2, 1, 5, 3

WIN BY A KNOCK-OUT

3, 2, 1, 8

BIT OF A NUISANCE
MAN IN A THOUSAND
ONE IN A THOUSAND
PUT ON A PEDESTAL
PUT UP A STRUGGLE

3, 2, 2, 3, 4

GET IT IN THE NECK
PUT IT TO THE TEST
PUT IT TO THE VOTE

3, 2, 2, 7

PUT IT IN WRITING
RUN UP AN ACCOUNT

3, 2, 3, 3, 3

DAY IN AND DAY OUT

3, 2, 3, 6

AIM AT THE TARGET
CAT ON HOT BRICKS
DOG IN THE MANGER
EAR TO THE GROUND
END OF ALL THINGS
END OF THE MATTER
END OF THE STREET
LAW OF THE JUNGLE
MAN IN THE STREET
MAN OF THE MOMENT
MAN OF THE PEOPLE
ONE OF THE FAMILY
ONE OF THE PEOPLE
PUT IN THE STOCKS
PUT ON THE MARKET
RUN IN THE FAMILY
SIT IN THE CORNER
SIT ON THE GROUND
SIT ON THE THRONE
TIP OF THE TONGUE
TOP OF THE CHARTS
TOP OF THE LEAGUE
WAR OF THE WORLDS
WIN ON THE HORSES

3, 2, 4, 5

ACT IN GOOD FAITH
DIE IN ONES SHOES

```
DIG   IN   ONES   HEELS
GET   ON   ONES   HORSE
HOT   ON   ONES   HEELS
HOT   ON   ONES   TRAIL
MAN   OF   MANY   PARTS
OUT   OF   ONES   DEPTH
OUT   OF   ONES   SHELL
OUT   OF   THIS   WORLD
PUT   IN   ONES   PLACE
SET   OF   GOLF-CLUBS
TOP   OF   ONES   VOICE
TOP   UP   ONES   GLASS
```

3, 2, 5, 4

```
ONE   OF   THESE   DAYS
```

3, 2, 6, 3

```
LOT   TO   ANSWER   FOR
```

3, 2, 9

```
ACT   AS   GUARANTOR
AGE   OF   INNOCENCE
ALL-IN   WRESTLING
ASK   NO   QUESTIONS
BAR   OF   CHOCOLATE
CUP   OF   HAPPINESS
DAY   OF   ATONEMENT
DAY   OF   CHRISTMAS
DAY   OF   JUDGEMENT
DAY   OF   RECKONING
GET   AN   EXTENSION
JAR   OF   MARMALADE
LAY   ON   TRANSPORT
MAN   OF   CHARACTER
MAN   OF   INTEGRITY
MAN   OF   SUBSTANCE
MAN   ON   HORSEBACK
NOD   IN   AGREEMENT
OUT   OF   CHARACTER
OUT   OF   CONDITION
PAY   NO   ATTENTION
POT   OF   MARMALADE
WAR   OF   ATTRITION
```

3, 3, 1, 7

```
ONE   AND   A   QUARTER
TWO   AND   A   QUARTER
```

3, 3, 2, 3, 3

```
GET   OUT   OF   THE   WAY
OLD   MAN   OF   THE   SEA
THE   END   OF   THE   DAY
```

3, 3, 2, 6

```
PUT   OUT   OF   ACTION
RUN   OUT   OF   PETROL
TOO   HOT   TO   HANDLE
```

3, 3, 3, 5

```
CUT   OFF   THE   WATER
FOR   ALL   THE   WORLD
GET   OFF   THE   POINT
HOT   OFF   THE   PRESS
OUT   FOR   THE   COUNT
OUT-AND-OUT   CROOK
OUT-AND-OUT   ROGUE
PUT   OFF   THE   SCENT
THE   OLD   OLD   STORY
TRY   AND   TRY   AGAIN
TRY,TRY,TRY   AGAIN
```

3, 3, 4, 2, 2

```
FOR   THE   LIFE   OF   ME
GET   THE   BEST   OF   IT
GET   THE   HANG   OF   IT
YOU   CAN   BANK   ON   IT
```

3, 3, 4, 4

```
ART   FOR   ARTS   SAKE
CUT   OFF   ONES   NOSE
FOR   THE   HIGH   JUMP
FOR   THE   LAST   TIME
FOR   THE   MOST   PART
GET   OFF   SCOT-FREE
GET   THE   WHIP-HAND
HOW   THE   LAND   LIES
LET   THE   SIDE   DOWN
NOW   THE   GOOD   NEWS
RUN   FOR   DEAR   LIFE
RUN   FOR   ONES   LIFE
THE   OLD   GREY   MARE
```

3, 3, 5, 3

```
ALL   THE   KINGS   MEN
DOT   AND   CARRY   ONE
HIT   THE   BULLS-EYE
HOW   NOW   BROWN   COW
NOT   THE   LEAST   BIT
WIN   THE   WORLD   CUP
```

3, 3, 6, 2

```
GET   THE   BETTER   OF
GET   THE   BREEZE   UP
PUT   THE   CLOCKS   ON
PUT   THE   KETTLE   ON
PUT   THE   KIBOSH   ON
```

3 . 3 . 8

BAD FOR BUSINESS
BAR THE SHOUTING
BEG THE QUESTION
EYE FOR BUSINESS
FIT THE OCCASION
FOR THE DURATION
HIT THE CROSSBAR
HOT AND BOTHERED
MAN AND SUPERMAN
MAY THE ELEVENTH
OFF THE PREMISES
ONE AND SIXPENCE
ONE-MAN BUSINESS
POP THE QUESTION
PUT THE QUESTION
RUN FOR CONGRESS
RUN THE GAUNTLET
SEE FOR YOURSELF
TEA AND BISCUITS
TEA AND SYMPATHY
TWO AND SIXPENCE
WIN THE NATIONAL

3 . 4 . 1 . 6

FLY INTO A TEMPER

3 . 4 . 2 . 2 . 3

FOR SALE OR TO LET

3 . 4 . 2 . 5

FOR LOVE OR MONEY
PUT DOWN ON PAPER
ROD, POLE OR PERCH
YOU MARK MY WORDS!

3 . 4 . 3 . 1 . 3

FOR EVER AND A DAY

3 . 4 . 3 . 4

ALL ONES OWN WORK
ALL OVER THE SHOP
ALL WELL AND GOOD
FOR EVER AND EVER
FOR ONES OWN GOOD
GET ONES OWN BACK
GOD SAVE THE KING!
HIT OVER THE HEAD
LET THEM EAT CAKE
OFF WITH HER HEAD
OFF WITH HIS HEAD
OLD BULL AND BUSH
ONE THAT GOT AWAY
PAY OVER THE ODDS
RUN LIKE THE WIND

RUN WITH THE PACK
THE GOOD OLD DAYS
THE PROS AND CONS
TWO TWOS ARE FOUR

3 . 4 . 4 . 3

CRY ONES EYES OUT
GET ONES FEET WET

3 . 4 . 5 . 2

DIG ONES HEELS IN
GET ONES HANDS ON
PIN ONES FAITH ON
PIN ONES HOPES ON
PUT ONES SPOKE IN
PUT YOUR HANDS UP

3 . 4 . 7

AIR ONES OPINION
AIR VICE-MARSHAL
AIR-RAID SHELTER
AIR-RAID WARNING
BID GOOD EVENING
BID GOOD MORNING
BIG GAME HUNTING
FOR GOOD MEASURE
GET INTO TROUBLE
GET ONES DESERTS
LET DOWN LIGHTLY
NEW YORK YANKEES
NON-FAST COLOURS
OLD BOYS REUNION
OLD-TIME DANCING
ONE FINE MORNING
ROW OVER NOTHING
RUN INTO TROUBLE
SAY GOOD EVENING
SAY GOOD MORNING
SAY ONES PRAYERS
SEE WHAT HAPPENS
SIR JOHN GIELGUD
THE BEST CIRCLES
THE BODY POLITIC
THE FOUR SEASONS
THE STAR CHAMBER
THE TIME MACHINE
TRY ONES HARDEST
WET ONES WHISTLE

3 . 5 . 2 : 4

ALL HANDS ON DECK
NEW LEASE OF LIFE
THE AKOND OF SWAT
THE CRACK OF DAWN
THE FIRST OF MANY
THE FLESH IS WEAK
THE THIEF OF TIME

THE WORLD OF GOOD
THE WORST IS OVER
WIN, PLACE OR SHOW

3 , 5 , 3 , 3

MAD ABOUT THE BOY
NEW LAMPS FOR OLD
THE GRAND OLD MAN
TWO FIVES ARE TEN

3 , 5 , 6

ALL-ROUND PLAYER
CUP FINAL TICKET
FAR-FLUNG EMPIRE
FUR-LINED GLOVES
HOT-WATER BOTTLE
HOT-WATER SUPPLY
ICE-CREAM CORNET
ICE-CREAM SUNDAE
ILL-TIMED REMARK
NEW WORLD RECORD
ONE-ARMED BANDIT
PRE-NATAL CLINIC
PUT UNDER ARREST
RUN RINGS AROUND
SEA-GOING VESSEL
SIR HENRY IRVING
SIR ISAAC NEWTON
THE ARMED FORCES
THE BLACK FOREST
THE BLACK PRINCE
THE CROWN JEWELS
THE FIRST CUCKOO
THE FIRST PERSON
THE GREAT DIVIDE
THE GREAT GATSBY
THE GREAT PLAGUE
THE LORDS PRAYER
THE SEVEN DWARFS
THE THIRD PERSON
THE WATER BABIES

3 , 6 , 5

CUT-THROAT RAZOR
GUY FAWKES NIGHT
HOB-NAILED BOOTS
ILL-GOTTEN GAINS
LET THINGS SLIDE
MAN-EATING SHARK
MAN-EATING TIGER
NON-SAFETY MATCH
OLD MOTHER RILEY
PUT THINGS RIGHT
SET THINGS RIGHT
SIR ADRIAN BOULT
SIR EDWARD ELGAR
SIR WALTER SCOTT
THE BEATEN TRACK

THE COMMON TOUCH
THE POLICE FORCE
TWO-HANDED SWORD
WIN SECOND PRIZE

3 , 7 , 4

BED-SITTING ROOM
FOR HEAVENS SAKE!
NEW-FANGLED IDEA
NOT ANOTHER WORD
OLD PEOPLES HOME
SEE JUSTICE DONE
SIR ROWLAND HILL
SIX WICKETS DOWN
THE EMERALD ISLE
THE FORSYTE SAGA
THE HIGHWAY CODE
THE MISSING LINK
THE SHINING HOUR
THE WINTERS TALE
THE WRITTEN WORD
TWO WICKETS DOWN

3 , 8 , 3

PRE-CAMBRIAN AGE
THE FAITHFUL FEW

3 , 11

ACT ACCORDINGLY
ACT IMMEDIATELY
ANY SUGGESTIONS?
ASK FORGIVENESS
AUF WIEDERSEHEN
BAD HANDWRITING
BEG FORGIVENESS
BOA CONSTRICTOR
GUN EMPLACEMENT
HIP MEASUREMENT
LAW ENFORCEMENT
LEG MEASUREMENT
LOW TEMPERATURE
NIL DESPERANDUM
ONE TEASPOONFUL
RAY ILLINGWORTH
SIX CENTIMETRES
TEN CENTIMETRES
THE CRUCIFIXION
THE DARDANELLES
THE FLINTSTONES
THE INQUISITION
THE NETHERLANDS
THE PHILLIPINES
THE PLANETARIUM
THE REFORMATION
THE RENAISSANCE
THE RESTORATION
THE UNDERGROUND
THE UNDERSIGNED

TWO CENTIMETRES

4 , 1 , 3 , 3 , 3

GIVE A MAN HIS DUE

4 , 1 , 3 , 4 , 2

TAKE A TIP FROM ME

4 , 1 , 3 , 6

MAKE A BIG SPLASH

4 , 1 , 4 , 2 , 3

HAVE A BITE TO EAT

4 , 1 , 4 , 3 , 2

MAKE A BOLT FOR IT
MAKE A DASH FOR IT

4 , 1 , 4 , 5

FLOG A DEAD HORSE
HAVE A GOOD NIGHT
HAVE A WHIP-ROUND
KEEP A GOOD TABLE
MAKE A GOOD START
RIDE A COCK-HORSE
ROCK 'N' ROLL MUSIC
TELL A GOOD STORY
TELL A TALL STORY
WITH A GOOD GRACE

4 , 1 , 5 , 2 , 2

MAKE A NIGHT OF IT
MAKE A POINT OF IT

4 , 1 , 5 , 4

DEAL A DEATH BLOW
HALF A DOZEN EGGS
HAVE A ROUGH TIME
KEEP A CLEAR HEAD
KEEP A TIGHT REIN
MAKE A LOCAL CALL
MAKE A WRONG MOVE
NINE O CLOCK NEWS
TAKE A WRONG TURN

4 , 1 , 6 , 3

INTO A COCKED HAT

4 , 1 , 9

FIRE A BROADSIDE
HALF A KILOMETRE
HALF A SOVEREIGN
HAVE A NIGHTMARE
MAKE A BEGINNING
MAKE A COMPLAINT
MAKE A DISCOVERY
MAKE A STATEMENT
ROLL A CIGARETTE
SEND A MESSENGER
WITH A BARGEPOLE
WITH A VENGEANCE

4 , 2 , 1 , 3 , 4

PICK UP A FEW TIPS

4 , 2 , 1 , 4 , 3

COME TO A DEAD END

4 , 2 , 1 , 7

FLAT AS A PANCAKE
GIRL IN A MILLION
GIVE IT A THOUGHT
HEIR TO A FORTUNE
LIVE TO A HUNDRED
MAKE UP A QUARREL
TALK IN A WHISPER
VAIN AS A PEACOCK
WIND UP A COMPANY

4 , 2 , 2 , 6

TAKE UP AN OPTION

4 , 2 , 3 , 3 , 2

COME UP AND SEE ME

4 , 2 , 3 , 5

BEST OF THE BUNCH
BOOK OF THE MONTH
BURN AT THE STAKE
CAST TO THE WINDS
COIN OF THE REALM
COME ON THE SCENE
COME TO THE FRONT
COME TO THE POINT
DEAD TO THE WORLD
DEAR AT THE PRICE
DIEU ET MON DROIT
DOWN IN THE DUMPS
DOWN IN THE MOUTH
DOWN IN THE WORLD
DROP IN THE OCEAN
DUEL TO THE DEATH

ENDS	OF	THE	EARTH
FACE	OF	THE	EARTH
FACE	OF	THE	GLOBE
FOAM	AT	THE	MOUTH
FOOT	OF	THE	TABLE
GIVE	IT	THE	WORKS
GIVE	UP	THE	BOOZE
GIVE	UP	THE	GHOST
GOAL	OF	THE	MONTH
GONE	BY	THE	BOARD
HEAD	OF	THE	HOUSE
HEAD	OF	THE	TABLE
HOME	ON	THE	RANGE
KEEP	TO	THE	POINT
KEEP	TO	THE	RIGHT
KEEP	TO	THE	RULES
LADY	OF	THE	HOUSE
LADY	OF	THE	NIGHT
LAST	IN	THE	QUEUE
LEAD	TO	THE	ALTAR
LEFT	IN	THE	LURCH
LEFT	ON	THE	SHELF
LINK	IN	THE	CHAIN
LONG	IN	THE	TOOTH
LOOK	IN	THE	GLASS
LOOK	IN	THE	MOUTH
LORD	OF	THE	FLIES
LORD	OF	THE	ISLES
LORD	OF	THE	MANOR
LORD	OF	THE	RINGS
LOST	TO	THE	WORLD
LUCK	OF	THE	DEVIL
LUCK	OF	THE	IRISH
MELT	IN	THE	MOUTH
MILL	ON	THE	FLOSS
MORE	TO	THE	POINT
NEWS	OF	THE	WORLD
PICK	OF	THE	BUNCH
PILE	ON	THE	AGONY
PLAY	TO	THE	CROWD
RAKE	IN	THE	MONEY
ROOF	OF	THE	MOUTH
ROOF	OF	THE	WORLD
SALT	OF	THE	EARTH
SCUM	OF	THE	EARTH
SEAT	IN	THE	HOUSE
SEAT	IN	THE	LORDS
SEAT	ON	THE	BOARD
SELL	UP	THE	RIVER
SIGN	OF	THE	CROSS
SIGN	OF	THE	TIMES
SINS	OF	THE	FLESH
SOLD	UP	THE	RIVER
STEP	ON	THE	JUICE
TAKE	TO	THE	HILLS
TAKE	TO	THE	WATER
TAKE	TO	THE	WOODS
TAKE	UP	THE	SLACK
TALK	OF	THE	DEVIL
TURN	OF	THE	SCREW
TURN	ON	THE	LIGHT

TURN	ON	THE	POWER
TURN	TO	THE	RIGHT
VEER	TO	THE	RIGHT
WALK	ON	THE	WATER
WARD	OF	THE	COURT
WARS	OF	THE	ROSES
WEAK	AT	THE	KNEES
WHAT	DO	YOU	THINK?
WHAT	IN	THE	WORLD?

4, 2, 4, 2, 2

TELL IT LIKE IT IS

4, 2, 4, 4

BALL	OF	ONES	FOOT
CAPE	OF	GOOD	HOPE
DOWN	ON	ONES	LUCK
EASY	IN	ONES	MIND
FAIL	IN	ONES	DUTY
FALL	ON	DEAF	EARS
FALL	ON	ONES	FEET
FLAT	ON	ONES	BACK
FLAT	ON	ONES	FACE
GAME	OF	ONES	LIFE
GIVE	UP	ONES	SEAT
GOOD	AS	ONES	WORD
HAVE	IT	BOTH	WAYS
HOLD	UP	ONES	HEAD
LAND	ON	ONES	FEET
LEND	ME	YOUR	EARS
LIFT	UP	ONES	HEAD
LIVE	ON	ONES	WITS
LOVE	OF	ONES	LIFE
MADE	IN	HONG	KONG
MAKE	UP	ONES	MIND
MISS	AN	OPEN	GOAL
OVER	MY	DEAD	BODY
PALM	OF	ONES	HAND
PATÉ	DE	FOIE	GRAS
PREY	ON	ONES	MIND
REST	ON	ONES	OARS
RING	IN	ONES	EARS
RISE	TO	ONES	FEET
STAY-AT-HOME			TYPE
TAKE	IN	GOOD	PART
TAKE	IT	FROM	HERE
THIS	IS	YOUR	LIFE
TIME	OF	ONES	LIFE
TOAD	OF	TOAD	HALL
TURN	ON	ONES	HEEL
TURN	UP	ONES	NOSE
WEAK	ON	ONES	PINS
WITH	AN	IRON	HAND

4, 2, 5, 3

PLAY IT AGAIN, SAM

4, 2, 8

ARMS OF MORPHEUS
AWAY ON BUSINESS
BAND OF HOODLUMS
BAND OF PILGRIMS
BAND OF SOLDIERS
BANK OF SCOTLAND
BILL OF EXCHANGE
BIRD OF PARADISE
BOOK OF PROVERBS
BOWL OF CHERRIES
CALL IN QUESTION
CASH ON DELIVERY
DEED OF COVENANT
DOSE OF MEDICINE
DUKE OF MONMOUTH
EASE OF HANDLING
FAIR TO MIDDLING
FAIR TO MODERATE
FEAT OF STRENGTH
FIVE OF DIAMONDS
FLOW OF REPARTEE
FOUR OF DIAMONDS
FREE OF INTEREST
FULL OF INCIDENT
FULL OF MISCHIEF
FULL OF VITALITY
FULL TO BURSTING
FULL TO CAPACITY
GAIN IN STRENGTH
GAME OF DRAUGHTS
GAME OF FOOTBALL
GAME OF SKITTLES
GIVE AN AUDIENCE
GIVE UP DRINKING
GROW UP TOGETHER
HARD TO DESCRIBE
HAVE NO SCRUPLES
HIVE OF ACTIVITY
HIVE OF INDUSTRY
HOLD AN ELECTION
HOLD IN ABEYANCE
HOLD IN CONTEMPT
HOLD IN SUSPENSE
HOUR OF DECISION
JACK OF DIAMONDS
JOIN IN MARRIAGE
KEEP IN SUSPENSE
KING OF DIAMONDS
KNOW BY INSTINCT
LACK OF EVIDENCE
LACK OF INTEREST
LACK OF JUDGMENT
LACK OF PRACTICE
LACK OF STRENGTH
LACK OF TRAINING
LINE OF APPROACH
LINE OF BUSINESS
LOAD OF COBBLERS
LORD OF CREATION

LOSS OF INTEREST
LOSS OF STRENGTH
LOVE OF PLEASURE
MAKE AN ENTRANCE
MAKE AN ESTIMATE
MAKE NO PROGRESS
MILK OF MAGNESIA
MOVE TO LAUGHTER
MUCH IN EVIDENCE
NINE OF DIAMONDS
OPEN TO ARGUMENT
OPEN TO QUESTION
PAIR OF BREECHES
PAIR OF CALIPERS
PAIR OF CRUTCHES
PAIR OF SCISSORS
PAIR OF SLIPPERS
PAIR OF TROUSERS
PAIR OF TWEEZERS
PEAL OF LAUGHTER
PLAN OF CAMPAIGN
PLAY AT SOLDIERS
RATE OF EXCHANGE
RATE OF INTEREST
RATE OF PROGRESS
RICH IN VITAMINS
ROAR OF LAUGHTER
SACK OF POTATOES
SEAL OF APPROVAL
SEAT OF LEARNING
SEND TO COVENTRY
SENT TO COVENTRY
SHOW OF STRENGTH
SHOW OF SYMPATHY
SIGN OF STRENGTH
SIGN OF WEAKNESS
TAKE AN INTEREST
TAKE BY SURPRISE
TAKE IN MARRIAGE
TEST OF PATIENCE
TEST OF STRENGTH
WANT OF PRACTICE
WAVE OF VIOLENCE
WORK IN PROGRESS
WORK TO SCHEDULE

4, 3, 1, 6

CALL FOR A REPORT
GIVE ONE A ROCKET
GONE FOR A BURTON
MARK OUT A COURSE
TAKE OUT A POLICY
WORK FOR A LIVING

4, 3, 2, 5

DEAR SIR OR MADAM
DROP OFF TO SLEEP
FISH OUT OF WATER
FROM BAD TO WORSE

GOOD - BYE	MR .	CHIPS
HARD NUT	TO	CRACK
JUST OUT	OF	REACH
KEEP OUT	OF	SIGHT
PULL OUT	OF	SHAPE
RULE OUT	OF	ORDER
WITH ALL	MY	HEART

4 . 3 . 3 . 2 . 2

HEAR THE END OF IT

4 . 3 . 3 . 4

BLOW HOT AND COLD
BLOW THE MAN DOWN
GIVE ONE HIS HEAD
GIVE ONE THE BIRD
GIVE ONE THE PUSH
GIVE ONE THE SLIP
GOOD FOR THE MIND
GOOD FOR THE SOUL
HAVE ONE TOO MANY
HOLD OUT FOR MORE
HOPE FOR THE BEST
JOBS FOR THE BOYS
JOIN THE RAT - RACE
LIVE AND LET LIVE
MADE FOR THE PART
MAKE FOR THE DOOR
SHOW ONE THE DOOR
SHOW THE RED CARD
TURN OFF THE HEAT

4 . 3 . 4 . 3

GIVE THE GLAD EYE
KEEP THE COLD OUT
PULL THE CORK OUT
PUSH THE BOAT OUT
READ THE RIOT ACT
TAKE THE EDGE OFF
TAKE THE WEEK OFF
WASH AND BLOW - DRY

4 . 3 . 5 . 2

READ ALL ABOUT IT
WASH AND BRUSH - UP

4 . 3 . 7

BLOW THE EXPENSE
BLOW THE WHISTLE
BURY THE HATCHET
COPS AND ROBBERS
DEEP SEA FISHING
DOWN THE CHIMNEY
DRAW THE CURTAIN
DROP THE SUBJECT
EACH FOR HIMSELF

FACT AND FICTION
FAME AND FORTUNE
FAST AND FURIOUS
FEED THE ANIMALS
FEEL THE BENEFIT
FEEL THE DRAUGHT
FEND FOR ONESELF
FILL THE VACANCY
FLEE THE COUNTRY
FOOD FOR THOUGHT
GOOD FOR NOTHING
HALF - DAY HOLIDAY
HANG THE EXPENSE
HEAD FOR FIGURES
HEAD FOR HEIGHTS
HELL FOR LEATHER
HELP ONE ANOTHER
HUNT THE SLIPPER
HUNT THE THIMBLE
INTO THE BARGAIN
JOHN THE BAPTIST
JUDE THE OBSCURE
JULY THE SEVENTH
JULY THE TWELFTH
JUNE THE SEVENTH
JUNE THE TWELFTH
KEEP - FIT FANATIC
KING AND COUNTRY
KNOW FOR CERTAIN
LATH AND PLASTER
LEAD THE FASHION
LOOK FOR TROUBLE
MAKE THE RUNNING
MODS AND ROCKERS
NAME AND ADDRESS
NEAR THE KNUCKLE
NUTS AND RAISINS
ONLY TOO PLEASED
OPEN THE BATTING
OPEN THE BIDDING
OPEN THE INNINGS
OPEN - AIR CONCERT
OPEN - AIR MEETING
OPEN - AIR SERVICE
OPEN - AIR THEATRE
OVER THE COUNTER
OVER THE RAINBOW
PAST AND PRESENT
PINS AND NEEDLES
PITT THE YOUNGER
PLAY FOR ENGLAND
PLAY THE VILLAIN
POST - WAR CREDITS
PULL THE STRINGS
PULL THE TRIGGER
RAGS AND TATTERS
READ THE MINUTES
REAP THE BENEFIT
REAP THE HARVEST
RING THE CHANGES
ROOM FOR DISPUTE

SALT AND VINEGAR
SEND ONE PACKING
SEND THE MESSAGE
SHOT-GUN WEDDING
SPIT AND SAWDUST
SWIM THE CHANNEL
TAKE FOR GRANTED
TAKE THE AVERAGE
TAKE THE BISCUIT
TAKE THE LIBERTY
TAKE THE TROUBLE
TOIL AND TROUBLE
TOUR THE COUNTRY
TOWN AND COUNTRY
WANT FOR NOTHING
WHAT THE DICKENS?
WIND AND WEATHER
WITH DUE RESPECT
WITH THE CURRENT

4, 4, 1, 5

MORE THAN A MATCH
SINK LIKE A STONE
WAKE WITH A START
WALK INTO A PUNCH
WORK LIKE A CHARM
WORK LIKE A HORSE
WORK LIKE A SLAVE

4, 4, 2, 1, 3

LIKE PEAS IN A POD

4, 4, 2, 4

BOYS WILL BE BOYS
COME FACE TO FACE
FROM EAST TO WEST
FROM HAND TO HAND
FROM HEAD TO FOOT
FROM HEAD TO TAIL
FROM SIDE TO SIDE
FROM TIME TO TIME
FROM YEAR TO YEAR
HELL HATH NO FURY
KEEP WELL IN HAND
KNOW WHEN TO STOP
WALK HAND IN HAND
WILD SIDE OF LIFE

4, 4, 3, 3

FIVE TWOS ARE TEN
HAVE ONES OWN WAY
HUNT HIGH AND LOW
LEFT HIGH AND DRY
LOOK HIGH AND LOW
MAKE LOVE NOT WAR
TAKE ONES HAT OFF
TURN DOWN THE GAS

TURN TAIL AND RUN
WAIT TILL THE END

4, 4, 4, 2

EASY COME, EASY GO
HOLD ONES HEAD UP
KEEP ONES CHIN UP
KEEP ONES HAIR ON
KEEP ONES HAND IN
KEEP YOUR HAIR ON!
MAKE ONES MIND UP
POKE ONES NOSE IN
TURN ONES NOSE UP

4, 4, 6

ALAS POOR YORICK
BACK-SEAT DRIVER
BARE-BACK RIDING
BEAT ONES BRAINS
BEAT ONES BREAST
BITE ONES TONGUE
BURY ONES TALENT
CLAP INTO PRISON
COME FROM BEHIND
COME FULL CIRCLE
COME INTO FAVOUR
CURB ONES TEMPER
DEAD MANS HANDLE
DING-DONG BATTLE
DUTY-FREE DRINKS
EARN ONES LIVING
FALL INTO DISUSE
FIVE PAST ELEVEN
FIVE PAST TWELVE
FREE FROM DANGER
GIVE ONES ASSENT
GIVE ONES NOTICE
GLOW WITH HEALTH
GOOD TIME-KEEPER
HAVE ONES DOUBTS
HOLD ONES BREATH
HOLD ONES HORSES
HOLD ONES TONGUE
HYDE PARK CORNER
JEAN-PAUL SARTRE
JUST THIS MOMENT
KEEP ONES TEMPER
KNOW ONES ONIONS
LICK ONES WOUNDS
LONG JOHN SILVER
LONG-LOST FRIEND
LONG-TERM POLICY
LOSE ONES MEMORY
LOSE ONES REASON
LOSE ONES TEMPER
LOSE ONES TONGUE
MANS BEST FRIEND
MIND OVER MATTER
MISS ONES CHANCE
MORE THAN ENOUGH

MOVE DOWN-MARKET
NEWS FROM ABROAD
NINE DAYS WONDER
NINE MENS MORRIS
OPEN-CAST MINING
OPEN-DOOR POLICY
PALE BLUE YONDER
PLOT ONES COURSE
PULL ONES WEIGHT
REAR-VIEW MIRROR
RIDE SIDE-SADDLE
RUSH ONES FENCES
RUSH-HOUR TRAVEL
SAVE ONES BREATH
SHOW ONES TICKET
SIGH WITH RELIEF
SLIP ONES MEMORY
STAY ONES GROUND
STIR ONES STUMPS
TAKE ONES CHANCE
TAKE ONES CHOICE
TAKE YOUR CHOICE
VERY BEST WISHES
VERY MUCH INDEED
VIEW WITH FAVOUR
WALK INTO DANGER
WELL-KEPT SECRET
WELL-WORN PHRASE
WILD BILL HICKOK
WORK ONES TICKET

4, 5, 2, 3

COLD LIGHT OF DAY

4, 5, 5

BLOW SMOKE-RINGS
COME ROUND AGAIN
DAME EDITH EVANS
DRAW FIRST BLOOD
FORD MADOX BROWN
FULL SPEED AHEAD
FULL STEAM AHEAD
FULL-SCALE MODEL
HAVE FORTY WINKS
HEAD ABOVE WATER
HIGH COURT JUDGE
HIGH-LEVEL TALKS
JOHN LOGIE BAIRD
LATE NIGHT FINAL
LONG WHITE BEARD
LOOK RIGHT AGAIN
MALE VOICE CHOIR
TAKE FIRST PRIZE
TEST MATCH SCORE
TURN RIGHT ROUND
WELL WORTH WHILE
WILD GOOSE CHASE

4, 6, 4

DOWN MEMORY LANE
FIVE-BARRED GATE
FIVE-COURSE MEAL
FIVE-DOLLAR BILL
FOOD,LOVELY FOOD
FOUR-COURSE MEAL
FOUR-LETTER WORD
FOUR-MINUTE MILE
GRUB-STREET HACK
HIGH-OCTANE FUEL
JOHN BROWNS BODY
JOHN STUART MILL
LORD MAYORS SHOW
MAKE DOUBLY SURE
MOCK TURTLE SOUP
PLAY INJURY TIME
TAKE THINGS EASY
TURN UPSIDE DOWN
WELL-EARNED REST
WITH EFFECT FROM

4, 7, 3

BEST DRESSED MAN
ROAD TRAFFIC ACT
TAKE ONESELF OFF
WELL-DRESSED MAN

4, 8, 2

GOOD GRACIOUS ME!
KEEP STRAIGHT ON

4, 10

ARMY MANOEUVRES
BARE ESSENTIALS
BEAT GENERATION
BEST ENDEAVOURS
BEST INTENTIONS
BOLD EXPERIMENT
BOON COMPANIONS
CALM REFLECTION
CAMP COMMANDANT
CAST ASPERSIONS
CLUB MEMBERSHIP
COIN COLLECTING
DARK COMPLEXION
DEEP DEPRESSION
DROP EVERYTHING
ELLA FITZGERALD
EVIL REPUTATION
FAIR COMPARISON
FAIR COMPLEXION
FALL DOWNSTAIRS
FIRE PROTECTION
FIRM COMMITMENT
FIRM CONVICTION

FIRM	FOUNDATION	LIVE	AMMUNITION
FIRM	GOVERNMENT	LONG	ENGAGEMENT
FIRM	OPPOSITION	LORD	CARRINGTON
FIVE	KILOMETRES	LORD	CHANCELLOR
FLAG	LIEUTENANT	LORD	PALMERSTON
FOOD	PRODUCTION	LORD	RUTHERFORD
FORT	LAUDERDALE	LOSE	CONFIDENCE
FOUR	KILOMETRES	LOSE	EVERYTHING
FREE	ADMITTANCE	LOST	GENERATION
FREE	ENTERPRISE	MAIN	ATTRACTION
FULL	COMPLEMENT	MAIN	INGREDIENT
FULL	EMPLOYMENT	MAKE	DELIVERIES
FULL	MEMBERSHIP	MAKE	PROVISIONS
FULL	SETTLEMENT	MAKE	SACRIFICES
GAIN	ADMITTANCE	MASS	PRODUCTION
GAIN	CONFIDENCE	MOST	HONOURABLE
GAIN	EXPERIENCE	NEAR	NEIGHBOURS
GAIN	POSSESSION	NEXT	GENERATION
GIVE	ASSISTANCE	NINE	KILOMETRES
GIVE	ASSURANCES	OPEN	DISCUSSION
GIVE	GENEROUSLY	OPEN	PARLIAMENT
GIVE	PERMISSION	OPEN	UNIVERSITY
GOOD	BACKGROUND	PAST	EXPERIENCE
GOOD	COMPANIONS	PAST	PARTICIPLE
GOOD	CONSCIENCE	PLAY	GOOSEBERRY
GOOD	DISCIPLINE	PLEA	BARGAINING
GOOD	INTENTIONS	POOR	VISIBILITY
GOOD	INVESTMENT	POOR	VOCABULARY
GOOD	MANAGEMENT	PURE	CONJECTURE
GOOD	NEIGHBOURS	RAPT	EXPRESSION
GOOD	REPUTATION	RARE	ATMOSPHERE
GOOD	TIMEKEEPER	RARE	OCCURRENCE
GOOD	UPBRINGING	RICH	VOCABULARY
GOOD	VISIBILITY	RISK	EVERYTHING
GROW	VEGETABLES	RUMP	PARLIAMENT
HARD	TASKMASTER	SHOW	COMPASSION
HAVE	COMPASSION	SHOW	MODERATION
HAVE	CONFIDENCE	SHOW	REPENTANCE
HAVE	MISGIVINGS	SOFT	FURNISHING
HIGH	CASUALTIES	SOLE	POSSESSION
HIGH	COMMISSION	SOLE	PROPRIETOR
HIGH	PERCENTAGE	SORE	AFFLICTION
HOLD	EVERYTHING	STAR	ATTRACTION
HOME	DEPARTMENT	TAKE	POSSESSION
IDLE	COMPLIMENT	TAKE	PRECEDENCE
IGOR	STRAVINSKY	TAKE	PUNISHMENT
JOAN	SUTHERLAND	TELL	EVERYTHING
JOHN	BARLEYCORN	TIME	IMMEMORIAL
JOHN	GALSWORTHY	TOWN	COUNCILLOR
JOHN	STONEHOUSE	TRUE	CONFESSION
LADY	CHATTERLEY	TRUE	REPENTANCE
LAKE	WINDERMERE	TURF	ACCOUNTANT
LAST	APPEARANCE	UPON	REFLECTION
LAST	COLLECTION	VAST	DIFFERENCE
LAST	GENERATION	VAST	EXPERIENCE
LAST	INSTALMENT	WARM	FRIENDSHIP
LEFT	SPEECHLESS	WELL	ACQUAINTED
LEFT	UNFINISHED	WIDE	VOCABULARY
LEND	ASSISTANCE	WILD	ACCUSATION
LIFE	EXPECTANCY	WILD	EXCITEMENT
LIFE	MEMBERSHIP	WIND	INSTRUMENT

277

WITH PERMISSION	BRING UP THE REAR
YALE UNIVERSITY	BROAD IN THE BEAM
YOUR EXCELLENCY	CHEER TO THE ECHO
	CLOSE TO THE WIND
5, 1, 3, 2, 3	CRACK OF THE WHIP
	CREST OF THE WAVE
WORTH A BOB OR TWO	CROWN OF THE HEAD
	DRIVE TO THE WALL
5, 1, 3, 5	DWELL ON THE PAST
	FACTS OF THE CASE
CARRY A BIG STICK	FIRST ON THE LIST
	GENIE OF THE LAMP
5, 1, 5, 3	GOING TO THE DOGS
	GRIST TO THE MILL
CARRY A TORCH FOR	GROPE IN THE DARK
SCORE A BULLS EYE	HORSE OF THE YEAR
	HOUSE OF THE LORD
5, 1, 8	IRONS IN THE FIRE
	KNOCK AT THE DOOR
BREAK A CONTRACT	KNOCK ON THE DOOR
CAUSE A NUISANCE	KNOCK ON THE HEAD
CAUSE A STOPPAGE	LEAVE AT THE POST
CLIMB A MOUNTAIN	LEAVE IN THE DARK
GIVEN A REPRIEVE	MONEY IN THE BANK
PAINT A PORTRAIT	NIGHT ON THE TOWN
RAISE A QUESTION	ORDER OF THE BATH
REACH A DECISION	ORDER OF THE BOOT
REPAY A MORTGAGE	PEACE IN OUR TIME
SERVE A SENTENCE	PENNY IN THE SLOT
STAGE A COMEBACK	PUNCH ON THE NOSE
UNDER A HANDICAP	QUEER IN THE HEAD
	QUICK ON THE DRAW
5, 2, 1, 3, 3	RELIC OF THE PAST
	RULES OF THE GAME
CLEAN AS A NEW PIN	SHAKE OF THE HEAD
STORM IN A TEA-CUP	SHAKE UP AND DOWN
	SLEEP OF THE JUST
5, 2, 1, 6	SMALL OF THE BACK
	STAND IN THE DOCK
BRING IN A PROFIT	STARE IN THE FACE
BURNT TO A CINDER	STING IN THE TAIL
DIARY OF A NOBODY	STRAW IN THE WIND
FIGHT TO A FINISH	TAXED TO THE HILT
GHOST OF A CHANCE	TEETH OF THE WIND
SHARP AS A NEEDLE	THING OF THE PAST
STICK UP A NOTICE	THORN IN THE SIDE
STUCK IN A GROOVE	THROW OF THE DICE
THINK OF A NUMBER	THROW TO THE DOGS
	TOAST OF THE TOWN
5, 2, 2, 5	WRATH OF THE GODS
SWIFT AS AN ARROW	**5, 2, 4, 3**
5, 2, 3, 4	APPLE OF ONES EYE
	CLASS OF ONES OWN
BABES IN THE WOOD	HOUSE OF ONES OWN
BACKS TO THE WALL	PLACE OF ONES OWN
BELLE OF THE BALL	THROW IN ONES LOT
BLACK IN THE FACE	WORLD OF ONES OWN
BRING TO THE BOIL	
BRING TO THE FORE	

5, 2, 5, 2

QUICK TO CATCH ON

5, 2, 7

APPLE OF DISCORD
BABES IN TOYLAND
BADGE OF COURAGE
BLACK AS THUNDER
BOARD OF CONTROL
BOARD OF ENQUIRY
BRING TO ACCOUNT
BRING TO JUSTICE
BROOK NO REFUSAL
BUNCH OF BANANAS
BUNCH OF FLOWERS
CARRY IT THROUGH
CHAIN OF COMMAND
CHAIN OF THOUGHT
CHEST OF DRAWERS
CHILD OF FORTUNE
CLASH OF COLOURS
CLASH OF CYMBALS
CLEAR AS CRYSTAL
COURT OF ASSIZES
COURT OF JUSTICE
CRASH OF THUNDER
CRIME OF PASSION
CRUMB OF COMFORT
DEATH BY BURNING
DEATH BY HANGING
DEPTH OF FEELING
DREGS OF SOCIETY
DRIVE TO DESPAIR
EMPTY OF MEANING
ENEMY OF FREEDOM
ENEMY OF MANKIND
FEAST OF STEPHEN
FIFTH OF JANUARY
FIFTH OF OCTOBER
FIRST OF JANUARY
FIRST OF OCTOBER
FLOCK OF PIGEONS
FORCE OF GRAVITY
GOODS IN TRANSIT
GRAIN OF COMFORT
GROUP OF ISLANDS
HEART OF ENGLAND
HOUSE OF COMMONS
HOUSE OF HANOVER
HOUSE OF WINDSOR
LEAVE NO ADDRESS
LEAVE OF ABSENCE
MEANS OF SUPPORT
MONTH OF SUNDAYS
NINTH OF JANUARY
NINTH OF OCTOBER
NORTH OF ENGLAND
OFFER AN OPINION
ORDER IN ADVANCE
PIECE OF HISTORY

PLACE IN HISTORY
PLACE OF WORSHIP
PLUCK UP COURAGE
POINT OF CONTACT
PROOF OF POSTING
QUEEN OF ENGLAND
QUICK AS THOUGHT
RAISE AN EYEBROW
ROSES OF PICARDY
ROUND IN CIRCLES
RULES OF CRICKET
SCALE OF CHARGES
SENSE OF BALANCE
SENSE OF DECENCY
SENSE OF HEARING
SENSE OF HISTORY
SENSE OF LOYALTY
SENSE OF PURPOSE
SIXTH OF JANUARY
SIXTH OF OCTOBER
SLAVE TO FASHION
SMELL OF BURNING
SOUTH OF ENGLAND
SPARE NO EXPENSE
SPEAK IN RIDDLES
SPEED OF THOUGHT
SPRAY OF FLOWERS
SPRIG OF HEATHER
STATE OF AFFAIRS
STATE OF DENMARK
STICK AT NOTHING
STICK OF RHUBARB
SWARM OF INSECTS
SWARM OF LOCUSTS
SWORN TO SECRECY
TENTH OF JANUARY
TENTH OF OCTOBER
THICK AS THIEVES
THIEF OF BAGHDAD
THIRD OF JANUARY
THIRD OF OCTOBER
TOKEN OF RESPECT
TOUGH AS LEATHER
TRAIN OF THOUGHT
WALLS OF JERICHO
WHEEL OF FORTUNE
WORLD OF FASHION

5, 3, 1, 5

DYING FOR A DRINK
PAUSE FOR A WHILE
SPOIL FOR A FIGHT
TOOTH FOR A TOOTH

5, 3, 2, 1, 3

THREE MEN IN A TUB

5 , 3 , 2 , 4

EVERY BIT AS GOOD
NASTY BIT OF WORK
PRIME CUT OF MEAT
SPEAK OUT OF TURN

5 , 3 , 3 , 3

BLOCK OUT THE SUN
PENNY FOR THE GUY
POINT OUT THE WAY
REACH FOR THE SKY
ROSES ALL THE WAY

5 , 3 , 6

ABOVE THE GROUND
AFTER THE DELUGE
APPLY THE BRAKES
APRIL THE EIGHTH
APRIL THE FOURTH
APRIL THE SECOND
BELOW THE GROUND
BLOCK AND TACKLE
BOUND AND GAGGED
BREAD AND BUTTER
BREAD AND CHEESE
BREAK NEW GROUND
BREAK THE RECORD
BREAK THE THREAD
BREAK THE WICKET
BURST THE BUBBLE
CATCH RED-HANDED
CAUSE AND EFFECT
CAUSE FOR REGRET
CHALK AND CHEESE
CHEAP-DAY RETURN
CLAIM THE REWARD
CLAIM THE THRONE
CLEAN THE SILVER
CLEAR THE GROUND
CLEAR THE THROAT
CLIMB THE LADDER
CLOAK AND DAGGER
CLOSE THE WINDOW
CLUBS ARE TRUMPS
COACH AND HORSES
COVER THE GROUND
CROOK THE FINGER
CROSS THE BORDER
CROSS THE STREAM
CROSS THE STREET
CROWN AND ANCHOR
DEBIT AND CREDIT
DRESS FOR DINNER
DUCKS AND DRAKES
ENTER THE CHURCH
FIGHT FOR BREATH
FIRST AND SECOND
GRASP THE NETTLE

GUESS THE ANSWER
HENRY THE EIGHTH
HENRY THE FOURTH
HENRY THE SECOND
HERBS AND SPICES
HOPES AND DREAMS
HORSE AND HOUNDS
JAMES THE SECOND
LEAPS AND BOUNDS
LIVER AND ONIONS
LORDS AND LADIES
MARCH THE EIGHTH
MARCH THE FOURTH
MARCH THE SECOND
MILES PER GALLON
MOUNT THE THRONE
PAUSE FOR BREATH
PAUSE FOR EFFECT
PEACE AND PLENTY
PINCH AND SCRAPE
PLAIN AND SIMPLE
PLEAD NOT GUILTY
PLUMB THE DEPTHS
POINT THE FINGER
PRESS FOR ACTION
PRESS THE BUTTON
READY FOR ACTION
READY FOR BATTLE
RENEW THE ATTACK
RHYME NOR REASON
ROMEO AND JULIET
ROUGH AND TUMBLE
ROUND THE CORNER
ROUND THE HOUSES
ROUND THE WICKET
SEIZE THE CHANCE
SHAKE THE BOTTLE
SHARE THE SPOILS
SHOOT THE RAPIDS
SHORT AND STOCKY
SIXES AND SEVENS
SLUGS AND SNAILS
SOLED AND HEELED
SOLVE THE RIDDLE
SOUTH SEA BUBBLE
SPOIL THE EFFECT
STAND THE STRAIN
STEAK AND KIDNEY
STEAK AND ONIONS
STOCK-CAR RACING
STOKE THE BOILER
STRIP FOR ACTION
SWEEP THE BOARDS
SWORD AND SHIELD
TABLE AND CHAIRS
THATS THE SPIRIT
THATS THE TICKET
THROW THE HAMMER
THROW THE SWITCH
TOUCH THE GROUND
TREAD THE BOARDS

TRIED AND TESTED
TRIED FOR MURDER
TROOP THE COLOUR
UNDER THE BONNET
UNDER THE CARPET
UNDER THE GROUND
UNDER THE HAMMER
USURP THE THRONE
WAIFS AND STRAYS
WATCH THE BIRDIE
WATER THE GARDEN
WATER THE HORSES
WATER THE WICKET
WHATS THE DAMAGE?
WHATS THE MATTER?
WHIGS AND TORIES
WIDEN THE BREACH
WIELD THE WILLOW
WORDS PER MINUTE
WORTH THE BOTHER
WORTH THE EFFORT
YOUNG AND TENDER

5, 4, 1, 4

BREAK INTO A TROT
CHOKE BACK A TEAR
DRINK LIKE A FISH
EIGHT DAYS A WEEK
SERVE WITH A WRIT
SHAKE LIKE A LEAF
SLEEP LIKE A BABY

5, 4, 2, 3

OTHER FISH TO FRY
SAINT JOAN OF ARC
SEVEN AGES OF MAN

5, 4, 5

ABUSE ONES POWER
BLESS THIS HOUSE
BREAK ONES HEART
BREAK-EVEN POINT
BRING GOOD CHEER
BRING INTO BEING
BRUSH ONES TEETH
BURST INTO FLAME
BURST INTO TEARS
CALFS-FOOT JELLY
CATCH ONES DEATH
CLEAN ONES TEETH
CLICK ONES HEELS
CLOSE ONES MOUTH
COUNT ONES MONEY
CRAMP ONES STYLE
CROSS ONES HEART
FIFTY-FIVE PENCE
FIFTY-FOUR PENCE
FIFTY-NINE PENCE

FIRST TIME LUCKY
FIRST TIME ROUND
FIRST-BORN CHILD
FIRST-RATE ACTOR
FLUSH WITH ANGER
FLUSH WITH MONEY
FORTY-FIVE PENCE
FORTY-FOUR PENCE
FORTY-NINE PENCE
FRONT-PAGE STORY
GNASH ONES TEETH
HEAVY WITH SLEEP
IRISH FREE STATE
KNOCK INTO SHAPE
KNOCK DOWN PRICE
LEAVE WELL ALONE
LOWER ONES VOICE
LUNCH-TIME SCORE
MAJOR ROAD AHEAD
MINCE ONES WORDS
MONEY WELL SPENT
PRESS ONES CLAIM
PROVE ONES POINT
PUPPY-DOGS TAILS
QUICK LOOK ROUND
RAISE ONES GLASS
RAISE ONES VOICE
RIGHT FROM WRONG
RIGHT-HAND DRIVE
RIGHT-HAND SCREW
ROUGH-HEWN STONE
ROYAL TANK CORPS
SHAKE LIKE JELLY
SIXTY-FIVE PENCE
SIXTY-FOUR PENCE
SIXTY-NINE PENCE
SMALL-BORE RIFLE
SMALL-TIME CROOK
SPLIT ONES SIDES
STAKE ONES CLAIM
STARE INTO SPACE
STEAL ONES HEART
STILL-LIFE STUDY
STONE-COLD SOBER
STRUT ONES STUFF
SUGAR-PLUM FAIRY
SWELL WITH PRIDE
THESE FOUR WALLS
THIRD TIME LUCKY
THREE-CARD TRICK
UNCLE TOMS CABIN
UNDER ONES THUMB
WASTE GOOD MONEY
WASTE ONES MONEY
WASTE ONES WORDS
WATCH THIS SPACE
WEIGH ONES WORDS
WORTH ONES WHILE
WRING ONES HANDS
YOUNG MANS FANCY

5, 5, 2, 2

FIRST THING TO DO

5, 5, 4

BURST WATER MAIN
FANCY-DRESS BALL
FIRST CLASS MAIL
FIRST CLASS POST
FIRST-CLASS SHOT
FIRST-FLOOR FLAT
GOING GREAT GUNS
GOING, GOING, GONE
GREAT NORTH ROAD
GREAT WHITE HOPE
GREEN CROSS CODE
JOINT-STOCK BANK
NEVER-NEVER LAND
RIGHT ABOUT TURN
RIGHT FIRST TIME
SWEAR UNDER OATH
THIRD-PARTY RISK
THREE BLIND MICE
THREE-PIECE SUIT
THREE-SPEED GEAR
THROW LIGHT UPON
WOMAN ABOUT TOWN
WORTH DOING WELL

5, 6, 3

AFTER-DINNER NAP
CRIME DOESNT PAY
EVERY SECOND DAY
INDIA-RUBBER MAN
PRIZE-GIVING DAY
RHODE ISLAND RED
SAINT DAVIDS DAY
STARK RAVING MAD
THINK THINGS OUT
THREE-BOTTLE MAN
ULTRA-VIOLET RAY
UNDER TWENTY-ONE

5, 7, 2

THINK NOTHING OF
YOURE TELLING ME!

5, 9

ABOVE CRITICISM
ABOVE SUSPICION
AFTER BREAKFAST
AFTER CHRISTMAS
ANNUS MIRABILIS
APPLE CHARLOTTE
ARMED BODYGUARD
AVOID BLOODSHED
BARRY HUMPHRIES

BASIC SUBSTANCE
BASIL DOLIVEIRA
BIJOU RESIDENCE
BLACK STOCKINGS
BLANK CARTRIDGE
BLIND IGNORANCE
BLOND BOMBSHELL
BLOOD POISONING
BLUNT STATEMENT
BOXER REBELLION
BRIEF ENCOUNTER
BRIEF INTERLUDE
BROAD SHOULDERS
BRUTE IGNORANCE
CAUSE CONFUSION
CHEAP EXCURSION
CHIEF CONSTABLE
CHIEF EXECUTIVE
CHIEF INSPECTOR
CHILD ALLOWANCE
CHUCK OVERBOARD
CIVIC RECEPTION
CIVIL LIBERTIES
CLAIM ATTENTION
CLASS CONSCIOUS
CLASS PREJUDICE
CLEAR FAVOURITE
CLEAR STATEMENT
CLOSE ATTENTION
CLOSE ENCOUNTER
CLOSE PROXIMITY
CLOUD FORMATION
COMIC INTERLUDE
COURT PROCEDURE
CRASS IGNORANCE
CRASS STUPIDITY
CREWE ALEXANDRA
CRIME DETECTION
CROSS REFERENCE
DAILY CHRONICLE
DAILY HAPPENING
DAILY NEWSPAPER
DAILY TELEGRAPH
DEREK UNDERWOOD
DEVIL INCARNATE
DIZZY GILLESPIE
DOLLS FURNITURE
DRESS REHEARSAL
DRIVE CAREFULLY
EARLY BREAKFAST
EARLY VICTORIAN
ELDER STATESMAN
ELIZA DOOLITTLE
EMILY DICKINSON
ENEMY TERRITORY
EVERY WEDNESDAY
EXERT AUTHORITY
EXERT INFLUENCE
FAIRY GODMOTHER
FALSE EYELASHES
FALSE MOUSTACHE

ALSE PRETENCES	LIGHT PROGRAMME
ALSE REASONING	LOCAL AUTHORITY
ALSE STATEMENT	LOCAL NEWSPAPER
IELD AMBULANCE	LOFTY AMBITIONS
INAL RECKONING	LORDS SPIRITUAL
IRST DIMENSION	LORDS TAVERNERS
IRST MAGNITUDE	LOUIS ARMSTRONG
IXED ALLOWANCE	LOYAL SUPPORTER
LORA MACDONALD	MADAM BUTTERFLY
LOYD PATTERSON	MAJOR OPERATION
RANK STATEMENT	MERRY CHRISTMAS
RONT ELEVATION	MINOR OPERATION
ULLY CONSCIOUS	MODEL AEROPLANE
ULLY DEVELOPED	MODEL BEHAVIOUR
ULLY FURNISHED	MODEL HOUSEHOLD
UNNY PROGRAMME	MORAL CERTAINTY
RAVE ADMISSION	MORAL CHARACTER
RAVE SITUATION	MORAL COWARDICE
RAVE STATEMENT	MORAL PRINCIPLE
RAVE SUSPICION	MORAL TURPITUDE
REAT INJUSTICE	MUSIC PUBLISHER
REAT SACRIFICE	NEGRO SPIRITUAL
REAT STATESMAN	NEVER SATISFIED
REEN VEGETABLE	NOISE ABATEMENT
ROSS INJUSTICE	NORTH AUSTRALIA
UEST CELEBRITY	NORTH YORKSHIRE
ALLÉ ORCHESTRA	NYLON STOCKINGS
APPY CHILDHOOD	PARTY POLITICAL
APPY CHRISTMAS	PARTY PROGRAMME
ARRY BELAFONTE	PENAL SERVITUDE
ARSH TREATMENT	PETTY GRIEVANCE
EART CONDITION	PITCH OVERBOARD
EAVY ARTILLERY	PLAIN CHOCOLATE
EMEL HEMPSTEAD	PLEAD IGNORANCE
OTEL DETECTIVE	PRICE REDUCTION
OTLY CONTESTED	PRIMA BALLERINA
OUSE DECORATOR	PRIME CONDITION
OUSE DETECTIVE	QUEEN ELIZABETH
OUSE PHYSICIAN	QUEEN GUINEVERE
UMAN ENDEAVOUR	QUEER SITUATION
UMAN RELATIONS	QUITE DIFFERENT
UMAN SACRIFICE	RADIO ANNOUNCER
DEAL COMPANION	RADIO ASTRONOMY
NNER SANCTUARY	RADIO FREQUENCY
RISH WOLFHOUND	RADIO PROGRAMME
AMES CALLAGHAN	RADIO TELEPHONE
OINT LIABILITY	RADIO TELESCOPE
OINT OPERATION	RAPID PROMOTION
OINT OWNERSHIP	REACH AGREEMENT
INGS MESSENGER	RIGHT DIRECTION
NOWN CHARACTER	ROBIN REDBREAST
EARN SHORTHAND	ROCKY COASTLINE
EGAL AUTHORITY	ROCKY MOUNTAINS
EGAL CHICANERY	ROGER BANNISTER
EGAL FORMALITY	ROUGH TREATMENT
EGAL LIABILITY	ROUND SHOULDERS
EGAL OWNERSHIP	ROYAL ARTILLERY
EGAL STATEMENT	ROYAL ENCLOSURE
IGHT ARTILLERY	ROYAL ENGINEERS
IGHT BREAKFAST	ROYAL FUSILIERS
IGHT FANTASTIC	ROYAL HOUSEHOLD

ROYAL RESIDENCE
SAINT AUGUSTINE
SALES PROMOTION
SARAH BERNHARDT
SCOTS FUSILIERS
SHADY CHARACTER
SHARP REJOINDER
SHEER STUPIDITY
SHEET LIGHTNING
SHIPS CARPENTER
SHOCK TREATMENT
SHORT PARAGRAPH
SHORT STATEMENT
SLIDE PROJECTOR
SOUND CHARACTER
SOUND EDUCATION
SOUND PRINCIPLE
SOUND REASONING
SOUND RECORDING
SOUTH AUSTRALIA
SOUTH GLAMORGAN
SOUTH YORKSHIRE
SPACE PROGRAMME
SPACE TRAVELLER
SPENT CARTRIDGE
STAGE CARPENTER
STAGE DIRECTION
STAMP COLLECTOR
STAND CONVICTED
STAND CORRECTED
START SOMETHING
STEEL ENGRAVING
STONY STRATFORD
STORE DETECTIVE
STUDY CAREFULLY
SUSAN HAMPSHIRE
SWEET SUBSTANCE
SWEET SURRENDER
SWORD SWALLOWER
SYBIL THORNDIKE
TEACH LANGUAGES
TENSE SITUATION
THINK CAREFULLY
THIRD DIMENSION
THIRD PROGRAMME
THREE FARTHINGS
THREE SHILLINGS
THREE SYLLABLES
THROW OVERBOARD
TOTAL BLACKNESS
TOTAL IGNORANCE
TREAD UNDERFOOT
UNDER DETENTION
UNDER GUARANTEE
UNDER RESTRAINT
UNDER SUSPICION
UNDER TREATMENT
UNDUE INFLUENCE
USUAL SIGNATURE
VAGUE SUSPICION
VITAL PRINCIPLE

WATCH CAREFULLY
WATCH COMMITTEE
WELSH MOUNTAINS
WHITE CHRISTMAS
WHITE CORPUSCLE
WORLD SITUATION
WREAK VENGEANCE
WRONG DIRECTION
YOUNG PRETENDER
YOUNG SHOULDERS
YOURS SINCERELY

6, 1, 4, 3

COMMIT A FAUX PAS

6, 1, 7

CHOOSE A HUSBAND
CONVEY A MEANING
CREATE A SCANDAL
DEMAND A HEARING
DEMAND A RECOUNT
FOLLOW A CALLING
FOLLOW A PATTERN
FULFIL A PROMISE
LYNDON B. JOHNSON
REFUSE A HEARING
RENDER A SERVICE
RETURN A VERDICT
SECURE A VICTORY
SETTLE A QUARREL
STRIKE A BALANCE
STRIKE A BARGAIN
THANKS A MILLION

6, 2, 1, 5

CLUTCH AT A STRAW
SHADOW OF A DOUBT
THINGS OF A CHILD

6, 2, 2, 4

WALTER DE LA MARE

6, 2, 3, 3

BEWARE OF THE DOG
BOTTOM OF THE SEA
CALLED TO THE BAR
CASTLE IN THE AIR
CAUGHT IN THE ACT
CAUGHT ON THE HOP
FINGER IN THE PIE
ISLAND IN THE SUN
LETTER OF THE LAW
MEMBER OF THE BAR
MIDDLE OF THE DAY
NIPPED IN THE BUD

SPIRIT OF THE LAW
SPRING IN THE AIR
STROKE OF THE PEN
STRONG IN THE ARM
WANTED BY THE LAW

6, 2, 4, 2

LOVELY TO LOOK AT

6, 2, 6

APPEAL TO REASON
APPEAR IN PUBLIC
ATTACK OF NERVES
BEREFT OF REASON
BOTTLE OF BRANDY
BOTTLE OF CLARET
BOTTLE OF SCOTCH
BOTTLE OF WHISKY
BREATH OF SPRING
BRIGHT AS SILVER
BUNDLE OF NERVES
BUNDLE OF STICKS
BUREAU DE CHANGE
CHANGE OF COURSE
CLUTCH AT STRAWS
COILED TO STRIKE
COMEDY OF ERRORS
COMMIT TO MEMORY
COMMON OR GARDEN
COURSE OF ACTION
COURSE OF EVENTS
CREATE AN EFFECT
CREATE AN UPROAR
DECIDE IN FAVOUR
DEMAND AN ENCORE
DEPTHS OF MISERY
DINNER IS SERVED
DIVIDE BY ELEVEN
DIVIDE BY TWELVE
DIVIDE BY TWENTY
DOZENS OF PEOPLE
EIGHTH OF AUGUST
ELEVEN OR TWELVE
ENGAGE IN BATTLE
ENOUGH IS ENOUGH
EXPOSE TO DANGER
FIGURE OF SPEECH
FILLET OF PLAICE
FLIGHT OF STAIRS
FOLLOW MY LEADER
FOURTH OF AUGUST
GALLON OF PETROL
GUIDED BY REASON
GUILTY OF MURDER
HEIGHT OF GENIUS
HEIGHT OF SUMMER
HONORÉ DE BALZAC
INSULT TO INJURY
INVENT AN EXCUSE

KILLED IN ACTION
KNIGHT IN ARMOUR
LAUNCH AN ATTACK
LEGION OF HONOUR
LETTER OF ADVICE
LETTER OF CREDIT
LIGHTS OF LONDON
LISTEN TO REASON
LITTLE BY LITTLE
LITTLE IN COMMON
MARGIN OF SAFETY
MASTER OF HOUNDS
MATTER OF CHOICE
MATTER OF COURSE
MATTER OF REGRET
OBJECT OF DESIRE
PACKET OF CRISPS
PACKET OF TWENTY
PEARLS OF WISDOM
PERSON OF REPUTE
PERSON TO PERSON
PHRASE OR SAYING
PIECES OF SILVER
PILLAR OF WISDOM
PLAGUE OF LONDON
PLEASE BE SEATED
POETRY IN MOTION
POISED TO STRIKE
PRINCE OF ORANGE
RECOIL IN HORROR
REDUCE IN NUMBER
REDUCE TO POWDER
RETURN TO NORMAL
RETURN TO SENDER
RICHER OR POORER
SADDLE OF MUTTON
SCHEME OF THINGS
SCHOOL OF WHALES
SCORES OF PEOPLE
SCROLL OF HONOUR
SECOND OF AUGUST
SERIES OF EVENTS
SMOOTH AS MARBLE
SMOOTH AS VELVET
SOURCE OF DANGER
SOURCE OF INCOME
STANDS TO REASON
STREAK OF HUMOUR
STRING OF ONIONS
STRING OF PEARLS
STROKE OF GENIUS
SUBMIT TO DEFEAT
TROPIC OF CANCER
TROUPE OF ACTORS
TWENTY OR THIRTY
WALLOW IN LUXURY
WALLOW IN MISERY
WORTHY OF ESTEEM
WORTHY OF PRAISE

6, 3, 1, 4

POLISH OFF A MEAL

6, 3, 5

ACROSS THE OCEAN
ACROSS THE RIVER
ACTION FOR LIBEL
ALCOCK AND BROWN
ALFRED THE GREAT
APPEAL FOR FUNDS
APPEAL FOR MERCY
APPLES AND PEARS
AROUND THE WORLD
ASSUME THE WORST
AUGUST THE FIFTH
AUGUST THE FIRST
AUGUST THE NINTH
AUGUST THE SIXTH
AUGUST THE TENTH
AUGUST THE THIRD
BEFORE AND AFTER
BEHIND THE CLOCK
BEHIND THE TIMES
BEHIND THE WHEEL
BESIDE THE POINT
BEYOND ALL DOUBT
BEYOND THE GRAVE
BEYOND THE LIMIT
BLOUSE AND SKIRT
BOSTON TEA PARTY
BRIGHT AND EARLY
BUCKET AND SPADE
CANCEL ALL LEAVE
CHANGE THE ORDER
CHANGE THE RULES
CHARGE THE EARTH
CHEESE AND ONION
CIRCLE THE EARTH
COMING-OUT PARTY
COMMIT FOR TRIAL
CURDLE THE BLOOD
CUSTOM AND USAGE
DEFEAT THE ENEMY
DINNER AND DANCE
DURING THE NIGHT
EDWARD THE FIFTH
EDWARD THE FIRST
EDWARD THE SIXTH
EDWARD THE THIRD
EIGHTY-ONE PENCE
EIGHTY-SIX PENCE
EIGHTY-TWO PENCE
ELICIT THE TRUTH
ENGAGE THE ENEMY
EXCEED THE LIMIT
FOLLOW THE CROWD
FOLLOW THE SCENT
FOLLOW THE TRAIL
GEORGE THE FIFTH

GEORGE THE FIRST
GEORGE THE SIXTH
GEORGE THE THIRD
HAMMER AND TONGS
HEAVEN AND EARTH
KNIVES AND FORKS
LABOUR THE POINT
LATTER-DAY SAINT
LAUREL AND HARDY
LITTLE AND LARGE
LITTLE AND OFTEN
MOTHER AND CHILD
NEARER THE TRUTH
NINETY-ONE PENCE
NINETY-SIX PENCE
NINETY-TWO PENCE
NUMBER ONE COURT
PENCIL AND PAPER
PHRASE AND FABLE
PLAICE AND CHIPS
POUNDS AND PENCE
POWDER AND PAINT
PUSHED FOR MONEY
QUIVER AND SHAKE
RATTLE THE SABRE
REALLY AND TRULY
ROBERT THE BRUCE
SCOTCH AND WATER
SEARCH FOR TRUTH
SHAGGY-DOG STORY
SHIVER AND SHAKE
THIRST FOR BLOOD
THIRST FOR POWER
THIRTY-ONE PENCE
THIRTY-SIX PENCE
THIRTY-TWO PENCE
TRAVEL THE WORLD
TWENTY NEW PENCE
TWENTY-ONE PENCE
TWENTY-ONE YEARS
TWENTY-SIX PENCE
TWENTY-SIX WEEKS
TWENTY-TWO CARAT
TWENTY-TWO PENCE
TWENTY-TWO YARDS
TWISTS AND TURNS

6, 4, 1, 3

SPOKEN LIKE A MAN

6, 4, 4

ANSWER ONES NAME
BEFORE ONES EYES
BEFORE ONES TIME
BEHIND ONES BACK
BETTER THAN EVER
BETTER THAN MOST
BILLIE JEAN KING
CHANGE ONES LUCK

CHANGE ONES MIND
CHANGE ONES NAME
CHANGE ONES TUNE
CHANGE ONES WAYS
CLENCH ONES FIST
COMMIT HARA-KIRI
CORDON BLEU CHEF
DARKEN ONES DOOR
DESERT ONES POST
FOLLOW ONES NOSE
GREASE ONES PALM
HANDLE WITH CARE
HOLIER THAN THOU
INSURE ONES LIFE
LARGER THAN LIFE
LIVING NEXT DOOR
MURDER MOST FOUL
NATION-WIDE HUNT
PLEASE TURN OVER
PLEDGE ONES WORD
PLUNGE INTO DEBT
RACKED WITH PAIN
SECOND-HAND BOOK
SECOND-HAND SHOP
STRAIN ONES EYES
STRIKE WITH FEAR
TAILOR-MADE SUIT
THANKS VERY MUCH
TWENTY-FIVE PAST
VACATE ONES POST
VACATE ONES SEAT
WHITER THAN SNOW

6, 5, 3

ANDREW BONAR LAW
BULLET-PROOF CAR
LITTLE BLACK BOX
LITTLE BROWN JUG
LITTLE GREEN MAN
REDUCE SPEED NOW
SECOND WORLD WAR
TWELVE ANGRY MEN
WINNER TAKES ALL

6, 8

ACTION PAINTING
ACTION STATIONS
ACTIVE INTEREST
AGATHA CHRISTIE
AIRING CUPBOARD
ALBERT EINSTEIN
ALBERT MEMORIAL
ALFRED TENNYSON
ALSACE LORRAINE
ANDREW CARNEGIE
ANGELA MORTIMER
ANIMAL CRACKERS
ANNUAL TURNOVER
ARABIC NUMERALS

ARETHA FRANKLIN
ARTHUR GRIFFITH
AURORA BOREALIS
BALLET MISTRESS
BALTIC EXCHANGE
BANNER HEADLINE
BARELY POSSIBLE
BATTLE STATIONS
BAYEUX TAPESTRY
BECOME AIRBORNE
BECOME CHAMPION
BEFORE DAYLIGHT
BEFORE MIDNIGHT
BEHIND SCHEDULE
BETTER JUDGMENT
BEYOND REPROACH
BISHOP AUCKLAND
BITTER MEMORIES
BITTER STRUGGLE
BODILY STRENGTH
BODILY WEAKNESS
BOILED POTATOES
BONNIE SCOTLAND
BORDER SKIRMISH
BRIGHT PROSPECT
BRIGHT SUNSHINE
BROKEN CONTRACT
BROKEN MARRIAGE
BUDGET ESTIMATE
BURIED TREASURE
BUTTER MOUNTAIN
CALVIN COOLIDGE
CARBON MONOXIDE
CARPET SLIPPERS
CASUAL LABOURER
CAUGHT UNAWARES
CHANGE PARTNERS
CHEESE OMELETTE
CHEESE SANDWICH
CHURCH DOCTRINE
CHURCH MILITANT
COARSE LANGUAGE
COFFEE STRAINER
COLOUR MAGAZINE
COLOUR QUESTION
COLOUR SERGEANT
COMMON ANCESTOR
COMMON COURTESY
COMMON CURRENCY
COMMON ENTRANCE
COMMON FRONTIER
COMMON INTEREST
COMMON MULTIPLE
COMMON NUISANCE
COMMON PARLANCE
COMMON PRACTICE
COMMON PROPERTY
COMMON SERGEANT
COPPER SULPHATE
COTTON INDUSTRY
CRADLE SNATCHER
CREDIT CUSTOMER

CREDIT	FACILITY	FRENCH	VERMOUTH
CREDIT	TRANSFER	FRINGE	BENEFITS
DECENT	INTERVAL	GAELIC	LANGUAGE
DECREE	ABSOLUTE	GATHER	MOMENTUM
DEEPLY	OFFENDED	GATHER	STRENGTH
DEFRAY	EXPENSES	GATHER	TOGETHER
DENTAL	PRACTICE	GENTLE	HANDLING
DEPUTY	CHAIRMAN	GENTLE	REMINDER
DEVILS	ADVOCATE	GEORGE	GERSHWIN
DIRECT	APPROACH	GEORGE	HARRISON
DIRECT	OPPOSITE	GEORGE	LANSBURY
DIRECT	QUESTION	GEORGE	MEREDITH
DIRECT	TAXATION	GERARD	HOFFNUNG
DOCTOR	BARNARDO	GERMAN	LANGUAGE
DOCTOR	DOLITTLE	GIANTS	CAUSEWAY
DONALD	CAMPBELL	GIFTED	COMPOSER
DOUBLE	EIGHTEEN	GLOOMY	FORECAST
DOUBLE	ENTENDRE	GLOOMY	PROSPECT
DOUBLE	EXPOSURE	GLOSSY	MAGAZINE
DOUBLE	FOURTEEN	GOLDEN	PHEASANT
DOUBLE	NEGATIVE	GOLDEN	TREASURY
DOUBLE	NINETEEN	GORDON	RICHARDS
DOUBLE	QUANTITY	GROUSE	SHOOTING
DOUBLE	STANDARD	HARDLY	ANYTHING
DOUBLE	THIRTEEN	HEARTY	APPETITE
DRYING	CUPBOARD	HEARTY	LAUGHTER
EASTER	HOLIDAYS	HEATED	ARGUMENT
EASTER	VACATION	HEATED	EXCHANGE
EIGHTH	SYMPHONY	HERMAN	MELVILLE
EIGHTY	THOUSAND	HIDDEN	RESERVES
ELDEST	DAUGHTER	HIDDEN	TREASURE
ELEVEN	THOUSAND	HIGHLY	ESTEEMED
ELEVEN	TWELFTHS	HIGHLY	ORIGINAL
ENFANT	TERRIBLE	HIGHLY	POLISHED
EVERLY	BROTHERS	HIGHLY	SEASONED
FAMILY	BUSINESS	HOLLOW	LAUGHTER
FAMILY	HEIRLOOM	HOLLOW	PRETENCE
FAMILY	LIKENESS	HUDDLE	TOGETHER
FAMILY	PLANNING	HUMBLE	DWELLING
FAMILY	PORTRAIT	IMPURE	THOUGHTS
FELLOW	CREATURE	INDIAN	ELEPHANT
FILTHY	LANGUAGE	INLAND	WATERWAY
FINGER	EXERCISE	INSIDE	POSITION
FINITE	QUANTITY	ISLAND	PARADISE
FLARED	TROUSERS	JESSIE	MATTHEWS
FLIGHT	MECHANIC	JOSHUA	REYNOLDS
FLIGHT	SERGEANT	JOSIAH	WEDGWOOD
FLYING	BUTTRESS	JULIAN	CALENDAR
FLYING	DUTCHMAN	KILLER	INSTINCT
FLYING	FORTRESS	KINDLY	DISPOSED
FLYING	SCOTSMAN	LABOUR	EXCHANGE
FLYING	SQUIRREL	LABOUR	MAJORITY
FORCED	MARRIAGE	LABOUR	MOVEMENT
FORMAL	APPROACH	LANDED	INTEREST
FORMAL	OCCASION	LATEST	BULLETIN
FOSTER	DAUGHTER	LEAGUE	FOOTBALL
FOURTH	DIVISION	LEONID	BREZHNEV
FOURTH	SYMPHONY	LITTLE	CHILDREN
FRENCH	CANADIAN	LITTLE	INTEREST
FRENCH	DRESSING	LITTLE	LEARNING
FRENCH	LANGUAGE	LITTLE	PITCHERS

LITTLE PROGRESS	PRINCE CHARMING
LITTLE RESPONSE	PRISON GOVERNOR
LIVING LANGUAGE	PRISON SENTENCE
LIVING QUARTERS	PROMPT DECISION
LIVING REMINDER	PROMPT DELIVERY
LIVING STANDARD	PROPER FRACTION
LLOYDS REGISTER	PROVEN INNOCENT
LOADED QUESTION	PUBLIC DISGRACE
LONDON SCOTTISH	PUBLIC EXPOSURE
LONDON TERMINUS	PUBLIC FESTIVAL
LOVING KINDNESS	PUBLIC FOOTPATH
MANUAL LABOURER	PUBLIC INTEREST
MARKET BOSWORTH	PUBLIC NUISANCE
MARKET GARDENER	PUBLIC PROPERTY
MARKET RESEARCH	PUBLIC SPIRITED
MASHED POTATOES	QUEENS BIRTHDAY
MASTER SERGEANT	QUEENS EVIDENCE
MAUNDY THURSDAY	QUEENS PLEASURE
MEDIUM WAVEBAND	QUEENS SHILLING
MENTAL ATTITUDE	RACING CALENDAR
MENTAL CAPACITY	RAGING HEADACHE
MENTAL CONFLICT	RAISED EYEBROWS
MENTAL EXERCISE	RAISED PLATFORM
MENTAL HOSPITAL	RANDOM SAMPLING
MENTAL SICKNESS	REFUSE DISPOSAL
MENTAL WEAKNESS	REMOTE ANCESTOR
MIDDLE DISTANCE	REMOTE LIKENESS
MIDDLE REGISTER	REPORT VERBATIM
MODERN LANGUAGE	RHESUS NEGATIVE
MONKEY BUSINESS	RIDING BREECHES
MORRIS NUFFIELD	ROBERT BROWNING
MOTHER SUPERIOR	ROBERT HELPMANN
MOVING PAVEMENT	ROBERT ROBINSON
MOVING PICTURES	ROLLED UMBRELLA
MUSEUM SPECIMEN	ROVING REPORTER
MUTUAL GOODWILL	RUGGED FEATURES
MUTUAL SYMPATHY	SACRED WRITINGS
MUZZLE VELOCITY	SAFETY MEASURES
NARROW MAJORITY	SALINE SOLUTION
NATIVE LANGUAGE	SAMUEL PICKWICK
NATIVE QUARTERS	SAMUEL PLIMSOLL
NICELY BALANCED	SCHOOL BUILDING
NINETY THOUSAND	SCHOOL GOVERNOR
NORMAN CONQUEST	SCHOOL HOLIDAYS
NUMBER THIRTEEN	SCHOOL MAGAZINE
OBTAIN JUDGMENT	SCRAPE TOGETHER
OFFICE BUILDING	SEALED ENVELOPE
OFFSET PRINTING	SECOND DIVISION
OLDEST DAUGHTER	SECOND ENGINEER
OLDHAM ATHLETIC	SECOND LANGUAGE
OLIVER CROMWELL	SECOND MARRIAGE
OXYGEN CYLINDER	SECOND SYMPHONY
PANZER DIVISION	SECOND THOUGHTS
PARISH REGISTER	SECRET IDENTITY
PATENT MEDICINE	SENIOR WRANGLER
PETROL SHORTAGE	SERENE HIGHNESS
PINCER MOVEMENT	SEVERE SENTENCE
POLICE SERGEANT	SHADOW MINISTER
POSTAL DELIVERY	SHEEPS CLOTHING
POSTAL DISTRICT	SHREWD OBSERVER
POWDER MAGAZINE	SILENT REPROACH

SILVER BRACELET
SILVER PHEASANT
SIMPLE ADDITION
SIMPLE EQUATION
SIMPLE FRACTION
SIMPLE FRACTURE
SIMPLE INTEREST
SIMPLE MAJORITY
SIMPLE PLEASURE
SIMPLE SOLUTION
SMOOTH CROSSING
SOCIAL ACTIVITY
SOCIAL DEMOCRAT
SOCIAL POSITION
SOCIAL SCIENCES
SOCIAL SECURITY
SOCIAL STANDING
SOCIAL SUPERIOR
SODIUM CHLORIDE
SOLEMN ENTREATY
SOLEMN OCCASION
SPEECH TRAINING
SPEEDY RECOVERY
SPOKEN LANGUAGE
SPORTS PAVILION
SPORTS REPORTER
SPRING CLEANING
SPRING MATTRESS
SQUARE BRACKETS
SQUASH RACQUETS
STAPLE INDUSTRY
STEADY INCREASE
STEADY PROGRESS
STOLEN PROPERTY
STREET FIGHTING
STREET MUSICIAN
STRICT TRAINING
STRING TOGETHER
STRONG ARGUMENT
STRONG FEELINGS
STRONG LANGUAGE
STRONG MEASURES
STRONG POSITION
STRONG SOLUTION
STUDIO AUDIENCE
STUPID QUESTION
SUDDEN DOWNPOUR
SUDDEN MOVEMENT
SUMMER HOLIDAYS
SUMMER VACATION
TARGET PRACTICE
TARTAN TROUSERS
TENDER FEELINGS
THIRTY THOUSAND
THOMAS CROMWELL
THREAD TOGETHER
THROAT PASTILLE
TIMBER MERCHANT
TIMELY REMINDER
TRAVEL BROCHURE
TRIBAL CONFLICT

TRICKY QUESTION
TRUMAN DOCTRINE
TWELVE APOSTLES
TWELVE MIDNIGHT
TWELVE THOUSAND
TWENTY THOUSAND
ULSTER UNIONIST
UNITED SERVICES
UPHILL STRUGGLE
URGENT TELEGRAM
UTMOST CELERITY
VASLAV NIJINSKY
VASTLY SUPERIOR
VERBAL ARGUMENT
VERBAL CONTRACT
VESTED INTEREST
VIOLIN CONCERTO
VULGAR FRACTION
VULGAR LANGUAGE
WARNER BROTHERS
WARREN HASTINGS
WARSAW CONCERTO
WEEKLY MAGAZINE
WEIGHT TRAINING
WILLIE WHITELAW
WINDOW DRESSING
WINDOW ENVELOPE
WINDOW SHOPPING
WINTER CLOTHING
WINTER QUARTERS
WOMENS SUFFRAGE
WORTHY CHAMPION
WORTHY OPPONENT
WRIGHT BROTHERS
YELLOW JAUNDICE

7 , 1 , 6

CONDUCT A SEARCH
DELIVER A SERMON
DELIVER A SPEECH
DICTATE A LETTER
DOROTHY L.SAYERS
ENCLOSE A CHEQUE
PRESENT A CHEQUE
PROPOSE A MOTION
RECEIVE A LEGACY
RECEIVE A LETTER
SCRATCH A LIVING
SUPPORT A FAMILY
WITHOUT A CHANCE
WITHOUT A PADDLE

7 , 2 , 1 , 4

CHAINED TO A DESK

7 , 2 , 2 , 3

BELIEVE IT OR NOT

7 , 2 , 5

AFFAIRS OF STATE
ARBITER OF TASTE
BALANCE OF POWER
BALANCE OF TRADE
BERWICK ON TWEED
BROUGHT TO LIGHT
CAPITAL OF ITALY
CAPITAL OF SPAIN
CASTLES IN SPAIN
CLUBBED TO DEATH
CLUSTER OF STARS
COMMAND OF WORDS
CONDEMN TO DEATH
DECLINE IN VALUE
DEGREES OF FROST
DRESSED IN BLACK
ECONOMY OF WORDS
ELEMENT OF DOUBT
ELEMENT OF SKILL
EMPEROR OF INDIA
EMPEROR OF JAPAN
ENGAGED IN TRADE
GARLAND OF ROSES
GOODBYE MR. CHIPS
LACKING IN POISE
LACKING IN SENSE
MATTERS OF STATE
MISSION OF MERCY
NOTHING TO OFFER
OFFICER OF STATE
PARTNER IN CRIME
PICTURE OF GLOOM
PLASTER OF PARIS
PLEASED AS PUNCH
PORTION OF CHIPS
PURSUIT OF POWER
QUALITY OF MERCY
QUARTER TO EIGHT
QUARTER TO SEVEN
QUARTER TO THREE
RESTORE TO POWER
REVENGE IS SWEET
ROLLING IN MONEY
SEVENTH OF APRIL
SEVENTH OF MARCH
SILENCE IN COURT
STABBED TO DEATH
STRAITS OF DOVER
TICKLED TO DEATH
TORRENT OF ABUSE
TRICKLE OF BLOOD
TRICKLE OF WATER
TRISTAN DA CUNHA
TROUBLE IN STORE
TRUMPED-UP STORY
TUMBLER OF WATER
TWELFTH OF APRIL
TWELFTH OF MARCH
WORRIED TO DEATH

7 , 3 , 1 , 3

FOREVER AND A DAY

7 , 3 , 4

ABANDON ALL HOPE
AGAINST ALL ODDS
AGAINST THE ODDS
AGAINST THE TIDE
AGAINST THE WALL
AGAINST THE WIND
ATTEMPT TOO MUCH
BANGERS AND MASH
BETWEEN THE EYES
BROADEN THE MIND
BUTTONS AND BOWS
CALLING ALL CARS
CATHODE-RAY TUBE
DECLINE AND FALL
DEVELOP THE MIND
EDUCATE THE MIND
ENLARGE THE MIND
FIFTEEN PER CENT
FINGERS AND TOES
GLUTTON FOR WORK
HOLDING THE BABY
HUNDRED AND FIVE
HUNDRED AND FOUR
HUNDRED AND NINE
HUNDRED PER CENT
HUSBAND AND WIFE
LIGHTEN THE LOAD
MACHINE-GUN FIRE
MACHINE-GUN POST
NEEDLES AND PINS
PRESSED FOR TIME
PROTEST TOO MUCH
SAUSAGE AND MASH
SEVENTY PER CENT
SHUFFLE THE PACK
SIXTEEN PER CENT
STRANGE BUT TRUE
SWALLOW THE BAIT
SWALLOW THE PILL
THOUGHT AND DEED
THROUGH THE AGES
THROUGH THE CARD
THROUGH THE NOSE
THROUGH THE TOWN
TOASTED TEA-CAKE
TREASON AND PLOT
UNLUCKY FOR SOME
VINCENT VAN GOGH
VIOLETS ARE BLUE
WILLIAM AND MARY
WILLING AND ABLE

7 , 4 , 3

ACHIEVE ONES AIM
ACHIEVE ONES END
HEAVIER THAN AIR
¬INCLINE ONES EAR
LIGHTER THAN AIR
NUCLEAR TEST BAN
OUTSIDE ONES KEN
QUARTER PAST ONE
QUARTER PAST SIX
QUARTER PAST TEN
QUARTER PAST TWO

7 , 5 , 2

NOTHING SHORT OF

7 , 7

ABRAHAM LINCOLN
ACHIEVE VICTORY
ADDRESS UNKNOWN
ADELPHI THEATRE
ADVANCE BOOKING
ALCOHOL CONTENT
AMATEUR COMPANY
AMONGST FRIENDS
ANCIENT BRITAIN
ANCIENT BRITONS
ANCIENT HISTORY
ANCIENT MARINER
ANOTHER VERSION
APPLIED PHYSICS
APPLIED SCIENCE
AWKWARD SILENCE
BACKING BRITAIN
BALLIOL COLLEGE
BARGAIN COUNTER
BARRAGE BALLOON
BATHING COSTUME
BATHING MACHINE
BATTING AVERAGE
BEDTIME READING
BENEATH CONCERN
BETWEEN FRIENDS
BLAZING INFERNO
BLOWING BUBBLES
BOOMING ECONOMY
BOROUGH COUNCIL
BOWLING AVERAGE
BOWLING FIGURES
BRACING CLIMATE
BREATHE HEAVILY
BRIGHTS DISEASE
BRISTOL CHANNEL
BRISTOL FASHION
BRITISH AIRWAYS
BRITISH BULLDOG
BRITISH COUNCIL
BRITISH EMBASSY

BRITISH LEYLAND
BRITISH SUBJECT
BROUGHT FORWARD
BUSMANS HOLIDAY
CABINET MEETING
CAMPING HOLIDAY
CANNING FACTORY
CAPITAL LETTERS
CAPITAL OFFENCE
CARAVAN HOLIDAY
CARDIAC DISEASE
CAREFUL THOUGHT
CARRIED FORWARD
CAUSTIC COMMENT
CAVALRY OFFICER
CENTRAL AMERICA
CENTRAL HEATING
CENTRAL STATION
CERTAIN VICTORY
CHAMOIS LEATHER
CHANNEL ISLANDS
CHANNEL STEAMER
CHANNEL SWIMMER
CHAPTER HEADING
CHARLES CHAPLIN
CHARLES DICKENS
CHARLES PARNELL
CHARLIE CHAPLIN
CHARLIE CHESTER
CHARRED REMAINS
CHEWING TOBACCO
CHICKEN NOODLES
CHINESE LANTERN
CHINESE LAUNDRY
CHINESE SNOOKER
CHINESE TORTURE
CHOPPED PARSLEY
CHRISTS COLLEGE
CHRONIC INVALID
CLASSIC EXAMPLE
CLASSIC QUALITY
CLEMENT WEATHER
CLOSELY GUARDED
COASTAL COMMAND
COLLEGE PUDDING
COLLEGE STUDENT
COMMAND RESPECT
COMMAND SUPPORT
COMPANY MEETING
COMPASS READING
COMPOSE ONESELF
CONCERT PIANIST
CONTAIN ONESELF
CONTROL ONESELF
COOKING UTENSIL
CORDIAL WELCOME
COUNCIL CHAMBER
COUNCIL HOUSING
COUNCIL MEETING
COUNTRY BUMPKIN
COUNTRY COTTAGE

COUNTRY	RETREAT	FACTORY	CHIMNEY
COVERED	WALKWAY	FALSELY	ACCUSED
CROSSED	FINGERS	FATALLY	WOUNDED
CRYPTIC	COMMENT	FIFTEEN	MINUTES
CURIOUS	MIXTURE	FIFTEEN	SECONDS
CURRENT	ACCOUNT	FIGHTER	COMMAND
CURRENT	AFFAIRS	FILLING	STATION
CURRENT	EDITION	FINDERS	KEEPERS
CURRENT	FASHION	FINGERS	BREADTH
CURRENT	OPINION	FISHING	LICENCE
CURRIED	CHICKEN	FISHING	VILLAGE
CURTAIN	LECTURE	FLATTER	ONESELF
CUSTOMS	BARRIER	FOREIGN	AFFAIRS
CUSTOMS	OFFICER	FOREIGN	CAPITAL
DANCING	ACADEMY	FOREIGN	COUNTRY
DANCING	DERVISH	FOREIGN	STATION
DANCING	PARTNER	FRANKIE	VAUGHAN
DEBASED	COINAGE	FREDDIE	TRUEMAN
DECEIVE	ONESELF	FREEDOM	FIGHTER
DECIMAL	COINAGE	FUNERAL	ORATION
DEFENCE	COUNSEL	FUNERAL	PARLOUR
DEFENCE	MEASURE	FURTHER	DETAILS
DEFENCE	WITNESS	GALLANT	SOLDIER
DEPOSIT	ACCOUNT	GARBLED	MESSAGE
DEVOTED	ADMIRER	GARBLED	VERSION
DEVOTED	HUSBAND	GATWICK	AIRPORT
DIAMOND	JUBILEE	GENERAL	CONSENT
DIAMOND	WEDDING	GENERAL	COUNCIL
DISTANT	HORIZON	GENERAL	MANAGER
DIVIDED	LOYALTY	GENERAL	MEETING
DOCTORS	DILEMMA	GENERAL	OUTLOOK
DOCTORS	MANDATE	GENERAL	RELEASE
DOWAGER	DUCHESS	GENERAL	RESERVE
DOWNING	COLLEGE	GENERAL	SERVICE
DRIVING	GLASSES	GENUINE	ARTICLE
DRIVING	LICENCE	GENUINE	RESPECT
DUBIOUS	COMPANY	GEORGES	SIMENON
EMINENT	SOLDIER	GHASTLY	MISTAKE
EMINENT	SPEAKER	GILBERT	HARDING
ENCLOSE	PAYMENT	GLARING	MISTAKE
ENDLESS	TROUBLE	GLASGOW	RANGERS
ENGLISH	CHANNEL	GLOWING	ACCOUNT
ENGLISH	GRAMMAR	GLOWING	COLOURS
ENGLISH	HISTORY	GRADUAL	DECLINE
ENGLISH	MUSTARD	GRAPHIC	ACCOUNT
ENGLISH	TEACHER	GROWING	ANXIETY
EQUABLE	CLIMATE	HANDELS	MESSIAH
EQUALLY	DIVIDED	HANGING	GARDENS
ERRATIC	CONDUCT	HAPPILY	MARRIED
ESCAPED	CONVICT	HEALTHY	OUTLOOK
EVENING	CLOTHES	HEALTHY	RESPECT
EXPENSE	ACCOUNT	HEATHER	MIXTURE
EXPLAIN	ONESELF	HERBERT	ASQUITH
EXPRESS	COMMAND	HERMANN	GOERING
EXPRESS	ONESELF	HIGHEST	CIRCLES
EXPRESS	REGRETS	HIGHWAY	ROBBERY
EXTINCT	VOLCANO	HISTORY	TEACHER
EXTREME	DISLIKE	HOLDING	COMPANY
EXTREME	MEASURE	HOLIDAY	COTTAGE
EXTREME	PENALTY	HOLIDAY	TRAFFIC
EXTREME	POVERTY	HOSTILE	COUNTRY

HOSTILE	WITNESS
HOUSING	PROBLEM
HOWLING	SUCCESS
HUNDRED	DOLLARS
HUNDRED	GUINEAS
ILLEGAL	TRAFFIC
IMMORAL	CONDUCT
IMPLIED	CONSENT
IMPROVE	MATTERS
IMPROVE	ONESELF
INSPIRE	RESPECT
INSTANT	DISLIKE
INTENSE	DISLIKE
INTENSE	FEELING
JEALOUS	HUSBAND
JIMMINY	CRICKET
KENNETH	GRAHAME
KITCHEN	CABINET
KITCHEN	DRESSER
KITCHEN	UTENSIL
LASTING	QUALITY
LEADING	ACTRESS
LEADING	ARTICLE
LEARNED	COUNSEL
LEEWARD	ISLANDS
LEGALLY	BINDING
LENDING	LIBRARY
LIAISON	OFFICER
LIBERAL	HELPING
LIBRARY	EDITION
LIMITED	COMPANY
LIMITED	EDITION
LITERAL	ACCOUNT
LITERAL	MEANING
LOGICAL	PROCESS
MALCOLM	SARGENT
MASSAGE	PARLOUR
MATTHEW	BOULTON
MAXIMUM	BENEFIT
MEDICAL	COLLEGE
MEDICAL	HISTORY
MEDICAL	OFFICER
MEDICAL	SCIENCE
MEDICAL	STUDENT
MERMAID	THEATRE
MICHAEL	BENTINE
MICHAEL	COLLINS
MILKING	MACHINE
MILLION	DOLLARS
MINCING	MACHINE
MINERAL	DEPOSIT
MONTHLY	ACCOUNT
MONTHLY	PAYMENT
MOROCCO	LEATHER
MOTHERS	MEETING
MUSICAL	ABILITY
MUSICAL	EVENING
MUSICAL	PRODIGY
MUSICAL	QUALITY
MUSICAL	TRIBUTE
NATURAL	ENEMIES
NATURAL	HARBOUR
NATURAL	HISTORY
NATURAL	PROCESS
NATURAL	SCIENCE
NERVOUS	TENSION
NEUTRAL	COUNTRY
NEWNHAM	COLLEGE
NOMINAL	CAPITAL
NOMINAL	DAMAGES
NOTHING	DAUNTED
NUCLEAR	FISSION
NUCLEAR	PHYSICS
NUCLEAR	REACTOR
NUCLEAR	WARFARE
NUCLEAR	WEAPONS
OEDIPUS	COMPLEX
OMNIBUS	EDITION
OPENING	BATSMAN
ORDERLY	CONDUCT
ORDERLY	OFFICER
ORDINAL	NUMBERS
OSTRICH	FEATHER
OUTDOOR	MEETING
OUTSIDE	FORWARD
OVERARM	BOWLING
OVERDUE	ACCOUNT
PACKAGE	HOLIDAY
PANCAKE	TUESDAY
PARKING	OFFENCE
PARKING	PROBLEM
PARTIAL	ECLIPSE
PARTIAL	SUCCESS
PARTICK	THISTLE
PARTING	PRESENT
PASSING	THOUGHT
PERFECT	DARLING
PERFECT	EXAMPLE
PERFECT	HUSBAND
PERFECT	SETTING
PERFECT	SILENCE
PERSONS	UNKNOWN
PICTURE	GALLERY
PILGRIM	FATHERS
PLANNED	ECONOMY
PLASTIC	SURGEON
PLASTIC	SURGERY
POLLING	STATION
POPULAR	CONCERT
POPULAR	EDITION
POPULAR	REQUEST
POPULAR	SCIENCE
POPULAR	VERDICT
PRECISE	MEANING
PREPARE	ONESELF
PRESENT	ADDRESS
PRESENT	COMPANY
PRIVATE	ADDRESS
PRIVATE	CITIZEN
PRIVATE	COMPANY
PRIVATE	HEARING
PRIVATE	OPINION

PRIVATE QUARREL	SHOTGUN WEDDING
PRIVATE REASONS	SHUTTLE SERVICE
PRIVATE SOLDIER	SIGNALS OFFICER
PRIVATE TEACHER	SINCERE APOLOGY
PRIVATE TUITION	SINKING FEELING
PRODUCE RESULTS	SKILLED WORKMAN
PROSPER MERIMÉE	SMOKING CONCERT
PROTEST AGAINST	SNOZZLE DURANTE
PROTEST MEETING	SOBERLY DRESSED
PROVOST MARSHAL	SOCIETY JOURNAL
PYRAMID SELLING	SOCIETY WEDDING
PYRRHIC VICTORY	SOLOMON ISLANDS
QUALITY CONTROL	SPECIAL EDITION
RAILWAY COMPANY	SPECIAL EFFECTS
RAILWAY CUTTING	SPECIAL FEATURE
RAILWAY SLEEPER	SPECIAL LICENCE
RAILWAY STATION	SPECIAL MENTION
RAILWAY VIADUCT	SPECIAL REQUEST
READING GLASSES	STANLEY BALDWIN
REGULAR SERVICE	STEPHEN LEACOCK
REGULAR SOLDIER	STOMACH TROUBLE
RESPECT ONESELF	STRANGE FEELING
RESTORE HARMONY	STUFFED CHICKEN
REVENUE OFFICER	SULPHUR DIOXIDE
REVISED EDITION	SUMMARY JUSTICE
REVISED VERSION	SUPREME COMMAND
RHYMING COUPLET	SUPREME CONTROL
RICHARD MURDOCH	SUPREME COUNCIL
RICHARD RODGERS	SURFACE TENSION
RICHARD STRAUSS	SUSPEND PAYMENT
ROARING FORTIES	SYSTEMS ANALYST
ROARING SUCCESS	TALKING PICTURE
ROLLING EXPANSE	TAPIOCA PUDDING
RUDOLPH NUREYEV	TESTIFY AGAINST
RUDYARD KIPLING	THIEVES KITCHEN
RUINOUS EXPENSE	TOBACCO PLANTER
RUNAWAY VICTORY	TOPICAL SUBJECT
RUNNING REPAIRS	TORTURE CHAMBER
SALIENT COMMENT	TOURING COMPANY
SALIENT FEATURE	TRADING STATION
SATANIC MAJESTY	TRAFFIC BOLLARD
SAVELOY SAUSAGE	TRAFFIC CONTROL
SAVINGS ACCOUNT	TRAFFIC DENSITY
SCIENCE FICTION	TRAFFIC PROBLEM
SCIENCE SUBJECT	TRAINED SOLDIER
SCIENCE TEACHER	TREACLE PUDDING
SERIOUS AILMENT	TRINITY COLLEGE
SERIOUS ATTEMPT	TROUBLE BREWING
SERIOUS ILLNESS	TUESDAY EVENING
SERIOUS MISTAKE	TUESDAY MORNING
SERIOUS OFFENCE	TURKISH DELIGHT
SERIOUS STUDENT	TWELFTH CENTURY
SERIOUS SUBJECT	TWINKLE TWINKLE
SERIOUS TROUBLE	TYPICAL EXAMPLE
SERVICE STATION	UNDERGO REPAIRS
SETTLED WEATHER	UNDRESS UNIFORM
SEVENTH CENTURY	UNEQUAL CONTEST
SEVENTY DOLLARS	UNKNOWN COUNTRY
SHANNON AIRPORT	UNKNOWN SOLDIER
SHINING EXAMPLE	UNKNOWN WARRIOR
SHOCKED SILENCE	VANILLA FLAVOUR

VARIETY THEATRE
VARIOUS COLOURS
VARYING SUCCESS
VATICAN COUNCIL
VENDING MACHINE
VIOLENT QUARREL
VISIBLE EXPORTS
WAGGING TONGUES
WARRANT OFFICER
WASHING MACHINE
WEALTHY PARENTS
WEATHER BALLOON
WEATHER OUTLOOK
WEATHER PROPHET
WEATHER STATION
WEDDING MORNING
WEDDING PRESENT
WEIGHTY PROBLEM
WEMBLEY STADIUM
WHITSUN HOLIDAY
WILFRED PICKLES
WILLIAM COBBETT
WILLIAM GOLDING
WILLIAM HOGARTH
WILLIAM TYNDALE
WILLIAM WALLACE
WITHOUT BLEMISH
WITHOUT CEASING
WITHOUT PURPOSE
WITHOUT RESERVE
WITHOUT RESPECT
WITHOUT RESPITE
WITHOUT STRINGS
WITHOUT WARNING
WOOLLEN SWEATER
WORKING CAPITAL
WORKING CLASSES
WORKING CLOTHES
WORKING HOLIDAY
WOUNDED SOLDIER
WRITTEN APOLOGY
WRITTEN CONSENT
YOUNGER BROTHER

8, 2, 1, 3

STRAIGHT AS A DIE

8, 2, 4

ATTITUDE OF MIND
BACHELOR OF ARTS
BROTHERS IN ARMS
BUSINESS IS GOOD
BUSINESS ON HAND
COMRADES IN ARMS
CONSIDER IT DONE
DESPATCH BY MAIL
DIVISION OF WORK
ELEVENTH OF JULY
ELEVENTH OF JUNE

FAREWELL TO ARMS
INTERVAL OF TIME
LIGHTING-UP TIME
MINISTRY OF FOOD
MULTIPLY BY FIVE
MULTIPLY BY FOUR
MULTIPLY BY NINE
OVERCOME BY FEAR
PRESENCE OF MIND
PRESSURE OF WORK
QUESTION OF TIME
RELEASED ON BAIL
RHAPSODY IN BLUE
SHOULDER OF LAMB
STOCKTON ON TEES
STRENGTH OF MIND
STRENGTH OF WILL

8, 3, 3

INFRINGE THE LAW
OFFICERS AND MEN
THOUSAND AND ONE
WHATEVER YOU SAY

8, 6

ABSOLUTE DECREE
ABSOLUTE MASTER
ABSOLUTE PIFFLE
ABSTRACT DESIGN
ACCUSING FINGER
ACHILLES TENDON
ADEQUATE INCOME
ADEQUATE REASON
ADEQUATE SUPPLY
ADOPTION PAPERS
AFFECTED MANNER
AFFECTED SPEECH
AIRBORNE TROOPS
ALLOTTED SPHERE
AMERICAN ACCENT
AMERICAN INDIAN
AMERICAN PATROL
AMERICAN TROOPS
ANGLICAN CHURCH
APPROVED SCHOOL
ARISTIDE BRIAND
ARMCHAIR CRITIC
ARROGANT MANNER
ARTISTIC EFFECT
ATHLETIC SPORTS
AUGUSTUS CAESAR
AVIATION SPIRIT
AVOGADRO NUMBER
BACKWARD GLANCE
BALANCED BUDGET
BALMORAL CASTLE
BAREBACK RIDING
BATHROOM SCALES

BILLIARD MARKER	CRITICAL MOMENT
BILLIARD PLAYER	CRITICAL PERIOD
BLENHEIM ORANGE	CRUSHING DEFEAT
BLENHEIM PALACE	CRUSHING REMARK
BOARDING SCHOOL	CRUSHING RETORT
BREEDING GROUND	DAMAGING REPORT
BRIGITTE BARDOT	DAYLIGHT SAVING
BROOKLYN BRIDGE	DAZZLING BEAUTY
BRUSSELS CARPET	DECIDING FACTOR
BUILDING BRICKS	DECISIVE FACTOR
BUSINESS CAREER	DEFERRED SHARES
BUSINESS LETTER	DEFINITE FIGURE
BUSINESS MATTER	DELICATE HEALTH
BUSINESS TYCOON	DEPARTED SPIRIT
CALAMINE LOTION	DETACHED MANNER
CARDINAL NUMBER	DETAILED REPORT
CARDINAL POINTS	DISABLED PERSON
CARDINAL VIRTUE	DISCOUNT BROKER
CARDINAL WOLSEY	DISTRESS SIGNAL
CARLISLE UNITED	DIVORCED PERSON
CHAMPION GOLFER	DOMESTIC DRUDGE
CHAMPION JOCKEY	DOMESTIC POLICY
CHARCOAL BURNER	DOMINION STATUS
CHARLTON HESTON	DOUBTFUL ORIGIN
CHARMING FELLOW	DOUBTING THOMAS
CHARMING MANNER	DOWNHILL SKIING
CHEMICAL CHANGE	DOWNWARD STROKE
CHEMICAL ENERGY	DRAMATIC CRITIC
CHESHIRE CHEESE	DRAMATIC EFFECT
CHIPPING BARNET	DRAMATIC FINISH
CHIPPING NORTON	DRINKING TROUGH
CIRCULAR LETTER	DRINKING VESSEL
CIRCULAR TICKET	DUELLING PISTOL
CITIZENS ARREST	ECONOMIC CRISIS
CLASSICS MASTER	ECONOMIC GROWTH
CLERICAL DUTIES	EIGHTEEN MONTHS
CLERICAL WORKER	EIGHTEEN POUNDS
COCKTAIL SHAKER	ELECTION RESULT
COHERENT MANNER	ELECTRIC CHARGE
COLONIAL OFFICE	ELECTRIC COOKER
COLORADO BEETLE	ELECTRIC GUITAR
COMBINED EFFORT	ELECTRIC HEATER
COMBINED FORCES	ELECTRIC KETTLE
COMPLEAT ANGLER	ELECTRIC SHAVER
COMPLETE ANSWER	EMPHATIC DENIAL
COMPLETE CHANGE	ENGAGING MANNER
COMPUTER DATING	ENORMOUS NUMBER
CONJUGAL RIGHTS	ESPRESSO COFFEE
CONSTANT STRAIN	EXCHANGE VISITS
CONSTANT SUPPLY	EXCITING CLIMAX
CONSUMER DEMAND	EXTENDED CREDIT
CONTRACT BRIDGE	FABULOUS WEALTH
COURTING COUPLE	FAITHFUL FRIEND
COVERING LETTER	FAMILIAR FIGURE
COWARDLY STREAK	FAMILIAR MANNER
CREATIVE ARTIST	FAREWELL SPEECH
CREATIVE GENIUS	FEATURES EDITOR
CREATIVE WRITER	FEMININE APPEAL
CRIMINAL CHARGE	FEMININE GENDER
CRIMINAL LAWYER	FIGHTING CHANCE
CRIMINAL RECORD	FIGHTING SPIRIT

FILLETED PLAICE	IMPOSING FIGURE
FIREMANS HELMET	INDIRECT EFFECT
FIREMANS LADDER	INDIRECT OBJECT
FLAGRANT BREACH	INDIRECT SPEECH
FLASHING THIGHS	INFERIOR NATURE
FLEETING GLANCE	INFERIOR STATUS
FLIPPANT SPEECH	INFINITE NUMBER
FLOATING BRIDGE	INFORMAL SPEECH
FLOATING CHARGE	INNOCENT ABROAD
FOOTBALL COUPON	INNOCENT REMARK
FOOTBALL GROUND	INNOCENT VICTIM
FOOTBALL LEAGUE	INTERNAL STRIFE
FOOTBALL PLAYER	INTIMATE FRIEND
FOOTBALL SEASON	INVERTED COMMAS
FOUNDERS SHARES	JACOBITE RISING
FOUNDING FATHER	JONATHAN MILLER
FOURTEEN OUNCES	JUDICIAL MURDER
FOURTEEN POUNDS	KEYSTONE COMEDY
FRIENDLY CRITIC	KNITTING NEEDLE
FRIENDLY DEBATE	LANGUAGE MASTER
FRIENDLY NATION	LAUGHING MATTER
GENEROUS AMOUNT	LAWFULLY WEDDED
GENEROUS NATURE	LEMONADE POWDER
GENEROUS PRAISE	LIFELONG FRIEND
GLORIOUS MUDDLE	LITERARY CRITIC
GLORIOUS SUNSET	LITERARY DIGEST
GRACIOUS LIVING	LITERARY EDITOR
GRUDGING PRAISE	LUNCHEON BASKET
GUTTURAL ACCENT	MACARONI CHEESE
GUTTURAL SPEECH	MAGELLAN STRAIT
HANDSOME MARGIN	MAGNETIC NEEDLE
HANDSOME PROFIT	MANAGING EDITOR
HANDSOME SALARY	MANDARIN ORANGE
HARDENED SINNER	MARATHON RUNNER
HAUNTING MELODY	MARCHING ORDERS
HEADACHE POWDER	MARITIME NATION
HEADLONG FLIGHT	MARRIAGE BROKER
HELPLESS VICTIM	MARRIAGE BUREAU
HERALDIC DEVICE	MATERIAL WEALTH
HERALDIC SHIELD	MEDICINE BOTTLE
HEREFORD UNITED	MERCHANT BANKER
HERNANDO CORTEZ	MERCHANT PRINCE
HIGHLAND CATTLE	MERCHANT SEAMAN
HISTORIC MOMENT	MERCHANT TAILOR
HOLLOWAY PRISON	MILITARY CAREER
HOMELESS PERSON	MILITARY ESCORT
HONORARY DEGREE	MILITARY GENIUS
HONORARY MEMBER	MILITARY PARADE
HONORARY STATUS	MILITARY POLICE
HOPELESS MISFIT	MILITARY SCHOOL
HOSPITAL MATRON	MILITARY TATTOO
HOSPITAL PORTER	MODERATE HEALTH
HUMPBACK BRIDGE	MODERATE HEIGHT
HUMPHREY BOGART	MODERATE INCOME
HYPNOTIC TRANCE	MODERATE TALENT
IDENTITY PARADE	MODERATE WEIGHT
IGNORANT MASSES	MOUNTAIN RESORT
IGNORANT PERSON	MOUNTAIN STREAM
IMMINENT DANGER	MOUNTING LOSSES
IMPERIAL GALLON	NAMELESS HORROR
IMPERIAL WEIGHT	NAMELESS TERROR

NAPOLEON BRANDY	POSITIVE DEGREE
NATIONAL ANTHEM	POSITIVE MENACE
NATIONAL CRISIS	POWERFUL SPEECH
NATIONAL EMBLEM	PRECIOUS LITTLE
NATIONAL FIGURE	PREPARED SPEECH
NATIONAL HEALTH	PRESSURE COOKER
NATIONAL INCOME	PRIMROSE YELLOW
NATIONAL WEALTH	PROFOUND EFFECT
NEGATIVE CHARGE	PROGRESS REPORT
NEGATIVE RESULT	PROLIFIC WRITER
NINETEEN EIGHTY	PUNITIVE ACTION
NINETEEN NINETY	QUESTION MASTER
NINETEEN POUNDS	RANDOLPH TURPIN
NINETEEN THIRTY	RAVENOUS HUNGER
NINETEEN TWENTY	RECKLESS DRIVER
NOBLESSE OBLIGE	RECKLESS GAMBLE
NORTHERN ACCENT	REFORMED CHURCH
NORTHERN COUNTY	REGISTRY OFFICE
NORTHERN LIGHTS	REPORTED SPEECH
OBITUARY NOTICE	RESEARCH WORKER
OFFICIAL CENSUS	RESIDENT ABROAD
OFFICIAL NOTICE	RESTLESS NATURE
OFFICIAL SECRET	ROBINSON CRUSOE
OFFICIAL SOURCE	ROMANTIC COMEDY
OFFICIAL STRIKE	SALUTARY LESSON
OPPOSITE NUMBER	SCATHING ATTACK
ORDINARY SEAMAN	SCOTTISH ACCENT
ORDINARY SHARES	SCOTTISH BORDER
ORDNANCE SURVEY	SCOTTISH CHURCH
ORTHODOX CHURCH	SCOTTISH OFFICE
PARALLEL COURSE	SEASONED TIMBER
PARMESAN CHEESE	SECLUDED CORNER
PATHETIC EFFORT	SECURITY PRISON
PAVEMENT ARTIST	SEPARATE TABLES
PECULIAR PERSON	SHEEPDOG TRIALS
PEDIGREE CATTLE	SHERLOCK HOLMES
PERSONAL APPEAL	SHERWOOD FOREST
PERSONAL ATTACK	SHIPPING CENTRE
PERSONAL COLUMN	SHIPPING OFFICE
PERSONAL ESTATE	SHOCKING TEMPER
PERSONAL FAVOUR	SHOOTING RIGHTS
PERSONAL LETTER	SHOOTING SEASON
PERSONAL MATTER	SHOPPING ARCADE
PERSONAL REASON	SHOPPING BASKET
PERSONAL REMARK	SHOPPING CENTRE
PHYSICAL BEAUTY	SKITTLES PLAYER
PICKWICK PAPERS	SLEEPING BEAUTY
PIERCING GLANCE	SLEEPING TABLET
PITCAIRN ISLAND	SOUTHEND UNITED
PLATFORM TICKET	SOUTHERN ACCENT
PLATINUM BLONDE	SOUTHERN AFRICA
PLEASANT DREAMS	SOUTHERN COUNTY
PLEASANT MANNER	SOUTHERN REGION
PLEASANT PERSON	SOUTHERN STATES
PLEASURE CRUISE	SPEAKERS CORNER
PLEASURE GROUND	SPECIFIC OBJECT
PLEASURE SEEKER	SPECIFIC REMEDY
PLYMOUTH ARGYLE	SPEEDWAY RACING
PORTLAND CEMENT	SPELLING LESSON
POSITIVE ACTION	SPINNING MOTION
POSITIVE CHARGE	SPIRITED ATTACK

SPITEFUL PERSON	UNEARNED INCOME
SPLENDID CHANCE	UNSALTED BUTTER
SPORTING CHANCE	UNSIGNED CHEQUE
SQUADRON LEADER	VENETIAN SCHOOL
STAFFORD CRIPPS	VENETIAN WINDOW
STAMFORD BRIDGE	VERBATIM REPORT
STAMPING GROUND	VICTORIA PALACE
STANDARD BEARER	VIRULENT STRAIN
STANDARD WEIGHT	WATERLOO BRIDGE
STANDING ORDERS	WORMWOOD SCRUBS
STARTERS ORDERS	WRONGFUL ARREST
STARTING HANDLE	YOUNGEST SISTER
STARTING PISTOL	
STEERING COLUMN	**9 , 1 , 4**
STERLING SILVER	
STINGING NETTLE	DISCHARGE A DEBT
STINGING REBUKE	ENTERTAIN A HOPE
STIRLING ALBION	GUARANTEE A LOAN
STIRRING SPEECH	
STRAIGHT ANSWER	**9 , 2 , 3**
STRAIGHT COMEDY	ACCORDING TO LAW
STRAINED MUSCLE	APARTMENT TO LET
STRICTLY KOSHER	BREAKFAST IN BED
STRIKING EFFECT	CHECKMATE IN ONE
STRONGLY WORDED	CHECKMATE IN TWO
STUBBORN FELLOW	FIFTEENTH OF MAY
SUITABLE TENANT	SIXTEENTH OF MAY
SUPERIOR NATURE	SOMETHING TO EAT
SUPERIOR PERSON	SOMETHING TO SAY
SUPERIOR STATUS	THIRTIETH OF MAY
SURGICAL SPIRIT	TWENTIETH OF MAY
SURPRISE ATTACK	
SURPRISE PACKET	**9 , 5**
SWEEPING ACTION	
SWEEPING REMARK	ADMIRALTY CHART
SWIMMING LESSON	ADVANCING YEARS
SWIMMING TRUNKS	ADVENTURE STORY
TACTICAL WEAPON	AESTHETIC TASTE
TANGIBLE OBJECT	ALCOHOLIC DRINK
TERRIBLE ORDEAL	ALEXANDRE DUMAS
THIEVING MAGPIE	ANONYMOUS DONOR
THIRTEEN OUNCES	ANTARCTIC OCEAN
THIRTEEN POUNDS	APARTMENT HOUSE
THIRTEEN TRICKS	ASCENDING ORDER
THOROUGH SEARCH	ASSENTING PARTY
THOUSAND METRES	AUSTRALIA HOUSE
THOUSAND POUNDS	AUTOGRAPH ALBUM
THREATEN DANGER	AUTOMATIC RIFLE
THRILLER WRITER	BADMINTON COURT
TIRELESS WORKER	BALANCING TRICK
TRACTION ENGINE	BEAUTIFUL VOICE
TRAINING GROUND	BEAUTIFUL WOMAN
TRANMERE ROVERS	BLACKPOOL TOWER
TREASURE ISLAND	BLEACHING AGENT
TRIFLING AMOUNT	BREAKFAST TABLE
TRIFLING MATTER	BREAKNECK SPEED
TRISTRAM SHANDY	BREATHING SPACE
TROUBLED WATERS	BURNISHED BRASS
ULTERIOR MOTIVE	CATHERINE WHEEL
ULTIMATE RESULT	CHALLENGE ROUND
UNBROKEN SPIRIT	CHAMPAGNE GLASS

CHAMPAGNE LUNCH	EXECUTIVE SUITE
CHARACTER ACTOR	EXQUISITE TASTE
CHARACTER STUDY	FALTERING STEPS
CHARLOTTE RUSSE	FAVOURITE PIECE
CHILDRENS NANNY	FIFTEENTH ROUND
CHILDRENS PARTY	FINANCIAL TIMES
CHILDRENS STORY	FINANCIAL WORRY
CHOCOLATE CREAM	FINISHING TOUCH
CHRISTMAS BONUS	FIVEPENNY PIECE
CHRISTMAS CAROL	FLOWERING PLANT
CHRISTMAS CHEER	FLOWERING SHRUB
CHRISTMAS PARTY	FLYWEIGHT TITLE
CHROMATIC SCALE	FORBIDDEN FRUIT
CIGARETTE PAPER	FORMATIVE YEARS
CIGARETTE SMOKE	FRIGHTFUL SIGHT
CIVILIZED WORLD	FURNISHED HOUSE
CLASSICAL MUSIC	FURNITURE STORE
CLASSICAL OFFER	GALLOPING MAJOR
CLOCKWORK TRAIN	GATHERING STORM
CLOUDLESS SKIES	GENTLEMAN CROOK
COLLECTED POEMS	GENTLEMAN USHER
COLLECTED WORKS	GRADUATED SCALE
COMMITTEE STAGE	GRENADIER GUARD
COMMUNIST CHINA	GREYHOUND DERBY
COMMUNIST PARTY	GREYHOUND TRACK
COMMUNITY CHEST	HALFPENNY STAMP
COMPANION PIECE	HALLOWEEN PARTY
COMPONENT PARTS	HAMPSTEAD HEATH
CONJURING TRICK	HONEYMOON HOTEL
CONTRALTO VOICE	HOUSEHOLD GOODS
COUNTLESS TIMES	HOUSEHOLD LINEN
CRANBERRY SAUCE	HYDRAULIC PRESS
CRINOLINE DRESS	IDENTICAL TWINS
CROCODILE TEARS	IMMEDIATE REPLY
DEAFENING NOISE	IMPENDING STORM
DEAFENING SOUND	IMPERFECT TENSE
DEBATABLE POINT	IMPORTANT EVENT
DECLINING YEARS	INCLUSIVE TERMS
DELICIOUS TASTE	INCREASED FARES
DEPARTING GUEST	INCREASED SPEED
DESIRABLE ASSET	INNERMOST BEING
DESPERATE STATE	INSURANCE AGENT
DETECTIVE NOVEL	INSURANCE CLAIM
DETECTIVE STORY	INTENSIVE STUDY
DETENTION ORDER	INTRINSIC VALUE
DICTATION SPEED	INTRINSIC WORTH
DIFFERENT STORY	INVISIBLE TRADE
DIFFICULT CATCH	LANCASTER HOUSE
DIFFICULT TIMES	LEASEHOLD HOUSE
DISTILLED WATER	LIGHTNING FLASH
DISTORTED IMAGE	LIGHTNING SPEED
DUPLICATE SHEET	LINGERING DEATH
EDITORIAL STAFF	LIVERPOOL DOCKS
EDWARDIAN HOUSE	MARKETING BOARD
ELABORATE STYLE	MEZZANINE FLOOR
ELOCUTION CLASS	MIDSUMMER NIGHT
EMOTIONAL WRECK	MOONLIGHT NIGHT
ENDEARING SMILE	NARRATIVE VERSE
EVERGREEN PLANT	NUMERICAL ORDER
EXCITABLE STATE	OCCUPYING FORCE
EXECUTION BLOCK	OPERATING TABLE

PASSENGER	PLANE
PASSENGER	TRAIN
PATCHWORK	QUILT
PATRIOTIC	FRONT
PERFECTLY	FRANK
PERPETUAL	WORRY
PERTINENT	REPLY
PETROLEUM	JELLY
PINEAPPLE	JUICE
PLAUSIBLE	DEVIL
PLOUGHING	MATCH
PNEUMATIC	BRAKE
PNEUMATIC	DRILL
POISONOUS	PLANT
POISONOUS	SNAKE
POLITICAL	AGENT
POLITICAL	PARTY
POLITICAL	TOPIC
PRACTICAL	JOKER
PRESERVED	FRUIT
PRESIDENT	ELECT
PRESIDING	JUDGE
PRIMITIVE	TRIBE
PROMISING	PUPIL
PROMISING	START
PUBLICITY	AGENT
QUOTATION	MARKS
RECEIVING	ORDER
RECEPTION	CLERK
RECORDING	ANGEL
REFLECTED	GLORY
REFLECTED	IMAGE
RELIGIOUS	FAITH
RELIGIOUS	MANIA
RELIGIOUS	ORDER
RELIGIOUS	TRACT
REPEATING	RIFLE
REVOLVING	DOORS
REVOLVING	STAGE
RHEUMATIC	FEVER
SALISBURY	PLAIN
SATELLITE	STATE
SATURDAYS	CHILD
SCRUBBING	BRUSH
SEBASTIAN	CABOT
SELECTION	BOARD
SENSITIVE	PAPER
SEVENTEEN	MILES
SEVENTEEN	PENCE
SHEFFIELD	STEEL
SHEPHERDS	CROOK
SHEPHERDS	PURSE
SHORTHAND	SPEED
SICKENING	SIGHT
SLEEPLESS	NIGHT
SOMETHING	EXTRA
SOMETHING	FISHY
SOMEWHERE	ABOUT
SOVEREIGN	POWER
SOVEREIGN	STATE
SPIRITUAL	NEEDS

SPIRITUAL	POWER
STAINLESS	STEEL
STRATEGIC	SKILL
STUMBLING	BLOCK
SUMPTUOUS	FEAST
SURRENDER	VALUE
TARPAULIN	SHEET
TECHNICAL	HITCH
TECHNICAL	SKILL
TELEPHONE	BOOTH
TELEPHONE	KIOSK
TEMPORARY	ABODE
TEMPORARY	LEASE
THURSDAYS	CHILD
TRANSPORT	HOUSE
TREMBLING	HANDS
TREMBLING	VOICE
TUNBRIDGE	WELLS
UNINVITED	GUEST
UNIVERSAL	PEACE
UNLIMITED	SCOPE
UNMARRIED	WOMAN
UNWELCOME	GUEST
VANISHING	CREAM
VANISHING	POINT
VANISHING	TRICK
VEGETABLE	CURRY
VEGETABLE	SALAD
VERSATILE	ACTOR
VOLUNTEER	CORPS
WALPURGIS	NIGHT
WEDNESDAY	NIGHT
WHOLEMEAL	BREAD
WHOLESALE	PRICE
WITHERING	STARE
WONDERFUL	SIGHT
WONDERFUL	WORLD
WORCESTER	SAUCE
WRESTLING	MATCH
YELLOWISH	BROWN
YESTERDAY	NIGHT
YORKSHIRE	DALES
YORKSHIRE	MOORS

10, 4

ACCESSIBLE	SPOT
ACCUSATIVE	CASE
AMMUNITION	DUMP
ANGLEPOISE	LAMP
ARTIFICIAL	FOOD
ARTIFICIAL	HAND
ARTIFICIAL	LAKE
ARTIFICIAL	LIMB
ARTIFICIAL	SILK
BANQUETING	HALL
BASKETBALL	TEAM
BENEVOLENT	FUND
BESEECHING	LOOK
BIRMINGHAM	CITY
BITUMINOUS	COAL

BORDERLINE	CASE
CALCULATED	ODDS
CALCULATED	RISK
CANTERBURY	BELL
CAUTIONARY	TALE
CHARITABLE	GIFT
COLLECTIVE	FARM
COLLECTIVE	NOUN
COLLECTORS	ITEM
COMMANDING	LEAD
COMMANDING	VIEW
CONFERENCE	PEAR
CONFERENCE	ROOM
CONIFEROUS	TREE
CONQUERING	HERO
CONSUMMATE	EASE
CONTINUITY	GIRL
CONTROLLED	RENT
CORRUGATED	IRON
CULTIVATED	LAND
CULTIVATED	MIND
DEPRESSING	NEWS
DEROGATORY	TERM
DICTIONARY	WORD
DIMINUTIVE	SIZE
DIPLOMATIC	MOVE
DISCORDANT	NOTE
DOWNSTAIRS	ROOM
EIGHTEENTH	HOLE
ELDERBERRY	WINE
ELECTRICAL	UNIT
ELEMENTARY	RULE
ENGAGEMENT	RING
EUCALYPTUS	TREE
EVAPORATED	MILK
EVERYTHING	GOES
EXPURGATED	BOOK
FAVOURABLE	WIND
FICTITIOUS	NAME
FISHERMANS	YARN
FORMIDABLE	TASK
FRACTIONAL	PART
FRESHWATER	FISH
GALVANIZED	IRON
GENTLEMANS	CLUB
GOOSEBERRY	BUSH
GOVERNMENT	LOAN
GOVERNMENT	POST
GOVERNMENT	WHIP
GRANDSTAND	VIEW
GROUNDLESS	FEAR
HEREDITARY	PEER
HISTORICAL	PLAY
HISTORICAL	WORK
HORIZONTAL	BARS
HORIZONTAL	LINE
HOUSEMAIDS	KNEE
IMPERATIVE	MOOD
IMPOSSIBLE	TASK
INCENDIARY	BOMB
INDICATIVE	MOOD
INDUSTRIAL	AREA
UNITIATIVE	TEST
INTERNMENT	CAMP
INVETERATE	LIAR
INVINCIBLE	ARMY
MANCHESTER	CITY
MECHANISED	ARMY
MEERSCHAUM	PIPE
MEMBERSHIP	CARD
MICHAELMAS	TERM
MIDSHIPMAN	EASY
MINESTRONE	SOUP
MISSIONARY	WORK
NAPOLEONIC	WARS
NATIONWIDE	HUNT
NOMINATIVE	CASE
ORNAMENTAL	POND
PADDINGTON	BEAR
PARLIAMENT	HILL
PEPPERCORN	RENT
PERFORMING	BEAR
PERFORMING	FLEA
PERFORMING	SEAL
PICCADILLY	LINE
POLICEMANS	BEAT
PONTEFRACT	CAKE
POSSESSIVE	CASE
POSTHUMOUS	FAME
PREVAILING	WIND
PRODUCTION	LINE
PROFITLESS	TASK
PROMISSORY	NOTE
PUBLISHERS	NOTE
REASONABLE	TIME
RECREATION	ROOM
REFLECTIVE	MOOD
REGIMENTAL	BAND
REGISTERED	MAIL
REGISTERED	POST
REGULATION	SIZE
REMARKABLE	GIRL
REPUBLICAN	ARMY
RESISTANCE	UNIT
RESTRICTED	AREA
RETROGRADE	STEP
SABBATICAL	YEAR
SEASONABLE	GIFT
SECONDHAND	SHOP
SHATTERING	BLOW
SHREWSBURY	TOWN
STAGGERING	BLOW
STARVATION	DIET
STARVATION	WAGE
STOCKINGED	FEET
STRAWBERRY	FAIR
STRAWBERRY	MARK
STRAWBERRY	TART
SUPPORTERS	CLUB
SUPPORTING	CAST
SUPPORTING	PART
SUPPORTING	ROLE

SUSPICIOUS MIND
SWELTERING HEAT
TELESCOPIC LENS
TELESCOPIC VIEW
TELEVISION FILM
TELEVISION MAST
TELEVISION PLAY
TELEVISION STAR
THOUGHTFUL MOOD
TORRENTIAL RAIN
TRANSITIVE VERB
TRAVELLING TIME
UNBALANCED MIND
UNFAMILIAR WORD
UNFINISHED WORK
UNIVERSITY TERM
UNIVERSITY TOWN
UNPLEASANT DUTY
UNREQUITED LOVE
UNSETTLING NEWS
VAUDEVILLE SHOW
VEGETARIAN DIET
VEGETARIAN DISH
VULNERABLE SPOT
WASHINGTON POST
WELLINGTON BOOT
WHISPERING DOME
WIDDICOMBE FAIR
YESTERDAYS DATE

11, 3

BULLETPROOF CAR
CAULIFLOWER EAR
CHRISTOPHER FRY
CHRISTOPHER LEE
COMFORTABLY OFF
CORPORATION TAX
DANGEROUSLY ILL
DEERSTALKER HAT
EDUCATIONAL TOY
ELECTRICITY CUT
ELIZABETHAN AGE
ELIZABETHAN ERA
ENLIGHTENED AGE
GINGERBREAD MAN
LONDONDERRY AIR
LUBRICATING OIL
NEANDERTHAL MAN
OBSERVATION CAR
PENSIONABLE AGE
PREHISTORIC AGE
REFRESHMENT BAR
REMEMBRANCE DAY
RESPONSIBLE MAN
SUBSTANTIAL SUM

1, 3, 2, 6, 3

A LOT TO ANSWER FOR

1, 4, 2, 3, 5

A DROP IN THE OCEAN

1, 5, 3, 1, 5

A TOOTH FOR A TOOTH

1, 6, 2, 6

A COMEDY OF ERRORS

1, 6, 4, 1, 3

I CANNOT TELL A LIE

1, 6, 8

A LITTLE LEARNING

1, 9, 5

A CHRISTMAS CAROL

2, 1, 4, 3, 5

AT A LOSS FOR WORDS

2, 1, 6, 2, 4

AS A MATTER OF FACT

2, 1, 6, 6

TO A LESSER DEGREE
TO A LESSER EXTENT

2, 1, 7, 5

DO A ROARING TRADE

2, 1, 12

AT A DISADVANTAGE

2, 2, 3, 4, 4

BE ON THE SAFE SIDE

2, 2, 3, 6, 2

DO AS THE ROMANS DO

2, 2, 3, 8

GO TO THE SCAFFOLD
UP TO THE EYEBROWS

2, 2, 8, 3

DO-IT-YOURSELF KIT

2, 2, 11

AS AN ALTERNATIVE
GO BY UNDERGROUND
OF NO CONSEQUENCE

2, 3, 2, 1, 7

GO OFF AT A TANGENT

2, 3, 2, 3, 3, 2

AS FAR AS YOU CAN GO

2, 3, 2, 3, 5

AS OLD AS THE HILLS
ON TOP OF THE WORLD

2, 3, 2, 8

AS FAR AS POSSIBLE
BY WAY OF CONTRAST
GO OUT OF BUSINESS
MY WAY OF THINKING

2, 3, 3, 4, 3

GO OFF THE DEEP END

2, 3, 4, 1, 5

GO OUT LIKE A LIGHT

2, 3, 4, 2, 1, 3

AT THE DROP OF A HAT

2, 3, 4, 2, 4

IN THE LINE OF DUTY
IN THE LINE OF FIRE
IN THE NICK OF TIME
ON THE ROAD TO RUIN

2, 3, 4, 4, 2

IF YOU CANT BEAT EM

2, 3, 4, 6

IN THE NEAR FUTURE
IN THE SAME BASKET
IN THE SAME BREATH

2, 3, 5, 2, 3

IN THE LIGHT OF DAY

2, 3, 5, 5

AT THE CROSS-ROADS
BY THE SHORT HAIRS
DO THE CIVIL THING
DO THE RIGHT THING
DO THE WRONG THING
IN THE FIRST PLACE
IN THE RIGHT PLACE
IN THE SMALL HOURS
OF THE FIRST WATER
ON THE NEVER-NEVER
ON THE RIGHT LINES
ON THE RIGHT SCENT
ON THE RIGHT TRACK
ON THE RIGHT TRAIL
ON THE WRONG LINES
ON THE WRONG SCENT
ON THE WRONG TRACK

2, 3, 6, 4

AS THE SAYING GOES
HE WHO LAUGHS LAST
ON THE BRIGHT SIDE
ON THE CREDIT SIDE
ON THE DOTTED LINE
TO THE MANNER BORN
UP THE GARDEN PATH

2, 3, 7, 3

IN THE MELTING-POT
IN THE WITNESS-BOX

2, 3, 10

DO THE CHARLESTON
IN ALL CONSCIENCE
IN THE ACCUSATIVE
IN THE ALTOGETHER
IN THE BACKGROUND
IN THE FOREGROUND
IN THE NOMINATIVE
IN THE VERNACULAR
IN THE WILDERNESS
ON THE BORDERLINE
ON THE TELEVISION

2, 4, 2, 2, 5

BY HOOK OR BY CROOK

2, 4, 2, 3, 4

AS GOOD AS ONE GETS

2, 4, 2, 7

AS KEEN AS MUSTARD

2, 4, 3, 2, 4

TO HAVE AND TO HOLD

2, 4, 3, 6

BY FITS AND STARTS
GO OVER THE GROUND
GO WITH THE STREAM
IN FITS AND STARTS
MY LIPS ARE SEALED
ON WITH THE MOTLEY
SO MUCH THE BETTER

2, 4, 4, 5

IN ONES GOOD BOOKS
ON ONES HIGH HORSE

2, 4, 5, 4

DO ONES LEVEL BEST
IN ONES RIGHT MIND

2, 4, 9

GO INTO ECSTASIES
IN FULL AGREEMENT
ON GOOD AUTHORITY

2, 5, 2, 1, 5

AS FRESH AS A DAISY
AS QUIET AS A MOUSE
AS STIFF AS A POKER
AS WHITE AS A SHEET

2, 5, 3, 5

GO ROUND THE WORLD
IN BLACK AND WHITE
IN DRIBS AND DRABS
IT TAKES ALL SORTS
ON HANDS AND KNEES

2, 5, 4, 4

TO SPITE ONES FACE

2, 5, 8

AT CLOSE QUARTERS
IN BROAD DAYLIGHT
IN SHARP CONTRAST
IN SHORT TROUSERS
NO STONE UNTURNED

2, 6, 2, 1, 4

AS GENTLE AS A LAMB

2, 6, 2, 5

DO THINGS IN STYLE
IN SEARCH OF TRUTH

2, 6, 7

ON ACTIVE SERVICE
ON-COURSE BETTING
TO LITTLE PURPOSE

2, 7, 1, 5

GO THROUGH A PHASE

2, 7, 2, 4

NO CONCERN OF MINE

2, 7, 4, 2

GO THROUGH WITH IT

2, 7, 6

BY POPULAR DEMAND
GO FIFTEEN ROUNDS
GO WITHOUT SAYING
MY LEARNED FRIEND
TO FORGIVE DIVINE

2, 8, 2, 3

NO DISTANCE AT ALL

2, 8, 5

ON INTIMATE TERMS
ON SPEAKING TERMS

2, 9, 4

DR.BARNARDOS HOME

2, 10, 3

ST.VALENTINES DAY

2, 13

IN CONSIDERATION
IN JUXTAPOSITION

3, 1, 4, 7

SET A GOOD EXAMPLE

3, 1, 5, 6

CUT A SORRY FIGURE

3 , 1 , 6 , 5

NOT A LIVING THING

3 , 1 , 11

RUN A TEMPERATURE
WIN A SCHOLARSHIP

3 , 2 , 1 , 4 , 2 , 3

PUT IN A WORD OR TWO

3 , 2 , 1 , 4 , 5

NOT BY A LONG CHALK
OFF TO A FINE START
OFF TO A GOOD START
PUT UP A GOOD FIGHT

3 , 2 , 1 , 5 , 4

MAD AS A MARCH HARE
PUT ON A BRAVE FACE
WIN BY A SHORT HEAD

3 , 2 , 1 , 9

BET ON A CERTAINTY

3 , 2 , 2 , 3 , 5

GET ON IN THE WORLD

3 , 2 , 2 , 8

GET UP TO MISCHIEF
NOT TO BE EXPECTED

3 , 2 , 3 , 2 , 2 , 3

PUT AN END TO IT ALL

3 , 2 , 3 , 3 , 2 , 2

AND SO SAY ALL OF US

3 , 2 , 3 , 3 , 4

OUT-OF-THE-WAY SPOT

3 , 2 , 3 , 4 , 3

OFF AT THE DEEP END

3 , 2 , 3 , 7

COG IN THE MACHINE
DIE IN THE ATTEMPT
END OF THE CENTURY

END OF THE CHAPTER
END OF THE RAINBOW
NOT IN THE RUNNING
OUT OF THE COUNTRY
OUT OF THE PICTURE
OUT OF THE RUNNING
PIT OF THE STOMACH
PUT IN THE PICTURE
PUT UP FOR AUCTION
TOP OF THE MORNING

3 , 2 , 4 , 3 , 3

GET ON WITH THE JOB

3 , 2 , 4 , 6

BEE IN ONES BONNET
END OF ONES TETHER
GET ON ONES NERVES
OLD AS TIME ITSELF
OUT OF ONES SENSES
PUT ON ONES ARMOUR
TIP OF ONES TONGUE

3 , 2 , 5 , 5

SET OF FALSE TEETH

3 , 2 , 7 , 3

PUT IT ANOTHER WAY

3 , 2 , 10

ACT OF AGGRESSION
ACT OF FRIENDSHIP
ACT OF PARLIAMENT
ACT OF PROVIDENCE
ACT OF SETTLEMENT
AIR OF DETACHMENT
BOX BF CHOCOLATES
FIT OF DEPRESSION
FIT OF GENEROSITY
GET ON SWIMMINGLY
GUY DE MAUPASSANT
MAN IN POSSESSION
MAN OF EXPERIENCE
OLD AS METHUSELAH
OUT OF COMMISSION
OUT OF PROPORTION
PUT IN QUARANTINE
SIN OF COMMISSION
TWO OF EVERYTHING

3 , 3 , 2 , 3 , 4

NOT OUT OF THE WOOD
THE END OF THE ROAD
THE FUN OF THE FAIR
THE LAP OF THE GODS

THE MAN IN THE MOON

3, 3, 2, 4, 3

GET OUT OF ONES WAY

3, 3, 2, 7

GET OUT OF TROUBLE
ONE WAY OR ANOTHER

3, 3, 3, 4, 2

SEE THE NEW YEAR IN

3, 3, 3, 6

ALL ONE CAN MANAGE
CAT AND THE FIDDLE
FLY OFF THE HANDLE

3, 3, 4, 2, 3

ONE MAN WENT TO MOW

3, 3, 4, 3, 2

NOT THE WORD FOR IT
PUT THE EVIL EYE ON

3, 3, 4, 5

ALL THE YEAR ROUND
ASK FOR MORE MONEY
ASK FOR ONES CARDS
CUT AND COME AGAIN
FOR ALL ONES WORTH
FOR THE TIME BEING
HIT THE HIGH SPOTS
HOT AND COLD WATER
NOT THE SAME THING
RUN FOR ONES MONEY

3, 3, 5, 2, 2

GET THE WORST OF IT

3, 3, 5, 4

ACT THE GIDDY GOAT
ALL THE WORLD OVER
EGG-AND-SPOON RACE
FOR OLD TIMES SAKE
FOR THE FIRST TIME
GET THE UPPER HAND
PUT THE CLOCK BACK
SAY THE MAGIC WORD
SEE THE FUNNY SIDE
THE SUN NEVER SETS

3, 3, 6, 3

THE OLD SCHOOL TIE
TOM,THE PIPERS SON

3, 3, 9

ALL THE TRIMMINGS
ASK THE QUESTIONS
BED AND BREAKFAST
HIT THE HEADLINES
HOG THE LIMELIGHT
MAY THE FIFTEENTH
MAY THE SIXTEENTH
MAY THE THIRTIETH
MAY THE TWENTIETH
MID-AIR COLLISION
OLD-AGE PENSIONER
RUN FOR PRESIDENT
SUM AND SUBSTANCE
THE LOW COUNTRIES
THE NEW STATESMAN
THE OLD PRETENDER

3, 4, 1, 4, 3

FOR MANY A LONG DAY

3, 4, 2, 1, 5

ANY PORT IN A STORM

3, 4, 2, 2, 4

TOO GOOD TO BE TRUE

3, 4, 2, 3, 3

GET DOWN TO THE JOB

3, 4, 2, 6

FOR WANT OF TRYING
THE BACK OF BEYOND
THE BEST OF HEALTH
THE COST OF LIVING
THE MOOR OF VENICE
THE TOWN OF TITIPU
YOU MUST BE JOKING

3, 4, 3, 3, 2

SEE WHAT YOU CAN DO

3, 4, 3, 5

ALL OVER THE PLACE
DIG ONES OWN GRAVE
DOG WITH TWO TAILS
FAR FROM THE TRUTH
FOR WHAT ITS WORTH

GET INTO HOT WATER
GOD SAVE THE QUEEN
HOT FROM THE PRESS
ITS THAT MAN AGAIN
ONE OVER THE EIGHT
PUT BACK THE CLOCK
SAY WHAT ONE MEANS
SEE ONES WAY CLEAR
SIX TENS ARE SIXTY
SUN, MOON AND STARS
THE LONG WAY ROUND
THE SAME OLD THING
THE SKYS THE LIMIT
TOM, DICK AND HARRY

3, 4, 4, 2, 2

PUT ONES FOOT IN IT
THE SHOW MUST GO ON

3, 4, 4, 4

GET INTO ONES HEAD
LAY DOWN ONES ARMS
LAY DOWN ONES LIFE
LET DOWN ONES HAIR
LET ONES HAIR DOWN
PUT ONES FOOT DOWN
PUT ONES NAME DOWN
SOW ONES WILD OATS
THE MICE WILL PLAY
THE TIME WILL COME

3, 4, 5, 3

EAT ONES HEART OUT
PUT THAT LIGHT OUT

3, 4, 6, 2

GET ONES SKATES ON
GET YOUR SKATES ON
PUT ONES SKATES ON

3, 4, 8

ALL THAT GLITTERS
DIE WITH LAUGHTER
PAY ONES RESPECTS
PUT INTO PRACTICE
ROB WITH VIOLENCE
SAY ONES GOODBYES
SIR ALEC GUINNESS
SIR JOHN BETJEMAN
THE COLD SHOULDER
THE HOME STRAIGHT
THE LATE-LAMENTED
THE LONG VACATION
THE PLOT THICKENS
THE UGLY DUCKLING
THE VERY REVEREND

TRY ONES PATIENCE
TRY ONES STRENGTH
TRY YOUR STRENGTH

3, 5, 2, 1, 4

ONE STAGE AT A TIME
ONE THING AT A TIME

3, 5, 2, 5

LET THERE BE LIGHT
PER ARDUA AD ASTRA
THE COAST IS CLEAR
THE SOUND OF MUSIC
THE WORLD AT LARGE

3, 5, 3, 4

ALL ALONG THE LINE
HIT BELOW THE BELT
RED, WHITE AND BLUE
THE DEVIL YOU KNOW
THE WORSE FOR WEAR
YOU NEVER CAN TELL

3, 5, 7

AIR CHIEF MARSHAL
ALL SOULS COLLEGE
ALL-NIGHT SESSION
ALL-NIGHT SITTING
ALL-ROUND ABILITY
ALL-ROUND ATHLETE
ICE-CREAM PARLOUR
KID-GLOVE METHODS
NEW YEARS HONOURS
ONE AFTER ANOTHER
SIR FRANK WHITTLE
SIR JACOB EPSTEIN
TEN GREEN BOTTLES
THE BLACK COUNTRY
THE ELGIN MARBLES
THE FIRST MILLION
THE KINGS ENGLISH
THE MERRY MONARCH
THE PEARL FISHERS
THE THREE SISTERS
TOP-LEVEL MEETING

3, 6, 2, 4

THE FOURTH OF JULY
THE GARDEN OF EDEN
TOO CLEVER BY HALF

3, 6, 3, 3

SEE NAPLES AND DIE
TWO THREES ARE SIX

3 , 6 , 4 , 2

THE POWERS THAT BE

3 , 6 , 6

ALL-COMERS RECORD
BOW-STREET RUNNER
FAN-TAILED PIGEON
HEY DIDDLE DIDDLE
LEE HARVEY OSWALD
LEG BEFORE WICKET
NON COMPOS MENTIS
NOT STRONG ENOUGH
OLD FATHER THAMES
OUR MUTUAL FRIEND
SIR HAROLD WILSON
THE ARTFUL DODGER
THE COMMON MARKET
THE COMMON PEOPLE
THE FOURTH ESTATE
THE GOLDEN FLEECE
THE LITTLE PEOPLE
THE LITTLE PRINCE
THE MOVING FINGER
THE QUEENS SPEECH
THE SECOND PERSON
THE TREBLE CHANCE
TWO-STROKE ENGINE

3 , 7 , 2 , 3

THE DESCENT OF MAN

3 , 7 , 5

CUT ONESELF LOOSE
EAT BETWEEN MEALS
HIS MASTERS VOICE
NET PRESENT VALUE
NEW ENGLISH BIBLE
RED-CURRANT JELLY
SIR FRANCIS DRAKE
SIX HUNDRED MILES
THE ANCIENT WORLD
THE BEGGARS OPERA
THE MORNING AFTER
TWO HUNDRED MILES

3 , 8 , 4

AIR MINISTRY ROOF
FOR GOODNESS SAKE!
GOD-FORSAKEN HOLE
HER MAJESTYS SHIP
HIS MAJESTYS SHIP
NEW SCOTLAND YARD
NOT STRICTLY TRUE
SIR HUMPHREY DAVY
TEN-SHILLING NOTE
THE ELEVENTH HOUR

THE KEYSTONE COPS
THE MULBERRY BUSH
THE PROMISED LAND
TRY ANYTHING ONCE

3 , 9 , 3

THE INVISIBLE MAN

3 , 12

AIR CONDITIONING
DUE DELIBERATION
OLD ACQUAINTANCE
OLD CONTEMPTIBLE
PAY COMPENSATION
TEN COMMANDMENTS
THE COMMONWEALTH
THE MARSEILLAISE
THE SUBCONSCIOUS
THE SUPERNATURAL
THE UNTOUCHABLES

4 , 1 , 4 , 2 , 4

HAVE A BONE TO PICK

4 , 1 , 4 , 4 , 2

HAVE A GOOD MIND TO

4 , 1 , 4 , 6

TAKE A DEEP BREATH

4 , 1 , 5 , 2 , 3

KNOW A THING OR TWO
KNOW A TRICK OR TWO

4 , 1 , 5 , 5

HAVE A SWEET TOOTH
KEEP A CLEAN SHEET
LEAD A MERRY DANCE
LIKE A HOUSE AFIRE
MAKE A CLEAN SWEEP
MAKE A FRESH START
RIDE A HOBBY-HORSE

4 , 1 , 6 , 4

JUST A PRETTY FACE
LEAD A DOUBLE LIFE
TAKE A SECOND LOOK
WITH A LITTLE LUCK
WITH A SINGLE BLOW

4 , 1 , 10

DRAW A COMPARISON
DRAW A CONCLUSION

FORM A GOVERNMENT
GAIN A REPUTATION
MAKE A CONFESSION
MAKE A PREDICTION
MAKE A RESOLUTION
MAKE A SUGGESTION
PASS A RESOLUTION
RIDE A BROOMSTICK
SEEK A COMPROMISE
TAKE A COLLECTION
TAKE A PERCENTAGE
TAKE A PHOTOGRAPH
WITH A DIFFERENCE

4, 2, 1, 4, 4

CALM AS A MILL-POND
COME TO A DEAD STOP
COME TO A FULL STOP
ONCE IN A BLUE MOON

4, 2, 1, 8

COME TO A DECISION
COOL AS A CUCUMBER
DEAD AS A DOORNAIL
HANG UP A STOCKING
KEEP AT A DISTANCE
MUCH OF A MUCHNESS
ONCE IN A LIFETIME

4, 2, 2, 3, 4

TAKE IT ON THE CHIN

4, 2, 2, 5, 2

TAKE IT OR LEAVE IT

4, 2, 2, 7

COME UP TO SCRATCH
LAND OF MY FATHERS

4, 2, 3, 2, 4

TELL IT NOT IN GATH

4, 2, 3, 3, 3

STOP ME AND BUY ONE

4, 2, 3, 6

BATS IN THE BELFRY
CALL IN THE POLICE
COME TO THE RESCUE
COME TO THE THRONE
CRUX OF THE MATTER
DASH TO THE GROUND
DEAF TO ALL ADVICE

DOWN IN THE VALLEY
DOWN TO THE GROUND
DRUG ON THE MARKET
FACT OF THE MATTER
FALL TO THE GROUND
FEET ON THE GROUND
FILL IN THE CRACKS
FOND OF THE BOTTLE
FROG IN THE THROAT
GIST OF THE MATTER
HEAD IN THE CLOUDS
HEAD OF THE FAMILY
HEAD OF THE SCHOOL
HEAT OF THE MOMENT
HEIR TO THE THRONE
HOLE IN THE GROUND
JACK OF ALL TRADES
JOIN IN THE CHORUS
JUMP AT THE CHANCE
KEEP ON THE COURSE
KING OF THE BEASTS
KING OF THE CASTLE
KING OF THE JUNGLE
LAND OF THE LIVING
LILY OF THE VALLEY
LOOK TO THE FUTURE
LOSE ON THE SWINGS
LUMP IN THE THROAT
OPEN TO THE PUBLIC
PICK UP THE PIECES
PICK UP THE THREAD
RAZE TO THE GROUND
ROOT OF THE MATTER
SEND TO THE BOTTOM
SIGN OF THE ZODIAC
SINK TO THE BOTTOM
SLIP OF THE TONGUE
SLOW ON THE UPTAKE
SPUR OF THE MOMENT
STAY AT THE HILTON
STIR UP THE EMBERS
TAKE TO THE BOTTLE
TALE OF TWO CITIES
THIN ON THE GROUND
TRUE TO THE LETTER
TURN UP THE VOLUME

4, 2, 4, 2, 3

LOVE ME, LOVE MY DOG

4, 2, 4, 5

BLOW TO ONES PRIDE
CASH IN ONES CHIPS
DRAW IN ONES HORNS
DROP OF HARD STUFF
FALL ON HARD TIMES
GIRD UP ONES LOINS
HALF AS MUCH AGAIN
HAND-TO-HAND FIGHT

311

HOLD	UP	YOUR	HANDS
KILL	IN	COLD	BLOOD
LACK	OF	WILL	POWER
LIFT	UP	ONES	HEART
LIFT	UP	ONES	VOICE
MELT	IN	ONES	MOUTH
PLUM	IN	ONES	MOUTH
PULL	UP	ONES	SOCKS
SINK	TO	ONES	KNEES
SKIN	OF	ONES	TEETH
SURE	OF	ONES	FACTS
TAKE	IT	FROM	THERE
TALK	IN	ONES	SLEEP
TILL	WE	MEET	AGAIN
TIME	ON	ONES	HANDS
TURN	IN	ONES	GRAVE

4, 2, 5, 1, 3

ROOM TO SWING A CAT

4, 2, 5, 2, 2

COME TO THINK OF IT

4, 2, 5, 4

COME	TO	TERMS	WITH
HOPE	IT	KEEPS	FINE
TAKE	IT	LYING	DOWN

4, 2, 6, 3

FREE OF INCOME-TAX

4, 2, 9

BODY	OF	KNOWLEDGE
BOOK	OF	REFERENCE
CALL	AN	AMBULANCE
CASE	OF	CHAMPAGNE
CAST	OF	THOUSANDS
CODE	OF	BEHAVIOUR
COME	TO	ATTENTION
DAYS	OF	CHRISTMAS
DEBT	OF	GRATITUDE
DRAW	AN	INFERENCE
DUKE	OF	EDINBURGH
FULL	OF	SURPRISES
GAME	OF	BILLIARDS
HAVE	AN	INTERVIEW
HEAD-ON		COLLISION
JOIN	IN	MATRIMONY
KEEP	IN	IGNORANCE
LACK	OF	EDUCATION
LACK	OF	KNOWLEDGE
LIVE	IN	SECLUSION
LOVE	OF	ADVENTURE
MAKE	AN	ASSERTION
MAKE	AN	EXCEPTION
MARK	OF	AUTHORITY

MODE	OF	BEHAVIOUR
ODDS-ON		FAVOURITE
OPEN	TO	CRITICISM
OPEN	TO	SUSPICION
PAIR	OF	CALLIPERS
PAIR	OF	COMPASSES
PAIR	OF	PLIMSOLLS
PAIR	OF	STOCKINGS
PINK	OF	CONDITION
ROCK	OF	GIBRALTAR
ROLL	OF	WALLPAPER
ROOM	TO	MANOEUVRE
SLAB	OF	CHOCOLATE
STAR	OF	BETHLEHEM
STAY	OF	EXECUTION
TERM	OF	REFERENCE
TEST	OF	ENDURANCE
TIME	OF	DEPARTURE
TREE	OF	KNOWLEDGE
TURN	TO	ADVANTAGE
WORK	OF	REFERENCE

4, 3, 1, 3, 4

GIVE ONE A BAD TIME

4, 3, 1, 7

TIME AND A QUARTER

4, 3, 2, 3, 3

KEEP	OUT	OF	THE	WAY
LONG	ARM	OF	THE	LAW

4, 3, 2, 6

COME	OUT	ON	STRIKE
FROM	TOP	TO	BOTTOM
WORD	OUT	OF	SEASON

4, 3, 3, 5

GAME, SET	AND	MATCH
GIVE	THE	ALL-CLEAR
GOOD	FOR	THE	BRAIN
HEAD	FOR	THE	HILLS
HOLD	ALL	THE	CARDS
JOIN	THE	AIR	FORCE
KEEP	OFF	THE	GRASS
LAST	BUT	NOT	LEAST
LONG	AND	THE	SHORT
NONE	BUT	THE	BRAVE
PASS	THE	HAT	ROUND
PLAY	CAT	AND	MOUSE
PULL	OUT	THE	STOPS
RIDE	OUT	THE	STORM
SEEN	AND	NOT	HEARD
SKIM	OFF	THE	CREAM
SWIM	FOR	THE	SHORE
TURN	FOR	THE	WORSE

TURN OFF THE LIGHT
TURN OFF THE POWER
TURN OUT THE LIGHT

4, 3, 4, 2, 2

HAVE THE BEST OF IT
MAKE THE BEST OF IT
MAKE THE MOST OF IT

4, 3, 4, 4

FEAR FOR ONES LIFE
FISH AND CHIP SHOP
FROM THE ROOF-TOPS
GIVE THE GAME AWAY
GIVE THE SHOW AWAY
HARD AND FAST RULE
HAVE THE LAST WORD
HAVE THE WHIP-HAND
HOLD OUT ONES HAND
HOLD THE WHIP-HAND
KEEP THE DOOR OPEN
KNOW HIM FROM ADAM
LOAD OFF ONES MIND
NECK-AND-NECK RACE
OPEN-AND-SHUT CASE
OVER AND DONE WITH
REAR ITS UGLY HEAD
TAKE OFF ONES COAT
WHEN THE CATS AWAY
WISH YOU WERE HERE

4, 3, 5, 3

FACE THE WRONG WAY
GAME AND FIRST SET
LOOK THE OTHER WAY
PULL THE OTHER ONE
SONG AND DANCE MAN
TAKE THE BLOOM OFF
TAKE THE CHILL OFF
TURN THE LIGHT OFF
TURN THE LIGHT OUT

4, 3, 6, 2

TURN THE VOLUME UP

4, 3, 8

ARTS AND SCIENCES
BEER AND SKITTLES
CALL THE REGISTER
DOWN THE STRAIGHT
DRAW THE CURTAINS
GAME FOR ANYTHING
GIVE ONE PLEASURE
GIVE THE PASSWORD
GOOD FOR BUSINESS
HAIL AND FAREWELL
HALF THE DISTANCE

HARE AND TORTOISE
HAVE THE PLEASURE
IVAN THE TERRIBLE
JULY THE ELEVENTH
JUNE THE ELEVENTH
LIFT THE RECEIVER
LIKE THE CLAPPERS
LORD GOD ALMIGHTY
LOSE THE ELECTION
MARK THE OCCASION
OPEN THE THROTTLE
PLAY THE BAGPIPES
POMP AND CEREMONY
PULL THE CURTAINS
ROOM FOR ARGUMENT
ROSS AND CROMARTY
SIGN THE REGISTER
STOP THE BLEEDING
SUIT THE OCCASION
TAKE THE SHILLING
WEAR THE TROUSERS
WEEK-END SHOPPING
WIFE AND CHILDREN
YEAR TWO THOUSAND

4, 4, 1, 6

FACE LIKE A FIDDLE
LIVE LIKE A PAUPER
WORK LIKE A TROJAN

4, 4, 2, 3, 2

MIND ONES PS AND QS

4, 4, 2, 5

COME DOWN TO EARTH
COME HOME TO ROOST
FAIR MAID OF PERTH
FROM HAND TO MOUTH
FROM LEFT TO RIGHT
FROM STEM TO STERN
HAVE WHAT IT TAKES
LOOK BACK IN ANGER
SLOW BOAT TO CHINA
SOME TIME OR OTHER

4, 4, 3, 4

BIND HAND AND FOOT
BOLT FROM THE BLUE
COME INTO THE OPEN
FAIR WEAR AND TEAR
GIFT FROM THE GODS
GONE WITH THE WIND
JUMP OVER THE MOON
KNOW ONES OWN MIND
LINK WITH THE PAST
LONG LIVE THE KING!
MEAN WHAT ONE SAYS

PASS AWAY THE TIME
PLAY HIDE-AND-SEEK
RAIN CATS AND DOGS
RISE FROM THE DEAD
RISE WITH THE LARK
SAIL INTO THE WIND
SAIL NEAR THE WIND
SWIM WITH THE TIDE
TAKE ONES OWN LIFE
WORK REST AND PLAY

4, 4, 4, 3

BITE ONES HEAD OFF
COME INTO ONES OWN
HOLD ONES HAND OUT
TAKE ONES COAT OFF
TAKE ONES MIND OFF

4, 4, 5, 2

KEEP ONES SHIRT ON
PULL ONES SOCKS UP

4, 4, 7

ANTE POST BETTING
BEST FOOT FORWARD
BODY-LINE BOWLING
BORN INTO SLAVERY
BURN ONES BRIDGES
BURN ONES FINGERS
COME INTO CONTACT
DAME EDNA EVERAGE
GIVE FULL DETAILS
GIVE ONES CONSENT
HALF-TERM HOLIDAY
HAVE ONES REVENGE
HERE GOES NOTHING
JUST GOOD FRIENDS
KEEP ONES BALANCE
KEEP ONES COUNSEL
KEEP ONES PROMISE
KERB-SIDE PARKING
LEND ONES SUPPORT
LESS THAN NOTHING
LICK ONES FINGERS
LIFE-BOAT STATION
LINE ONES POCKETS
LOCH NESS MONSTER
LORD HIGH ADMIRAL
LOSE ONES BALANCE
LOSE ONES FOOTING
LOSE ONES HUSBAND
MAIN LINE STATION
MAKE ONES FORTUNE
MIND ONES MANNERS
MISS ONES FOOTING
MORE THAN WELCOME
PASS WITH HONOURS
PULL ONES PUNCHES

RUIN ONES CHANCES
SEEK ONES FORTUNE
SELL INTO SLAVERY
SHOW ONES COLOURS
SHOW SOME RESPECT
SINK ONES CAPITAL
SNAP ONES FINGERS
SOFT-SHOE SHUFFLE
SOLD INTO SLAVERY
STAY WITH FRIENDS
TAKE INTO ACCOUNT
TAKE INTO CUSTODY
TEAR ONES CLOTHES
TELL ONES FORTUNE
WALK INTO TROUBLE
WORK ONES PASSAGE

4, 5, 1, 5

FALL UNDER A SPELL

4, 5, 2, 4

FAIR MEANS OR FOUL
FROM FIRST TO LAST
GOOD PIECE OF WORK
MAIN CLAIM TO FAME
NEAT PIECE OF WORK

4, 5, 3, 3

PASS ROUND THE HAT
STAY WHERE YOU ARE

4, 5, 4, 2

MAKE SHORT WORK OF

4, 5, 6

ANTE-NATAL CLINIC
DAME FLORA ROBSON
DAVY JONES LOCKER
DIRT-TRACK RACING
EVEN MONEY CHANCE
FULL SPEED ASTERN
FULL-DRESS DEBATE
GILT-EDGED STOCKS
HOLY ROMAN EMPIRE
JUST ABOUT ENOUGH
KEEP UNDER ARREST
LAND SPEED RECORD
LORD BADEN-POWELL
POST-DATED CHEQUE
SODA-WATER SYPHON
SUCH SWEET SORROW
WITH BATED BREATH

4, 6, 2, 3

GIVE THANKS TO GOD
GOOD ENOUGH TO EAT

4, 6, 5

DAME NELLIE MELBA
DEAR LITTLE THING
GATE-LEGGED TABLE
GOOD NIGHTS SLEEP
JOHN PHILIP SOUSA
JOHN QUINCY ADAMS
KEEP THINGS GOING
LONG-WINDED STORY
LORD GEORGE BROWN
LORD MAYORS COACH
MAKE THINGS CLEAR
MAKE THINGS WORSE
MUCH SOUGHT AFTER
ONES STRONG POINT
ROCK-BOTTOM PRICE
SHED BITTER TEARS
TAKE SECOND PRIZE
THIS LITTLE PIGGY
VERY LITTLE POINT

4, 7, 4

ALEC DOUGLAS-HOME
COLD COMFORT FARM
FIVE WICKETS DOWN
FOUR WICKETS DOWN
GIVE ONESELF AIRS
GIVE ONESELF AWAY
HIGH-PROTEIN DIET
HOLD NOTHING BACK
HOPE AGAINST HOPE
KEEP NOTHING BACK
MAKE FRIENDS WITH
NINE WICKETS DOWN
RACE AGAINST TIME
RAIN STOPPED PLAY
SELF-IMPOSED TASK
SING ANOTHER SONG
TEAR ONESELF AWAY
TELL SOMEONE FLAT
WHAT HAPPENS NEXT?

4, 8, 3

ANTI-AIRCRAFT GUN
DUAL CARRIAGE-WAY
LOVE CONQUERS ALL

4, 9, 2

CALL ATTENTION TO

4, 11

BARE SUBSISTENCE
BEAR RESEMBLANCE
BODY TEMPERATURE
CASH TRANSACTION
CITY CORPORATION
DICK WHITTINGTON
DRAW CONCLUSIONS
DRAW INSPIRATION
DUAL CARRIAGEWAY
DUAL PERSONALITY
EARL MOUNTBATTEN
FEEL COMFORTABLE
FIRM UNDERTAKING
FIVE CENTIMETRES
FOUR CENTIMETRES
FREE ASSOCIATION
FULL EXPLANATION
GAIN INFORMATION
GALA PERFORMANCE
GIVE PARTICULARS
GOOD CONNECTIONS
GOOD HANDWRITING
GOOD HOUSEKEEPER
HEIR PRESUMPTIVE
HIDE UNDERGROUND
HIGH TEMPERATURE
KEEN COMPETITION
LIVE DANGEROUSLY
LORD BEAVERBROOK
LORD CHAMBERLAIN
LORD MOUNTBATTEN
LORD WILBERFORCE
LOSE COUNTENANCE
LOST OPPORTUNITY
MAKE ALTERATIONS
MAKE COMPARISONS
MAKE CORRECTIONS
MALE SUPERIORITY
MERE COINCIDENCE
MORE COMFORTABLE
MOST INTERESTING
MOST RESPECTABLE
NEAT HANDWRITING
NINE CENTIMETRES
OBEY REGULATIONS
OPEN COMPETITION
OPEN HOSTILITIES
OPEN SCHOLARSHIP
ORAL EXAMINATION
POOR HANDWRITING
PURE COINCIDENCE
PURE MATHEMATICS
RARE OPPORTUNITY
ROOM TEMPERATURE
SEEK INFORMATION
SHOW FAVOURITISM
SOLO PERFORMANCE
STAY UNDERGROUND
TAKE PRECAUTIONS

VAIN   EXPECTATION
VAST   IMPROVEMENT
VERY   INTERESTING
WELL   REPRESENTED
WILL   SHAKESPEARE
WIND   INSTRUMENTS
WITH   COMPLIMENTS
WORD   ASSOCIATION
XMAS   DECORATIONS

5, 1, 5, 4

NEVER   A   CROSS   WORD
UNDER   A   FALSE   NAME

5, 1, 9

CAUSE   A   SENSATION
ISSUE   A   CHALLENGE
LODGE   A   COMPLAINT
NURSE   A   GRIEVANCE
QUITE   A   CHARACTER
SMOKE   A   CIGARETTE
UTTER   A   FALSEHOOD

5, 2, 1, 7

AGREE   ON   A   VERDICT
BIRDS   OF   A   FEATHER
BRING   IN   A   VERDICT
BURNT   TO   A   FRAZZLE
CHALK   UP   A   VICTORY
CLEAN   AS   A   WHISTLE
HAPPY   AS   A   SANDBOY
LIGHT   AS   A   FEATHER
PATCH   UP   A   QUARREL
PROUD   AS   A   PEACOCK
SPEAK   IN   A   WHISPER

5, 2, 2, 6

LEAVE   IT   TO   CHANCE
POINT   OF   NO   RETURN

5, 2, 3, 5

AFTER   MY   OWN   HEART
ALONE   IN   THE   WORLD
ARMED   TO   THE   TEETH
BIRTH   OF   THE   BLUES
BLACK   AS   THE   DEVIL
BLUES   IN   THE   NIGHT
BURNT   AT   THE   STAKE
BURST   AT   THE   SEAMS
CARES   OF   THE   WORLD
CHEAP   AT   THE   PRICE
CLERK   OF   THE   COURT
CLERK   OF   THE   HOUSE
CLERK   OF   THE   WORKS
CLOSE   TO   THE   SHORE
DEATH   ON   THE   ROADS

DRINK   ON   THE   HOUSE
FIGHT   TO   THE   DEATH
FIRST   IN   THE   FIELD
FIRST   IN   THE   QUEUE
FLICK   OF   THE   WRIST
FLOOR   OF   THE   HOUSE
HOVER   ON   THE   BRINK
KNOCK   TO   THE   FLOOR
LEAVE   IN   THE   LURCH
LIGHT   OF   THE   WORLD
MOUTH   OF   THE   RIVER
NIGHT   AT   THE   OPERA
NIGHT   ON   THE   TILES
NORTH   OF   THE   RIVER
PEACE   AT   ANY   PRICE
PENCE   IN   THE   POUND
PENNY   IN   THE   POUND
POWER   OF   THE   PRESS
PUNCH   IN   THE   MOUTH
QUEEN   OF   THE   SOUTH
RIGHT   TO   THE   POINT
SCENE   OF   THE   CRIME
SHIPS   IN   THE   NIGHT
SNAKE   IN   THE   GRASS
SOUTH   OF   THE   RIVER
SPEAK   OF   THE   DEVIL
STAND   IN   THE   QUEUE
STICK   TO   THE   FACTS
STICK   TO   THE   POINT
STICK   TO   THE   RULES
STILL   OF   THE   NIGHT
SWEAR   ON   THE   BIBLE
SWEET   TO   THE   TASTE
SWORD   IN   THE   STONE
THORN   IN   THE   FLESH
THROW   IN   THE   TOWEL
TOOLS   OF   THE   TRADE
TREND   OF   THE   TIMES
TRICK   OF   THE   TRADE
WATER   ON   THE   BRAIN
WOMAN   OF   THE   WORLD

5, 2, 4, 4

CLEAR   IN   ONES   MIND
HAPPY   IN   ONES   WORK
MUSIC   TO   ONES   EARS
PIECE   OF   GOOD   NEWS
PIECE   OF   ONES   MIND
PRICE   ON   ONES   HEAD
PRICK   UP   ONES   EARS
STAND   IN   FULL   VIEW
STAND   ON   ONES   HEAD
STAND   ON   ONES   TOES
STICK   TO   ONES   GUNS
SWEAT   OF   ONES   BROW
THORN   IN   ONES   SIDE
THROW   IN   ONES   HAND
WORLD   AT   ONES   FEET

5 , 2 , 5 , 3

CATCH AS CATCH CAN
FIRST IN FIRST OUT
WHIFF OF FRESH AIR

5 , 2 , 8

ABUSE OF LANGUAGE
AGREE TO DISAGREE
AHEAD OF SCHEDULE
BRING TO FRUITION
BROOD OF CHICKENS
BURST OF APPLAUSE
BURST OF LAUGHTER
CLASH OF OPINIONS
CLEAR AS DAYLIGHT
COURT OF JUDGMENT
CURSE OF SCOTLAND
DEATH BY DROWNING
EIGHT OF DIAMONDS
ERROR OF JUDGMENT
FIELD OF ACTIVITY
FIFTH OF DECEMBER
FIFTH OF FEBRUARY
FIFTH OF NOVEMBER
FIRST OF DECEMBER
FIRST OF FEBRUARY
FIRST OF NOVEMBER
FORCE AN ENTRANCE
HOURS OF BUSINESS
KNAVE OF DIAMONDS
LEAVE IN SUSPENSE
LIONS OF LONGLEAT
MARCH OF PROGRESS
MEANS OF APPROACH
NINTH OF DECEMBER
NINTH OF FEBRUARY
NINTH OF NOVEMBER
NURSE AN AMBITION
OFFER IN EXCHANGE
PIECE OF EVIDENCE
PIECE OF NONSENSE
PLACE OF BUSINESS
POWER OF ATTORNEY
POWER OF RECOVERY
PROOF OF DELIVERY
PROOF OF PURCHASE
QUEEN OF DIAMONDS
ROUND OF APPLAUSE
SENSE OF PLEASURE
SENSE OF SECURITY
SEVEN OF DIAMONDS
SHORT OF PRACTICE
SHRED OF EVIDENCE
SIEGE OF MAFEKING
SIMON DE MONTFORT
SIXTH OF DECEMBER
SIXTH OF FEBRUARY
SIXTH OF NOVEMBER
STAMP OF APPROVAL

STAND NO NONSENSE
STAND ON CEREMONY
STAND UP STRAIGHT
START AN ARGUMENT
STATE OF COLLAPSE
STATE OF SOBRIETY
STICK OF DYNAMITE
STORM OF APPLAUSE
SWORD OF DAMOCLES
TABLE OF CONTENTS
TEARS OF LAUGHTER
TENTH OF DECEMBER
TENTH OF FEBRUARY
TENTH OF NOVEMBER
THIRD OF DECEMBER
THIRD OF FEBRUARY
THIRD OF NOVEMBER
THREE OF DIAMONDS
TOWER OF STRENGTH
TRIAL OF STRENGTH
TROOP OF SOLDIERS
UNITY IS STRENGTH
WORLD OF LEARNING
YIELD TO PRESSURE

5 , 3 , 1 , 6

CARRY OUT A CENSUS
PAUSE FOR A MOMENT
THROW OUT A FEELER

5 , 3 , 2 , 1 , 4

THREE MEN IN A BOAT

5 , 3 , 2 , 5

DRIVE ONE TO DRINK
LAUGH OUT OF COURT
THROW OUT OF COURT
TOUGH NUT TO CRACK

5 , 3 , 3 , 4

BREAK THE BAD NEWS
BRING AND BUY SALE
BRING OUT THE BEST
EVERY NOW AND THEN
FEAST FOR THE GODS
FIRST THE BAD NEWS
MONEY FOR OLD ROPE
PETER AND THE WOLF
QUICK OFF THE MARK
REACH FOR THE MOON
READY FOR THE FRAY
THANK GOD FOR THAT
THROW OFF THE YOKE

5 , 3 , 4 , 3

ANNIE GET YOUR GUN
LAUGH AND GROW FAT

LEARN	THE	HARD	WAY
PAINT	THE	TOWN	RED
SINCE	THE	YEAR	DOT
WASTE	NOT	WANT	NOT

5, 3, 5, 2

THROW	NEW	LIGHT	ON
THROW	THE	TOWEL	IN

5, 3, 7

ABOVE THE AVERAGE
ABOVE THE SURFACE
ALIVE AND KICKING
APRIL THE SEVENTH
APRIL THE TWELFTH
BEGIN THE BEGUINE
BELOW THE HORIZON
BELOW THE SURFACE
BLOOD AND THUNDER
BOARD AND LODGING
BREAK THE BARRIER
BREAK THE SILENCE
CHEAT THE GALLOWS
CLAIM THE VICTORY
CLEAN THE WINDOWS
COUNT FOR NOTHING
COUNT THE MINUTES
COUNT THE TAKINGS
CROSS THE CHANNEL
CROSS THE RUBICON
DAVID AND GOLIATH
FACTS AND FIGURES
FIGHT FOR FREEDOM
FIRST-AID STATION
HENRY THE SEVENTH
JOINT AND SEVERAL
JUDGE FOR ONESELF
LEAVE THE COUNTRY
LORDS AND COMMONS
LOWER THE CURTAIN
MARCH THE SEVENTH
MARCH THE TWELFTH
MARKS AND SPENCER
NORTH SEA FISHING
PRESS FOR PAYMENT
PRESS THE TRIGGER
QUEEN AND COUNTRY
QUITE THE REVERSE
RAISE THE CURTAIN
RAISE THE SUBJECT
READY AND WILLING
ROYAL AND ANCIENT
SERVE TWO MASTERS
SHORT AND CURLIES
SOLVE THE PROBLEM
SORRY FOR ONESELF
SOUND THE RETREAT
SOUTH SEA ISLANDS
SPEAK FOR ONESELF

STAND AND DELIVER
STARS AND STRIPES
START THE BIDDING
STEAL THE THUNDER
SWEEP THE CHIMNEY
THROW OUT FEELERS
UNDER THE COUNTER
UNDER THE SURFACE
UNDER THE WEATHER
WATER THE FLOWERS
WHATS THE PROBLEM?
WINES AND SPIRITS
WOULD YOU BELIEVE?
YOUNG AND HEALTHY

5, 4, 1, 5

BLOOD FROM A STONE
LAUGH LIKE A DRAIN
LAUGH LIKE A HYENA
NEVER CAST A CLOUT
SHAKE LIKE A JELLY

5, 4, 2, 4

FIRST PORT OF CALL

5, 4, 3, 3

THREE TWOS ARE SIX
UNDER LOCK AND KEY

5, 4, 4, 2

PRICK ONES EARS UP

5, 4, 6

BRING INTO ACTION
BURST INTO FLAMES
CATCH ONES BREATH
CLEAR ONES THROAT
CLOAK-ROOM TICKET
COUNT ONES CHANGE
COVER ONES TRACKS
DRINK ONES HEALTH
ENJOY GOOD HEALTH
HORSE-SHOE MAGNET
JELLY ROLL MORTON
JOLLY GOOD FELLOW
LEARN ONES LESSON
LOWER ONES SIGHTS
MUSIC-HALL ARTIST
PEACE WITH HONOUR
QUOTE FROM MEMORY
RAISE ONES SIGHTS
REACH ROCK-BOTTOM
READY MADE EXCUSE
SHORT-TERM POLICY
SOUTH-WEST AFRICA
SPEED-BOAT RACING

SPOIL ONES RECORD
STAGE-DOOR JOHNNY
STAND ONES GROUND
STUNT ONES GROWTH
THREE EASY STAGES
THREE MILE ISLAND
THROW INTO PRISON
TIGHT-ROPE WALKER
TOUCH ROCK-BOTTOM
UNDER ONES BREATH
WASTE ONES BREATH
WATCH ONES WEIGHT
WATCH WITH MOTHER
WHATS YOUR POISON?
WHITE MANS BURDEN
WRONG WAVE-LENGTH

5, 5, 2, 3

CRAZY MIXED-UP KID
MERRY MONTH OF MAY

5, 5, 5

CROSS ENEMY LINES
EIGHT SCORE-DRAWS
FANCY-DRESS PARTY
FIFTY-EIGHT PENCE
FIFTY-SEVEN PENCE
FIFTY-THREE PENCE
FIRST-CLASS HOTEL
FIRST-CLASS MATCH
FORTY-EIGHT HOURS
FORTY-EIGHT PENCE
FORTY-SEVEN PENCE
FORTY-THREE PENCE
GOING THREE TIMES
GRAND UNION CANAL
HEAVY-METAL MUSIC
JERRY-BUILT HOUSE
MONEY MAKES MONEY
MONTE CARLO RALLY
MONTH AFTER MONTH
NIGHT AFTER NIGHT
NOBEL PEACE PRIZE
OCEAN-GOING LINER
POINT-BLANK RANGE
ROYAL OPERA HOUSE
SHARE PRICE INDEX
SHEER BRUTE FORCE
SIXTY-EIGHT PENCE
SIXTY-SEVEN PENCE
SIXTY-THREE PENCE
SOUND-PROOF WALLS
STAND STOCK-STILL
STILL, SMALL VOICE
SWEET FANNY ADAMS
THREE-PIECE SUITE
UNDER CLOSE GUARD
UNDER-COVER AGENT

5, 6, 2, 2

THINK BETTER OF IT

5, 6, 4

CLOUD-CUCKOO LAND
EXTRA STRONG MINT
MARYS LITTLE LAMB
NEVER-ENDING TASK
ROYAL ALBERT HALL
SEVEN DEADLY SINS
SIGHT-SEEING TOUR
THEIR FINEST HOUR
THINK THINGS OVER
THREE LITTLE PIGS
THREE-COURSE MEAL
THREE-LEGGED RACE
THREE-LETTER WORD
ULTRA-VIOLET RAYS
WHERE THERES LIFE
WHERE THERES MUCK
WHILE THERES LIFE

5, 7, 3

CROSS-COUNTRY RUN
EARLY CLOSING DAY
EVERY MOTHERS SON
LEAVE NOTHING OUT
PLAIN-CLOTHES MAN
SAINT GEORGES DAY
SOUTH AFRICAN WAR
STARK STARING MAD

5, 10

ABOVE EVERYTHING
ADDED ATTRACTION
ADMIT EVERYTHING
AGREE BEFOREHAND
ARMED NEUTRALITY
ASCOT RACECOURSE
BASIC INGREDIENT
BLUNT INSTRUMENT
BRASS INSTRUMENT
CARRY CONVICTION
CHEAP RESTAURANT
CHIEF MAGISTRATE
CHILD PSYCHOLOGY
CHRIS BONNINGTON
CLEAR CONSCIENCE
CLEAR REFLECTION
CLOSE COMPANIONS
CLOSE FRIENDSHIP
CROWD PSYCHOLOGY
CUBIC CENTIMETRE
DAILY OCCURRENCE
DRILL INSTRUCTOR
DRIVE RECKLESSLY
EIGHT KILOMETRES

ENTER PARLIAMENT	PARTY CONFERENCE
EPSOM RACECOURSE	PEACE CONFERENCE
FALSE ACCUSATION	PETER OOSTERHUIS
FALSE IMPRESSION	PIOUS SENTIMENTS
FALSE REPUTATION	POLAR EXPEDITION
FATAL ATTRACTION	PRESS CONFERENCE
FIFTY KILOMETRES	PRICE COMMISSION
FIRST APPEARANCE	PRICE REGULATION
FIRST IMPORTANCE	PRIOR ENGAGEMENT
FIRST IMPRESSION	PRIVY COUNCILLOR
FIRST LIEUTENANT	PROVE ACCEPTABLE
FIRST PRINCIPLES	QUICK SUCCESSION
FIXED IMPRESSION	QUITE DELIGHTFUL
FORTY KILOMETRES	RADIO JOURNALISM
FRESH COMPLEXION	RAISE OBJECTIONS
FULLY GUARANTEED	RALPH RICHARDSON
GRAND INQUISITOR	RAPID SUCCESSION
GRAVE MISGIVINGS	RIGHT HONOURABLE
GREAT ASSISTANCE	RIGHT WAVELENGTH
GREAT EXCITEMENT	RIGID DISCIPLINE
GREAT EXHIBITION	ROBIN GOODFELLOW
GREAT IMPORTANCE	ROYAL COMMISSION
GREAT POPULARITY	ROYAL TOURNAMENT
GREEK RESTAURANT	RUDDY COMPLEXION
GREEN CHARTREUSE	RURAL POPULATION
GROSS NEGLIGENCE	SALES RESISTANCE
HARSH PUNISHMENT	SCOTT FITZGERALD
HEART TRANSPLANT	SEVEN KILOMETRES
HEAVY CASUALTIES	SHADY REPUTATION
HEAVY PUNISHMENT	SHARP IMPRESSION
HENRY LONGFELLOW	SIXTY KILOMETRES
HOTEL PROPRIETOR	SLANG EXPRESSION
HUMAN EXPERIENCE	SMALL PERCENTAGE
HUMID ATMOSPHERE	SMOKY ATMOSPHERE
IRISH SWEEPSTAKE	SOLID FOUNDATION
JOINT GOVERNMENT	SOUND INVESTMENT
JOINT POSSESSION	SOUTH KENSINGTON
JONAH BARRINGTON	SPLIT INFINITIVE
KEITH WATERHOUSE	SPOIL EVERYTHING
LARGE PERCENTAGE	STAGE DIRECTIONS
LEAST RESISTANCE	STAMP COLLECTING
LEAVE FOOTPRINTS	STAMP COLLECTION
LEAVE UNFINISHED	STATE DEPARTMENT
LEGAL DEPARTMENT	STATE ENTERPRISE
LEGAL PROFESSION	SUGAR PLANTATION
LEGAL SETTLEMENT	SWEAR ALLEGIANCE
LIGHT LITERATURE	TEMPT PROVIDENCE
LOCAL GOVERNMENT	TENSE ATMOSPHERE
LOCAL INHABITANT	THREE KILOMETRES
MANIC DEPRESSION	THREE MUSKETEERS
MANIC DEPRESSIVE	TITUS ANDRONICUS
MARIE ANTOINETTE	TOTAL ABSTINENCE
MORAL OBLIGATION	TOUGH ASSIGNMENT
MORAL PHILOSOPHY	TRADE DELEGATION
MORAL STANDPOINT	TRADE SUPPLEMENT
NAVAL ENGAGEMENT	UNDER COMPULSION
NAVAL OPERATIONS	UNDER DISCIPLINE
NIGHT MANOEUVRES	UNDER DISCUSSION
NOBLE SENTIMENTS	UNDER OBLIGATION
NOVEL EXPERIENCE	URBAN POPULATION
OLDER GENERATION	VICHY GOVERNMENT

VITAL STATISTICS
WATCH TELEVISION
WHITE CORPUSCLES
WORLD GOVERNMENT
WRONG ASSUMPTION
YIELD GRACEFULLY
YOUNG GENERATION
YOURS FAITHFULLY
YOURS OBEDIENTLY
YOUTH HOSTELLING

6, 1, 8

ACCEPT A PROPOSAL
ASSUME A DISGUISE
EDWARD G. ROBINSON
SPRING A SURPRISE

6, 2, 1, 3, 3

BRIGHT AS A NEW PIN

6, 2, 1, 6

BRIGHT AS A BUTTON
PUPPET ON A STRING

6, 2, 3, 4

BATTLE OF THE NILE
BEATEN AT THE POST
BELONG TO THE PAST
BEWARE OF THE BULL
BOTTOM OF THE FORM
BOTTOM OF THE HILL
BRIDGE OF THE NOSE
CUCKOO IN THE NEST
DRIVEN UP THE WALL
HANGED BY THE NECK
HARROW ON THE HILL
KEEPER OF THE KEYS
KITTEN ON THE KEYS
KNIGHT OF THE BATH
KNIGHT OF THE ROAD
LEADER OF THE BAND
MIDDLE OF THE ROAD
MONTHS OF THE YEAR
PATRON OF THE ARTS
PIPPED AT THE POST
RETURN TO THE FOLD
RETURN TO THE PAST
ROOTED TO THE SPOT
ROTTEN TO THE CORE
SCRUFF OF THE NECK
SOAKED TO THE SKIN
STRAWS IN THE WIND
STRIKE UP THE BAND
TARZAN OF THE APES
WHITES OF THE EYES

6, 2, 7

ASCENT OF EVEREST
BARBER OF SEVILLE
BATTLE OF BRITAIN
BOTTLE OF PERFUME
BOTTLE OF VINEGAR
BREACH OF PROMISE
BREAST OF CHICKEN
BREATH OF SCANDAL
CENTRE OF GRAVITY
CHANCE OF SUCCESS
CHANGE OF ADDRESS
CHANGE OF CLIMATE
CHANGE OF CLOTHES
CHANGE OF COSTUME
CHANGE OF OPINION
CHANGE OF PURPOSE
CHANGE OF SCENERY
CHANGE OF SUBJECT
CHANGE OF TACTICS
CHOICE OF COLOURS
CHOICE OF WEAPONS
CHURCH OF ENGLAND
CIRCLE OF FRIENDS
COLOUR BY NUMBERS
COMMIT AN OFFENCE
COMMIT TO WRITING
CREATE AN OPENING
DAPHNE DU MAURIER
DEPTHS OF DESPAIR
DEVOID OF MEANING
DOCTOR OF SCIENCE
DOUBLE OR NOTHING
EIGHTH OF JANUARY
EIGHTH OF OCTOBER
FOURTH OF JANUARY
FOURTH OF OCTOBER
FRUITS OF VICTORY
GEORGE DU MAURIER
HAUNCH OF VENISON
HAZARD AN OPINION
HEAVEN BE PRAISED
HEIGHT OF FASHION
HIDING TO NOTHING
JOINED-UP WRITING
LADIES IN WAITING
LEADER OF SOCIETY
LEAGUE OF NATIONS
LENGTH OF SERVICE
LITTER OF PUPPIES
LITTLE OR NOTHING
MASTER OF SCIENCE
MATTER OF OPINION
MEMBER OF SOCIETY
MINUTE OF SILENCE
MOMENT OF MADNESS
MUSTER UP COURAGE
OBJECT OF DISLIKE
OBJECT OF WORSHIP
ORIGIN OF SPECIES

PEOPLE	IN	GENERAL	BUBBLE	AND	SQUEAK
PEOPLE	OF	QUALITY	CASTOR	AND	POLLUX
PILLAR	OF	SOCIETY	CAUGHT	AND	BOWLED
PLAGUE	OF	LOCUSTS	CAUGHT	RED-HANDED	
PRINCE	OF	DENMARK	CHARGE	TOO	LITTLE
PURSUE	AN	INQUIRY	CHEESE	AND	PICKLE
REDUCE	TO	NOTHING	CLOSER	AND	CLOSER
REDUCE	TO	POVERTY	CORNER	THE	MARKET
RENDER	AN	ACCOUNT	DEMAND	AND	SUPPLY
REPENT	AT	LEISURE	DENNIS	THE	MENACE
RETURN	IN	TRIUMPH	DOUBLE	THE	STAKES
SAFETY	IN	NUMBERS	DOZENS	AND	DOZENS
SCALES	OF	JUSTICE	EDWARD	THE	EIGHTH
SCHOOL	OF	DANCING	EDWARD	THE	FOURTH
SCHOOL	OF	THOUGHT	EDWARD	THE	SECOND
SECOND	IN	COMMAND	EXPORT	AND	IMPORT
SECOND	OF	JANUARY	FASTER	AND	FASTER
SECOND	OF	OCTOBER	FATHER	AND	MOTHER
SHIVER	ME	TIMBERS!	FOLLOW	THE	LEADER
SLOUGH	OF	DESPOND	FOLLOW	THE	PLOUGH
SOURCE	OF	TROUBLE	GEORGE	THE	FOURTH
SPEECH	IS	SILVERN	GEORGE	THE	SECOND
SPOILS	OF	VICTORY	GREASE	THE	WHEELS
STATUE	OF	LIBERTY	GUILTY	BUT	INSANE
STREAM	OF	THOUGHT	HAMMER	AND	SICKLE
STREAM	OF	TRAFFIC	HANGED	FOR	MURDER
SUFFER	IN	SILENCE	HANSEL	AND	GRETEL
SYMBOL	OF	JUSTICE	HEALTH	AND	WEALTH
TRAVEL	IN	COMFORT	HEARTS	ARE	TRUMPS
TREATY	OF	LOCARNO	HIGHER	AND	HIGHER
VOLLEY	OF	THUNDER	HUNGER	AND	THIRST
WEALTH	OF	NATIONS	INCOME-TAX	DEMAND	
WEIGHT	OF	NUMBERS	INCOME-TAX	RELIEF	
WEIGHT	OF	OPINION	INCOME-TAX	RETURN	
WISDOM	OF	SOLOMON	JOCKEY	FOR	PLACES
WORTHY	OF	COMMENT	LOAVES	AND	FISHES
			LOCKED	AND	BOLTED

6 , 3 , 3 , 3

LOUISA MAY ALCOTT
MIDDLE-AGE SPREAD

PRAYER FOR THE DAY

MONTHS AND MONTHS
MOTHER AND FATHER

6 , 3 , 6

NEARER AND NEARER
NEEDLE AND COTTON

ACROSS	THE	STREET	NEEDLE	AND	THREAD
AROUND	THE	CORNER	PESTLE	AND	MORTAR
ASCEND	THE	THRONE	PLOUGH	THE	FIELDS
AUGUST	THE	EIGHTH	POISON-PEN	LETTER	
AUGUST	THE	FOURTH	POPEYE	THE	SAILOR
AUGUST	THE	SECOND	PREACH	THE	GOSPEL
BARNUM	AND	BAILEY	PURELY	AND	SIMPLY
BARRED	AND	BOLTED	PURSUE	THE	MATTER
BEHIND	THE	SCENES	REASON	FOR	LIVING
BETRAY	THE	SECRET	REMOVE	ALL	TRACES
BETTER	AND	BETTER	REOPEN	OLD	WOUNDS
BEYOND	ALL	BOUNDS	REPAIR	THE	DAMAGE
BEYOND	THE	FRINGE	RIGHTS	AND	WRONGS
BIGGER	AND	BETTER	SAVILE	ROW	TAILOR
BIGGER	AND	BIGGER	SCOTCH	AND	GINGER
BOLTED	AND	BARRED	SCRAPE	THE	BARREL
BRICKS	AND	MORTAR	SETTLE	OLD	SCORES
BRIGHT	AND	BREEZY	SETTLE	THE	MATTER

SLINGS AND ARROWS
SLOWLY AND SURELY
SLOWLY BUT SURELY
SPADES ARE TRUMPS
SPREAD THE GOSPEL
SQUARE-LEG UMPIRE
STACKS AND STACKS
STICKS AND STONES
STOCKS AND SHARES
STRESS AND STRAIN
STRIVE FOR EFFECT
SUPPLY AND DEMAND
TICKLE THE PALATE
WANTED FOR MURDER

6, 4, 1, 4

BELLOW LIKE A BULL
SEALED WITH A KISS
WADDLE LIKE A DUCK

6, 4, 5

BETRAY ONES TRUST
BEYOND ONES GRASP
BEYOND ONES MEANS
BEYOND ONES PRIME
BEYOND ONES REACH
BEYOND THIS POINT
CHANGE ONES VIEWS
CHOOSE ONES WORDS
CLENCH ONES FISTS
CLENCH ONES TEETH
DINING-ROOM TABLE
DOUBLE YOUR MONEY
EIGHTY-FIVE PENCE
EIGHTY-FOUR PENCE
EIGHTY-NINE PENCE
FAMOUS LAST WORDS
FASTER THAN LIGHT
FASTER THAN SOUND
HARDEN ONES HEART
HASTEN ONES DEATH
HEAVEN UPON EARTH
INDIAN ROPE-TRICK
INVEST WITH POWER
LOADED WITH MONEY
LOUDER THAN WORDS
MIDDLE-AGED WOMAN
NINETY-FIVE PENCE
NINETY-FOUR PENCE
NINETY-NINE PENCE
ORANGE FREE STATE
PLIGHT ONES TROTH
PRETTY MUCH ALIKE
SEARCH ONES HEART
SECOND TIME ROUND
SPLASH ONES MONEY
SPRAIN ONES ANKLE
SPREAD ONES WINGS
STRAIN ONES LUNGS

STRONG WILL-POWER
THINGS LOOK BLACK
THIRTY-FOUR PENCE
THIRTY-NINE PENCE
THIRTY-NINE STEPS
TICKLE ONES FANCY
TWENTY-FIVE MILES
TWENTY-FIVE PENCE
TWENTY-FOUR CARAT
TWENTY-FOUR HOURS
TWENTY-FOUR PENCE
TWENTY-NINE PENCE
WHITER THAN WHITE
WITHIN EASY REACH
WITHIN ONES GRASP

6, 5, 4

BULLET-PROOF VEST
DEVILS PUNCH BOWL
DOUBLE WHITE LINE
DRINKA PINTA MILK
FRENCH ONION SOUP
GROUND-FLOOR FLAT
LITTLE-KNOWN FACT
SECOND CLASS MAIL
SECOND CLASS POST
TWENTY-EIGHT DAYS

6, 6, 3

PUBLIC-SCHOOL BOY

6, 9

ABRUPT DEPARTURE
ACTIVE SUPPORTER
ALFRED HITCHCOCK
ANIMAL MAGNETISM
BANNER HEADLINES
BARBRA STREISAND
BEAUTY TREATMENT
BECOME ENAMOURED
BECOME INVISIBLE
BEFORE BREAKFAST
BEFORE CHRISTMAS
BEHAVE NATURALLY
BENITO MUSSOLINI
BEYOND CRITICISM
BEYOND ENDURANCE
BLONDE BOMBSHELL
BOLTON WANDERERS
BONDED WAREHOUSE
BRIGHT YOUNGSTER
BRONZE MEDALLIST
BUDGET ESTIMATES
BUTTON MUSHROOMS
CASUAL REFERENCE
CHANCE DISCOVERY
CHANCE ENCOUNTER

CHANGE	DIRECTION
CHILLY	RECEPTION
COLOUR	BLINDNESS
COLOUR	PREJUDICE
COMMON	COMPLAINT
COMMON	KNOWLEDGE
COMMON	OWNERSHIP
COUNTY	CRICKETER
COUNTY	FERMANAGH
CREASE	RESISTANT
DECENT	BEHAVIOUR
DEMAND	ATTENTION
DENTAL	TREATMENT
DEVILS	COMPANION
DEVILS	PUNCHBOWL
DIRECT	INFLUENCE
DIVINE	MESSENGER
DJANGO	REINHARDT
DONALD	PLEASANCE
DOUBLE	SEVENTEEN
DOUBLE	STANDARDS
ERNEST	HEMINGWAY
ESCAPE	DETECTION
EVONNE	GOOLAGONG
EXPECT	OTHERWISE
EXPERT	KNOWLEDGE
FAMILY	GATHERING
FAMILY	SOLICITOR
FATHER	CHRISTMAS
FATHER	CONFESSOR
FEEBLE	IMITATION
FELLOW	TRAVELLER
FENCED	ENCLOSURE
FOLLOW	PRECEDENT
FORGED	SIGNATURE
FORKED	LIGHTNING
FORMAL	AGREEMENT
FORMAL	COMPLAINT
FORMAL	STATEMENT
FOURTH	DIMENSION
FRENCH	BREAKFAST
FRENCH	DICTATION
FRIDAY	AFTERNOON
FUTURE	EXISTENCE
FUTURE	REFERENCE
GARDEN	FURNITURE
GOLDEN	DELICIOUS
GOLDEN	HANDSHAKE
GOLDEN	RETRIEVER
GOLDEN	SOVEREIGN
GOSSIP	COLUMNIST
GROVER	CLEVELAND
GUILTY	BEHAVIOUR
HAROLD	MACMILLAN
HEARTY	BREAKFAST
HEROIC	QUALITIES
HIGHER	EDUCATION
HIGHLY	COMMENDED
HIGHLY	CONNECTED
HIGHLY	DELIGHTED
HIGHLY	EFFICIENT
HIGHLY	ORGANISED
HIGHLY	QUALIFIED
HIGHLY	RESPECTED
INDOOR	FIREWORKS
INFANT	MORTALITY
ISLAND	CONTINENT
JOHNNY	DANKWORTH
KEENLY	CONTESTED
LABOUR	CANDIDATE
LABOUR	RELATIONS
LABOUR	SUPPORTER
LADIES	COMPANION
LATEST	INVENTION
LIONEL	BARRYMORE
LIQUID	RESOURCES
LITTLE	ENGLANDER
LITTLE	KNOWLEDGE
LIVING	STANDARDS
LIVING	TESTIMONY
LONDON	TRANSPORT
LONDON	WEIGHTING
MARINE	INSURANCE
MASTER	CARPENTER
MASTER	CRAFTSMAN
MENTAL	BREAKDOWN
MENTAL	DEFECTIVE
MENTAL	FACULTIES
MENTAL	TREATMENT
MODEST	BEHAVIOUR
MONDAY	AFTERNOON
MORBID	CURIOSITY
MOTLEY	GATHERING
MOVING	SPECTACLE
MOVING	STAIRCASE
MUTUAL	AFFECTION
MUTUAL	AGREEMENT
MUTUAL	HOSTILITY
MUTUAL	SUSPICION
NORMAL	BEHAVIOUR
NORMAL	PROCEDURE
OLIVER	GOLDSMITH
ORANGE	MARMALADE
PENCIL	SHARPENER
PERIOD	FURNITURE
PETROL	RATIONING
POLICE	CONSTABLE
POLICE	INSPECTOR
PUBLIC	CHARACTER
PUBLIC	EDUCATION
PUBLIC	ENCLOSURE
PUBLIC	EXECUTION
PUBLIC	KNOWLEDGE
PUBLIC	OWNERSHIP
PUBLIC	RELATIONS
PUBLIC	TRANSPORT
QUEENS	MESSENGER
RACIAL	PREJUDICE
RACIAL	TOLERANCE
RACING	CERTAINTY
RAMSAY	MACDONALD
RECENT	DISCOVERY

REFUSE COLLECTOR
ROGETS THESAURUS
RUBBER TRUNCHEON
SAMSON AGONISTES
SCHOOL INSPECTOR
SECOND CHILDHOOD
SECOND DIMENSION
SECOND FAVOURITE
SECRET COURTSHIP
SECRET INFLUENCE
SECRET STAIRCASE
SECURE ADMISSION
SELECT COMMITTEE
SEVERE THRASHING
SHABBY TREATMENT
SILVER MEDALLIST
SLIGHT VARIATION
SOCIAL GATHERING
SPEECH THERAPIST
SPIRAL STAIRCASE
SPORTS EQUIPMENT
SQUARE SHOULDERS
STABLE COMPANION
STEADY BOYFRIEND
STICKY SITUATION
STRONG INFLUENCE
STRONG OBJECTION
STRONG WILLPOWER
SUDDEN DEPARTURE
SUDDEN ULTIMATUM
SUMMER LIGHTNING
SUMMER RESIDENCE
SUNDAY AFTERNOON
SUNDAY NEWSPAPER
SUNDAY TELEGRAPH
SUNSET BOULEVARD
SUTTON COLDFIELD
THOMAS JEFFERSON
TICKET COLLECTOR
TICKET INSPECTOR
TIPPED CIGARETTE
TRAVEL INCOGNITO
TRICKY SITUATION
TWELVE DISCIPLES
TWENTY QUESTIONS
TWENTY SHILLINGS
UNFAIR ADVANTAGE
UNFAIR TREATMENT
UNTRUE STATEMENT
VERBAL AGREEMENT
VERBAL CRITICISM
VIRGIN TERRITORY
WALRUS MOUSTACHE
WASHED OVERBOARD
WEEKLY NEWSPAPER
WIENER SCHNITZEL
WILSON COMMITTEE
WOMANS INTUITION
WOMENS INSTITUTE
WOODEN PARTITION
WORTHY ADVERSARY

7, 1, 7

WITHOUT A PURPOSE
WITHOUT A SCRATCH

7, 2, 2, 4

QUARTER OF AN HOUR

7, 2, 3, 3

CASTLES IN THE AIR
ECLIPSE OF THE SUN
HOLIDAY BY THE SEA
HOLIDAY IN THE SUN
OFFICER OF THE DAY
OFFICER OF THE LAW

7, 2, 6

ANXIOUS TO PLEASE
BENEFIT OF CLERGY
BOTTLED UP INSIDE
BREADTH OF VISION
CAPITAL OF FRANCE
CHARLES DE GAULLE
COUNCIL OF EUROPE
COUNTRY OF ORIGIN
EXPENSE NO OBJECT
EXPOSED TO DANGER
FRANCIS OF ASSISI
FREEDOM OF ACCESS
FREEDOM OF ACTION
FREEDOM OF CHOICE
FREEDOM OF SPEECH
GENERAL DE GAULLE
HANDFUL OF SILVER
HONOURS OF BATTLE
IMPROVE IN HEALTH
KINGDOM OF HEAVEN
MEASURE OF LENGTH
MEASURE OF WEIGHT
NOTHING IN COMMON
NOTHING TO CHOOSE
OFFICER IN CHARGE
PARAGON OF VIRTUE
PAYABLE ON DEMAND
PICTURE OF HEALTH
QUARTER TO ELEVEN
QUARTER TO TWELVE
RESERVE OF ENERGY
RESTORE TO HEALTH
RESTORE TO SANITY
SEVENTH OF AUGUST
SILENCE IS GOLDEN
STRANGE TO RELATE
TRUMPED-UP CHARGE
TWELFTH OF AUGUST
WILLIAM OF ORANGE
WILLING TO PLEASE

7 , 3 , 3 , 2

BETWEEN YOU AND ME

7 , 3 , 5

AGAINST   THE   CLOCK
AGAINST   THE   GRAIN
AGAINST   THE   RULES
BALANCE   THE   BOOKS
BETWEEN   THE   LINES
CHAPTER   AND   VERSE
CHARLES   AND   DIANA
CHARLES   THE   FIRST
CHARLES   THE   THIRD
CONFUSE   THE   ISSUE
DELIVER   THE   GOODS
DEVALUE   THE   POUND
DISPUTE   THE   FACTS
DISTORT   THE   TRUTH
DISTURB   THE   PEACE
DOLLARS   AND   CENTS
ENGLAND   AND   WALES
HUNDRED   AND   EIGHT
HUNDRED   AND   FIFTY
HUNDRED   AND   FORTY
HUNDRED   AND   SEVEN
HUNDRED   AND   SIXTY
HUNDRED   AND   THREE
JANUARY   THE   FIFTH
JANUARY   THE   FIRST
JANUARY   THE   NINTH
JANUARY   THE   SIXTH
JANUARY   THE   TENTH
JANUARY   THE   THIRD
JUMPING-OFF   PLACE
MUSTARD   AND   CRESS
OCTOBER   THE   FIFTH
OCTOBER   THE   FIRST
OCTOBER   THE   NINTH
OCTOBER   THE   SIXTH
OCTOBER   THE   TENTH
OCTOBER   THE   THIRD
PEACHES   AND   CREAM
PERSONA   NON   GRATA
PRESSED   FOR   MONEY
PRESSED   FOR   SPACE
PROLONG   THE   AGONY
QUICKEN   THE   PULSE
RECOVER   THE   ASHES
RICHARD   THE   FIRST
RICHARD   THE   THIRD
ROMULUS   AND   REMUS
SAUSAGE   AND   CHIPS
SEVENTY-ONE   PENCE
SEVENTY-SIX   PENCE
SEVENTY-TWO   PENCE
SHUFFLE   THE   CARDS
STRETCH   THE   POINT
THROUGH   THE   YEARS
TOSSING   THE   CABER

VANILLA   ICE-CREAM
VIOLATE   THE   TERMS
WAITING   FOR   GODOT
WEATHER   THE   STORM
WILLIAM   THE   FIRST
WILLIAM   THE   THIRD

7 , 4 , 4

ABANDON   ONES   POST
ACHIEVE   ONES   GOAL
AGAINST   ONES   WILL
ANOTHER   FINE   MESS
BREATHE   ONES   LAST
BROADEN   ONES   MIND
CARDIFF   ARMS   PARK
CHINESE   TAKE-AWAY
CLOSING-DOWN   SALE
COULDNT   CARE   LESS
DECLARE   ONES   LOVE
FEATHER   ONES   NEST
FREEDOM   FROM   FEAR
FREEDOM   FROM   WANT
NEGLECT   ONES   DUTY
NOTTING   HILL   GATE
POURING   WITH   RAIN
QUARTER   PAST   FIVE
QUARTER   PAST   FOUR
QUARTER   PAST   NINE
RELEASE   ONES   HOLD
SCRATCH   ONES   HEAD
SHARPEN   ONES   WITS
SLACKEN   ONES   PACE
STRETCH   ONES   LEGS
SUSPECT   FOUL   PLAY
TEEMING   WITH   RAIN
TIGHTEN   ONES   BELT
TIGHTEN   ONES   GRIP
TIGHTEN   ONES   HOLD
TREATED   LIKE   DIRT
TREMBLE   WITH   FEAR
VARSITY   BOAT-RACE
WHISTLE-STOP   TOUR
WORKING-MANS   CLUB
WROUGHT-IRON   GATE

7 , 5 , 3

CAPITAL   GAINS   TAX
HUNDRED   YEARS   WAR
PRESTON   NORTH   END
SPANISH   CIVIL   WAR

7 , 6 , 2

STRANGE   GOINGS-ON

7 , 8

ABERFAN   DISASTER
ACCOUNT   RENDERED

ADOPTED	DAUGHTER	DELAYED	REACTION
AFRICAN	ELEPHANT	DELIVER	JUDGMENT
AMATEUR	CHAMPION	DIAMOND	MERCHANT
AMATEUR	FOOTBALL	DIAMOND	NECKLACE
AMERIGO	VESPUCCI	DISTANT	RELATIVE
ANCIENT	LANGUAGE	DRASTIC	MEASURES
ANCIENT	MONUMENT	DRAUGHT	EXCLUDER
ANTHONY	TROLLOPE	DUBIOUS	BLESSING
AVERAGE	CONTENTS	EARNING	CAPACITY
AWKWARD	CUSTOMER	EASTERN	COUNTIES
AWKWARD	POSITION	ENDLESS	ARGUMENT
AWKWARD	QUESTION	ENGLISH	LANGUAGE
BARGAIN	BASEMENT	ENTENTE	CORDIALE
BEDROOM	SLIPPERS	ESCAPED	PRISONER
BENEATH	CONTEMPT	ETERNAL	TRIANGLE
BERMUDA	TRIANGLE	EVENING	STANDARD
BINDING	CONTRACT	EXALTED	POSITION
BOWLING	ANALYSIS	EXPOSED	POSITION
BRAILLE	ALPHABET	EXPRESS	CONTEMPT
BRITISH	CHAMPION	EXPRESS	DELIVERY
BRITISH	COLUMBIA	EXTREME	MEASURES
BRITISH	HONDURAS	EXTREME	PATIENCE
BRITISH	PASSPORT	EXTREME	POSITION
BROADLY	SPEAKING	EYEBROW	TWEEZERS
BUDDING	CHAMPION	FEDERAL	REPUBLIC
BURNING	QUESTION	FESTIVE	OCCASION
CABINET	MINISTER	FIFTEEN	THOUSAND
CAPITAL	EMPLOYED	FINANCE	MINISTER
CAPITAL	SENTENCE	FISHING	INDUSTRY
CAPITAL	TRANSFER	FLAMING	NUISANCE
CAPTIVE	AUDIENCE	FOREIGN	CURRENCY
CENTRAL	POSITION	FOREIGN	EXCHANGE
CERTAIN	QUANTITY	FOREIGN	LANGUAGE
CHANNEL	CROSSING	FOREIGN	MINISTER
CHARLES	KINGSLEY	FORWARD	MOVEMENT
CHARLES	LAUGHTON	FRANKLY	SPEAKING
CHICKEN	MARYLAND	FUNERAL	CEREMONY
CHICKEN	SANDWICH	FUNERAL	DIRECTOR
CHINESE	TAKEAWAY	GENERAL	ASSEMBLY
CHIPPED	POTATOES	GENERAL	ELECTION
CLAPHAM	JUNCTION	GENERAL	FACTOTUM
COLLECT	EVIDENCE	GENERAL	HOSPITAL
COLLECT	MATERIAL	GENERAL	INTEREST
COMPANY	DIRECTOR	GENERAL	OVERHAUL
COMPARE	FINDINGS	GENERAL	PRACTICE
CONCERT	PLATFORM	GEORGES	POMPIDOU
COOKING	UTENSILS	GIRLISH	LAUGHTER
CORDIAL	GREETING	GISCARD	DESTAING
CORRECT	ESTIMATE	GLARING	OMISSION
COTTAGE	HOSPITAL	GRADUAL	PROGRESS
COTTAGE	INDUSTRY	GREATLY	INDEBTED
CRAMPED	QUARTERS	GREATLY	SUPERIOR
CREAMED	POTATOES	GRILLED	SAUSAGES
CRICKET	PAVILION	GRILLED	TOMATOES
CROOKED	SIXPENCE	GUARDED	LANGUAGE
CRUCIAL	QUESTION	GUSTAVE	FLAUBERT
CURTAIN	MATERIAL	HACKNEY	CARRIAGE
CUSTOMS	OFFICIAL	HAILING	DISTANCE
DAMNING	EVIDENCE	HARBOUR	FEELINGS
DANCING	MISTRESS	HARVEST	FESTIVAL
DEFENCE	MINISTER	HEALTHY	APPETITE

HEALTHY	ATTITUDE
HEALTHY	EXERCISE
HEARSAY	EVIDENCE
HOUSING	MINISTER
HOUSING	SHORTAGE
HUMANLY	POSSIBLE
HUNDRED	THOUSAND
INJURED	INNOCENT
INNINGS	DECLARED
INSTANT	RESPONSE
INTERIM	DIVIDEND
INVALID	CARRIAGE
INVITED	AUDIENCE
ITALIAN	VERMOUTH
JACQUES	COUSTEAU
JOBBING	GARDENER
KITCHEN	UTENSILS
KNIGHTS	TEMPLARS
LASTING	MONUMENT
LEADING	NOVELIST
LEADING	QUESTION
LEATHER	TROUSERS
LENGTHY	ARGUMENT
LENGTHY	BUSINESS
LIBERAL	MINORITY
LOGICAL	ARGUMENT
LOGICAL	SEQUENCE
MALCOLM	CAMPBELL
MANILLA	ENVELOPE
MARLENE	DIETRICH
MARRIED	QUARTERS
MARTHAS	VINEYARD
MAUREEN	CONNOLLY
MEDICAL	PRACTICE
MESSAGE	RECEIVED
MICHAEL	FLANDERS
MICHAEL	REDGRAVE
MIDLAND	COUNTIES
MOLOTOV	COCKTAIL
MONTHLY	MAGAZINE
MONTHLY	PAYMENTS
MUSICAL	DIRECTOR
MUSICAL	FESTIVAL
NATURAL	APTITUDE
NATURAL	INSTINCT
NAUGHTY	NINETIES
NEAREST	RELATIVE
NERVOUS	DISORDER
NOBODYS	BUSINESS
NOTHING	VENTURED
OFFICER	MATERIAL
OPENING	CEREMONY
OPENING	SENTENCE
OPTICAL	ILLUSION
ORDERLY	CORPORAL
ORDERLY	SERGEANT
OUTDOOR	CLOTHING
OUTSIDE	ESTIMATE
OUTSIDE	INTEREST
OVERALL	MAJORITY
PASSING	INTEREST
PASSIVE	INTEREST
PELICAN	CROSSING
PEOPLES	REPUBLIC
PERFECT	LIKENESS
PERFECT	NUISANCE
PERFECT	SPECIMEN
PERFECT	STRANGER
PERFECT	TREASURE
PICTURE	POSTCARD
PLAYERS	ENTRANCE
POINTED	REMINDER
POPULAR	DECISION
POPULAR	LANGUAGE
PRIMARY	ELECTION
PRIVATE	CARRIAGE
PRIVATE	DEVOTION
PRIVATE	HOSPITAL
PRIVATE	PRACTICE
PRIVATE	PROPERTY
PRIVATE	QUARTERS
PRIVATE	TEACHING
PROBLEM	CHILDREN
PROPOSE	MARRIAGE
PROVIDE	EVIDENCE
QUARTER	SESSIONS
RADICAL	SOLUTION
RAILWAY	ACCIDENT
RAILWAY	CARRIAGE
RAILWAY	ENGINEER
RAILWAY	JUNCTION
RAILWAY	TERMINUS
REGULAR	CUSTOMER
REGULAR	EXERCISE
REGULAR	FEATURES
REGULAR	PRACTICE
RESERVE	STRENGTH
RICHARD	DIMBLEBY
RICHARD	SHERIDAN
ROUGHLY	SPEAKING
RUFFLED	FEATHERS
RUFFLED	FEELINGS
RUNAWAY	MARRIAGE
RUSSIAN	ALPHABET
RUSSIAN	LANGUAGE
RUSSIAN	ROULETTE
SAILORS	HORNPIPE
SAVOURY	OMELETTE
SCALENE	TRIANGLE
SEATING	CAPACITY
SERIOUS	ACCIDENT
SERIOUS	QUESTION
SERVICE	INCLUDED
SERVICE	REVOLVER
SEVENTH	SYMPHONY
SEVENTY	THOUSAND
SHOTGUN	MARRIAGE
SIXTEEN	THOUSAND
SPANISH	CHESTNUT
SPANISH	LANGUAGE
SPANISH	OMELETTE
SPECIAL	DELIVERY

SPECIAL OCCASION
STANLEY HOLLOWAY
STANLEY MATTHEWS
STOMACH DISORDER
STRINGS ATTACHED
SUSPEND SENTENCE
SUSTAIN INJURIES
TALKING PICTURES
TAPERED TROUSERS
TERENCE RATTIGAN
TITANIC STRENGTH
TOPICAL INTEREST
TOURIST INDUSTRY
UMPIRES DECISION
UNDERGO TRAINING
UNEQUAL STRUGGLE
UNHAPPY MEMORIES
UNKNOWN QUANTITY
UPRIGHT CARRIAGE
UPRIGHT POSITION
VANESSA REDGRAVE
VAUGHAN WILLIAMS
VIOLENT CONTRAST
VIOLENT EXERCISE
VIOLENT OUTBURST
VIOLENT REACTION
VIOLENT STRUGGLE
WALKING DISTANCE
WEATHER FORECAST
WEDDING CEREMONY
WELCOME STRANGER
WHITSUN VACATION
WILLIAM CONGREVE
WINNING POSITION
WINNING SEQUENCE
WISHFUL THINKING
WITCHES CAULDRON
WITHOUT CEREMONY
WITHOUT INCIDENT
WITHOUT INTEREST
WITHOUT PARALLEL
WITHOUT THINKING
WOOLLEN INDUSTRY
WORKERS PLAYTIME
WORKING MAJORITY
WRITING MATERIAL
WRITTEN CONTRACT
WRITTEN EVIDENCE
WRITTEN LANGUAGE
YOUNGER DAUGHTER

8, 1, 6

COMPOUND A FELONY
DESCRIBE A CIRCLE

8, 2, 1, 4

PORTRAIT OF A LADY
STUBBORN AS A MULE

8, 2, 2, 3

SLIPPERY AS AN EEL

8, 2, 5

ACCIDENT OF BIRTH
ADVANCED IN YEARS
AMERICAN IN PARIS
ARTICLES OF FAITH
BACHELOR OF MUSIC
BUSINESS AS USUAL
CHERCHEZ LA FEMME
CONTEMPT OF COURT
CREATURE OF HABIT
CRIMINAL AT LARGE
ELEVENTH OF APRIL
ELEVENTH OF MARCH
EXCHANGE OF VIEWS
FOUNTAIN OF YOUTH
JUDGMENT OF PARIS
KINDNESS OF HEART
LEONARDO DA VINCI
MINISTER OF STATE
MINISTER OF WORKS
MINISTRY OF STATE
MINISTRY OF WORKS
MULTIPLY BY EIGHT
MULTIPLY BY SEVEN
MULTIPLY BY THREE
PARTNERS IN CRIME
PETITION OF RIGHT
POSITION OF POWER
POSITION OF TRUST
PREPARED TO FIGHT
PRINCESS OF WALES
PRISONER OF STATE
PRISONER OF ZENDA
REGIMENT OF WOMEN
SARDINES ON TOAST
SENTENCE TO DEATH
SOMEBODY OR OTHER
SPOONFUL OF SUGAR
SQUEEZED TO DEATH
SURPRISE IN STORE

8, 3, 4

BRIGHTON AND HOVE
CARRIAGE AND PAIR
CRIPPLED FOR LIFE
EIGHTEEN PER CENT
EXCHANGE AND MART
EXERCISE THE MIND
EXERCISE THE VETO
FOURTEEN PER CENT
HEREWARD THE WAKE
MILITARY TWO-STEP
NINETEEN PER CENT
OVERSTEP THE MARK
SAUSAGES AND MASH

TATTERED AND TORN
THIRTEEN PER CENT
WHATEVER YOU WANT

8, 4, 3

COMPLETE WASH-OUT
WRINKLED WITH AGE

8, 7

ABERDEEN TERRIER
ABRIDGED VERSION
ABSOLUTE MINIMUM
ABSTRACT PAINTER
ACADEMIC CIRCLES
ACCEPTED MEANING
ADJUTANT GENERAL
ADVANCED STUDENT
AFFLUENT SOCIETY
AIRCRAFT CARRIER
AIREDALE TERRIER
AMERICAN EMBASSY
AMERICAN HISTORY
ANNOUNCE ONESELF
ARTISTIC ABILITY
ASSISTED PASSAGE
ATTORNEY GENERAL
AUTUMNAL EQUINOX
BALLROOM DANCING
BENJAMIN BRITTEN
BERTRAND RUSSELL
BIRTHDAY HONOURS
BIRTHDAY PRESENT
BOARDING OFFICER
BODLEIAN LIBRARY
BRUSSELS SPROUTS
BUILDING SOCIETY
BUSINESS ADDRESS
BUSINESS AFFAIRS
BUSINESS CONTACT
BUSINESS FOOTING
BUSINESS MANAGER
BUSINESS MEETING
BUSINESS METHODS
BUSINESS VENTURE
CARDINAL NUMBERS
CARELESS DRIVING
CARELESS RAPTURE
CASUALTY STATION
CHANGING FASHION
CHEMICAL FORMULA
CHEMICAL PROCESS
CHEMICAL WARFARE
CHIPPING SODBURY
CIVILIAN CLOTHES
CLASSICS SCHOLAR
COCKTAIL CABINET
COLORADO SPRINGS
COMMUNAL KITCHEN
COMPLETE ABANDON

COMPLETE CONTROL
COMPLETE FAILURE
COMPLETE SILENCE
COMPLETE VICTORY
CONSTANT ANXIETY
CORONERS INQUEST
CORONERS VERDICT
CREATIVE WRITING
CREATURE COMFORT
CRIMINAL NEGLECT
CRIMINAL OFFENCE
CRITICAL OPINION
CRUSHING VICTORY
DAMPENED SPIRITS
DAYLIGHT ROBBERY
DECISIVE VICTORY
DECLARED MISSING
DEFERRED PAYMENT
DEFINITE ARTICLE
DELAYING TACTICS
DELICATE BALANCE
DELIRIUM TREMENS
DESOLATE COUNTRY
DETACHED OPINION
DETAILED ACCOUNT
DEVILLED KIDNEYS
DIRECTOR GENERAL
DISGUISE ONESELF
DISPENSE JUSTICE
DISTRICT COUNCIL
DISTRICT OFFICER
DIVIDEND WARRANT
DOMESTIC AFFAIRS
DOMESTIC ECONOMY
DOMESTIC PROBLEM
DOMESTIC SCIENCE
DOMESTIC SERVANT
DOMESTIC SERVICE
DOUBTFUL STARTER
DRAMATIC GESTURE
DRAMATIC SETTING
DRAMATIC SOCIETY
DRESSING STATION
DROOPING SPIRITS
DUELLING PISTOLS
EBENEZER SCROOGE
ECONOMIC MIRACLE
ECONOMIC WARFARE
ELECTION ADDRESS
ELECTION RESULTS
ELECTRIC BLANKET
ELECTRIC CIRCUIT
ELECTRIC CURRENT
ELECTRIC RAILWAY
ELECTRIC TOASTER
ELEVATED WALKWAY
ELEVENTH CENTURY
EMMANUEL COLLEGE
EXCHANGE CONTROL
EXCHANGE GLANCES
EXCHANGE LETTERS

EXERCISE	CONTROL
FAITHFUL	HUSBAND
FAITHFUL	SERVANT
FALKLAND	ISLANDS
FAREWELL	ADDRESS
FEDERICO	FELLINI
FINISHED	PRODUCT
FIREWORK	DISPLAY
FLAGGING	SPIRITS
FLAWLESS	DIAMOND
FLEETING	GLIMPSE
FLOATING	CAPITAL
FOOTBALL	FIXTURE
FOOTBALL	RESULTS
FORCIBLE	FEEDING
FORENSIC	CHEMIST
FOURTEEN	MINUTES
FREEHAND	DRAWING
FRENZIED	EFFORTS
FREQUENT	VISITOR
FRIENDLY	FEELING
FRIENDLY	GESTURE
FRIENDLY	RIVALRY
FRIENDLY	SOCIETY
GENEROUS	GESTURE
GENEROUS	HELPING
GENEROUS	MEASURE
GEOFFREY	BOYCOTT
GEOFFREY	CHAUCER
GLORIOUS	HOLIDAY
GLORIOUS	TWELFTH
GLORIOUS	VICTORY
GORGEOUS	WEATHER
GOTTLIEB	DAIMLER
GOVERNOR	GENERAL
GRACEFUL	GESTURE
GREATEST	RESPECT
GUERILLA	WARFARE
HANDSOME	APOLOGY
HANDSOME	FORTUNE
HAUNTING	REFRAIN
HEATHROW	AIRPORT
HEINRICH	HIMMLER
HIGHLAND	COSTUME
HIGHLAND	TERRIER
HISTORIC	PRESENT
HOMEWARD	JOURNEY
HOPELESS	FAILURE
HORRIBLE	WEATHER
HOSPITAL	ALMONER
HOSPITAL	GROUNDS
IMPERIAL	COLLEGE
IMPERIAL	MEASURE
IMPROVED	VERSION
INCOMING	BATSMAN
INFAMOUS	CONDUCT
INFERIOR	ARTICLE
INFERIOR	QUALITY
INFERIOR	VERSION
INFERNAL	MACHINE
INFERNAL	REGIONS
INFORMED	OPINION
INTERNAL	AFFAIRS
KATHLEEN	FERRIER
KNITTING	MACHINE
KNITTING	NEEDLES
KNITTING	PATTERN
LANGUAGE	BARRIER
LANGUAGE	PROBLEM
LANGUAGE	TEACHER
LAUGHING	JACKASS
LAURENCE	OLIVIER
LEIGHTON	BUZZARD
LEISURED	CLASSES
LITERARY	CIRCLES
LITERARY	SUBJECT
LUNCHEON	VOUCHER
MAGAZINE	ARTICLE
MAGDALEN	COLLEGE
MAGNETIC	COMPASS
MAJORITY	VERDICT
MARGINAL	COMMENT
MARRIAGE	ADVISER
MARRIAGE	LICENCE
MARRIAGE	PARTNER
MARRIAGE	PORTION
MATERIAL	BENEFIT
MATERNAL	FEELING
MEMORIAL	SERVICE
MIDNIGHT	MATINÉE
MILITARY	ACADEMY
MILITARY	ATTACHÉ
MILITARY	BEARING
MILITARY	COLLEGE
MILITARY	FUNERAL
MILITARY	HISTORY
MILITARY	HONOURS
MILITARY	SERVICE
MILITARY	STATION
MILITARY	TACTICS
MODERATE	DEMANDS
MODERATE	DRINKER
MODERATE	SUCCESS
MORTALLY	WOUNDED
MOTORING	OFFENCE
MOUNTAIN	RAILWAY
NATIONAL	COLOURS
NATIONAL	COSTUME
NATIONAL	DEFENCE
NATIONAL	GALLERY
NATIONAL	HOLIDAY
NATIONAL	LIBRARY
NATIONAL	LOTTERY
NATIONAL	PRODUCT
NATIONAL	SAVINGS
NATIONAL	SERVICE
NATIONAL	THEATRE
NINETEEN	HUNDRED
NINETEEN	SEVENTY
NORTHERN	IRELAND
OBEDIENT	SERVANT
OFFICIAL	INQUIRY

OFFICIAL SECRETS
OPPOSITE EXTREME
OPPOSITE MEANING
OPPOSITE PARTIES
ORDNANCE OFFICER
ORIGINAL MEANING
OVERHEAD CHARGES
OVERHEAD RAILWAY
PARALLEL PASSAGE
PARENTAL CONSENT
PARENTAL CONTROL
PATENTLY OBVIOUS
PATERNAL FEELING
PATHETIC ATTEMPT
PEMBROKE COLLEGE
PERILOUS VENTURE
PERSONAL ACCOUNT
PERSONAL EFFECTS
PERSONAL OPINION
PERSONAL PRONOUN
PERSONAL REASONS
PERSONAL SERVICE
PHEASANT PLUCKER
PHYSICAL CULTURE
PHYSICAL FATIGUE
PHYSICAL FITNESS
PHYSICAL SCIENCE
PIERCING WHISTLE
PLEASANT EVENING
PLEASANT FLAVOUR
PLEASURE GARDENS
PLEASURE GROUNDS
PLEASURE STEAMER
PLYMOUTH HARBOUR
POLISHED MANNERS
PORTRAIT GALLERY
PORTRAIT PAINTER
PREVIOUS OFFENCE
PROFOUND THINKER
PROFOUND THOUGHT
PROGRESS PAYMENT
PROPERLY DRESSED
REIGNING MONARCH
RELATIVE PRONOUN
RELIABLE SERVICE
REMEMBER NOTHING
RESEARCH CHEMIST
RESTRICT IMPORTS
SALVADOR ALLENDE
SANDWICH ISLANDS
SATURDAY EVENING
SATURDAY MORNING
SCOTTISH TERRIER
SCOTTISH THISTLE
SECURITY COUNCIL
SECURITY MEASURE
SEMOLINA PUDDING
SHETLAND ISLANDS
SHIPPING COMPANY
SHIPPING MAGNATE
SHOCKING WEATHER

SHOOTING GALLERY
SICKNESS BENEFIT
SKELETON SERVICE
SLEEPING DRAUGHT
SLEEPING PARTNER
SLIPPERY SURFACE
SOBERING THOUGHT
SOMERSET MAUGHAM
SPARRING PARTNER
SPECIFIC GRAVITY
SPELLING MISTAKE
SPLENDID VICTORY
SPLENDID WEATHER
SPORTING FIXTURE
SPORTING GESTURE
SPRINGER SPANIEL
STANDARD EDITION
STANDARD ENGLISH
STANDARD VERSION
STANDING OVATION
STICKING PLASTER
STRAIGHT ACTRESS
STRAIGHT DEALING
STRAINED SILENCE
STRICTLY ILLEGAL
STRICTLY NEUTRAL
STRICTLY PRIVATE
STRIKING SUCCESS
STRUGGLE THROUGH
SUITABLE PARTNER
SUPERIOR NUMBERS
SUPERIOR OFFICER
SUPERIOR QUALITY
SUSPENSE ACCOUNT
SWEEPING CHANGES
SWEEPING REFORMS
SWEEPING SUCCESS
SWEEPING VICTORY
SWIMMING COSTUME
SWINGING SIXTIES
SYMPHONY CONCERT
TABLEAUX VIVANTS
TERMINAL ILLNESS
TERRIBLE TRAGEDY
TERRIBLE WEATHER
THATCHED COTTAGE
THIRTEEN MINUTES
THOUSAND DOLLARS
THOUSAND GUINEAS
THURSDAY EVENING
THURSDAY MORNING
TOMORROW MORNING
TOWERING PASSION
TRAINING COLLEGE
TROPICAL CLIMATE
UNDERARM BOWLING
UNSEEMLY CONDUCT
UNSOLVED MYSTERY
VICTORIA STATION
VIRGINIA CREEPER
WALTZING MATILDA

WATERLOO STATION
WEIGHING MACHINE
WHIRLING DERVISH
WINDMILL THEATRE
WIRELESS MESSAGE
WITHHOLD PAYMENT
YOUNGEST BROTHER
ZIEGFELD FOLLIES

9, 1, 5

CULTIVATE A HABIT
ESTABLISH A CLAIM

9, 2, 2, 2

SOMETHING TO GO ON

9, 2, 4

ABUNDANCE OF FOOD
ACCORDING TO PLAN
COMPANION IN ARMS
DELIVERED BY HAND
ENDEAVOUR TO HELP
FIFTEENTH OF JULY
FIFTEENTH OF JUNE
NEWCASTLE ON TYNE
PLAYTHING OF FATE
SIXTEENTH OF JULY
SIXTEENTH OF JUNE
SOMETHING IN HAND
STATEMENT OF FACT
STATEMENT ON OATH
STRATFORD ON AVON
THIRTIETH OF JUNE
TWENTIETH OF JULY
TWENTIETH OF JUNE
UNTOUCHED BY HAND
VENGEANCE IS MINE!

9, 3, 3

BEGINNING AND END

9, 6

AFTERNOON SIESTA
ALEXANDRA PALACE
AMBITIOUS SCHEME
AMBULANCE DRIVER
AMUSEMENT ARCADE
ANONYMOUS LETTER
ANTARCTIC CIRCLE
APPEALING MANNER
ASSISTANT MASTER
ASSURANCE POLICY
ATTEMPTED MURDER
AUTOGRAPH HUNTER
AUTOMATIC PISTOL
AUXILIARY FORCES

AUXILIARY TROOPS
BALACLAVA HELMET
BATTERSEA BRIDGE
BEAUTIFUL FIGURE
BEVERIDGE REPORT
BLACKBURN ROVERS
BLACKWALL TUNNEL
BOTANICAL GARDEN
BOUNDLESS ENERGY
BREAKFAST CEREAL
BUTTERFLY STROKE
BYZANTINE EMPIRE
CAMBRIDGE CIRCUS
CAMBRIDGE UNITED
CAMEMBERT CHEESE
CATALOGUE NUMBER
CEASELESS ENERGY
CELESTIAL SPHERE
CHAMPAGNE SUPPER
CHARACTER SKETCH
CHARLOTTE BRONTË
CHEQUERED CAREER
CHILDHOOD FRIEND
CHILDRENS CORNER
CHOCOLATE ECLAIR
CHOCOLATE SUNDAE
CHRISTIAN MARTYR
CHRISTMAS DINNER
CHRISTMAS ISLAND
CHRISTMAS SEASON
CHRISTMAS SPIRIT
CIGARETTE COUPON
CIGARETTE HOLDER
CIGARETTE PACKET
CLASSICAL BALLET
CLASSICAL WRITER
COLERIDGE TAYLOR
COLLISION COURSE
COLOURING MATTER
COMMUNITY CENTRE
COMPANION VOLUME
CONCERTED ACTION
CONCERTED EFFORT
CONDITION POWDER
CORRECTED PROOFS
CREDULOUS PERSON
CROSSWORD PUZZLE
DANGEROUS CORNER
DANGEROUS PERSON
DANGEROUS VOYAGE
DANGEROUS WEAPON
DEAFENING CHEERS
DEFECTIVE MEMORY
DEFECTIVE VISION
DEFENSIVE WEAPON
DEPARTURE LOUNGE
DESIRABLE OBJECT
DESPERATE PLIGHT
DESPERATE REMEDY
DETENTION CENTRE
DETERRENT EFFECT

DIFFERENT	TASTES	IMMEDIATE	ACTION
DIFFERING	TASTES	IMMERSION	HEATER
DIFFICULT	CHOICE	IMMOVABLE	OBJECT
DIFFICULT	MATTER	IMPENDING	DANGER
DIFFICULT	PERSON	IMPORTANT	MATTER
DIFFIDENT	MANNER	IMPORTANT	PERSON
DIRECTION	FINDER	IMPULSIVE	NATURE
DISCHARGE	PAPERS	INAUGURAL	SPEECH
DISPLACED	PERSON	INCREASED	DEMAND
DONCASTER	ROVERS	INDELIBLE	PENCIL
DORMITORY	SUBURB	INGENIOUS	DEVICE
EDINBURGH	CASTLE	INSURANCE	BROKER
EDINBURGH	TATTOO	INSURANCE	OFFICE
EDITORIAL	COLUMN	INSURANCE	POLICY
ELABORATE	DESIGN	INVENTIVE	GENIUS
ELABORATE	DETAIL	INVISIBLE	EXPORT
ELECTORAL	DEFEAT	LANDSCAPE	ARTIST
ELECTORAL	REFORM	LEICESTER	SQUARE
ELECTORAL	SYSTEM	LIGHTNING	SKETCH
ELIZABETH	TAYLOR	LIGHTNING	STRIKE
ELOCUTION	LESSON	LIVERPOOL	STREET
EMERGENCY	POWERS	LUXURIANT	GROWTH
EMERGENCY	RATION	MALIGNANT	GROWTH
ENDOWMENT	POLICY	MASCULINE	GENDER
ENERGETIC	PERSON	MERCENARY	TROOPS
ERRONEOUS	BELIEF	MINIATURE	POODLE
EXCELLENT	CHANCE	MISERABLE	SINNER
EXCELLENT	RESULT	MOONLIGHT	SONATA
EXCESSIVE	CHARGE	MOTHERING	SUNDAY
EXCESSIVE	HEIGHT	NEWCASTLE	UNITED
EXCESSIVE	WEIGHT	NEWSPAPER	REPORT
EXCLUSIVE	REPORT	NEWSPAPER	SELLER
EXCLUSIVE	RIGHTS	NUREMBERG	TRIALS
EXPENSIVE	TASTES	OFFENSIVE	MANNER
EXPLOSIVE	CHARGE	OFFENSIVE	REMARK
EXPLOSIVE	DEVICE	OFFENSIVE	WEAPON
EXTENSIVE	DAMAGE	OPPORTUNE	MOMENT
FEATHERED	FRIEND	ORCHESTRA	STALLS
FENCHURCH	STREET	ORGANISED	LABOUR
FINANCIAL	CRISIS	PARACHUTE	TROOPS
FINANCIAL	WIZARD	PARKHURST	PRISON
FINISHING	SCHOOL	PEREGRINE	FALCON
FORGIVING	NATURE	PERFECTLY	HONEST
FRIEDRICH	ENGELS	PERMANENT	CREASE
FRUITLESS	EFFORT	PERMANENT	RECORD
FRUITLESS	SEARCH	PERPETUAL	MOTION
FURNITURE	POLISH	PERTINENT	REMARK
GATHERING	CLOUDS	PETRIFIED	FOREST
GENTLEMAN	FARMER	PLANETARY	SYSTEM
GEOGRAPHY	LESSON	POLITICAL	ASYLUM
GEOGRAPHY	MASTER	POLITICAL	CAREER
GRENADIER	GUARDS	POLITICAL	EVENTS
GREYHOUND	RACING	POLITICAL	OFFICE
GROSVENOR	SQUARE	POLITICAL	SPEECH
HACKNEYED	PHRASE	POLITICAL	THEORY
HACKNEYED	SAYING	POLITICAL	WEAPON
HOMICIDAL	MANIAC	POLITICAL	WRITER
HONEYMOON	COUPLE	POTENTIAL	DANGER
HOUSEHOLD	CHORES	POTENTIAL	ENERGY
HOUSEHOLD	DRUDGE	PRACTICAL	RESULT
HOUSEHOLD	TROOPS	PREFERRED	SHARES

PRESERVED GINGER
PRESIDENT NASSER
PRINCIPAL PERSON
PROGRAMME SELLER
PRONOUNCE GUILTY
QUALIFIED PERSON
QUALIFIED PRAISE
QUARTERLY REVIEW
REARGUARD ACTION
RECEPTION CENTRE
RECORDING STUDIO
REFRESHER COURSE
RELIGIOUS BELIEF
RELIGIOUS MANIAC
ROTHERHAM UNITED
SCHEDULED FLIGHT
SCHOOLBOY HOWLER
SEAFARING NATION
SEARCHING GLANCE
SEAWORTHY VESSEL
SECONDARY MODERN
SECONDARY PICKET
SECONDARY SCHOOL
SENSITIVE MARKET
SENSITIVE NATURE
SEVENTEEN POUNDS
SHEEPSKIN JACKET
SHEFFIELD UNITED
SHORTHAND TYPIST
SHORTHAND WRITER
SHRINKING VIOLET
SITUATION COMEDY
SITUATION VACANT
SITUATION WANTED
SLAPSTICK COMEDY
SOMETHING ROTTEN
SQUATTING RIGHTS
STARBOARD ENGINE
STOCKPORT COUNTY
STRAPPING FELLOW
STRENUOUS EFFORT
STRETCHER BEARER
STROLLING PLAYER
SUSTAINED EFFORT
TATTENHAM CORNER
TELEGRAPH OFFICE
TELEPHONE NUMBER
TELEPHONE SYSTEM
TEMPORARY RELIEF
THRILLING CLIMAX
THUMBNAIL SKETCH
TONSORIAL ARTIST
TOOTHSOME MORSEL
TRAFALGAR SQUARE
TRANSPORT SYSTEM
TREASURED MEMORY
TURBULENT PRIEST
UNANIMOUS CHOICE
UNBRIDLED TONGUE
UNFROCKED PRIEST
UNGUARDED MOMENT

UNGUARDED REMARK
UNMARRIED MOTHER
UNSKILLED LABOUR
VEGETABLE GARDEN
VEGETABLE MARKET
VEGETABLE MATTER
VICTORIAN PERIOD
WAISTCOAT POCKET
WHISTLING KETTLE
WHOLESALE MURDER
WIMBLEDON COMMON

10, 2, 3

CONTRABAND OF WAR
EIGHTEENTH OF MAY
FOURTEENTH OF MAY
NINETEENTH OF MAY
THIRTEENTH OF MAY

10, 5

ACCIDENTAL DEATH
ALIMENTARY CANAL
ARTIFICIAL LIGHT
ARTIFICIAL STONE
ARTIFICIAL TEETH
ASTRONOMER ROYAL
AUTOMOBILE CRASH
BACKGROUND MUSIC
BANKRUPTCY COURT
BEETHOVENS FIFTH
BEETHOVENS NINTH
BLISSFULLY HAPPY
BOTTOMLESS PURSE
CALEDONIAN CANAL
CAMBERWELL GREEN
CANTERBURY BELLS
CANTERBURY TALES
CAPABILITY BROWN
CENTIGRADE SCALE
CHARITABLE CAUSE
CINDERELLA DANCE
COLLECTION PLATE
COLLECTORS PIECE
COLOURLESS FLUID
COMMANDING VOICE
COMMERCIAL COURT
COMMERCIAL RADIO
COMMERCIAL VALUE
COMMISSION AGENT
COMPULSORY GAMES
CONCLUSIVE PROOF
CONFERENCE TABLE
CONFIDENCE TRICK
CONGENITAL IDIOT
CONSCIENCE MONEY
CONSENTING ADULT
CONSENTING PARTY
CONSUMMATE SKILL
CONTROLLED PRICE

CONVENIENT PLACE
CONVERSION TABLE
CORONATION COACH
CORONATION ROBES
CORRUGATED PAPER
CULTIVATED TASTE
DEMOCRATIC PARTY
DEMOLITION SQUAD
DEPARTMENT STORE
DESCENDING ORDER
DEVONSHIRE CREAM
DIPLOMATIC STAFF
DISLOCATED ELBOW
DISORDERED BRAIN
DISORDERLY HOUSE
DISPOSABLE GOODS
DISSENTING PARTY
DORCHESTER HOTEL
EIGHTEENTH GREEN
ELECTRICAL FAULT
ELECTRONIC BRAIN
ELECTRONIC MUSIC
EXHAUSTION POINT
EXORBITANT PRICE
FATHERLESS CHILD
FAVOURABLE REPLY
FAVOURABLE TERMS
FIGURATIVE SENSE
FORWARDING AGENT
FOUNDATION CREAM
FOUNDATION STONE
FRIGHTENED CHILD
GARGANTUAN FEAST
GENERATING PLANT
GLITTERING PRIZE
GOVERNMENT GRANT
GRANULATED SUGAR
GRAPEFRUIT JUICE
GREENHOUSE PLANT
HEARTBREAK HOTEL
HEARTBREAK HOUSE
HERBACEOUS PLANT
HEREDITARY TITLE
HIERONYMUS BOSCH
HISTORICAL NOVEL
HORIZONTAL PLANE
IMMACULATE STYLE
IMPROBABLE STORY
INCIDENTAL MUSIC
INDIVIDUAL STYLE
INDUSTRIAL PLANT
INORDINATE PRIDE
INSTRUMENT PANEL
INTANGIBLE ASSET
INTERESTED PARTY
INVESTMENT TRUST
LEGITIMATE CHILD
LEGITIMATE STAGE
LEGUMINOUS PLANT
MAGNIFYING GLASS
MAGNIFYING POWER

MECHANICAL MEANS
MICHAELMAS DAISY
MOTHERLESS CHILD
MOTIVATING FORCE
NOMINATION PAPER
NUTCRACKER SUITE
OPPOSITION BENCH
OPPOSITION PARTY
ORCHESTRAL MUSIC
PADDINGTON GREEN
PERCENTAGE BASIS
PERFORMING FLEAS
PERISHABLE GOODS
PHOTOGRAPH ALBUM
PLOUGHMANS LUNCH
PRECARIOUS STATE
PREFERENCE SHARE
PREVAILING TASTE
PROTESTANT FAITH
PROVINCIAL PAPER
PURCHASING POWER
REASONABLE DOUBT
REASONABLE TERMS
RECRUITING DRIVE
REGIMENTAL BADGE
REGIMENTAL MARCH
RELATIVELY QUIET
REMARKABLE SIGHT
REMARKABLE WOMAN
REPUBLICAN PARTY
ROCKABILLY REBEL
ROUNDABOUT ROUTE
SATURATION POINT
SOLICITORS CLERK
SPOTLESSLY CLEAN
STENTORIAN VOICE
SUCCESSFUL WOMAN
SUPERSONIC SPEED
SURPRISING THING
TELESCOPIC SIGHT
TELEVISION TABLE
TEMPERANCE HOTEL
THREEPENNY OPERA
THREEPENNY PIECE
THREEPENNY STAMP
TRANSISTOR RADIO
TRAVELLERS TALES
TRAVELLING CLOCK
TRAVELLING LIGHT
UNDERCOVER AGENT
UNDERWATER CRAFT
UNEXPECTED VISIT
UNFINISHED STATE
UNIVERSITY GRANT
UNIVERSITY SLANG
UNLEAVENED BREAD
UNSOCIABLE HOURS
UNTROUBLED SLEEP
VULNERABLE POINT
WEDNESDAYS CHILD
WELLINGTON BOOTS

WINCHESTER RIFLE
WINDSCREEN WIPER
YESTERDAYS PAPER

11, 4

ALTERNATIVE PLAN
ALTERNATIVE VOTE
ANNIVERSARY DATE
APPLICATION FORM
BULLETPROOF VEST
CALCULATING MIND
CHRISTOPHER WREN
COMBINATION LOCK
COMFORTABLE SEAT
CONDITIONAL MOOD
CONSIGNMENT NOTE
CONSOLATION RACE
COUNTERFEIT COIN
COUNTERFEIT NOTE
DEVELOPMENT AREA
DISTRESSING NEWS
DOCUMENTARY FILM
ELECTRICITY BILL
ENGLISHMANS HOME
EVERLASTING FAME
EXAGGERATED IDEA
EXAMINATION ROOM
EXCLAMATION MARK
FASHIONABLE AREA
FLAMBOROUGH HEAD
HIPPOCRATIC OATH
HOMOGENISED MILK
HONEYSUCKLE ROSE
HUCKLEBERRY FINN
ILLUSTRATED WORK
ILLUSTRIOUS PAST
INFORMATION DESK
INTELLIGENT LIFE
INTELLIGENT TALK
IRREPARABLE HARM
IRREPARABLE LOSS
LEGISLATIVE BODY
MOUNTAINOUS AREA
NORTHAMPTON TOWN
OBSERVATION POST
OUTSTANDING DEBT
PASTEURISED MILK
PAWNBROKERS SIGN
PENETRATING LOOK
PERSONALITY CULT
PRELIMINARY HEAT
PROHIBITION ZONE
PUNCTUATION MARK
REFRESHMENT ROOM
REFRESHMENT TENT
RESIDENTIAL AREA
RESTORATION PLAY
RESTRAINING HAND
SENSATIONAL NEWS
SIGHTSEEING TOUR

STOCKTAKING SALE
SUBJUNCTIVE MOOD
SUBSISTENCE WAGE
SUBSTANTIAL MEAL
SUBTRACTION SIGN
TERRITORIAL ARMY
THREATENING LOOK
TRADITIONAL FARE
TRADITIONAL JAZZ
UNCIVILIZED RACE
UNFURNISHED FLAT
UNPUBLISHED WORK
WESTMINSTER HALL
WHISTLESTOP TOUR
YELLOWSTONE PARK

12, 3

CONSIDERABLE SUM
DISAPPEARING ACT
EXTORTIONATE FEE
EXTORTIONATE SUM
INDEPENDENCE DAY
MARRIAGEABLE AGE
MILLIONAIRES ROW
NEWFOUNDLAND DOG
PALAEOLITHIC AGE
PREMEDITATED ACT
PROFESSIONAL AIR
PROFESSIONAL MAN
REGISTRATION FEE
THANKSGIVING DAY
UNEMPLOYMENT PAY